Handbook of Research on Advancements of Swarm Intelligence Algorithms for Solving Real-World Problems

Shi Cheng
Shaanxi Normal University, China

Yuhui Shi
Southern University of Science and Technology, China

A volume in the Advances in Computational Intelligence and Robotics (ACIR) Book Series

Published in the United States of America by
    IGI Global
    Engineering Science Reference (an imprint of IGI Global)
    701 E. Chocolate Avenue
    Hershey PA, USA 17033
    Tel: 717-533-8845
    Fax: 717-533-8661
    E-mail: cust@igi-global.com
    Web site: http://www.igi-global.com

Library of Congress Cataloging-in-Publication Data

Names: Cheng, Shi, 1983- editor. | Shi, Yuhui, editor.
Title: Handbook of research on advancements of swarm intelligence
   algorithms for solving real-world problems / Shi Cheng and Yuhui Shi,
   editors.
Description: Hershey, PA : Engineering Science Reference, an imprint of IGI
   Global, [2020] | Includes bibliographical references and index. |
   Summary: "This book explores various concepts, principles, and
   applications of swarm intelligence algorithms"-- Provided by publisher.
Identifiers: LCCN 2019049633 (print) | LCCN 2019049634 (ebook) | ISBN
   9781799832225 (hardcover) ISBN 9781799832249 (ebook)
Subjects: LCSH: Swarm intelligence.
Classification: LCC Q337.3 .H358 2020 (print) | LCC Q337.3 (ebook) | DDC
   006.3/824--dc23
LC record available at https://lccn.loc.gov/2019049633
LC ebook record available at https://lccn.loc.gov/2019049634

This book is published in the IGI Global book series Advances in Computational Intelligence and Robotics (ACIR) (ISSN: 2327-0411; eISSN: 2327-042X)

British Cataloguing in Publication Data
A Cataloguing in Publication record for this book is available from the British Library.

The views expressed in this book are those of the authors, but not necessarily of the publisher.

For electronic access to this publication, please contact: eresources@igi-global.com.

Advances in Computational Intelligence and Robotics (ACIR) Book Series

Ivan Giannoccaro
University of Salento, Italy

ISSN:2327-0411
EISSN:2327-042X

Mission

While intelligence is traditionally a term applied to humans and human cognition, technology has progressed in such a way to allow for the development of intelligent systems able to simulate many human traits. With this new era of simulated and artificial intelligence, much research is needed in order to continue to advance the field and also to evaluate the ethical and societal concerns of the existence of artificial life and machine learning.

The **Advances in Computational Intelligence and Robotics (ACIR) Book Series** encourages scholarly discourse on all topics pertaining to evolutionary computing, artificial life, computational intelligence, machine learning, and robotics. ACIR presents the latest research being conducted on diverse topics in intelligence technologies with the goal of advancing knowledge and applications in this rapidly evolving field.

Coverage

- Cyborgs
- Brain Simulation
- Fuzzy Systems
- Agent technologies
- Automated Reasoning
- Computational Intelligence
- Artificial Life
- Cognitive Informatics
- Intelligent control
- Computational Logic

IGI Global is currently accepting manuscripts for publication within this series. To submit a proposal for a volume in this series, please contact our Acquisition Editors at Acquisitions@igi-global.com or visit: http://www.igi-global.com/publish/.

Titles in this Series

For a list of additional titles in this series, please visit:
https://www.igi-global.com/book-series/advances-computational-intelligence-robotics/73674

IoT and Cloud Computing Advancements in Vehicular Ad-Ho Networks
Ram Shringar Rao (Ambedkar Institute of Advanced Communication Technologies and Research, India) Vishal Jain (Bharati Vidyapeeth's Institute of Computer Applications and Management, New Delhi, India) Omprakash Kaiwartya (School of Science and Technology, Nottingham Trent University, UK) and Nanhay Singh (Ambedkar Institute of Advanced Communication Technologies and Research, India)
Engineering Science Reference • © 2020 • 330pp • H/C (ISBN: 9781799825708) • US $215.00

Emerging Capabilities and Applications of Artificial Higher Order Neural Networks
Ming Zhang (Christopher Newport University, USA)
Engineering Science Reference • © 2020 • 346pp • H/C (ISBN: 9781799835639) • US $225.00

Applications of Advanced Machine Intelligence in Computer Vision and Object Recognition Emerging Research and Opportunities
Shouvik Chakraborty (University of Kalyani, India) and Kalyani Mali (University of Kalyani, India)
Engineering Science Reference • © 2020 • 270pp • H/C (ISBN: 9781799827368) • US $195.00

Smart Systems Design, Applications, and Challenges
João M.F. Rodrigues (Universidade do Algarve, Portugal & LARSyS, Institute for Systems and Robotics, Lisbon, Portugal) Pedro J.S. Cardoso (Universidade do Algarve, Portugal & LARSyS, Institute for Systems and Robotics, Lisbon, Portugal) Jânio Monteiro (Universidade do Algarve, Portugal & INESC-ID, Lisbon, Portugal) and Célia M.Q. Ramos (Universidade do Algarve, Portugal & CIEO, Portugal)
Engineering Science Reference • © 2020 • 459pp • H/C (ISBN: 9781799821120) • US $245.00

Deep Learning Applications and Intelligent Decision Making in Engineering
Karthikrajan Senthilnathan (VIT University, India) Balamurugan Shanmugam (Quants IS & CS, India) Dinesh Goyal (Poornima Institute of Engineering and Technology, India) Iyswarya Annapoorani (VIT University, India) and Ravi Samikannu (Botswana International University of Science and Technology, Botswana)
Engineering Science Reference • © 2020 • 335pp • H/C (ISBN: 9781799821083) • US $245.00

Implementing Computational Intelligence Techniques for Security Systems Design
Yousif Abdullatif Albastaki (Ahlia University, Bahrain) and Wasan Awad (Ahlia University, Bahrain)
Information Science Reference • © 2020 • 332pp • H/C (ISBN: 9781799824183) • US $195.00

701 East Chocolate Avenue, Hershey, PA 17033, USA
Tel: 717-533-8845 x100 • Fax: 717-533-8661
E-Mail: cust@igi-global.com • www.igi-global.com

List of Contributors

Abeyrathna, Kuruge Darshana / *Department of Information and Communication Technology, University of Agder, Norway* 63

Alfimtsev, Alexander / *Bauman Moscow State Technical University, Russia* 116

Chen, Junfeng / *Hohai University, China* 27, 277

Cheng, Shi / *Shaanxi Normal University, China* 217, 247, 277, 312, 345

Desai, Veena / *KLS Gogte Institute of Technology, India* 415

Dif, Nassima / *EEDIS Laboratory, Djillali Liabes University, Sidi Bel Abbes, Algeria* 43

Elberrichi, Zakaria / *EEDIS Laboraory, Djillali Liabes University, Sidi Bel Abbes, Algeria* 43

Giuliani, Donatella / *University of Bologna, Italy* 78

Hazra, Sunanda / *Central Institute of Plastics Engineering and Technology, India* 1

J., Sharon Moses / *Vellore Institute of Technology, India* 195

Jeenanunta, Chawalit / *School of Management Technology, Sirindhorn International Institute of Technology, Thammasat University, Thailand* 63

Kalgin, Yuri / *Bauman Moscow State Technical University, Russia* 116

Kareem, Shahab Wahhab / *Erbil Polytechnic University, Iraq* 139

Kulkarni, Raghavendra V. / *M. S. Ramaiah University of Applied Sciences, India* 415

Kulkarni, Vaishali Raghavendra / *M. S. Ramaiah University of Applied Sciences, India* 415

L. D., Dhinesh Babu / *Vellore Institute of Technology, India* 195

M., Nirmala / *Vellore Institute of Technology, India* 195

Mandal, Barun / *Kalyani Government Engineering College, India* 160

Okur, Mehmet Cudi / *Yaşar University, Turkey* 139

Pal, Tandra / *National Institute of Technology, Durgapur, India* 382

Pradhan, Moumita / *Dr. B. C. Roy Engineering College, India* 382

Qin, Quande / *Shenzhen University, China* 277, 312, 345

Roy, Provas Kumar / *Kalyani Government Engineering College, India* 1, 160, 382

Sakulin, Sergey / *Bauman Moscow State Technical University, Russia* 116

Shi, Yuhui / *Southern University of Science and Technology, China* 217, 247, 277, 312, 345

Shindo, Takuya / *Nippon Institute of Technology, Japan* 100

Sikarwar, Akash / *M. S. Ramaiah University of Applied Sciences, India* 415

Srinivasan, Santhoshkumar / *Vellore Institute of Technology, India* 195

Wu, Zhou / *ChongQing University, China* 247

Xue, Xingsi / *Fujian University of Technology, China* 27

Table of Contents

Preface.. xvi

Chapter 1
Newly-Developed Swarm Intelligence Algorithms Applied to Renewable Energy-Based Load
Dispatch Real-World Problems 1
    Sunanda Hazra, Central Institute of Plastics Engineering and Technology, India
    Provas Kumar Roy, Kalyani Government Engineering College, India

Chapter 2
Semi-Automatic Sensor Ontology Matching Based on Interactive Multi-Objective Evolutionary
Algorithm... 27
    Xingsi Xue, Fujian University of Technology, China
    Junfeng Chen, Hohai University, China

Chapter 3
A Comparative Study Among Recursive Metaheuristics for Gene Selection 43
    Nassima Dif, EEDIS Laboratory, Djillali Liabes University, Sidi Bel Abbes, Algeria
    Zakaria Elberrichi, EEDIS Laboraory, Djillali Liabes University, Sidi Bel Abbes, Algeria

Chapter 4
Training Artificial Neural Networks With Improved Particle Swarm Optimization: Case of
Electricity Demand Forecasting in Thailand 63
    Kuruge Darshana Abeyrathna, Department of Information and Communication Technology,
        University of Agder, Norway
    Chawalit Jeenanunta, School of Management Technology, Sirindhorn International Institute
        of Technology, Thammasat University, Thailand

Chapter 5
Segmentation and Edge Extraction of Grayscale Images Using Firefly and Artificial Bee Colony
Algorithms 78
    Donatella Giuliani, University of Bologna, Italy

Chapter 6
Analysis of the Dynamic Characteristics of the Firefly Algorithm 100
    Takuya Shindo, Nippon Institute of Technology, Japan

Chapter 7
Nature-Inspired Usability Optimization..116
    Sergey Sakulin, Bauman Moscow State Technical University, Russia
    Alexander Alfimtsev, Bauman Moscow State Technical University, Russia
    Yuri Kalgin, Bauman Moscow State Technical University, Russia

Chapter 8
Evaluation of Bayesian Network Structure Learning Using Elephant Swarm Water Search
Algorithm...139
    Shahab Wahhab Kareem, Erbil Polytechnic University, Iraq
    Mehmet Cudi Okur, Yaşar University, Turkey

Chapter 9
Multi-Objective Optimal Power Flow of Integrated Renewable Systems Using a Novel
Evolutionary Algorithm...160
    Barun Mandal, Kalyani Government Engineering College, India
    Provas Kumar Roy, Kalyani Government Engineering College, India

Chapter 10
Genetic Algorithm-Influenced Top-N Recommender System to Alleviate the New User Cold Start
Problem..195
    Sharon Moses J., Vellore Institute of Technology, India
    Dhinesh Babu L. D., Vellore Institute of Technology, India
    Santhoshkumar Srinivasan, Vellore Institute of Technology, India
    Nirmala M., Vellore Institute of Technology, India

Chapter 11
Experimental Study on Boundary Constraints Handling in Particle Swarm Optimization...............217
    Shi Cheng, Shaanxi Normal University, China
    Yuhui Shi, Southern University of Science and Technology, China

Chapter 12
Contour Gradient Optimization 247
    Zhou Wu, ChongQing University, China
    Shi Cheng, Shaanxi Normal University, China
    Yuhui Shi, Southern University of Science and Technology, China

Chapter 13
An Analysis of Fireworks Algorithm Solving Problems With Shifts in the Decision Space and
Objective Space...277
    Shi Cheng, Shaanxi Normal University, China
    Junfeng Chen, Hohai University, China
    Quande Qin, Shenzhen University, China
    Yuhui Shi, Southern University of Science and Technology, China

Chapter 14
Population Diversity of Particle Swarm Optimization Algorithm on Solving Single and Multi-Objective Problems 312
    Shi Cheng, Shaanxi Normal University, China
    Yuhui Shi, Southern University of Science and Technology, China
    Quande Qin, Shenzhen University, China

Chapter 15
A Study of Normalized Population Diversity in Particle Swarm Optimization 345
    Shi Cheng, Shaanxi Normal University, China
    Yuhui Shi, Southern University of Science and Technology, China
    Quande Qin, Shenzhen University, China

Chapter 16
Multi-Objective Short-Term Hydro-Thermal Scheduling Using Meta-Heuristic Approaches 382
    Moumita Pradhan, Dr. B. C. Roy Engineering College, India
    Provas Kumar Roy, Kalyani Government Engineering College, India
    Tandra Pal, National Institute of Technology, Durgapur, India

Chapter 17
Mobile Anchor-Assisted Localization Using Invasive Weed Optimization Algorithm 415
    Vaishali Raghavendra Kulkarni, M. S. Ramaiah University of Applied Sciences, India
    Veena Desai, KLS Gogte Institute of Technology, India
    Akash Sikarwar, M. S. Ramaiah University of Applied Sciences, India
    Raghavendra V. Kulkarni, M. S. Ramaiah University of Applied Sciences, India

Compilation of References 437

About the Contributors 476

Index 481

Detailed Table of Contents

Preface.. xvi

Chapter 1
Newly-Developed Swarm Intelligence Algorithms Applied to Renewable Energy-Based Load
Dispatch Real-World Problems 1

Sunanda Hazra, Central Institute of Plastics Engineering and Technology, India
Provas Kumar Roy, Kalyani Government Engineering College, India

Swarm intelligence is a promising field of biologically-inspired artificial intelligence, which is based on the behavioral models of social insects. This article covers Swarm Intelligence Algorithm, i.e., grasshopper optimization algorithm (GOA) which is based on the social communication nature of the grasshopper, applied to renewable energy based economic and emission dispatch problems. Based on Weibull probability density function (W-pdf), the stochastic wind speed including optimization problem is numerically solved for a 2 renewable wind energy incorporating 6 and 14 thermal units for 3 different loads. Moreover, to improve the solution superiority and convergence speed, quasi oppositional based learning (QOBL) is included with the main GOA algorithm. The performance of GOA and QOGOA is evaluated and the simulation results as well as statistical results obtained by these methods along with different other algorithms available in the literature are presented to demonstrate the validity and effectiveness of the proposed GOA and QOGOA schemes for practical applications.

Chapter 2
Semi-Automatic Sensor Ontology Matching Based on Interactive Multi-Objective Evolutionary
Algorithm 27

Xingsi Xue, Fujian University of Technology, China
Junfeng Chen, Hohai University, China

Since different sensor ontologies are developed independently and for different requirements, a concept in one sensor ontology could be described with different terminologies or in different context in another sensor ontology, which leads to the ontology heterogeneity problem. To bridge the semantic gap between the sensor ontologies, authors propose a semi-automatic sensor ontology matching technique based on an Interactive MOEA (IMOEA), which can utilize the user's knowledge to direct MOEA's search direction. In particular, authors construct a new multi-objective optimal model for the sensor ontology matching problem, and design an IMOEA with t-dominance rule to solve the sensor ontology matching problem. In experiments, the benchmark track and anatomy track from the Ontology Alignment Evaluation Initiative (OAEI) and two pairs of real sensor ontologies are used to test performance of the authors' proposal. The experimental results show the effectiveness of the approach.

Chapter 3

A Comparative Study Among Recursive Metaheuristics for Gene Selection 43

Nassima Dif, EEDIS Laboratory, Djillali Liabes University, Sidi Bel Abbes, Algeria

Zakaria Elberrichi, EEDIS Laboraory, Djillali Liabes University, Sidi Bel Abbes, Algeria

This chapter compares 4 variants of metaheuristics (RFA, EMVO, RPSO, and RBAT). The purpose is to test the impact of refinement on different types of metaheuristics (FA, MVO, PSO, and BAT). The refinement helps to enhance exploitation and to speed up the search process in multidimensional spaces. Moreover, it presents a powerful tool to solve different issues such as slow convergence. The different methods have been used for gene selection on 11 microarrays datasets to solve their various issues related to the presence of irrelevant genes. The obtained results reveal the positive impact of refinement on FA, MVO, and PSO, where all performances have been improved. On the other hand, this process harmed the BAT algorithm. The comparative study between the 4 variants highlights the efficiency of EMVO and FA in terms of precision and dimensionality reduction, respectively. Overall, this study suggests drawing attention to the choice of embedded metaheuristics in the refinement procedure, where powerful methods in exploration are recommended. Moreover, metaheuristics that risk form fast convergence are not advised.

Chapter 4

Training Artificial Neural Networks With Improved Particle Swarm Optimization: Case of Electricity Demand Forecasting in Thailand 63

Kuruge Darshana Abeyrathna, Department of Information and Communication Technology, University of Agder, Norway

Chawalit Jeenanunta, School of Management Technology, Sirindhorn International Institute of Technology, Thammasat University, Thailand

Particle Swarm Optimization (PSO) is popular for solving complex optimization problems. However, it easily traps in local minima. Authors modify the traditional PSO algorithm by adding an extra step called PSO-Shock. The PSO-Shock algorithm initiates similar to the PSO algorithm. Once it traps in a local minimum, it is detected by counting stall generations. When stall generation accumulates to a prespecified value, particles are perturbed. This helps particles to find better solutions than the current local minimum they found. The behavior of PSO-Shock algorithm is studied using a known: Schwefel's function. With promising performance on the Schwefel's function, PSO-Shock algorithm is utilized to optimize the weights and bias of Artificial Neural Networks (ANNs). The trained ANNs then forecast electricity consumption in Thailand. The proposed algorithm reduces the forecasting error compared to the traditional training algorithms. The percentage reduction of error is 23.81% compared to the Backpropagation algorithm and 16.50% compared to the traditional PSO algorithm.

Chapter 5

Segmentation and Edge Extraction of Grayscale Images Using Firefly and Artificial Bee Colony Algorithms 78

Donatella Giuliani, University of Bologna, Italy

This chapter proposes an unsupervised grayscale image segmentation method based on the Firefly and Artificial Bee Colony algorithms. The Firefly Algorithm is applied in a histogram-based research of cluster centroids to determine the number of clusters and the gray levels, successively used in the initialization step for the parameter estimation of a Gaussian Mixture Model. The coefficients of the linear superposition of Gaussians can be thought of as prior probabilities of each component. Applying the Bayes rule, the posterior probabilities of the grayscale intensities are evaluated and their maxima are used to assign each pixel to clusters. Subsequently, region spatial information is extracted to form homogeneous regions through ABC algorithm. Initially, scout bees are moving on the search space describing random paths, with food sources given by the detected homogeneous regions. Then onlooker bees rush to scouts' aid proportionally to unclassified pixels enclosed into the bounded boxes of the discovered regions.

Chapter 6

Analysis of the Dynamic Characteristics of the Firefly Algorithm 100
Takuya Shindo, Nippon Institute of Technology, Japan

The firefly algorithm is a meta-heuristic algorithm, the fundamental principle of which mimics the characteristics associated with the blinking of natural fireflies. This chapter presents a rigorous analysis of the dynamics of the firefly algorithm, which the authors performed by applying a deterministic system that removes the stochastic factors from the state update equation. Depending on its parameters, the individual deterministic firefly algorithm exhibits chaotic behavior. This prompted us to investigate the relationship between the behavior of the algorithm and its parameters as well as the extent to which the chaotic behavior influences the searching ability of the algorithm.

Chapter 7

Nature-Inspired Usability Optimization 116
Sergey Sakulin, Bauman Moscow State Technical University, Russia
Alexander Alfimtsev, Bauman Moscow State Technical University, Russia
Yuri Kalgin, Bauman Moscow State Technical University, Russia

Nature-inspired algorithms have come into use to solve more and more optimization tasks of high dimension when classical optimization algorithms do not apply. The task of user interface usability optimization becomes the one to be solved by nature-inspired algorithms. Usability optimization suggests a choice of interface design out of a large number of variants. At that, there is no common technique to determine the objective function of such optimization that would lead to the invitation of highly qualified specialists to implement it. The chapter presents a new approach of automatic interface usability optimization. The approach is based on the template employment as well as nature-inspired algorithms such as genetic algorithm (GA), artificial bee colony (ABC) algorithm, and charged system search (CSS) algorithm, bacterial foraging optimization (BFO) algorithm, and cuckoo search (CS) algorithm that are analyzed in the chapter. The results of the experiments have discovered research prospects and new features of the algorithms' application for the set task.

Chapter 8

Evaluation of Bayesian Network Structure Learning Using Elephant Swarm Water Search
Algorithm 139
Shahab Wahhab Kareem, Erbil Polytechnic University, Iraq
Mehmet Cudi Okur, Yaşar University, Turkey

Bayesian networks are useful analytical models for designing the structure of knowledge in machine learning which can represent probabilistic dependency relationships among the variables. The authors present the Elephant Swarm Water Search Algorithm (ESWSA) for Bayesian network structure learning. In the algorithm; Deleting, Reversing, Inserting, and Moving are used to make the ESWSA for reaching the optimal structure solution. Mainly, water search strategy of elephants during drought periods is used in the ESWSA algorithm. The proposed method is compared with Pigeon Inspired Optimization, Simulated Annealing, Greedy Search, Hybrid Bee with Simulated Annealing, and Hybrid Bee with Greedy Search using BDeu score function as a metric for all algorithms. They investigated the confusion matrix performances of these techniques utilizing various benchmark data sets. As presented by the results of evaluations, the proposed algorithm achieves better performance than the other algorithms and produces better scores as well as the better values.

Chapter 9
Multi-Objective Optimal Power Flow of Integrated Renewable Systems Using a Novel
Evolutionary Algorithm 160
    Barun Mandal, Kalyani Government Engineering College, India
    Provas Kumar Roy, Kalyani Government Engineering College, India

This chapter introduces an approach to explain optimal power flow (OPF) for stochastic wind and conventional thermal power generators-based system. In this chapter, grasshopper optimization algorithm (GOA) is implemented to efficiently prove its superiority for solving wind-based OPF problem. Diminishing carbon emissions is a significant goal for the entire world; a tremendous penetration of unpredictable wind energy can assist in reducing emissions. In the previous decade, the access of renewable energy opening for energy production has improved significantly. WE has become an important source that has begun to be used for energy all over the world in recent years. The optimal dispatch between thermal and wind units to minimize the total generating costs and emission are considered as multi-objective (MO) model. In MO optimization, whole electrical energy generation costs and burning emissions are concurrently minimized. The performance of aforesaid approach is exercised and it proves itself as a superior technique as compared to other algorithms revealed in the literature.

Chapter 10
Genetic Algorithm-Influenced Top-N Recommender System to Alleviate the New User Cold Start
Problem 195
    Sharon Moses J., Vellore Institute of Technology, India
    Dhinesh Babu L. D., Vellore Institute of Technology, India
    Santhoshkumar Srinivasan, Vellore Institute of Technology, India
    Nirmala M., Vellore Institute of Technology, India

Most recommender systems are based on the familiar collaborative filtering algorithm to suggest items. Quite often, collaborative filtering algorithm fails in generating recommendations due to the lack of adequate user information resulting in new user cold start problem. Cold start problem is one of the prevailing issues in recommendation system where the system fails to render recommendation. To overcome the new user cold start issue, demographical information of the user is utilised as the user information source. Among the demographical information, the impact of user gender is less explored when compared with other information like age, profession, region, etc. In this chapter, genetic algorithm influenced gender-based top-n recommender algorithm is proposed to address the new user cold start problem. The algorithm utilises the evolution concepts of genetic algorithm to render top-n recommendations to a new user. The evaluation of the proposed algorithm using real world datasets proved that the algorithm has a better efficiency than the state-of-art approaches.

Chapter 11
Experimental Study on Boundary Constraints Handling in Particle Swarm Optimization 217
Shi Cheng, Shaanxi Normal University, China
Yuhui Shi, Southern University of Science and Technology, China

With an improper boundary constraints handling method, particles may get "stuck in" the boundary. Premature convergence means that an algorithm has lost its ability of exploration. Population diversity (PD) is an effective way to monitor an algorithm's ability for exploration and exploitation. Through the PD measurement, useful search information can be obtained. PSO with a different topology structure and different boundary constraints handling strategy will have a different impact on particles' exploration and exploitation ability. In this chapter, the phenomenon of particles gets "stuck in" the boundary in PSO and is experimentally studied and reported. The authors observe the position diversity time-changing curves of PSOs with different topologies and different boundary constraints handling techniques and analyze the impact of these strategies on the algorithm's ability of exploration and exploitation.

Chapter 12
Contour Gradient Optimization 247
Zhou Wu, ChongQing University, China
Shi Cheng, Shaanxi Normal University, China
Yuhui Shi, Southern University of Science and Technology, China

Inspired by local cooperation in the real world, a new evolutionary algorithm, Contour Gradient Optimization algorithm (CGO), is proposed for solving optimization problems. CGO is a new type of population-based algorithm that emulates the cooperation among neighbors. Each individual in CGO evolves in its neighborhood environment to find a better region. Each individual moves with a velocity measured by the field of its nearest individuals. The field includes the attractive forces from its better neighbor in the higher contour level and the repulsive force from its worse neighbor in the lower contour level. In this chapter, CGO is compared with six different widely used optimization algorithms, and comparative analysis shows that CGO is better than these algorithms in respect of accuracy and effectiveness.

Chapter 13
An Analysis of Fireworks Algorithm Solving Problems With Shifts in the Decision Space and Objective Space 277
Shi Cheng, Shaanxi Normal University, China
Junfeng Chen, Hohai University, China
Quande Qin, Shenzhen University, China
Yuhui Shi, Southern University of Science and Technology, China

Fireworks algorithms for solving problems with the optima shifts in the decision space and/or objective space are analyzed. The standard benchmark problems have several weaknesses in the research of swarm intelligence algorithms for solving single-objective problems. The optimum shift in decision space and/or objective space will increase the difficulty of problem-solving. Modular arithmetic mapping is utilized in the original fireworks algorithm to handle solutions out of the search range. The solutions are implicitly guided to the center of search range for problems with symmetrical search range via this strategy. The optimization performance of the fireworks algorithm on shift functions may be affected by this strategy. Four kinds of mapping strategies are compared with different problems. The fireworks algorithms with mapping to the boundary or mapping to a limited stochastic region obtain good performance on problems with the optimum shift.

Chapter 14
Population Diversity of Particle Swarm Optimization Algorithm on Solving Single and Multi-
Objective Problems 312

Shi Cheng, Shaanxi Normal University, China
Yuhui Shi, Southern University of Science and Technology, China
Quande Qin, Shenzhen University, China

Premature convergence occurs in swarm intelligence algorithms searching for optima. A swarm intelligence algorithm has two kinds of abilities: the exploration of new possibilities and the exploitation of old certainties. The exploration ability means that an algorithm can explore more search places to increase the possibility that the algorithm can find good enough solutions. In contrast, the exploitation ability means that an algorithm focuses on the refinement of found promising areas. An algorithm should have a balance between exploration and exploitation, that is, the allocation of computational resources should be optimized to ensure that an algorithm can find good enough solutions effectively. The diversity measures the distribution of individuals' information. From the observation of the distribution and diversity change, the degree of exploration and exploitation can be obtained.

Chapter 15
A Study of Normalized Population Diversity in Particle Swarm Optimization 345

Shi Cheng, Shaanxi Normal University, China
Yuhui Shi, Southern University of Science and Technology, China
Quande Qin, Shenzhen University, China

The values and velocities of a Particle swarm optimization (PSO) algorithm can be recorded as a series of matrix and its population diversity can be considered as an observation of the distribution of matrix elements. Each dimension is measured separately in the dimension-wise diversity. On the contrary, the element-wise diversity measures all dimensions together. In this chapter, the PSO algorithm is first represented in the matrix format. Then, based on the analysis of the relationship between pairs of vectors in the PSO solution matrix, different normalization strategies are utilized for dimension-wise and element-wise population diversity, respectively. Experiments on benchmark functions are conducted. Based on the simulation results of 10 benchmark functions (including unimodal/multimodal function, separable/non-separable function), the properties of normalized population diversities are analyzed and discussed.

Chapter 16
Multi-Objective Short-Term Hydro-Thermal Scheduling Using Meta-Heuristic Approaches 382

Moumita Pradhan, Dr. B. C. Roy Engineering College, India
Provas Kumar Roy, Kalyani Government Engineering College, India
Tandra Pal, National Institute of Technology, Durgapur, India

Every day humans face new challenges to survive in this world. It is a big challenge to utilize hydro and thermal generating unit properly. Researchers are trying to explore new techniques to improve scheduling of generating units. Environmental matter is a big issue to modern society. This chapter suggests a well-organized and effective approach using concept of grey wolf optimization (GWO) to deal with non-linear, multi-objective, short-term, hydro-thermal scheduling (MOHTS) problem. Moreover, authors have incorporated oppositional based learning (OBL) to enhance characteristics of GWO to achieve solution more consistently and accurately. To explore authenticity of our proposed algorithms, GWO and OGWO (oppositional based GWO) are applied to multi-chain cascade of 4-hydro and 3-thermal test system.

Effective constraints like valve-point loading, water discharge, water storage, etc., are considered here. Statistical comparisons with other enlisted heuristic methods are done. The projected methods solve MOHTS problem quickly and efficiently.

Chapter 17
Mobile Anchor-Assisted Localization Using Invasive Weed Optimization Algorithm......................415
    Vaishali Raghavendra Kulkarni, M. S. Ramaiah University of Applied Sciences, India
    Veena Desai, KLS Gogte Institute of Technology, India
    Akash Sikarwar, M. S. Ramaiah University of Applied Sciences, India
    Raghavendra V. Kulkarni, M. S. Ramaiah University of Applied Sciences, India

Sensor localization in wireless sensor networks has been addressed using mobile anchor (MA) and a metaheuristic algorithm. The path of a MA plays an important role in localizing maximum number of sensor nodes. The random and circle path planning methods have been presented. Each method has been evaluated for number of localized nodes, accuracy, and computing time in localization. The localization has been performed using trilateration method and two metaheuristic stochastic algorithms, namely invasive weed optimization (IWO) and cultural algorithm (CA). Experimental results indicate that the IWO-based localization outperforms the trilateration method and the CA-based localization in terms of accuracy but with higher computing time. However, the computing speed of trilateration localization is faster than the IWO- and CA-based localization. In the path-planning algorithms, the results show that the circular path planning algorithm localizes more nodes than the random path.

Compilation of References 437

About the Contributors 476

Index..481

Preface

Optimization, in general, is concerned with finding "best available" solution(s) for a given problem. An optimization problem in R^n, or simply an optimization problem is a mapping $f: R^n \rightarrow R^m$, where R^n is termed as decision space (or parameter space, problem space), and R^m is termed as objective space. Each solution in decision space is associated with a fitness value or a vector of fitness values in objective space.

Optimization problems can be divided into different categories according to the value of m. When $m=1$, this kind of problem is called a single objective problem, when $m=2$ or $m=3$, this is called multi-objective problem, and when $m \geq 4$, this is called many-objective optimization problems. Single-objective optimization problems can be simply divided into unimodal problems and multimodal problems. As the name indicated, the unimodal problem has only one optimum solution, on the contrary, multi-modal functions have several or numerous optimum solutions, of which many are local optimal solutions. It is difficult for optimization algorithms to find the global optimum solution.

The optimization problems also could be divided into categories differently, such as multimodal optimization, dynamic optimization, discrete optimization, multiobjective optimization, etc. The term "multimodal" or "multimode" has a different meaning in single-objective optimization and multimodal optimization. Single objective optimization problems concerns finding the maximum or minimum of a fitness function. A multimodal problem in single-objective optimization indicates that a problem has multiple local optima and one global optimum. Solving a multimodal problem is to find the global optimum, and to jump out of local optima. Unlike the single-objective optimization, the goal of multimodal optimization is to track multiple global/local optima in a single run. These found optima should be maintained until the end of a run (Parrott, 2006; Rönkkönen, 2009; Li, 2010). The search strategy from solving one kind of optimization problem could be transferred to other kinds of optimization problems. For example, a multimodal optimization problem could be solved as a multiobjective problem (Song, 2015; Wang, 2015) and the strategy in the multimodal optimization could be used in the large-scale optimization. New problems, which combine the multimodal optimization and other kinds of optimization, are more difficult to solve with current techniques. For example, the solutions for multimodal multiobjective problems should have good distributions in both the objective and the decision spaces (Yue, 2018).

THE CHALLENGES

Many real-world problems could be modeled as optimization problems and solved by using optimization algorithms. These problems often have several conflicting objectives to be optimized. For example, different factors, which include economic benefits, production efficiency, energy consumption, and environmental protection, need to be optimized simultaneously in the steel production industry (Tang, 2014). Having many factors makes an optimization problem difficult to solve. For example, such challenges can be listed as follows:

- The functions have non-linear, non-quadratic, non-convex, non-smooth, discontinuous, multi-modal, and/or noisy environment properties;
- The dimensionality of optimization problems is extremely large. In addition, the non-separability dependencies or partially non-separability dependencies between the variables for problems with a huge number of dimensions;
- Several conflicted objectives are needed to be optimized for optimization problems to be solved simultaneously.

SEARCHING FOR A SOLUTION

Swarm intelligence, which studies the collective intelligence in a population of simple individuals, is a group of nature-inspired searching and optimization techniques (Kennedy, 2001). The swarm intelligence algorithms are inspired by the interaction among individuals within a group or several groups, which involves the patterns of competition and cooperation. Especially, the interactive behaviors of individuals in the group, such as a flock of birds or a cluster of ants, are modeled as an optimization process.

A set of successful swarm intelligence algorithms have been proposed, promising examples being the particle swarm optimization (PSO) algorithm (Kennedy, 1995), which was originally designed for solving continuous optimization problems, and the ant colony system (ACS) algorithm, which was originally designed for discrete optimization problems (Dorigo, 1997).

Taking a brain storm optimization (BSO) algorithm as an example, the BSO algorithm is not only a simple optimization method but also could be viewed as a framework of optimization technique (Shi, 2011; Cheng, & Shi, 2019). The BSO algorithm has a similar framework with the genetic algorithm. The differences are solution grouping (solution clustering/classification) strategy and solution generation strategy. The BSO algorithm could be simplified as a framework with two basic operations: the converging operation and the diverging operation. Solutions are diverged into the decision space by diverging operation while clustered together by converging operation. Based on performing these two operations iteratively, more representative solutions could be obtained to reveal the landscapes of the solved problems.

Different algorithms could be summarized as a framework to analyze their common properties. Based on the framework, it could give a better understanding of algorithms and guide designing or implementing a new strategy. There are several most used frameworks, such as memetic computing methodologies, cultural algorithms, and developmental swarm intelligence (DSI) algorithms (Shi, 2014), etc. A developmental swarm intelligence algorithm is defined as a swarm intelligence algorithm with both capability learning ability and capacity developing ability (Shi, 2014).

This book aims to present a collection of recent advances in swarm intelligence algorithms for solving real-world optimization problems. Based on a peer-review process, seventeen chapters were accepted to be included in the book, covering various topics ranging from variants of swarm intelligence algorithms, theoretical analysis, and applications.

ORGANIZATION OF THE BOOK

To enhance the diversity of research topics, seventeen chapters from nine countries are selected in this collection book. Most chapters have been published in the 2017, 2018, and 2019 volume years of the International Journal of Swarm Intelligence Research. Each selected chapter has been revised and enhanced to give an illustration of the advancements of swarm intelligence algorithms on solving real-world problems. The book is organized into seventeen chapters. A brief description of each of the chapters follows:

Chapter 1 introduces newly developed swarm intelligence algorithms on solving renewable energy-based load dispatch real-world problems. This chapter covers the Swarm Intelligence Algorithm i.e. grasshopper optimization algorithm (GOA) which is based on the social communication nature of the grasshopper, applied to renewable energy-based economic and emission dispatch problems. Based on the Weibull probability density function (W-pdf), the stochastic wind speed including the optimization problem is numerically solved for two renewable wind energy incorporating six and fourteen thermal units for three different loads.

Chapter 2 designs a semi-automatic sensor ontology matching based on an interactive multi-objective evolutionary algorithm. To bridge the semantic gap between the sensor ontologies, in this work, a semi-automatic sensor ontology matching technique was proposed based on an Interactive MOEA (IMOEA), which can utilize the user's knowledge to direct MOEA's search direction. In particular, a new multi-objective optimal model was constructed for the sensor ontology matching problem, and design an IMOEA with the t-dominance rule to solve the sensor ontology matching problem.

Chapter 3 takes a comparative study between recursive metaheuristics for gene selection. In this chapter, four variants of metaheuristics (RFA, EMVO, RPSO, and RBAT) are compared. The purpose of this investigation is to test the impact of refinement on different types of metaheuristics (FA, MVO, PSO, and BAT). The refinement helps to enhance exploitation and to speed up the search process in multidimensional spaces. The different methods have been used for gene selection on 11 microarrays datasets to solve their various issues related to the presence of irrelevant genes.

Chapter 4 reports using an improved particle swarm optimization for training artificial neural networks, and a case of electricity demand forecasting in Thailand is stated. A modified particle swarm optimization (PSO) algorithm by adding an extra step and called PSO-Shock was proposed in this chapter. The PSO-Shock algorithm initiates similar to the PSO algorithm. Once it traps at a local minimum, it is detected by counting stall generations. When stall generation accumulates to a prespecified value, particles are perturbed. This helps particles to find better solutions than the current local minimum they found. The behavior of the PSO-Shock algorithm is studied using a known Schwefel's function. With promising performance on the Schwefel's function, PSO-Shock algorithm is utilized to optimize the weights and bias of Artificial Neural Networks (ANNs). The trained ANNs then forecast electricity consumption in Thailand. The proposed algorithm is able to reduce the forecasting error compared to the traditional training algorithms.

Chapter 5 introduces the using firefly and artificial bee colony algorithms for segmentation and edge extraction of grayscale images. In this chapter, an unsupervised grayscale image segmentation method was proposed based on the Firefly and Artificial Bee Colony algorithms.

Chapter 6 reports the analysis of the dynamical characteristics of the firefly algorithm. The firefly algorithm is a meta-heuristic algorithm, the fundamental principle of which mimic the characteristics associated with the blinking of natural fireflies. This chapter presents a rigorous analysis of the dynamics of the firefly algorithm, which the authors performed by applying a deterministic system that removes the stochastic factors from the state update equation.

Chapter 7 reviews the nature-inspired usability optimization. Nature-inspired algorithms have come in use to solve more and more optimization tasks of high dimension when classical optimization algorithms are not applicable. The task of user interface usability optimization becomes the one to be solved by nature-inspired algorithms. Usability optimization suggests a choice of interface design out of a big number of variants. At that, there is no common technique to determine the objective function of such optimization that would lead to the invitation of highly qualified specialists to implement it. The chapter presents a new approach to automatic interface usability optimization. The approach is based on the template employment as well as nature-inspired algorithms, such as genetic algorithm (GA), artificial bee colony (ABC) algorithm, charged system search (CSS) algorithm, bacterial foraging optimization (BFO) algorithm, and cuckoo search (CS) algorithm that are analyzed in the chapter.

Chapter 8 reports using an elephant swarm water search algorithm on the evaluation of bayesian network structure learning. Bayesian networks are useful analytical models for designing the structure of knowledge in machine learning which can represent probabilistic dependency relationships among the variables. The Elephant Swarm Water Search Algorithm (ESWSA) was proposed for Bayesian network structure learning. In the algorithm, Deleting, Reversing, Inserting, and Moving are used to make the ESWSA for reaching the optimal structure solution. Mainly, the water search strategy of elephants during drought periods is used in the ESWSA algorithm. The proposed method is compared with Pigeon Inspired Optimization, Simulated Annealing, Greedy Search, Hybrid Bee with Simulated Annealing, and Hybrid Bee with Greedy Search using BDe score function as a metric for all algorithms.

Chapter 9 designs an evolutionary algorithm for solving multi-objective optimal power flow of an integrated renewable system. This chapter introduces an approach to explain optimal power flow (OPF) for stochastic wind and conventional thermal power generators based system. In this study, the grasshopper optimization algorithm (GOA) is implemented to efficiently prove its superiority for solving wind-based OPF problem.

Chapter 10 designs a genetic algorithm based top-N recommender system to alleviate new user cold-start problems. Most recommender systems are based on the familiar collaborative filtering algorithm to suggest items. Quite often, a collaborative filtering algorithm fails in generating recommendations due to the lack of adequate user information resulting in a new user cold-start problem. Cold start problem is one of the prevailing issues in the recommendation system where the system fails to render a recommendation. To overcome the new user cold start issue, demographical information of the user is utilized as the user information source. Among the demographical information, the impact of user gender is less explored when compared with other information like age, profession, region, etc. In this work, a genetic algorithm influenced gender-based top-N recommender algorithm is proposed to address the new user cold start problem. The algorithm utilises the evolution concepts of genetic algorithm to render top-N recommendations to a new user.

Chapter 11 gives an experimental study on boundary constraints handling in particle swarm optimization algorithms. In this chapter, the position diversity time-changing curves of PSOs with different topologies and different boundary constraints handling techniques are monitored and analyzed. From the experimental studies, an algorithm's ability to explore and exploit can be observed and the search information obtained; therefore, more effective algorithms can be designed to solve problems.

Chapter 12 presents the advancements of contour gradient optimization (CGO) algorithms. In this Chapter, CGO is compared with six different widely used optimization algorithms, and comparative analysis shows that CGO is better than these algorithms in the respect of accuracy and effectiveness.

Chapter 13 gives an analysis of fireworks algorithms on solving problems with shifts in the decision space and objective space. Four kinds of mapping strategies are compared on problems with different dimensions and different optimum shift ranges in this Chapter. From experimental results, the fireworks algorithms with mapping to the boundary or mapping to a limited stochastic region obtain good performance on problems with the optimum shift.

Chapter 14 discusses the population diversity definitions and measurements of particle swarm optimization algorithms for solving single and multi-objective problems. The population diversity of particle swarm optimizer for solving both single objective and multiobjective problems was analyzed in this chapter. The population diversity of solutions is used to measure the goodness of a set of solutions. This metric may guide the search in problems with numerous objectives.

Chapter 15 presents a study of normalized population diversity in particle swarm optimization. In this chapter, the PSO algorithm is first represented in the matrix format, then based on the analysis of the relationship between pairs of vectors in the PSO solution matrix, different normalization strategies are utilized for dimension-wise and element-wise population diversity, respectively. Experiments on benchmark functions are conducted. Based on the simulation results of ten benchmark functions (include unimodal/multimodal function, separable/non-separable function), the properties of normalized population diversities are analyzed and discussed.

Chapter 16 introduces using meta-heuristic approaches for solving multi-objective short-term hydro-thermal scheduling *(MOHTS)* problems. In this chapter, a well-organized and effective approach using the concept of grey wolf optimization (GWO) is suggested to deal with non-linear multi-objective short-term hydro-thermal scheduling problems.

Chapter 17 presents using an invasive weed optimization (IWO) algorithm for solving mobile anchor assisted localization problems. The random and circle path planning methods have been presented. Each method has been evaluated for a number of localized nodes, accuracy and computing time in localization. The localization has been performed using the trilateration method and two metaheuristic stochastic algorithms namely, invasive weed optimization and cultural algorithm (CA). Experimental results indicate that the IWO-based localization outperforms the trilateration method and the CA-based localization in terms of accuracy but with higher computing time.

We wish to express our sincere gratitude to all the authors of this book who have put in so much effort to prepare their manuscripts, sharing their research findings as a chapter in this book. Based on a compilation of chapters in this book, it is clear that the authors have done a stupendous job, each chapter directly or indirectly hitting on the spot certain pertinent aspects of swarm intelligence algorithms. As editors of this book, we have been very fortunate to have a team of Editorial Board members who besides offering useful suggestions and comments, helped to review manuscripts submitted for consideration. Finally, we would like to put in no definitive order our acknowledgments of the various parties who played a part in the successful production of this book:

- Authors who contributed insightful and technically engaging chapters in this book;
- The panel of experts in swarm intelligence algorithms that form editorial board members.
- The publisher, who has been very helpful and accommodating, making our tasks a little easier.

This work was supported by National Natural Science Foundation of China (Grant Nos. 61806119, 61761136008, and 61773103), and Natural Science Basic Research Plan In Shaanxi Province of China (Grant No. 2019JM-320)

Shi Cheng
Shaanxi Normal University, China

Yuhui Shi
Southern University of Science and Technology, China

REFERENCES

Cheng, S., & Shi, Y. (2019). Brain Storm Optimization Algorithms: Concepts, Principles and Applications, ser. Adaptation, Learning, and Optimization. Springer International Publishing AG, 2019, vol. 23.

Dorigo, M., & Gambardella, L. M. (1997). Ant colony system: A cooperative learning approach to the traveling salesman problem. *IEEE Transactions on Evolutionary Computation*, *1*(1), 53–66. doi:10.1109/4235.585892

Kennedy, J., & Eberhart, R. (1995). Particle swarm optimization. *Proceedings of IEEE International Conference on Neural Networks*, pp. 1942-1948. 10.1109/ICNN.1995.488968

Kennedy, J., Eberhart, R., & Shi, Y. (2001). *Swarm Intelligence*. San Francisco, CA: Morgan Kaufmann.

Li, X. (2010). Niching without niching parameters: Particle swarm optimization using a ring topology. *IEEE Transactions on Evolutionary Computation*, *14*(1), 150–169. doi:10.1109/TEVC.2009.2026270

Parrott, D., & Li, X. (2006). Locating and tracking multiple dynamic optima by a particle swarm model using speciation. *IEEE Transactions on Evolutionary Computation*, *10*(4), 440–458. doi:10.1109/TEVC.2005.859468

Rönkkönen, J. (2009). Continuous Multimodal Global Optimization with Differential Evolution-Based Methods. [Ph.D. thesis], Lappeenranta University of Technology.

Shi, Y. (2011). An optimization algorithm based on brainstorming process. [IJSIR]. *International Journal of Swarm Intelligence Research*, *2*(4), 35–62. doi:10.4018/ijsir.2011100103

Shi, Y. (2014). Developmental swarm intelligence: Developmental learning perspective of swarm intelligence algorithms. [IJSIR]. *International Journal of Swarm Intelligence Research*, *5*(1), 36–54. doi:10.4018/ijsir.2014010102

Song, W., Wang, Y., Li, H.-X., & Cai, Z. (2015). Locating multiple optimal solutions of nonlinear equation systems based on multiobjective optimization. *IEEE Transactions on Evolutionary Computation*, *19*(3), 414–431. doi:10.1109/TEVC.2014.2336865

Tang, L., Zhao, Y., & Liu, J. (2014). An improved differential evolution algorithm for practical dynamic scheduling in steelmaking-continuous casting production. *IEEE Transactions on Evolutionary Computation*, *18*(2), 209–225. doi:10.1109/TEVC.2013.2250977

Wang, Y., Li, H.-X., Yen, G. G., & Song, W. (2015). MOMMOP: Multiobjective optimization for locating multiple optimal solutions of multimodal optimization problems. *IEEE Transactions on Cybernetics*, *45*(4), 830–843. doi:10.1109/TCYB.2014.2337117 PMID:25099966

Yue, C., Qu, B., & Liang, J. (2018). A multiobjective particle swarm optimizer using ring topology for solving multimodal multiobjective problems. *IEEE Transactions on Evolutionary Computation*, *22*(5), 805–817. doi:10.1109/TEVC.2017.2754271

Chapter 1
Newly–Developed Swarm Intelligence Algorithms Applied to Renewable Energy–Based Load Dispatch Real–World Problems

Sunanda Hazra
Central Institute of Plastics Engineering and Technology, India

Provas Kumar Roy
 https://orcid.org/0000-0002-3433-5808
Kalyani Government Engineering College, India

ABSTRACT

Swarm intelligence is a promising field of biologically-inspired artificial intelligence, which is based on the behavioral models of social insects. This article covers Swarm Intelligence Algorithm, i.e., grasshopper optimization algorithm (GOA) which is based on the social communication nature of the grasshopper, applied to renewable energy based economic and emission dispatch problems. Based on Weibull probability density function (W-pdf), the stochastic wind speed including optimization problem is numerically solved for a 2 renewable wind energy incorporating 6 and 14 thermal units for 3 different loads. Moreover, to improve the solution superiority and convergence speed, quasi oppositional based learning (QOBL) is included with the main GOA algorithm. The performance of GOA and QOGOA is evaluated and the simulation results as well as statistical results obtained by these methods along with different other algorithms available in the literature are presented to demonstrate the validity and effectiveness of the proposed GOA and QOGOA schemes for practical applications.

DOI: 10.4018/978-1-7998-3222-5.ch001

INTRODUCTION

The addition of renewable energy sources in power systems is rising, with the increase in fossil fuel prices and due to excessive environmental degradation from the greenhouse gases i.e. global warming. Wind energy is a nondepleting, low cost and environment friendly source of renewable energy.

Economic load dispatch (ELD) is a technique to allocate the generating units according to the load demand and to minimize operating cost. ELD (Hazra et al. 2015) with consideration of carbon emission tax and integration of renewable source is a recent trend and an emerging technology. In this paper, economic load dispatch of six and fourteen conventional thermal generators under different loading condition is performed, with and without tax imposed on carbon emission. Afterward, two windmills are included in the system and ELD is performed with and without considering carbon emission tax. Wind power is readily available in nature, but due to its uncertain and stochastic characteristics, it creates challenges in the load dispatch model. As wind speed variation controls windmill outputs, so wind power forecasting errors will bring a major problem while estimating system reserve margin to provide the guarantee of secure and reliable operation. The uncontrolled penetration of wind power is risky for a power system as it may bring out difficulties. If the errors of forecasting generated by different methods have a low degree of correlation among each other, the random error from the individual forecasts will tend to offset each other with the result thus forecasting will have very fewer errors than individual forecast. Wind power generally follows Weibull distribution shown in so many papers (Roy et al. 2015). In several articles (Liu, and Xu, 2010; Hetzer et al. 2008), probabilistic optimization strategies are used to deal with wind power uncertainty.

Ero glu et al. (2013) implemented wind farm layout optimization by using particle filtering (PF) and ant colony optimization (ACO) approach accordingly. Chen et al. (2015) propose distribution management oriented renewable energy generation using different interval optimization. Hazra et al. (2019) approaches towards the economical operation of a hybrid systems which consist of conventional thermal generators and renewable energy sources. Jin et al. (2016) proposed optimal day-ahead scheduling of integrated urban energy systems considering the reconfigurable capability.

A meta-heuristic is an iterative technique that helps to find out the near-optimal solution in a more efficient way. The objective of this method is to enlarge the aptitude of heuristics by joining more and more heuristic method. Due to the significant achievements of meta-heuristics approaches in solving different kinds of non-linear optimization problems, interest has been gradually shifted to applications of population-based approaches to handling the complexity involved in the nonlinear problem. It is proved that population based metaheuristics method is used to speed up the search process as well as to get optimal solution. Recently, so many researchers have expressed their interest in solving load dispatch problems with constraint using evolutionary algorithms such as differential evolution (DE) (Bhattacharya & Chattopadhyay, 2010), genetic algorithm(GA) (Chung, & Chan, 2012), Particle swarm optimization PSO (Meng et al. 2010), evolutionary programming (EP) (Vlachogiannis, & Lee, 2008), pattern search(PS) (Al-Sumait et al. 2007), simulated annealing (SA) (Precup et al. 2012) and tabu search(TS) (Lin, 2010).

HS is a recently developed meta-heuristic optimization strategy which is inspired by musicians to improve the harmony their instruments. HS algorithm has several impressive advantages, such as easy implementation, less adjustable parameters, and quick convergence. But HS algorithm still has some defects such as premature convergence and slow convergence speed (Seok & Woo, 2017). The authors of the paper (Qu et al., 2017) implemented HSA in finding out the effect of fuel cell units in the economic and environmental dispatch of a Microgrid with penetration of photovoltaic and micro-turbine units. TS is a meta-heuristic approach which is based on the method of adaptive memory and responsive exploration that starts searching the solution space economically and efficiently until any improvement is reached. The advantage of TS technique is that, it can have explicit memory as well as it can be applied to the discrete and continuous type variable. Disadvantages of this method is that it is depended on technique for tabu list manipulation, and often makes the search heuristic converge prematurely, or get stuck in local minima, but to find the global optimum a single generation with the maximum possible number of evaluations or reliable parameter setting is preferred. In the paper (Golshan, & Arefifar, 2006), Golshan used TS algorithm in the field of Distributed generation, reactive sources and network-configuration planning for power and energy-loss reduction. Ant colony optimization (ACO) is inspired by the socio-economic behavior of insects such as ants in order to find their food. The benefit of ACO method is that, it can have inherent parallelism and positive feedback accounts for rapid discovery of good solutions as well as it can be used in dynamic applications also. Some disadvantages are that probabilistic distribution may be changed for each iteration, and theoretical analysis is very difficult (Dorigo & Stutzle, 2004).In the paper (Falaghi & Haghifam, 2007) authors have applied ACO algorithm for the allocation of distributed generation sources and sizing in distribution systems. PSO is inspired by the social behavior of bird flocking and fish schooling. Its advantages are, PSO have no overlapping and mutation calculation that's why speed of the execution is very fast and calculation in PSO is very simple. The main disadvantages of old methods are that,final solution is dependent on the initially chosen random solution,that's why old techniquesdoes not usually produce an optimal solution because initial parameters cannot work out the complex problems. In this paper (Mohamed et al. 2017), authors present a proposed particle swarm optimization (PSO) algorithm for an optimized design of grid-dependent hybrid photovoltaic-wind energy systems.

Recently, Wu et al. (Wu et al., 2013) addressed a stochastic framework considering the uncertainties of wind power generation as well as the statistical plug-in electric vehicles driving patterns. Firouzi et al. (Firouzi, Farjah, & Abarghooee, 2013) applied the dynamic economic emission dispatch problem by incorporating wind power plant with the power system. To evaluate the feasibility and efficiency of the suggested framework, it was applied to a small and a large-scale power system. Bai et al. in their current research work proposed artificial bee colony (ABC) (Bai & Lee, 2016) to tackle the uncertainty of wind power in order to solve ELD problem. Arabali et al. (Arabali, Ghofrani, & Amoli, 2013) examined the storage application and its optimal placement for the social cost and transmission congestion relief of wind integration. The proposed method was successfully applied to carry out a cost-benefit analysis of the IEEE 24-bus system. Hetzer et al. (Hetzer, Yu, & Bhattrarai, 2008) briefly discussed the overestimation cost and underestimation cost of available wind power generation. Zhao et al. developed a new algorithm based on the well-established particle swarm optimization (PSO) and interior point method to solve the economic dispatch model (Zhao, et al., 2012), and the mathematical expectations of the generation costs of wind power and V2G (vehicle to grid) power are then derived analytically. Alham et al. (Alham, et al. 2016) proposed a dynamic economic emission dispatch (DEED) model incorporating high wind penetration uncertainty. Dubey et al. (Dubey, Pandit, & Panigrahi, 2015)studied hybrid flower pollination algorithm (HFPA)to solve dynamic multi-objective optimal dispatch (DMOOD) for the wind-based hybrid power system. Chen et al.(Chen et al.,2016)studied a robust hydro-thermal-wind economic dispatch (HTW-ED) method to enhance the flexibility and reliability of power system operation. The proposed HTW-ED was found to be superior to the existing hydro-thermal-wind economic dispatch approach. Hu et al.(Hu et al. 2016) applied a new formulation for the dynamic economic emission dispatch (DEED) based on robust optimization (RO) and bi-level programming (BLP) in the background of large-scale wind power connected into the power grid. The proposed solution methodology was applied to three cases with different ratios of wind power to evaluate their feasibility and efficiency. Morshed et al. (Morshed, Hmida, & Fekih, 2018)introduced a probabilistic optimal power flow approach (POPF) for a hybrid power system that includes plug-in electric vehicles (PEV), photovoltaic (PV) and wind energy (WE) sources. The performance of the proposed approach was implemented on the IEEE 30-bus, 57-bus and 118-bus power systems. Arabali et al. (Arabali, Ghofrani, & Amoli, 2013) examined the storage application and its optimal placement for the social cost and transmission congestion relief of wind integration. Krishnasamy et al. (Krishnasamy, & Nanjundappan, 2016) applied a hybridized version of weighted probabilistic neural network and biogeography-based optimization to solve ELD of hybrid wind–thermal system. The effectiveness of the approach was verified by comparing the results of the present method with that of the existing methodologies available in the literature of the power system and may be implemented in operational conditions of energy suppliers. Mondal et al. (Mondal, Bhattacharya, & Dey, 2013) invented gravitational search algorithm (GSA) to solve an economic emission load dispatch problem in order to minimize the emission of nitrogen oxides (NOX) and fuel cost, considering both thermal generators and wind turbines.

In recent times, several evolutionary algorithms, such as ant lion optimization (ALO) (Dubey et al., 2016), genetic algorithm (GA) (Yuan et al., 2015), predator- prey optimization (PPO) (Hazra & Roy, 2015) and particle swarm optimization (PSO) (Wang et al., 2013) are applied to solve the renewable wind energy-oriented thermal power load transmits problem.

Though aforementioned algorithms offer a significant performance of the system, they still have some drawback. Most of the aforesaid algorithms suffer from slow convergence rate, poor local optima avoidance, & require large computation time. For GOA, it not only modifies the position of grasshoppers by changing its current position and global best but also by the position of all other grasshoppers. It indicates that GOA involves all of its agents in the optimization process thus GOA has very high search efficiency (Saremi, & Mirjalili, 2017). The purpose of this paper is to provide an effective, robust, and intelligent computational algorithm namely grasshopper optimization algorithm (GOA) to overcome the abovementioned shortcomings. GOA is a newly developed algorithm based on the social interaction nature of the grasshopper. In the present work, opposition-based learning (OBL) concept proposed by Tizhoosh (Tizhoosh, 2005) is integrated with GOA to progress the convergence speed of the normal GOA method and offer global optimal result. OBL is an effective method to speed up the convergence of conventional population- based techniques. It has been used in various evolutionary algorithms to create a new population during the learning process to improve their search ability. A quasi-oppositional based learning (QOBL) introduced by Rahnamayan (Rahnamayan et al., 2007) is usually performs better than OBL approach. In recent times, QOBL approach has been used to raise the convergence speed. The recent study introduces quasi-oppositional grasshopper optimization algorithm (QOGOA) method for solving renewable energy incorporating load dispatch problem with non-convex cost functions. An innovative quasi-oppositional nature-inspired population-based grasshopper optimization algorithm (GOA) is a new optimization technique developed by (Saremi & Mirjalili, 2017) and it has hardly been used to solve power system optimization problem. This article presents the QOGOA algorithm to solve renewable energy based economic load dispatch problem having several equality and non-equality constraints. To demonstrate the effectiveness of the proposed QOGOA algorithm, the two different cases namely, ELD without renewable energy and ELD with renewable energy have been considered. The potential and effectiveness of the proposed approach are demonstrated. Additionally, the results are compared to those reported in the literature. The proposed QOGOA along with basic GOA is applied on 6-unit, and 14-unit test systems incorporating two wind plant in two different cases. Moreover, to authenticate the superiority of the proposed technique, its simulation outcome is compared with the newly available different optimization techniques results available in the literature.

The rest of the research work is focused as follows: Section 2 which shows the mathematical problem formulation of thermal and renewable wind energy. Thermal and wind constraints are described in section 3. The basic GOA (Grasshoppers optimization algorithm)quasi oppositional grasshoppers optimization algorithm (QOGOA)model is formulated in Section 4 in brief. Article 5, describes different steps of QOGOA technique. In Section 6, simulation result of GOA and QOGOA is demonstrated through a mathematical model. Section 7 summarized the conclusions.

MATHEMATICAL PROBLEM FORMULATION

The actual functions of the renewable energy incorporating economic load dispatch problem is to minimize the total thermal power fuel cost and pollutant emission using the accessible renewable wind. The objective function is to minimize total operating coast of the system, formulated as below (Roy & Hazra, 2015):

$$\Gamma = Min\left(C_{TOTAL}\right) = \sum_{i=1}^{M} C_T\left(P_{gi}\right) + \sum_{i=1}^{M} C_{pi} + \sum_{i=1}^{N} E\left(X_{OE}\right) + \sum_{i=1}^{N} E\left(X_{UE}\right) \tag{1}$$

Γ is denoting total cost. C_{TOTAL} is the total cost incorporating M number of thermal generator cost including carbon emission tax and N number of wind power plant. $C_T(P_{gi})$ is the thermal generator cost; C_{pi} is the cost related to emission; $E(X_{OE})$ is the wind power overestimation cost; $E(X_{UE})$ is the wind power underestimation cost.

Mathematical Analysis of Cost Model of Thermal Power Generators

The relation between fuel cost in (\$) and generating power (MW) is given by a quadratic relationship (Dubey, Pandit, & Panigrahi, 2015):

$$C_T\left(P_{gi}\right) = \sum_{i=1}^{N_{TG}} \alpha_i + \beta_i P_{TGi} + \gamma_i P_{TGi}^2 \tag{2}$$

$\alpha_i, \beta_i, \gamma_i$ are the thermal unit's cost coefficients for the ith units. N_{TG} is the number of thermal power units. P_{TGi} is the actual power generated by the ith thermal unit.

Valve point effect is included for more realistic and precise modeling of cost function. The valve loading effects of multi valve steam turbines is modeled as sinusoidal function (Yao et al., 2012) and it's absolute vale is added to the basic cost function of equation(2)

$$C_T\left(P_{gi}\right) = \sum_{i=1}^{N_{TG}} \alpha_i + \beta_i P_{TGi} + \gamma_i P_{TGi}^2 + \left| f_i \times \sin\left(g_i \times \left(P_{TGi}^{\min} - P_{TGi}\right)\right)\right| \tag{3}$$

f_i, g_i are thermal unit's co-efficient for valve-point effects of ith thermal unit.

The carbon emission tax is expressed as below (Masters, 2004):

$$C_{Pi} = \sum_{i=1}^{M} EM_i\left(P_{TGi}\right) \times C_{TAX} \tag{4}$$

$$EM_i\left(P_{TGi}\right) = ef_i \times \left(a_i + b_i P_{TGi} + c_i P_{TGi}^2\right) \tag{5}$$

C_{TAX} is a tax levied on the carbon content of fuels. This Carbon tax (C_{TAX}) is determined by governments regulation and market $EM_i(P_{TGi})$ is carbon emission by the ith thermal unit calculated by equation (5). cf_i is the fuel emission factors of CO_2 from thermal generators. a_i, b_i, c_i are fuel consumption coefficients.

Probabilistic Analysis of Wind Power/Wind Power Cost Calculation

The wind power output follows nonlinear relationship with its input wind speed. The model is (Hetzer et al., 2008):

$$P_W = 0.5 \rho A_s v_W^3 \tag{6}$$

Where P_w is the input wind power(watt), ρ is the air density (kg/m^3), A_s is the cross-sectional area through which the wind passes, v_w is the wind speed which is a random variable. It has been shown in various papers that wind speed follows Weibull distribution (Roy & Hazra, 2015), with the cumulative distribution Function(CDF):

$$F_V\left(V_W\right) = 1 - \exp\left[-\left(\frac{v_W}{c}\right)^k\right] \tag{7}$$

probability density function (pdf) of V:

$$f_V\left(V_W\right) = \frac{k}{c}\left[\left(\frac{v_W}{c}\right)^{k-1}\right] \exp\left[-\left(\frac{v_W}{c}\right)^k\right] \tag{8}$$

Where, v_w is the wind speed which is a random variable, ($c>0$) is the scale factor and k ($k>0$) is the shape factor. For wind turbine a simplified model is used to established relation between wind power (WP) and wind speed (Leon, 2008; Liu, & Xu, 2010). These are followings:

$$W_P = \begin{cases} 0; \left(V_W < v_w^{in} \ or \ V_W > v_w^{out}\right) \\ 0.5\rho A_s v_W^3; \left(v_w^{in} \leq V_W > v_w^{rated}\right) \\ w_{rated}; \left(v_w^{rated} \leq V_W > v_w^{out}\right) \end{cases} \tag{9}$$

$v_w^{in}, v_w^{rated}, v_w^{out}$ are cut-in, rated, and cut-out wind speeds respectively.

According to the theory of random variables (Liu & Xu, 2010), in the interval $v_w^{in} \leq V_W > v_w^{rated}$, the pdf is

$$f_{WP}\left(W_P\right) = \frac{k \times h \times v_w^{in}}{c \times w_{rated}} \left[\frac{\left(1 + \dfrac{h \times w_p}{w_{rated}}\right) \times v_w^{in}}{c}\right]^{k-1} \times \exp\left\{-\left[\frac{\left(1 + \dfrac{h \times w_p}{w_{rated}}\right) \times v_w^{in}}{c}\right]^{k}\right\} \tag{10}$$

Where $h = \dfrac{v_w^{rated}}{v_w^{in}} - 1$

Owing to stochastic nature of the wind power, the mathematical representation between the actual wind power output and the wind speed (Liu & Xu, 2010) is presented and according to (9) two discrete probabilities are (Bai & Lee, 2016):

Case 1: $V_W < v_w^{in} \ or \ V_W > v_w^{out}$

$$P_{rw}\left(W_P = 0\right) = P_{rw}\left(V_W < v_w^{in}\right) + P_{rw}\left(V_W > v_w^{out}\right)$$
$$= \exp\left[-\left(\frac{v_w^{rated}}{c}\right)^k\right] + \exp\left[-\left(\frac{v_w^{out}}{c}\right)^k\right] \tag{11}$$

Case 2: $v_w^{rated} \leq V_W > v_w^{out}$

$$P_{rw}\left(W_P = w_{rated}\right) = P_{rw}\left(v_w^{out}\right) - P_{rw}\left(v_w^{rated}\right)$$
$$= \exp\left[-\left(\frac{v_w^{rated}}{c}\right)^k\right] - \exp\left[-\left(\frac{v_w^{out}}{c}\right)^k\right] \tag{12}$$

Wind power cost has been calculated by applying the aforementioned equation.

Underestimation and Overestimation Cost of Wind Power

The wind power generating cost, namely, overestimation, underestimation and direct cost for the wind power may be presented when the schedule wind power doesn't match to the genuine value. Wind power is termed as overestimated, if the real wind power is a smaller amount than the scheduled value, and the worker desires to acquire some energy from the different source to fulfill the load requirement. Wind power is termed as underestimated cost, when the actual renewable wind power is higher than the schedule value, and the user needs to reimburse the renewable wind power production cost. Direct electrical power cost is set to zeroin this research work.

Wind power availability is random in nature due to the uncertain behavior of wind speed, so the operator may overestimate or underestimates the wind power (WP) availability.

Overestimation cost included when the actual WP is wrongly predicted as a less amount that actually are needed so operators have to purchase power from another source, so certain cost is indulged in this process (Dubey, Pandit, & Panigrahi, 2015).

$$E\left(X_{OE}\right) = w_{j} \times P_{rw}\left(W_{P} = 0\right) + C_{pwj} \times \left[\int_{0}^{w_{rated}} \left(w_{1} - w_{p}\right) \times f_{w}\left(w_{p}\right) dw_{p}\right] \tag{13}$$

Where, w_{j} is the scheduled power output from jth wind mill; C_{pwj} is the cost coefficient of over estimation case. w_{rated} rated power for the jth wind turbine. w_{1} is predicted power in the jth windmill.

Underestimation occurs when the actual wind power (WP) is wrongly predicted as a more amount that actually are needed so operators have to compensate the excess power, so certain cost is indulged in this process (Firouzi, Farjah, & Abarghooee, 2013).

$$E\left(X_{uE}\right) = w_{j} \times P_{rw}\left(W_{P} = w_{rated}\right) + C_{rwj} \times \left[\int_{0}^{w_{rated}} \left(w_{p} - w_{j}\right) \times f_{w}\left(w_{p}\right) dw_{p}\right] \tag{14}$$

Where, w_{j} is the scheduled power output from jth wind mill; C_{rwj} is the cost coefficient of under estimation case.

In renewable wind and fossil fuel energy penetration, the major aim is to minimize generation cost and other costs related to renewable wind power. The main objective function can be given as:

$$FC_{total} = C_{T}\left(P_{gi}\right) + C_{Pi} + \left[E\left(X_{OE}\right) + E\left(X_{uE}\right)\right] \tag{15}$$

SYSTEM CONSTRAINTS

$$P_{i,\min} \leq P_{i} \leq P_{i,\max} \tag{16}$$

8

$$0 \leq w_{av,j} \leq w_{r,j} \tag{17}$$

$$\sum_{i}^{M} P_i + \sum_{i=1}^{N} w_{av,j} = P_{idemand} + P_{loss} \tag{18}$$

Thermal unit's lower and upper bounds, wind power output limitation, power balance equation are defined by the constraint equations (Dubey, Pandit, & Panigrahi, 2015).

$P_{i,\min}$ and $P_{i,\max}$ are the minimum and maximum limit of thermal power generation. $P_{idemand}$ is the total demand of the system. P_{loss} is transmission losses of the system.

GOA ALGORITHM

An innovative quasi-oppositional nature-inspired population-based grasshopper optimization algorithm (GOA)is a new optimization technique developed by (Saremi, & Mirjalili, 2017) and it has hardly been used to solve power system optimization problem. Grasshoppers have the carnivorous strategy based on a specific social network which connects them in a way that their positions can be harmonized (Saremi, & Mirjalili, 2017). Grasshoppers can decide the direction by the group recognition in the network. There are two types of forces existing among them: repulsion and attraction forces, the first one allows them to explore search space, later one revitalizes them to destroy the promising regions. The comfort zone is the zone where two forces become equal. As the target position is unknown to us, the location of the grasshopper with the best fitness value will be considered as the nearest one to the target. With the updating location of grasshopper in the social interaction network to make balance between global and local search the grasshopper will move along the target and converges to the best solution (Saremi, & Mirjalili, 2017). Nature-inspired swarm-based GOA algorithms are most popular among stochastic optimization approaches. The main advantage of GOA method is that all creatures in nature is to survive and to achieve this goal they intend to evolve and modify as well as adapt different ways. GOA has a superior probability to be nearer to the global optimum solution than a random candidate solution, which can be effectively used to solve nonlinear and non-continuous optimization problems. Pseudo code of GOA is given below:

```
Initialize the swarm Xi (i=1,2,...,n)
Initialize cmax, cmin, and maximum number of iterations
Evaluate the fitness of search agent
T= best search agent
while (1<Max number of iterations)
update α using equation no. 20
for each search agent
standardize the distances between grasshoppers in [1,4]
update the position of current search agent by the equation no. 18
fetch the current search agent reverse if it goes exterior the limitations
end for
```

```
Update T if there is a enhanced solution
l= the attractive length scale.
l=l+1
end while
Return T
```

The Mathematical Model of GOA

Let there are M number of grasshoppers in the swarm $S_i^e \left(i = 1, 2, ..., M \right)$, the position of the ith grasshopper in the e-dimension is given by

$$S_i^e \left(i = 1, ..., M \right). \tag{19}$$

Where

$$h\left(r \right) = \exp\left(\frac{-z}{m_h} \right) - \exp\left(-z \right) \tag{20}$$

where t is the present iteration; h defines the toughness of social forces(reputation and social forces);*g, h* indicates strength of attraction m_h denote the attractive length scale; $\max_e$, $\min_e$ denote the upper and lower limits respectively in the e dimension; e_{ij} is the distance between the ith and the jth grasshoppers; T_e is the e-dimensional location of the target (i.e. best solution till now); k is the shrink factor; If k is large then search activity of GOA is exploration i.e. global search activity, when k is small then local search activity exploitation i.e. local search activity, *p* is the set following forms for shrinking the comfort zone adaptively:

$$\alpha\left(t \right) = \alpha_{\max} - t \times \frac{\alpha_{\max} - \alpha_{\min}}{t_{\max}} \tag{21}$$

Where $\alpha_{\max}$, $\alpha_{\min}$ are the maximum and minimum values respectively; $t_{\max}$ is the value of maximum iteration.

Opposition-Based Learning

Opposition-based learning (OBL) is a novel thought in optimization intelligence (Tizhoosh, 2005), which depends on existing estimate and its opposite estimate at the same cases to get an improved approximation for an existing candidate resolution. It has been proved that an opposition candidate result has a better possibility to be nearer to the global optimum result than an arbitrary candidate result. Opposite number and quasi-opposite number is distinct as the mirror point of the solution from the centre of the search space.

Opposition Number

In a one-dimensional search space, if X_r be any real number between $[q_o m, q_o n]$, its opposite number X_o, may be defined as follows:

$$X_o = [q_o m + q_o n - X_r] \tag{22}$$

Where X_r is the real number. Limitation of real number is in between $[q_o m, q_o n]$.

Opposition Point

For n-dimensional search space, the opposite point may be mathematically expressed as follows:

$$D_{o,j} = \left[\left(q_o m \right)_j + \left(q_o n \right)_j - D_j \right]; D_j \in \left[q_o m, q_o n \right]; j = 1, 2......, d. \tag{23}$$

Where d is the dimension of search space. $D_{o,j}$ is the opposite point.

Opposition Based Optimization

It can be classified into opposition-based initialization and generation jumping. Opposite population $O^{\neq}$ may be described as follows:

```
for  i = P_S, P_S = population size
for  j = P_C, P_C = Control variable
O#_{i,j} = F_j + E_j - P_{i,j}
end
end
```

Opposition based generation jumping may be described as follows based on jumping rate J^r:

```
if  rand(0,1) < J^r
for  i = 1 : P_S
for  i = 1 : P_C
O#_{i,j} = F_j + E_j - P_{i,j}
end
end
end
```

Where E and F are extreme point of search space. J^r is the jumping rate. P_S is the population size and P_C is the control variable.

Quasi-Opposition Number

Quasi-opposite number (X_o^q) may be clarified as the quantity between the centre of the search space and the opposite quantity. It may be represented as follows:

$$X_0^q = rand\left[\left(\frac{q_o m + q_o n}{2}\right), \left(q_o m + q_o n - X_r\right)\right] \tag{24}$$

Where X_r is the real number. Limitation of real number is in between $[q_o m, q_o n]$.

Quasi-Opposition Point

The quasi-opposite point for n-dimensional search space is mathematically expressed as follows:

$$D_{0,j}^q = rand\left[\left(\frac{\left(q_o m\right)_j + \left(q_o n\right)_j}{2}\right), \left(\left(q_o m\right)_j + \left(q_o n\right)_j - X_r\right)\right]; j = 1.2, ..., d \tag{25}$$

$q_o m, q_o n$, are the real number exists between two number; X_r is the real number and d is the dimension of search space; j is the search space index.

PROCEDURE OF QOGOA FOR RENEWABLE ECONOMIC LOAD DISPATCH PROBLEM

The search procedure of the proposed GOA for ELD problem is described as follows:

Step 1. Specify the lower and upper bound generation power of every unit. Randomly generate the initial positions of all the grasshoppers in the search space. The active power generation of wind turbines and active power generation of all thermal units except slack unit are randomly generated between their operating limits. The thermal generation of the last unit is calculated using the equality constraint (18) and its feasibility is checked using the inequality constraints (16-17). If the infeasible solution is generated, the corresponding solution is discarded and a new feasible solution set is generated. Among all the initial solutions, the solutions which satisfy all constraints are considered as the feasible solution. Depending upon the population size initial feasible solutions are generated. Each solution represents grasshoppers' individual positions that satisfy the practical operation constraints of ELD.

Step 2. Set the generation counter to zero, i.e. $n=0$.

Step 3. Opposite population $O^{\#}_{i,j}$ is shaped using (25) and initialize every factor of a given molecule set.

$$O^{\#}_{i,j} = F_j + E_j - P_{i,j} \tag{25}$$

Where, $P_{i,j}$ is the jth independent variables of the ith vector of the population. $i=1,2,\ldots,P_S$ and$^{j=1,2,\ldots,PC}$. E and F are extreme point of search space

Step 4. Depending upon the quasi-opposite population (QOP) while fulfilling different constraints and evaluate the fitness value. Evaluate fitness of each individual of the population.

Step 5. Sort the population from best to worst fitness value. Few elite solutions are identified.

Step 6. Modify all the independent variables (i.e. active power of wind turbines and thermal power generation of all the units except the slack unit) of all non-elite population string based on GOA position updating equation (19).

Step 7. If active power generation of any unit is less than the minimum level it is made equal to minimum value and if it is greater than the maximum level it is made equal to maximum level. The thermal generation of the slack unit is evaluated and this must be checked by the inequality constraints. The infeasible solutions are replaced by randomly generated new feasible solutions.

Step 8. Evaluate fitness of each grasshopper of current population by using the fitness function and store the solution corresponding to the best-fit.

Step 9. Apply the replacement operator to replace worse solution with the elite solutions.

Step 10. Increase the generation counter by one, i.e. $n=n+1$.

Step 11. Check for the convergence criterion: if current generation number n is equal to gen max, stop and print the results such as unit thermal generations, wind generation, overestimation cost, underestimation cost, loss, fuel cost, etc. corresponding to the best fit vector of the population. Otherwise, go to step 4.

SIMULATIONS RESULT AND DISCUSSION

The performance of the proposed QOGOA method is explained by applying economic load dispatch problem without wind and ELD with the wind for two different test systems and its results are compared with existing techniques. The generators parameters and the emission factors of the thermal generator for six unit and fourteen unit are taken from (Venkatesh & Lee, 2008) and (Mandal & Chakraborty, 2008). The cost and emission coefficients for six and fourteen units are furnished in Table 1 and Table 2. Two windmills are incorporated on the system. The wind plant parameters (Masters, 2004) and speed data (Australian Bureau of Meteorology, last accessed 2012) are given in Table 3. For each case study, a population dimension of 50 and iteration cycles of 100 are considered. This computational algorithm is implemented and is executed on 4.0 GHz core i3 processor with 2GB RAM in MATLAB system with a 30 independent runs concerning 50 dissimilar initial trial solutions. To check the usefulness of the proposed method, two case studies have been replicated i.e. without wind/renewable energy and with wind/renewable energy.

Table 1. System data for 6 unit test system

Unit	Pg^{min} (MW)	Pg^{max} (MW)	Cost Coefficients					Emission Coefficients		
			a ($/MW²hr)	b ($/MWhr)	c ($/hr)	d ($/hr)	e (rad/MW)	α (ton/MW²hr)	β (ton/MWhr)	γ (ton/hr)
1	20	110	0.002	10.0	2000	0.08	200	0.00004	0.2	40
2	20	100	0.0025	15.0	2500	0.04	300	0.00005	0.3	50
3	120	600	0.0018	9.0	6000	0.04	400	0.000024	0.12	80
4	110	520	0.00315	18.0	923.4	0.06	150	0.0084	48	2462.4
5	110	500	0.0032	20.0	950	0.08	100	0.009	50	2500
6	40	200	0.003432	23.4	124.8	0.10	80	0.0000343	0.234	1.248

Table 2. System data for 14 unit test system

Unit	Min and Max Limit		Cost Coefficient					Emission Coefficient		
	Pgmin (MW)	Pgmax (MW)	Gama	Beta	Alpha	Sin1	Sin2	Gama1	Beta1	Alpha1
1	150	455	150	1.8900	0.0050	300	0.0350	23.3330	-1.5000	0.0160
2	150	455	115	2.0000	0.0055	200	0.0420	21.0220	-1.8200	0.0310
3	20	130	40	3.5000	0.0060	200	0.0420	22.0500	-1.2490	0.0130
4	20	130	122	3.1500	0.0050	150	0.0630	22.9830	-1.3550	0.0120
5	150	470	125	3.0500	0.0050	150	0.0630	21.3130	-1.9000	0.0200
6	135	460	120	2.7500	0.0070	150	0.0630	21.9000	0.8050	0.0070
7	135	465	70	3.4500	0.0070	150	0.0630	23.0010	-1.4000	0.0150
8	60	300	70	3.4500	0.0070	150	0.0630	24.0030	-1.8000	0.0180
9	25	162	130	2.4500	0.0050	150	0.0630	25.1210	-2.0000	0.0190
10	25	160	130	2.4500	0.0050	100	0.0840	22.9900	-1.3600	0.0120
11	20	80	135	2.3500	0.0055	100	0.0840	27.0100	-2.1000	0.0330
12	20	80	200	1.6000	0.0045	100	0.0840	25.1010	-1.8000	0.0180
13	25	85	70	3.4500	0.0070	100	0.0840	24.3130	-1.8100	0.0180
14	15	55	45	3.8900	0.0060	100	0.0840	27.1190	-1.9210	0.0300

Table 3. The wind plants parameters and speed data

Wind Plant Data	Wind Plant 1	Wind Plant Data	Wind Plant 2	Wind Plant Data	Wind Plant 1	Wind Plant Data	Wind Plant 2
No of WP	30	No of WP	20	υ_{out}	25	υ_{out}	25
C	4.6024	C	4.4363	$C_{p,j}$	30	$C_{p,j}$	20
K	1.8862	K	1.7128	$C_{r,j}$	5	$C_{r,j}$	5
υ_{in}	4	υ_{in}	3	$C_{w,j}$	0	$C_{w,j}$	0
υ_{rated}	16	υ_{rated}	13	w_{rated}	3	w_{rated}	3

Test System 1

Test System 1 consists of six thermal units and subdivided in two cases i.e. ELD without wind (case 1) and ELD with the wind (case 2) and its results are compared with QPSO.

Case 1

The effectiveness of the proposed QOGOA method for without wind and without carbon tax is verified by applying it to 30-bus test system without carbon tax for three different load demands i.e. 1200MW, 1400MW, 1600MW. 100 trials with different populations are carried out to test the robustness of the QOGOA algorithm. The results in Table 4 clearly indicate that the proposed QOGOA algorithm gives more reduction in total cost (29109.6744, 33132.933, 37503.7216) as compared to GOA (29536.2 $/h, 33222.5 $/h, 37527.7 $/h) and QPSO (29556.7 $/h, 33686.8 $/h, 37841.9 $/h) for three different loads.

Table 4. Comparison of optimal thermal power generation of 6 unit for cost minimization for without renewable energy and without carbon tax

Unit	1200 MW			1400 MW			1600 MW		
	QOPSO	GOA	QOGOA	QOPSO	GOA	QOGOA	QOPSO	GOA	QOGOA
G1 (MW)	107.7300	109.8962	98.5398	108.6000	101.8259	98.5398	109.9400	109.7128	110.0000
G2(MW)	99.9200	20.0000	98.5398	99.6300	100.0000	98.5398	99.3400	100.0000	100.0000
G3(MW)	582.5400	600.0000	591.2389	588.7300	594.0227	591.2389	578.7800	600.0000	600.0000
G4(MW)	259.0300	320.1038	261.6815	416.1600	372.2747	424.1008	509.3400	520.0000	482.8720
G5(MW)	110.4200	110.0000	110.0000	146.8600	191.8767	147.5807	259.7200	230.2872	267.1280
G6(MW)	40.3600	40.0000	40.0000	40.0100	40.0000	40.0000	42.8800	40.0000	40.0000
Cost($)	29556.7	29536.2	29109.6744	33686.8	33222.5	33132.933	37841.88	37527.7	37503.7216
Computational time (sec)	NA	27.74	25.97	NA	30.77	28.02	NA	32.48	29.18

When carbon tax is considered, it is observed from the simulation results that minimized total cost using QOGOA for 1200MW, 1400MW and 1600MW loads are 48528.8752 $, 53035.7214 $, 57835.0465 $whereas for GOA and QPSO these costs are (48568.2$, 53233.9$, 57935.8 $) and (48669.39$, 53346.7$,58035.9$) for 1200MW, 1400MW and 1600MW load, respectively. This result is shown in Table 5. Figure (1) demonstrates the convergence profile of six-unit system without renewable energy and without emission tax for 1200 MW loads using QOGOA and GOA. A comparison of each unit for 1600MW load without renewable wind energy and with carbon tax using QOGOA and GOA are made in figure (2).

Table 5. Comparison of optimal thermal power generation of 6 unit for cost minimization for without renewable energy and with carbon tax

Unit	1200 MW			1400 MW			1600 MW		
	QOPSO	GOA	QOGOA	QOPSO	GOA	QOGOA	QOPSO	GOA	QOGOA
G1 (MW)	23.01	59.7447	61.7617	29.4400	20.6745	98.5398	23.01	100.1909	98.5398
G2(MW)	21.7400	20.0000	20.0000	22.4500	20.0000	20.0000	21.7400	21.3154	20.0000
G3(MW)	569.4400	600.0000	594.2801	570.1200	592.5451	591.2389	569.4400	590.2075	591.2389
G4(MW)	404.0800	370.2553	373.9582	511.2800	414.3555	424.1593	506.1200	474.9951	476.5191
G5(MW)	137.8100	110.0000	110.0000	226.0700	312.4249	226.0620	369.5000	372.9821	373.7021
G6(MW)	40.9300	40.0000	40.0000	40.6400	40.0000	40.0000	43.2300	40.3117	40.0000
Cost($)	48669.39	48568.2	48528.8752	53346.7	53233.9	53035.7214	58035.9	57935.8	57835.0465
Computational time (sec)	NA	28.92	27.00	NA	33.13	31.24	NA	32.05	31.07

Figure 1. Convergence graph for 1200 MW load without wind and without renewable energy for six-unit system using QOGOA and GOA

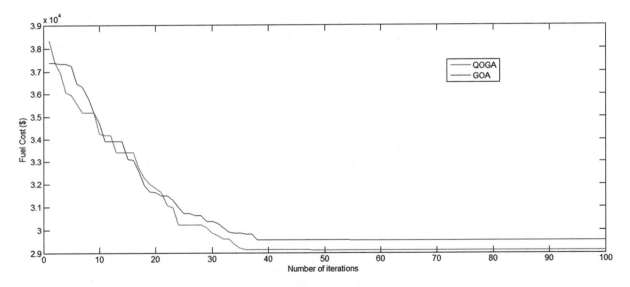

Case 2

For case 2, renewable wind energy is introduced and the proposed QOGOA method for with wind and without carbon tax is verified by applying it to 30-bus test system without carbon tax for three different load demands i.e. 1200MW, 1400MW, 1600MW.The simulation results of QOGOA, GOA and QPSO are given in Table 6.

Cost obtained incorporating QOGOA are 27858.59 $, 31755.4255$, and 35875.2512 $. The total cost for QPSO are found to be 29513.5 $, 33259.6 $, 37601.7 $ and these costs using GOA are 27927.80$/h, 31874.4002$, 36071.2002$ for 1200MW, 1400MW, 1600MW loads, respectively. It can be observed from the simulation study that the suggested QOGOA algorithm provides better performance as compared

Figure 2. Generation comparison using QOGOA and GOA for 1600 MW load without wind and tax

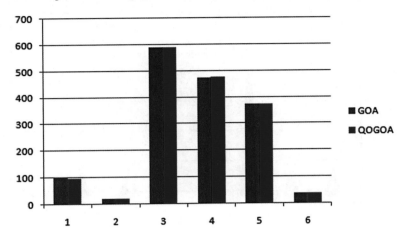

Table 6. Comparison of optimal thermal power generation of 6 unit and 2 wind unit for cost minimization for with renewable energy and without carbon tax

Unit	1200 MW			1400 MW			1600 MW		
	QOPSO	GOA	QOGOA	QOPSO	GOA	QOGOA	QOPSO	GOA	QOGOA
G1 (MW)	103.5600	96.4979	100.2213	94.3900	96.2270	98.5426	95.2700	102.2086	106.0620
G2(MW)	99.0900	100.0000	98.5398	96.5300	100.0000	98.5366	97.9500	100.0000	100.0000
G3(MW)	567.6600	593.5021	591.2389	594.2400	590.7879	591.2393	568.8700	600.0000	591.2389
G4(MW)	211.6400	110.0000	110.0000	319.9600	315.0956	319.4401	452.1300	473.8040	424.1593
G5(MW)	138.0500	110.0000	110.0000	117.1600	110.0000	110.0000	266.2300	136.9874	188.5398
G6(MW)	40.2500	40.0000	40.0000	43.9500	40.0000	40.0000	49.5200	40.0000	40.0000
W7(MW)	8.318	90.0000	90.0000	15.8000	90.0000	82.2414	1.9100	89.0000	90.0000
W8(MW)	31.42	60.0000	60.0000	58.4700	57.8894	60.0000	59.1200	58.0000	60.0000
Fuel Cost($)	29513.46	26267.6	26198.06	33259.6	30214.2	30207.0345	37601.7	34411.0	34215.0981
Total Cost($)	**29513.46**	**27927.80**	**27858.59**	**33259.6**	**31874.4002**	**31755.4255**	**37601.7**	**36071.2002**	**35875.2512**
Computational time (sec)	**NA**	**27.52**	**25.10**	**NA**	**36.53**	**33.72**	**NA**	**32.55**	**30.14**

to GOA and QPSO method. Generation of each unit for 1200 MW load with renewable wind energy and without carbon tax using QOGOA is represented in figure (3). The cost convergence characteristics of GOA and QOGOA approaches for 1600MW load with wind and with carbon tax are illustrated in figure (4). Figure (5) depicts the variation of total cost for the QOGOA algorithm for 1400 MW load with wind and with carbon tax.

In order to investigate further, the efficiency of the proposed QOGOA method, it is applied to the same 30-bus renewable system to minimize total cost of operation, including the carbon tax. Table 7 shows the simulation results and the corresponding cost of QOGOA (46760.015 $, 51247.7955 $, 55857.0768 $)GOA (47104.3 $/h, 51472.3 $/h, 55994 $/h) and QPSO (48527.4 $/h, 55628 $/h, and 57699.2 $/h) for 1200MW, 1400MW and 1600MW load, respectively. It is confirmed from the simulation result that QOGOA is the best comparing to other methods.

Figure 3. Generation of each unit using QOGOA with wind and without tax for 1200 MW load

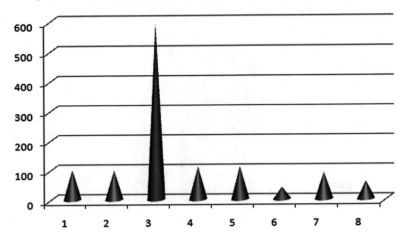

Figure 4. Convergence graph of 1600 MW load with wind and with carbon for six unit system using QOGOA and GOA

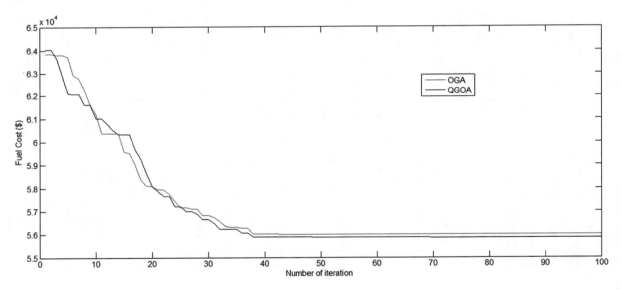

Test System 2

In order to confirm the usefulness of QOGOA and GOA further, a little more complex system considering nonlinearities of valve-point loading effect consisting of 14 thermal units for solving single-objective cost minimization problem. The load demand equivalent to this generating station is 1800 MW, 2000 MW, and 2200 MW. This test system is subdivided in two cases i.e. ELD without wind (case 1) and ELD with the wind (case 2).

Figure 5. Cost Comparison for 1400 MW load using QOGOA with wind and tax

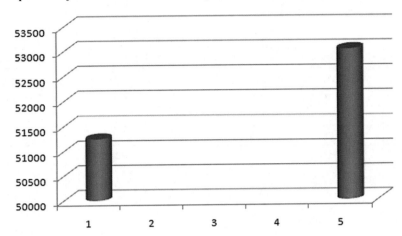

Table 7. Comparison of optimal thermal power generation of 6 unit and 2 wind unit for cost minimization for with renewable energy and with carbon tax

Unit	1200 MW			1400 MW			1600 MW		
	QOPSO	GOA	QOGOA	QOPSO	GOA	QOGOA	QOPSO	GOA	QOGOA
G1 (MW)	55.4900	20.6482	20.0000	63.5900	59.2558	20.0155	20.6482	48.5314	98.5397
G2(MW)	20.9200	21.3966	20.0000	20.2100	20.0000	20.0000	21.3966	20.0000	20.0000
G3(MW)	563.3600	600.0000	591.2389	568.8700	591.2532	591.2712	600.0000	591.1547	591.2389
G4(MW)	355.1200	273.5901	268.7611	472.0800	376.4179	425.0887	273.5901	476.5313	476.5191
G5(MW)	110.4400	110.0000	110.0000	132.4800	212.6576	153.6245	110.0000	293.6334	223.7023
G6(MW)	47.7400	40.0000	40.0000	42.8800	40.0000	40.0000	40.0000	40.0000	40.0000
W7(MW)	5.2500	82.2808	90.0000	40.8800	42.0162	90.0000	36.6100	50.0078	90.0000
W8(MW)	41.6800	52.0843	60.0000	59.0100	58.3993	60.0000	59.3000	80.1414	60.0000
Fuel Cost($)	NA	NA	45100.7310	NA	NA	49588.0003	NA	NA	54197.5673
Total Cost($)	48527.4	47104.3	46760.015	55628	51472.3	51247.7955	57699.2	55994.0	55857.0768
Computational time (sec)	NA	29.01	28.65	NA	30.34	28.14	NA	29.84	29.07

Case 1

Firstly, individually minimized the thermal generator fuel cost using the proposed GOA and QOGOA algorithms. The optimal values of the control variables and fuel cost of individual units for 1800 MW, 2000 MW, and 2200 MW are listed in Table 8. From Table 8, it is considered that among all other methods, the proposed QOGOA method outcomes the best fuel price i.e. 8211.2854$, 9294.4168 and 10327.0531$. To verify the usefulness of the projected GOA and QOGOA algorithm, their numerical results of best, worst and average values of fitness function by different methods are shown in Table 9. It is observed from Table 9 that best, mean and worst costs produced by QOGOA method are better than the results obtained by DE (Mandal & Chakraborty, 2008), PSO (Roy et al., 2010), GA(Roy et al., 2010), BBO (Roy et al., 2010), CIHSA[64], and GOA.

Table 8. Comparison of optimal thermal power generation of 14 unit for cost minimization for without renewable energy

Unit	Cost Minimization					
	1800MW		2000MW		2200MW	
	GOA	QOGOA	GOA	QOGOA	GOA	QOGOA
P_{T1} (MW)	328.2367	329.5196	419.2794	329.4228	329.5218	419.3958
P_{T2} (MW)	297.4223	299.5997	299.5997	373.3814	374.3986	375.3946
P_{T3} (MW)	20.0000	20.0000	95.1347	20.0000	94.8069	95.6576
P_{T4} (MW)	120.3688	119.7331	119.7331	125.5708	119.7359	120.4458
P_{T5} (MW)	150.0000	150.0000	150.0000	254.5298	150.0000	150.0000
P_{T6} (MW)	135.0000	135.0000	135.0000	135.0000	184.8677	135.0000
P_{T7} (MW)	135.0000	135.0000	135.0000	135.0000	135.0000	135.0000
P_{T8} (MW)	60.0000	60.0000	60.0000	109.5204	209.6001	209.9845
P_{T9} (MW)	162.0000	124.7331	126.2532	126.3169	162.0000	162.0000
P_{T10} (MW)	137.0732	137.1997	160.0000	159.5421	160.0000	137.3723
P_{T11} (MW)	59.7095	80.0000	80.0000	57.0965	80.0000	80.0000
P_{T12} (MW)	80.0000	80.0000	80.0000	56.9662	80.0000	59.9853
P_{T13} (MW)	60.1895	74.2148	85.0000	62.6532	65.0691	66.8391
P_{T14} (MW)	55.0000	55.0000	55.0000	55.0000	55.0000	52.9249
FC($)	8220.3673	8211.2854	9298.6963	9294.4168	10332.489	10327.0531
Computational time (sec)	31.88	30.00	31.94	28.56	32.28	30.52

Table 9. Statistical results obtained by different algorithms for 14-unit system without renewable wind energy for 2000MW load

Algorithms	Best	Mean	Worst	Computational time
PSO (Roy et al, 2010)	10166.0	NA	NA	NA
GA(Roy et al, 2010)	9889.3	NA	NA	NA
BBO(Roy et al, 2010)	9874.3	NA	NA	NA
CIHSA(Rezaie et al, 2018)	9809.08	NA	NA	NA
DE (Mandal& Chakraborty, 2008)	9592.4	NA	NA	NA
GOA	**9298.6963**	**9338.0051**	**9367.0992**	**31.94**
QOGOA	**9294.4168**	**9321.0101**	**9344.8750**	**28.56**

Case 2

In order to judge the performance of the proposed GOA and QOGOA methods for solving wind-based load dispatch problem, the same 14-unit system is customized by adding two more wind units. For the sake of simplicity, wind farm related data of this case are remained same as the previous test system.

In this process, the GOA and QOGOA approaches are implemented on a 14-unit test system to find the optimal solution of individual cost minimization problem. The optimal scheduling of the generation, cost obtained by the proposed QOCRO and CRO methods for 1800 MW, 2000 MW, and 2200 MW are provided in Table 10. It can be observed that after introducing wind generator for 1800 MW, 2000 MW, and 2200 MW that cost of the electrical energy is reduced from 8211.2854\$ to 8140.2665\$, 9294.4168\$ to 9067.1461\$, 10327.0531\$ to 10283.449\$ using QOGOA method. The simulation results reveal that the proposed QOCRO technique renders the better fitness values as compared to those obtained by GOA technique. Generation comparison of each unit for 1800 MW load with renewable wind energy using QOGOA and GOA is represented in figure (6). The cost convergence characteristic of QOGOA technique for 2200MW load with renewable wind energy is illustrated in figure (7).

Table 10. Comparison of optimal thermal power generation of 14 unit and 2 wind unit for cost minimization for with renewable energy

Unit	Cost Minimization					
	1800MW		2000MW		2200MW	
	GOA	QOGOA	GOA	QOGOA	GOA	QOGOA
P_{T1} (MW)	239.7598	329.5195	329.4790	329.5352	329.5196	419.2794
P_{T2} (MW)	224.7998	299.6001	299.7045	299.6601	374.3990	374.3995
P_{T3} (MW)	94.7998	20.0000	94.7319	94.7626	94.7996	94.7998
P_{T4} (MW)	119.7331	119.7329	119.7384	119.7786	119.7337	119.7331
P_{T5} (MW)	150.0000	150.0000	199.9845	249.6307	299.5989	150.0000
P_{T6} (MW)	135.0000	135.0000	135.0000	234.6622	135.0000	135.0000
P_{T7} (MW)	135.0000	135.0000	135.0000	135.0000	135.0000	135.0000
P_{T8} (MW)	109.8666	60.0000	159.7105	60.0000	159.7330	209.5996
P_{T9} (MW)	162.0000	162.0000	124.7423	124.7245	162.0000	162.0000
P_{T10} (MW)	160.0000	137.2000	160.0000	137.1364	160.0000	160.0000
P_{T11} (MW)	57.3999	57.4031	57.5658	57.3450	57.3999	57.3999
P_{T12} (MW)	80.0000	57.4015	57.4381	57.6950	80.0000	57.3999
P_{T13} (MW)	62.3999	62.4001	62.3706	25.0000	25.0000	62.3999
P_{T14} (MW)	52.3999	52.4004	55.0000	55.0000	55.0000	52.3999
W7(MW)	8.1813	0	0	11.2426	4.6922	0
W8(MW)	8.6599	22.3424	9.5343	8.8270	8.1243	10.5889
Overestimation Cost ($)	49.8263	129.7509	28.9167	69.9596	31.3511	34.9242
Underestimation Cost ($)	30.5452	26.5135	37.8097	27.8429	34.5730	36.4720
FC($/h)	8066.9067	7984.00211	9006.1780	8969.3030	10225.0118	10212.0528
TC ($)	**8147.2782**	**8140.2665**	**9072.9044**	**9067.1461**	**10290.9359**	**10283.449**
Computational time (sec)	**35.29**	**32.76**	**36.02**	**34.48**	**36.98**	**32.10**

Figure 6. Generation comparison of QOGOA and GOA for 1800 MW load with wind

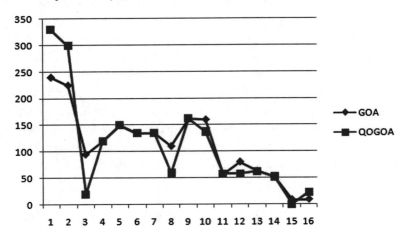

Figure 7. Convergence graph for 14-unit system of 2200 MW lead using QOGOA

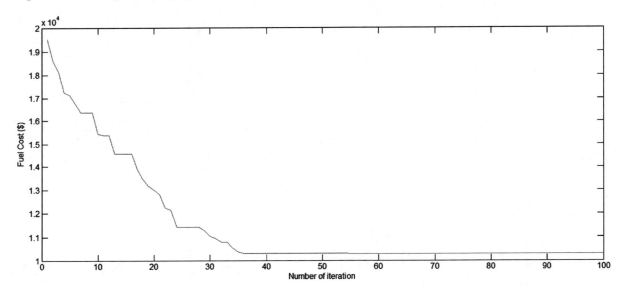

CONCLUSION

With the expansion of new technologies in the field of wind hybrid renewable energy system, a new problem arises, which become much more charming to be solved. A real-time economic load dispatch with wind power participation method is developed in this paper. The solution of such problem is done using swarm intelligence algorithm i.e. QOBL. So, it is comprehensible that QOGOA algorithm gives the best global optimum solution and it performs better than other reported algorithm in terms of the solution superiority, robustness, and computational efficiency. Simulation results powerfully suggest that the proposed QOGOA method is competent and encouraging to advance the systems. Application of swarm intelligence algorithm is more useful than traditional algorithm to attain the optimal solution for real world problem.

REFERENCES

Al-Sumait, J. S., AL-Othman, A. K., & Sykulski, J. K. (2007). Application of pattern search method to power system valve-point economic load dispatch. *Electr. Power Energy Syst*, *29*(10), 720–730. doi:10.1016/j.ijepes.2007.06.016

Alham, M. H., Elshahed, M., Ibrahim, D. H., Din, E. E., & Zahab, A. E. (2016). A dynamic economic emission dispatch considering wind power uncertainty incorporating energy storage system and demand side management. *Renewable Energy*, *96*, 800–811. doi:10.1016/j.renene.2016.05.012

Arabali, A., Ghofrani, M., & Amoli, M. E. (2013). Cost analysis of a power system using probabilistic optimal power flow with energy storage integration and wind generation. *Electrical Power and Energy Systems*, *53*, 832–841. doi:10.1016/j.ijepes.2013.05.053

Australian Bureau of Meteorology. Last accessed 2012. [Online]. Available at http://www.bom.gov.au

Bai, W., & Lee, Y. (2016) Modified Optimal Power Flow on Storage Devices and Wind Power Integrated System. *Proceedings IEEE International Conference on Power and Energy Society General Meeting(PESGM)*, Boston, USA. IEEE.

Bhattacharya, A., & Chattopadhyay, P. K. (2010). Hybrid differential evolution with biogeography-based optimization for solution of economic load dispatch. *IEEE Transactions on Power Systems*, *25*(4), 1955–1964. doi:10.1109/TPWRS.2010.2043270

Chen, C., Wang, F., Zhou, B., Chan, K. W., Cao, Y., & Tan, Y. (2015). An interval optimization-based day-ahead scheduling scheme for renewable energy management in smart distribution systems. *Energy Conversion and Management*, *106*, 584–596. doi:10.1016/j.enconman.2015.10.014

Chen, Y., Wei, W., Liu, F., & Mei, S. (2016). Distributionally robust hydro-thermal-wind economic dispatch. *Applied Energy*, *173*, 511–519. doi:10.1016/j.apenergy.2016.04.060

Chung, S. H., & Chan, H. K. (2012). A two-level genetic algorithm to determine production frequencies for economic lost scheduling problem. *IEEE Transactions on Industrial Electronics*, *59*(1), 611–619. doi:10.1109/TIE.2011.2130498

Dorigo, M., & Stutzle, T. (2004). Ant Colony Optimization. Cambridge: The MIT Press.

Dubey, H., Panigrahi, B. K., & Pandit, M. (2014). Bio-inspired optimisation for economic load dispatch: A review. *International Journal of Bio-Inspired Compu.*, *6*(1), 7–21. doi:10.1504/IJBIC.2014.059967

Dubey, H. M., Pandit, M., & Panigrahi, B. K. (2015). Hybrid flower pollination algorithm with time-varying fuzzy selection mechanism for wind integrated multi-objective dynamic economic dispatch. *Renewable Energy*, *83*, 188–202. doi:10.1016/j.renene.2015.04.034

Ero_glu Y, & S. U. Seçkiner. (2013). Wind farm layout optimization using particle filtering approach. *Renew Energy, 58*, pp. 95-107.

Falaghi, H., & Haghifam, M.-R. (2007). ACO based algorithm for distributed generation sources allocation and sizing in distribution systems. Power Tech, Lausanne. doi:10.1109/PCT.2007.4538377

Firouzi, B. B., Farjah, E., & Abarghooee, R. A. (2013). An efficient scenario-based and fuzzy self-adaptive learning particle swarm optimization approach for dynamic economic emission dispatch considering load and wind power uncertainties. *Energy, 50*(1), 232–244. doi:10.1016/j.energy.2012.11.017

Golshan, M. E. H., & Arefifar, S. A. (2006). Distributed generation, reactive sources and network-configuration planning for power and energy-loss reduction. *IEEE Proceedings-Generation, Transmission, and Distribution 153*(2), pp. 127-136. IEEE.

Hazra, S., Pal, T., & Roy, P. K. (2019). Renewable Energy Based Economic Emission Load Dispatch Using Grasshopper Optimization Algorithm. *International Journal of Swarm Intelligence Research, 10*(1), 38–57. doi:10.4018/IJSIR.2019010103

Hazra, S., & Roy, P. (2015). Economic Load Dispatch considering non-smooth cost functions using Predator Prey Optimization. *Intelligent Computing and Applications-SPRINGER., 343*, 67–78. doi:10.1007/978-81-322-2268-2_8

Hazra, S., & Roy, P. (2015). Economic Load Dispatch considering non-smooth cost functions using Predator Prey Optimization. *Intelligent Computing and Applications-SPRINGER, 343*, 67–78. doi:10.1007/978-81-322-2268-2_8

Hazra, S., Roy, P. K., & Sinha, A. (2015). An Efficient Evolutionary algorithm applied to Economic load dispatch problem. IEEE Computer, Communication, Control and Information Technology-C3IT. pp. 1-6. doi:10.1109/C3IT.2015.7060129

Hetzer, J., Yu, D. C., & Bhattrarai, K. (2008). An economic dispatch model incorporating wind power. *IEEE Transactions on Energy Conversion, 23*(2), 603–611. doi:10.1109/TEC.2007.914171

Hu, Z., Zhang, M., Wang, X., Li, C., & Hu, M. (2016). Bi-level robust dynamic economic emission dispatch considering wind power uncertainty. *Electric Power Systems Research, 135*, 35–47. doi:10.1016/j.epsr.2016.03.010

Jin, X., Mu, Y., Jia, H., Wu, J., Xu, X., & Yu, X. (2016). Optimal day-ahead scheduling of integrated urban energy systems. *Applied Energy, 180*, 1–13. doi:10.1016/j.apenergy.2016.07.071

Krishnasamy, U., & Nanjundappan, D. (2016). Hybrid weighted probabilistic neural network and biogeography-based optimization for dynamic economic dispatch of integrated multiple-fuel and wind power plants. *Electrical Power and Energy Systems, 77*, 385–394. doi:10.1016/j.ijepes.2015.11.022

Lin, X. N., Ke, S. H., Li, Z. T., Weng, H. L., & Han, X. H. (2010). A fault diagnosis method of power systems based on improved objective function and genetic algorithm-tabu search. *IEEE Transactions on Power Delivery, 25*(3), 1268–1274. doi:10.1109/TPWRD.2010.2044590

Liu, X., & Xu, W. (2010). Minimum emission dispatch constrained by stochastic wind power availability and cost. *IEEE Transactions on Power Systems, 25*(3), 1705–1713. doi:10.1109/TPWRS.2010.2042085

Mandal, K. K., & Chakraborty, N. (2008). Effect of control parameters on differential evolution based combined economic emission dispatch with valve-point loading and transmission loss. *Int. J. Emerg. Electric Power Syst., 9*(4), 1–18. doi:10.2202/1553-779X.1918

Masters, G. M. (2004). *Renewable and Efficient Electric Power Systems*. New York: Wiley. doi:10.1002/0471668826

Meng, K., Wang, H. G., Dong, Z. Y., & Wong, K. P. (2010). Quantum-inspired particle swarm optimization for valve-point economic load dispatch. *IEEE Transactions on Power Systems*, 25(1), 215–222. doi:10.1109/TPWRS.2009.2030359

Mohamed, A. M., Ali, M. E., & Abdulrahman, I. A. (2017, September). Swarm intelligence-based optimization of grid-dependent hybrid renewable energy system. *Renewable & Sustainable Energy Reviews*, 77, 515–524. doi:10.1016/j.rser.2017.04.048

Mondal, S., Bhattacharya, A., & Dey, S. H. (2013). Multi-objective economic emission load dispatch solution using gravitational search algorithm and considering wind power penetration. *Electrical Power and Energy Systems*, 44(1), 282–292. doi:10.1016/j.ijepes.2012.06.049

Precup, R. E., David, R. C., Petriu, E. M., Preitl, S., & Radac, M. B. (2012). Fuzzy control systems with reduced parametric sensitivity based on simulated annealing. *IEEE Transactions on Industrial Electronics*, 59(8), 3049–3061. doi:10.1109/TIE.2011.2130493

Qu, B. Y., Liang, J. J., Zhu, Y. S., Wang, Z. Y., & Suganthan, P. N. (2017). Economic emission dispatch problems with stochastic wind power using summation based multi-objective evolutionary algorithm. *Information Sciences*, 351, 48–66. doi:10.1016/j.ins.2016.01.081

Rahnamayan, S., Tizhoosh, H. R., & Salama, M. M. A. (2007). Quasi oppositional differential evolution. *Proceedings of IEEE Congress on Evolu. Comput.* pp. 2229–36. 10.1109/CEC.2007.4424748

Rezaie,, H., & Kazemi-Rahbar,, M. H., Vahidi, B., & Rastegar, H. (2018). Solution of combined economic and emission dispatch problem using a novel chaotic improved harmony search algorithm. *Journal of Computational Design and Engg.*, 6(3), 447–467.

Roy, P. K., Ghoshal, S. P., & Thakur, S. S. (2010). Combined economic and emission dispatch problems using biogeography-based optimization. *Electrical Engineering*, 92, pp. 4-5, 173-184.

Seok, L. K., & Woo, G. Z. (2017). A new structural optimization method based on the harmony search algorithm. *ComputStruc April 2004; 82*(9–10), pp. 781-798.

Tizhoosh, H. (2005). Opposition-based learning: A new scheme for machine intelligence. *Proceedings of the Int Conference on Computational Intelligence for Modelling Control and Automation*, pp. 695–701. 10.1109/CIMCA.2005.1631345

Venkatesh, P., & Lee, K. Y. (2008). Multi-objective evolutionary programming for economic emission dispatch problem. *Proc. IEEE PES Gen. Meeting*, Pittsburgh, PA, Jul. 2008. 10.1109/PES.2008.4596896

Vlachogiannis, G., & Lee, K. Y. (2008). Quantum-inspired evolutionary algorithm for real and reactive power and reactive power dispatch. *IEEE Transactions on Power Systems*, 23(4), 1627–1636. doi:10.1109/TPWRS.2008.2004743

Wang, K. Y., Luo, X. J., Wu, L., & Liu, X. C. (2013). Optimal coordination of wind-hydro-thermal based on water complementing wind. *Renewable Energy*, 60, 169–178. doi:10.1016/j.renene.2013.04.015

Wu, T., Yang, Q., Bao, Z., & Yan, W. (2013). Coordinated Energy Dispatching in Microgrid With Wind Power Generation and Plug-in Electric Vehicles. *IEEE Transactions on Smart Grid*, *4*(3), 1453–1463. doi:10.1109/TSG.2013.2268870

Yao, F., Dong Z. Y., Xu, Z., Iu, H. H.-C., & Wong, K. P. (2012). Quantum-Inspired Particle Swarm Optimization for Power System Operations Considering Wind Power Uncertainty and Carbon Tax in Australia. IEEE Transactions on Industrial Informatics, 8(4), pp. 880-888.

Yuan, X., Tian, H., Yuan, Y., Huang, Y., & Ikram, R. M. (2015). An extended NSGA-III for solution multi-objective hydro-thermal-wind scheduling considering wind power cost. *Energy Conversion and Management*, *96*, 568–578. doi:10.1016/j.enconman.2015.03.009

Zhao, J. H., Fushuan Dong, W. Z. Y., Xue, Y., & Wong, K. P. (2012). Optimal Dispatch of Electric Vehicles and Wind Power Using Enhanced Particle Swarm Optimization. *IEEE Transactions on Industrial Informatics*, *8*(4), 889–899. doi:10.1109/TII.2012.2205398

Chapter 2
Semi–Automatic Sensor Ontology Matching Based on Interactive Multi–Objective Evolutionary Algorithm

Xingsi Xue
Fujian University of Technology, China

Junfeng Chen
iD https://orcid.org/0000-0002-3642-007X
Hohai University, China

ABSTRACT

Since different sensor ontologies are developed independently and for different requirements, a concept in one sensor ontology could be described with different terminologies or in different context in another sensor ontology, which leads to the ontology heterogeneity problem. To bridge the semantic gap between the sensor ontologies, authors propose a semi-automatic sensor ontology matching technique based on an Interactive MOEA (IMOEA), which can utilize the user's knowledge to direct MOEA's search direction. In particular, authors construct a new multi-objective optimal model for the sensor ontology matching problem, and design an IMOEA with t-dominance rule to solve the sensor ontology matching problem. In experiments, the benchmark track and anatomy track from the Ontology Alignment Evaluation Initiative (OAEI) and two pairs of real sensor ontologies are used to test performance of the authors' proposal. The experimental results show the effectiveness of the approach.

1. INTRODUCTION

A sensor ontology provides a formal specification on the sensor concepts and their relationships, which is a state-of-the-art technique for addressing the data heterogeneity issue in the semantic sensor web (Xue et al., 2019c). In particular, a sensor ontology can be defined as 3-tuple (C,P,R), where C, P, and

DOI: 10.4018/978-1-7998-3222-5.ch002

R are respectively the set of classes, properties and relationships, which can describe the sensors' capabilities, performance, and usage conditions that allow the discovery of different data depending on the purpose and context (Xue et al., 2019d). Since different sensor ontologies are developed independently and for different requirements, a concept in one sensor ontology could be described with different terminologies or in different context in another sensor ontology, which raises the heterogeneity problem to a higher level. Ontology matching is an effective technique to solve the sensor ontology heterogeneity problem by determining the semantically identical entities in heterogeneous sensor ontologies (Xue, & Wang, 2016). The obtained sensor ontology alignment A is a correspondence set, and each correspondence inside is a 4-tuple (e, e', n, r), where e and e' are the entities of two sensor ontologies. $n \in [0,1]$ is a confidence value holding for the correspondence between e and e', and r is the relationship between e and e', which refers to equivalence in this work.

Due to the complex nature of the ontology matching process, Evolutionary Algorithm (EA) has become a state-of-the-art methodology for matching the ontologies. However, there existing different aspects of solution that are partially or wholly in conflict, and the single-objective EA may lead to unwanted bias to one of them and reduce the solution's quality. Multi-objective EA (MOEA) can estimate different aspect of solutions simultaneously, and produce a set of solutions which contains a number of non-dominated solutions, none of which can be further improved on any one objective without degrading it in another. MOEA based ontology matching technique is a recently introduced, innovative, and efficient methodology to address the ontology matching problem (Acampora et al., 2014). However, due to the complexity of the ontology matching process, ontology alignments generated by an automatic matcher should be checked by users to ensure their quality (Shvaiko & Euzenat, 2013). To improve the quality of sensor ontology alignment, in this work, we propose an Interactive MOEA (IMOEA)-based semi-automatic ontology matching technique. In particular, our contributions are as follows:

1. A semi-automatic ontology matching framework is proposed for matching sensor ontologies;
2. A multi-objective optimal model is constructed for the sensor ontology matching problem;
3. A t-dominance rule is proposed and a problem-specific IMOEA is designed to effectively solve the sensor ontology matching problem.

The rest of the paper is organized as follows. Section 2 describes related works. Section 3 defines the ontology matching problem. Section 4 provides the details of IMOEA. Section 5 shows the experimental results, and section 6 relates our conclusions.

2. RELATED WORK

2.1 Multi-Objective Evolutionary Algorithm Based Ontology-Matching Techniques

Since a suitable computation of parameters could be better performed by evaluating the right compromise among different objectives involved in the matching process, approaches based on MOEAs are emerging as an innovative and efficient methodology to address the ontology matching problem.

Acampora et al. first propose to use Non-dominated Sorting Genetic Algorithm II (NSGA-II) (Deb et al., 2002) to tune the appropriate values for an ontology matching system's parameters. NSGA-II enables the determination of high-quality ontology alignments. Xue et al. also propose to use NSGA-II to determine various non-dominated ontology matching system parameters in terms of recall and precision (Xue et al., 2015). They further propose the novel ontology alignment quality measures that do not require experts to provide a reference alignment (Xue et al., 2014), and on this basis, a novel optimal model was constructed for ontology matching. Xue et al. also try to use the multi-objective evolutionary algorithm based on decomposition (MOEA/D) (Zhang, & Li, 2007) to improve the performance of ontology-matching technique based on NSGA-II (Xue et al., 2014b). They present the decomposition approach of the objective, the encoding mechanism, the problem-specific evolutionary operators and the principle of selecting the representative solutions for different decision-makers. A more recent study (Acampora et al., 2014) compare the performance of NSGA-II, SPEA2 (Zitzler et al., 2001), PESA-II (Corne et al., 2001), OMPPSO (Sierra, & Coello, 2005), and DENSEA (Greiner et al., 2006) when solving the ontology-matching problem; proposed a novel optimal model using different ontology alignment measures, and evaluated the algorithms based on three metrics. More recently, Xue et al. propose a compact MOEA/D (Xue et al., 2017a) and metamodel-assisted compact MOEA/D (Xue et al., 2017b) to improve the performance of MOEA/D based ontology matcher. Similar idea is also introduced into the work of improving NSGA-II based ontology matching process (Xue et al., 2017c). They also propose a hybrid NSGA-II to solve biomedical ontology matching problem (Xue et al., 2019), which is an open challenge in the ontology matching domain.

In all these existing approaches, the requirement of an exponentially increasing population to explore the Pareto-optimal front leads to huge computational expense (Sinha et al., 2014). Our approach employs the user's knowledge to guide the algorithm to focus on the user's preferred parts of the Pareto front and use computational resources more effectively. Since the effort concentrates on looking just for the solutions in the preferred region of the Pareto front, our approach can determine the sensor ontology alignment more efficiently than MOEA-based approach.

2.2 Semi-Automatic Ontology-Matching

To obtain a high quality-ontology alignment, a user must be required to cooperate with the automatic ontology matchers (Dragisic et al., 2016). Thus, in recent years, many semi-automatic ontology matching systems have been developed to exploit user interventions in the different processes of ontology matching to obtain high-quality ontology alignments.

AML (Faria et al., 2015) combines its design principles (flexibility and extensibility) with a strong focus on efficiency and scalability. AML employs an interactive selection algorithm, which utilized the matching results returned by various ontology matchers to detect suspicious mappings. Above the high similarity threshold of 70%, AML queries the user for suspicious mappings, and accepts all other mappings as true. Below this threshold, AML automatically rejects suspicious mappings, and queries the user for all other mappings, until the minimum threshold of 45% is reached, the limit of consecutive negative answers is reached, or the query limit is reached. It ensures that the reasonable workload for the user by setting the query limit as 45% of the determined correspondences for small scale ontology matching tasks, and 15% for the others.

Alin (Dragisic et al., 2016) is another state-of-the-art semi-automatic ontology matching system, which primarily utilizes the linguistic matching techniques and uses the Wordnet as external resource. After generating an initial set of candidate correspondences, which are the correspondences being selected to receive the feedback from the expert, alin requires the user to validate these candidate mappings. When the user accepts a candidate mapping, it is moved to the final alignment. After that, Alin checks the correspondences related to the accepted mappings, adds them to the candidate mappings list and removes all the candidate mappings that are not consistent with the approved correspondences. The interactions continue until there are no more candidate correspondences left.

LogMap (Jimenez-Ruiz et al., 2016) identifies reliable and non-reliable mappings using lexical, structural, and reasoning-based techniques. It removes reliable mappings and most of the non-reliable mappings, and presents the rest to the users for validation. The user feedback is utilized to detect conflicts with previously found mappings, which are rejected. LogMap allows interrupting user interaction, which means using heuristics to deal with remaining mapping suggestions, and it also allow to pause the user interaction (save current status of system) and continue user's validation work in the future.

XMap (Dragisic et al., 2016) also makes use of user interactions in the post-matching steps to filter its candidate mappings. It uses two thresholds to implement this procedure, i.e. the upper threshold and lower threshold. Upper threshold is set for those mappings that can be directly added to the final alignment and lower threshold is set for those that should be presented to the user for validation. The mappings accepted by the user are moved to the final alignment.

Xue et al. (Xue et al., 2017d) propose a collaborative ontology matching framework, which asks multiple users to work together to reduce the error rate. Later, they introduce a partial reference alignment, which works as a history document, into this framework to improve the efficiency of matching process (Xue et al., 2018). They further utilize this technique to match the biomedical ontologies (Xue et al., 2019b).

All the semi-automatic ontology matching systems mentioned above make use of the user involvement exclusively in pre-matching or post-matching steps to filter their candidate mappings, present all the mappings at a time to the user. Different from these approaches, we utilize EA to implement an iterative semi-automatic ontology matching process and get user involved to improve the previous alignment in each generation, which is regarded as the most effective approach to implement the semi-automatic ontology matching (Dragisic et al., 2016).

3. ONTOLOGY-MATCHING PROBLEM

An ontology matcher takes as input two ontologies O_1 and O_2, and outputs an $|O_1 \times O_2|$ similarity matrix S, whose elements s_{ij} are the similarity values between the i-th entity in O_1 and j-th entity in O_2. Basic ontology matchers can generally be divided into the four categories of syntactic-, linguistic-, structure- and instance-based similarity matchers (Xue, & Wang, 2015a). Since different ontology matchers do not necessarily determine the same correct correspondences, several competing matchers are usually applied to the same pair of entities to increase the evidence pointing towards a potential match or mismatch (Nguyen, & Conrad, 2015). How to select, combine and tune various ontology matchers to obtain a high-quality ontology alignment is one of the main challenges in ontology matching (Shvaiko, & Euzenat, 2013). Moreover, the quality of the alignments clearly is strongly dependent on the selection of an appropriate aggregation strategy. Among different compositions, the parallel composition of basic matchers, due to its ability to dynamically tune the basic matchers to obtain high-quality output, is a key breakthrough in attaining first-rate matching performance (Gulic et al., 2016). In this work, we choose the weighted average strategy to aggregate different ontology matchers, and further utilize IMOEA to automatically find the best manner of aggregating various similarity matrices into one.

Given n ontology matchers, suppose the golden alignment is one-to-one, i.e., one entity in the source ontology is matched with only one entity in the target ontology and vice versa, based on the observation that the more correspondences found and the higher the mean similarity values of the correspondences, the better the alignment quality (Bock, & Hettenhausen, 2012), the optimal model of the ontology matching problem is defined as:

$$
\begin{aligned}
&\max f\left(X\right) = \left(MC\left(X\right), I\left(X\right)\right) \\
&s.t.\, X = \left(x_1, x_2, \ldots x_n, x_{n+1}\right)^T \\
&\sum_{i=1}^{n} x_i = 1 \\
&x_i \in [0,1], i = 1, 2, \ldots, n+1
\end{aligned}
\tag{1}
$$

where the decision variable X represents the parameter set, i.e., the weights for aggregating various ontology matchers (x_i, i=1,2,..,n), and a threshold x_{n+1} for filtering the aggregated alignment to obtain the final one. Supposing some solution X corresponding to an ontology alignment A, $MC(X)$ and $MR(X)$ calculate A's MatchCoverage and MatchRatio (Xue, & Wang, 2015b), and

$$
I\left(X\right) = 0.5 \times MR\left(X\right) + 0.5 \times \frac{\sum_{i=1}^{|A|} \delta_i}{|A|},
$$

where $|A|$ is the number of correspondences in A, and δ_i is the similarity value of the i-th correspondence in A.

4. INTERACTIVE MULTI-OBJECTIVE EVOLUTIONARY ALGORITHM

Incorporating the user's knowledge on the solution quality into the intermediate generations of NSGA-II, IMOEA can lead the algorithm to progress towards the user's most preferred point. Given an ideal point in the objective space, whose objective values are the best values that each objective function can achieve, if the Euclidean distance between the elite and the ideal point in the objective space remains unchanged for ε generation, IMOEA involves the user in guiding the algorithm. After the user picks the most preferred point from the Pareto front, a triangle in the objective space will be constructed to express the user's preference region. Based on that triangle in the objective space, a new Pareto domination rule, t-dominance, is proposed to implement a new fast non-dominated sorting procedure.

Next, we will present three basic components of IMOEA, chromosome encoding, evolutionary operators, and t-dominance.

4.1 Chromosome Encoding Mechanism for Weighted-Average Sum Combination

In this work, we use binary encoding where the parameter set, which includes several weights of similarity measures and one threshold, is encoded in a solution. Therefore, a solution can be divided into two parts: one for several weights and the other for a threshold. The weighted-average approach combines various similarity measures whose weights sum to 1. Our encoding mechanism indirectly represents them through numbers in the interval $[0,1]$. If p is the number of weights required, the number set can be represented as $c_1, c_2, \ldots, c_p$, and the chromosome decoding is carried out by dividing the numbers by their sum, resulting in the parameter set

$$\left\{ \frac{c_1}{\sum_{i=1}^{p} c_i}, \frac{c_2}{\sum_{i=1}^{p} c_i}, \ldots \frac{c_p}{\sum_{i=1}^{p} c_i} \right\}.$$

4.2 Evolutionary Operators

In this paper, to balance the diversity of the population and the algorithm's convergence, the selection operator first sorts the chromosomes of the population in descending order according to their crowding distances which estimate the density of the solutions. Then we select the chromosomes from the top half of the population, and randomly copy one each time to form a new population.

The crossover operator takes two chromosomes called parents and generates two children chromosomes, which are obtained by mixing the genes of the parents. Crossover is applied with a certain probability, a parameter of EA. In this work, we use the common one-cut-point method to carry out the crossover operation on the population. First, a cut position in two parents is randomly determined and this position is a cut point which cuts each parent into two parts: the left part and the right part. Then, the right parts of them are switched to form two children.

Mutation operator assures diversity in the population and prevents premature convergence. In our work, for each bit in the chromosome we check if the mutation could be applied according to the mutation probability and if it is, the value of that bit is then flipped.

4.3 *T*-Dominance Rule

First, we combine the current and new populations and remove redundant chromosomes. Then, the fast, non-dominated sorting approach is applied to the population to obtain different non-domination levels. After that, from the Pareto front, IMOEA picks as best chromosome (elite) which is closest to the ideal point in terms of Euclidean distance, and tries to update the historical elite by comparing their Euclidean distances to the ideal point. If the elite remains unchanged for ε generations, IMOEA requires the user to guide the algorithm.

After the user determines a preferred solution in the Pareto front, two solutions with the best $MC()$ and $I()$respectively are selected one after another among the remaining solutions. These three solutions' corresponding points in the objective space form the apexes to construct a triangle, and on this basis, we propose a t-dominance rule to emphasize and create preferred solutions. Using the t-dominance-based fast non-dominated sorting, the population can be partitioned into different triangular-non-domination levels. Two sides of a triangle, originating from the user's preferred point, are used to eliminate regions, whose equations are $p_i^T f + q_i = 0$, $i=1,2$. They specifically divide the region into two half-spaces, $p_i^T f + q_i \geq 0$ and $p_i^T f + q_i < 0$, $i=1,2$, to focus the search entirely on the user's preferred region. The region represented by $p_i^T f + q_i < 0$ is assumed to be less preferred than that represented by $p_i^T f + q_i \geq 0$. Therefore, the intersection of the regions represented by $p_i^T f + q_i \geq 0$ gives the preferred region in which we perform a focused search after user interaction. Based on this idea, we propose a triangle-domination criterion.

Once the triangle set is known, two feasible solutions x_1 and x_2 can be compared with their corresponding objective function values f_1 and f_2 through the following domination criterion:

1. If $p_i^T f_1 + q_i \geq 0$ and $p_i^T f_2 + q_i \geq 0$, $i=1,2$, two solutions are compared based on the usual Pareto-domination rule;
2. If $p_i^T f_1 + q_i < 0$ and $p_i^T f_2 + q_i < 0$ for at least one $i=1,2$, two solutions are compared based on the usual Pareto-domination rule;
3. If $p_i^T f_1 + q_i \geq 0$ and $p_i^T f_2 + q_i < 0$ for at least one $i=1,2$, then the former dominates the latter.

An example of T-dominance rule is shown in Fig1. As shown in the figure, x_2 dominates x_3 according to the criterion (1); x_1 dominates x_4 according to the criterion (2) x_2 and x_3 dominates x_1 and x_4 according to the criterion (3).

Figure 1. An example of T-dominance rule

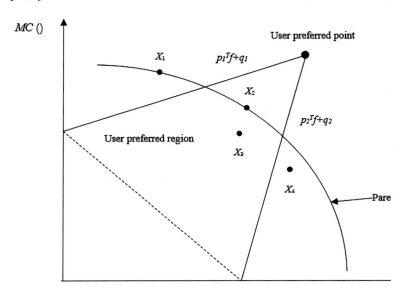

5. EXPERIMENTAL RESULTS AND ANALYSIS

In the experiments, the benchmark track and anatomy track provided by the Ontology Alignment Evaluation Initiative (OAEI)[1] and two pairs of real sensor ontologies, i.e., CSIRO sensor ontology[2] vs SSN ontology[3] and MMI Device ontology[4] vs SSN ontology, were used to test our approach. In the following, we present the experimental configuration and compare our approach with the participants of OAEI 2016 (Dragisic et al., 2016) and the state-of-the-art sensor ontology matching systems (Fernandez et al., 2013). The obtained alignments are assessed by means of the standard evaluation metrics, i.e., recall, precision and fmeasure (Rijsberge, 1975). Our approach's results are the average of 10 independent runs and the user is simulated by using an all-knowing oracle that can identify the quality of various solutions.

5.1 Experiment Configuration

The ontology matchers used in this work are as follows:

1. Syntactic-based ontology matcher using SMOA (Stoilos et al., 2005);
2. Linguistic-based ontology matcher using WordNet-based similarity measure (Miller, 1995);
3. Taxonomy-based ontology matcher using similarity flooding based similarity measure (Melnik et al., 2002);
4. Instance-based ontology matcher using soft TFIDF based similarity measure (Xue & Wang, 2015a).

In our work, IMOEA uses the following parameters which represent a tradeoff setting obtained empirically to achieve the highest average alignment quality on all test cases.

Through the configuration of parameters chosen in this way, it has been justified by the experiments in this paper that parameters chosen are robust for all the heterogeneous problems presented in the test cases, and are hoped to be robust for common heterogeneous situations in the real world.

1. Numerical accuracy: 0.01;
2. Population size: 50;
3. Crossover probability: 0.6;
4. Mutation probability: 0.02;
5. Generation threshold ε of involving user: 20;
6. Maximum number of generations: 300.

In addition, in order to compare with the participants of OAEI 2016, we run the testing cases on a Debian Linux virtual machine configured with four processors and 8GB of RAM running under a Dell PowerEdge T610 with 2*Intel Xeon Quad Core 2.26GHz E5607 processors and 32GB of RAM, under Linux ProxMox 2 (Debian). The softwares we used are JDK 1.8 and AlignmentAPI 4.9[5].

5.2 Benchmark Track

A benchmark consists of a set of small-scale ontologies built around a seed ontology and many variations. A brief description of the benchmark is presented in Table 1. Table 2 and Table 3 respectively show the statistical comparisons among three classic EA based approaches and IMOEA, the configurations of

Table 1. Brief description of benchmarks. 1XX, 2XX and 3XX denote test cases with ID beginning with the prefix digit 1, 2 and 3, respectively

ID	Brief Description
1XX	Ontologies under alignment have the same lexical, linguistic, or structure features.
2XX	Ontologies under alignment have different lexical, linguistic, or structure features.
3XX	Ontologies under alignment are from real-world cases.

these EA based approaches are referred to their corresponding literatures. Table 4 compares IMOEA with the participants in OAEI 2016.

We first carry out the statistical comparison on the alignment's quality in terms of f-measure among Genetic Algorithm (GA) based (Martinez-Gil et al., 2008), Memetic Algorithm (MA) based (Acampora et al., 2012), Particle Swarm Optimization (PSO) based (Bock et al., 2012) ontology meta-matching approaches and IMOEA. The comparison is formally carried out by means of a multiple comparison procedure which consists of two steps: in the first one, a statistical technique, i.e. the Friedman's test (Friedman, 1937), is used to determine whether the results provided by various approaches present any difference; in the second one, which method is outperformed is determined by carrying out a post-hoc test, i.e. Holm's test (Holm, 1979), only if in the first step an difference is found.

As can be seen from Table 2, in the Friedman's test, the computed

$$\chi_r^2 = 17.0612 > \chi_{0.05}^2 = 7.815 \,.$$

In the Holm's test, as shown in Table 3, our approach statistically outperforms other EA based ontology meta-matching approaches on the alignment's quality at 0.05 significance level.

We can see from Table 4 that our approach outperforms all participants in OAEI 2016 in terms of recall, precision and fmeasure. Compared with our approach's non-interactive version, i.e., NSGA-II based approach, the utilization of user's knowledge can significantly improve the quality of the alignment, especially in terms of precision. Therefore, our approach is effective for small-scale ontology-matching problem.

5.3 Anatomy Track

The anatomy real-world track is a large ontology matching task concerning the matching of Adult Mouse Anatomy (2,744 classes) and part of the NCI Thesaurus (3,304 classes), describing the human anatomy. The results of our approach and the participants in OAEI 2016 on anatomy track are shown in Table 5.

We can see from Table 5 that our approach attains the highest fmeasure among all the participants in OAEI 2016, and the recall, precision and fmeasure of our approach are highly improved over the NSGA-II based approach. Thus, user's knowledge can help the algorithm to find a better solution in the large search space.

To conclude, the fmeasure of our approach is higher than those of other systems, demonstrating that the tradeoff between two objectives enables our approach to determine a greater number of correct correspondences. Moreover, the iterative utilization of the user's knowledge can guide the algorithm

Table 2. Friedman's test on the alignment's quality obtained by three EA based ontology approaches and IMOEA. Each value represents the fmeasure, and the number in round parentheses is the corresponding computed rank.

ID	GA	MA	PSO	IMOEA
101	1.00 (2.5)	1.00 (2.5)	1.00 (2.5)	1.00 (2.5)
103	0.99 (4)	1.00 (2)	1.00 (2)	1.00 (2)
104	0.99 (4)	1.00 (2)	1.00 (2)	1.00 (2)
201	0.50 (3)	0.52 (2)	0.42 (4)	0.58 (1)
203	0.97 (3)	0.96 (4)	1.00 (1)	0.99 (2)
204	0.94 (4)	0.97 (3)	0.98 (1.5)	0.98 (1.5)
205	0.83 (2)	0.79 (3)	0.73 (4)	0.93 (1)
206	0.84 (4)	0.88 (2)	0.85 (3)	0.90 (1)
221	0.99 (3.5)	0.99 (3.5)	1.00 (1.5)	1.00 (1.5)
222	0.99 (3)	0.99 (3)	0.99 (3)	1.00 (1)
223	0.99 (2.5)	0.99 (2.5)	0.99 (2.5)	0.99 (2.5)
224	1.00 (2.5)	1.00 (2.5)	1.00 (2.5)	1.00 (2.5)
225	0.99 (4)	1.00 (2)	1.00 (2)	1.00 (2)
228	0.99 (3)	0.99 (3)	0.99 (3)	1.00 (1)
230	0.93 (3.5)	0.93 (3.5)	0.98 (2)	1.00 (1)
231	0.99 (3)	0.99 (3)	0.99 (3)	1.00 (1)
301	0.70 (2.5)	0.70 (2.5)	0.64 (4)	0.72 (1)
302	0.61 (3)	0.63 (2)	0.04 (4)	0.65 (1)
304	0.83 (3)	0.87 (2)	0.72 (4)	0.88 (1)
Average	0.90 (3.16)	0.91 (2.63)	0.86 (2.71)	**0.92 (1.5)**

Table 3. Holm's test on the alignment's quality obtained by three EA based ontology matching approaches and IMOEA

	Approach	z Value	Unadjusted p Value	$\frac{a}{k-i}$, $\alpha=0.05$
3	MA	2.6978	0.0070	0.05
2	PSO	2.8888	0.0039	0.025
1	GA	3.9631	$7.3983*e^{-5}$	0.0166

Table 4. Comparison of our approach with participants in the OAEI 2016 on benchmark

Systems	Recall	Precision	f-Measure
AML	0.24	1.00	0.38
CroMatch	0.83	0.96	0.89
Lily	0.83	0.97	0.89
LogMap	0.39	0.93	0.55
LogMapLt	0.50	0.43	0.46
PhenoMF	0.01	0.03	0.01
PhenoMM	0.01	0.03	0.01
PhenoMP	0.01	0.02	0.01
XMap	0.40	0.95	0.56
LogMapBio	0.24	0.48	0.32
NSGA-II based Approach	0.78	0.82	0.80
IMOEA	**0.87**	**0.98**	**0.92**

Table 5. Comparison of our approach with the participants in OAEI 2016 on benchmark

Systems	Recall	Precision	f-Measure
AML	0.93	0.95	0.94
LPHOM	0.72	0.70	0.71
Lily	0.79	0.87	0.83
DKP-AOM	0.13	**0.99**	0.23
XMap	0.86	0.92	0.89
DKP-AOM-Lite	0.13	**0.99**	0.23
FCA_Map	0.83	0.93	0.88
Alin	0.33	**0.99**	0.50
LogMap	0.84	0.91	0.88
LogMapBio	0.89	0.88	0.89
LYAM	0.87	0.86	0.86
LogMapLite	0.72	0.96	0.82
CroMatcher	0.90	0.94	0.92
FuzzyAlign	0.89	0.94	0.91
NSGA-II based Approach	0.87	0.73	0.79
IMOEA	**0.94**	0.97	**0.95**

to significantly improve the solution quality. Experimental results also show that our approach can effectively match ontologies with various scales and under different heterogeneous situations.

5.4 Real Sensor Ontologies

We now test our approach on two pairs of real sensor ontologies: CSIRO sensor ontology vs SSN ontology and MMI Device ontology vs SSN ontology. Since SSN is the most used global reference ontology that has been developed in the domain of sensor networks, the goal of this experiment is to align the CSIRO sensor ontology and MMI Device ontology to SSN ontology. We compare our approach with state-of-the-art sensor ontology-matching systems ASMOV (Noessner et al., 2010), CODI (Jean-Mary et al., 2009), SOBOM (Xu et al., 2010), and FuzzyAlign (Fernandez et al., 2013), on two pairs of real sensor ontologies in terms of recall, precision and fmeasure. The comparative results are shown in Table 6.

We can see that the values of recall, precision and fmeasure obtained by our approach are better than those of the other approaches, which demonstrates the effectiveness of the proposed method when matching ontologies in the semantic sensor web domain.

Table 6. Comparison of our approach with the sensor ontology matchers on two pairs of real sensor ontologies

Systems	CSIRO vs SSN			MMI Device vs SSN		
	Recall	Precision	f-Measure	Recall	Precision	f-Measure
ASMOV	0.78	0.72	0.75	0.65	0.84	0.73
CODI	0.78	0.81	0.79	0.83	0.78	0.80
SOBOM	0.81	0.76	0.78	0.74	0.81	0.77
FuzzyAlign	0.82	0.95	0.88	0.84	0.92	0.88
IMOEA	**0.85**	**0.96**	**0.90**	**0.89**	**0.95**	**0.92**

6. CONCLUSION

To match the heterogeneous sensor ontologies, we propose an interactive multi-objective evolutionary algorithm (IMOEA)-based semi-automatic ontology-matching technique. Our proposal utilizes the user's knowledge to guide the algorithm, and it can self-adaptively determine when to involve the user, constructing triangular region in the Pareto front and selecting the next generation's population using a novel *t*-dominance rule. The experimental results show that IMOEA can effectively match ontologies with various scales and under different heterogeneous situation.

ACKNOWLEDGMENT

This work is supported by the National Natural Science Foundation of China (Nos. 61503082 and 61403121), the Natural Science Foundation of Fujian Province (No. 2016J05145), the Fundamental Research Funds for the Central Universities (No. 2019B22314), the Program for New Century Excellent

Talents in Fujian Province University (No. GY-Z18155), the Program for Outstanding Young Scientific Researcher in Fujian Province University (No. GY-Z160149) and the Scientific Research Foundation of Fujian University of Technology (Nos. GY-Z17162 and GY-Z15007).

REFERENCES

Acampora, G., Ishibuchi, H. H., & Vitiello, A. (2014). A comparison of multi-objective evolutionary algorithms for the ontology meta-matching problem. *Proceedings IEEE Congress on Evolutionary Computation (CEC 2014)*, (pp. 413-420). Beijing, China. 10.1109/CEC.2014.6900544

Acampora, G., Kaymak, U., Loia, V., & Vitiello, A. (2013). Applying NSGA-II for solving the Ontology Alignment Problem. *Proceedings 2013 IEEE International Conference on Systems, Man, and Cybernetics (SMC 2013)*, (pp. 1098-1103). Manchester, UK: IEEE. 10.1109/SMC.2013.191

Acampora, G., Loia, V., Salerno, S., & Vitiello, A. (2012). A hybrid evolutionary approach for solving the ontology alignment problem. *International Journal of Intelligent Systems*, *27*(3), 189–216. doi:10.1002/int.20517

Bock, J., & Hettenhausen, J. (2012). Discrete particle swarm optimisation for ontology alignment. *Information Sciences*, *192*, 152–173. doi:10.1016/j.ins.2010.08.013

Corne, D. W., Jerram, N. R., Knowles, J. D., & Oates, M. J. (2001) PESA-II: Region-based selection in evolutionary multiobjective optimization, *Proceedings of the 3rd Annual Conference on Genetic and Evolutionary Computation*. San Francisco, CA: Morgan Kaufmann, (pp. 283-290).

Deb, K., Pratap, A., Agarwal, S., & Meyarivan, T. (2002). A fast and elitist multiobjective genetic algorithm: NSGA-II. *IEEE Transactions on Evolutionary Computation*, *6*(2), 182–197. doi:10.1109/4235.996017

Dragisic, Z., Ivanova, V., Lambrix, P., Faria, D., Jimenez-Ruiz, E., & Pesquita, C. (2016). User validation in ontology alignment. *Proceedings 15th International Semantic Web Conference 2016*. Kobe, Japan. Berlin, Germany: Springer. (pp. 200-217). 10.1007/978-3-319-46523-4_13

Falconer, M. S., & Noy, F. N. (2011). Schema Matching and Mapping, Data-Centric Systems and Applications. Berlin, Germany: Springer.

Faria, D., Martins, C., Nanavaty, A., Oliveiraand, D., Balasubramani, B. S., Taheri, A., . . . Cruz, I. F. (2015). AML results for OAEI 2015. *Proceedings 10th International Workshop on Ontology Matching*, (pp. 116-123). Bethlehem, PA. Academic Press.

Friedman, M. (1937). The use of ranks to avoid the assumption of normality implicit in the analysis of variance. *Journal of the American Statistical Association*, *32*(200), 675–701. doi:10.1080/01621459.1937.10503522

Greiner, D., Winter, G., & Emperador, J. M. (2006). Enhancing the multiobjective optimum design of structural trusses with evolutionary algorithms using DENSEA. *Proceedings 44th AIAA (American Institute of Aeronautics and Astronautics) Aerospace Sciences Meeting and Exhibit*. Reno, Nevada. Berlin, Germany: Springer. (pp. 1474). 10.2514/6.2006-1474

Gulic, M., Vrdoljak, B., & Banek, M. (2016). CroMatcher: An ontology matching system based on automated weighted aggregation and iterative final alignment. *Journal of Web Semantics*, *41*, 50–71. doi:10.1016/j.websem.2016.09.001

Holm, S. (1979). A simple sequentially rejective multiple test procedure. *Scandinavian Journal of Statistics*, 65–70.

Jean-Mary, Y. R., Shironoshita, E. P., & Kabuka, M. R. (2009). Ontology matching with semantic verification. *Journal of Web Semantics*, *7*(3), 235–251. doi:10.1016/j.websem.2009.04.001 PMID:20186256

Jimenez-Ruiz, E., Grau, B. C., & Cross, V. (2016). LogMap family participation in the OAEI 2016. *Proceedings 11th International Workshop on Ontology Matching*, (pp. 185-189). Kobe, Japan.

Martinez-Gil, J., Alba, E., & Montes, J. F. A. (2008). Optimizing ontology alignments by using genetic algorithms. *Proceedings of the First International Conference on Nature Inspired Reasoning for the Semantic Web*, (pp. 1-15). Berlin, Germany.

Nguyen, T. T. A., & Conrad, S. (2015). Ontology Matching using multiple similarity measures. *Proceedings 7th International Joint Conference on Knowledge Discovery, Knowledge Engineering and Knowledge Management (IC3K 2015)*, (pp. 603-611). Lisbon, Portugal: IEEE.

Noessner, J., Niepert, M., Meilicke, C., & Stuckenschmidt, H. (2010) Leveraging terminological structure for object reconciliation. *Proceedings 7th Extended Semantic Web Conference*, (pp. 334-348). Heraklion, Greece: Springer.

Shvaiko, P., & Euzenat, J. (2013). Ontology matching: State of the art and future challenges. *IEEE Transactions on Knowledge and Data Engineering*, *25*(1), 158–176. doi:10.1109/TKDE.2011.253

Sierra, M. R., & Coello, C. A. C. (2005). Improving PSO-based multi-objective optimization using crowding, mutation and -dominance. *Proceedings International Conference on Evolutionary Multi-Criterion Optimization (EMO 2005)*, (pp. 505-519). Guanajuato, Mexico. Berlin, Germany: Springer. 10.1007/978-3-540-31880-4_35

Sinha, A., Korhonen, P., Wallenius, J., & Deb, K. (2014). An interactive evolutionary multi-objective optimization algorithm with a limited number of decision maker calls. *European Journal of Operational Research*, *233*(3), 647–688. doi:10.1016/j.ejor.2013.08.046

Van Rijsberge, C. J. (1975). *Information Retrieval*. Butterworth, UK: University of Glasgow.

Xu, P., Wang, Y., Cheng, L., & Zhang, T. (2010). Alignment Results of SOBOM for OAEI 2010. *Proceedings of the 5th International Conference on Ontology Matching (OM-2010)*, (pp. 203-211). Shanghai, China: CEUR-WS.org.

Xue, X., Chen, J., & Yao, X. (2019). Efficient User Involvement in Semi-automatic Ontology Matching, IEEE Transactions on Emerging Topics in Computational Intelligence, pp. 1-11.

Xue, X., & Chen, J. (2019c). Using Compact Evolutionary Tabu Search Algorithm for Matching Sensor Ontologies. *Swarm and Evolutionary Computation*, *48*, 25–30. doi:10.1016/j.swevo.2019.03.007

Xue, X., & Chen, J. (2019d). Optimizing Ontology Alignment Through Hybrid Population-based Incremental Learning Algorithm. *Memetic Computing*, *11*(2), 209–217. doi:10.100712293-018-0255-8

Xue, X., Hang, Z., & Tang, Z. (2019b). Interactive Biomedical Ontology Matching. *PLoS One*, *14*(4), 1–13. doi:10.1371/journal.pone.0215147 PMID:30995257

Xue, X., & Liu, J. (2017a). Optimizing Ontology Alignment through Compact MOEA/D. *International Journal of Pattern Recognition and Artificial Intelligence*, *31*(4). doi:10.1142/S0218001417590042

Xue, X., & Liu, J. (2017d). Collaborative Ontology Matching Based on Compact Interactive Evolutionary Algorithm. *Knowledge-Based Systems*, *137*, 94–103. doi:10.1016/j.knosys.2017.09.017

Xue, X., Tsai, P., & Feng, G. (2017b). Efficient Ontology Meta-Matching Based on Metamodel-assisted Compact MOEA/D. *Journal of Information Hiding and Multimedia Signal Processing*, *8*(5), 1021–1028.

Xue, X., & Wang, Y. (2015a). Ontology alignment based on instance using NSGA-II. *Journal of Information Science*, *41*(1), 58–70. doi:10.1177/0165551514550142

Xue, X., & Wang, Y. (2015b). Optimizing Ontology Alignments through a Memetic Algorithm Using both MatchFmeasure and Unanimous Improvement Ratio. *Artificial Intelligence*, *223*, 65–81. doi:10.1016/j.artint.2015.03.001

Xue, X., & Wang, Y. (2016). Using Memetic Algorithm for Instance Coreference Resolution. *IEEE Transactions on Knowledge and Data Engineering*, *28*(2), 580–591. doi:10.1109/TKDE.2015.2475755

Xue, X., & Wang, Y. (2017c). Improving the Efficiency of NSGA-II based Ontology Aligning Technology. *Data & Knowledge Engineering*, *108*, 1–14. doi:10.1016/j.datak.2016.12.002

Xue, X., Wang, Y., & Hao, W. (2014b). Using MOEA/D for optimizing ontology alignments. *Soft Computing*, *18*(8), 1589–1601. doi:10.100700500-013-1165-9

Xue, X., Wang, Y., & Hao, W. (2015). Optimizing ontology alignments by using NSGA-II. *The International Arab Journal of Information Technology*, *12*(2), 175–181.

Xue, X., Wang, Y., Hao, W., & Hou, J. (2014a). Optimizing Ontology Alignments through NSGA-II without Using Reference Alignment. *Computer Information*, *33*(4), 857–876.

Xue, X., & Yao, X. (2018). Interactive Ontology Matching based on Partial Reference Alignment. *Applied Soft Computing*, *72*, 355–370. doi:10.1016/j.asoc.2018.08.003

Zhang, Q., & Li, H. (2007). MOEA/D: A multiobjective evolutionary algorithm based on decomposition. *IEEE Transactions on Evolutionary Computation*, *11*(6), 712–731. doi:10.1109/TEVC.2007.892759

Zitzler, E., Laumanns, M., & Thiele, L. (2002). SPEA2: Improving the strength Pareto evolutionary algorithm. Optimization and Control with Applications to Industrial Problems. (pp. 95-100). Berlin, Germany: Springer.

Zitzler, E., & Thiele, L. (1999). Multiobjective evolutionary algorithms: A comparative case study and the strength Pareto approach. *IEEE Transactions on Evolutionary Computation*, *3*(4), 257–271. doi:10.1109/4235.797969

ENDNOTES

[1]   http://oaei.ontologymatching.org/2016

[2]   https://www.w3.org/2005/Incubator/ssn/wiki/SensorOntology2009

[3]   https://www.w3.org/TR/vocab-ssn

[4]   https://marinemetadata.org/

[5]   http://alignapi.gforge.inria.fr/

Chapter 3
A Comparative Study Among Recursive Metaheuristics for Gene Selection

Nassima Dif

(iD) https://orcid.org/0000-0002-8683-3163

EEDIS Laboratory, Djillali Liabes University, Sidi Bel Abbes, Algeria

Zakaria Elberrichi

(iD) https://orcid.org/0000-0002-3391-6280

EEDIS Laboraory, Djillali Liabes University, Sidi Bel Abbes, Algeria

ABSTRACT

This chapter compares 4 variants of metaheuristics (RFA, EMVO, RPSO, and RBAT). The purpose is to test the impact of refinement on different types of metaheuristics (FA, MVO, PSO, and BAT). The refinement helps to enhance exploitation and to speed up the search process in multidimensional spaces. Moreover, it presents a powerful tool to solve different issues such as slow convergence. The different methods have been used for gene selection on 11 microarrays datasets to solve their various issues related to the presence of irrelevant genes. The obtained results reveal the positive impact of refinement on FA, MVO, and PSO, where all performances have been improved. On the other hand, this process harmed the BAT algorithm. The comparative study between the 4 variants highlights the efficiency of EMVO and FA in terms of precision and dimensionality reduction, respectively. Overall, this study suggests drawing attention to the choice of embedded metaheuristics in the refinement procedure, where powerful methods in exploration are recommended. Moreover, metaheuristics that risk form fast convergence are not advised.

DOI: 10.4018/978-1-7998-3222-5.ch003

1. INTRODUCTION

The DNA microarrays technology helps researchers to measure the expression level of thousands of genes(Harrington et al., 2000). Cancer identification is among the most important applications in the microarrays field (Almugren, & Alshamlan, 2019). The extracted biomarkers assist in diagnosis, prognosis, and treatment (Baliarsingh et al., 2019). In such applications, machine learning (ML) methods are exploited to analyze the generated biomedical datasets and to extract meaningful knowledge. However, these datasets suffer from the curse of dimensionality and the presence of redundant and irrelevant genes, which can result false diagnoses because of the presence of indiscriminate features. This issue becomes crucial especially for some machine learning algorithms that don't perform feature selection during training. Moreover, these datasets can result overfitting during training because of the large difference between the number of genes and samples. Thus to handle these volumes effectively, preprocessing techniques such as gene selection have been largely exploited.

The feature selection process set out to select M relevant subset of features from the initial set N (M <= N). The purpose of this method is to reduce the computational complexity of the ML algorithm and to enhance its precision.

Feature (gene) selection techniques are categorized into four strategies: filters(Hancer et al., 2018), wrappers (Jiang et al., 2019), embedded (Zhu et al., 2007) and hybrid methods (Alomari et al., 2018). Filters are based on statistic methods to evaluate the selected set. Whereas, wrappers depend on the performance of the machine learning algorithm, where a training step is required for each subset, which makes them computationally expensive compared to filters but more accurate (Inza et al., 2004). To take advantage of these two methods, hybrid approaches between filters and wrappers are proposed. In general, a filter strategy is performed first to reduce the high-dimensional space, and then the wrapper method is applied to the obtained result to select effectively the relevant subset. Last, embedded methods are characterized by their embedded future selection process within the training process.

For feature selection, first, a subset generation process is performed to generate the candidate subsets. Then, theses subsets are evaluated according to the cited strategies above. In exact methods, the generation step generates 2^N subset for N features in the initial set, and then these subsets are evaluated to select finally the best one among all possibilities. This procedure is computationally expensive, especially for high-dimensional datasets. As a solution, stochastic methods have been largely exploited such as probabilistic (Roffo et al., 2017), heuristic (Min, & Xu, 2016) and metaheuristic (Gu et al., 2018) strategies.

Metaheuristics are stochastic methods that have received considerable attention in several optimization problems: feature selection (Gu et al., 2018), classification (Abd-Alsabour, & Ramakrishnan, 2016), parameters and hyper-parameters optimization (Rojas-Delgado et al., 2019). The main purpose of these methods is to find good solutions in a reasonable run time complexity compared to exact methods. We should note that metaheuristics do not guarantee to find the best global solution as exact methods but it helps to find good solutions close to the best global one. Traditionally, genetic algorithm (GA) (Holland et al., 1992), particle swarm optimization (PSO) (Eberhart, & Kennedy, 1995) and ant colony optimization (ACO) (Dorigo et al., 1996) metaheuristics have been used in various classic studies to solve different NP-hard problems. Lately, there has been a large amount of publication on recent metaheuristics such as: cuckoo search (CS) (Yang, & Deb, 2009), firefly algorithm (FA) (Yang, 2009), bat algorithm (BAT) (Yang, 2010) and seven-spot ladybird optimization (SLO) (Wang et al., 2013).

These methods can be categorized into two groups: evolutionary and swarm intelligence algorithms (Fister et al., 2013). The first category points out on the exploration of the search space due to the evolutionary operations (selection, crossover, and mutation). Whereas, the second category focuses on the communication and co-operation between individuals whose strength generally their exploitation. To solve the different issues related to the lack of exploitation and exploration for some metaheuristics, variants of metaheuristics (Jayabarathi et al., 2018) and hybrid methods (DIF et al., 2018) have been proposed.

The purpose of this chapter is to detail the related literature on gene selection methods and to determine the impact of refinement of the search space on BAT and PSO metaheuristics. We should note that this process has been introduced previously and performed on the multi-verse Optimizer (MVO) and the firefly algorithm (FA) (DIF et al., 2017; DIF et al., 2019). The refinement helps to speeds up the search progression for dimensionality reduction, especially for high-dimensional data such as microarray datasets.

This chapter is organized as follows. Section 2 presents related works. Section 3 explains the principle of enhanced metaheuristics. Section 4 presents the experimentations and discuss the obtained results. The last part concludes this works and discusses some of the perspectives.

2. RELATED WORKS

Methods for feature selection have been focused on metaheuristics due to their capacity in the resolution of NP-hard problems. These methods can be used for the search process in both filters (Bala et al., 1995) and wrappers (Xue et al., 2012; Singh et al., 2015; Emary et al., 2015; Faris et al., 2018; Dif et al. (b), 2018). Previously, numerous studies have attempted to solve the feature selection process based on classical metaheuristics such as GA (Bala et al., 1995) and PSO (Chuang et al., 2008). Recent advances in metaheuristics methods have encouraged the machine learning community to exploit these new algorithms for feature selection. For instance, (Emary et al., 2015) used the FA algorithm to solve this task, their purpose was to take advantage of the capacity of FA in the generation of optimal subsets. In another research, (Faris et al., 2018) employed the MVO for both feature selection and parameter optimization. Another recent investigation conducted by (Dif et al. (b), 2018) examined the emerging role of MVO for instance and feature selection. The use of metaheuristics covered several domains such as the medical (Alaoui et al., 2018) and the biomedical (Bidi et al., 2018; Tarik et al., 2019) fields. For more details on metaheuristics for feature selection, several reviews have been published in the literature (Brezočnik et al., 2018; Yusup et al., 2019). This chapter focuses on their use in the biomedical domain and particularly the gene selection process in microarray datasets. This process has attracted considerable attention due to the challenging nature of microarray datasets and the sensitivity of the cancer classification task. The main purpose of all contributions was to enhance the machine learning algorithms' precision by reducing the number of genes. For instance, (Chen et al., 2014) proposed the exploitation of PSO for gene selection. In another investigation, (Deepthi et al., 2016) highlighted the efficiency of FA compared to random projection and PCA methods. Besides, (Begum et al., 2018) used the memetic algorithm (MA) for gene selection due to its specificity in escaping from premature convergence compared to GA. Their comparative study reports the effectiveness of MA compared to GA, SA, and TS metaheuristics.

Other researches propose to hybridize between filters- and wrappers-based metaheuristics to optimize the computational cost. For instance, (Dashtban et al., 2017) proposed to combine the filter method that uses the Laplacian and fisher score concepts and GA. A more recent investigation has examined the hybridization between the emperor penguin optimization (EPO) algorithm and chaos (MOCEPO) (Baliarsingh et al., 2019).

To solve the different issues related to the lack of exploitation and exploration, the proposition of hybrid metaheuristics received increased attention. The main purpose was to create a co-operation between these two concepts and to overcome the slow, premature convergence and the fact of getting trapped in a local optimum. The combination of the exploitation of PSO and the exploration of GA presented one of the classical hybridizations (Talbi et al., 2008). Other recent investigations tested the impact of combination with other more recent swarm intelligence methods such as Artificial Bee Colony (ABC) (Alshamlan et al., 2015) and music-based metaheuristic (Harmony Search) (Das et al., 2016). For more details on hybrid metaheuristics for gene selection, various surveys have been published (Ang et al., 2015; Almugren et al., 2019). Despite the considerable literature on hybrid methods, (DIF et al., 2018) highlighted the efficiency of a variant of the penguin search optimization metaheuristic (PeSOA-C) compared to the two sequential hybridizations FA-DE and BAT-AIS for gene selection. Moreover, (Piotrowski et al., 2018) demonstrated that some hybridizations become unnecessarily complicated due to their computational cost. These findings suggest the consideration of variants of metaheuristics instead of their hybridizations to optimize the run time complexity for high dimensional problems. Moreover, despite the large use of metaheuristics, there are no theoretical rules on their behavior and adaptation to all domains of applications.

Several variants of metaheuristics have been proposed in the literature. The main purpose was to enhance the efficiency of the proposed framework and to adapt them to the application domain. In general, the proposed methods incorporate a new or existed function in a metaheuristic into another one. For instance, (Vieira et al., 2013) introduced the local search and the mutation into PSO to overcome premature convergence and to enhance exploitation. Besides, (Xue et al., 2012) introduced the ideas of crowding, mutation, and dominance into PSO. In another research, (Prasad, & Biswas, 2015) exploited the principle of refinement for PSO. Their investigations aim to reduce the search space for the high dimensional dataset. To sum up, various recent investigations encouraged the exploitation of enhanced metaheuristics such as BAT (Jayabarathi et al., 2018), and grey wolf optimizer (Faris et al. (b), 2018).

3. METHODS

The purpose of this section is to details the related principles to the metaheuristics (MVO, FA, BAT, and PSO) and their variants (EMVO, RFA, RBAT, RSPO).

3.1. Multi-Verse Optimizer (MVO)

The multi-verse optimizer (MVO) takes its inspiration from the multi-verse theory (Mirjalili et al., 2016). It is based on three concepts: black holes, white holes, and wormholes. Black holes attract everything with their gravitational force. On the other hand, white holes are produced from collisions between parallel universes. Wormholes present time and space travel tunnels that join the different parts of a universe. Each universe is characterized by an inflation rate and an Inflation speed.

In the multi-verse algorithm, each solution is a universe and the variables present its components. To make a tradeoff between exploitation and exploration, this algorithm uses black and white holes for explorations. On the other hand, wormholes are employed for exploitation and to exchange objects between universes. The process of exchange is modeled by the roulette wheel selection method and it depends on the inflation rate value (equation1: U_i is the universe, $x_i^j \in U_i$, x_k^j is selected by the roulette wheel selection, NI normalized inflation rate and r_1 is a random number), where universes with small values have more probability to send objects.

$$x_i^j = \begin{cases} x_k^j & r_1 < NI\left(U_i\right) \\ x_i^j & r_1 \geq NI\left(U_i\right) \end{cases} \tag{1}$$

To ensure the diversity, each universe transports also its objects randomly and separately to the inflation rate value (equation 2:

$$X_j \in U_{best}, x_i^j \in U_i, ub_j, and\, lb_j$$

upper and lower bounds, and r_2, r_3, r_4 are random numbers).

$$x_i^j = \begin{cases} \begin{cases} X_j + TDR \times \left(\left(ub_j - lb_j\right) \times r_4 + lb_j\right) & r_3 < 0.5 \\ X_j - TDR \times \left(\left(ub_j - lb_j\right) \times r_4 + lb_j\right) & r_3 \geq 0.5 \end{cases} & r_2 < WEP \\ x_i^j & r_2 \geq WEP \end{cases} \tag{2}$$

WEP is the wormhole existence probability (equation 3: min and max are the minimum and the maximum wormhole existence probabilities)

$$WEP = \min + l \times \left(\frac{\max - \min}{L}\right) \tag{3}$$

TDR is the traveling distance rate (equation 4: l is the current iteration, L is the maximum number of iterations and p is the exploitation accuracy). WEP is used to measure the variation between an object and the best universe. Whereas, TDR set out to improve the exploitation close to the best solution.

$$TDR = 1 - \frac{l^{1/p}}{L^{1/p}} \tag{4}$$

For gene selection, a universe U_i is presented as a combination of genes, where each object x_i^j is a gene. The inflation rate $NI(U_i)$ is the f-measure value achieved by the 10-cross-validation evaluation method and the SVM classifier on the preprocessed dataset by the generated vector. $lb=1$ and ub_j is the total number of genes in the initial set. Algorithm 1 explains the multi-verse optimizer process for gene selection.

This algorithm was exploited in several optimization problems such as classification (Faris et al., 2016), feature selection and parameters optimization (Faris et al., 2018). To enhance the exploitation of

MVO, (Jangir et al., 2017) proposed to combine it with PSO (HPSO-MVO). In another investigation, (DIF et al., 2017) introduced the principle of refinement into MVO.

Algorithm 1. *MVO for feature selection*

Inputs: Dataset, Number of iterations l, Number of universes M, max_number_of_
genes
Outputs: Best
Function MVO
       Initialize a random set of M universes.
       Best = All genes
       Initialize WEP and TDR (equations 3 and 4).
       While (i <= l**)do**
            Foreach ($U_i \in universes$) **do**
                  Evaluate (U_i, Dataset, SVM, 10-cross-validation).
                  Update Best, WEP and TDR.
                  Foreach ($x_i^j \in U_i$) **do**
                       update x_i^j (equation 1)
                       update x_i^j (equation 2)
                  End For
            End For
            Select the Best solution.
       End While
       Return Best
End Function

3.2. Firefly Algorithm (FA)

The firefly algorithm (FA) (Yang et al., 2009) is a bio-inspired algorithm from the behavior of fireflies. The fireflies produce flashlights for various functions such as communication and to attract prey. FA is based on three main principles: (a) fireflies are unisex, (b) attractiveness correlated to brightness, and (c) brightness and the fitness function are proportional. For maximization problems, the brightness is presented by the fitness function. Whereas, the attractiveness β depends on the distance r_{ij} between two fireflies (i,j) and also on the light intensity of the other firefly. Equation 5 illustrates the light intensity update, where β_0 is the initial attractiveness and γ is the light absorption coefficient.

$$\beta\left(r\right) = \beta_0 e^{-\gamma r^2} \tag{5}$$

The distant r_{ij} between two fireflies x_i and x_j is computed according to the equation 6 and equation 7 presents the movement process of the firefly i to another one j, where α is a randomization parameter, rand is a random number and n is the dimensionality of the firefly.

$$r_{ij} = \sqrt{\sum_{k=1}^{d} \left(x_{i,k} - x_{j,k} \right)^2} \tag{6}$$

$$x_i^{(t)} = x_i^{(t-1)} + \beta \left(r_{ij} \right) \left(x_j^{(t)} - x_i^{(t-1)} \right) + \alpha \left(rand - 0.5 \right) \tag{7}$$

For gene selection, a firefly x_i is presented as a combination of genes, where each component x_i^j is a gene. The light intensity rate I_i is the f-measure value achieved by the 10-cross-validation evaluation method and the SVM classifier on the preprocessed dataset by the generated vector. Algorithm 2 explains the firefly algorithm process for gene selection.

The FA is characterized by its capacity to explore the search space (Zhang et al., 2016), which makes it prone to slow convergence and local optimums. To solve the different related issue to FA, (Zhang et al., 2016) proposed to combine between FA and differential evolution (DE). In another investigation, (Mazen et al., 2016) proposed to hybridize between FA and GA.

Algorithm 2. *FA for feature selection*

```
Inputs: Dataset, Number of iterations l, Number of fireflies M, fitness func-
tion f
Outputs: Best
Function FA
        Initialize a random set of M fireflies
        Best = All genes
        While (i <= l)do
                Foreach ( xᵢ ∈ fireflies )  do
                        Foreach ( xⱼ ∈ fireflies )  do
                                If ( f(xⱼ) > f(xᵢ) )  then
                                        update  xᵢ   (equation 7)
                                f ( xᵢ ) = Evaluate ( xᵢ , Dataset, SVM, 10-cross-valida-
tion)
                                End For
                End For
                Select the Best solution
        End While
        Return Best
End Function
```

3.3. BAT Algorithm (BAT)

The Bat algorithm (BAT) (Yang et al., 2010) is inspired by the behavior of microbats in their search process on prey and their practice to avoid obstacles. Microbats listen for echolocation and emit pulse for communication. They can distinguish between distant prey and barriers. Virtual bats are characterized by a position x_i and a velocity υ_i, which are updated according to equations 9 and 10. The new velocity is computed based on the frequency, the best solution x_*, the current position, and velocity. In BAT, the frequency is initialized randomly (f $\in [0, f_{max}]$) and then updated according to equation 8 (β is a random vector).

$$f_i = f_{min} + \left(f_{max} - f_{min}\right)\beta \tag{8}$$

$$v_i^t = v_i^{t-1} + \left(x_i^t - x_*\right)f_i \tag{9}$$

$$x_i^t = x_i^{t-1} + v_i^t \tag{10}$$

Next, new random solutions are generated based on a random walk (equation 11), where A^t is the average of loudness at the current iteration and ϵ is a random number.

$$x_{new} = x_{old} + \epsilon A^t \tag{11}$$

Finally, loudness $A_i \in [A_{min}, A_{max}]$ and emission rate r_i are updated when the new solution is improved (equations 12 and 13), where α, γ are constants and t is the current iteration. We should note that the loudness decreases when the bat reaches its objective. Whereas the emission rate increase.

$$A_t^{t+1} = \alpha A_t^{t+1} \tag{12}$$

$$r_i^{t+1} = r_i^0 \left[1 - \exp\left(-\gamma t\right)\right] \tag{13}$$

For gene selection, a bat x_i is presented as a combination of genes, where each component x_i^j is a gene. For evaluation, we used the f-measure value achieved by the 10-cross-validation evaluation method and the SVM classifier on the preprocessed dataset by the generated vector. To simplify the process, we used the loudness A and the pulse rate r as constant (fixed to 0.5). Algorithm 3 explains the bat algorithm process for gene selection.

The BAT algorithm was exploited in various data mining applications such as clustering (Ashish et al., 2018), neural network training (Jaddi et al., 2015) and feature selection. Despite the advantages of BAT, this metaheuristic risks from a fast convergence in the multi-dimensional tasks (Fister et al., 2013).

Algorithm 3. *BAT for feature selection*

```
Inputs: Dataset, Number of iterations l, Number of bats M, max_number_of_genes,
pulse rate A, loudness r, fitness function f
Outputs: Best
Function BAT
```

```
        Initialize a random set of M bats
        Initialize frequencies f_i
        Best = All genes
        While (i <= l) do
                Foreach (b_i ∈ bats) do
                        update f_i,v_i,x_i (equations 8, 9 and 10)
                        f(x_i) = Evaluate (x_i, Dataset, SVM, 10-cross-valida-
tion)
                        generate a random number rand        ∈ [0,1]
                        If (rand > r) Then
                                Generate x_new around the best solution
                        Generate x_new (equation 11)
                        f(x_i) = Evaluate (x_new, Dataset, SVM, 10-cross-valida-
tion)
                        If (rand < A & f(x_new) > f(x_i)) Then
                                x_i = x_new
                        End If
                End For.
                Select the Best solution
        End While
        Return Best
End Function
```

3.4. Particle Swarm Optimization Algorithm (PSO)

The particle swarm optimization (PSO) (Eberhart et al., 1995) is a bio-inspired algorithm from the behavior of swarms in their cooperation to reach an objective. This metaheuristic is characterized by its simple concepts compared to the other metaheuristics (FA, MVO, and BAT). The simple operators make it less expensive in terms of computational complexity and memory requirements. In the PSO process, particles are initialized randomly and each solution has a position x_i and a velocity v_i to fly in the search space. These two variables are updated according to equations 14 and 15.

$$v_i^{(t+1)} = \left(1 - Q\right)v_i^{(t)} + Qc\left(r_1\left(pbest_i^{(t)} - x_i^{(t)}\right) + r\left(lbest_i^{(t)} - x_i^{(t)}\right)\right) \tag{14}$$

$$x_i^{(t+1)} = x_i^{(t)} + v_i^{(t+1)} \tag{15}$$

The velocity v_i is computed according to: the best position $pbest_i^{(t)}$ in the history of the particle i, the current position $x_i^{(t)}$, the current velocity $v_i^{(t)}$, the acceleration constant c to weight between gbest and lbest, the velocity weight Q, and the best position in the history of its informants or neighborhood

$lbest_i^{(t)}$. Other previous variants of PSO uses the global best solution (gbest) instead of lbest. The purpose of the local best solution (lbest) is to improve diversity and to prevent local optimums.

For gene selection, a particle p_i is presented as a combination of genes, where each component x_i^j of its position x_i is a gene. For evaluation, we used the f-measure value achieved by the 10-cross-validation evaluation method and the SVM classifier on the preprocessed dataset by the generated vector. To prevent local optimums, we used the informant's particles and we fixed their number 4. Algorithm 4 explains the PSO algorithm process for gene selection.

Algorithm 4. *PSO for feature selection*

```
Inputs: Dataset, Number of iterations l, Number of particles M, max_number_of_
genes, fitness function f
Outputs: Best.
Function PSO
        Initialize a random set of M particles
        Initialize velocities vᵢ
        Best = All genes
        While (i<= l)do
                Foreach ( pᵢ ∈ particles ) do
                        update vᵢ,xᵢ (equations 14 and 15)
                        f(xᵢ) = Evaluate (xᵢ, Dataset, SVM, 10-cross-valida-
tion).
                End For.
                Select the Best solution
        End While
        Return Best
End Function
```

3.5. Recursive Variants

The enhanced variants of metaheuristics attracted significant interest in the literature. The main purpose was to resolve the different issues related to metaheuristics. For instance, the FA algorithm risks form slow convergence and the fact of getting trapped into a local minimum (Mazen et al., 2016). Besides, BAT is prone to fast convergence for multi-dimensional problems (Fister et al., 2013).

To solve the different issues related to the use of metaheuristics in multidimensional problems. (DIF et al., 2017; DIF et al., 2019) proposed to introduce a recursive behavior on the metaheuristics MVO and FA respectively, which is based on the refinement of the search space. The purpose of this process is to enhance the exploitation, to limit the search space close to the promising areas and especially to accelerate convergence on high dimensional microarray datasets. The purpose of this chapter is to examine the process of refinement on other metaheuristics such as BAT and PSO. Algorithm 5 presents the overall process of the recursive variants.

Algorithm 5. *Recursive variants*

```
Inputs: Dataset, Number of iterations (Nmax, N), Number of solutions M, fit-
ness function f, metaheuristic ∈{FA, MVO, PSO, BAT}
Outputs: Best
Initialize a random set of M solutions
Best = All genes
Seed = 0
While (n<Nmax)do
        Best 2 = metaheuristic (solutions, parameters, N, Seed)
        If ((f (Best 2) >f (Best)) or(f(Best 2) = f(Best) and | Best | > |
Best 2|) Then
                Best = Best 2
        Else if (f (Best 2) <f (Best 1)) Then
                Seed = Seed +1
        End If
        Select the Best solution.
        End While.
        Return Best.
End.
```

First, the algorithm initializes a random set of solutions and initializes the best solution to all genes. Each solution S = {$X_1, X_2, ..., X_n$} is presented as a set of integers X_i, where X_i is the index of the selected gene. In the recursive variants, each variable belongs to the best solution ($X_i \in Best$). Whereas, in the classic version this variable belongs to any point in the search space (X_i [0, *Number_of_genes*]). This property helps to refine this space over iterations. Then, the metaheuristic is performed for a number of iterations (N). Next, the new best solution is selected and the metaheuristic is applied to the new best solution. The variable seed is used for initialization and updated if the best solution is not changed to prevent redundant initializations. Finally, The overall process is repeated for a fixed number of iterations (Nmax).

4. EXPERIMENTAL STUDY

In this section, we tested the framework of recursive metaheuristics on 11 microarray datasets [1](Table 1). These datasets are categorized into two groups. The first category distinguishes between normal and abnormal profiles such as Colon Tumor, Breast Cancer and Ovarian Cancer. Whereas, the second category classifies different types of tumors. For instance, SRBCT differentiates between four similar types of childhood tumors: Ewing's sarcoma, Neuroblastoma, and Burkitt's lymphoma. Besides, Lung cancer dataset classifies samples into normal profiles and four lung cancers. Lymphoma distinguishes between three lymphatic system cancers (CLL, FL, DLBC). The datasets Leukemia, Leukemia_3c, Leukemia_4c, and MLL-leukemia distinguish between different types of leukemia cancers and differs in the number of classes.

Table 1. Microarrays datasets description

Dataset	Genes	Samples	Classes
Colon tumor	2000	62	2
CNS	7129	60	2
Leukemia	7129	72	2
Breast cancer	24481	97	2
Ovarian cancer	15154	253	2
MLL	12582	72	3
SRBCT	2308	83	4
Lung cancer	12533	181	5
Prostate	12600	102	2
Leukemia_3c	7129	72	3
Leukemia_4c	7129	72	4
Lymphoma	4026	66	3

For evaluation, we used the support vector machine algorithm and the 10-cross-validation evaluation method. For all experiments, we select methods that maximize the f-measure value as the most accurate and secondly we choose among the selected ones the strategy that minimizes the number of selected genes. Table 2 summarizes the parameters of metaheuristics and their recursive versions.

The first set of analyses examined the impact of the classic metaheuristics FA, MVO, PSO and BAT on gene selection. Table 3 provides the obtained results in terms of f-measure and the number of selected genes. The comparative study between the states before and after the gene selection process reveals that all results have been improved. Which indicates the importance of gene selection and its positive impact on performance. The table shows that FA achieved the best f-measure results on the datasets: Colon tumor, CNS, Breast cancer and it was more promising in dimensionality reduction for the datasets: MLL, SRBCT, and Leukemia_4c. On the other hand, PSO selected a reduced number of genes for the datasets Ovarian cancer and Lymphoma. Whereas, MVO and BAT were more accurate for the datasets Leukemia_3c and SRBCT respectively. Overall, the initial analysis highlights the efficiency of FA in both performance and dimensionality reduction.

Secondly, we examined the recursive variants (RFA, EMVO, RPSO, and RBAT) of the metaheuristics (FA, MVO, PSO, and BAT) on the same microarray datasets (Table 4). We should note that the EMVO and RFA results are retrieved from (DIF et al., 2017) and (DIF et al., 2019) investigations. (DIF et al., 2017) highlighted the superiority of EMVO in terms of the f-measure value on the datasets: CNS, Breast cancer, MLL and lung cancer and in terms of dimensionality reduction on the remaining datasets. Besides, (DIF et al., 2019) showed the efficiency of RFA compared to FA in terms of f-measure value for the dataset: CNS, breast cancer and lung cancer and in terms of the number of genes in the remaining cases. To sum up, the comparative study between the metaheuristics (MVO, FA) and their recursive version (EMVO and RFA) identifies the importance of the introduced recursive behavior, especially in dimensionality reduction.

The comparison between PSO and RPSO indicates the positive impact of recursion on the datasets: CNS, Breast cancer and lung cancer, where we observe a significant improvement for the datasets CNS

Table 2. The parameters of metaheuristics

Metaheuristic	Parameter	Value
PSO	Informant particles size	4
	Acceleration constant(c)	2.05
	Velocity weight (Q)	0.73
	Frequency min (f_{min})	0
	Frequency max (f_{max})	2
MVO	Constants (α, γ)	0.9
	Wormhole existence probability (min)	0
	Wormhole existence probability (max)	2
	Exploitation accuracy (p)	6
FA	Randomization parameter (Seed)	1
	Initial attractiveness (β0)	0.2
	Max attractiveness (βmax)	1
	Randomization parameter (α)	0.5
	Light absorption coefficient (γ)	1
Number of solutions (M)		100
Total number of iterations (N)		50
Recursive metaheuristics	Number of iterations (N)	5
	Number of iterations in the embedded metaheuristics (Nmax)	5

(from 0.798 to 0.867) and Breast cancer (from 0.798 to 0.867). On the other hand, there is a remarkable reduction in dimensionality for all datasets especially for the MLL, were only 8% of informative genes have been selected. Overall, these results indicate the superiority of RPSO over PSO.

The comparative study between BAT and RBAT indicates the superiority of BAT over RBAT for the datasets: Colon tumor, CNS, Leukemia, MLL, and Leukemia_3. The obtained results reveal a significant decrease in terms of the f-measure value for the colon tumor dataset (from 0.919 to 0.856). Which implicates the negative impact of refinement on BAT.

Turning now to the comparative study between the variants RFA, EMVO, RPSO, and RBAT. It reveals the efficiency of RFA on the datasets Colon tumor and CNS. Besides, RMVO was more promising in the remaining cases. Which highlights the powerful effect of refinement on MVO compared to the other variants. Figure 1 highlights the dimensionality reduction rate of these variants. It indicates the efficiency of EMVO compared to the other variants.

Overall, these findings show the powerful effect of refinement upon the metaheuristics: FA, MVO, and PSO. The variants were more promising compared to their classical versions in terms of precision on the datasets: CNS, breast cancer, and lung cancer. On the other hand, they almost achieved the same precision with a good reduction in dimensionality in the remaining cases. We should note that the refinement was more promising on FA and MVO compared to PSO. Evidence propose that this process is positively related to powerful metaheuristics in term of exploration (FA, MVO). This helps to make cooperation between their exploration and the exploitation of refinement. The obtained results reveal

Table 3. The obtained results by metaheuristics

Dataset	Before	FA	MVO	PSO	BAT
Colon tumor	0.854 (2000)	0.920 (127)	0.919 (331)	0.903 (140)	0.919 (128)
CNS	0.677 (7129)	0.831 (884)	0.8 (978)	0.798 (471)	0.816 (412)
Leukemia	0.958 (7129)	1.0 (880)	1.0 (484)	1.0 (754)	1.0 (143)
Breast cancer	0.681 (24481)	0.804 (3052)	0.803 (3597)	0.794 (768)	0,763 (1404)
Ovarian cancer	1 .0 (15154)	1.0 (581)	1.0 (341)	1 .0 (86)	1.0 (15086)
MLL	0.972 (12582)	1.0 (555)	0.986 (415)	1.0 (924)	0.986 (589)
SRBCT	0.988 (2308)	1.0 (85)	1.0 (152)	1.0 (105)	1.0 (699)
Lung cancer	0.954 (12533)	0.970 (1691)	0.965 (1267)	0.970 (1416)	0.9701 (330)
Leukemia_3c	0.972 (7129)	0.986 (892)	0.986 (619)	0.986 (786)	0.986 (1767)
Leukemia_4c	0.927 (7129)	0.971 (1562)	0.971 (2569)	0.971 (2053)	0.958 (2112)
Lymphoma	1.0 (4026)	1.0 (105)	1.0 (97)	1.0 (28)	1.0 (1776)

that refinement impacts negatively on BAT. We suggest that this metaheuristic has been trapped into a local minimum in the first iterations because of its fast convergence. One of the limits of the proposed refinement method is that the search process of each iteration (Nmax) depends on the best solution of the previous one which can cause worse results if this solution is distant to the best global one. To overcome this drawback, we recommend to increase the number of iterations (N) of the embedded metaheuristic to develop the search process on the best solution. To sum up, the majority of the best solutions have been achieved by the EMVO metaheuristic. Besides, the RFA method was more accurate in the dimensionality reduction task. Although, refinement was less promising on PSO and BAT. Evidence suggests that the choice of embedded metaheuristics is among the most important factors to ensure the success of refinement. This process succeeds on the efficient metaheuristics in exploration rather than exploitation. Moreover, we should make attention to metaheuristics that risks form fast convergence.

5. CONCLUSION

In this investigation, we compared four variants of metaheuristics (RFA, EMVO, RPSO, RBAT). These variants introduce a recursive behavior to the classical metaheuristics (FA, MVO, PSO, BAT). This process is based on the principle of refinement. it proposes to refine the search space near to the best solution after a number of iterations instead of the classic iterative process. In the proposed variant, the embedded metaheuristic is applied recursively on the best solution. The purpose of refinement is

Table 4. The obtained results by recursive metaheuristics

Dataset	RFA	EMVO	RPSO	RBAT
Colon tumor	0.920 (87)	0.919 (73)	0.903 (52)	0.856 (55)
CNS	0.917 (79)	0.883 (107)	0.867 (190)	0.794 (465)
Leukemia	1.0 (187)	0.986 (6)	1.0 (60)	1.0 (219)
Breast cancer	0.845 (61)	0.887 (186)	0.866 (127)	0.784 (39)
Ovarian cancer	1.0 (19)	1.0 (15)	1.0 (19)	1.0 (4620)
MLL	0.986 (139)	1.0 (80)	1.0 (86)	0.972 (1661)
SRBCT	1.0 (33)	1.0 (26)	1.0 (58)	1.0 (49)
Lung cancer	0.979 (251)	0.980 (90)	0,980 (483)	0.975 (198)
Leukemia_3c	0.986 (585)	0.986 (93)	0.986 (261)	0.972 (1950)
Leukemia_4c	0.971 (448)	0.971 (177)	0.971 (891)	0.958 (250)
Lymphoma	1.0 (9)	1.0 (7)	1.0 (10)	1.0 (17)

Figure 1. The dimensionality reduction rate achieved by RBAT, RPSO, EMVO, RFA

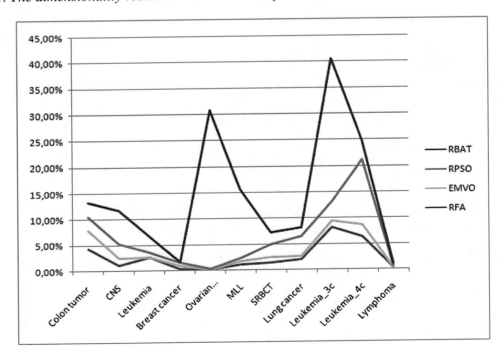

to reduce the search process and thus to speed up the processing time for high dimensional problems. These variants have been tested on the microarray datasets to selected the relevant genes and to enhance performance. The obtained results showed the superiority of EMVO, RFA, and RPSO upon their classic versions in terms of both precision and dimensionality reduction. Whereas, RBAT was less promising compared to BAT.

Among the perspectives of this work is to perform the process of refinement on other characterized metaheuristics by explorations (GA, DE) and to solve the different issues of refinement related to metaheuristics with fast convergence such as BAT.

REFERENCES

Abd-Alsabour, N., & Ramakrishnan, S. (2016). *Hybrid metaheuristics for classification problems*. Pattern Recognition-Analysis and Applications. doi:10.5772/65253

Alaoui, A., & Elberrichi, Z. (2018). Feature Subset Selection Using Ant Colony Optimization for a Decision Trees Classification of Medical Data. *International Journal of Information Retrieval Research*, *8*(4), 39–50. doi:10.4018/IJIRR.2018100103

Almugren, N., & Alshamlan, H. (2019). A Survey on Hybrid Feature Selection Methods in Microarray Gene Expression Data for Cancer Classification. *IEEE Access: Practical Innovations, Open Solutions*, *7*, 78533–78548. doi:10.1109/ACCESS.2019.2922987

Alomari, O. A., Khader, A. T., Al-Betar, M. A., & Awadallah, M. A. (2018). A novel gene selection method using modified MRMR and hybrid bat-inspired algorithm with β-hill climbing. *Applied Intelligence*, *48*(11), 4429–4447. doi:10.100710489-018-1207-1

Alshamlan, H. M., Badr, G. H., & Alohali, Y. A. (2015). Genetic Bee Colony (GBC) algorithm: A new gene selection method for microarray cancer classification. *Computational Biology and Chemistry*, *56*, 49–60. doi:10.1016/j.compbiolchem.2015.03.001 PMID:25880524

Ang, J. C., Mirzal, A., Haron, H., & Hamed, H. N. A. (2015). Supervised, unsupervised, and semi-supervised feature selection: A review on gene selection. *IEEE/ACM Transactions on Computational Biology and Bioinformatics*, *13*(5), 971–989. doi:10.1109/TCBB.2015.2478454 PMID:26390495

Ashish, T., Kapil, S., & Manju, B. (2018). Parallel bat algorithm-based clustering using mapreduce. In *Networking Communication and Data Knowledge Engineering* (pp. 73–82). Singapore: Springer. doi:10.1007/978-981-10-4600-1_7

Bala, J., Huang, J., Vafaie, H., DeJong, K., & Wechsler, H. (1995, August). Hybrid learning using genetic algorithms and decision trees for pattern classification. In IJCAI (1) (pp. 719-724).

Baliarsingh, S. K., Vipsita, S., Muhammad, K., & Bakshi, S. (2019). Analysis of high-dimensional biomedical data using an evolutionary multi-objective emperor penguin optimizer. *Swarm and Evolutionary Computation*, *48*, 262–273. doi:10.1016/j.swevo.2019.04.010

Begum, S., Chakraborty, S., Banerjee, A., Das, S., Sarkar, R., & Chakraborty, D. (2018). Gene selection for diagnosis of cancer in microarray data using memetic algorithm. In *Intelligent Engineering Informatics* (pp. 441–449). Singapore: Springer. doi:10.1007/978-981-10-7566-7_43

Bidi, N., & Elberrichi, Z. (2018). Best Features Selection for Biomedical Data Classification Using Seven Spot Ladybird Optimization Algorithm. [IJAMC]. *International Journal of Applied Metaheuristic Computing*, *9*(3), 75–87. doi:10.4018/IJAMC.2018070104

Brezočnik, L., Fister, I. Jr, & Podgorelec, V. (2018). Swarm intelligence algorithms for feature selection: A review. *Applied Sciences (Basel, Switzerland)*, *8*(9), 1521. doi:10.3390/app8091521

Chen, K. H., Wang, K. J., Tsai, M. L., Wang, K. M., Adrian, A. M., Cheng, W. C., ... Chang, K. S. (2014). Gene selection for cancer identification: A decision tree model empowered by particle swarm optimization algorithm. *BMC Bioinformatics*, *15*(1), 49. doi:10.1186/1471-2105-15-49 PMID:24555567

Chuang, L. Y., Chang, H. W., Tu, C. J., & Yang, C. H. (2008). Improved binary PSO for feature selection using gene expression data. *Computational Biology and Chemistry*, *32*(1), 29–38. doi:10.1016/j.compbiolchem.2007.09.005 PMID:18023261

Das, K., Mishra, D., & Shaw, K. (2016). A metaheuristic optimization framework for informative gene selection. *Informatics in Medicine Unlocked*, *4*, 10–20. doi:10.1016/j.imu.2016.09.003

Dashtban, M., & Balafar, M. (2017). Gene selection for microarray cancer classification using a new evolutionary method employing artificial intelligence concepts. *Genomics*, *109*(2), 91–107. doi:10.1016/j.ygeno.2017.01.004 PMID:28159597

Deepthi, P. S., & Thampi, S. M. (2016). A metaheuristic approach for simultaneous gene selection and clustering of microarray data. In *Intelligent Systems, Technologies, and Applications* (pp. 449–461). Cham, Switzerland: Springer. doi:10.1007/978-3-319-23258-4_39

Dif, N., Walid Attaoui, M., & Elberrichi, Z. (2018, December). Gene Selection for Microarray Data Classification Using Hybrid Meta-Heuristics. *Proceedings International Symposium on Modelling and Implementation of Complex Systems* (pp. 119-132). Cham, Switzerland: Springer.

Dif, N., & Elberrichi, Z. (2017, December). Microarray Data Feature Selection and Classification Using an Enhanced Multi-Verse Optimizer and Support Vector Machine. In 3rd International Conference on Networking and Advanced Systems. Academic Press.

Dif, N., & Elberrichi, Z. (2019). An Enhanced Recursive Firefly Algorithm for Informative Gene Selection. [IJSIR]. *International Journal of Swarm Intelligence Research*, *10*(2), 21–33. doi:10.4018/IJSIR.2019040102

Dif (b), N., & Elberrichi, Z. (2018). A Multi-Verse Optimizer Approach for Instance Selection and Optimizing 1-NN Algorithm. *International Journal of Strategic Information Technology and Applications (IJSITA), 9*(2), 35-49.

Dorigo, M., Maniezzo, V., & Colorni, A. (1996). Ant system: Optimization by a colony of cooperating agents. *IEEE Transactions on Systems, Man, and Cybernetics. Part B, Cybernetics*, *26*(1), 29–41. doi:10.1109/3477.484436 PMID:18263004

Eberhart, R., & Kennedy, J. (1995, October). A new optimizer using particle swarm theory. *MHS'95. Proceedings of the Sixth International Symposium on Micro Machine and Human Science* (pp. 39-43). IEEE. 10.1109/MHS.1995.494215

Emary, E., Zawbaa, H. M., Ghany, K. K. A., Hassanien, A. E., & Pârv, B. (2015, September). Firefly optimization algorithm for feature selection. *Proceedings of the 7th Balkan Conference on Informatics Conference* (p. 26). ACM.

Faris, H., Aljarah, I., & Mirjalili, S. (2016). Training feedforward neural networks using multi-verse optimizer for binary classification problems. *Applied Intelligence, 45*(2), 322–332. doi:10.100710489-016-0767-1

Faris, H., Hassonah, M. A., Ala'M, A. Z., Mirjalili, S., & Aljarah, I. (2018). A multi-verse optimizer approach for feature selection and optimizing SVM parameters based on a robust system architecture. *Neural Computing & Applications, 30*(8), 2355–2369. doi:10.100700521-016-2818-2

Faris (b), H., Aljarah, I., Al-Betar, M. A., & Mirjalili, S. (2018). Grey wolf optimizer: a review of recent variants and applications. *Neural computing and applications, 30*(2), 413-435.

Fister, I., Jr., Fister, D., & Yang, X. S. (2013). A hybrid bat algorithm. *arXiv preprint arXiv:1303.6310.*

Gu, S., Cheng, R., & Jin, Y. (2018). Feature selection for high-dimensional classification using a competitive swarm optimizer. *Soft Computing, 22*(3), 811–822. doi:10.100700500-016-2385-6

Hancer, E., Xue, B., & Zhang, M. (2018). Differential evolution for filter feature selection based on information theory and feature ranking. *Knowledge-Based Systems, 140*, 103–119. doi:10.1016/j.knosys.2017.10.028

Harrington, C. A., Rosenow, C., & Retief, J. (2000). Monitoring gene expression using DNA microarrays. *Current Opinion in Microbiology, 3*(3), 285–291. doi:10.1016/S1369-5274(00)00091-6 PMID:10851158

Holland, J. H. (1992). *Adaptation in natural and artificial systems: an introductory analysis with applications to biology, control, and artificial intelligence.* MIT Press. doi:10.7551/mitpress/1090.001.0001

Inza, I., Larrañaga, P., Blanco, R., & Cerrolaza, A. J. (2004). Filter versus wrapper gene selection approaches in DNA microarray domains. *Artificial Intelligence in Medicine, 31*(2), 91–103. doi:10.1016/j.artmed.2004.01.007 PMID:15219288

Jaddi, N. S., Abdullah, S., & Hamdan, A. R. (2015). Multi-population cooperative bat algorithm-based optimization of artificial neural network model. *Information Sciences, 294*, 628–644. doi:10.1016/j.ins.2014.08.050

Jangir, P., Parmar, S. A., Trivedi, I. N., & Bhesdadiya, R. H. (2017). A novel hybrid particle swarm optimizer with multi verse optimizer for global numerical optimization and optimal reactive power dispatch problem. *Engineering Science and Technology, an International Journal, 20*(2), 570-586.

Jayabarathi, T., Raghunathan, T., & Gandomi, A. H. (2018). The bat algorithm, variants and some practical engineering applications: a review. In *Nature-Inspired Algorithms and Applied Optimization* (pp. 313–330). Cham: Springer. doi:10.1007/978-3-319-67669-2_14

Jiang, L., Kong, G., & Li, C. (2019). Wrapper Framework for Test-Cost-Sensitive Feature Selection. *IEEE Transactions on Systems, Man, and Cybernetics. Systems*, 1–10. doi:10.1109/TSMC.2019.2904662

Mazen, F., AbulSeoud, R. A., & Gody, A. M. (2016). Genetic algorithm and firefly algorithm in a hybrid approach for breast cancer diagnosis. [IJCTT]. *International Journal of Computer Trends and Technology*, *32*(2), 62–68. doi:10.14445/22312803/IJCTT-V32P111

Min, F., & Xu, J. (2016). Semi-greedy heuristics for feature selection with test cost constraints. *Granular Computing*, *1*(3), 199–211. doi:10.100741066-016-0017-2

Mirjalili, S., Mirjalili, S. M., & Hatamlou, A. (2016). Multi-verse optimizer: A nature-inspired algorithm for global optimization. *Neural Computing & Applications*, *27*(2), 495–513. doi:10.100700521-015-1870-7

Piotrowski, A. P., & Napiorkowski, J. J. (2018). Some metaheuristics should be simplified. *Information Sciences*, *427*, 32–62. doi:10.1016/j.ins.2017.10.039

Prasad, Y., & Biswas, K. K. (2015, March). Gene selection in microarray datasets using progressively refined PSO scheme. *Proceedings Twenty-Ninth AAAI Conference on Artificial Intelligence*. Academic Press.

Roffo, G., Melzi, S., Castellani, U., & Vinciarelli, A. (2017). Infinite latent feature selection: A probabilistic latent graph-based ranking approach. *Proceedings of the IEEE International Conference on Computer Vision* (pp. 1398-1406). 10.1109/ICCV.2017.156

Rojas-Delgado, J., Trujillo-Rasúa, R., & Bello, R. (2019). A continuation approach for training Artificial Neural Networks with meta-heuristics. *Pattern Recognition Letters*, *125*, 373–380. doi:10.1016/j.patrec.2019.05.017

Singh, D. A. A. G., Leavline, E. J., Valliyappan, K., & Srinivasan, M. (2015). Enhancing the performance of classifier using particle swarm optimization (PSO)-based dimensionality reduction. *International Journal of Energy, Information, and Communications*, *6*(5), 19–26.

Talbi, E. G., Jourdan, L., Garcia-Nieto, J., & Alba, E. (2008, March). Comparison of population based metaheuristics for feature selection: Application to microarray data classification. *Proceedings 2008 IEEE/ACS International Conference on Computer Systems and Applications* (pp. 45-52). IEEE. 10.1109/AICCSA.2008.4493515

Tarik, B., & Zakaria, E. (2019). Best Feature Selection for Horizontally Distributed Private Biomedical Data Based on Genetic Algorithms. [IJDST]. *International Journal of Distributed Systems and Technologies*, *10*(3), 37–57. doi:10.4018/IJDST.2019070103

Vieira, S. M., Mendonça, L. F., Farinha, G. J., & Sousa, J. M. (2013). Modified binary PSO for feature selection using SVM applied to mortality prediction of septic patients. *Applied Soft Computing*, *13*(8), 3494–3504. doi:10.1016/j.asoc.2013.03.021

Wang, P., Zhu, Z., & Huang, S. (2013). Seven-spot ladybird optimization: A novel and efficient metaheuristic algorithm for numerical optimization. *The Scientific World Journal*, *2013*. doi:10.1155/2013/378515 PMID:24385879

Xue, B., Zhang, M., & Browne, W. N. (2012). Particle swarm optimization for feature selection in classification: A multi-objective approach. *IEEE Transactions on Cybernetics*, *43*(6), 1656–1671. doi:10.1109/TSMCB.2012.2227469 PMID:24273143

Yang, X. S. (2009, October). Firefly algorithms for multimodal optimization. *Proceedings International symposium on stochastic algorithms* (pp. 169-178). Berlin, Germany: Springer.

Yang, X. S. (2010). A new metaheuristic bat-inspired algorithm. Proceedings *Nature inspired cooperative strategies for optimization (NICSO 2010)* (pp. 65–74). Berlin, Germany: Springer. doi:10.1007/978-3-642-12538-6_6

Yang, X. S., & Deb, S. (2009, December). Cuckoo search via Lévy flights. *Proceedings 2009 World Congress on Nature & Biologically Inspired Computing (NaBIC)* (pp. 210-214). IEEE. 10.1109/NABIC.2009.5393690

Yusup, N., Zain, A. M., & Latib, A. A. (2019, March). A review of Harmony Search algorithm-based feature selection method for classification. [IOP Publishing.]. *Journal of Physics: Conference Series*, *1192*(1). doi:10.1088/1742-6596/1192/1/012038

Zhang, L., Liu, L., Yang, X. S., & Dai, Y. (2016). A novel hybrid firefly algorithm for global optimization. *PLoS One*, *11*(9). doi:10.1371/journal.pone.0163230 PMID:27685869

Zhu, Z., Ong, Y. S., & Dash, M. (2007). Markov blanket-embedded genetic algorithm for gene selection. *Pattern Recognition*, *40*(11), 3236–3248. doi:10.1016/j.patcog.2007.02.007

ENDNOTE

[1]   http://csse.szu.edu.cn/staff/zhuzx/Datasets.html

Chapter 4
Training Artificial Neural Networks With Improved Particle Swarm Optimization:
Case of Electricity Demand Forecasting in Thailand

Kuruge Darshana Abeyrathna

Department of Information and Communication Technology, University of Agder, Norway

Chawalit Jeenanunta

iD https://orcid.org/0000-0002-1932-9776

School of Management Technology, Sirindhorn International Institute of Technology, Thammasat University, Thailand

ABSTRACT

Particle Swarm Optimization (PSO) is popular for solving complex optimization problems. However, it easily traps in local minima. Authors modify the traditional PSO algorithm by adding an extra step called PSO-Shock. The PSO-Shock algorithm initiates similar to the PSO algorithm. Once it traps in a local minimum, it is detected by counting stall generations. When stall generation accumulates to a prespecified value, particles are perturbed. This helps particles to find better solutions than the current local minimum they found. The behavior of PSO-Shock algorithm is studied using a known: Schwefel's function. With promising performance on the Schwefel's function, PSO-Shock algorithm is utilized to optimize the weights and bias of Artificial Neural Networks (ANNs). The trained ANNs then forecast electricity consumption in Thailand. The proposed algorithm reduces the forecasting error compared to the traditional training algorithms. The percentage reduction of error is 23.81% compared to the Backpropagation algorithm and 16.50% compared to the traditional PSO algorithm.

DOI: 10.4018/978-1-7998-3222-5.ch004

1. INTRODUCTION

Current effective data harvesting tools have shifted the data scarcity issue we had a few decades back to new challenges where we need new methods or improve the existing methods to analyze those data. However, Artificial Neural Networks (ANNs) or ANN-based techniques are still powerful enough to work with those data, but slight modifications can be made to improve its performances. As a result, the architecture of the ANNs has evolved over the years from Feed Forward NN and will continue to change until we find a new method that can outperform ANNs.

Due to the highly nonlinear patterns appearing in the electricity consumption data, usage of ANNs to forecast electricity consumption is ample. The superior performances of ANNs over other methods to forecast future electricity consumption have been shown in many studies (Singh & Sahay, 2018; Chakravorty, Shah, & Nagraja, 2018). ANNs have both advantages and disadvantages (Hippert, Pedreira, & Souza, 2001). Computational complexity, the amount of data and time required during the training phase to learn the patterns, that performances depend on the random initialization of weights and bias, and that training is likely to stop in local minima are considered as the highlighted limitations of the ANNs.

In this study, we address one of these issues, where ANNs can trap in local minima during the training phase, by introducing a new training algorithm to train the ANNs. The conventional training algorithm to adjust the weights and bias in ANNs is Backpropagation. However, researchers have already found the above issue of Backpropagation and suggested alternative methods to train ANNs (Jeenanunta & Abeyrathn, 2017; Shayeghi, Shayanfar & Azimi, 2009; Jeenanunta & Abeyrathn, 2019). They highlight the importance of metaheuristic approaches for training ANNs. Particle Swarm Optimization (PSO) and Genetic Algorithm (GA) are popular among researchers due to their ability to solve complex nonlinear optimization problems (Subbaraj & Rajasekaran, 2019). PSO has been successfully applied to train ANNs and shown that it outperforms the traditional training algorithm, Backpropagation on a number of occasions (Jeenanunta & Abeyrathn, 2017; Das, 2017; Asar, Hassnain, & Khan, 2007; Mishra & Patra, 2008). Simultaneously, GA has also set better weights in ANNs compared to Backpropagation in electricity forecasting research (Mishra & Patra, 2008; Heng, Srinivasan & Liew, 1998).

Nevertheless, these metaheuristics are also unable to perform deftly when the complexity of the data pattern goes higher and ANNs have a large number of weight parameters to be optimized. However, the advantage of using metaheuristic approaches is that they can be adjusted to increase the performances. One of the examples is the PSO algorithm. Its performances can be further improved by changing it slightly or adding some extra steps. In our previous attempt (Abeyrathna & Jeenanunta, 2019), we introduced the PSO+GA algorithm. In that, we modified the PSO algorithm by introducing GA operations into the traditional PSO workflow. However, in this study, we make even simpler modifications to the traditional PSO algorithm in order to obtain on par or better performances while training ANNs. The new modifications are not only intelligible but also have computational advantages. The proposed algorithm is perfect for the considered application where it is used to train ANNs with complex data such as historical electricity consumption in Thailand.

The paper is organized as follows. In Section 2, we briefly discuss how PSO can be used to train ANNs. In Section 3, modifications on the PSO algorithm to train ANNs are discussed. In this section, we present both our previous and new PSO based algorithms. The behavior of the proposed algorithm is also emphatically analyzed using a known function. The basics of the application, procedure of applying proposed algorithm on above application, and results are discussed in Section 4. We conclude our findings in Section 7.

2. TRAINING ARTIFICIAL NEURAL NETWORKS WITH PARTICLE SWARM OPTIMIZATION

When PSO is used for training ANNs, each particle represents a weight set that creates different solutions for different training samples. Together, these particles create a bunch of weight sets for the ANNs at each training iteration. The performance of each weight set at each training iteration is assessed by calculating the training error for that specific weight set. The weight sets or the particles that create minimum training error at that specific training iteration are considered as the best weight sets or the particles. The best particle from all the particles for all the generations is the global best solution (g). Simultaneously, each particle maintains its best solution for all the generations and called personal best (p). The velocities and positions of particles for the next training iteration are calculated with the aid of g and p as given in Equation(1) and (2).

$$V^i\left(t+1\right) = w \times V^i\left(t\right) + c1 \times rand1 \times \left(p - X^i\left(t\right)\right) + c2 \times rand2 \times \left(g - X^i\left(t\right)\right) \tag{1}$$

$$X^i\left(t+1\right) = X^i\left(t\right) + V^i\left(t+1\right) \tag{2}$$

According to the Equation (1), the velocity of the ith particle at $(t+1)^{th}$ generation, $V^i(t+1)$ is a combination of the current velocity and positions of the same particle and the positions of the global best and personal best particles. The weights of these individual components decide by the random values; rand1 and rand2 and learning factors; c1, and c2. The position of the ith particle at the $(t+1)^{th}$ generation is calculated using the updated velocity and the position at the current generation as given in Equation (2).

3. PARTICLE SWARM OPTIMIZATION ALGORITHMS TO TRAIN ARTIFICIAL NEURAL NETWORKS

In PSO, although particles rapidly converge to an optimum point, the chance of trapping all particles in a local minimum is high. This happens since all particles follow the global best solution with a slight ability to expand the solution space with the help of personal best solutions and current positions. Therefore, not only has it a chance of getting stuck in local minima but also once they are trapped in local minima, they cannot find the way out from the trap on their own. Consequently, we modify the PSO algorithm by adding extra steps to the algorithm so that particles escape local minima when they trap in. This occasion in the training phase is identified when particles cannot find a better solution than the current best solution over a certain number of consecutive training iterations. In the following two sections, previous (PSO+GA) and current (PSO-Shock) modifications for the PSO algorithm are discussed, respectively.

3.1 PSO+GA Algorithm

Previously, we introduced the PSO+GA algorithm which has GA operations in PSO to help to find better solutions once its particles trap in local minima (Abeyrathna & Jeenanunta, 2019). When the fitness value shows minor or no improvements over successive generations, we assume that it has reached a local minimum or the global minimum and stars counting the stall generations. When stall generations reach to 20, GA operations are applied to perturb the particles of PSO. From a total number of particles, 50% of mutation and 50% of crossover children are produced. 50% of the particles from the last generation are selected randomly for producing the mutation children. Random values between -1 and 1 are added to the randomly selected 5 elements of each selected particle. For producing crossover children, we merge a random number of genes of a randomly selected particle from the previous generation and remaining genes from another randomly selected particle.

GA operations help PSO to create a completely different particle set while they keep the previous personal best and global best values. In case newly created particles can beat the current personal best or the global best, these values are updated and carried to the next generation. After applying these GA operations, PSO starts performing its regular activities for finding the global best. Likewise, GA operations are applied two times in PSO over one training period in order to minimize the training error without stopping it at a local minimum. An ANN is trained with the PSO+GA algorithm and used to forecast the Thailand electricity consumption for the year 2013. The results of the proposed algorithm are compared with the results from the Backpropagation training algorithm and the traditional PSO algorithm. More details about the procedure, experiments, and performance can be found in original PSO+GA article (Abeyrathna & Jeenanunta, 2019).

3.2 PSO-Shock Algorithm

In this research, we propose simpler perturbation to the traditional PSO algorithm in order to obtain on par or better performance compared to PSO+GA algorithm. The motivation behind the current endeavor is introducing a computationally feasible and less complicated algorithm.

3.2.1 Theoretical Overview

Parameters of the PSO algorithm can be changed to find a completely new particle set while saving the previous best particles. However, at this stage, we just focus on changing the learning factors (c1 and c2) of the Equation (1) to perturb the particles. This helps particles to find better solutions than the current global best and to reach the global minimum solution, consequently.

A similar way to the traditional PSO algorithm, the proposed algorithm starts generating random solutions to the ANNs. The fitness value of each particle is the error that a specific weight set obtains for the training data. However, since the objective is to minimize the training error, the best particles (g and p) are the particles that create the lowest training errors. Once the global best g and personal bests p are updated, they are used to find the velocities and positions of all particles for the next generation using Equation (1) and (2). The traditional PSO iterates until it meets one of the stopping conditions:

1. Reached the minimum training error,
2. Reached the maximum training iterations,
3. Reached the maximum stall generations.

Stall generations are the training iterations that do not improve the current global best solution, g. Therefore, when there is no improvement in the global best solution continuously for a specific number of training iterations, the training process is ended assuming that it has reached the global minimum.

Nevertheless, difficult problems have more local minima in the solution space. Therefore, the algorithm can show no or minor improvements when it sticks in local minima as well. However, there is no way to identify exactly whether it is in a local minimum or the global minimum when there is no improvement to the global best solution. Therefore, we perturb all particles assuming that they trap in a local minimum when the number of stall generation reaches to 15 while saving the current best solutions in case it is the global minimum, i.e. apply Shock on PSO particles. We do this merely by changing the learning factors c1 and c2 in Equation (1). This additional step is applied two times to the traditional PSO during the complete training iterations. The stages of the proposed algorithm can be clarified clearly with the flowchart given in Figure 1.

Hyperparameters w, c1, and c2 in Equation (1) should be decided for two stages: initial and perturbation. The effect of these hyperparameters has been studied with a different combination for them to optimize complex objective functions in Trelea (2003). Considering its findings, the inertia weight w is fixed at 0.6 and learning factors are fixed at 1.7 (c1 = c2 = 1.7) at the initial stage. A secondary experiment is arranged to identify the best learning factors to perturb the particles when they trap in local minima.

3.2.2 Behavior of the PSO-Shock Algorithm: Experiment Setup

The behavior of the PSO-Shock algorithm is analyzed utilizing a function with multiple local minima, which is famous in terms of its toughness to find the global optimum (Whitley, Gordon & Mathias, 1995): Schwefel's function. Schwefel's function is mathematically expressed in Equation (3).

$$f(R) = 418.9829 \times d - \sum_{i=1}^{d} r_i \times \sin\left(\sqrt{|r_i|}\right) \tag{3}$$

The global minimum of the above function is 0. The function value f (R) reaches 0 when R is optimum,

R*: $R^* = (r_1, r_2, \ldots\ldots r_d) = (420.9687, 420.9687, \ldots\ldots 420.9687)$.

Figure 1. Training ANNs with the improved PSO algorithm

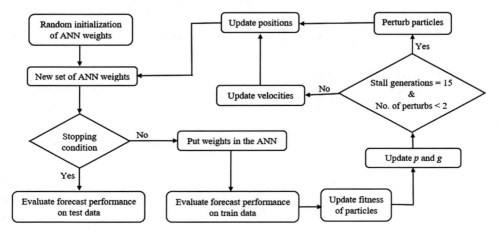

Figure 2. Schwefel's function for two variables

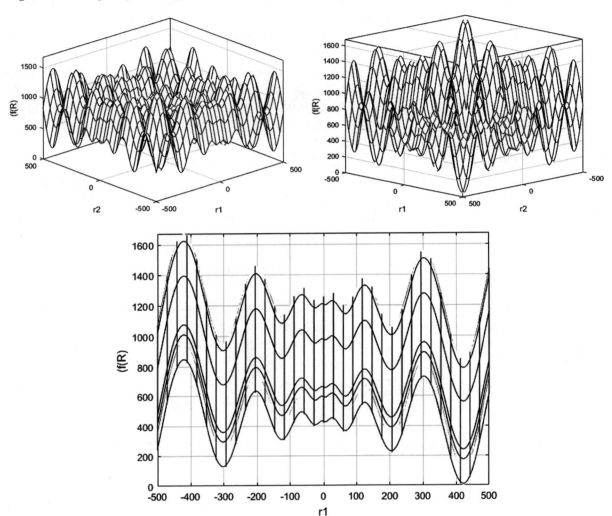

In order to grasp the idea better, Figure 2 illustrates the top, bottom, and side view of Schwefel's function for two variables (d = 2).

However, to increase the challenge further for the PSO-Shock algorithm, it is asked to find the global minimum of the Schwefel's function when it has four variables (d = 4). The algorithm initiates similar to the traditional PSO algorithm. The number of particles is set to 100 and the constraint for the variables is $r_i \in$ [-500, +500]. Velocities and positions of the particles are computed as in Equation1 and 2 after analyzing the global best, g and personal best, p. The other hyperparameters, inertia weight w and learning factors, c1 and c2 are fixed at 0.6 and 1.7 (c1 = c2 = 1.7), respectively according to the findings of Trelea (2003). When there is no improvement of the global best, g for 15 consecutive iterations, the traditional PSO operation is interrupted and all particles are perturbed. In this experiment, we merely focus on changing the learning factors to perturb the particles. Since the exact value for learning factors is unknown to make a reasonable ruffle, the effect is monitored by changing the learning factor values starting from 2 (c1 = c2 = 2, which is slightly higher than the initial value, 1.7). The other values selected for learning factors are 10, 20, 50, 100, 500, and 1000. The results obtained with these changes are presented and discussed in the next section.

3.2.3 Behavior of the PSO-Shock Algorithm: Results

Since the variables are randomly initialized, the fitness of most of the particles is high (low is better since this is a minimization problem) during the first training iterations. However, the fitness of the particles decreases over training iterations and researches to a minimum point. Nevertheless, this is not guaranteed to be the global minimum always. As illustrated by Figure 3, particles can also trap in local minima during the global minimum quest of traditional PSO.

Figure 3. Evolution of fitness of particles over training iterations

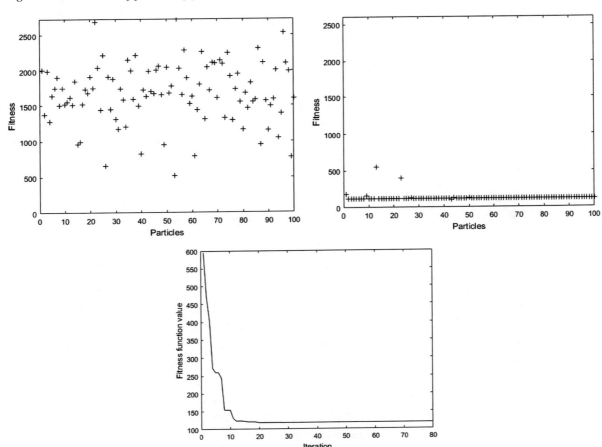

When the particles are trap in a local minimum, the improvement of the global best is zero or considerably low as we can see in Figure 3c. All particles are then perturbed in the PSO-Shock algorithm. Resulting variation of fitness of the particles can be seen in Figure 4.

Figure 4. Perturb particles to get out from the local minimum

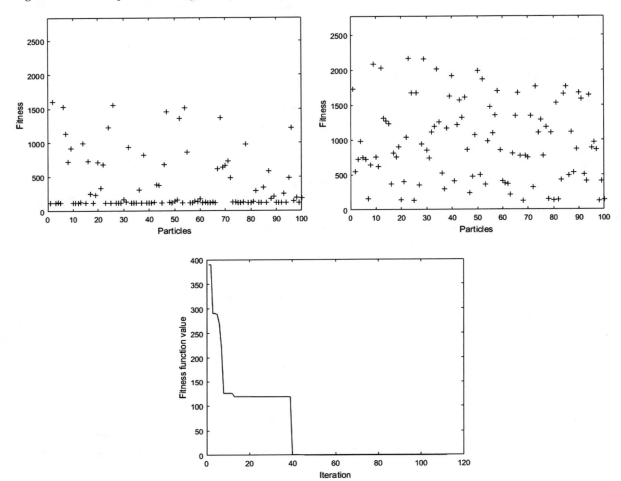

The effect of the value of the learning factors can be clearly seen in Figure 4a and 4b. The impact made when the particles are perturbed with $c1 = c2 = 500$ (Figure 4b) is higher than when the particles are perturbed with $c1 = c2 = 10$ (Figure 4a). Figure 4c illustrates an example where perturbances help particles to escape local minima and consequently find the global minimum. First, it traps at a local minimum around the fitness value of 120. That local minimum can also be seen in 2c when r1 is -300. However, as we saw in these figures, the effect of the perturbances depends on the values of the used learning factors. Table 1 provides an overview of the average minimum values of each training algorithm (traditional PSO and proposed algorithm with different learning factor values) obtained after 30 attempts and number of times each algorithm reaches the global minimum.

Table 1 reveals that at 2 out of 3 attempts, PSO traps in local minima. Even though the global minimum is 0, the average of minimum values obtained for 30 attempts by PSO is 93.87. Which means they trap not only in the local minimum around 120 but also somewhere higher, since 93.87 is higher than 120_20=30. However, perturbances made with trivial learning factors do not make a significant effect to reduce the average of minimum values obtained by the PSO algorithm. Up to $c1 = c2 = 100$,

Table 1. Average of the minimum values given by different algorithms with different parameters

	PSO	Proposed Algorithm With $c1 = c2 =$						
		2	10	20	50	100	500	1000
No. of global minimum findings (out of 30)	10	9	10	10	12	14	19	21
Average of minimum values	93.87	97.80	90.07	101.47	85.73	77.87	50.73	35.40

the percentage reduction of the average of minimum values is less than 20%. the percentage reduction of the average of minimum values when c1 = c2 = 500 and 1000 are 45.96% and 62.29%, respectively. When the learning factors equal to these two values, they find the global minimum almost at 2 out of 3 attempts. However, a secondary experiment finds that further increase of learning factor values does not make significant differences to the average of minimum values.

4. TRAIN ARTIFICIAL NEURAL NETWORKS WITH PSO-SHOCK FOR FORECASTING ELECTRICITY DEMAND IN THAILAND

With above changes for the PSO algorithm, it is used to train ANNs to forecast future electricity consumption in Thailand, as discussed in the following sections.

4.1 Thailand Power Grid Data

Contemplating the significance of Short-Term Load Forecasting (STLF), we apply our proposed PSO algorithm with ANNs to forecast future electricity consumption in Thailand. STLF is an input to make important decisions related to fuel purchasing, security analysis, maintenance schedules, and generator scheduling (Rana & Koprinska, 2016). Therefore, accurate forecasting outcomes are important and bring the attention of researchers and engineers in the field. Simultaneously, STLF is an arduous task since the time series is highly nonlinear and controlled by many external factors: commercial and social activities, human behavior, weather conditions, etc. (Singh & Singh, 2001).

The data gathered by the Electricity Generating Authority of Thailand (EGAT) has data from March 2009 to December 2013. The data has been gathered at every 30-minute for five regions in Thailand for the mentioned period. Electricity consumption in the Bangkok region is selected for the experiment since it has a higher variation over time compared to the other regions where they have nearly flat curves due to the population difference. Outliers of the selected dataset are removed using a sliding window filtering band as discussed in (Jeenanunta, Abeyrathna, Dilhani, Hnin & Phyo, 2018). Temperature variation for the same time period is also considered to forecast future electricity consumption.

Therefore, the objective of the proposed method is to forecast the next day's electricity consumption for every 30-minute in advance. The history of the electricity consumption and temperature variation and the forecasted temperature for the forecasting day can be used to reach the above objective. The data, ANN, and training algorithm preparation to complete the above task are discussed in the following section.

4.2 Experiment Setup

Instead of adding different inputs to identify the days of the week and the time period of the day, which put the ANN in more trouble during the pattern learning phase, we divide all data into separate days and separate time intervals. Therefore, in our attempt, each time period of each testing day is forecasted separately. This lessens the number of inputs to the ANN. To forecast the electricity consumption on day d at time t, (Lt (d)), four inputs are arranged using the historical electricity data and temperature data:

1. Electricity consumption history of the previous day at same time period, (Lt (d-1)),
2. Electricity consumption history of the previous week same day at the same time period, (Lt (d+7)),
3. Forecasted temperature for the same day at same time period, (Tt (d)),
4. Temperature variation history of the previous day at the same time period (Tt (d-1)).

To forecast each time period of each day separately, the selected ANN is trained with one-year data. As an example, to forecast electricity consumption on the 1st of May 2013 (Wednesday), training dataset starts from 2nd of May 2012(Wednesday). This arrangement, just to forecast the above day, is well presented in Table 2. Likewise, all the days in 2013 are forecasted using the concept of walking-forward testing routine, where the same amount of training data is used to forecast each time period of each day in 2013.

Table 2. Sample data arrangement to forecast time-period t on the 1ˢᵗ of May 2013

	$L_t(d-1)$	$L_t(d-7)$	$T_t(d)$	$T_t(d-1)$	$L_t(d)$
Training Data	$L_t(8.5.2012)$	$L_t(2.5.2012)$	$T_t(9.5.2012)$	$T_t(8.5.2012)$	$L_t(9.5.2012)$
	$L_t(15.5.2012)$	$L_t(9.5.2012)$	$T_t(16.5.2012)$	$T_t(15.5.2012)$	$L_t(16.5.2012)$
	$\vdots$	$\vdots$	$\vdots$	$\vdots$	$\vdots$
	$L_t(23.4.2013)$	$L_t(17.4.2013)$	$T_t(24.4.2013)$	$T_t(23.4.2013)$	$L_t(24.4.2013)$
Testing Data	$L_t(30.4.2013)$	$L_t(24.4.2013)$	$T_t(1.5.2013)$	$T_t(30.4.2013)$	$L_t(1.5.2013)$

Since the number of input and output nodes of the ANN has been already defined with the above data arrangement (4input nodes and 1 output node), just the hidden parameters have to be set. In one of our previous research, the effect of hidden parameters was studied (Jeenanunta & Abeyrathna, 2016). Considering the number of input and output nodes and to keep the network simple, one hidden layer with 4 neurons is added to the network as given in Figure 5.

All the nodes in the input layer make connections with all neurons in the hidden layer. This makes 16 weight connections between them. Each neuron in the hidden layer has a bias. The neurons in the hidden layer make connections with the output node which also has a bias in it. Therefore, the proposed ANN has 25 parameters (16+4+4+1) in total to be optimized with the proposed training algorithm. Hence, each particle in PSO is a collection of these parameters and they make different solutions for the input data.

These parameters then should be encoded into the particles. Encoding gives the above parameters specific places in the particles. The first 16 positions of all particles compute the values for 16 weight

Figure 5. The proposed ANN with its inputs and output

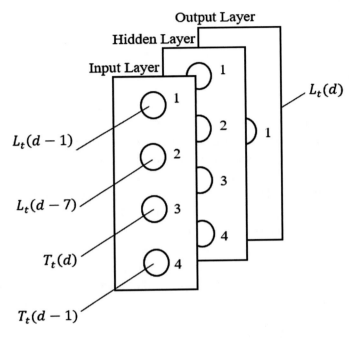

connections between input and hidden layers. The next four positions determine the bias of the hidden neurons. Positions from 20 to 24 belong to the weight connections between the hidden and output layers. The last position of all particles reckons the value of the bias of hidden neurons. Mean Squared Error (MSE) between the target and training outputs is computed as the fitness of each particle. Therefore, weights and bias in each particle are updated to minimize the MSE, which at the end provides the optimum parameters that give the minimum MSE for training data.

Similar to work with Schwefel's function (Equation 3), 100 particles (population) are assigned to find the best weight and bias setting for the ANN. Unlike in the Schwefel's function, there are no constraints for the weight and bias values. Particles start with random weights and bias. Velocities and positions of particles are updated according to Equation (1) and (2). Parameters in the Equation (1) are initialized with 0.6 and 1.7 for the inertia weight, w and learning factors, c1 and c2, respectively. When there is no or minor improvement of MSE of the global best for 15 iterations (15 stall generations), learning factors are changed to 1000 in order to perturb the particles. Results for the same experiment are obtained with three other training algorithms: traditional PSO, PSO+GA, and Backpropagation. These results are presented and discussed in the following section.

4.3 Results and Discussion

Mean Absolute Percentage Error (MAPE) is used to measure the performance of each algorithm as in Equation (5). Once the ANN is trained, each day in the testing dataset is predicted and compared with the actual data. The MAPE for each day is then calculated.

$$e_t(d) = L_t(d) - F_t(d) \tag{4}$$

$$MAPE(d) = \left[\left(\frac{1}{48} \right) \sum_{t=1}^{48} \left| \frac{e_t(d)}{L_t(d)} \right| \right] \times 100 \tag{5}$$

The error between the forecasted load value for time t of day d (Ft (d)) and actual load value for time t of day d (Lt (d)) is identified as et (d). Since each day has 48-time intervals, MAPE for day d (MAPE(d)) is calculated using the errors of all 48 values of the considered day.

Each experiment is conducted 15 times to get the average MAPE. Table 3 summarizes the average monthly MAPE for each training algorithm when they are used to train ANNs to forecast load demand in Thailand. The minimum and maximum monthly average MAPE obtained by the proposed PSO-Shock algorithm are 2.033 (in August) and 6.705 (in December), respectively. PSO+GA algorithm acquires its best MAPE in April (2.164) and the worst MAPE in December (6.761). However, MAPE of each month by PSO-Shock algorithm is somewhat similar to MAPE obtained by PSO+GA algorithm. Backpropagation (BP) and traditional PSO algorithms struggle in the process of finding the best weights and bias parameters for the ANN, in order to forecast future electricity consumption in Thailand. The minimum and maximum MAPE obtained by Backpropagation training algorithm are 2.655 (September) and 8.466 (December), respectively. The traditional PSO algorithm procures these values in November (2.556) and December (8.636), respectively. Out of these minimum and maximum MAPEs, both minimum of the minimum MAPE and minimum of the maximum MAPE secure by PSO-Shock algorithm.

Table 3. Monthly average MAPE by different training algorithms

	Monthly Average MAPE			
	BP-ANN	**PSO-ANN**	**PSO+GA**	**PSO-Shock-ANN**
January	3.837	3.139	2.638	2.642
February	3.480	3.215	2.836	2.838
March	4.253	3.492	2.887	2.889
April	3.398	2.604	2.155	2.092
May	3.416	2.938	2.412	2.452
June	3.591	3.200	2.843	2.881
July	3.173	2.932	2.394	2.437
August	2.541	2.574	2.171	2.033
September	2.653	2.611	2.268	2.349
October	3.388	3.257	2.737	2.744
November	2.914	2.554	2.293	2.300
December	8.470	8.637	6.762	6.705

Only December has higher than 3.00 average monthly MAPE when the ANN trains with the PSO+GA and PSO-Shock algorithms. Average monthly MAPE in January, February, March, June, October, and December are over 3.00 when ANN uses traditional PSO for training weights and bias while only August, September, and November have less than 3.000 MAPE when ANN uses Backpropagation training algorithm to optimize the ANN parameters. Regardless of the training algorithm, the average monthly MAPE in December is higher compared to the other months. The reason is, although holidays, bridging holidays, and outliers are replaced with the estimated data, still the load consumption in December is much lower compared to the other months. When the ANN is trained with higher consumption values from other months, it forecasts assuming that December has also similar consumption values as in other months.

As a summary, the mean of the monthly MAPE of each training algorithm is computed. This can also be considered as the mean forecasting error for the entire testing dataset or the forecasting error for the year 2013 by ANN when it is trained with different training algorithms. Mean MAPE for the year 2013 with the Backpropagation training algorithm is 3.759. Mean MAPE for the year 2013 with the traditional PSO algorithm is 3.430. This value with the PSO+GA and PSO-Shock algorithms are 2.867 and 2.864, respectively. The total error for the entire testing dataset with PSO+GA and PSO-Shock algorithms have no significant difference. However, the percentage reductions of the error for the year 2013 when PSO-Shock algorithm used to train the ANN compared to Backpropagation and traditional PSO algorithms are 23.81% and 16.50%, respectively. This is a significant improvement of the results compared to the traditional training algorithms while obtaining on par performance compared to PSO+GA algorithm.

5. CONCLUSION

In this study, we proposed a solution to one of the inherent issues of the traditional PSO algorithm where it easily traps in local minima and cannot find the way out from the local minima once they stuck. The behavior of the proposed algorithm was studied with a known function. With the promising performance of the proposed algorithm on the known function, it was utilized to update the weights in ANNs in order to forecast the future electricity consumption in Thailand. The proposed algorithm shows significantly better performance compared to the traditional training algorithms of ANN. However, compared to the previously introduced PSO+GA algorithm, PSO-Shock algorithm demonstrates on par performance. Nevertheless, the PSO-Shock algorithm has trouble-free operations in the modification phase, fewer parameters to be decided, and is easy to understand compared to the PSO+GA algorithm and can still provide on par accuracy for the testing data.

REFERENCES

Abeyrathna, K. D., & Jeenanunta, C. (2019). Hybrid particle swarm optimization with genetic algorithm to train artificial neural networks for short-term load forecasting. [IJSIR]. *International Journal of Swarm Intelligence Research*, *10*(1), 1–14. doi:10.4018/IJSIR.2019010101

Asar, A. U., Hassnain, S. R. U., & Khan, A. (2007). Short-Term Load Forecasting Using Particle Swarm Optimization Based ANN Approach. *Proceedings 2007 International Joint Conference on Neural Networks*, 1476–1481. (IEEE). 10.1109/IJCNN.2007.4371176

Chakravorty, J., Shah, S., & Nagraja, H. M. (2018). ANN and ANFIS for Short Term Load Forecasting. *Engineering, Technology, & Applied Scientific Research*, 8(2), 2818–2820.

Das, G. S. (2017). Forecasting the energy demand of Turkey with a NN based on an improved particle swarm optimization. *Neural Computing & Applications*, 28(S1), 539–549. doi:10.100700521-016-2367-8

Heng, E. T., Srinivasan, D., & Liew, A. (1998). Short term load forecasting using genetic algorithm and neural networks. *Proceedings of EMPD'98 1998 International Conference on Energy Management and Power Delivery*, 2, 576–581 (IEEE). 10.1109/EMPD.1998.702749

Hippert, H. S., Pedreira, C. E., & Souza, R. C. (2001). Neural networks for short-term load forecasting: A review and evaluation. *IEEE Transactions on Power Systems*, 16(1), 44–55. doi:10.1109/59.910780

Jeenanunta, C., & Abeyrathn, K. D. (2017). Combine particle swarm optimization with artificial neural networks for short-term load forecasting. [ISJET]. *International Scientific Journal of Engineering and Technology*, 1, 25–30.

Jeenanunta, C., & Abeyrathna, K. D. (2016). The study of artificial neural network parameters for electricity forecasting. *Proceedings International Conference on Applied Statistics*, pp. 105–111. Phuket, Thailand, July 13-15. Academic Press.

Jeenanunta, C., & Abeyrathna, K. D. (2019). Neural network with genetic algorithm for forecasting short-term electricity load demand. *International Journal of Energy Technology and Policy*, 15(2/3), 337–350. doi:10.1504/IJETP.2019.098957

Jeenanunta, C., Abeyrathna, K. D., Dilhani, M. H. M. R. S., Hnin, S. W., & Phyo, P. P. (2018). Time series outlier detection for short-term electricity load demand forecasting. [ISJET]. *International Scientific Journal of Engineering and Technology*, 2(1), 37–50.

Mishra, S., & Patra, S. K. (2008). Short term load forecasting using neural network trained with genetic algorithm & particle swarm optimization. *Proceedings 2008 First International Conference on Emerging Trends in Engineering and Technology*, 606–611 (IEEE). 10.1109/ICETET.2008.94

Rana, M., & Koprinska, I. (2016). Forecasting electricity load with advanced wavelet neural networks. *Neurocomputing*, 182, 118–132. doi:10.1016/j.neucom.2015.12.004

Shayeghi, H., Shayanfar, H., & Azimi, G. (2009). STLF based on optimized neural network using PSO. *Iranian Journal of Electrical and Computer Engineering*, 4, 1190–1199.

Singh, A., & Sahay, K. B. (2018). Short-Term Demand Forecasting by Using ANN Algorithms. *Proceedings International Electrical Engineering Congress (iEECON)*. IEEE. 10.1109/IEECON.2018.8712265

Singh, D., & Singh, S. P. (2001). A self-selecting neural network for short-term load forecasting. *Electric Power Components and Systems*, 29(2), 117–130. doi:10.1080/153250001300003386

Subbaraj, P., & Rajasekaran, V. (2008). Evolutionary techniques based combined artificial neural networks for peak load forecasting. *World Academy of Science, Engineering, and Technology*, 45, 680–686.

Trelea, I. C. (2003). The particle swarm optimization algorithm: Convergence analysis and parameter selection. *Information Processing Letters, 85*(6), 317–325. doi:10.1016/S0020-0190(02)00447-7

Whitley, D., Gordon, V. S., & Mathias, K. (1995). Lamarckian evolution, the Baldwin effect and function optimization. *Proceedings International Conference on Parallel Problem Solving from Nature*, 5–15 (Springer).

Chapter 5

Segmentation and Edge Extraction of Grayscale Images Using Firefly and Artificial Bee Colony Algorithms

Donatella Giuliani

University of Bologna, Italy

ABSTRACT

This chapter proposes an unsupervised grayscale image segmentation method based on the Firefly and Artificial Bee Colony algorithms. The Firefly Algorithm is applied in a histogram-based research of cluster centroids to determine the number of clusters and the gray levels, successively used in the initialization step for the parameter estimation of a Gaussian Mixture Model. The coefficients of the linear super-position of Gaussians can be thought of as prior probabilities of each component. Applying the Bayes rule, the posterior probabilities of the grayscale intensities are evaluated and their maxima are used to assign each pixel to clusters. Subsequently, region spatial information is extracted to form homogeneous regions through ABC algorithm. Initially, scout bees are moving on the search space describing random paths, with food sources given by the detected homogeneous regions. Then onlooker bees rush to scouts' aid proportionally to unclassified pixels enclosed into the bounded boxes of the discovered regions.

INTRODUCTION

Firefly Algorithm and Gaussian Mixture Model

Image segmentation is the process of partitioning a digital image into multiple segments of pixels. The goal of image segmentation is to simplify the representation of an image in one more meaningful and easier to understand. It is often an essential step in image analysis, object representation, visualization, and many other image processing issues and it is aimed at facilitating the tasks at higher levels, such as

DOI: 10.4018/978-1-7998-3222-5.ch005

object detection and recognition. Image segmentation is a preliminary step in image processing, playing a role of great relevance in object recognition and classification, machine learning, image learning and understanding (Gonzalez & Wood, 2007).

In this work, we propose a method for grayscale image segmentation and edge extraction that is composed of two different phases in which are applied two bio-inspired algorithms (Osuna-Enciso, 2014) Firefly and the Artificial Bee Colony algorithms. In the first phase, a pixel-based segmentation is performed applying the FA algorithm and the Gaussian Mixture Model. Classification of pixels in different gray levels is obtained through a histogram-based segmentation approach. To do so, we utilize the nature-inspired FA algorithm for defining automatically the number of clusters given by histogram maxima.

Artificial Bee Colony Algorithm

After assigning all pixels to the corresponding gray classes, we carry out the second step with a region-based segmentation. For this purpose, the ABC algorithm was performed to complete the segmentation process, which resulted greatly simplified since there are only a few levels of gray. The region growing technique is implemented using randomly generated scout bees as initial seed points. The scout bees are moving on the search space, i.e. the gray image, describing random paths. The food sources are defined by homogeneous regions. Once a region of a specific gray intensity has been found, the scout bee comes back to the hive for executing the waggle dance in order to involve onlooker bees in the exploitation phase. Then onlooker bees give rise to a local search, rushing to scouts' aid proportionally to the size the of the bounded boxes of regions discovered by scout bees and to the number of unclassified pixels included into them.

BACKGROUND

The basic goal of any image segmentation process is to subdivide an image into components belonging to different objects or to different parts of an object. Theoretically, pixels derived by the same component should have similar intensities, forming a connected region (Russ & Neal, 2015). During the last decades many segmentation methods have been proposed in literature, for an in-depth overview of clustering techniques refer to (Nikhil & Sankar,1993; Jain, Murry, & Flynn., 1999; Herbert & Pantofaru, 2005; Zaitoun & Musbah, 2015). The segmentation techniques are categorized into three main classes: pixel-based, region-based and edge-based schemes (Haralick & Shapiro, 1985). The threshold-based segmentation approach belongs to the first category, it is one of the simplest and widely used in computer vision. In thresholding methods, pixels are partitioned depending on their intensity levels, recurring to global thresholding, with a single threshold T, or to variable thresholding if T changes over the image, or to multiple thresholding values $T_1, \ldots T_n$. Global thresholding maps a gray-valued image into a binary image, hence it can be suitable to segment an image into objects and background. Threshold segmentation can be extended to use multiple thresholds to decompose an image into more than two segments. Many methods exist to select threshold values for a segmentation task, among them we could mention the image histogram-based approaches, which are often valuable tools in establishing suitable thresholding values (Ridler & Calvard, 1978; Chen & Chen, 2009).

Region-based segmentation algorithms operate iteratively by grouping together pixels that have neighbours with similar values and splitting groups of pixels that are dissimilar.

In edge-based segmentation, an edge operator is applied to the image for detecting meaningful discontinuities in intensity values. The ascertained edges are assumed to be object or region boundaries, therefore pixels are classified in such a way that those which are not separated by an edge are assigned to the same region or category (Bresson et al., 2007; Mahmoud & Marshall, 2008).

More specifically, edge-based techniques attempt to find object boundaries and then to allocate pixels by filling them in. Region-based techniques apply an opposite approach by starting in a specific position of a region from which pixels are adjoined outward until boundaries are met (Gould, Fulton, & Koller, 2009; Gu, Lim, Arbelaez, & Malik, 2009).

Another category of clustering methods performs an image partition trying to minimize the intra-cluster differences and maximize the inter-cluster differences. These approaches are usually classified into two types; hierarchical clustering and partitional clustering. Hierarchical clustering produces a nested series of partitions based on a criterion for splitting or merging clusters. On contrast, partitional clustering segmentation is carried out by partitioning the data into a fixed number of clusters, using similarity measures. A commonly used partitional clustering method is the K-means algorithm (Frigui & Krishnapuram, 1999; Senthilnath, Omkar, & Mani, 2011; Senthilnath, Das, Omkar, & Mani, 2012). Traditional K-means clustering algorithms have the drawback of being strongly affected by predefinition of the number of clusters and the initial values of centroids, thus the results will generally depend on the initialization parameters.

GRAY IMAGE SEGMENTATION AND EDGE EXTRACTION

Pixel-Based Segmentation With Firefly Algorithm and Gaussian Mixture Model

Over the last few decades, researchers started to use metaheuristic algorithms for clustering to overcome the limitations of the existing conventional, generally deterministic, clustering algorithms (Osman & Laporte, 1996; Zheng, Pan, Li, & Liang, 2009). Metaheuristic algorithms are a class of approximate methods that allow to discover possible solutions exploring the search space in order to find near-optimal solutions. Shortly, metaheuristic algorithms are iterative processes developed to search for a solution that is good enough in a time that is small enough (Blum & Roli, 2003). These algorithms are frequently nature-inspired, they have the advantages of finding global optima due to the action of multiple search agents, randomly generated (Rothlauf, 2011).

The solution of an optimization problem with a metaheuristic process implies an initialization step generating one or more random solutions.

In each iteration step, the current solution is then changed by a new one, created by search operators, with a global optimization approach composed by two schemes: the *exploitation* of new solutions with the goal of improving the quality of solutions and the *exploration* of the entire search space to prevent the selection of local optima.

The two main families of metaheuristic algorithms are the Evolutionary Computing and the Swarm Intelligence (SI) algorithms, the former is based on the principles of biological evolution, such as natural selection and genetic inheritance, the latter is founded on the characteristics and behavior of biological swarms, for instance, ants, bees, birds, and fishes (Parpinelli & Lopes, 2011),

In order to solve optimization problems, previous scientific literature has proposed many heuristic algorithms, including for instance: a) Differential Evolution (DE) algorithms, namely computational methods able to optimize a problem iteratively, trying to improve a candidate solution through a given measure of quality (Storn & Price K, 1997; Goldberg, 1989), which works by choosing solutions from the current population and applying them genetic operators; b) Ant Colony Optimization (ACO) algorithms that emulate the behavior of real ants in finding the shortest path from the food source to their nest (Bilchev & Parmee, 1995); c) Bees Algorithms (BA) that mimic the food foraging behavior of swarms of honey bees (Pham et al., 2006); d) Particle Swarm Optimization (PSO), that are optimization methods based on the social comportment of groups, such as flocks of birds or schools of fish (Kennedy & Eberhart, 1995; Kennedy, Eberhart, & Shi, 2001). Clustering techniques based on Evolutionary Computing and Swarm Intelligence algorithms have outperformed many classical methods of clustering (Abshouri & Bakhtiary, 2012).

In this chapter, the number of clusters and the cluster means have been evaluated automatically by means a histogram-based segmentation approach applying the Firefly Algorithm (Giuliani, 2017). The Firefly Algorithm was developed by Yang X.S. (2008; 2010a; 2010b; Fong, Deb, Yang, & Zhuang, 2014), it employs fireflies as search agents making use of their idealized flashing characteristics. In describing the Firefly Algorithm, three fundamental rules may be delineated:

1. All fireflies are unisex so that one firefly will be attracted to other fireflies regardless of their sex;
2. Attractiveness is proportional to their brightness, thus for any two flashing fireflies, the less bright one will move towards the brighter one. The attractiveness is proportional to brightness, decreasing as their distance increases. If there is no brighter one, a generic firefly will move randomly in the search space;
3. The brightness of a firefly is determined by an objective function. For a maximization problem, the brightness can simply be proportional to the objective function.

The attractiveness $\beta(r)$ of a firefly is proportional to the brightness and decreases with distance r monotonically and exponentially, because the luminosity becomes weaker with the distance from its source and light is absorbed in the media, so we have:

$$\beta(r) = \beta_0 \cdot e^{-\gamma r^2}$$

where β_0 is the attractiveness at $r=0$ and γ is the light absorption coefficient. As a firefly i is attracted to another brighter j, its movement is described at time t by:

$$x_i^{t+1} = x_i^t + \beta_0 \cdot e^{-\gamma r_{ij}^2} \cdot \left(x_j^t - x_i^t\right) + \alpha_t \cdot \epsilon_i^t \tag{1}$$

where r_{ij} represents the distance between the two fireflies. The second term is due to the attraction, while the third term defines the random component through the vector of casual values ϵ_i, drawn from a Gaussian or uniform distribution at a given iteration. Thus, if $\beta_0=0$ it describes a simple random walk. The value of γ expresses the variation of attractiveness, the use of $\gamma = 0$ corresponds to constant attractiveness and conversely if $\gamma \to \infty$ the attractiveness tends to zero, which is equivalent to a totally random search.

Given the significant level of variability of the gray level histograms for real images. the choice of FA algorithm is particularly suitable for finding global optima. In this unsupervised clustering method, we have adopted as objective function the percentage increase of pixel frequency.

In the following applications, the fireflies used as search agents are 30, the average scale L is set equal to 256 that are the number of gray levels, the light absorption coefficient γ is set equal to $1/\sqrt{L}$, the random vectors ϵ_i^t have been reduced during iterations, in order to avoid an excessive erratic motion in the search space.

After evaluating automatically the number K of clusters through the global maxima derived by the FA algorithm, the corresponding gray-levels intensities have been assigned as initial means μ_k, $k=1,...$,K to the Gaussian Mixture Model (Lindsay, 1995; McLachlan & Basford, 1988). The initial standard deviations σ_k are approximately evaluated by the intensity distribution.

A Gaussian Mixture Model (GMM) is a parametric probability density function represented as a weighted sum of Gaussian component densities. In this work GMM parameters are estimated from training data using the iterative Expectation-Maximization (EM) algorithm.

Let us recall that a univariate Gaussian density distribution is expressed by:

$$p\left(x\mid\mu,\sigma^2\right) = N\left(x\mid\mu,\sigma^2\right) = \frac{1}{\sigma\sqrt{2\pi}}\exp\left(-\frac{\left(x-\mu\right)^2}{2\sigma^2}\right)$$

where $N(x\mid\mu,\sigma^2)$ represents the Gaussian or Normal distribution of mean μ and standard deviation σ. A Gaussian mixture model is a weighted sum of K components of Gaussian densities, analytically given by:

$$p\left(x\right) = \sum_{k=1}^{K}\pi_k \cdot N\left(x\mid\mu_k,\sigma_k^2\right) \tag{2}$$

Equation (2) represents a linear superposition of Gaussian probability densities and the *mixing coefficients* π_k indicates the weight of each distribution. As a consequence of the first and second axiom of the probability theory, these coefficients must satisfy the following relations:

$$0 \leq \pi_k \leq 1, \sum_{k=1}^{K}\pi_k = 1$$

The first axiom states that all the probabilities are nonnegative real numbers, the second axiom attributes a probability of unity to the universal event, providing a normalization of the probability. Thus the complete Gaussian mixture model is parameterized by means μ_k, variances σ_k^2 and mixture weights π_k of all components. We can think of the mixing coefficients as prior probabilities for each component:

$$\pi_k = \frac{N_k}{N}$$

where N is the number of data points and N_k, $k=1,\dots,K$ are the numbers of data belonging to the k-th cluster.

The GMM parameters have been calculated using the Expectation Maximization (EM) algorithm. This algorithm is an iterative optimization technique that starts from some initial estimation of parameters and then proceeds to iteratively update them until convergence is detected, in short it consists of four basic steps:

1. The Initialization Step: define initial guesses for parameters, in this context they have been derived by the FA algorithm
2. The Expectation Step: compute the *responsibilities* γ_k Equation (3), namely the posterior probabilities of a given gray intensity x to belong to the k-th cluster, according to the Bayes rule we have:

$$\gamma_k\left(x\right) = p\left(k|x\right) = \frac{\pi_k \cdot N\left(x \mid \mu_k, \sigma_k^2\right)}{\sum_{i=1}^{K} \pi_i \cdot N\left(x \mid \mu_i, \sigma_i^2\right)} \tag{3}$$

3. The Maximization Step: re-estimate the parameters using Equation (4). (5) and the current responsabilities, given -by Equation (3):

$$\hat{\mu}_k = \frac{\sum_{i=1}^{N} \gamma_k\left(x_i\right) \cdot x_i}{\sum_{i=1}^{N} \gamma_k\left(x_i\right)} \tag{4}$$

$$\hat{\sigma}_k^2 = \frac{\sum_{i=1}^{N} \gamma_k\left(x_i\right) \cdot \left(x_i - \hat{\mu}_k\right)^2}{\sum_{i=1}^{N} \gamma_k\left(x_i\right)}$$

$$\hat{\pi}_k = \frac{\sum_{i=1}^{N} \gamma_k\left(x_i\right)}{N} \tag{5}$$

4. Compute convergence by the value of log likelihood after each iteration, halting if it does not change in a significant manner from one iteration to the next:

$$\ln\left(p\left(X|\mu,\sigma,\pi\right)\right) = \sum_{i=1}^{N} \ln\left(\sum_{k=1}^{K} \pi_k \cdot N\left(x_i \mid \mu_k, \sigma_k^2\right)\right)$$

Iterate Expectation Step (2) and Maximization Step (3) until convergence.

After determining the parameter values with the EM technique, we have proceeded to the assignment of pixels of a given gray level x_i to the cluster $\tilde{k}$ by means the evaluation of the maximum value of responsibilities:

$$\gamma_{\tilde{k}}\left(x_i\right) = \max_{k \in K}\left\{\gamma_k\left(x_i\right)\right\}$$

all the pixels with gray level x_i are attributed to the $\tilde{k}$-th cluster, given that, by definition, $\gamma_k(x_i)$ represents the probability of the k-th GMM's component to have generated the value x_i. The proposed segmentation method performs classification of pixels in a straightforward and effective way reducing greatly the computational costs.

For testing the performance of this segmentation approach based on FA, we have computed several standard measures, more precisely: the Root Mean Square Error (RMSE), the Structural Content (SC), the Normalized Correlation Coefficient (NK) and finally the Davies-Bouldin (DB) index (Jaskirat, Sunil, & Renu, 2012), (Nihar, Bikram, & Amiya, 2013). The RMSE is the simplest image quality measurement, a large value of RMSE means the image is of poor quality, given an image I_{ij} $i=1,\ldots,m; j=1,\ldots,n$ and the segmented image Is_{ij} $i=1,\ldots,m; j=1,\ldots,n$, it is defined as:

$$RMSE = \sqrt{\frac{\sum_{i=1}^{m}\sum_{j=1}^{n}\left|I_{ij}\right|^2}{n \cdot m \sum_{i=1}^{m}\sum_{j=1}^{n}\left|I_{ij} - Is_{ij}\right|^2}} \tag{6}$$

The structural content measure is computed by the following formula:

$$SC = \frac{\sum_{i=1}^{m}\sum_{j=1}^{n}\left|I_{ij}\right|^2}{\sum_{i=1}^{m}\sum_{j=1}^{n}\left|Is_{ij}\right|^2} \tag{7}$$

even in this case a smaller value of SC corresponds to a better quality of the segmented image. The normalized correlation coefficient (NK) quantifies in percentage the level of correlation between the two images and it is so expressed:

$$NK = \frac{\sum_{i=1}^{m}\sum_{j=1}^{n}I_{ij} \cdot Is_{ij}}{\sum_{i=1}^{m}\sum_{j=1}^{n}\left|I_{ij}\right|^2} \tag{8}$$

Finally, to test the consistency of each application, we have calculated the Davies-Bouldin index, that is based on similarity measure of clusters R_{ij} obtained through the dispersion S_i of a cluster and the dissimilarity measure D_{ij}. Usually, given a partition of the initial dataset I in disjoint clusters $C_i, i=1,\ldots,k$ of cardinality n_i, R_{ij} is defined in the following way:

$$R_{ij} = \frac{S_i}{D_{ij}} \tag{9}$$

where

$$S_i = \left(\frac{1}{n_i} \cdot \sum_{I_{ij} \in C_i} \left| I_{ij} - \mu_i \right|^2 \right)^{\frac{1}{2}}$$

represents the intra-cluster standard deviation and $D_{ij} = \left(\left| \mu_i - \mu_j \right|^2 \right)^{\frac{1}{2}}$ measures the distance between two different clusters C_i and C_j through the distance of their centre points. The Davies-Bouldin index estimates the average of similarity between each cluster:

$$DB = \frac{1}{k} \sum_{i=1}^{k} \max_{j=1,..k;k \neq j} \frac{S_i + S_j}{D_{ij}} \tag{10}$$

even with this validation index a lower value implies a better clustering segmentation.

Regional-Based Segmentation and Edge Extraction With Artificial Bee Colony Algorithm

After assigning each pixels to the corresponding gray class, we proceed to a region-based segmentation. The first step in region growing is to select a set of seed points. The region begins to grow at the location of these seeds. Then regions are expanding from them to adjacent points depending on a specific criterion, which may be pixel intensity for grayscale images or texture, color for color images. In the present work, the selection of initial seed points was achieved through the Artificial Bee Colony algorithm.

The ABC algorithm is a swarm-based meta-heuristic algorithm that was introduced by Karaboga in 2005 (Karaboga, 2005) for optimizing numerical problems. It was inspired by the intelligent foraging behavior of honey bees in nature. The algorithm is specifically based on the model for the foraging behavior of honey bee colonies (Lučić & Teodorović, 2003; Pham et al., 2006). In ABC algorithm the colony of artificial bees consists of three groups: employed bees, onlookers and scouts (Karaboga, Gorkemli, Orzturk, & Karaboga, 2014). Employed bees are those who have discovered a food source. Every food source is associated to only one employed bee. The employed bee whose food source is abandoned becomes a scout bee, starting new random research around the hive. The exchange of information among bees is the most important occurrence in the formation of collective knowledge. Communication among bees related to the quality of food sources takes place in the dancing area of the hive, this dance is called the waggle dance. After localizing a source, employed bees share nectar and position information of the food sources with onlooker bees executing the waggle dance. An onlooker bee evaluates nectar information taken from employed bees and decides to employ herself at the most profitable source, with a probability related to the nectar amount (Nikolić & Teodorović, 2013).

In this chapter, initially scout bees are moving on the search space, i.e. the gray image, describing random paths each of which is a piecewise linear curve, composed by a connected sequence of M arbitrary line segments. The trajectories of scout bees are defined by the following parametric equations:

$$\vec{X}_{k+1}\left(t\right) = \vec{X}_{k}\left(t\right) + \vec{v}_{k}\left(t\right)\cdot t$$
$$t \in \left[0;1\right], k = 1, \dots M \tag{11}$$

More explicitly, for each scout bee Equation (11) is expressed as:

$$\begin{cases} x_{k+1}\left(t\right) = x_{k}\left(t\right) + v_{0}\cdot rand\left(1\right)\cdot \cos\left(rand\left(1\right)\cdot\theta\right) \\ y_{k+1}\left(t\right) = y_{k}\left(t\right) + v_{0}\cdot rand\left(1\right)\cdot \sin\left(rand\left(1\right)\cdot\theta\right) \end{cases} \tag{12}$$

where v_0 is the initial velocity, $\theta \in [0;2\pi]$ and rand(1) is a generator of random numbers uniformly distributed in the interval [0;1], the endpoints of each line segment determine the positions of unemployed bees during their flights. The paths will result confined inside the image space, so as not to go beyond edges. If along the path a scout bee finds a food source, i.e. zones with not classified pixels, the growing process will be activated starting from the actual position, otherwise the bee keeps going undisturbed. Once the region with uniform gray intensity is outlined, its edges are extracted and the bounded box of boundaries is determined. At this point, employed bees share their food source information with onlooker bees waiting in the hive and then onlooker bees probabilistically choose their food sources depending on this information. The scout bees come back to the hive for executing the waggle dance in order to involve onlooker bees in the exploitation phase. In the present application of ABC algorithm, the fitness values are computed through the percentage of pixels not yet assigned and included inside the bounded box of the extracted regions. Then onlooker bees give rise to a local search, rushing to scouts' aid proportionally to the number of unclassified pixels and to the size of the rectangle containing the extracted boundary.

SOLUTIONS AND RECOMMENDATIONS

Till date many unsupervised clustering methods have been used for segmenting images. After all separation of an image into a set of disjoint regions is a fundamental task for automated image recognition systems. Since it is widely known that a unique segmentation of an image does not exist, many different types of segmentation techniques have been developed. For example, two people may perceive differently the same scene and the relative principal components, depending on their own predominant interests or their level of accuracy in observing it. Thus, the choice of a method based on metaheuristic algorithms could be going in the right direction, because, at any rate, the discovered solution will be a good solution among all the other possible ones. In this section we analyse in details the results obtained with some test images.

The first image we have processed is extracted by ALL-IDB database (Labati, Donida, Piuri, & Scotti, 2011), it reproduces blood cells (Figure 1). In this context we have used a combination of nature inspired algorithms and a classic technique based on the Gaussian Mixture Model, without recurring to the evaluation of threshold points for the grayscale histogram (Osuna-Enciso, Cuevas, & Sossa, 2013).

As outlined above, the pixel assignment to clusters has directly performed through the highest level of the posterior probabilities defined by Bayes rule, consequently, this approach implies a consistent reduction of the computational costs and of the error level in the step of attribution of each element to the corresponding cluster. Figure 2 displays the segmented image, Table 1 shows the GMM parameters and the estimated error values. We point out that the final values of standard deviations of the first four clusters are quite different respect to the initial values, as we can see in Figure 5, we recall that the standard deviations were not evaluated by a metaheuristic algorithm but minimizing the deviations from the initial means.

Figure 1. Original image: blood cells

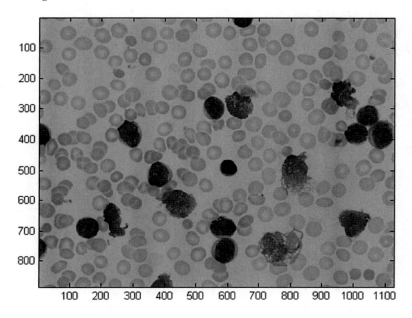

Figure 2. Segmented image: blood cells

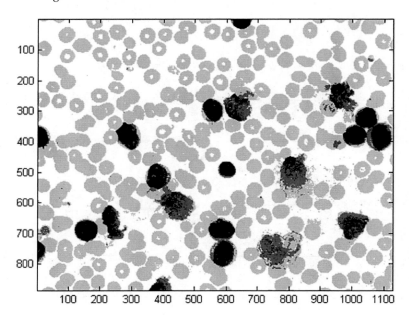

Table 1. Parameter values of FA and GMM and validation indices (Blood Cells) (K = 3)

N. Pixels = 998280 = 885x1128	Data Clusters (N. Iterations EM =10)		
μ_k initial	47.87	134.20	166.29
μ_k final	60.82	135.74	164.29
σ_k initial	5.28	6.54	3.58
σ_k final	20.41	10.44	3.29
N_k	85995	413481	498804
π_k final	0.096	0.447	0.456
RMSE	**SC**	**NK**	**DB**
0.0156	1.0088	0.9936	0.4521

Figure 3. Initial values derived by FA Algorithm and Gaussian Mixture Model

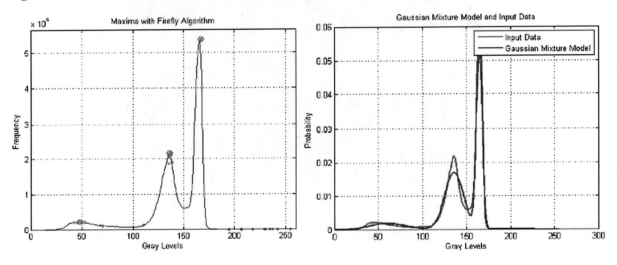

Figure 4. GMM parameters computed by EM algorithm (blood cells)

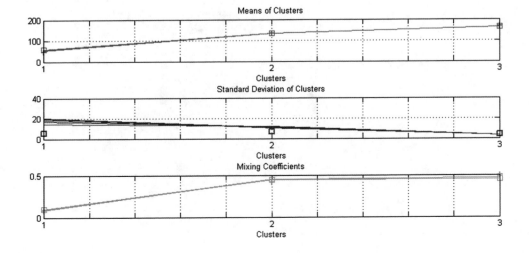

Clustering is an intrinsically difficult task, to this regards the three main challenges concern: the number of clusters of the data set, the initial values of centroids and the quality of the segmented data. In particular, evaluating the quality of results in determining the number of clusters and their initial centres is a crucial issue. In the method hereby presented, to ensure that the choice of the number of clusters and value of centroids was adequate and justifiable, we have executed the algorithm multiple times for the image of Figure 1. These multiple executions allowed to analyze the distribution of optima generated by FA algorithm (Figure 5).

Figure 5. Distribution of centroids evaluated by FA after 20 executions (blood cells)

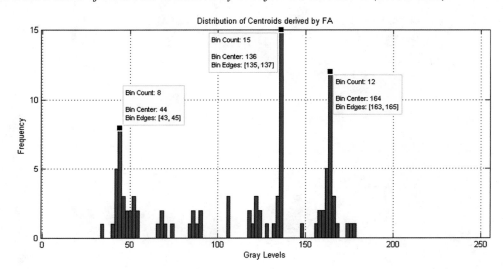

Observing Figure 5, we infer that the values of centroids are basically concentrated around the grayscale levels 44, 136 and 164. Actually, during the segmentation process of image in Figure 1, the gray levels derived by the initialization step are 47.87, 134.20 and 166.29, while the final values generated by GMM are 60.82, 135.74, and 164.29 respectively. The difference between the corresponding values associated to the first cluster is affected by the difference between the original histogram and the distribution obtained by GMM in the interval

[0, 100], as we can see in Figure 3. At any rate though, the clustering algorithm is not influenced by variations of initial centroids in a limited range, in any case the GMM converges to the final solution with a different number of iterations. The model parameters appear rather stable regardless of the starting gray levels. Regarding the validation tests, we refer to the validity indices discussed above. Analysing Table 1, we could observe that the quality of segmentation is very high, for example, the normalized correlation coefficient (NK) is 0.9936 out 1.00.

After finishing the pixel-based segmentation, we proceed to the regional segmentation by applying the ABC algorithm. In Figure 6 the random paths of scout bees are shown, they are generated during two different iterations. Figure 7 displays examples of the local search activated by onlookers coming to help the employed bees in the exploitation phase of this metaheuristic algorithm. All the classified pixels are excluded by successive researches, consequently, computational time decreases as the number of iterations increases. For partitioning the image of Figure 2, we have performed 8 iterations, with 25

Figure 6. Random paths of scout bees generated during two different iterations

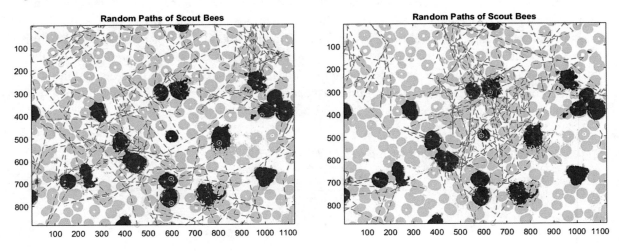

Figure 7. Random paths of onlookers inside the bounded boxes

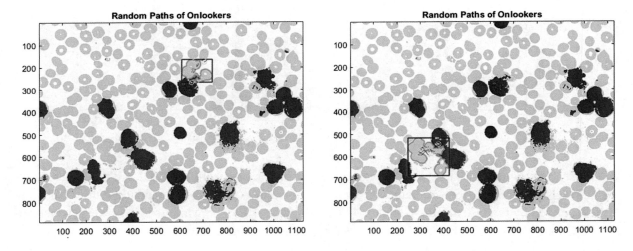

scout bees and 40 onlookers in total staying in the hive, of which only a percentage will be engaged by employed bees.

The general structure of the ABC optimization method is given as follows:

Initialization Phase

```
REPEAT Employed Bees Phase (Random Search all over the image)
    If Scout bee finds out a source food
     Start local search: Onlooker Bees Phase
    Else
     Continue global search
    end
```

```
    Memorize the solution achieved so far
UNTIL (Maximum Number of Iterations or All pixels are assigned to regions or a
Maximum CPU time)
```

The number of onlookers varies with the percentage of pixels that remains to be classified belonging to the bounded box of the extracted edge and with the size of the researching area. The algorithm carries out all the cell edges, drawn with red lines, as we can see in Figure 8. After 8 iterations, only two red blood cells (in light gray) are not captured during the exploration phase, the first one is located nearby the left upper corner, and the second one nearby the left lower corner, whereas all the cells' nucleuses (darker blobs) are detected.

Figure 8. Edges of cells extracted by ABC algorithm

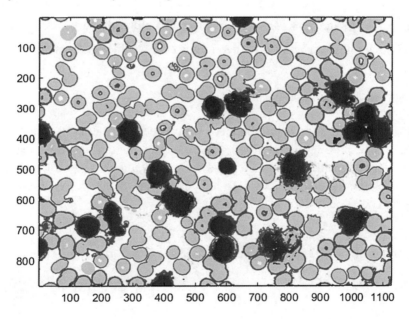

As a second test image, we have processed the image 260058 selected by the Berkeley Segmentation Dataset BSDS300 (Figure 9, on left). Initially, we started with a pre-processing step, during which the original colour image has been projected on the principal component $\vec{v}_1$, recurring to the Principal Component Analysis (Dikbas S., Arici T., Altunbasak Y., 2007). Applying PCA, the image dimensionality has been reduced from the three-dimensional Hue-Saturation-Value (HSV) colour space to the one-dimensional gray representation (Figure 9, on right). This preliminary phase of elaboration enhances the contrast between pixel intensities (Giuliani D.,2018). To perform PCA technique, we need to compute the covariance matrix. For a given colour image:

$$\vec{I}\left(i, j\right), i = 1,..m; j = 1,..n$$

with components $\vec{I} = \left(I_1, I_2, I_3\right)$, let be $\vec{\bar{I}}$ the vector mean:

$$\vec{\bar{I}} = \frac{1}{m \times n} \sum_{i=1}^{m} \sum_{j=1}^{n} \vec{I}\left(i, j\right) \tag{13}$$

the associated covariance matrix 3×3 C is evaluated as:

$$C = \frac{1}{m \times n} \sum_{i=1}^{m} \sum_{j=1}^{n} \left(\vec{I}\left(i, j\right) - \vec{\bar{I}}\right) \cdot \left(\vec{I}\left(i, j\right) - \vec{\bar{I}}\right)^{T} \tag{14}$$

Let $\lambda_1 \geq \lambda_2 \geq \lambda_3$ and $\vec{v}_1, \vec{v}_2, \vec{v}_3$ be the eigenvalues of C in decreasing order and relative eigenvectors, respectively. The colour image $\vec{I} = \left(I_1, I_2, I_3\right)$ is projected along the direction of the principal component $\vec{v}_1$, in which the highest variability has been registered, by means the matrix product:

$$I = \vec{v}_1^{T} \cdot \vec{I} \tag{15}$$

Once the intensity image I has been obtained, we proceed in evaluating automatically the number of clusters and the associated representative levels through a histogram-based segmentation approach recurring to the Firefly Algorithm. Table 2 reports the mean values of the 7 different clusters, the GMM parameters and the estimated error values with indices RMSE, SC, NK, DB, even in this case the normalized correlation coefficient (NK) is 0.9990 out 1.00.

Figure 9. Colour image of BSDS300 Dataset and gray image obtained with PCA

At the end of the pixel-based segmentation, we proceed with regional segmentation by applying the ABC algorithm. The random paths of scout bees generated during two different iterations are displays in Figure 12.

In Figure 13 and Figure 14, four examples of local research executed by onlookers are shown, the employed bees rush to aid scout bees for completing the exploitation phase of this metaheuristic algorithm. Their number depends on both the size of the rectangle delimiting the extracted region and the number of internal points that remain to be classified.

Table 2. Parameter values of FA and GMM and validation indices (K = 7)

N. Pixels = 153920 = 320x481	Data Clusters (N. Iterations EM =10)						
μ_k initial	53.96	79.78	113.36	137.05	163.02	212.19	239.00
μ_k final	52.86	78.77	113.34	136.40	175.27	217.28	233.80
σ_k initial	4.07	2.35	2.02	1.27	2.48	4.55	4.14
σ_k final	11.14	8.28	9.80	7.21	15.11	11.93	5.99
N_k	1246	694	570	355	151	1516	4395
π_k final	0.1869	0.0718	0.0795	0.0300	0.0407	0.2308	0.3603
	RMSE	SC		NK		DB	
	0.0588	1.0002		0.9990		0.6864	

Figure 10. Initial values derived by FA algorithm and Gaussian Mixture Model

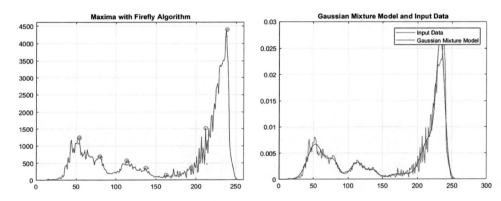

The extracted edges are shown in Figure 15. The algorithms, developed with Matlab, are able to detect even low significant regions that eventually could be excluded on basis of the measure of their area or perimeter length. In any case, if a more detail is needed, the image with the remaining components (Figure 16) could be elaborated, at the end of the process.

FUTURE RESEARCH DIRECTIONS

In future works, we will explore new methodologies for extending metaheuristic approaches to clustering of color images. For this purpose, generally, the HSV color space is more suitable, since it structures any color in the same way in which it is perceived by human eyes. The regional segmentation based on ABC algorithm could be implemented on components of the vector space HSV in order to have a significant reduction of color levels appearing in the image. As already asserted, this preliminary phase is of fundamental importance, thus, it must be robust and effective in order to apply efficiently the differential operators on whatever three-dimensional color vector space should be used.

Figure 11. Gray Segmented Image

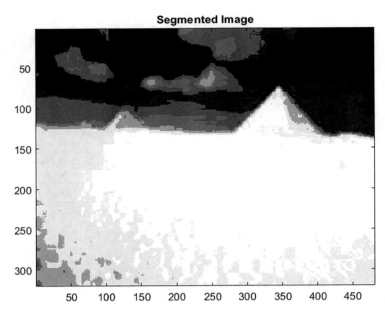

Figure 12. Random paths of scout bees generated during two different iterations

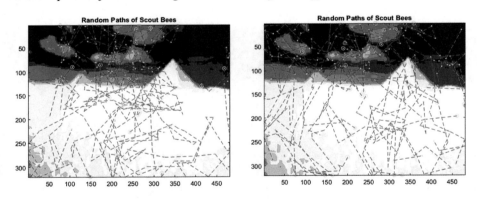

Figure 13. Random paths of onlookers inside the bounded boxes

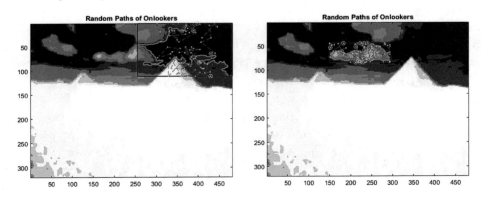

Figure 14. Random paths of onlookers inside the bounded boxes

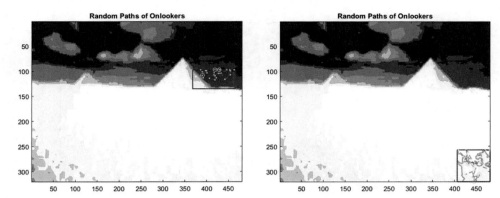

Figure 15. Random paths of scout bees generated during two different iterations

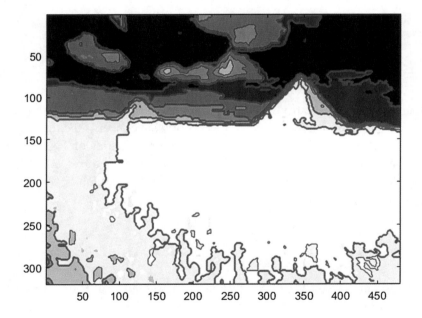

CONCLUSION

This research has addressed image segmentation, one of the fundamental tasks of image processing, recurring to a nature-inspired and population-based algorithm. The algorithm, developed in this application, can automatically find the number of groups in which an image may be partitioned and the initial centroids. Subsequently these values, outcomes of a metaheuristic approach, are used as initial means for the estimation of a Gaussian Mixture Model. The approach previously outlined appears fairly solid and reliable, the validation analysis has been performed by using different standard measures, more precisely: the Root Mean Square Error (RMSE), the Structural Content (SC), the Normalized Correlation Coefficient (NK) and finally the Davies-Bouldin (DB) index. The achieved results have strongly confirmed the robustness of this gray scale segmentation method. Another noteworthy advantage of

Figure 16. Residual regions excluded by edge extraction

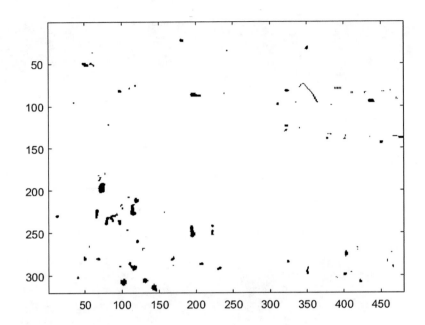

the proposed methodology derives from the use of maxima of responsibilities for pixel assignment that implies a consistent reduction of computational costs. For what concerns the regional segmentation, the application of the probabilistic ABC algorithm carries out boundaries of segmented regions in a fast way. The erratic motion of scout bees is able to detect edges even if the size of regions is very small, hence negligible. This is basically due to the local search activated by onlookers rushing to scouts' aid that makes the research more effective and detailed.

REFERENCES

Abshouri, A. A., & Bakhtiary, A. (2012). A New Clustering Method Based on Firefly and KHM. *Journal of Communication and Computer, 9,* 387–391.

Bilchev, G., & Parmee, I. C. (1995). The Ant Colony Metaphor for Searching Continuous Design Spaces. *Selected Papers from AISB Workshop on Evolutionary Computing*, pp. 25-39. Berlin, Germany: Springer.

Blum, C., & Roli, A. (2003). Metaheuristics in combinatorial optimization: Overview and conceptual comparison. *ACM Computing Surveys, 35*(3), 268–308. doi:10.1145/937503.937505

Bresson, X., Esedoglu, S., Vandergheynst, P., Thiran, J. P., & Osher, S. (2007). Fast global minimization of the active contour/snake model. *Journal of Mathematical Imaging and Vision, 28*(2), 151–167. doi:10.100710851-007-0002-0

Chen, Y. B., & Chen, O. T. (2009). Image Segmentation Method Using Thresholds Automatically Determined from Picture Contents, *Journal on Image and Video Processing*, EURASIP.

Dikbas, S., Arici, T., & Altunbasak, Y. (2007). Chrominance Edge preserving Grayscale Transformation with approximate First Principal Component for Colour Edge Detection. *Proceedings of IEEE Conference of Image Processing (ICIP'07)*, 9, pp. 497-500. IEEE.

Fong, S., Deb, S., Yang, X. S., & Zhuang, Y. (2014). Towards Enhancement of Performance of K-Means Clustering Using Nature-Inspired Optimization Algorithms. *The Scientific World Journal, 2014*, 1–16. doi:10.1155/2014/564829 PMID:25202730

Frigui, H., & Krishnapuram, R. (1999). A Robust Competitive Clustering Algorithm with Applications. *Computer Vision Journal. IEEE Transactions on Pattern Analysis and Machine Intelligence, 21*(5), 450–465. doi:10.1109/34.765656

Giuliani, D. (2017). A Grayscale Segmentation Approach using the Firefly Algorithm and the Gaussian Mixture Model. International Journal of Swarm Intelligence Research, 9(1). IGI Global.

Giuliani, D. (2018). Colour Image Segmentation based on Principal Component Analysis with application of Firefly Algorithm and Gaussian Mixture Model. *International Journal of Image Processing, 12*(4).

Goldberg, D. E. (1989). *Genetic Algorithms in Search, Optimization and Machine Learning*. Reading: Addison-Wesley Longman.

Gonzalez, R. C., & Wood, R. E. (2007). *Digital Image Processing* (3rd ed.). Prentice Hall.

Gould, S., Fulton, R., & Koller, D. (2009). Decomposing a scene into geometric and semantically consistent regions. *Proceedings, ICCV*. Academic Press.

Gu, C., Lim, J. J., Arbelaez, P., & Malik, J. (2009). Recognition using regions. *Proceedings CVPR 2009*. Academic Press.

Haralick, R. M., & Shapiro, L. G. (1985). Image Segmentation Techniques. *Computer Vision Graphics and Image Processing, 29*(1), 100–132. doi:10.1016/S0734-189X(85)90153-7

Herbert, M., & Pantofaru, C. (2005). *A comparison of segmentation algorithms, Report of Robotic Institute*. Pittsburgh, PA: Carnegie Mellon University.

Jain, A. K., Murry, M. N., & Flynn, P. J. (1999). Data Clustering a review. *ACM Computing Surveys, 31*(3).

Jaskirat, K., Sunil, A., & Renu, V. (2012). A comparative analysis of thresholding and edge detection segmentation techniques. *International Journal of Computers and Applications, 39*.

Karaboga, D. (2005). *An idea based on honey bee swarm for numerical optimization, Technical Report*. Computer Engineering Department, Engineering Faculty, Erciyes University.

Karaboga, D., Gorkemli, B., Orzturk, C., & Karaboga, N. (2014). A comprehensive survey: Artificial Bee Colony algorithm and applications. *Artificial Intelligence Review, 42*(1), 21–57. doi:10.100710462-012-9328-0

Kennedy, J., & Eberhart, R. (1995). Particle Swarm Optimization. *Proceedings of the IEEE International Conference on Neural Networks*, 4, pp. 1942–1948. 10.1109/ICNN.1995.488968

Kennedy, J., Eberhart, R., & Shi, Y. (2001). *Swarm intelligence*. Academic Press.

Labati, R. D., Donida, R., Piuri, V., & Scotti, F. (2011). All-IDB: The acute lymphoblastic leukemia image database for image processing. Proceedings 2011 18th IEEE International Conference on Image Processing (pp. 2045-2048). IEEE.

Lindsay, B. G. (1995). *Mixture Models: Theory, Geometry, and Applications*. NFS-CBMS Regional Conference Series in Probability and Statistics.

Lučić, P., & Teodorović, D. (2003). Computing with bees: Attacking complex transportation engineering problems. *International Journal of Artificial Intelligence Tools*, *12*(3), 375–394. doi:10.1142/S0218213003001289

Mahmoud, T. M., & Marshall, S. (2008). Edge-Detected Guided Morphological Filter for Image Sharpening, *Journal on Image and Video Processing*, EURASIP.

McLachlan, G. J., & Basford, K. E. (1988). Mixture Models: Inference and Applications to Clustering. New York: Marcel Dekker.

Nihar, R. N., Bikram, K. M., & Amiya, K. R. (2013). A Time Efficient Clustering Algorithm for Gray Scale Image Segmentation. *International Journal of Computer Vision and Image Processing*, *3*(1), 22–32. doi:10.4018/ijcvip.2013010102

Nikhil, R. P., & Sankar, K. P. (1993). A Review on Image Segmentation Techniques. *Pattern Recognition*, *26*(29).

Nikolić, M., & Teodorović, D. (2013). Empirical study of the Bee Colony Optimization (BCO) algorithm. *Expert Systems with Applications*, *40*(11), 4609–4620. doi:10.1016/j.eswa.2013.01.063

Osman, I. H., & Laporte, G. (1996). Metaheuristics: A bibliography. *Annals of Operations Research*, *63*(5), 511–623. doi:10.1007/BF02125421

Osuna-Enciso, V. (2014). *Bioinspired metaheuristics for image segmentation* (Vol. 13, p. 2). Electronic Letters on Computer Vision and Analysis.

Osuna-Enciso, V., Cuevas, E., & Sossa, H. (2013). *A Comparison of Nature Inspired Algorithms for Multi-Threshold Image Segmentation, 40*(4), pp. 1213-1219.

Parpinelli, R. S., & Lopes, H. S. (2011). New inspirations in swarm intelligence: A survey. *International Journal of Bio-inspired Computation*, *3*(1), 1–16. doi:10.1504/IJBIC.2011.038700

Pham, D. T., Ghanbarzadeh, A., Koc, E., Otri, S., Rahim, S., & Zaidi, M. (2006). The Bees Algorithm: A Novel Tool for Complex Optimisation Problems. *Proceedings of IPROMS 2006 Conference*. 10.1016/B978-008045157-2/50081-X

Pham, D. T., Ghanbarzadeh, A., Koc, E., Otri, S., Rahim, S., & Zaidi, M. (2006). The Bees Algorithm–A Novel Tool for Complex Optimisation, *Proceedings of the 2nd International Virtual Conference on Intelligence Production Machines and Systems*, pp. 454-459. 10.1016/B978-008045157-2/50081-X

Ridler, T. W., & Calvard, S. (1978). Picture thresholding using an iterative selection method. *IEEE Transactions on Systems, Man, and Cybernetics*, *8*(8), 630–632. doi:10.1109/TSMC.1978.4310039

Rothlauf, F. (2011). Design of Modern Heuristics Principles and Application. Springer.

Russ, J. C., & Neal, F. B. (2015). *The image processing handbook* (7th ed.). Boca Raton, FL: CRC Press.

Senthilnath, J., Omkar, S. N., & Mani, V. (2011). Clustering using firefly algorithm: Performance study. *Swarm and Evolutionary Computation, Elsevier, 1*(3), 164–171. doi:10.1016/j.swevo.2011.06.003

Senthilnath, J., Vipul, D., Omkar, S. N., & Mani, V. (2012). Clustering using levy flight cuckoo search. *Proceedings 7th International Conference on Bio-Inspired Computing: Theories and Applications, Advances in Intelligent Systems and Computing*, pp. 65–75. LNCS, Springer India.

Storn, R., & Price, K. (1997). Differential Evolution – A Simple and Efficient Heuristic for global Optimization over Continuous Spaces. *Journal of Global Optimization, 11*(4), 341–359. doi:10.1023/A:1008202821328

Yang, X. S. (2008). *Nature-inspired Metaheuristic Algorithms*. UK: Luniver Press.

Yang, X. S. (2010a). Firefly Algorithm, Stochastic Test Functions, and Design Optimization. *International Journal of Bio-inspired Computation, 2*(2), 78–84. doi:10.1504/IJBIC.2010.032124

Yang, X. S. (2010b). In M. Bramer, R. Ellis, & M. Petridis (Eds.), Firefly Algorithm, Levy Flights, and Global Optimization. Research and Development, Intelligent Systems XXVI (pp. 209–218). London, UK: Springer. doi:10.1007/978-1-84882-983-1_15

Zaitoun, N. M., & Musbah, J. A. (2015). Survey on Image Segmentation Techniques. *Proceedings of International Conference on Communication, Management, and Information Technology*. Elsevier.

Zheng, L., Pan, A., Li, G., & Liang, J. (2009). Improvement of Grayscale Segmentation based on PSO Algorithm. *Proceedings of IEEE 4th Int. Conference on Computer Science and Convergence Information Technology*. 10.1109/ICCIT.2009.68

Chapter 6
Analysis of the Dynamic Characteristics of the Firefly Algorithm

Takuya Shindo

Nippon Institute of Technology, Japan

ABSTRACT

The firefly algorithm is a meta-heuristic algorithm, the fundamental principle of which mimics the characteristics associated with the blinking of natural fireflies. This chapter presents a rigorous analysis of the dynamics of the firefly algorithm, which the authors performed by applying a deterministic system that removes the stochastic factors from the state update equation. Depending on its parameters, the individual deterministic firefly algorithm exhibits chaotic behavior. This prompted us to investigate the relationship between the behavior of the algorithm and its parameters as well as the extent to which the chaotic behavior influences the searching ability of the algorithm.

INTRODUCTION

Under the given constraints, the Optimization Problem is to find a solution that a certain objective function gives the maximum value or the minimum value. The optimization problem has been studied in various fields such as engineering, economics, and et al.

In recent years, many researchers pay attention to swarm intelligence as the application of the optimization problem solver. The swarm intelligence algorithm is between agents to emerge the behavior by local interaction (Krishnanand and Ghose, 2008). For example, some methods are based on the behavior of ants colony, slime mold colony, fish flock, and so on, (Dorigo, Maniezzo and Colorni, 1996)(Zengin and Tuncel, 2010).

A number of meta-heuristic algorithms with diverse applications have been proposed. These algorithms are continuously being improved and studies are also underway to enhance the solution search performance of the algorithm. When considering such performance improvements, an analysis of the characteristics of the algorithm is very important. In general, the theoretical analysis of meta-heuristic

DOI: 10.4018/978-1-7998-3222-5.ch006

algorithms is highly challenging because most of these algorithms contain stochastic factors, (Clerc & Kennedy, 2002; Koguma & Aiyoshi, 2010). Therefore, stochastic analysis of the operation of meta-heuristic algorithms is considered very difficult. Therefore, to analyze the dynamics of the firefly algorithm, the authors proposed a deterministic firefly algorithm.

The firefly algorithm (FA) is one of these meta-heuristic algorithms, (Yang, 2010; Yang, Ed. 2013). The FA was developed by Xin-She Yang et al. and is based on the characteristics of the blinking of a natural firefly. Many performance improvement methods and application fields have already been studied for the FA (Cai, Niu, & Yang, 2018; Alor, Mota, Olmos, & Rodas, 2019; Wang *et al.*, 2018). The original FA expresses the dynamics of the firefly by a simple update equation; however, apart from this, the behavior of the FA is very complex.

The conventional FA is based on the following three rules, (Yang, 2010; Yang, Ed. 2013):

1. Fireflies are unisex creatures such that one firefly will be attracted to other fireflies regardless of their sex.
2. The attractiveness is of a firefly proportional to its brightness, with both of these properties decreasing as the distance between individual fireflies increases. Thus, for any two flashing fireflies, the less bright one would be expected to move towards the brighter one. In the absence of any firefly brighter than itself, it will move randomly.
3. The brightness of a firefly is determined by the landscape of the objective function.

In the work presented in this chapter, the stochastic factors are removed from the update equation. Furthermore, the authors investigate and confirm the effect of the solution search performance of the FA when it exhibits chaotic behavior (Yang, 2013).

FIREFLY ALGORITHM

The dynamics of the FA are described by the following equation.

$$x_i^{t+1} = x_i^t + \beta\left(x_j^t - x_i^t\right) + \alpha_t \varepsilon_i^t,$$

(1)

where x_i^t denotes the position of the i-th firefly on the t-th iteration, β denotes the attractiveness of the i-th firefly as perceived by the j-th fireflies, α_t represents the variation of the randomness with t and ε_i^t denotes a random number vector on the t-th iteration.

Light Intensity and Attractiveness

The following two points have a significant effect on the solution search performance of the FA.

- Variation of light intensity
- Formulation of attractiveness

The distance between the i-th firefly and the j-th firefly is

$$r_{ij}^t = x_i^t - x_j^t = \sqrt{\sum_{d=1}^{n} \left(x_{i,d}^t - x_{j,d}^t \right)^2}.$$

(2)

In the case of a simple maximization problem, the brightness I of the firefly is in proportion to the evaluation function value at position x.

$$I(x) \propto f(x)$$

(3)

Each firefly is attracted to other firefly with a strong intensity of brightness. The intensity of the brightness is inverse proportion to the distance between two fireflies

$$I = I_0 e^{-\gamma r^2}.$$

(4)

Equation (4) can be approximated as follows.

$$I = \frac{I_0}{1 + \gamma r^2},$$

(5)

where I_0 denotes the light intensity at the light source, γ denotes a scaling constant, and r_{ij}^t represents the distance between itself and the other firefly. Compared with Eqs. (4) and (5), the computational amount of Equation (5) is smaller than that of Equation (4).

Similarly, the attractiveness is in proportion to the light intensity seen in the adjacent firefly. The attractiveness of the firefly β is defined as follows.

$$\beta = \beta_0 e^{-\gamma r^2}.$$

(6)

Equation (6) can be approximated by

$$\beta = \frac{\beta_0}{1 + \gamma r^2},$$

(7)

where β_0 denotes the attractiveness of the case of $r=0$. In addition, the computational effort required for Equation (7) is less than for Equation (6). Therefore, Equation (7) is recommended.

If $\beta_0=0$ in Equation (1), the behavior of Equation (1) corresponds to a simple random walk. On the other hand, in the case of $\gamma=0$, the system represented by Equation (1) is regarded as a kind of particle swarm optimization (PSO), (Yang, 2013; Kennedy & Eberhart, 1995; Kennedy, 1997; Gandomi, Yang, Talatahari & Alavi, 2013).

Parameter Setting

Parameter α_t controls the randomness. This parameter can be varied by the status update. For example, the parameter is defined as

$$\alpha_t = \alpha_0 \delta^t, 0 < \delta < 1, \tag{8}$$

where, α_0 is an initial random scale factor, and δ is the attenuation coefficient. In many applications, the parameter δ is assigned a value in the interval from 0.95 to 0.97.

The initial randomness parameter α_0 is set as $\alpha_0=0.01L$, where L denotes the width of the search range. On the other hand, if the randomness parameter is small, the step size of the random walk becomes small, thereby enabling the system to conduct a local search. The balance between a global search and a local search is maintained by setting the randomness parameter as above. Figure 1 shows the results of a solution search simulation when α_0 is varied. The simulation uses a two-dimensional sphere function, which is the most simple benchmark function. The parameter ε is assigned a uniform random number in the range [-0.5,+0.5]. If α_0 is small, the step of the initial search is small. On the other hand, if α_0 is large, the random walk is observed in the initial stage of the search.

Figure 1. State of searching for solutions by setting α_0. (a) $\alpha_0=0.01L$, (b) $\alpha_0=0.05L$, (c) $\alpha_0=0.1L$, (Sphere function two-dimensional, initialization area (-600: 600). number of individuals n=10, $\beta_0=1.0$, $\gamma=1/L$, L=1200, maximum iteration $t_{max}=5000$.

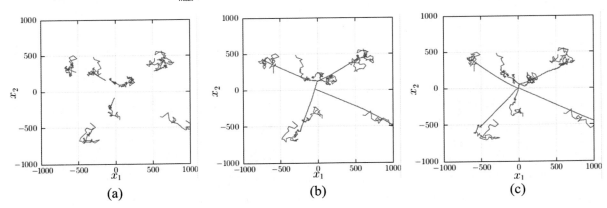

The parameter β controls the attractiveness. In general, $\beta_0=1$ is applied. The parameter γ is a coefficient representing the attenuation of the light intensity and is related to the scale of L. In general, it is possible to set $\gamma = 1/\sqrt{L}$. Figure 2 represents the solution search when β_0 is varied. As β_0 is small, the attractiveness of the other firefly is small; hence, the attraction force is weak. In other words, the closest firefly is initially attracted. Therefore, all individuals accumulate in a certain area.

Figure 2. State of searching for solutions by setting β_0. (a) $\beta_0=0.1$, (b) $\beta_0=1.0$, (c) $\beta_0=2.0$, (Sphere function two-dimensional, initialization area (-600: 600), number of individuals n=10, $\beta_0=1.0$, $\gamma=1/L$, L=1200, maximum iteration $t_{max}=5000$.

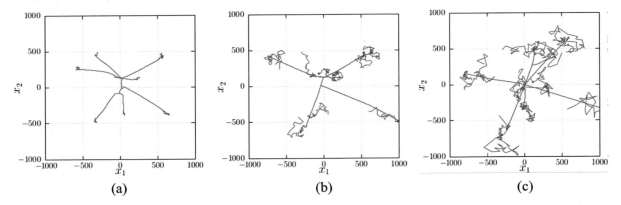

(a)   (b)   (c)

DETERMINISTIC FIREFLY ALGORITHM

The deterministic FA is applied to analyze the dynamics of this algorithm, (Shindo, Xiao, Kurihara, Morita & Jin'no, 2015). Without loss of generality, the authors can consider the one-dimensional case. The authors assume that the j-th firefly found the optimal solution, which is located at the origin. In addition, the initial positions of the other fireflies are located randomly except at the origin. The authors consider the following case of $\alpha_i=0$ of Equation (1) as follows;

$$x_i^{t+1} = x_i^t - \beta_0 e^{-\gamma\left(x_i^t\right)^2} x_i^t ..$$ (9)

Since the system described by Equation (9) does not contain stochastic factors, it can be regarded as a deterministic system. Thus, the authors refer to this system as the deterministic FA. The dynamics of the i-th firefly of the deterministic FA are described by a one-dimensional return map as shown in Figure 3, which shows the effect of varying the parameters γ and β_0. Figure 3 indicates that the characteristic of the one-dimensional return map is dependent on the parameter γ. In the case where γ is large, most of the domain is mapped to itself. On the other hand, when γ becomes small, the return map is varied depending on γ. This enlarges the search range, which is therefore determined by γ. In addition, as the attractiveness of β_0 is large, the amount of movement in the vicinity of the j-th firefly increases, indicating that β_0 controls the search range around $x_j=0$. Here, x_j represents the position of the other firefly. The authors consider the slope of the one-dimensional return map.

$$\frac{dx_i^{t+1}}{dx_i^t} = 1 + \beta_0\left[2\gamma\left(x_i^t\right)^2 - 1\right] - \beta_0 e^{-\gamma\left(x_i^t\right)^2} .$$ (10)

In this case, the authors assume the optimal position is the origin. If the absolute value of the slope of the origin is greater than 1, the dynamics around the origin is expanded. On the other hand, if the absolute slope around the origin is less than 1, the trajectory converges to the origin. From Equation (10), the slope of the origin is. $\left.\dfrac{dx_i^{t+1}}{dx_i^t}\right|_{x_i^t=0} = 1 - \beta_0$. Therefore, if $\beta_0 > 2$, the map is expandable. In addition, if $0 < \beta_0 < 2$, the map is regarded as a contraction map.

Figure 3. Individual behavior determined by the absorption coefficient γ and attractiveness α_0. (a) $\gamma=1.0$, (b) $\gamma=0.1$, (c) $\gamma=0.001$.

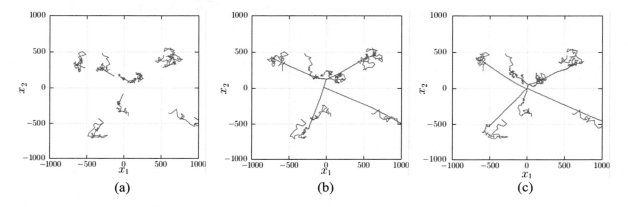

(a)   (b)   (c)

CHAOTIC BEHAVIOR OF FIREFLY

The authors used the deterministic FA to clarify the detailed behavior of each parameter. Figure 4 illustrates the bifurcation diagram of Equation (9). The horizontal axis denotes parameter β_0, and the vertical axis denotes the search position. In this case, γ is set as 0.1, and the initial position x^0 is set to 0.01. Moreover, elimination of the transient state depends on the parameter β_0. For example, when β_0 is set to 7.0, the firefly exhibits chaotic motion during a search. The corresponding return map is shown in Figure 5 and confirms the same tendency as in Figure 3. In addition, the sensitivity to the initial conditions is shown in Figure 6. Sensitivity to initial conditions is confirmed that one of the characteristics of chaos. Time series is shown in Figure 6 when the x^0 is changed minutely. Initially, the position x is almost the same. From around $t=30$, the difference becomes large.

Figure 7 illustrates the time evolution of the search position depending on the parameters. Figure 7(a) that the parameter is $\beta_0=1.0$, the search point is monotonously attenuated, and all fireflies converge to the origin which corresponds to the optimal position. Figure 7(b) that the parameter is $\beta_0=2.5$, the search point converges to the two periodic points. In this case, the firefly to search for only two points. Figure. 7(c) that the parameter is $\beta_0=7.0$, the time-series of the search point exhibits non-periodic motion.

Figure 4. Bifurcation diagram, $\gamma=0.1$, $x^0=0.01$

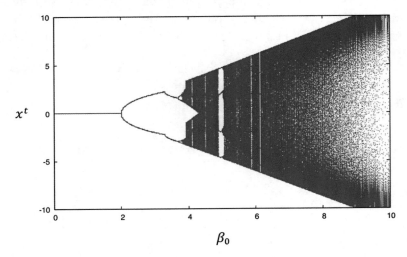

Figure 5. Return map, $\gamma=0.1$, $\beta_0=7.0$, $x^0=0.01$

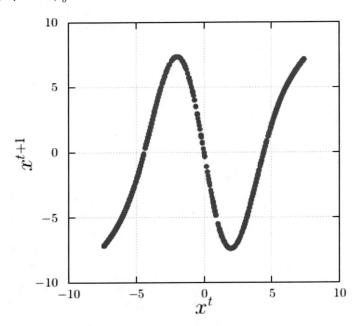

Figure 8 illustrates the time evolution of the search position on the return map depending on the parameters. In Figure 8(a), the search points are monotonously attenuated and are converged. In Figure 8(b), the search points oscillate between two points, whereas in Figure 8(c), the search point exhibits a chaotic non-periodic motion. The Lyapunov exponent is shown in Figure 9. In deterministic FA, the Lyapunov exponent λ is calculated by the following equation.

Figure 6. Sensitivity to initial conditions, γ=0.1, β₀=7.0, x⁰=-5.0, Δ=1e–12

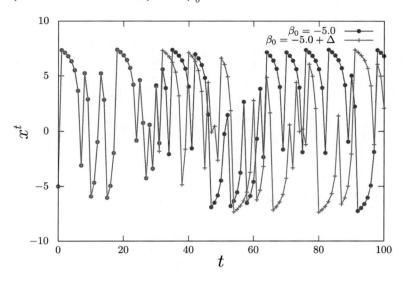

Figure 7. Time series of search position according to the attractiveness of β₀. (a) β₀=1.0, (b) β₀=2.5, (c) β₀=7.0.

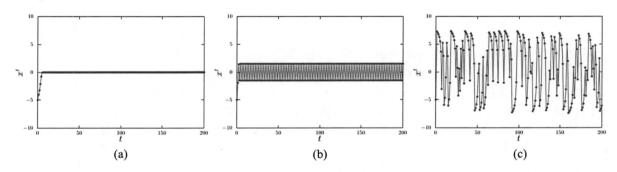

Figure 8. Individual behavior according to the attractiveness β₀: (a) β₀=1.0, (b) β₀=2.5, (c) β₀=7.0.

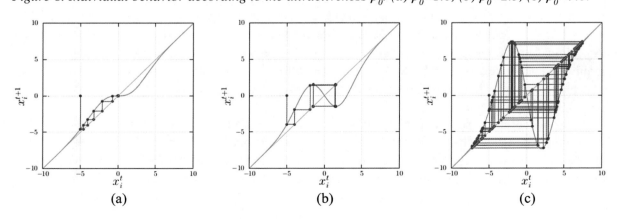

Figure 9. Lyapunov Exponent, γ=0.1, x⁰=0.01, t=100000

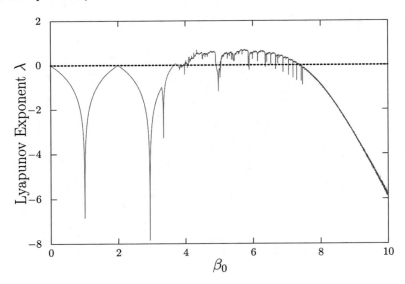

$$\lambda = \lim_{n \to \infty} \frac{1}{t} \sum_{i=0}^{t-1} \ln \left| f'\left(x_i^t\right) \right| \tag{11}$$

Here, $x_i^{t+1} = f\left(x_i^t\right)$ and t is the number of mappings. Generally, when $\lambda > 0$, the trajectory is one of the chaotic conditions (Pecora, Carroll, Johnson, Mar and Heagy, 1997).

These figures indicate this system has an invariant interval. Moreover, Figure 8(c) indicates the trajectory of the map diverges. Therefore, this system generates a chaotic non-periodic motion (Guckenheimer & Holmes, 2013). The behavior of the chaotic motion is different from the random walk (Nara, Davis & Totsuji, 1993). There are several studies that focus on non-linearity of such a system. Such chaotic motion improves the solution search performance of the artificial neural network and the genetic algorithm (Chen & Amhara, 1995).

Conventionally, the system obtains diversity by employing a random number (Yang, Ed. 2013). Injection of chaotic perturbation to ε in Equation (1) has also been proposed (Gandomi, Yang, Talatahari & Alavi, 2013). However, the chaotic behavior of deterministic FA is not an added function. It exists from the original in the system of the conventional FA. The deterministic FA produces the chaotic motion required to generate the diversity to search for the optimal solution. In other words, by using the original chaotic behavior included in FA system, the solution search performance can be improved without including random factors.

In the numerical experiment shown previously, β=7.0 is used as a representative value of the chaos generating parameter. The parameter β can be adjusted to change the search width or to merge individuals. According to the parameter β, individuals are dispersed in the region where chaos occurs. On the other hand, individuals merge in the region where periodic solutions are obtained.

Table 1. Benchmark functions

Function		Optimal Value
Rosenbrock's Function	$f_1\left(x\right) = \sum_{d=1}^{N-1}\left(100\left(x_{d+1} - x_d^2\right)^2 + \left(x_d - 1\right)^2\right)$	$f_1(1,1,1,\ldots,1)=0$
Rastrigin's Function	$f_2\left(x\right) = 10N + \sum_{d=1}^{N}\left(\left(x_d\right)^2 - 10\cos\left(2\pi x_d\right)\right)$	$f_2(0,0,0,\ldots,0)=0$

Figure 10. Solution search performance by β_0 using (a) Rastrigin's function, (b) Rosenbrock's function. The value of trial max is 30 and the dimension of function is 10.

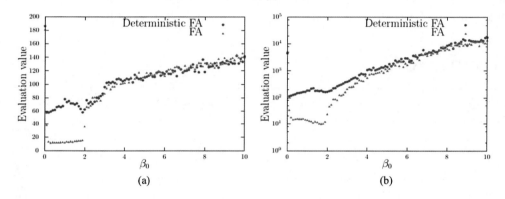

(a)   (b)

Figure 11. Search characteristics resulting from the setting of β_0 using (a) Rastrigin's function, (b) Rosenbrock's function. The value of trial max is 100 and the dimension of the function is 10.

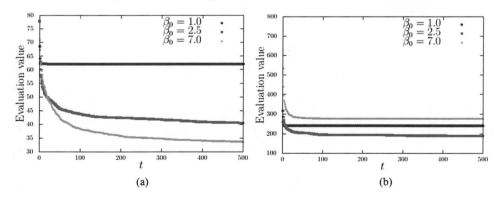

(a)   (b)

NUMERICAL SIMULATIONS

The authors carried out numerical simulations to confirm the extent to which the solution search performance depends on the parameter β_0. The numerical simulations were performed by using the well-known benchmark functions presented in Table 1. The number of trials is 100, the parameter γ is set as $1/\sqrt{L}$, and δ of the conventional FA is 0.97. A uniform distributed random number from the range is [-0.5,+0.5], is applied to ε.

Figures 10 and 11 show the solution search performance for the standard FA and the deterministic FA, respectively. These results, which are obtained by varying the parameter β_0, are excellent results in the range from $\beta_0=0$ to $\beta_0=2$ for either of the FA function. However, for $\beta_0>2$, the solution search performance becomes worse, and the firefly does not converge in this range. Chaotic oscillation is effective for the global search; however, it has no effect on a local search. Thus, controlling of parameter such that the global search shifts to a local search is expected to lead to an improvement in the solution

Table 2. CEC'14 Test Suite

	No.	Functions	$F_i^* = F_i(x^*)$
Unimodal functions	1	Rotated High Conditioned Function	100
	2	Rotated Bent Cigar Function	200
	3	Rotated Discus Function	300
Simple multimodal functions	4	Shifted and Rotated Rosenbrock's Function	400
	5	Shifted and Rotated Ackley's Function	500
	6	Shifted and Rotated Weierstrass Function	600
	7	Shifted and Rotated Griewank's Function	700
	8	Shifted Rastrigin's Function	800
	9	Shifted and Rotated Rastrigin's Function	900
	10	Shifted Schwefel's Function	1000
	11	Shifted and Rotated Schwefel's Function	1100
	12	Shifted and Rotated Katsuura Function	1200
	13	Shifted and Rotated HappyCat Function	1300
	14	Shifted and Rotated HGBat Function	1400
	15	Shifted and Rotated Expanded Griewank's plus Rosenbrock's Function	1500
	16	Shifted and Rotated Expanded Schaffer's F6 Function	1600
Hybrid functions	17	Hybrid Function 1 (N=3)	1700
	18	Hybrid Function 2 (N=3)	1800
	19	Hybrid Function 3 (N=4)	1900
	20	Hybrid Function 4 (N=4)	2000
	21	Hybrid Function 5 (N=5)	2100
	22	Hybrid Function 6 (N=5)	2200

search performance. A comparison between the standard FA and the deterministic FA indicates that the third term of Equation (1) is responsible for performing the initial global search.

The effect of chaotic oscillations in the solution search process was confirmed by using the function of the CEC'14 Test Suite (Liang, Qu, Suganthan and Hernández-Díaz, 2013) for numerical experiments. The functions that were used are listed in Table 2 and the search range is $[-100, 100]^D$. The number of trials is 30 times, the number of state updates according to the criterion is 3000 times, and each dimension of the benchmark function is 10. The population size is set as 10. The settings for the other parameters were the same as those in previous experiments. The results are presented in Table 3. The result for each parameter is given in the form of the mean value and standard deviation of the number of trials. For all the test functions that were used, the best results were obtained for the parameter representing chaotic behavior. Therefore, chaotic behavior is an important factor determining the solution search performance. In other words, the individuals obtain a diversity depending on the chaotic behavior. Namely, each individual has a diversity without depending on the randomness.

Table 3. Simulation result using CEC'14 Test Suite

Func. No.	β0_1.0		β0_2.5		β0_7.0	
	Mean	Std. Dev.	Mean	Std. Dev.	Mean	Std. Dev.
1	4.517E+08	4.433E+08	6.975E+07	1.631E+08	8.958E+06	1.656E+07
2	9.154E+09	4.746E+09	4.329E+09	3.487E+09	6.145E+08	1.029E+09
3	3.593E+04	1.643E+04	2.064E+04	8.734E+03	1.135E+04	5.627E+03
4	4.077E+03	2.391E+03	1.659E+03	1.240E+03	562.72	172.31
5	520.51	0.09	520.29	0.09	520.19	0.08
6	611.41	1.13	610.96	1.62	609.19	2.07
7	901.02	81.10	834.02	75.93	718.89	27.62
8	900.71	21.34	873.97	27.25	865.66	23.95
9	990.89	19.63	970.00	19.17	959.41	22.08
10	2.925E+03	2.052E+02	2.644E+03	2.162E+02	2.414E+03	2.894E+02
11	3.082E+03	2.121E+02	2.832E+03	3.535E+02	2.503E+03	3.537E+02
12	1201.81	0.30	1200.83	0.35	1200.36	0.13
13	1304.81	1.33	1302.87	1.74	1300.69	0.64
14	1436.45	15.74	1418.97	13.63	1404.13	5.69
15	3.367E+04	7.663E+04	6.198E+03	6.753E+03	1509.53	16.90
16	1604.09	0.21	1604.05	0.21	1603.51	0.37
17	1.632E+06	1.890E+06	6.245E+04	1.129E+05	4.253E+03	4.519E+03
18	5.720E+06	1.024E+07	2.669E+03	1.430E+03	1.975E+03	1.282E+02
19	1958.45	33.23	1913.99	10.26	1905.34	2.02
20	2.102E+05	4.986E+05	7.197E+03	7.456E+03	2.708E+03	1.887E+03
21	8.423E+05	1.933E+06	2.493E+04	9.943E+04	3.076E+03	9.385E+02
22	2559.03	151.96	2497.61	105.68	2439.64	108.95

Figures 12, 13, and 14 show changes in the average evaluation value of each function. In each figure, the horizontal axis represents the number of iterations and the vertical axis represents the average evaluation value of the number of trials. A similar trend was shown in all of the unimodal, simple multimodal and hybrid functions. From these results, the best performance is shown for the parameters showing the chaotic behavior. In addition, such parameter setting is possible with finer solution finding higher than other parameter settings, with lesser iteration.

In numerical experiments, three values were confirmed as representative values for parameter β. In the case of setting parameter that give the best results, the individual moves chaotically. On the other hand, local search performance is not obtained. Therefore, the performance can be improved by adaptive parameter adjustment. For example, if parameter β_0 decreases gradually, the individual will transition to a local search. In other words, the search that maintains the diversity of individuals and the search that merges individuals can be switched.

Figure 12. Unimodal functions

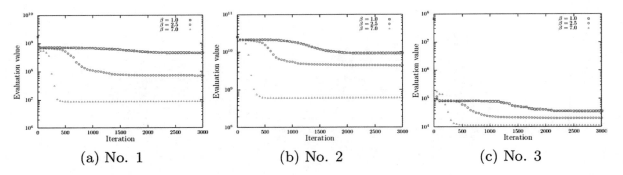

(a) No. 1   (b) No. 2   (c) No. 3

CONCLUSION

The authors clarified the dynamics of the FA by carrying out an analysis of the deterministic FA. Generally, parameter β_0 was set to approximately 1.0 as this configuration was determined to exhibit stable performance. However, the work in this chapter focused on the use of large values for parameter β_0, in which case the behavior of the fireflies was found to become chaotic, thereby resulting in an improvement in the solution search performance. In future, the authors plan to consider a method that would enable the convergence range parameters and chaotic parameters to be set adaptively. This technique is expected to improve the solution search performance of the deterministic FA. In such an approach, the computational cost of random number generation is reduced. In addition, this optimization technique has an advantage that the system does not depend on the initial individuals.

Figure 13. Simple multimodal functions

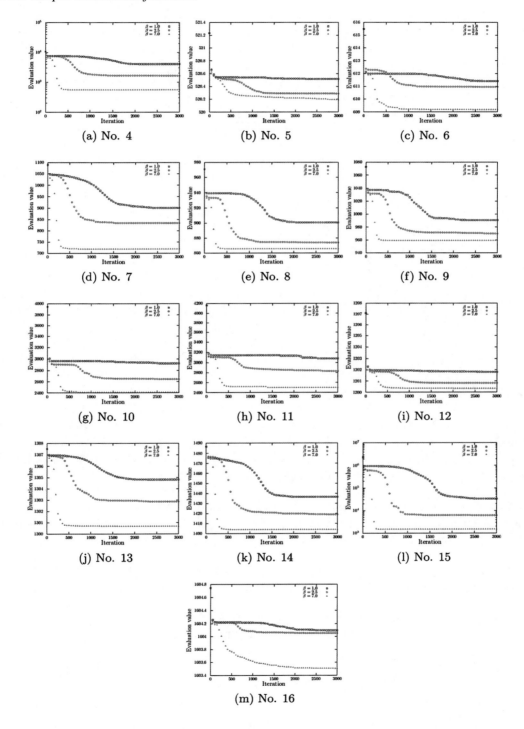

(a) No. 4

(b) No. 5

(c) No. 6

(d) No. 7

(e) No. 8

(f) No. 9

(g) No. 10

(h) No. 11

(i) No. 12

(j) No. 13

(k) No. 14

(l) No. 15

(m) No. 16

Figure 14. Hybrid functions

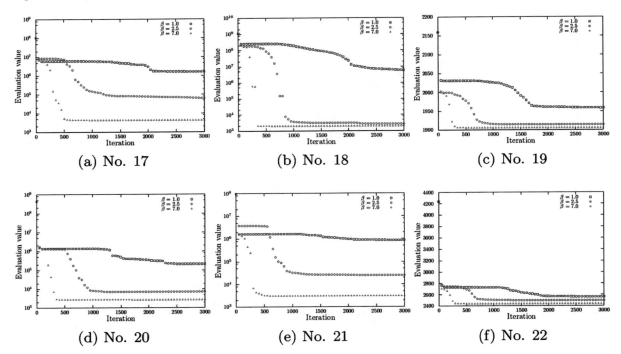

| (a) No. 17 | (b) No. 18 | (c) No. 19 |
| (d) No. 20 | (e) No. 21 | (f) No. 22 |

REFERENCES

Alor, A., Mota, D., Olmos-Sánchez, K., & Rodas-Osollo, J. (2019). An Order-Picking Model Associated With Hospital Components and Solved by a Firefly Algorithm. In *Handbook of Research on Metaheuristics for Order Picking Optimization in Warehouses to Smart Cities* (pp. 173–188). Hershey, PA: IGI Global. doi:10.4018/978-1-5225-8131-4.ch009

Cai, Z., Niu, J., & Yang, X. (2018, May). A Multi Measure Improved Firefly Algorithm. *Proceedings 2018 2nd IEEE Advanced Information Management, Communicates, Electronic, and Automation Control Conference (IMCEC)* (pp. 20-26). IEEE.

Chen, L., & Aihara, K. (1995). Chaotic simulated annealing by a neural network model with transient chaos. *Neural Networks*, 8(6), 915–930. doi:10.1016/0893-6080(95)00033-V

Clerc, M., & Kennedy, J. (2002). The particle swarm-explosion, stability, and convergence in a multidimensional complex space. *IEEE Transactions on* Evolutionary Computation, 6(1), 58–73.

Dorigo, M., Maniezzo, V., & Colorni, A. (1996). Ant system: optimization by a colony of cooperating agents. *IEEE Transactions on* Systems, Man, and Cybernetics, Part B: Cybernetics, 26(1), 29–41.

Gandomi, A. H., Yang, X. S., Talatahari, S., & Alavi, A. H. (2013). Firefly algorithm with chaos. *Communications in Nonlinear Science and Numerical Simulation*, 18(1), 89–98. doi:10.1016/j.cnsns.2012.06.009

Guckenheimer, J., & Holmes, P. J. (2013). *Nonlinear oscillations, dynamical systems, and bifurcations of vector fields* (Vol. 42). Springer Science & Business Media.

Kennedy, J. (1997). The particle swarm: social adaptation of knowledge. *Proceedings IEEE International Conference on Evolutionary Computation, 1997.* (pp. 303-308). IEEE. 10.1109/ICEC.1997.592326

Kennedy, J., & Eberhart, R. (1995). Particle swarm optimization. *Proceedings of ICNN'95 - International Conference on Neural Networks: Vol. 4.* (pp. 1942-1948). 10.1109/ICNN.1995.488968

Koguma, Y., & Aiyoshi, E. (2010). Stability analysis in consideration of random numbers for particle swarm optimization dynamics: The best parameter for sustainable search. *IEEJ Transactions on Electronics, Information Systems, 130*, 29–38.

Krishnanand, K. N., & Ghose, D. (2008). Theoretical foundations for rendezvous of glowworm-inspired agent swarms at multiple locations. *Robotics and Autonomous Systems, 56*(7), 549–569. doi:10.1016/j.robot.2007.11.003

Liang, J. J., Qu, B. Y., Suganthan, P. N., & Hernández-Díaz, A. G. (2013). Problem definitions and evaluation criteria for the CEC 2013 special session on real-parameter optimization. Computational Intelligence Laboratory, Zhengzhou University, China, and Nanyang Technological University, Singapore, Technical Report, 201212.

Nara, S., Davis, P., & Totsuji, H. (1993). Memory search using complex dynamics in a recurrent neural network model. *Neural Networks, 6*(7), 963–973. doi:10.1016/S0893-6080(09)80006-3

Pecora, L. M., Carroll, T. L., Johnson, G. A., Mar, D. J., & Heagy, J. F. (1997). Fundamentals of synchronization in chaotic systems, concepts, and applications. *Chaos (Woodbury, N.Y.), 7*(4), 520–543. doi:10.1063/1.166278 PMID:12779679

Shindo, T., Xiao, J., Kurihara, T., Morita, K., & Jin'no, K. (2015, May). Analysis of the dynamic characteristics of firefly algorithm. *Proceedings 2015 IEEE Congress on Evolutionary Computation (CEC),* (pp. 2647-2652). IEEE. 10.1109/CEC.2015.7257215

Wang, H., Wang, W., Cui, L., Sun, H., Zhao, J., Wang, Y., & Xue, Y. (2018). A hybrid multi-objective firefly algorithm for big data optimization. *Applied Soft Computing, 69*, 806–815. doi:10.1016/j.asoc.2017.06.029

Yang, X. S. (2010). *Nature-inspired metaheuristic algorithms.* Cambridge, UK: Luniver Press.

Yang, X. S. (Ed.). (2013). *Cuckoo search and firefly algorithm: Theory and applications* (Vol. 516). Springer.

Yang, X. S. (2013). *Recent Algorithms and Applications in Swarm Intelligence Research.* Hershey, PA: IGI Global.

Zengin, A., & Tuncel, S. (2010). A survey on swarm intelligence based routing protocols in wireless sensor networks. *International Journal of Physical Sciences, 5*(14), 2118–2126.

Chapter 7
Nature–Inspired Usability Optimization

Sergey Sakulin

https://orcid.org/0000-0001-9218-9725

Bauman Moscow State Technical University, Russia

Alexander Alfimtsev

https://orcid.org/0000-0002-3805-4499

Bauman Moscow State Technical University, Russia

Yuri Kalgin

Bauman Moscow State Technical University, Russia

ABSTRACT

Nature-inspired algorithms have come into use to solve more and more optimization tasks of high dimension when classical optimization algorithms do not apply. The task of user interface usability optimization becomes the one to be solved by nature-inspired algorithms. Usability optimization suggests a choice of interface design out of a large number of variants. At that, there is no common technique to determine the objective function of such optimization that would lead to the invitation of highly qualified specialists to implement it. The chapter presents a new approach of automatic interface usability optimization. The approach is based on the template employment as well as nature-inspired algorithms such as genetic algorithm (GA), artificial bee colony (ABC) algorithm, and charged system search (CSS) algorithm, bacterial foraging optimization (BFO) algorithm, and cuckoo search (CS) algorithm that are analyzed in the chapter. The results of the experiments have discovered research prospects and new features of the algorithms' application for the set task.

DOI: 10.4018/978-1-7998-3222-5.ch007

1. INTRODUCTION

Every day users deal with various unique web pages with different interfaces. Users spend time in surfing the Net for necessary information, comparing internet-store prices, studying with the use of the e-learning systems, etc. In addition, being on a new page users often display conservative attitude, which means leaving the page within first minutes due to unwillingness to waste time and feel mental workload of studying new interface. This can result in the reduction of resource audience and hence financial losses for its owners.

This problem can be solved by such interface usability optimization that would allow users to avoid discomfort and annoyance. According to this, developers should not design whatsoever interface but the one which would (because of its high usability) attract as many potential clients as possible. Moreover, modern search systems rank search results on the basis of evaluating of user behavior which additionally increase high-quality interfaced resources traffic value. Generally, high-quality interface cannot be design at the first attempt, a qualitative result can be reached only by a number of iterations. At the same time, interface usability optimization challenges some main difficulties.

Firstly, by the reason of unified approach to quantitative measurement of interface usability and connected with its usage mental workload absence, a need for objective function defensible choice for such optimization arises. Secondly, because of big amount of possible parameters and respectively, interface implementation variations, corresponding optimization problem will have high dimension. As a result, classical methods are not suitable for interface optimization. Thirdly, the people carrying out this optimization should have deep knowledge and experience in web interface development and modification, which is often impossible. Due to this, a question of the development of web interface optimization methods, which would let overcome the described difficulties or reduce their influence on the result, becomes actual.

One way to implement such methods is the use of nature inspired algorithms since they are preferable to classical ones in high-dimensional problems solution. The chapter is devoted to the use of such algorithms for user interface usability optimization.

Further chapter features the following structure. In section 2, a review of literature from the fields of interface usability optimization, web page users' behavior analysis are given; works devoted to nature inspired algorithms usage for user interface optimization problems solution are considered; a review of this algorithms and its practical application is provided. Section 3 considers implementation of the suggested approach on the basis of application of GA, ABC, CSS, BFO, CS algorithms. As the optimization objective interface approximation to the template was used which was pre-selected by heat maps corresponding to DOM interface models. Section 4 describes the above-mentioned algorithms, interface optimization experiments and the obtained results. In section 5, the conclusion based on the experiments results is given and further research is proposed.

2. BACKGROUND

Different technologies of visualization and analysis of users' behavior for the evaluation of interface usability are applied. Leading search systems provide journaling facilities of users' behavior on web pages. These systems provide more and more free software and shareware means of evaluation of various usability metrics as well as the parameters of users' interaction with the interface. In particular, Google

Analytics sets the most suitable interface metrics such as average page views per visit, percentage of click depth per visits, percentage of time spent for the visits.

One of the mostly registered parameters of users' behavior on the page is time needed to fulfill a task. Time spent on the page tells us indirectly about the level of usability of an interface (Paz et al., 2019). Also the user's repeated actions can show the places of the preferred location of interface elements and relocate the elements of the current interface so that its usability would increase as well as the speed of user's work (Chung et al., 2019).

Graphical representation of data in form of heat maps allows visual analysis of color mouse activity, mouse clicks, page scrolling, and path of user view movement on the interface (Deu-Pons et al., 2014). Certain places of the interface where users click, the number of such clicks (Kaur & Singh, 2016), information about page scrolling and path of user's view movement over the interface can be registered and used as usability metric (Menges et al., 2018). This data is shown by the web-page overlay of the graphical report about the click parameters such as an exact number of clicks, a country, a web-browser, time of the click, a type of the device as well as with the use of confetti cards where the clicks are depicted as points. Each point features its color that shows the information about the click parameters. This may help developers to find out unclicking interface elements that the users consider to be clickable ones.

To represent and analyze heat maps, specialized toolset such as Crazy Egg and Heat Map can be used (Babicki et al, 2016). Moreover, methods of objective data and expert knowledge display on the same heat map are developed (Danilov et al, 2016).

The data received by the above-mentioned ways is analyzed and interpreted that is not a simple task at all. Data analysis for compliance with usability criteria and decision making about necessary interface correction are carried out on the basis of checking recommendations related to usability (Dingli & Cassar, 2014). For instance such recommendations are graphics and text proportion (Lin et al, 2013), application of aggregation operators' hierarchy (Sakulin & Alfimtsev, 2017), correspondence to design recommendations (Aizpurua et al., 2016), taxonomy of menu properties (Bailly et al., 2016), interface optimization criteria such as efficiency of actions and responsiveness of the system (Feit et al., 2015), formal rules of interface distribution among several devices (Sakulin et al., 2019).

However, this approach is restricted by the requirement of experts' participation and the influence of certain subject field specificity on its result. In addition, every interface redesigning which compiles with special properties made takes significant amount of time. As it was mentioned, classical optimization algorithms are hardly suitable for solving high-dimensional problems. In this regard, to optimize the interfaces based on the data received from users, the approaches and methods of artificial intelligence, in particular, nature-inspired algorithms have recently become frequently applied.

The review of current developments concerned with genetic algorithm (GA) and applying different visualization methods to involve users in forming several interface generations notes big perspective for this research direction (Farooq & Siddique, 2014). One example of such application is interactive GA for user interface design (Quiroz, 2007). As inputs for GA, both measurable interface parameters and user data in the form of the worst and best interface from the suggested set are used. Adapting web page template to a particular user with the interactive method (Sorn & Rimcharoen, 2013) is also based on GA application. The user is suggested to estimate any given interface template element step by step. On the basis of these estimations the algorithm proposes new template design in accordance with user preferences.

Furthermore, a number of works are devoted to the problems of practical applications of GA to optimize interfaces, such as interface color palette definition with taking into account users with color vision deficiencies (Troiano et al., 2009); conversion rate optimization through evolutionary computation (Miikkulainen et al., 2017); interface segmentation in order to ensure compliance with segmentation principle and attainment of the acceptable complexity level (Romano et al., 2014); the implementation of interactive interface development system (Masson et al., 2010); the implementation of a distributed system for modifying markup styles based on user preferences (Park, 2007); computer-aided testing of web interfaces (Eladawy et al., 2018); optimization of the user interface layout with the use of eye tracking and screen-scraping (Diego-Mas et al., 2019); interactive composition of the web interface from simple component parts (Salem, 2017). In similar application, the ant colony algorithm for interactive optimization of complicated static menu systems is used (Bailly, 2013).

Nevertheless, the mentioned sources do not provide a full description and a comparison study of the application of other algorithms inspired by nature. Due to this, in this chapter the application of different nature inspired algorithms to optimize interface usability and a comparison study of obtained results are considered. The classification of nature inspired meta-heuristic methods includes algorithms based on evolution, swarm behavior and principles of physics (Rajakumar et al, 2016). As optimization algorithms for solving the posed problem the most popular algorithms from each of these classes were chosen: genetic algorithm (GA), artificial bee colony (ABC) algorithm, charged system search (CSS) algorithm, bacterial foraging optimization (BFO) algorithm, and cuckoo search (CS) algorithm.

ABC algorithm (Karaboga & Basturk, 2007) is efficient in solving problems of multi-criteria selection in the context of local and global optimization because of the used selection approach (Kar, 2016). In addition, this algorithm is defined by respectively well developed theoretical background and is intriguing in the context of its different applications (Chakraborty & Kar, 2017). The idea of ABC algorithm was borrowed from the model of bees' behavior when they are looking for places with the biggest volume of honeydew. The population of bees consists of two groups, namely employed bees and scout bees. At different stages of the algorithm the employed bees become scouts and vice versa so that the number of bees in each group of the populations remains equal. One employed bee is assigned to each source of honeydew. If a certain location with honeydew is no longer of bees' interest, the location is considered neglected and the employed bee becomes a scout. ABC algorithm contains the stage of population initialization and repeated iterations of searching process, with each iteration consisting of the following stages: location exploitation by employed bees, location exploitation by scout bees, new location search by scout bees, termination of the iteration.

The extensive overview of this algorithm practical application including software does not contain references to its application in solving interface optimization problem (Karaboga, 2014). Among the contributions which refer to this overview such references were not found as well.

CSS algorithm (Kaveh & Talatahari, 2010) is related to electromagnetic search algorithms based in electrostatics Coulomb's principles and Newton's laws of motion. In this algorithm, each population agent is interpreted as electrically charged particle with the charge proportional to the fitness function value in the search area where it is located. Population charge defines total force acting on the particle, the direction and the distance to which it moves at the current iteration. The total force is calculated as the vector sum of the attraction and repulsion forces from the other population particles. This algorithm is applied to solve design optimization problems for objects such as concrete walls (Kaveh & Behnam, 2013), frame structures (Kaveh & Talatahari, 2012), energy systems (Niknam et al., 2013) and water networks (Asadieh, & Afshar, 2019). Among the available contributions there was no mention of the application of this algorithm to the interface optimization.

BFO algorithm (Passino, 2010) is based on feeding bacteria behavior that can be watched in nature. Moving bacteria such as an intestinal bacterium or salmonella use flagellates to move. To move straight forward all the flagellates move in one certain directions. Such bacteria movement is called swimming. If the flagellates move in various directions, the bacteria tumble about randomly that leads to a new location in search space. The goal of the bacteria movement is the search of the most convenient conditions to live (wide assortment of nutritional support with the lack of toxins). In microbiology, such movement is called chemotaxis. Chemotaxis is a complex combination of swimming and tumbling that helps bacteria stay at the locations with high concentration of nutritional support and escape from the locations with inappropriate concentration of toxins. As for the tasks of search optimization, bacterial chemotaxis can be interpreted as bacteria optimization process of locations with high concentration of nutrition and search for new ones with higher concentrations.

BFO algorithm was offered by (Passino, 2002) and it has drawn the attention of researchers since then due to its effectiveness in optimization problem solutions. There are several examples of the algorithm implementation to solve the applied tasks of various scientific areas. In particular, this algorithm is applied to optimize PID controller settings (Ali & Majhi, 2006), with highly nonlinear parameters. The experiments carried out with a PID controller showed its better control that proved the effectiveness of the algorithm. Moreover, BFO algorithm was used to model solar photoelectric characteristics (Rajasekar et al., 2013); image segmentation (Rajini, 2019); troubleshooting in distributing networks (Fu et al., 2018).

The above-mentioned papers compare BFO algorithm with other optimization algorithms and show that BFO algorithm features high degree of convergence and accuracy. The available papers do not mention the application of this algorithm for user interface usability optimization (Sharma et al., 2012).

CS algorithm was offered by (Yang & Deb, 2009). It also has proved to be successful to solve various optimization tasks. The algorithm is based on imitation of cuckoo reproduction approach when it finds recently built nests by birds of other species and leaves its eggs there (or changes the present eggs for its ones) that can be thrown away by the nest owner. The algorithm is based on three rules. First, a cuckoo leaves one egg in a randomly chosen nest that represents a solution. Second, a part of the best solutions will be passed down to the next generation. Third, the number of nests is settled. Moreover, there is a probability that the nest owner will define an alien egg. In this case the nest owner will throw it away from the nest or leave the nest and build a new one. An important element of CS algorithm is the use of "Levi Flight" for local and global search. The process of Levi flight is a random movement that features a series of jumps, with probability of large deviations from the average being higher than of Gauss distribution.

The algorithm is known to have been applied for optimization of production processes (Yildiz, 2013); training of neural networks in classification tasks (Valian et al., 2011); parameters settings for power systems (Elazim & Ali, 2016); Twitter sentiment analysis (Pandey et al., 2017); optimization of the cropping pattern for effective distribution of water resources in agriculture (Rath et al., 2019). The experiments and statistical analysis described in (Pandey et al., 2017) prove that the technique based on CS is more accurate than the present techniques used for sentiment analysis. In (Elazim & Ali, 2016) it is shown that CS allows better optimization results for parameters adjustment of a power system in comparison with GA. Practical experience of CS application has shown that its parameters influence the convergence degree in a minor way. Therefore, these parameters are not adjusted when solving a certain optimization task. However, there are practical applications of this algorithm where such adjustments were carried out (Valian et al., 2011). In this chapter, the application of the algorithm is described without preliminary adjustment of the parameters.

3. NATURE INSPIRED OPTIMIZATION

3.1. Heat Maps, DOM-Model and Interface Optimization

Any web page interface can be represented as a tree in accordance with DOM model of corresponding web document, regardless of its format (Wood et al., 2004). This model contains the information about web document structure and the elements which define its design. Some elements can be changed dynamically by scripts which are executed while web page is loading. For this reason, DOM tree has to be obtained from the browser after all scripts have been loaded. Such a tree contains all the elements which users can observe when he visits the corresponding web page. With help of obtained elements their positioning and their sizes an interface layout can be represented in an abstract form where each element corresponds to a rectangular block. This approach allows stepping back from a particular appearance including content in the form of text and images. An example of the abstract interface layout for the element tree with a maximum depth of 5 (left) and 2 (right) is shown in Figure 1. According to DOM tree, some elements of this abstract interface are nested in its other elements. In Figure 1 elements located in the tree at a greater depth have a darker shade in the gray scale.

In general, the elements corresponding to the tree leaves carry the basic information for the user. The remaining elements are ancillary blocks used for positioning convenience. As already noted, usually the heat map method is applied to display mouse activity, clicks, page scrolling, and eye movement over it. On the other hand, information about the element nesting depth in the tree is also important when visualizing and analyzing interfaces. In this regard, in the chapter heat maps are built on the basis of elements relative arrangement, more precisely their nesting depth in the DOM tree. The elements corresponding to the tree leaves will have the "warmest" color. The continuous color range shown in Figure 2 was used to compile the heat maps.

Each element corresponds to a "heat zone" represented by a radial gradient which is scalable depending on the element size. For each element corresponding to the tree leaf, the zone of its "heat effect" was chosen with the maximum value of "heat" in the center of the element and the minimum value at

Figure 1. Abstract interface layouts with maximum tree depth of 5 (left) u 2 (right)

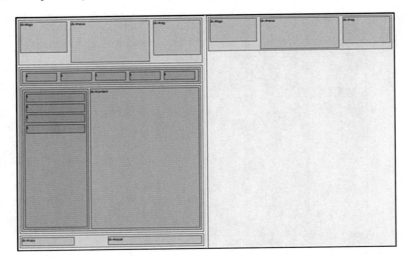

Figure 2. Heat map color range

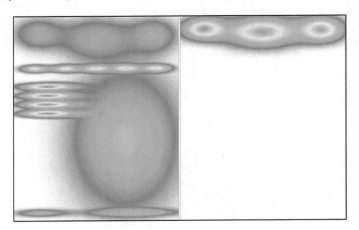

the distance of twice the element radius. The value of "heat" in the center of a particular element was chosen depending on the maximum tree depth and was calculated using the equation:

$$actual\_depth = depth + (6 - max\_depth), \tag{1}$$

where *actual_depth* is the actual depth value with taking into account maximum depth of source tree elements; *depth* is the depth of element in the source tree; *max_depth* is maximum depth of the elements source tree; *6* is the maximum depth value for a card of 7 colors.

In Figure 3 shows the corresponding abstract interface layouts. In case of the tree with depth of 2, the elements will have maximum possible "heat" in their center. For the interface having elements with depth of 5, the maximum "heat" will respectively be in the center of these elements.

This way of the interfaces visualizing makes it possible to display all the changes introduced to the interface and to apply numerous algorithms of image comparison for comparing the interfaces (Schmidt et al., 2013). In this case, the input data for such algorithms will be the matrices whose elements will be the values of the pixel colors on the heat map images corresponding to the interfaces.

In general, users like a certain style of interface for web pages. Moreover, the user gets used to buttons' layouts in the forms to perform certain sequences of actions on the page and tries to repeat the same actions on another page with similar theme. Such attempts do not always lead the user to the desired result, when visiting an unfamiliar page its interface seems unusual and uncomfortable for him/her. In this regard, many interface developers try to follow certain principles of building interfaces. These principles depend on the themes of the sites.

Figure 3. Heat maps of the interfaces with maximum tree depth of 5 (left) и 2 (right)

However, pages may have outdated or unique interfaces that require redesign. In this regard, it seems relevant to create a tool that enables successively approximating the design of one interface to the design of another (template) interface, preserving the tree structure of its elements. To create such a tool, the optimization algorithms described above are applied.

3.2. Genetic Algorithm for Usability Optimization

The iterative interface design approximation to the template was realized on the basis of GA. The fitness function for this algorithm was calculated as the second-order Minkowski metric (Minkowski, 1989) used as the distance between two images:

$$fitness = \sqrt{\sum_{i=1,j=1}^{i=n,j=m} \left(x_{ij} - y_{ij}\right)^2} \tag{2}$$

where *fitness* is the fitness function value or the fitness value; *n* is the width of the image in pixels; *m* is the height of the image in pixels; x_{ij} is the pixel color value with indices *i* by horizontal and *j* by vertical on the first heat map; y_{ij} is the pixel color value with indices *i* by horizontal and *j* by vertical on the second heat map.

Below one can find a description of the pseudo-code program, where *N* is the number of generated individuals within the population; *Model [N]* is a model that describes each individual of a population; *D* is the number of iterations on which the best solution is not found; *MaxD* is the maximum searching depth; *evolution(Model)* is a function that performs crossing-over and mutation of individuals within the population; *fitness[N]* are the fitness values for current populations.

```
// Population with zero index contents an information about
// the best found population.
1.          fitness[0] ← evolution(Model[0]);
2.          minFitness ← fitness[0];
3.       D ← 0;
4.              while (D <MaxD) {
5.              fitness[i] ← evolution(Model[i]), i ← 0..N;
6.              indexMin ← min(fitness), i ← 0..N;
7.              if (indexMin==0 || (fitness[IndexMin] == fitness[0]))
8.              then          D++;
9.              else {D ← 0; Model[0] ← Model[indexMin]; }}
```

The condition for the completion of the program is the achievement of a given iterations number, on which populations were obtained, inferior in quality to previously found or equal to it. One of the populations always stores the best result found at the moment. At the end of the program, this enables us to obtain interface version which is closest to the template.

3.3. Artificial Bee Colony Algorithm for Usability Optimization

The fitness function for ABC was calculated by equation 2. This function corresponds to the absolute value of the difference between the current bee-scout position and its possible best position. Below one can find a description of the pseudo-code program, where *ModelScouts* is a model describing the positions of the scout bees; *ModelWorkers* is a model describing the positions of employed bees; *D* is the number of iterations on which the best solution is not found; *MaxDis* the maximum searching depth; *migration(ModelScouts)* is the function that performs migration of scout bees within the search space; *fitnessScouts* is the fitness value for the current scout bees position; *fitnessWorkers* is the fitness value for the current employed bees position.

```
1.        D ← 0;
2.        ModelWorkers ← ModelScouts;
3.              while (D <MaxD) {
4.              fitnessScouts ← getFitness(ModelScouts);
5.              migration(ModelScouts);
6.              fitnessWorkers ← getFitness(ModelWorkers);
7.              if (fitnessScouts>= fitnessWorkers)
8.              then D++;
9.              else {D ← 0;         ModelWorkers ← ModelScouts;}}
```

3.4. Charged System Algorithm for Usability Optimization

Search restriction by the charged system algorithm is the preservation of the document tree DOM structure. In this case, all interface elements that are inside the parent can only change their positions within it, keeping the tree structure unchanged. The fitness function for the implementation of this algorithm was calculated in accordance with expression 3:

$$fitness = \sum_{i=1}^{n} fitness_i \tag{3}$$

where *fitness* is the general value of fitness function or general fitness value; $fitness_i$ is the fitness value for the ith interface element.

Fitness function for each interface element is written as in expression 4:

$$fitness_i = \sum_{j=1}^{n} \frac{q_i q_j}{r_{ij}^2} \tag{4}$$

where $fitness_i$ is the fitness value for the ith interface element; n is a number of interface elements; q_i is the value for the ith charge; r_{ij} is the destination between the ith and j^{th} charges. The charge value is calculated as an equation taking into account the element position depth in the DOM tree of the source web page and its sizes respectively to tree root element which is parent for all other elements and has the greatest size:

$$q_i = \frac{width_i * height_i * actual\_depth_i}{width_{view} * height_{view}} \qquad (5)$$

where q_i is the charge value for the ith interface element; $width_i$ is the value for the ith interface element width; $height_i$ is the value for the ith interface element height; $actual\_depth_i$ is the actual depth of the ith element position in the source web documentobject model, calculated by equation (1); $width_{view}$ is the width of the interface root element; $height_{view}$ is the height of the interface root element.

The value of the radius vector connecting the ith and jth charges is calculated as the equation:

$$r_{ij}\sqrt{\left(x_i + \frac{width_i}{2} - x_j - \frac{width_j}{2}\right)^2 + \left(y_i + \frac{height_i}{2} - y_j - \frac{height_j}{2}\right)^2} \qquad (6)$$

where r_{ij} is the radius vector between the ith and j^{th} elements; x_i is coordinate x of the upper left corner of the ith interface element, y_i is coordinate y of the upper left corner of the ith interface element; $width_i$ is the ith element length; $height_i$ is the ith interface element width.

Below one can find a description of the pseudo-code program, where *Model* is a model describing the positions of charged particles; *BestModel* is the best found model of the charged particles arrangement; *D* is the number of iterations on which the best solution is not found; *MaxD* is the maximum searching depth; *getDestination(Model)* is a function that determines the direction of charged particle motion under the influence of forces from all other particles; *moveCharges(Model)* is a function that moves charged particles; *prevFitness* is the fitness value for the charged particles position before the charges movement; *fitness* is the fitness value for the charged particles position after the charges movement.

```
1.        D ← 0;
2.        BestModel ← Model;
3.              while (D <MaxD) {
4.              prevFitness ← getTotalForce(Model);
5.              getDestination(Model);
6.              moveCharges(Model);
7.              fitness ← getTotalForce(Model);
6.              if (fitness >= prevFitness)
8.              then D++;
9.              else {D ← 0;BestModel ← Model;}}
```

3.5. Bacterial Foraging Optimization Algorithm for Usability Optimization

As well as for the usability optimization based on the algorithm of artificial bee colony, fitness function for the algorithm of bacterial foraging optimization was calculated according to expression (2). The starting population of moving bacteria consists of *N* bacteria, with each of them being correspondent to the interface under optimization. At the stage of chemotaxis, each specimen of the population is transformed that means interface elements move randomly. As a result, we have got an even number of randomly generated interfaces, with the fitness-function being rated for. At the stage of reproduction, we analyze the received values of the fitness-function for each specimen of the population. The values of the fitness-function turn to become a health condition of the moving bacterium. A half of the population with the highest value of the fitness-function that consists of healthy bacteria is deleted. Each of the remaining bacterium splits into two equal bacteria with equal values of the fitness-function. The result of the reproduction present the fact that the number of species in the population remains constant and equal to N. It is the replication scheme that sets the requirement for the even number of species in the initial population.

The stage of elimination and dissemination allows the species of the population to leave local maximums of the fitness-function. At the beginning of the stage, an amount of species is chosen in a random way and they are deleted from the population. A new bacterium is created instead of each randomly deleted species. In the context of interface usability optimization, this means new bacteria appear that correspond to the new interfaces. After that, for each new species the fitness-function is calculated. If the value of the fitness-function is equal to zero or less than the threshold for a certain bacterium, the optimization should be considered successfully finished. The result of the optimization is the location of the bacterium.

Below you can see the listing of the pseudo-code where N –number of generated species within the population. *Model* [N] is a model that describes each species of the population; K is a number of iterations until a better solution is found; *MaxD* – maximum search depth; *Bacterial(Model)* is a function that carries out chemotaxis, reproduction and elimination-dissemination of the population species; *fitness*[N] – values of the fitness-functions for the current populations.

```
1.        fitness[0] ← Bacterial(Model[0]);
2.        minFitness ← fitnessFunc[0];
3.        K ← 0;
4.        while (K <MaxD) {
5.        fitnessFunc[i] ← Bacterial (Model[i]), i = 0..N;
6.        indexMin ← min(fitnessFunc), i = 0..N;
7.        if (indexMin==0 || (fitness[IndexMin] == fitnessFunc[0]))
8.        then        K++;
9.        else {K ← 0; Model[0] ← Model[indexMin]; }}
```

3.6. Cuckoo Search Algorithm for Usability Optimization

As well as for the usability optimization on the basis of ABC and BFO algorithms, the fitness-function for CS algorithm is calculated by expression (2). The initial location of the cuckoo corresponds to the incipient interface. The initial population consists of evenly distributed species over the search space. Bird nests are assigned to these species. In the beginning, there is one egg in a nest and a cuckoo egg left there will bring us to a new solution where the interface elements move relatively and randomly. After that, on the basis of Levi flight we build a random vector of the cuckoo movement. Then, if the value of the fitness-function in the new location is higher than of the randomly chosen nest, the cuckoo leaves its egg in the nest which corresponds to one of the versions of the interface. At the nest stage, it is possible for the cuckoo egg to be found by the nest owner that destructs the nest. Then, we calculate the fitness-function for the each appeared solutions. If the value of the fitness-function is equal to zero or lower than a predetermined threshold for one of the solutions, the optimization is considered to be successfully finished. In other cases, the cuckoo repeats Levi flights until either an appropriate solution is found or a limited number of iterations is carried out.

Below you can see the listing of the pseudo-code where N – number of generated species within the population which we set for the optimization task. Model $[N]$ is a model that describes each species of the population; K is a number of iterations until a better solution is found; $MaxD$ – maximum search depth; *Cuckoo(Model)* is a function that initiates the species of the population, cuckoo flights and elimination of the population species; *fitness[N]* – values of the fitness-functions for the current populations.

```
1.          fitness[0] ← Cuckoo(Model[0]);
2.          minFitness ← fitness[0];
3.          K = 0;
4.          while (K <MaxD) {
5.          fitness[i] ← Cuckoo (Model[i]), i = 0..N;
6.          indexMin ← min(fitness[i]), i = 0..N;
7.          if (indexMin==0 || (fitness[IndexMin] ≤ fitnessFunc[0]))
8.          then        K++;
9.          else {K ← 0; Model[0] ← Model[indexMin]; }}
```

4. EXPERIMENTS AND RESULTS

To carry out the experiments the special software was developed (Sakulin et al., 2018). The input data for the experiments were JSON format files containing interface model description based on its DOM model. For interface optimization experiments two interfaces were used, with the layouts and heat maps being shown in Figure 4.

Figure 4. Layouts and heat maps of optimized interface (left) and template (right)

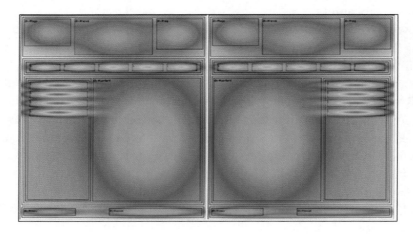

The positions of two blocks which are within the central block of optimized interface were changed in a mirror manner in regard to the template. Regardless the algorithm, optimization process will iteratively approximate the interface to the template.

The interface represented in Figure 4 (on the right) was sequentially approximated by using GA to the template represented in Figure 4 on the left. One of the algorithms application results is shown in Figure 5. The obtained interface is identical to the template. Notice that fitness function is set to zero, which is often impossible in practice due to the structure differences of the template and the optimized interface.

Figure 5. Result of GA application to optimize interface

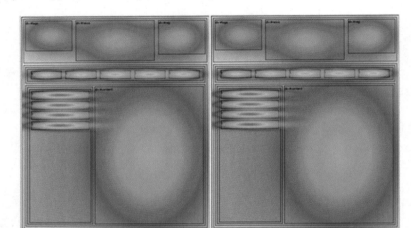

A series of optimizing experiments for interfaces shown in Figure 4 were carried out in order to obtain GA application results and its further comparison to other implemented algorithms. For this purpose, the following parameter values were used: maximum number of iterations is 100; maximum number of iterations on which the best solution is not found is 50; minimum allowed fitness function value is 10; mutation occurrence probability is 30%.

Another input for GA was an interface which cannot be precisely brought to the template. The layout and the heat map of such interface are shown in Figure 6 on the right; the template layout and the heat map are shown in Figure 6 on the left.

All twenty experiments of this interface optimization with the use of GA resulted in the same "the most optimized" interface. Corresponding layout and heat map are represented in Figure 7 on the right.

For experiments with ABC algorithm the same template and optimized interfaces as for GA were used. Twenty experiments were carried out for each of these two interfaces. The result in all the experiments was the same as the result of the GA. Besides, half of ABC algorithm executions leads to the result for less than twenty iterations, with no following search improving the result.

The experiments with CSS algorithm were carried out with the same interfaces as the experiments with GA and with ABC algorithm. For interface 1, nine out of 20 experiments led to the precise match of the resulting interface with the template. Based on the results of this algorithm, two new types of interfaces are formed and shown in Figures 8 and 9.

Figure 6. Layouts and heat maps of template (left) and optimized interface (right)

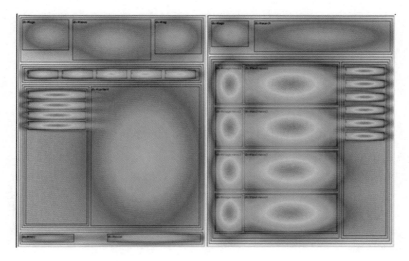

Figure 7. Layouts and heat maps of template (left) and the result (right)

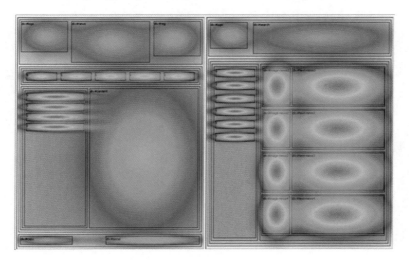

The interface layouts shown in Figures 8 and 9 on the right do not match with the interface shown in Figure 7 on the right, when GA and ABC algorithms were used. The variants in Figures 8 and 9 are "the closest to the template" not by heat maps but by the interaction potential of the charged system represented by the interface elements. On one hand, the obvious disadvantage of CSS algorithm is noticed in this example, since the result in Figure 7 is more "close" to the template. On the other hand, CSS algorithm makes it possible to obtain several interface options with a similar "interaction potential of the elements" which can be useful to provide the developer with the opportunity to choose.

For the experiments with BFO and CS algorithms, we used the same template and the same interfaces being optimized as for the above described algorithms. We carried out 20 experiments employing both BFO and CS algorithms for each of the two interfaces. The result of the optimization for all these experiments appeared identical and equal to that obtained with the help of GA and ABC algorithms.

Figure 8. Result of CSS algorithm application

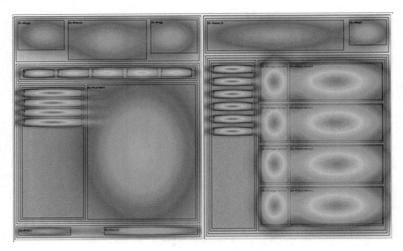

Figure 9. Result of CSS algorithm application

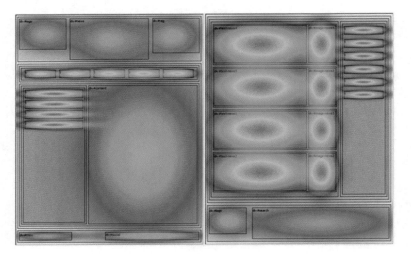

The dependences of the total iterations number for each of the considered algorithms are shown in Figure 10 (for interface 1) and Figure 11 (for interface 2). In Figure 12 and Figure 13, the curves of the iterations number before obtaining the result from the experiment number are shown for interfaces 1 and 2, respectively.

These graphics illustrate that for interface 1 which cannot be brought to the template, GA gives the best results for both the total algorithm iteration number and for the number of iterations necessary for the final result. Among the considered algorithms, GA gives the best results and the majority of the results are with the lowest value of the fitness function.

The average values of the parameters obtained from the experiments were calculated to compare. All the data about average values are presented in Table 1 and Table 2 for interface 1 and interface 2 respectively. Mentioned in Table 2 optimization percentage is calculated by equation 7:

Figure 10. Number of iterations for interface 1

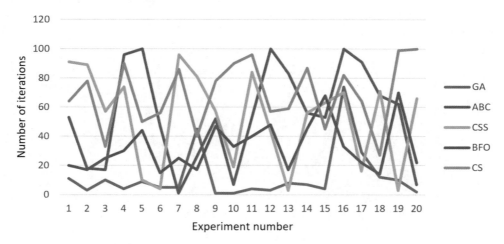

Figure 11. Number of iterations for interface 2

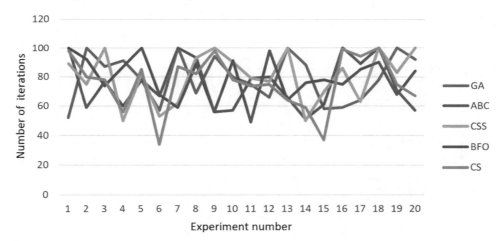

$$P = (1 - f_{\min}) * 100\% \tag{7}$$

where P is the variable expressing approximation of optimized interface to the template on a percentage base; $f_{\min}$ – minimum obtained fitness function value. *(исправил фитнес –функцию)*

Table 1 shows that GA is the quickest algorithm with the lowest average iteration number to obtain the final result with the best accuracy. Other two algorithms have the similar results but CSS algorithm is a little better on both the iteration number and result accuracy points.

Table 2 shows that the efficiency difference of the considered algorithms is less for interface 2. This is because interface 2 cannot be accurately approximated to the template until interface 1 is a modified template.

Figure 12. Number of iterations before obtaining the result for interface 1

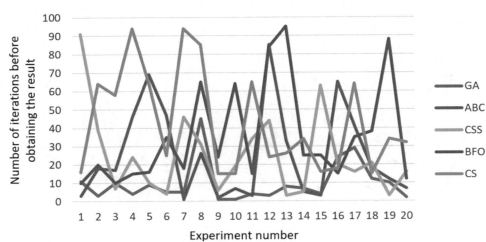

Figure 13. Number of iterations before obtaining the result for interface 2

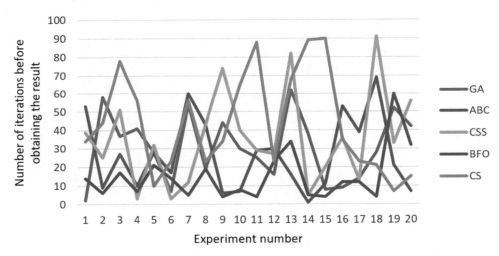

Table 1. Average values from the experiments for interface 1

Characteristic	GA	ABC	CSS	BFO	CS
Average iteration number	12,35	54,5	52,7	32,6	69,05
Average iteration number without result improving	2,5	29,1	27,6	17,3	35,2
Average iteration number before obtaining the final result	9,85	25,4	25,1	15,3	33,85
Number of precise approximations (fitness function value is 0)	19	7	9	16	13
Number of precise approximations (fitness function value is 0), %	95%	35%	45%	47%	23%

Table 2. Average values from the experiments for interface 2

Characteristic	GA	ABC	CSS	BFO	CS
Average iteration number	79,4	75,05	80,4	79,15	76
Average iteration number without result improving	48,7	48,25	45,05	50,7	49
Average iteration number before obtaining the final result	30,7	26,8	35,35	28,45	27
Optimization percentage, %	13,68%	13,68%	9,22%	10,17%	12,32%

CSS algorithm has the lowest approximation rate to the template because its fitness function differs from the ones of the other considered algorithms. This algorithm considers interface elements as a system of point charges. Calculating electrical potential of such system provides information about mutual positions of the optimized interface elements.

The selection of CSS algorithm solutions is based on the natural physical process of charged particles distribution. In this approach these particles are compared with interface elements. The "charge" of each interface element being proportional to its dimensions and the depth of its nesting in the DOM tree. This enables us to obtain several results. While carrying out the experiments two such results differing from two other algorithm results were obtained. The received "natural" interface variants may be analyzed for their usability as the first approximation. Then we choose the best variants for further selection and modification. The chosen best variants of interfaces may serve as the template to which some interface should be consistently reduced by GA, ABC, BFO and CS reduction algorithms.

These algorithms solve the task of reduction to the template with various efficiency.

All the algorithms produce similar iterations number whether before finishing or obtaining the best result. However, ABC algorithm has the lowest iteration number before obtaining the best result. The reason for this is local search for new interface options, when similar to the template result is obtained. In this case, other algorithms continue random search increasing working time and the iteration number.

GA provided the best result when the optimized interface structure is similar to the template structure. However, GA requires higher computing resources which are essential to new generation formation, storing data about each individual and fitness evaluation for each individual using the heat map. Judging by the results of other algorithms operating with a simple example, BFO algorithm is close to GA by the number of iterations, but it is not stable enough with the interface which could not be accurately referenced. CS algorithm is not stable enough with a simple example (fully reduced to the template), but with a complicated example (interface not fully reduced to the template) it shows the result close to the one of ABC algorithm. Each applied algorithm has its advantages and disadvantages in the context of the considered problem. GA provides the best result with the simple sample but requires the biggest amount of recourses and has no advantages with the complicated sample. ABC algorithm enables us to obtain the result in the shortest time but it is not stable enough on simple samples. CSS algorithm is based on physical principle of point charge system interaction and extends this principle to interface elements. This enables us to alternatively evaluate interface options comparing with GA and ABC algorithm. However, the results obtained with this algorithm require additional usability evaluation by an expert.

The initial interface that cannot be fully reduced to the template by GA, ABC, BFO and CS algorithms is consistently reduced to the template. Despite the fact that these interfaces are impossible to be fully reduced, some other variants of the interface may be obtained. These variants for each algorithm will depend on solution selection strategy that is based on the natural phenomena (genetics, behavior of a college of bees, eating behavior of bacteria, reproduction strategy of cuckoos).

These variants may be considered as the best in the sense of their closest reduction to the template and may be analyzed for their usability in the first approximation.

5. CONCLUSION

In the chapter usability optimization methods of web page interface on the basis of nature-inspired algorithms were considered. These methods take a basis of customary interface and approximate another interface to it using optimization. GA, ABC, CSS, BFO and CS algorithms were applied as optimization algorithms. Optimization was implemented by interfaces' heat maps which were built on the basis of its DOM-models.

The received "natural" interface variants may be analyzed for their usability as the first approximation. Then we choose the best variants for further selection and modification.

Such an approach may serve as optimization of creative activity of an interface designer. It is very effective to do research for interface design in "brainstorming session" while designing new interfaces and redesigning the current ones. If the optimal solution is not found quickly, the approach will at least offer the variants of sequential improvement of the current interface that can be obtained by heuristics based on nature-inspired swarm principles and objects.

Further research is the application of deep reinforcement learning methods in the context of the considered problem for the construction of user model and increasing number of optimization parameters. In addition, another formulation of the optimization problem is possible, e.g. when the sizes of the interface elements will be able to change, when interface has distributional nature, when multi agent systems collaborate.

ACKNOWLEDGMENT

This work was supported by Grant No. 2.5048.2017/8.9

REFERENCES

Aizpurua, A., Harper, S., & Vigo, M. (2016). Exploring the relationship between web accessibility and user experience. *International Journal of Human-Computer Studies*, *91*, 13–23. doi:10.1016/j.ijhcs.2016.03.008

Alfimtsev, A., Sakulin, S., & Levanov, A. (2016). Formalization of Expert Knowledge About the Usability of Web Pages Based on User Criteria Aggregation [IJSI]. *International Journal of Software Innovation*, *4*(3), 38–50. doi:10.4018/IJSI.2016070103

Ali, A., & Majhi, S. (2006). Design of optimum PID controller by bacterial foraging strategy. *Proceedings 2006 IEEE International Conference on Industrial Technology*, 601-605. 10.1109/ICIT.2006.372205

Asadieh, B., & Afshar, A. (2019). Optimization of Water-Supply and Hydropower Reservoir Operation Using the Charged System Search Algorithm. *Hydrology*, *6*(1), 5. doi:10.3390/hydrology6010005

Babicki, S., Arndt, D., Marcu, A., Liang, Y., Grant, J. R., Maciejewski, A., & Wishart, D. S. (2016). Heatmapper: Web-enabled heat mapping for all. *Nucleic Acids Research*, *44*(W1), W147–W153. doi:10.1093/nar/gkw419 PMID:27190236

Bailly, G., Lecolinet, E., & Nigay, L. (2016). Visual Menu Techniques [CSUR]. *ACM Computing Surveys*, *49*(4), 60. doi:10.1145/3002171

Bailly, G., Oulasvirta, A., Kötzing, T., & Hoppe, S. (2013). Menuoptimizer: Interactive optimization of menu systems. *Proceedings of the 26th annual ACM symposium on User interface software and technology*, 331-342. ACM.

Chakraborty, A., & Kar, A. K. (2017). Swarm intelligence: A review of algorithms. Nature-Inspired Computing and Optimization, 475-494. Springer International Publishing.

Chung, J., Hong, S., Kim, Y., Kang, S. J., & Kim, C. (2019). Layout placement optimization methods using repeated user interface sequence patterns for client applications. *Information Visualization*, *18*(3), 357–370. doi:10.1177/1473871618825334

Danilov, N., Shulga, T., Frolova, N., Melnikova, N., Vagarina, N., & Pchelintseva, E. (2016). Software Usability Evaluation Based on the User Pinpoint Activity Heat Map. In *Software Engineering Perspectives and Application in Intelligent Systems,* (pp. 217–225). Cham, Switzerland: Springer. doi:10.1007/978-3-319-33622-0_20

Diego-Mas, J. A., Garzon-Leal, D., Poveda-Bautista, R., & Alcaide-Marzal, J. (2019). User-interfaces layout optimization using eye-tracking, mouse movements and genetic algorithms. *Applied Ergonomics*, *78*, 197–209. doi:10.1016/j.apergo.2019.03.004 PMID:31046951

Dingli, A., & Cassar, S. (2014). An intelligent framework for website usability. *Advances in Human-Computer Interaction*, *2014*, 5. doi:10.1155/2014/479286

Eladawy, H. M., Mohamed, A. E., & Salem, S. A. (2018). A New Algorithm for Repairing Web-Locators using Optimization Techniques. *Proceedings 2018 13th International Conference on Computer Engineering and Systems (ICCES)*, 327-331.

Elazim, S. A., & Ali, E. S. (2016). Optimal power system stabilizers design via cuckoo search algorithm. *International Journal of Electrical Power & Energy Systems*, *75*, 99–107. doi:10.1016/j.ijepes.2015.08.018

Farooq, H., & Siddique, M. T. (2014). A Comparative Study on User Interfaces of Interactive Genetic Algorithm. *Procedia Computer Science*, *32*, 45–52. doi:10.1016/j.procs.2014.05.396

Feit, A. M., Bachynskyi, M., & Sridhar, S. (2015). Towards multi-objective optimization for ui design. In *CHI 2015 Workshop on Principles, Techniques, and Perspectives on Optimization and HCI*.

Fu, Y., Zheng, Z., Gao, X., Yang, Y., Lv, P., Wang, Z., & Zhao, W. (2018). Application of Modified BFA for Fault Location in Distribution Networks. In *2nd IEEE Conference on Energy Internet and Energy System Integration (EI2)*, 1-6.

Kar, A. K. (2016). Bio inspired computing–A review of algorithms and scope of applications. *Expert Systems with Applications*, *59*, 20–32. doi:10.1016/j.eswa.2016.04.018

Karaboga, D., & Basturk, B. (2007). A powerful and efficient algorithm for numerical function optimization: Artificial bee colony (ABC) algorithm. *Journal of Global Optimization*, *39*(3), 459–471. doi:10.100710898-007-9149-x

Karaboga, D., Gorkemli, B., Ozturk, C., & Karaboga, N. (2014). A comprehensive survey: Artificial bee colony (ABC) algorithm and applications. *Artificial Intelligence Review*, *42*(1), 21–57. doi:10.100710462-012-9328-0

Kaur, K., & Singh, H. (2016). Click analytics: What clicks on webpage indicates? In *2016 2nd International Conference on Next Generation Computing Technologies (NGCT)*, 608-614.

Kaveh, A., & Behnam, A. F. (2013). Charged system search algorithm for the optimum cost design of reinforced concrete cantilever retaining walls. *Arabian Journal for Science and Engineering*, *38*(3), 563–570. doi:10.100713369-012-0332-0

Kaveh, A., & Talatahari, S. (2010). A novel heuristic optimization method: Charged system search. *Acta Mechanica*, *213*(3), 267–289. doi:10.100700707-009-0270-4

Kaveh, A., & Talatahari, S. (2012). Charged system search for optimal design of frame structures. *Applied Soft Computing*, *12*(1), 382–393. doi:10.1016/j.asoc.2011.08.034

Lin, Y. C., Yeh, C. H., & Wei, C. C. (2013). How will the use of graphics affect visual aesthetics? A user-centered approach for web page design. *International Journal of Human-Computer Studies*, *71*(3), 217–227. doi:10.1016/j.ijhcs.2012.10.013

Longo, L., & Dondio, P. (2015). On the relationship between perception of usability and subjective mental workload of web interfaces. *Proceedings IEEE International Conference on Web Intelligence and Intelligent Agent Technology*, 1, 345-352. 10.1109/WI-IAT.2015.157

Masson, D., Demeure, A., & Calvary, G. (2010). Magellan, an evolutionary system to foster user interface design creativity. *Proceedings of the 2nd ACM SIGCHI symposium on Engineering interactive computing systems*, 87-92. 10.1145/1822018.1822032

Menges, R., Tamimi, H., Kumar, C., Walber, T., Schaefer, C., & Staab, S. (2018). Enhanced representation of web pages for usability analysis with eye tracking. *Proceedings of the 2018 ACM Symposium on Eye Tracking Research & Applications*, 18. 10.1145/3204493.3214308

Miikkulainen, R., Iscoe, N., Shagrin, A., Cordell, R., Nazari, S., Schoolland, C., ... Lamba, G. (2017). Conversion rate optimization through evolutionary computation. *Proceedings of the Genetic and Evolutionary Computation Conference*, 1193-1199. ACM. 10.1145/3071178.3071312

Minkowski, H. (1989). Volumen und oberfläche. *In Ausgewählte Arbeiten zur Zahlentheorie und zur Geometrie*. 146-192. Springer Vienna.

Niknam, T., Golestaneh, F., & Shafiei, M. (2013). Probabilistic energy management of a renewable microgrid with hydrogen storage using self-adaptive charge search algorithm. *Energy*, *49*, 252–267. doi:10.1016/j.energy.2012.09.055

Pandey, A. C., Rajpoot, D. S., & Saraswat, M. (2017). Twitter sentiment analysis using hybrid cuckoo search method. *Information Processing & Management*, *53*(4), 764–779. doi:10.1016/j.ipm.2017.02.004

Park, S. (2007). *Webpage design optimization using genetic algorithm driven CSS*. (Doctoral dissertation), Iowa State University.

Passino, K. M. (2002). Biomimicry of bacterial foraging for distributed optimization and control. *IEEE Control Systems Magazine*, *22*(3), 52–67. doi:10.1109/MCS.2002.1004010

Passino, K. M. (2010). Bacterial foraging optimization [IJSIR]. *International Journal of Swarm Intelligence Research*, *1*(1), 1–16. doi:10.4018/jsir.2010010101

Paz, F., Diaz, E., Paz, F. A., & Moquillaza, A. (2019). Application of the Usability Metrics of the ISO 9126 Standard in the E-Commerce Domain: A Case Study. *Proceedings International Conference on Intelligent Human Systems Integration*, 352-356. 10.1007/978-3-030-11051-2_54

Quiroz, J. C., Louis, S. J., Shankar, A., & Dascalu, S. M. (2007). Interactive genetic algorithms for user interface design. *Proceedings 2007 IEEE Congress on Evolutionary Computation, 1366-1373. IEEE*. 10.1109/CEC.2007.4424630

Rajakumar, R., Dhavachelvan, P., & Vengattaraman, T. (2016). A survey on nature inspired meta-heuristic algorithms with its domain specifications. *Proceedings Communication and Electronics Systems (IC-CES)*, 1-6.

Rajasekar, N., Kumar, N. K., & Venugopalan, R. (2013). Bacterial foraging algorithm based solar PV parameter estimation. *Solar Energy*, *97*, 255–265. doi:10.1016/j.solener.2013.08.019

Rajini, N. H. (2019). Image Segmentation for Diabetic Retinopathy Using Modified Bacterial Foraging Optimization Algorithm. *Indian Journal of Public Health Research & Development*, *10*(7), 1313–1319. doi:10.5958/0976-5506.2019.01769.8

Rath, A., Samantaray, S., & Swain, P. C. (2019). Optimization of the Cropping Pattern Using Cuckoo Search Technique. In *Smart Techniques for a Smarter Planet* (pp. 19–35). Cham, Switzerland: Springer. doi:10.1007/978-3-030-03131-2_2

Romano, D., Raemaekers, S., & Pinzger, M. (2014). Refactoring fat interfaces using a genetic algorithm. *Proceedings International Conference on Software Maintenance and Evolution (ICSME)*, 351-360. 10.1109/ICSME.2014.57

Sakulin, S., Alfimtsev, A., Solovyev, D., & Sokolov, D. (2018). Web page interface optimization based on nature-inspired algorithms [IJSIR]. *International Journal of Swarm Intelligence Research*, *9*(2), 28–46. doi:10.4018/IJSIR.2018040103

Sakulin, S., Alfimtsev, A., Tipsin, E., Devyatkov, V., & Sokolov, D. (2019). User Interface Distribution Method Based on Pi-Calculus [IJDST]. *International Journal of Distributed Systems and Technologies*, *10*(3), 1–20. doi:10.4018/IJDST.2019070101

Sakulin S. A., & Alfimtsev, A. N. (2017). Data fusion based on the fuzzy integral: Model, methods, and applications. *Data Fusion: Methods, Applications, and Research*, 1-64.

Salem, P. (2017). User Interface Optimization using Genetic Programming with an Application to Landing Pages. *Proceedings of the ACM on Human-Computer Interaction*, *1*(1), 13. 10.1145/3099583

Schmidt, J., Gröller, M. E., & Bruckner, S. (2013). VAICo: Visual analysis for image comparison. *IEEE Transactions on Visualization and Computer Graphics*, *19*(12), 2090–2099. doi:10.1109/TVCG.2013.213 PMID:24051775

Sharma, V., Pattnaik, S. S., & Garg, T. (2012). A review of bacterial foraging optimization and its applications [IJCA]. *International Journal of Computers and Applications*, 9–12.

Sorn, D., & Rimcharoen, S. (2013). Web page template design using interactive genetic algorithm *Proceedings Computer Science and Engineering Conference (ICSEC)*, 201-206. 10.1109/ICSEC.2013.6694779

Troiano, L., Birtolo, C., & Cirillo, G. (2009). Interactive Genetic Algorithm for choosing suitable colors in User Interface. *Proceedings of Learning and Intelligent Optimization, LION3*, 14–18.

Valian, E., Mohanna, S., & Tavakoli, S. (2011). Improved cuckoo search algorithm for feedforward neural network training. *Int. Jour. of Artif. Intellig. & Applications*, *2*(3), 36–43. doi:10.5121/ijaia.2011.2304

Wood, L., Nicol, G., Robie, J., Champion, M., & Byrne, S. (2004). *Document Object Model (DOM)*. Level 3 core specification.

Yang, X. S., & Deb, S. (2009). Cuckoo search via Lévy flights. *Proceedings World Congress on Nature & Biologically Inspired Computing (NaBIC)*, 210-214. 10.1109/NABIC.2009.5393690

Yildiz, A. R. (2013). Cuckoo search algorithm for the selection of optimal machining parameters in milling operations. *International Journal of Advanced Manufacturing Technology*, *64*(1-4), 55–61. doi:10.100700170-012-4013-7

Chapter 8
Evaluation of Bayesian Network Structure Learning Using Elephant Swarm Water Search Algorithm

Shahab Wahhab Kareem

https://orcid.org/0000-0002-7362-4653
Erbil Polytechnic University, Iraq

Mehmet Cudi Okur

https://orcid.org/0000-0002-0096-9087
Yaşar University, Turkey

ABSTRACT

Bayesian networks are useful analytical models for designing the structure of knowledge in machine learning which can represent probabilistic dependency relationships among the variables. The authors present the Elephant Swarm Water Search Algorithm (ESWSA) for Bayesian network structure learning. In the algorithm; Deleting, Reversing, Inserting, and Moving are used to make the ESWSA for reaching the optimal structure solution. Mainly, water search strategy of elephants during drought periods is used in the ESWSA algorithm. The proposed method is compared with Pigeon Inspired Optimization, Simulated Annealing, Greedy Search, Hybrid Bee with Simulated Annealing, and Hybrid Bee with Greedy Search using BDeu score function as a metric for all algorithms. They investigated the confusion matrix performances of these techniques utilizing various benchmark data sets. As presented by the results of evaluations, the proposed algorithm achieves better performance than the other algorithms and produces better scores as well as the better values.

DOI: 10.4018/978-1-7998-3222-5.ch008

INTRODUCTION

Probabilistic graphical models, have been to be valuable instruments as a description of ambiguous knowledge. The theory of probability presents methods to analyze how the components joined, guaranteeing that the system remains consistent. The combined results expected to be compatible and present new techniques to propose new interface models for observed data. The graph-theoretic side of graphical models presents both an appealing interface within which humans can create interacting collections of variables and a data structure that can use in powerful general-purpose algorithms (Friedman, Murphy, & Russell, 1998). Bayesian networks (Koski & Noble, 2009; Pourret & Naim, 2008) are such a kind of probabilistic graphical models.

Bayesian networks (BN) are one of the simplified analytical methods for constructing the probabilistic structure of knowledge in machine learning (Ji, Wei, Liu, 2012). They can be implemented universally in knowledge design, argumentation, and inference (Fortier, Sheppard & Pillai, 2013). The structure of Bayesian network is a direct acyclic graph (DAG) which formed concerning two significant parts; the parameters and the structure of the network. The parameters describe conditional probabilities, and the structure expresses dependencies among the variables. Solving the learning structure of a Bayesian network without a suitable search method is difficult. The challenges for learning the optimal structure of a Bayesian network (BN) from a dataset is an NP-hard optimization problem (Li & Chen, 2014); however, extensive research conducted to develop approximate strategies for learning network structure. Essentially, there are two procedures for Bayesian networks structural learning. The first is a constraint-based procedure while the second is score and search procedure (Margaritis, 2003). The score and search method is used to explore the space of BN structures and continuously evaluate all applicant network structures until the valid metric value achieved.

Score-based procedures rely on a function to evaluate the network, the available data, and they search for a structure that optimizes the score, which is the goal (Fast, 2010). The score function method implemented using two primary criteria: Bayesian score and information-theoretic score. The information-theoretic score has implemented in methods like; Log-likelihood (LL), Akaike information criterion (AIC), Bayesian Information Criterion (BIC), Minimum Description Length (MDL), Normalized Minimum Likelihood (NML), and Mutual Information Tests (MIT). The Bayesian score has implemented in other methods like; BD (Bayesian Dirichlet), BDeu (Bayesian Dirichlet ("e" for likelihood-equivalence)), BDeu (Bayesian Dirichlet equivalent uniform ("u" for uniform joint distribution)), and K2 (Cooper & Herskovits, 1992).

There are several methods of the search strategy for achieving the optimization of the structure learning problem. They include Particle Swarm Intelligence (Cowie, Oteniya, Coles, 2007), Ant Colony Optimization Algorithm (Salama & Freitas, 2012), Bee Colony (Li & Chen, 2014), Hybrid Algorithm (He & Gao, 2018; Li, & Wang, 2017; Kareem & Okur, 2018; Sun, Chen, Wang, Kang, Shen & Chen, 2019), Simulated Annealing Algorithm (Hesar, 2013), Bacterial Foraging Optimization (Yang, Ji, Liu, Liu & Yin, 2016), Genetic Algorithms (Larraiiaga & Poza, 1996), Gene-Pool Optimal Mixing Evolutionary Algorithm (GOMEA) (Orphanou, Thierens & Bosman, 2018), Breeding Swarm Algorithm (Khanteymoori, Olyaee, Abbaszadeh & Valian, 2018), Binary Encoding Water Cycle (Wang & Liu, 2018), Pigeon Inspired Optimization (Kareem & Okur, 2019), Tightening Bounds (Fan & Malone, 2014), A* Search Algorithms (Yuan, Malonean & Wu, 2011), Scatter Search Documents (Djan-Sampson & Sahin, 2004), Cuckoo Optimization Algorithm (Askari & Ahsaee, 2018), Quasi-Determinism Screening (Rahier, Marie, Girard, Forbes, 2019), parallel learning (Gao & Wei, 2018), continuous learning (Silva,

Bezerra, Perkusich, Gorgônio, Almeida, & Perkusich, 2018), The Two-Step Clustering-Based Algorithm (Zhang, Liu, & Liu, 2018), and Minimum Spanning Tree Algorithm (Sencer, Oztemel, Taskin, & Torkul, 2013). The search techniques used in these studies are essentially constrained optimization techniques searching for a solution to an optimization problem controlled through a set of constraints. This paper proposes the elephant swarm optimization algorithm as a novel approach to Bayesian network structure learning and presents a comparative evaluation of this method.

The models of BN are integrating with: administration for decision networks; fundamental formulation of causal systems; mixed continuous and discrete variables; quantum probability; Bayesian neural networks; state-and-transition standards; object-oriented and agent-based standards; geographic information systems; and other fields. BNs are becoming valuable mechanisms in risk management, risk analysis, and decision science for resource planning and environmental management. BNs are natural and compact graphical descriptions which can utilize to manage causal reasoning, risk evaluation examination and allow many benefits beyond regression-based approaches (Arora, Boyne, Slater, Gupta, Brenner, & Druzdzel, 2019). The Bayesian network used to present a short description of the relation between the appearance of many chronic diseases and patient-level risk circumstances across time (Faruqui, Alaeddini, Jaramillo, Potter, & Pugh, 2018). A structure learning challenge can be viewed as an inference problem where the variables define a selection of parents for any node within the graph. The major combinatorial problem arises from the global constraint that the graph structure has to be acyclic. We called the structure learning problem as a linear program over the polytope represented by valid acyclic structures. In decreasing this problem, we maintain an outer bound approximation to the polytope and imperatively stretch it by searching a new kind of validity constraints. If a full solution found, it is proven to be the optimal Bayesian network.

The organization of the remainder of this paper is as follows. Section 2 presents the concept of structure learning in Bayesian Networks. Section 3 includes a brief introduction of Elephant Swarm Water Search Algorithm. We discuss in detail the methodology and present the experimental result in section 4. The conclusions are in section 5.

STRUCTURE LEARNING OF BAYESIAN NETWORKS

Probabilistic graphical models (PGM) are a combination of graph theory and probability theory. They present a mechanism to deal with two important difficulties: complexity and uncertainty. Graphical Models are combined structures that represent conditional dependence structures between random variables. They play a major role in the analysis and designing of machine learning algorithms. Probabilistic graphical models are diagrams, where nodes express random variables, and edges describe dependencies between pairs of variables. These models produce a compressed description of joint probability distributions of random variables. There are two important types of PGMs. First, undirected graphical models, which are identified as Markov Random Fields (MRFs) or Markov Networks and second, directed graphical models also named Bayesian Networks.

Learning a BN from observational data is an essential difficulty that has been studied over the latest decade. The development of principles can be performed both by using expertise or observed data. Several kinds of research have been conducted on this subject, deriving on various approaches: Techniques to the development regarding conditional independence within the data to rebuild the graph to optimizing an actual function, namely a score. Optimization techniques aim to the development of a representation of the local structure based on a destination variable to rebuild the global structure of the network. Most of the researches have restricted the structure learning of Bayesian networks to static cases. The majority of these algorithms use a traditional approach which depended on scores.

If there are just a few variables, we can exhaustively calculate the probability of all DAG models as produced. We then pick the values of a stochastic random variable (gp) that maximize P(d|gp) (Note that there should be higher than one maximizing model.) If the number of variables is not few, to get the maximizing DAG models by considering every DAG models is computationally inconvenient. (Robinson, 1977) has shown the quantity of DAGs, including n nodes provided by the following equation:

$$f(n) = \sum_{i=1}^{n} (-1)^{i+1} \binom{n}{i} 2^{i(n-i)} f(n-i) \, \text{n>2} \tag{1}$$

f(0) = 1, f(1) = 1.

There are smaller DAG models than there are DAGs, but this number further is forbiddingly high (Gillispie & Pearlman, 2001). Chickering has proven that for certain classes of prior distributions, the difficulty of getting the usual probable DAG patterns is NP-complete (Chickering, 1996.). One way to manipulate a problem like this is to improve heuristic search algorithms.

Fundamentally the Bayesian Network can be expressed using two components: (G, P). The first one, G(V; E) is the DAG covering the calculable group of vertices (or nodes), V, interconnected over marked edges (or links), E . The second one, P = {P (X$_i$ | Pa (X$_i$))} represents the collection of conditional probabilistic distributions (CPD), individual to all variables X$_i$ (vertices from a graph). Moreover, Pa(X$_i$) represents the collection of parents of the node X$_i$ in G (Cowie, Oteniya, & Coles, 2007). Based on this model, a simple probabilistic combination for a (G; P) network can represent via:

$$P(X_i, \ldots X_n) = \prod_{i=1}^{n} P(X_i \mid Pa(X_i)) \tag{2}$$

A score function, on the other hand, depends on several criteria, including Bayesian approaches, information and entropy, and minimum description length (Campos, 2006). According to Bayesian inference rules, Bayesian - network posterior probability can express as:

$$P(G|D) = P(D|G) \cdot P(G) / \sum_{G'} P(D|G') P(G') \tag{3}$$

In (3), P(D|G) is a marginal likelihood, which is defined using the normalizing constant P(D) as:

$$P(D \mid G) = \int P(D \mid G, \theta) P(\theta \mid G) d\theta \tag{4}$$

P(D) is assumed to be independent of the structure of Bayesian network G. P(G') is the prior probability, and θ represents the parameter of the model. Consequently, as long as the marginal probability to all feasible structure is determined, the posterior distribution of the network structure can be calculated (Zhang & Liu, 2008). Structure learning methods use score-based techniques by comparing the current and previous scores of the structure. The ultimate expression of the score is (Heckerman, Geiger, & Chickering, 1995):

$$Score(G, D) = \sum Score\left(X_i, Pa\left(X_i\right), D\left(X_i, pa\left(X_i\right)\right)\right) \tag{5}$$

Score-based learning algorithms describe the utilization of heuristic optimization procedures to the difficulty of learning the structure of a BN. Every applicant BN has a network score reflecting its success of fit, which the algorithm later tries to maximize (Bouckaert, 1995).

The following forms a multinomial Bayesian network structure learning space:

1. A multinomial Bayesian network structure learning schema including the variables X1, X2,... Xn;
2. A stochastic variable GP whose scope comprises every DAG models including the n variables, and for any value gp of GP a prior probability P(gp);
3. A set D = {X(1), X(2), ... X(M)} of n-dimensional arbitrary vectors such that every $X_i^{(h)}$ has the equivalent space as Xi for any value gp of GP, D is a multinomial Bayesian network sample of size M with parameter (G, F(G)), where (G, F(G)) is the multinomial expanded Bayesian network comparing to gp in the schema's specification.

A scoring model for a DAG (or DAG model) is a role that selects a meaning to each DAG (or DAG model) depend on consideration based on the data. The formulation in Equation 5 is named as Bayesian scoring criterion score B and applied to score both DAGs and DAG models.

scoreB (d, gp) = scoreB(d, G) = P(d|G).

Note that in Equation 5, we used a DAG pattern to calculate the probability that D = d. Therefore, this structure was part of the prior experience learning to evolve in our definition space, also since we did not train on it. Consider, the conditional probability individually explained. That is a basis on a selection of DAGs for (G, F(G), ρ|G). Presented a multinomial Bayesian network structure learning data and space, model collection decomposed of picking and determining the DAG models, including highest probability conditional on the data. The goal of the model collection is to learn a DAG pattern subject to its parameter values (a model) that can apply to decision making and inference. We could enhance a Bayesian network, whose DAG is in the equality group described by gp1, to prepare inference including X1 and X2. Note that we grow the DAG model that is the one including the dependency because, in the data, the variables deterministically correlated. Learning from a Mixture of Observational and Experimental Data.

The Bayesian scoring criterion (Equation 5) regarding every case concerned and whose value corresponds to the equal probability distribution can use to learn and test the structure just when all the data is observational. That is if no values are available for every variable by conducting a randomized control experiment (RCE). As usual, we can own both observational data also temporary data (data collected of an RCE) for a presented collection of variables. For instance, in the medical area, it involves a large deal of observational data in routinely handled electronic medical records. For specific variables of high clinical importance, we sometimes own data collected from an RCE. Cooper and Yoo enhanced an approach for using Equation 5 to score DAGs by using a hybrid of observational and experimental data (Cooper & Yoo, 1999). The scoring method presented is applied in several algorithms and investigations (Tong & Koller, 2001; Pe'er, Regev, Elidan & Friedman, 2001). Cooper and Yoo (1999) present managing the situation in which the guidance is stochastic. Cooper represents learning from a composite of observational, experimental, and case-control (biased sample) data (Cooper, 2000).

NATURE INSPIRED ELEPHANT SWARM WATER SEARCH ALGORITHM

Metaheuristics are nature-inspired algorithms for finding approximate solutions to some computationally hard optimization problems. Swarming behaviors of animals including; Firefly-BAT (Reddy & Kare, 2016), Cuckoo (Gadekallu & Khare, 2017), ant, pigeon, fish, bee,...etc, have been used in metaheuristics (Gandomi, Yang, Marand, & Alavi, 2013). Some properties behind the metaheuristics include; homogeneity, adaptability, illation-free tools plus local optima eschewal ability (Mirjalili, Mirjalili, & Lewis, 2014). An interesting example is the swarm behaviour of the biggest terrestrial mammals, elephants. The trunk is the common representative characteristic of an elephant which is multi-objective, like respiration, following things and uplifting water (Wang, Deb, & Coelho, 2015). Swarm properties of water search of elephant herds have utilized to define metaheuristic algorithms (Wang, Deb, & Coelho, 2015). The following four idealizing assumptions utilized for describing swarm water search algorithm (Mandal, 2018). (i) Elephants walk nearby in exploration for water through dryness within various groups; this act is named elephant swarm. Every group operates concurrently for obtaining water. The leader from every organization (elderly elephant, matriarch) is qualified for using a choice for searching the biggest water source. (ii) While the elephant group discovers any resource of water, the matriarch shares with the nearby groups, the information about the quality and quantity of the resource. Good water level indicates the next valid move. (iii) Elephants hold pretty strong memory. Several elephant groups can retain information about some correct positions of the water supply that existed and recognized through its private group (local best solution). They can also remember the correct position of the best water source that found out through the entire flock of groups (global best solution). (iv) Local and global water exploration choices represent through a probabilistic constant P. Based on this value, the matriarch opts actions for switching between global and local search options. Because of certain physical and natural factors, water exploration in local may have a higher P value (Mandal, 2018). The elephant can distinguish and learn among several visual also some acoustic signals of discrimination. Several techniques including; acoustic, seismic, and chemical means used for communication among elephant groups in long-distance up to 10–12 km away.

The d-dimensional optimization problem can formulate using the location and velocity of the ith elephant group from a swarm(Composed of N members). In t^{th} iteration,the location can be represented by $X_{i,d}^t = (X_{i1}, X_{i2}, ..., X_{id})$. Similarly, the velocity can expresse using $V_{i,d}^t = (V_{i1}, V_{i2}, ..., V_{id})$. Based on these, the best local solution for i^{th} elephant group at the current iteration expressed as $P_{best\ i,d}^t = (P_{i1}, P_{i2}, ..., P_{id})$ and Gbest expresses the best global solution $G_{best\ i,d}^t = (G_1, G_2, ..., G_d)$. The starting velocity and position of elephant groups arbitrarily assigned within the exploration area. During iteration, the positions and velocities of the elephants renewed. Optimal water search decision actions should occur in both global and local scales. While iteration proceeds, the velocities from the members are renewed based on several techniques during local and global search according to the equations (6) and (7) below. The value of switching probability p determines the type of search:

$$V_{i,d}^{t+1} = V_{i,d}^t w^t + rand(1,d) . \left(G_{best,d}^t - X_{i,d}^t \right) \tag{6}$$

If rand>p [global search]

$$V_{i,d}^{t+1} = V_{i,d}^t w^t + rand(1,d) . \left(P_{best,d}^t - X_{i,d}^t \right) \tag{7}$$

If rand≤p [local search]

In (6) and (7), rand is a value that produces a d-dimensional array of random values in [0,1]. (.) Expresses element by element multiplication and w^t is the weight of inertia for compromising exploitation and exploration throughout the current iteration. Next, the location of the elephant group is adjusted as specified by the following formula (Mandal, 2018).

$$X_{i,d}^{t+1} = V_{i,d}^{t+1} + X_{i,d}^t \tag{8}$$

In (8), t_{max}, X_{max} and X_{min} indicate the maximum iteration number, lower and upper limits regarding positions. A search route is affected by three elements specifically: current velocity ($V_{i,d}^t$), current particle memory commands ($P_{best,d}^t$) and swarm memory commands ($G_{best,d}^t$) (Mandal, 2018). Nevertheless, in ESWSA, the new search route is determined through both current speed and current elephant memory and swarm memory effects. In the global search, the velocity update based on the elephant's best position, and the search continues to obtain the best global solution. In the case of Random Inertia Weight (RIW) (Yang, 2010), the weight of inertia values chosen randomly, which is extremely valuable for a dynamic system that tries to obtain the optima. The following formula used to select the weight of inertia in RIW:9 (Mandal, 2018).

$$w^t = 0.5 + \left(rand * 0.5 \right) \tag{9}$$

In (9), rand is a uniform random number in [0,1]. A successful procedure is the Linearly Decreasing Inertia Weight (LDIW) (Larraiiaga & Poza, 1996). This procedure can use in developing some good tuning properties concerning the optimization. In LDIW, the weight of inertia values depends on the value (w_{max}) and an ultimate small value (w_{min}), according to the following Equation (Xin, Chen & Hai, 2009):

$$w^t = w_{max} - \left\{ \frac{w_{max} - w_{min}}{t_{max}} \right\} * t \tag{10}$$

where the index of iteration is t, and the maximum number of iterations is t_{max}.

It should note that the PSO approach uses the random repair technique, which involves jumping randomly within the search space, while in ESWSA, the position change based on Equation (8).

ESWSA FOR BAYESIAN NETWORK STRUCTURE LEARNING

The proposed method uses ESWSA approach as a search method for structural learning of Bayesian networks. The BDeu metric used as a score function for assessing the Bayesian network structure. The ESWSA algorithm is effectively an iterated procedure that consists of a population of individuals where every elephant encodes a potential position and velocity in a given space. This space held to be the search area. The proposed method depends on two techniques. The first technique uses Equation (8) for local search through the necessary process if (rand$\leq$p). The second one uses Equation (7) for global search through the necessary process if (rand $>$ p). Figure 1 shows the pseudo code of this technique.

Figure 1.

Algorithm: Structure Learning of Bayesian Network based on elephant swarm water search algorithm

INPUT: - datasets
 NE: number of Elephant swarm
D: search space dimension
P: the switching probability p
Search range: the search space border
t_{max}: maximum number of iteration number; X_{max}: upper boundary, and X_{min}: - lower boundary
OUTPUT: - learning Bayesian Network

(1) *The initialized empty structure and initialize parameters of ESWSA algorithm (dimension space D, size of population NE, the switching probability p, the number of iteration number, upper boundary and lower boundary, ($G_{best,i,d}^{t}$). and $X_{max} > X_{min}$.*

(2) *Set the velocity and position for all Elephant randomly. Comparing each elephant by BDe score function, and find the best in the current position ($P_{best,i,d}^{t}$).*

(3) *Assign the value of w^{t} according to the weight update using Equations (9) or (10).*

(4) *Find a new best position by comparing the BDe score function of each elephant.*

(5) *If rand>p, update elephant velocity ($V_{i,d}$) using equation (6).*
else rand$\leq$ p update elephant velocity using Equation (7).

(6) *Update the position $X_{i,d}$ using Equation (8).*

(7) *Evaluate BDeu score function of new position ($X_{i,d}^{t}$)*

    a) *If current position ($X_{i,d}^{t}$) is better than the best position ($P_{best,i,d}^{t}$) then update the best position by (($P_{best,i,d}^{t}$)= ($X_{i,d}^{t}$))*

    b) *If (($G_{best,i,d}^{t}$)< current position then update the best solution for global by ($G_{best,i,d}^{t}=(X_{i,d})$)*

    c) *The best score value and solution are saved.*

    d) *If $X_{min} \geq X_{max}$, stop the iteration process, and the results are present. If not, move into Step 5.*

(8) *Return the maximum BDe score.*

ESWSA algorithm's solution construction utilizes different neighbourhood than local search. The expectation is high that the local search updates a solution formed by an elephant group. Structure learning Bayesian network solution area is formed for each potential DAG. Every elephant group inside the swarm initiates a possible solution which represents a DAG having empty arcs. An elephant later examines the exploration area for finding the approximately near-optimal or optimal solution, which is known as the BDeu score. Equation (6) used to calculate the BDeu score as the goal function of the optimization. The exploration aims for obtaining a higher BDeu score for the network structure. All initial solutions produced through iterative operations. Starting with a blank graph (G0), the arcs are appended one after another, provided that they not included in the current graph solution. The append operation performs if only if the score function of the new solution is higher than the current score and also the new solution satisfies the DAG constraint. This process continues until the quantity of the arcs equals the quantity defined in advance. In the model, the solution starts assigning a population for each operator and picks the solution, which has a higher score function. Elephant group continues according to the selected operator until the process has performed a maximum number of iterations or the BDeu score does not increase any more. Typically, the processes hold four separate operations in local optimization: Deletion, Addition, Reversion, Movement. The first three are-simple operations within this domain, involve just replacing an individual edge every time from a competitor solution. This allows the inclusion of a comparatively small area near the solution. With every movement operation, on the other hand, the existing edges change the set of parents, which can make a moderately big modification for the current solution. Therefore, if the solution not changed after applying simple operators, the move operator may improve it. Walking is the major force utilizing the chosen operation in local optimization, which grows further widespread while an elephant approaches the desirable solution. Walking directions, the switch with various local optimization operators, grows extra widespread as an elephant moves continuously from a solution through exploration toward a better one. Therefore, the current velocity renewed by either elephant's best global or best local solution based on the (p) value. The ESWSA based on the probability value p can switch off from global search into local or from local to global. The velocity of ESWSA is renewed based on the current best position of the elephant in the local search. On the other hand, the global velocity depends on the best global solution concerning elephants in a global search, near a global best position. As shown in Figure 2, an elephant G0, which describes a DAG with arcs, tries reversion, move, addition, and deletion, and reaches new solutions G1, G2, G3, and G4, respectively. Assuming the best score is in G3, it will select, and the elephant will proceed to examine some similar process to get G+3 as the new solution. If the BDeu score of G+3 is higher Than that of G+1, it will continue to perform the corresponding operator. The operations will repeat until the BDeu score stabilizes, or iteration loop reaches the maximum.

EXPERIMENTAL EVALUATION

Several approaches describe possibilities for traditional optimization, and they are well-developed for a class of optimization problems related to the increased optimization difficulties. Traditional optimization approaches further possess weaknesses, including those that not applicable to every optimization problem. There have been many substitutions approaches, during the last few decades and some of them are under improvement (Kulkarni, Krishnasamy, & Abraham, 2017).

Figure 2.

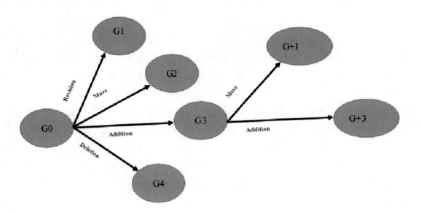

To evaluate algorithm performance (ESWSA), a standard assessment technique utilized by employing probabilistic datasets extracted from popular Bayesian networks benchmarks. The platform for experiments includes a PC having the following properties: Core i3, 2.1GHz CPU, 4GB RAM, Ubuntu 14.04 operating system and utilizes Java to implement the algorithm. We investigated the properties of proposed algorithm in several static datasets including; Asia (8 variables, 8 arcs, and 3000 instance), WDBC (9 variables and 1000 instance), Lucas01(10 variables and 10000 instance), Adult (16 variables and 30162 instance), Letter (17 variables and 20000 instance), Child (20 variables, 25 arcs, and 230 instance), Imports(22 variables and 205 instance), Heart(22 variables and 267 instance), Parkinsons (23 variables and 195 instance), Mushroom (23 variables and 1000 instance), Sensors(25 variables and 5456 instance), Insurance (27 variables, 52 arcs, and 3000 instance), Epigenetics (30 variable and 72228 instance), Water (32 variables, 66 arcs, and 10083 instance), Static Banjo (33 variables and 320 instance), Hepatitis(35 variables and 137 instance), Soybean (35 variables and 307 instance), Alarm (37 variables, 46 arcs, and 10000 instance), Hailfinder (56 variables, 66 arcs, and 2656 instance), Hepar (70 variables, 123 arcs, and 350 instance), win95pts (76 variables, 112 arcs, and 574 instance), Andes (223 variables, 338 arcs, and 500 instance), and Lucap02 (143 variables and 10000 instance) (Nagarajan, Scutari & Lèbre, 2013). In the present form, this work based on stationary data assumption, and the learning datasets that we considered are stationery sets. Extending the ESWSA algorithm to sensor data sets or other forms of online stream data sets is a challenging task. It could attempt after assessing its performance over stationary data sets.

The results of ESWSA compared with Pigeon Inspired Optimization (PIO) (Kareem & Okur, 2019), Simulated Annealing (SA), Hybrid Bee with Simulated Annealing(BSA) (Kareem & Okur, 2017), Greedy Search (GS), and Hybrid Bee with Greedy search (BGS) (Kareem & Okur, 2018) methods by utilizing corresponding metrics for the datasets. All algorithms have evaluated under the same conditions. Choice of fitting parameters concerning ESWSA is an essential responsibility to produce the best achievements for real-world and statistical optimization challenges. Use of trial and error plan or a random choice of parameters for a real-life challenge may guide to high computational cost and less performance. After defining the parameters of ESWSA algorithm, local and global search applied to the datasets. In EWSA, three parameters used to control exploration performance. The first parameter randomly is chosen inertia weight (w^t), which indicates the speed of inertia at the current iteration. The second one is switching probability p, which is implemented as a constant parameter, i.e., the value remains constant during the entire search. This choice suggests that local and global water exploration can be changed based on the value of the parameter p. Based on this value; the matriarch opts actions for switching between global and local search options. Because of certain physical and natural factors, water exploration in local may have a higher P-value. In order to be able to decide on a reasonable P-value, alternatives from the set {0.1, 0.2, 0.3, 0.4, 0.5, 0.6, 0.7, 0.8, 0.9, 0.99} have been evaluated. We observed that P = 0.7 gave satisfactory results for most of the cases under the same evaluation criteria. Since the main aim of this paper was to evaluate the structure learning properties of ESWSA alongside with the others, no other values of p considered.

Nevertheless, if growing the number of population (elephant swarm) and the number of iteration, it is supposed the increasing the accuracy as well as increase the computational time consequently. Accordingly, optimization challenges in the real-life, number of iteration and enough population are needed to consider for better efficiency and accuracy.

For the experiments, the following fixed parameters used for ESWSA optimization: p=0.7, tmax =1000, population size N=50. The observing of the above parameters is favoured in this study work as well as for different real-life optimization challenges as it will balance computational time and accuracy.

The parameters of Simulated Annealing algorithms are as follows: Temperature of Reannealing = 500, cooling factor= 0.8, Initial temperature=1000. Greedy search parameters are as follows: Recommended minimum networks before reboot = 3000, minimum recommended networks after highest score = 1000, maximum recommended networks before reboot = 5000, the maximum parent count for operations Reboot=5, restart by random network = yes. The parameters of Bee algorithms are: Number of Scout Bees n= 200, Number of Sites m out of n visited sites=30, Number of best site e out of m selected site =7, Number of Bees recruited for best e site n2=90, Number of Bees recruited for the other site (m-e) (n1)=30, Initial size of patches ngh which includes site randomly selected=200, Number of algorithm steps repetitions imax=10000. The Pigeon parameters are Pigeons number (NP=300), search space dimension (D=20), the factor of the map and compass (P=0.3), the maximum number of iteration number for the map and compass operation (Nc1max=5000), the maximum number of iteration number for the landmark operation (Nc2max=10000). The algorithms have been implemented in three different execution times: 2 minutes, 5 minutes and 60 minutes.

As shown in Tables (1, 2, and 3), it can note that the proposed method produces better score values than other Algorithms for most situations. It indicates that the ESWSA finds the best score with the minimum time required. The authors calculate the score function in 3 different times, as shown in the tables. The score produced by the proposed method in 2 minutes is better than the score produced by Simulated Annealing and Greedy search in 60 minutes. The BDeu score function of the proposed method need implement the program more time to produce a score function in 2 minutes while other algorithms needed more time to produce a useful score function, so the proposed method offers higher speed for producing a better BDeu score function.

To evaluate the success of structure discovery, Confusion matrix values can compute for each algorithm and data set using known network structures. The general idea is to compare the known network structure with the produced network. To calculate the confusion matrix, first, we need to have a set of predictions network so that it can compare to the actual network. Each row in a confusion matrix represents an actual class, while each column represents a predicted class. To test the success of structure discovery, we have to compute the confusion matrix for each data set and its known network structure. We have calculated the metrics TP, TN, FN, and FP for each network per algorithm and the criteria (Sensitivity (SE), Accuracy (ACC), F1_Score, and AHD) which defined as:

Table 1. Score function the best of ESWSA, PIO, simulated annealing, hybrid bee with simulated annealing, greedy and hybrid bee with greedy in 2 minutes execution time

Dataset	2 Minutes					
	ESWSA	PIO	Simulated Annealing	Hybrid Bee With Simulated Annealing	Greedy	Hybrid Bee With Greedy
Asia	-54849.9	-55269.5	-56340.27	-56158.6	-56340.3	-56258.65
WDBC	-6660.43	-6666.04	-6682.716	-6675.42	-8089.41	-8080.83
lucas01	-11863.1	-11860	-12243.24	-12235.28	-13890.9	-13795.3
Adult	-207809	-207809	-211677.7	-211670	-211844	-211850
Letter	-175200	-175200	-178562.2	-178550.3	-184307	-184205
Child	-62365.7	-62362	-62343.73	-62341.82	-63336.6	-63325.15
Heart	-2426.42	-2423.8	-2432.188	-2423.8	-2576.93	-2570.56
Imports	-1811.99	-1811.99	-1828.906	-1820.259	-1994.15	-1982.59
spect.heart	-2141.53	-2142.5	-2141.468	-2141.23	-2144.65	-2144.2
Parkinsons	-1486.86	-1598.91	-1601.297	-1600.92	-1732.76	-1715.57
Mashroom	-3160.87	-3372.51	-3375.31	-3374.18	-3745.46	-3745.46
Sensors	-60343.3	-60343.3	-60710.5	-60508.7	-69200.3	-68962.5
insurance	-13895.1	-138997	-13872.33	-13870.59	-13904.6	-13904
Epigenetics	-176636	-176657	-179910.3	-179906	-225346	-225340
Water	-11562.7	-13269.5	-13290.83	-13262.58	-14619.1	-13262.83
static.data	-8409.42	-8425.72	-8451.495	-8449.49	-8585.21	-8570.26
Hepatitis	-1327.73	-1327.73	-1330.465	-1329.965	-1350.16	-1346.5
soybean	-2973.3	-2870.2	-2870.851	-2859.1344	-3021.41	-3025.82
Alarm	-105165	-105150	-104927.1	-104927.18	-105972	-105552.28
Hailfinder	-75583.9	-89521.6	-148192.9	-148179.96	-153602	-152037.97
Hepar	-160095	-160095	-161086.4	-161049.62	-169497	-161050.91
win95pts	-46779.5	-46779.5	-47085.1	-47032.38	-83749.3	-83650.82
Lucap2	-169582	-186368	-112260.5	-111413.33	-151215	-151242.78
Andes	-613180	-613197	-497353.3	-477461.41	-591871	-589927.23

$$sensitivity = \frac{TP}{TP + FN} \qquad (11)$$

$$accuracy = \frac{TP + TN}{TP + FP + TN + FN} \qquad (12)$$

$$F1\ Score = \frac{2 * TP}{2TP + FP + FN} \qquad (13)$$

Table 2. Score function the best of ESWSA, PIO, simulated annealing, hybrid bee with simulated annealing, greedy and hybrid bee with greedy in 5 minutes execution time

Dataset	5 Minutes					
	ESWSA	PIO	Simulated Annealing	Hybrid Bee With Simulated Annealing	Greedy	Hybrid Bee With Greedy
Asia	-54849.9	-55852.58	-56340.27	-56218.5	-56340.3	-56320.87
WDBC	-6660.43	-6666.04	-6682.716	-6675.52	-7954.65	-75236.65
lucas01	-11492.7	-11892.52	-12243.24	-12229.69	-12243.2	-12230.42
Adult	-207258	-207809	-211677.7	-211664	-211781	-211756
Letter	-175200	-175200	-178562.2	-178523.28	-184916	-182584
Child	-62365.7	-62369.2	-62343.73	-62140.72	-63799.4	-63235
Heart	-2426.42	-2423.8	-2423.804	-2423.8	-2560.43	-2545.2
Imports	-1811.99	-1811.99	-1828.906	-1824.3	-2012.21	-1950.3
spect.heart	-2128.82	-2132.823	-2143.731	-2140.852	-2142.89	-2141.25
Parkinsons	-1439.09	-1598.91	-1601.297	-1600.58	-1721.16	-1701
Mashroom	-3160.87	-3372.51	-3375.31	-3375.51	-3709.7	-3625.4
Sensors	-60343.3	-60343.3	-60710.5	-60642.2	-69150	-66250
insurance	13895.11	-13895.11	-13872.33	-13842.65	-13904.6	-13892.27
Epigenetics	-176628	-176657	-179300.2	-179295.54	-224172	-224162
Water	-11562.6	-13269.5	-13290.83	-13262.58	-14644.7	-13264.46
static.data	-8409.42	-8425.2	-8449.77	-8445.411	-8561.93	-8448.24
Hepatitis	-1327.73	-1327.73	-1330.465	-1328.62	-1350.16	-1340.3
soybean	-2973.3	-2973.3	-2857.82	-2863.82	-3011.38	-2991.81
Alarm	-105165	-105182	-104927.1	-104927.18	-106114	-106170.99
Hailfinder	-75583.9	-75698	-148188.2	-148178.65	-153075	-151863.2
Hepar	-160095	-160095	-161086.4	-161048.96	-169881	-163374.8
win95pts	-46779.5	-46779.5	-47085.1	-47023.68	-83150.7	-75201.54
Lucap2	-169582	-175635	-112217.4	-110834.29	-152092	-151912.8
Andes	-613180	-613180	-489795.7	-480065.27	-588503	-584604.8

$$AHD = \frac{FN + FP}{TP + TN + FP + FN} \tag{14}$$

The meanings of these metrics are as follows: A TP is an arc (vertex or edge) in the right position inside the learning network. TN is the arc inside neither the learning network nor the proper network. FP is the arc inside the learning network not in the actual network. The FN is the arc in the actual, however, not in the learning network.

The Sensitivity results for ESWSA, PIO, Simulated Annealing, Hybrid Simulated Annealing, Greedy and Hybrid Bee with Greedy, are shown in Figure 3. The proposed method produces better values than

Table 3. Score function the best of ESWSA, PIO, simulated annealing, hybrid bee with simulated annealing, greedy and hybrid bee with greedy in 60 minutes execution time

Dataset	60 Minutes					
	ESWSA	**PIO**	**Simulated Annealing**	**Hybrid Bee With Simulated Annealing**	**Greedy**	**Hybrid Bee With Greedy**
Asia	-29791	-30850	-56340.27	-56340	-56340.3	-56340
WDBC	-6660.43	-6666	-6682.716	-6679.632	-7841.35	-7752.35
lucas01	-11213.8	12115.38	-12243.24	-12212.92	-12243.2	-12236.4
Adult	-207258	-207809	-211677.7	-211664	-211762	-211739
Letter	-175200	-175200	-178562.2	-178509.62	-184118	-182269
Child	-62245.7	-62275.2	-62343.73	-62312.42	-63799.4	-63756.9
Heart	-2426.42	-2423.8	-2432.188	-2423.8	-2527.44	-2522395
Imports	-1811.99	-1812	-1828.906	-1824.3	-1995.76	-1950.2
spect.heart	-2128.82	-2135.4	-2144.128	-2144.1	-2142.24	-2142.24
Parkinsons	-1439.09	-1598.9	-1601.297	-1695.25	-1700.36	-1693.58
Mashroom	-3003.45	-3372.5	-3375.31	-3374.57	-3588.69	-3524.83
Sensors	-60343.3	-60343	-60710.5	-60612.521	-68364	-67825
insurance	-13895.1	-13950	-13872.3	-13850.62	-13904.6	-1385.62
Epigenetics	-176628	-176657	-179300.2	-179295.54	-217246	-217212
Water	-11562.6	-13270	-13290.83	-13262.2	-14272	-13262
static.data	-8317.87	-83268.4	-8445.356	-8552.374	-8556.7	-8552.4
Hepatitis	-1327.73	-1327.7	-1330.465	-1328.62	-1350.16	-1346.52
soybean	-2973.3	-2973.3	-2973.828	-2992.993	-3012.72	-2993
Alarm	-104865	-104915	-104927.1	-105270.7	-105377	-105271
Hailfinder	-75583.9	-78293	-148182.7	-151772.6	-152299	-151773
Hepar	-160095	-160095	-161086.4	-163230.9	-168871	-163231
win95pts	-46779.5	-46780	-47085.1	-470015.65	-83150.7	-80253.4
Lucap2	-105251	-105621	-111274.8	-151160.11	-150938	-151160
Andes	-469217	-469342	-480491.3	-480253.4	-586760	-587098

the Simulated Annealing, Hybrid Simulated Annealing, Greedy and Hybrid Bee with Greedy in the different datasets.

Similarly, the proposed method in the most dataset has high accuracy values than the Simulated Annealing, Hybrid Simulated Annealing, Greedy and Hybrid Bee with Greedy in the different datasets, as shown in Figure 4. The proposed ESWSA Learning Algorithm performs well in finding the appropriate structure. As a result, from the point of prediction accuracy, the Iterative ESWSA algorithm is the best algorithm compared to other algorithms in most datasets, and from the point of construction times also the ESWSA is better than the other algorithms. For performance metrics, in addition to the best score in Bayesian results, we used F1 as a metric of the model's accuracy.

Figure 3. Sensitivity for ESWSA, PIO, Simulated Annealing, Hybrid Simulated Annealing, Greedy and Hybrid Bee with Greedy

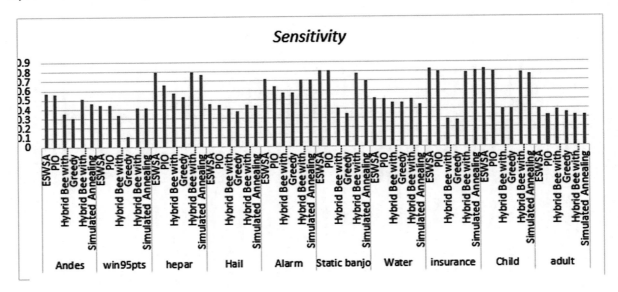

Figure 4. Accuracy for ESWSA, PIO, Simulated Annealing, Hybrid Simulated Annealing, Greedy and Hybrid Bee with Greedy

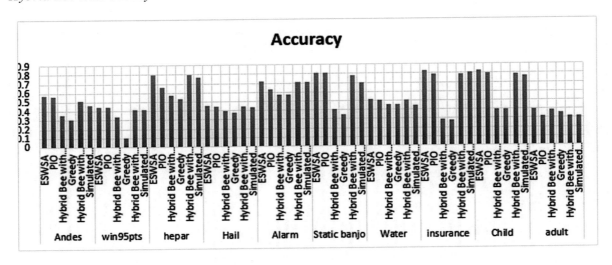

The F1- score, Precision, and Recall are used to evaluate the performance of the proposed algorithm. In these circumstances, Precision is the number of directed edges that found correctly divided by the number of all edges in the expected BN. The Recall represents the division of the number of directed edges that are found by the number of edges in the actual BN. It does know that F1 is the harmonic average of accuracy and Recall. Figure 5 presents a comparison of ESWSA with other mentioned algorithms. As presented in Figure 5, the proposed methods are successful than the other methods. Furthermore, the

Figure 5. F1_Score for ESWSA, PIO, Simulated Annealing, Hybrid Simulated Annealing, Greedy and Hybrid Bee with Greedy

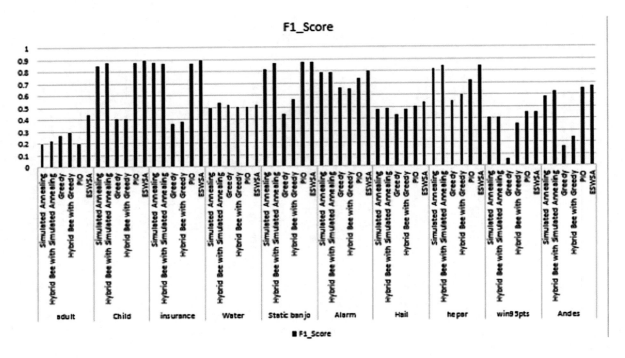

Figure 6. AHD for ESWSA, PIO, Simulated Annealing, Hybrid Simulated Annealing, Greedy and Hybrid Bee with Greedy

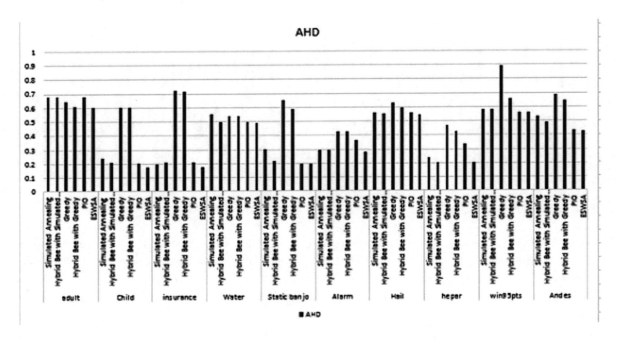

ultimate purpose of the model is to present a convenient representation of the real world, so accuracy is a useful measure of model performance evaluation.

The proposed algorithm is also preferable from the Hamming distances, which are always considerably lower than the ones obtained by using the DAG space. Hamming distances is one of the most widely used evaluation metrics for BN structure learning, which directly matches the structure of learners and local networks also are directed entirely towards exploration rather than inference. Figure 6 shows the Average Hamming Distances for the mentioned algorithms. The results demonstrate that the proposed method produces better performance values than the other methods that we have considered.

CONCLUSION

The Authors focused on Bayesian network structure learning problem and applied the elephant swarm inspired optimization as a novel approach to structure learning of Bayesian networks. The optimization method based on using ESWSA approach as the search technique and BDeu as the score function. ESWSA essentially is a method for searching a discrete solution space, and as such, it can adjust to suit for many other application areas. Concentration control in ESWSA presents quickened concentration to the global extremum by allowing the elephant to move to the shortest useful solution space. Evaluations of the ESWSA together with several alternatives have demonstrated that the proposed method has a higher ability for searching, which indicates it can detect better structure solution, calculate higher score function and excellent approximation to the network structure and the results are accurate. The algorithm improves the global search and leads rapidly to global convergence.

REFERENCES

Arora, P., Boyne, D., Slater, J. J., Gupta, A., Brenner, D. R., & Drudzel, M. J. (2019). Bayesian Networks for Risk Prediction Using Real-World Data: A Tool for Precision Medicine. Elsevier, 439- 445.

Askari, M. B., & Ahsaee, M. G. (2018). Bayesian network structure learning based on cuckoo search algorithm. *Proceedings 2018 6th Iranian Joint Congress on Fuzzy and Intelligent Systems (CFIS)*, pp. 127-130. IEEE. Kerman, Iran.

Bouckaert, R. R. (1995). *Bayesian belief networks: from construction to inference*. The Netherlands: Utrecht University.

Campos, L. M. (2006). A Scoring Function for Learning Bayesian Networks based on Mutual Information and Conditional Independence Tests. *Journal of Machine Learning Research*, (7), 2149–2187.

Chickering, D. (1996). *Learning Bayesian Networks is NP-Complete*. Springer-Verlag. doi:10.1007/978-1-4612-2404-4_12

Cooper, G. (2000). A Bayesian Method for Causal Modeling and Discovery Under Selection. *Proceedings of the Sixteenth conference on Uncertainty in artificial intelligence* (pp. 98-106). California: Morgan Kaufmann.

Cooper, G. F., & Herskovits, E. (1992). A Bayesian method for the induction of probabilistic networks from data. *Machine Learning*, *9*(4), 309–347. doi:10.1007/BF00994110

Cooper, G. F., & Yoo, C. (1999). Causal Discovery from a Mixture of Experimental and Observational Data. *Proceedings of the Fifteenth conference on Uncertainty in artificial intelligence* (pp. 116-125). California: Morgan Kaufmann.

Cowie, J., Oteniya, L., & Coles, R. (2007). *Particle Swarm Optimisation for learning Bayesian Networks*. Engineering and Physical Sciences Research Council.

Djan-Sampson, P. O., & Sahin, F. (2004). Structural Learning; of Bayesian Networks from Complete Data using the Scatter Search Documents. *Proceedings IEEE International Conference on Systems, Man, and Cybernetics*. 10.1109/ICSMC.2004.1400904

Fan, X., & Malone, C. Y. (2014). *Tightening Bounds for Bayesian Network Structure Learning*. Association for the Advancement of Artificial Intelligence.

Faruqi, S. H., Alaeddini, A., Jaramillo, C. A., Potter, J. S., & Pugh, M. J. (2018). Mining patterns of comorbidity evolution in patients with multiple chronic conditions using unsupervised multi-level temporal Bayesian network. *PLoS One*, *13*(7), 1–22. doi:10.1371/journal.pone.0199768 PMID:30001371

Fast, A. S. (2010). *Learning the Structure of Bayesian Networks with Constraint Satisfaction*. Massachusetts: (PHD Thesis), Department of Computer Science, University of Massachusetts, February 2010.

Fortier, N., Sheppard, J., & Pillai, K. G. (2013). Abductive Inference using Overlapping Swarm Intelligence. *Proceedings 2013 IEEE Symposium on Swarm Intelligence (SIS), pp. 263-270. IEEE.*.

Friedman, N., Murphy, K., & Russell, S. (1998). Learning the structure of dynamic probabilistic networks. *Proceedings 14th Conference on Uncertainty in Artificial Intelligence (UAI-98)*, 139-147. San Francisco, CA: Morgan Kaufmann.

Gadekallu, T. R., & Khare, N. (2017). Cuckoo search optimized reduction and fuzzy logic classifier for heart disease and diabetes prediction. [IJFSA]. *International Journal of Fuzzy System Applications*, *6*(2), 25–42. doi:10.4018/IJFSA.2017040102

Gandomi, A. H., Yang, X.-S., Marand, S. T., & Alavi, A. H. (2013). *Metaheuristic applications in structures and infrastructures*. USA: Elsevier.

Gao, T., & Wei, D. (2018). Parallel Bayesian Network Structure Learning. *35th International Conference on Machine Learning*. PMLR 80, 1685-1694. Stockholm, Sweden.

Gillispie, S. B., & Pearlman, M. D. (2001). Enumerating Markov Equivalence Classes of Acyclic Digraph Models. *Proceedings of the Seventeenth conference on Uncertainty in artificial intelligence* (pp. 171-177). California: Morgan Kaufmann.

He, C.-C., & Gao, X.-G. (2018, July 25-27). Structure Learning of Bayesian Networks Based On the LARS-MMPC Ordering Search Method. Wuhan, China: *Chinese Control Conference* 10.23919/ChiCC.2018.8483049

Heckerman, D., Geiger, D., & Chickering, D. M. (1995). Learning Bayesian networks: The combination of knowledge and statistical data. *Machine Learning, 20*(3), 197–243. doi:10.1007/BF00994016

Hesar, A. S. (2013). Structure Learning of Bayesian Belief Networks Using Simulated Annealing Algorithm. *Middle East Journal of Scientific Research, 18*, 1343–1348.

Ji, J., Wei, H., & Liu, C. (December 2012). An artificial bee colony algorithm for learning Bayesian networks. *Springer-Verlag Berlin Heidelberg*.

Kareem, S., & Okur, M. C. (2017). Evaluation Of Bayesian Network Structure Learning. *Proceedings 2nd International Mediterranean Science and Engineering Congress (IMSEC 2017)* (pp. 1313-1319). Adana, Turkey: Çukurova University.

Kareem, S., & Okur, M. C. (2018). *Bayesian Network Structure Learning Using Hybrid Bee Optimization and Greedy Search. Adana*, Turkey: Çukurova University.

Kareem, S. W., & Okur, M. C. (2019). Bayesian Network Structure Learning Based On Pigeon Inspired Optimization. *International Journal of Advanced Trends in Computer Science and Engineering, 8*(1.2), 131-137.

Khanteymoori, A., Olayee, M. H., Abbaszadeh, O., & Valian, M. (2018). A novel method for Bayesian networks structure learning based on Breeding Swarm algorithm. *Soft Computing*, 9.

Koski, T., & Noble, J. M. (2009). *Bayesian Networks-An Introduction.* Wiley series in probability and statistics.

Kulkarni, A. J., Krishasamy, G., & Abraham, A. (2017). *Cohort Intelligence: A Socio-inspired Optimization Method.* Springer. doi:10.1007/978-3-319-44254-9

Larraiiaga, P., & Poza, M. (1996). Structure Learning of Bayesian Networks by Genetic Algorithms. Berlin, Germany: Springer-Verlag.

Li, J., & Chen, J. (2014). A Hybrid Optimization Algorithm for Bayesian Network Structure Learning Based on Database. *Journal of Computers, 9.*

Li, S., & Wang, B. (2017). *A Method for Hybrid Bayesian Network Structure Learning from Massive Data Using MapReduce.* IEEE. doi:10.1109/BigDataSecurity.2017.42

Mandal, S. (2018). Elephant swarm water search algorithm for global optimization. Indian Academy of Sciences.

Margaritis, D. (2003). *Learning Bayesian Network Model Structure from Data.* Pittsburgh, PA. Available as Technical Report: Carnegie-Mellon University.

Mirjalili, S., Mirjalili, S. M., & Lewis, A. (2014). A grey wolf optimizer. *Advances in Engineering Software, 69*, 46–61. doi:10.1016/j.advengsoft.2013.12.007

Nagarajan, R., Scutari, M., & Lèbre, S. (2013). *Bayesian Networks in R with Applications in Systems Biology.* New York: Springer. doi:10.1007/978-1-4614-6446-4

Orphanou, K., Thierens, D., & Bosman, P. A. (2018). *Learning Bayesian Network Structures with GO-MEA. kyoto*. Japan: ACM.

Pe'er, D., Regev, A., Elidan, G., & Friedman, N. (2001.). Inferring Subnetworks from Perturbed Expression Profiles. *Ninth International Conference on Intelligent Systems for Molecular Biology (ISMB)*. Copenhagen, Denmark. Academic Press.

Pourret, O., & Naim, P. (2008). Bayesian networks: a practical guide to applications. UK: John Wiley & Sons, The Atrium, Southern Gate, Chichester, West Sussex PO19 8SQ. doi:10.1002/9780470994559

Reddy, T. G., & Kare, N. (2016). FFBAT-optimized rule based fuzzy logic classifier for diabetes. International Journal of Engineering Research in Africa Trans Tech Publications, 137-152.

Robinson, R. (1977). Counting Unlabeled Acyclic Digraphs. Springer- Verlag, 622.

Salama, K. M., & Freitas, A. A. (2012). ABC-Miner: An Ant-Based Bayesian Classification Algorithm.

Sencer, S., Oztemel, E., Taskin, H., & Torkul, O. (2013). Bayesian Structural Learning with Minimum Spanning Tree Algorithm. *Proceedings of the International Conference on Information and Knowledge Engineering (IKE) (p. 1). The Steering Committee of The World Congress in Computer Science, Computer Engineering and Applied Computing (WorldComp)*.

Silva, L. A., Bezzera, J. B., Perkusich, M. B., Gorgônio, K. C., Almeida, H. O., & Perkusich, A. (2018). Continuous Learning of the Structure of Bayesian Networks: A Mapping Study. In F. U. Grande (Ed.), *Bayesian Networks - Advances and Novel Applications* (pp. 1–15). Paraíba, Brazil: Intechopen.

Sun, X., Chen, C., Wang, L., Kang, H., Shen, Y., & Chen, Q. (2019). Hybrid Optimization Algorithm for Bayesian Network Structure Learning. *Information*, 1-16.

Tahier, T., Marie, S., Girard, S., & Forbes, F. (2019). Fast Bayesian Network Structure Learning using Quasi-Determinism Screening. *HAL*, *2*, 14–24.

Tong, S., & Koller, D. (2001). Active Learning for Structure in Bayesian Networks. *Proceedings International joint conference on artificial intelligence*, *17*(1), pp. 863-869. Lawrence Erlbaum Associates.

Wang, G.-G., Deb, S., & Coelho, L. (2015). *Elephant Herding Optimization*. IEEE. doi:10.1109/IS-CBI.2015.8

Wang, J., & Liu, S. (2018). Novel binary encoding water cycle algorithm for solving Bayesian network structures learning problem. *Knowledge-Based Systems*, *150*, 150. doi:10.1016/j.knosys.2018.03.007

Xin, J., Chen, G., & Hai, Y. (2009). A particle swarm optimizer with multistage linearly-decreasing inertia weight. *Proceedings International Joint Conference on Computational Sciences and Optimization*. 10.1109/CSO.2009.420

Yang, C., Ji, J., Liu, J., Liu, J., & Yin, B. (2016). Structural learning of Bayesian networks by bacterial foraging optimization. *International Journal of Approximate Reasoning*, *69*, 69. doi:10.1016/j.ijar.2015.11.003

Yang, S. X. (2010). New metaheuristic bat-inspired algorithm. *Nature Inspired Cooperative Strategies for Optimization*, *284*, 65–74. doi:10.1007/978-3-642-12538-6_6

Yuan, C., Malonean, B., & Wu, X. (2011). Learning Optimal Bayesian Networks Using A* Search. NSF grants IIS-0953723 and EPS-0903787, 21 IJCAI. Barcelona, Spain.

Zhang, S.-Z., & Liu, L. (2008). *Mcmc Samples Selecting for Online Bayesian Network Structure Learning*. Kunming: IEEE.

Zhang, Y., Liu, J., & Liu, Y. (2018). Bayesian Network Structure Learning: The Two-Step Clustering-Based Algorithm. Association for the Advancement of Artificial Intelligence, 8183-8184.

Chapter 9
Multi–Objective Optimal Power Flow of Integrated Renewable Systems Using a Novel Evolutionary Algorithm

Barun Mandal

Kalyani Government Engineering College, India

Provas Kumar Roy

 https://orcid.org/0000-0002-3433-5808

Kalyani Government Engineering College, India

ABSTRACT

This chapter introduces an approach to explain optimal power flow (OPF) for stochastic wind and conventional thermal power generators-based system. In this chapter, grasshopper optimization algorithm (GOA) is implemented to efficiently prove its superiority for solving wind-based OPF problem. Diminishing carbon emissions is a significant goal for the entire world; a tremendous penetration of unpredictable wind energy can assist in reducing emissions. In the previous decade, the access of renewable energy opening for energy production has improved significantly. WE has become an important source that has begun to be used for energy all over the world in recent years. The optimal dispatch between thermal and wind units to minimize the total generating costs and emission are considered as multi-objective (MO) model. In MO optimization, whole electrical energy generation costs and burning emissions are concurrently minimized. The performance of aforesaid approach is exercised and it proves itself as a superior technique as compared to other algorithms revealed in the literature.

DOI: 10.4018/978-1-7998-3222-5.ch009

1. INTRODUCTION

Presently, more than seventy percent of the world electricity requirements are supplied by heating fossil fuels, such as coal, natural gas and crude oil. Conventional fossil fuels are expected to be depleted due to growing demand and rapid industrialization. Bringing CO_2 emissions under control has motivated developing countries to invest in alternative energies. Conventional based thermal power station discharges carbon dioxide (CO_2), sulphur oxides (SOx) and nitrogen oxides (NOx) into the air. Furthermore, the polluted emission is the mainly preferred calculation as its ease of discharge. Energy may be obtained from conventional sources (fossil fuels such as coal, natural gas and oil), or from renewable sources (wind, solar, biomass, geothermal, etc.). Now, renewable energy resources have received considerable attention to achieve environmentally friendly power generation. Renewable energy based sources have many advantages, including sustainability, low pollution, and economic benefits. Furthermore, OPF is special of the primary comprehensive mechanism used in the power system planning, control, process and competitive electricity business market. Its primary objective is to propose high-class electrical power or energy at a nominal cost. In addition, the OPF problem has been considered in power system research because of the enhancement of classical mathematics methods. The main objective of the OPF problem is to find the optimal adjustments of the power system control variables to minimize the selected objective function while satisfying various equality and inequality constraints. However, the OPF problem is an optimization problem within general nonconvex, non-smooth, and non-differentiable objective functions. OPF is usually used for considering the most favourable settings of a known power system that combines various objectives, for example, fuel cost, emission, active power loss, etc. However, as power systems are getting more complex, the OPF problems turn to be more difficult to handle. Power system engineers need unique tools to optimally evaluate, control different aspects and monitor of power systems planning and operation. Although several of these approaches have good convergences' characteristics, few of their main drawbacks are associated with their convergence to local results rather than global ones, but the initial guess is situated within a confined solution neighbourhood.

Many traditional optimization techniques like linear programming (LP) (Mota, & Quintana, 1986), nonlinear programming (NLP) (Alsac, & Stott, 1974; Shoults, & Sun, 1982), quadratic programming (QP) (Burchett, Happ, & Vierath, 1984), Newton method and interior point method (IPM) (Wei, Sasaki, Kubokawa, & Yokoyama, 1998; Yan, & Quantana, 1999; Momoh, &Zhu, 1999) have already been employed to explain the OPF problem. Over the last three decades, many successful algorithms have been established (Momoh, EL-Hawary, & Adapa, 1999; Momoh, EL-Hawary, & Adapa, 1999) like successive linear programming, Newton method, generalized reduced gradient method, successive quadratic programming, etc. It objectives at optimizing few objectives by acting on accessible control should satisfy system load flow equations, operational and physical constraints. With the aim of overcome the boundaries of classical optimization methods, a wide diversity of the heuristic approaches have been proposed to explain OPF, such as genetic algorithm (GA) (Lai, Ma, Yokoyama, & Zhao, 1997; Bakirtzis, Biskas, Zoumas, & Petridis, 2002), simulated annealing (SA) (Roa-Sepulveda, & Pavez-Lazo, 2003; Sousa, Soares, Vale, Morais, & Faria, 2011), tabu search (TS) (Abido, 2002), differential evolution (DE) algorithm (Sayah, & Zehar, 2008; Nayak, Krishnanand, & Rout, 2011), harmony search (HS) algorithm (Sivasubramani, & Swarup, 2011), and biogeography based optimization (BBO) (Roy, Ghoshal, &Thakur, 2010; Rarick, Simon, Villaseca, & Vyakaranam, 2009). While evolutionary algorithms utilize a population of solutions, they can produce a feasible solution in order to maintain various set of solutions in the first run. Last few years, several evolutionary optimization methods have been applied to explain complex controlled optimization problems in the area of power systems. This condition arises when prohibited operating zones, piece-wise quadratic cost and valve-points unit characteristics are present (Sayah, & Zehar, 2008). Hence, none of the above techniques are able to provide an optimal solution. Different economic aspects of wind power integration have been considered in the current literature. Huge integrations of the wind energy production and full utilization of carbon detain facilities on coal-fired units can remarkably decrease the CO_2 emitted into the air. As compared to the usual generator, the wind-based turbine has the benefit of reducing the dependence on conventional fuels, pollutant emission and the transmission power losses. Increasing electrical power consumption often leads to upgrading and extending distribution networks and existing power transmission to deliver all customers effectively, economically and sufficiently. Widespread investigations have been devoted to the synchronized optimization difficulty in a hybrid generating station. Recently, wind energy has played a major role in the global energy transformation trend. A good suggestion, but the incorporation of a considerable amount of irregular natural sources like wind energy has carefully balanced full awareness for simple, fresh and economic aspects. Wind energy, a natural source of fresh energy and can reduces the consumptions of depleting energy sources and pollutant emissions. Although dissimilar usual power systems the natural random and inconsistency of wind power have most confused for the power system process (Su, Wang, & Roh, 2014). Besides, the operation of large-scale energy storage in the system to create use of excess energy by optimizing its discharge and renew cycles is a challenge. To minimize operating costs, it usually increases the application for more competent conventional generation groups, which can guidance to superior fuel consumption, lower level fuel usage, and substantial compact pollutants. Many researchers and practitioners have studied energy storage in power systems. With the expansion of science and technologies, the larger capacity of the modern wind power station can be as good as to that of traditional other units. Wind power integration and generation have confirmed to be one of the vital economic and established non-conventional energy technologies. The advancement of wind potential in the world has expanded exponentially in the previous decades. However, only a few numerous investigations have been made at the forecast of wind activity for service in controlling the possible wind capacity. The process requires definite hourly wind velocity data recorded over an extended phase for the particular geographic site to construct a wind speed simulation model for the specific site. Among the all renewable energy, the wind has shown massive penetration in power systems around the globe. The mixture of wind power production with higher than twenty percent entrance layers requires new administration and spinning reserve effects for grid constancy purposes. With the increase of wind acceleration, the power developed by the turbine will boost as the cubic of the wind velocity. However, the unpredictability environment of wind velocity follows to the intermittent of wind energy generation of wind turbines. Besides all the sustainable sources, the wind has owned strongly well-recognized it's as a wide spread opportunity for humankind (Council GWE, 2012). The original wind turbines to produce electricity in the countryside U.S.A. was installed in 1890. The majority of this renewable energy gets from wind as other renewable sources are not appropriate for mass power generation.

The Monte Carlo, interval and robust maximizations are amid the theoretical data processing methods which are projected in (Quan, Srinivasan, Khambadkone, & Khosravi, 2015; Shabanzadeh, Sheikh-El-Eslami, & Haghifam, 2015; Bai, Li, Cui, Jiang, Sun, & Zhu, 2016), to employ the unpredictability related close to wind power production, electricity market prices and load values. Incorporating wind power into the existing conventional units introduces various threats to the process, control and operating actions for all services. Throughout the world, projects connecting extensive penetration of wind potential toward the network additional offshore wind plant establishment are massively gaining attention (Bonou,

Laurent, & Olsen, 2016). The lesser value of wind penetration and exactly no polluted gas discharge are the main objectives of wind potential.

There is a specific necessitate in the effective optimization of the networks which can help in the minimization of operational expenditure as well as the total loss of the arrangement. Researchers across the globe have extensively studied OPF with only thermal power generators. Several conventional OPF techniques are linear programming, non-linear programming, Newton-Raphson, gradient methods, quadratic programming and interior point. Earlier, many traditional (mathematical based) methods like quadratic programming, gradient method, linear programming method, non-linear programming and mixed-integer linear programming methods are developed to answer the OPF problem (Monticelli, Pereira, & Granville,1987; Alsac, Bright, Prais, & Stott, 1990; Alsac, & Stott, 1974). However, for a big scale system, the usual techniques have oscillatory issues resulting in much more solution time. These methods frequently use approximations to range the difficulty of the problem and the solution obtained from these techniques is trapped in the local best possible. Recently, Majid et al. (Majid, & Louis, 2017), proposed a MO stochastic OPF which includes the operational amount, voltage stability index and pollutant discharge as the main purpose operations. The IEEE 39-bus verified these approaches.

Abarghooee et al (Abarghooee, Golestaneh, Gooi, Lin, Bavafa, & Terzija, 2016), presented a probabilistic unit commitment crisis with incentive-related demand response and more penetration of wind power. The proposed structure was applied to a very small test system with 10 units and as well to the IEEE 118-bus system to demonstrate its advantages in active scheduling of production in the power systems. Bai et al. (Bai, & Lee, 2016), in their paper tackled the capture the uncertainty of wind energy was by the purpose-based method and later the simulation based trouble became deterministic over each situation and artificial bee colony (ABC), was tested to exercise the modified IEEE 30-bus systems. Optis et al (Optis, Perr-Sauer, 2019), examined the issue of atmospheric stability inputs and turbulence on statistical model forecasts of wind farm power generation. Based on this job, they suggested that turbulence and stability variables turn into standard inputs into statistical structures of wind farm energy production. JunHua et al. (JunHua, Fushuan, Zhao, Yusheng, & Kit, 2012), proposed an optimization method by conventional particle swarm optimization (PSO) along with interior point mechanism to explain the profitable complete simulation. The mentioned methods were verified on IEEE 118-bus standard system in consideration of the unpredictability of plug-in electric conveyances and wind turbines. Khalid et al (Khalid, Aguilera, Savkin, & Agelidis, 2018), proposed a framework to extend an OPF strategy for grid-linked wind power plants consist of a battery energy storage system (BESS). Their obtained solutions depict the efficiency of the strategy to assist power system companies in ensuring cost-effectively optimal power dispatch. Rasoul et al. (Rasoul, Taher, Mohammad, & Mohsen, 2014), suggested a new algorithm named combined differential evolution and modified cuckoo search algorithm to take out the Pareto optimal surface for least cost and highest chance of taking the objective cost and joins just as the objectives. The proposed method was applied to six and forty unit standard systems. Zhang et al. (Zhang, Miao, Zhang, & Wang, 2018), proposed a parameter-adaptive variational mode decomposition method based on GOA to analyze vibration signals from rotating machinery. They demonstrated that the proposed method is effective to analyze machinery vibration signal for fault diagnosis. John et al. (John, David, & Kalu, 2008), presented the solutions of wind-based OPF problem, and these results demonstrated that the portion of power generation quantity might be motivated by multipliers connected to the safety of overestimation cost and underestimation cost of usable of wind energy generation. In (Yashen, Jeremiah, & Johanna, 2016), Yashen et al. analyzed the impacts of emission in a test system and identified important drivers that affect the environmental outcomes. In this paper, Morshed et al (Morshed,

Hmida, & Fekiha, 2018), formulated and explained a probabilistic optimal power flow (POPF) solution for a mixture power system that comprises photovoltaic (PV), wind energy (WE) and plug-in electric vehicles (PEV) sources. The achievement of the recommended approach was assessed using the IEEE 30-bus, IEEE 57-bus and IEEE118-bus power systems. Ting et al. (Ting, Qiang, Zhejing, & Wenjun, 2013), addressed a stochastic structure given the ambiguities of wind power formation as well as the analytical plug-in electric vehicles driving patterns. In (Morteza, Masoud, & Mahmud, 2015), Morteza et al. reviewed the probabilistic method analyzed for probabilistic OPF (P-OPF) problems and proposed a new and influential approach applying the unscented transformation (UT) technique. Adaryani et al. (Adaryani, & Karami, 2013), proposed artificial bee colony (ABC) approach was committed as the chief optimizer for optimal modifications of the power system regulated control variables of the OPF problem. The efficiency and validity of the projected method was verified with the IEEE 9-unit system, IEEE 30-unit system and IEEE 57-unit system. The analysis results were examined through the results established by other heuristic algorithms reported in the journal in recent past.

Alham et al. (Alham, Elshahed, Ibrahim, & Zahab, 2016), proposed a dynamic economic emission dispatch (DEED) form absorbing massive wind energy entrance taking into account peculiar intermittency and condition of unpredictability. Results of this paper showed the importance of using energy storage scheme and demand-side supervision in dropping fuel cost and pollutant emission equally and rising the wind power consumption. Rahman et al. (Rahman & Saleh, 2018) presented a summary of significant hybrid bio-inspired computational intelligence (CI) techniques for power system optimization problem. Amirsaman et al. (Amirsaman, Mahmoud, & Mehdi, 2013), examined the storage request and its best possible position for the community return and long transmission over crowding help of wind power regularity. This method was utilized to carry out a price based study of the IEEE 24-bus structure. Bahman et al. (Bahman, Ebrahim, & Rasoul, 2013), presented the dynamic economic emission dispatch issue by integrating wind power generation. To calculate the usefulness and capability of the suggested framework, the considered issue was tested to two studies with small-scale and large-scale. Biswas et al. (Biswas, Suganthan, & Amaratunga, 2017), proposed an efficient optimization approach to solve OPF connecting stochastic solar power and wind power with fossil fuel based thermal generators in the hybrid system. Basu (Basu, 2011), presented MODE to optimize generation cost, active power transmission loss and emission of flexible ac transmission systems (FACTS) device-equipped for power systems. The recommended approach was examined and verified on the revised IEEE 30-bus and 57-bus study systems.

Chang et al. (Chang, Lee, Chen, & Jan, 2014), studied an evolutionary particle swarm optimization (EPSO) method for the crisis of OPF. They used the load data and system data of newly adapted IEEE 30-bus system to analyze the latest method. Chen et al. (Chen, Wei, Liu, & Mei, 2016), suggested a distributionally healthy thermal-hydro-wind economic dispatch (DR-HTW-ED) scheme to progress the simplicity and consistency of power generation. The proposed DR-HTW-ED was verified with ARO set hydro-thermal-wind economic dispatch (AR-HTW-ED) problem. Dubey et al. (Dubey, Pandit, & Panigrahi, 2015), implemented a result of dynamic multi-objective optimal dispatch (DMO-OD) for the wind and thermal mixture arrangement using a recent approach hybrid flower pollination algorithm (HFPA). The proposed algorithm was verified on two thermal-wind assessment systems from popular literature. Chen et al. (Chen, Bo, & Zhu, 2014), proposed a multi-hive multi objective bee algorithm (M^{2}OBA) used for OPF in modern power systems. The IEEE 30-bus test system was explored to demonstrate the purpose of the projected algorithm. Hu et al. (Hu, Zhang, Wang, Li, & Hu, 2016), they presented an innovative idea on dynamic economic emission dispatch (DEED) approached on robust optimization (RO) and bi-level programming (BLP) in the other side of extensive wind potential associated into power system grid. The solution methodologies of the projected model were tested to three studies with unlike mixtures of wind based power to estimate their viability and efficiency. Morshed et al. (Morshed, Hmida, & Fekih, 2018), presented and solved a probabilistic OPF method (POPF) for a wind incorporating mixture power system which keeps wind energy (WE), photovoltaic (PV) and plug-in electric vehicles (PEV) sources. The credential of the presented access was applied with the IEEE 30-bus, IEEE 57-bus and IEEE 118-bus unit combinations. Reddy et al. (Reddy, & Bijwe, 2016) proposed the assessment of 'best-fit' membership portions by pleasing into the explanation of solar energy, wind energy and load demand for RT-OPF, and DA-OPF, over a specific time span due to the minute-to-minute variability. IEEE 30-bus combination was applied to check the success of the projected algorithm regarding system safety and economic benefit.

In this study, Ghasemi et al. (Ghasemi, Ghavidel, Ghanbarian, Gharibzadeh, & Vahed, 2014) presented an innovative Multi-Objective Modified Imperialist Competitive Algorithm (MOMICA) for the MOOPF problem. The utility of multi-objective algorithms was considered and checked on the regular IEEE 30-bus and IEEE 57-bus modern power systems. Amirsaman et al. (Amirsaman, Mahmoud, & Mehdi, 2013), examined the storage request and its perfect position for the community price and transmission blockage support of wind power integration. They were tested to bring out a financial-benefit study of the IEEE 24-bus scheme and determined the utmost reasonable technology. Krishnasamy et al. (Krishnasamy, & Nanjundappan, 2016), implemented dynamic ELD problem for minimizing the total cost per hour of generation of thermal wind hybrid system by utilizing the hybridized edition of the weighted probabilistic approach of neural network with the biogeography-based approach of optimization. The efficiency of the technique was verified by comparing the performances of the current mechanism with that of the presenting procedures presented in the research. Mandal et al. (Mandal & Roy, 2014) suggested quasi-oppositional teaching learning based optimization (QOTLBO) method was resolved on IEEE 30-bus system, Indian utility 62-bus system and IEEE 118-bus system to explain four different single objectives, namely system power loss, minimization fuel cost minimization, emission minimization and voltage stability index minimization. Their recommended approach presents superiority of the individual along with the compromising results than other methods. Lau et al. (Lau, Yang, Taylor, Forbes, Wright, & Livina, 2016) proposed the expenses and carbon compensating approach in the economic dispatch (ED) trouble of the entire process considering the difficulty and multiplicity of the power system. Lee et al. (Lee, Lin, Liao, & Tsao, 2011), proposed the quantum genetic algorithm (QGA) to explain the ELD problem that includes generation of wind capacity. Mondal et al. (Mondal, Bhattacharya, & Halder, 2013), applied gravitational search algorithm to economic emission load dispatch (EELD) approach to reducing the discharge of nitrogen oxides (NO_x) and combustible price, taking into consideration together thermal and wind generators.

A novel PV/wind/ battery mixture power source was designed by Fathabadi (Fathabadi, 2018) to change the internal combustion mechanism with a small-size photovoltaic (PV) module located on the top of the PHEV, and a micro wind turbine situated before the PHEV, last the condenser of the air conditioning arrangement. A prototype of the PV/wind/battery mixture power source was constructed and experimented verifications were explored that openly demonstrate utilizing the micro wind turbine and PV module. Mohammad et al. (Mohammad, & Alireza, 2014),demonstrated an advanced approach related to a combination approach adding of the sequential quadratic programming (SQP) algorithm and imperialist competitive algorithm (ICA) to answer the economic load dispatch (ELD) trouble of the power system. To calculate its efficiency, the proposed technique was verified on different power systems units like 6, 13, 15, and 40 units in the bus structure in addition to allowing for wind capability integration.

These methods can obtain the high quality of solutions by accumulating several complicated constraints. With the improvement of computer science and technology, innovative processes have been successfully utilized to resolve the OPF based problem. These approaches are able of providing good quality solutions in the lesser computational effort. Though, all those approaches discussed above generally offer quick and practical explanations but do not the assurance to obtain the optimal on the whole clarification.

In this article, a latest powerful optimization algorithm named grasshopper optimization (GO) is proposed to answer the OPF problem. Mirjalili et al (Mirjalili S, & Lewis A, 2016) proposed GO algorithm to determine optimal solution for optimization problem. GOA is a population based algorithm which is mimicking the behavior of grasshopper swarms and their social interaction. There life has two phases are nymph and adulthood. The nymph grasshoppers have no wings so they move slowly and eat all vegetation on their path. The unique aspect of the grasshopper swarm is that the swarming behavior is found in both nymph and adulthood. Food source seeking is another important characteristic of the swarming of grasshoppers by dividing the search process into two tendencies: exploration and exploitation.

Beside this, Saxena presented implications of different chaotic sequences on the performance of GOA (Saxena, 2019). Results revealed that the proposed variants exhibit better exploration and exploitation properties as compared to the parent algorithm. Buker et al (Bukar Tan, & Lau, 2019) proposed a latest nature-inspired metaheuristic optimization algorithm named GOA in the area of microgrid system sizing design problem and the effectiveness of the proposed GOA is solved and its performance is compared with literature. Ewees et al. (Ewees, Elaziz, & Houssein, 2018) presented an improved version of the original GOA using the OBL strategy for solving benchmark optimization functions and engineering problems. Mafarja et al. (Mafarja, Aljarah, Faris, Hammouri, Al-Zoubi, & Mirjalili, 2019) presented binary variants of GOA in their work and employed to select the optimal feature subset for classification purposes within a wrapper-based framework. Moreover, multi objective version of GOA was proposed by Tharwat et al. (Tharwat A, Houssein EH, Ahmed MM, Hassanien AE, & Gabel T, 2017).

The success of GOA algorithm in various area of optimization encourages the present authors to implement in renewable energy based OPF problem. In this article, the trade-off among emission and cost minimization objectives are proposed for mixing of the wind and thermal power system to solve the OPF problem. In view of the leading, this present work proposed GOA to solve multi-objective approach for power flow optimization in hybrid wind based power systems. This article aims to integrate wind-powered generators into the traditional OPF problem and to examine the problem via mathematical solutions. In this article, the GO method has been clarified to solve the OPF problem with a non-smooth cost formula. In the current work, the efficiency of the proposed GOA is verified for the explanation of OPF problem of IEEE 30-bus and IEEE 57-bus test power systems with two unlike individual objectives like the reduction of emission and fuel cost minimization. The formulated OPF problem and GO techniques are altogether verified through the IEEE 30-bus arrangement and IEEE 57-bus arrangement to prove its validness. The quality solution obtained by the announced finding is inspected with that of a few famous results to formulate it more practical and more justified.

The full of the manuscript is ordered as follows: Now, Section 2 presents complication methodology and constraints handling. In this section, wind energy modelings are also presented. The proposed GO principle for explaining the OPF problem is discussed in Section 3. Furthermore, in section 4, different categories are shown and programming outcomes are tabulated. Ultimately, the article concluded is in section 5. Finally, future scope of work is given in section 6.

2. PROBLEM FORMULATION

2.1 Modeling of Wind Energy Source

The multi-generation system is designed for various applications especially electricity, hydrogen and freshwater productions for sustainable development. A wind generator changes the kinetic energy of wind converted to mechanical energy, which is then harvested to generate electricity. In this article, wind energy has been used as suitable prime energy sources in this power system work. Since, the natural irregular nature of air, the productivity wind capability of a wind turbine is unpredicted. Due to the unpredictable and variable characteristics of wind power, its integration into the traditional thermal generation systems will incur the operator's concern on system security. Because of the irregular and changeable unique of wind based operating system and its addition to the conventional thermal generation power systems is very challenging. The aim of this recent research work is to resolve the highest penetration level of wind related formation, at the respective bus of the load distribution network, that reduces the total production cost and subject to the various power system constraints. Therefore, the most of the countries have produced considerable amount of wind power plant for dropping carbon productions and generation price for electrical energy production. Because of the inherent intermittent behavior of wind, the output power of a wind turbine is uncertain. Comparing with the traditional generator, the wind-based generator has the several advantages of decreasing the dependence on conventional fuels, pollutant emission and the transmission power losses, increasing the independence and improved changeability of large power system grid. The level of reactive and active powers for a particular purpose is balanced on the variable-speed expressions of the generator. Few researchers improve on the special things of up/down spinning reserves for covering the OPF of a thermal and wind mixture hybrid power plant or the effects of a wind operated generation system in OPF operations on the power generation system. As the wind power generation is free of charge source, its effective cost is so small which is carefully overlooked herein. Electric power and load demand must be balanced in real-time for the power system. Now, this has been a relevant field of research in some disciplines, such as marketing, policy, organizational behavior, economics, and the past of technology. This cost of wind drive is extremely competitive with the energy expenditure of the conventional power technologies.

2.1.1 Wind Energy

Wind power mixing is a crucial subject to address for achieving a reliable power system as well as wind power source. The fundamental basis of wind generated electrical power is transforming dynamic energy hence the wind to motor driven electrical operation applying wind turbines. As the wind velocity increases gradually, the power produced by the wind turbine will changes roughly proportional to the cubic factor of the wind velocity. The mechanical power captured by a wind turbine is proportional to the swept blade area (A), the air density (ρ), the wind velocity (υ) and the coefficient of power (Cp). A variation in the wind speed is common over the entire world; it can change in time, such as annual, inter-annual, diurnal and short-term. This method for calculating wind power generation from the wind power density (W/m2) considers wind power generation is proportional to the cubic of wind velocity i.e. υ^3. The wind power generated, W by the wind generator is formulated as a part of watts as follows:

$$W = \frac{1}{2}\rho A v^3 c_p \tag{1}$$

where A is the wind traversed area (m²); ρ is the density of air; υ denotes the velocity of air (m/s), where c_p is the value of power coefficient.

It is rightly established that probability apportionment of the uncertain wind velocity can be designed by the two-parameters of the Weibull distribution function. During any particular time period if the wind velocity 'υ_w' m/s may be described by Weibull distribution can be formulated as below (Yao, & Xu, 2012). The variations in wind speed are best formulated by the Weibull PDF 'f':

$$f(v_w) = \left(\frac{sf}{sp}\right)\left(\frac{v_w}{sf}\right)^{(k-1)} e^{-\left(\frac{v_w}{sf}\right)^k} \; for \; 0 < v_w < \infty \tag{2}$$

$$F(V_w) = 1 - e^{-(V_w/sf)k}, V_m > 0$$

Here 'sf' denotes scale ratio and 'sp' denotes shape parameters respectively, and the probability of wind speed being 'υ_w' during any time interval which collectively controls the extent of inconsistency and wind flow pattern.

2.1.2 Underestimation and Overestimation Cost

The wind is considered as the main factor that affects wind power. When the planned power is found to be less than the capacity of actual wind power available, the scenario is known as underestimation. There may be situations when the real available wind power could fall behind the planned value. The scenario is referred to as overestimation. In this situation, to moderate the power difference, extra costs are included to the objective purpose to manage the power difference during the underestimation (*UE*) and overestimation (*OE*) scenarios. Wind farm owners are remunerated depending upon the profit of the electricity market arrangement.

Present circumstance, to promote the power difference, extra costs are combined to the main desire function to handle the power inequality during the underestimation (UE) and overestimation (OE) purposes.

The straight cost formula of wind power plant of kth is computed, as follow (Morshed, Hmida, & Fekih, 2018):

$$Cost_{d,w}^k = d_w^k p_w^k \tag{3}$$

The under estimation cost and overestimation cost can be mathematical, determined as bellows (Morshed, Hmida, & Fekih, 2018):

$$Cost_{u,w}^k = K_{u,w}^k \int_{p_w^i}^{p_{w,r}^k} \left(p - p_{w,k} \right) f(p) dp \tag{4}$$

$$Cost_{o,w}^k = K_{o,w}^k \int_0^{p_{w,l}^k} \left(p_{w,k} - p \right) f(p) dp \tag{5}$$

Here $k=1,2,...,n_w$; $f(p)$ denotes the probability distribution function (PDF) of this estimated wind power generation.

The entire cost for the wind energy generation is calculated and formulated as given below for both the estimation (Morshed, Hmida, & Fekih, 2018):

$$COST_w^k = Cost_{d,w}^k + Cost_{u,w}^k + Cost_{o,w}^k \tag{6}$$

2.2 Objective Function

OPF crisis is one of the very significant problems in power system control and analysis. Solving the OPF difficulty consists of finding the most excellent operating levels used for electric power systems to meet up demand given all through a transmission network, mostly with the goal of minimizing operating cost and emission. As a result, all traditional generators can optimize nearby considering both the reserve and energy capacities to supervise the system wind velocity forecast uncertainties. At the present time, pollutants are the most important concerns when operating the fossil fuel operating power plants on the globe. There are different types of aims for which an OPF is determined and one of the most accepted objectives in the power system has been the emission minimisation, generation cost or a compromise solution among the two. The purpose of conventional OPF analysis is to reduce generation price for power production by determining a set of control variables although fulfilling network constraints and its operational requirements. It is well known to us that the total operating system loss is an objective of the electrical power output of all the operating generators. Majority of objectives of optimization is to take full advantage of the estimated profit or reduce the cost of the system fulfilling the system constraints of balance and irregularity at the equivalent time. In this article, the OPF issue includes wind generation units. Initially, the three objectives are taken to optimize independently using a single objective equation and later these objectives are optimized all together via the multi-objective equation.

In common, the OPF difficulty can be analytically explained as follows:

2.2.1 Single Objective Optimization

2.2.1.1 Fuel Cost Minimization

Although most OPF problems commit the total generation cost of the whole power system, a few cases having dissimilar objectives may be selected. It is expected that the OPF issue is a non-linear and non-convex type problem. But, the primary motto of the manuscript is to decrease the fuel cost by lessening the suitable values of the control parameters with respect to the different constraints like in-equal and equal conditions. The OPF is a practical non-straight, multimodal, non-convex and non-regular optimization issue which finds out the optimally suitable control variables for minimizing the specific objective functions subjected to some inequality and equality system constraints. In this manuscript, the costs of output power and pollutant emission are economized at the same time, subject to few inequality and equality constraints. The aim is to achieve the highest point allotment of power output within the existing generators with specified constraints. Three dissimilar equations of fuel expense function specifically, the quadratic price with valve-point effect, piecewise quadratic price expression and quadratic price express are taken in this consideration.

(A) Quadratic Fuel Cost Minimization

The generation cost expression (of kth production unit) is frequently formulated in a quadratic pattern of the operating power output. Mathematically, this target function is accepted as:

$$f_{FC} = Min\left[f(P_{Tgk}) + f(P_{Wgk})\right] = \sum_{k=1}^{NTG} f_k(P_{Tg_k}) + \sum_{k=1}^{NWG} f_k(P_{Wg_k})$$
$$= \sum_{k=1}^{NTG}(a_k + b_k P_{Tg_k} + c_k P_{Tg_k}{}^2) + \sum_{k=1}^{NWG} COST_{Wg_k} \tag{7}$$

here a_k, b_k as well as c_k are the cost-factors of the kth generating system; P_{Tg_k} is the operating generation of the kth thermal generator; P_{Wg_k} is the operating wind power at k^{th} wind generator; $COST_{Wg}$ is the total cost of wind generators as given in (6).

(B) Multi-Fuel Cost Objective

Practically, many generating units are equipped with various fuel connections that are coal, petroleum gas and crude oil and the production cost of operating units are calculated with only some piecewise quadratic cost equations. The consecutive equation represents the fuel for production cost expression of the operating generator worked in various types of fuel. By taking into consideration the multiple fuel function, the conventional quadratic fuel cost function modifies piecewise cost functions. The multi-fuel cost of OPFs can be written as follows:

$$f_{MFC} = \sum_{k=1}^{NTG} a_k + b_k P_{Tg_k} + c_k P_{Tg_k}{}^2 + \sum_{k=1}^{NWG} COST_{Wg_k} \text{ for fuel } k \text{ } P_{min}^{Tg_i} \le P_k \le P_{max}^{Tg_i} \tag{8}$$

(C) Valve-Point Effect Objective

In the practical procedure of thermal operated power plants, the output energy of generating units has been restricted by the closing or opening valves of steam running turbines. Approximate the cost plots by smooth quadratic formulas results in some errors due to not considering the ripples developed by the valve-point loading.

Working process of thermally generated industry, the active powers operation of thermal effecting systems have been guided by closing or opening gates of steam mechanisms. However, it is observed that the fuel cost obtains of any systems has non-differentiable marks suitable to the valve- point resolve and alteration of resources. To obtain a suitable model that it is to be considered of valve-point effect for the generator. The superimposed sinusoidal components signify the rippling effects created by the steam entrance valve openings. By taking into account the valve-loading effects of all physical system, a reappearing correcting sinusoidal part is accumulated to the primary quadratic fuel cost calculation, as below:

$$
\begin{aligned}
F_{VPE} &= Min\left(\sum_{k}^{m} F_k(P_k)\right) \\
&= Min\left(\sum_{k=1}^{NTG} a_k + b_k P_{Tg_k} + c_k P_{Tg_k}^2 + \left|e_k \times \sin\left\{f_k \times \left(P_{Tg_k}^{\min} - P_{Tg_k}\right)\right\}\right|\right) + \sum_{k=1}^{NWG} COST_{Wg_k}
\end{aligned}
\tag{9}
$$

2.2.1.2 Minimize the Real Power Losses

The control variable parameters are controlled in order to optimize the real power loss. Transmission line loss is a part of power loss which wastes because of the heat in transmission conductors. Solving load flow problems, the phase angle and voltage magnitude at every bus can be determined and these are optimized to attain the minimum active power losses.

The total associated resistance and the total associated conductance of respective transmission connected lines create ohmic losses and additional ohmic losses enhance the generated charges of power. Line loss is a part of the power which wastes as heat produce in transmission conductors. Using all load flow equations, the voltage magnitude in per unit and phase angle in radian for each bus can be calculated and these are solved to optimize to achieve the minimum true power losses. The entire MW true power waste in a long transmission system can be designated as formulates:

$$
f_{AL} = Min(TL_{Loss}) = Min\left[\sum_{i=1}^{NTL} g_i\left(V_j^2 + V_k^2 - 2V_j V_k \cos\alpha_{jk}\right)\right]
\tag{10}
$$

here, g_i is the magnitude of conductance associated with the kth and the jth connected bus of the ith transmission line; V_k, V_j are the values of voltage at the kth and the jth buses, correspondingly; NTL represents transmission lines numbers; α_{jk} is voltage angle in radian difference among the kth and the jth connected buses.

2.2.1.3 Emission Minimization Objective

The emission gasses produced by all generating units may be estimated by the addition of a quadratic function and an exponential function of the thermal plant output. Power generation presents itself today as a major challenge in terms of impact on the environment and human health. The atmospheric pollutants like nitrogen oxides (NOx) and sulfur oxides (SOx) created by the thermal plant can be modeled individually. In this article, SOx, NOx gases as the mainly pollutant gases are measured.

It is inevitable to produce electrical energy although emitting few harmful gases and increasing the atmospheric pollution. The total discharge of poisonous pollutants gases created by the process of exhausted-fueled based on steamy power manufacturing. The pollutants gases produce in the atmosphere by the conventional generators are the sulfur oxide (SO), nitrogen oxides (NOx) and sulfur oxides (SOx) produced can be designed individually. The pollutant emissions to the burning of fossil fuel like SO_2, SO_X and NO_X can be calculated through the equations that correlate emissions with power generation for every unit. Anyhow, for assessment ideas, the overall emission giving out during the operating phase can be formulated as observes:

$$f_E = \sum_{k=1}^{NTG} \alpha_k + \beta_k P_{Tg_k} + \gamma_k P_{Tg_k}^2 + \zeta_k \exp\left(\lambda_k P_{Tg_k}\right) \tag{11}$$

2.2.2.1 Multi-Objective Optimization

The majority of the real-world issues involve concurrently optimization of numerous objective functions. The objective of the MOOPF problem is to resolve the optimal control parameters for minimizing few objective functions comprising a set of inequality and equality constraints. In MOOPF we have few objective issues to be optimized simultaneously. In MO optimization, the objective is to determine the best probable trade-off between the objectives because, frequently, the single objective can be corrected simply at the price of worsening others. MO problems have a set of results because their optimality is that not anyone can be selected to be superior to anyone against every objective function. The MOOPF problem is complex to explain because it should consider the different complicated process and system constraints.

Within this section, the multi-objective OPF (MO-OPF) concern is also considered to minimize two challenging objective functions, that is to say, the cost of fuel and emission while fulfilling some equations ranges. In the real-life problem application, it frequently consists simultaneous equation of multiple-objectives functions, which generally clash with each of them. Multi-objective problem refers to the consecutive optimization of two or higher conflicting objectives that simulates well-set suitable solutions instead of the single particular solution whereas few constraints limits should be fulfilled. It aims is to optimize some chosen objective function concurrently through the best possible set of tuning control variables while achieving various inequality/equality constraints.

$$\text{Minimum}(F) = \text{Minimize}(foy_1, foy_2, \ldots, foy_t, \ldots foy_p), \, y = y_1, y_2, \ldots, y_n \tag{12}$$

With respect to the numerous equality and inequality limits:

$$y \in S \tag{13}$$

$$g_{ik}(y)=0; \, ik=1,2,\ldots,p \tag{14}$$

$$h_{jk}(y) \leq 0; \, jk=1,2,\ldots,q \tag{15}$$

where P is objective functions; $y_1, y_2, \ldots, y_n$ and $foy_1, foy_2, \ldots, foy_t, \ldots, foy_p$ are the control variables within the solution space S and the conflicting fitness, respectively. $h_j(y) \leq 0$ is the jth unlike equation, $g_i(y)=0$ is the ith similarity, q and p are the number of similar and dissimilar equation.

Multi-objective problem-based optimization is a very challenging and interesting job for new researchers to explain the optimization problem when concurrently satisfying many constraints. The objective of MO-OPF for the thermal-wind combined power plant is to catch the best match by conducting consecutive optimization of the three goals, i.e., overall generating cost and emission subject to many equations of different limits. In this case, fuel expenditure and emission are considered for solving OPF problem to simultaneously multi-objective function. Combining two functions with the fuel cost based desire operation and the emission development concern function look after the following problem to twofold object oriented function:

$$f_1 = f_{FC} + w_1 f_E \tag{16}$$

$$f_1 = \sum_{k=1}^{NTG} \left(a_k + b_k P_{Tg_k} + c_k P_{Tg_k}^2 \right) + w_1 \sum_{k=1}^{NTG} \alpha_k + \beta_k P_{Tg_k} + \gamma_k P_{Tg_k}^2 + \zeta_k \exp\left(\lambda_k P_{Tg_k} \right) \tag{17}$$

where w_1 acts a convenient equated weighting scale ratio, to be adjusted by the end user.

2.2.2.2 System Constraints

Power flow through every overhead line must be controlled by its physical capacity limits.

The OPF equality constraints follow the physics of the power system.

The system power balanced equation act as comply:

$$P_{Tg_i} + P_{Wg_i} - P_{d_i} - V_i \sum_{j=1}^{NB} V_j \left[g_{ij} \cos(\delta_i - \delta_j) + b_{ij} \sin(\delta_i - \delta_j) \right] = 0; i = 1,...,NB \tag{18}$$

$$Q_{Tg_i} + Q_{Wg_i} - Q_{d_i} - V_i \sum_{j=1}^{N_B} V_j \left[g_{ij} \sin(\delta_i - \delta_j) - b_{ij} \cos(\delta_i - \delta_j) \right] = 0; i = 1,...,NB \tag{19}$$

The in-equality constraints of the OPF overcome the restrictions on physical devices present in the power system as well as the limits created to guarantee system security.

The system generation limits are as follows:

$$P_{\min}^{T_{gi}} \leq P^{T_{gi}} \leq P_{\max}^{T_{gi}}; i = 1,...,NTG \tag{20}$$

$$P_{\min}^{Wg_i} \leq P^{Wg_i} \leq P_{\max}^{Wg_i}; i = 1,...,NWG \tag{21}$$

$$Q_{\min}^{Tg_i} \leq Q^{Tg_i} \leq Q_{\max}^{Tg_i}; i = 1,...,NTG \tag{22}$$

$$Q_{\min}^{Wg_i} \leq Q^{Wg_i} \leq Q_{\max}^{Wg_i}; i = 1,...,NWG \tag{23}$$

The system security constraints limits are as follows:

$$V_{\min}^{gi} \leq V^{gi} \leq V_{\max}^{gi}; i = 1, ..., NG \tag{24}$$

$$V_{\min}^{li} \leq V^{li} \leq V_{\max}^{li}; i = 1, ..., NL \tag{25}$$

$$T_{\min}^{i} \leq T^{i} \leq T_{\max}^{i}; i = 1, ..., NT \tag{26}$$

$$Q_{\min}^{ci} \leq Q^{ci} \leq Q_{\max}^{ci}; i = 1, ..., NC \tag{27}$$

$$S^{li} \leq S_{\max}^{li}; i = 1, ..., NTL \tag{28}$$

where g_{ij}, b_{ij} are the conductance and susceptance of the bus connected admittance elements in the matrix, successively, of the $(i,j)^{th}$ access; active power in watt and reactive power in volt-amp-reactive generation are P_{Tg_i}, Q_{Tg_i} of the ith thermal generator; active power in watt and reactive power in volt-amp-reactive generation are P_{Wg_i}, Q_{Wg_i} of the ith wind generator; $Q_{\min}^{Tg_i}$, $Q_{\max}^{Tg_i}$ are the generation of least and largest value of volt ampere reactive of the ith thermal generator; $Q_{\min}^{Wg_i}$, $Q_{\max}^{Wg_i}$ are the generation of least and largest value of reactive power of the ith wind turbine respectively; P_{di}, Q_{di}, are the true component of power and reactive component of power in load component of the ith bus; $V_{\min}^{gi}$ and $V_{\max}^{gi}$ are the ranges of voltages in least and largest value of the ith generator bus, correspondingly; $V_{\min}^{li}$, $V_{\max}^{li}$ are the limits of generator voltages of the ith load bus, respectively; $T_{\min}^{i}$, $T_{\max}^{i}$ are the higher and lower range of tap setting of transmission line of the ith transformer correspondingly; $Q_{\min}^{ci}$, $Q_{\max}^{ci}$ are the least and highest volt ampere reactive power injection range of the system of the ith shunt compensator, respectively; $S_{\max}^{li}$ is the highest volt ampere power flow in the ith transmission line.

3. GO ALGORITHM

GOA mimics the characteristic of grasshopper swarms in the environment for determining optimization problems. GOA is ready to develop the preliminary arbitrary population for various genuine problems. It shows excellent exploitation and exploration potentials for unidentified exploration spaces. Grasshoppers are pests, usually harmful in nature; they cause spoil to crop making and farming produce. The algorithm simulates attraction and repulsion forces among grasshoppers. Attraction forces allow grasshopper to exploit promising regions (local search), and the repulsion forces encourage them to explore the search space (global search). Grasshoppers execute these two movements along with natural looking for the objective (food source). The search freedom in the algorithm motivated from the environment is separated by two parts, namely, exploitation and exploration. The main characteristic of the swarm in the larval stage is the slow movement and tiny steps of the grasshoppers. The suggested approach has been used to solve the OPF issue for unlike cases with different objective functions with wind and without wind generation.

In this section, the latestswarm-based nature-inspired algorithm named grasshopper optimization (GO) proposed by Mirjalili et al (Mirjalili, & Lewis, 2016) is used. Grasshoppers are considered as one of the most harmful insect due to their damage to crop production and agriculture. The social interaction between grasshoppers is categorized into three zones, repulsion zone, comfort zone, and attraction zone. The target grasshopper starts attracting the other individual around its locations, and all grasshopper start moving towards the target grasshopper. There are two opposite forces between grasshoppers called attraction force and repulsion force. These two forces encourage exploring the search agent and exploiting promising regions respectively.

In the simulation study, GOA has been applied to answer the OPF issue of a hybrid power network. The authors in (Saremi, Mirjalili, & Lewis, 2017), proposed the GOA swarm algorithm, which emulates the behaviour of grasshopper insects. GOA inspired by nature latest method which imitates the swarming behavior of grasshopper in universal nature. The latest tools can make the superior answer and reach to its final value very fastly concerning conventional evolutionary methods. The brief overview of the algorithm is discussed below.

GO is a recently proposed evolutionary meta-heuristic algorithm motivated by the swarming activities of grasshoppers in the environment. In GO algorithm, a set of candidate solutions which represents a grasshopper are randomly calculated to make the initial artificial swarm. After that, all candidate agents calculated with viewed to the appropriateness values and the best look for the agent in the present swarm is considered as the target. Finally, target grasshopper is started to attracting the other individuals in the region of its position, and all grasshoppers initiate to moving towards the objective grasshopper.

The grasshopper swarm behaviour has been defined in two phases. First one, larval grasshoppers move slowly and with tiny steps, during the long range and no sequence movement drive adults. Next, seeking the process of the food source can be separated into two categories: exploration and exploitation. The individual positions of grasshopper express a complete candidate solution set of the OPF problem.

The progress of the ith grasshopper near the target grasshopper is represented as P_i and is mathematically calculated as in eqn (2) as follows (Mirjalili, & Lewis, 2016):

$$P_i = SA_i + GF_i + WA_i \qquad (29)$$

where SA_i the interaction of social; GF_i is the force of gravity on the ith grasshopper; WA_i is the wind advection and P_i describes the ith grasshopper the location or position.

From above the random behavior of the equation may be written as (Saremi, Mirjalili, & Lewis, 2017)

$$P_i = R_1 SA_i + R_2 GF_i + R_3 WA_i \qquad (30)$$

where R_1, R_2, and R_3 are randomly generated three numbers between [0,1].

The social interaction of the ith grasshopper (SA_i)is depended on the social two forces among two grasshoppers where an attraction force exists for aggregation purpose and a repulsion force to stop collisions over a small length scale and it is defined as (Saremi, Mirjalili, & Lewis, 2017):

$$SA_k = \sum_{\substack{l=1 \\ l \neq i}}^{N} SA(D_{kl})D_{kl} \tag{31}$$

here D_{kl} is the length of 'Euclidian' of the kth with the lth position grasshopper, and measured D_{kl} is $|X_k - X_l|$ and $\hat{D}_{lk} = \dfrac{X_k - X_l}{D_{lk}}$ is present unit vector between the kth with the lth grasshopper.

There are social interactions between grasshoppers that can be defined as attraction and repulsion. The 'SF' function is calculated as the strong point of social forces that can be considered as follows:

$$SF(R) = f_i e^{-R/L} - e^{-R} \tag{32}$$

where 'f_i' represents the intensity force of attraction and 'L' represents the length scale of attraction.

$$X_k^d = c \left(\sum_{\substack{l=1 \\ l \neq 1}}^{N} c \frac{U_B^d - L_B^d}{2} SF\left(\left|X_l^d - X_k^d\right|\right) \frac{X_l - X_k}{D_{lk}} \right) + \hat{T}_d$$

represents the intensities attraction strength and 'L' indicates the attractive force length of scale due to attraction. The 'SF' designated the force due to grasshopper on social interaction.

The 'GF' component is calculated as follows (Saremi, Mirjalili, & Lewis, 2017):

$$GF_i = -GF\hat{e}_g \tag{33}$$

where $\hat{e}_g$ represents a unity vector direction to the centre of earth and G_i is the constant of gravitational or gravity force.

The element WA_i is wind advection is designed as follows (Saremi, Mirjalili, & Lewis, 2017):

$$WA_i = U\hat{e}_g \tag{34}$$

where $\hat{e}_g$ represents a unity vector in associate with the wind and 'U' represents a constant drift.

The following equations can be obtained by substituting all components as follows (Saremi, Mirjalili, & Lewis, 2017):

$$X_k = \sum_{\substack{k=1 \\ k \neq 1}}^{N} SF\left(\left|X_l - X_k\right|\right) \frac{X_l - X_k}{D_{kl}} - GF\hat{e}_g + U\hat{e}_w \tag{35}$$

The eqn (35) is used and simulate the interactions connecting swarming of grasshoppers.

'N' express the number of grasshoppers and 'SF' is a function to defined as the generated strength of the social forces which used to describe the social forces (repulsion and attraction) of grasshopper which can be calculated and 'SF' function which used as the social forces (repulsion and attraction).

Here GOA, optimization methods are solved by a modified a new equation that designed excluding taking of gravity and wind assumption that is always towards the desired target.

Furthermore, this mathematical approach cannot be applied straightforward to explain optimization problems, mostly due to the grasshoppers speedily attain the comfort zone and the swarm doesn't converge to a particular point.

Now, the equation is utilized to calculate the connections among swarm grasshoppers.

$$x_l^d = c \left(\sum_{\substack{l=1 \\ l \neq 1}}^{N} c \frac{U_B^d - L_B^d}{2} SF\left(\left| X_k^d - X_l^d \right| \right) \frac{X_l - X_k}{D_{lk}} \right) + \hat{T}_d \tag{36}$$

where LB_d and UB_d are the lower limit and upper limit in the dth dimension respectively.

$\hat{T}_d$; acts target magnitude of dth dimension within objective grasshopper and 'c'; factor of reducing to the suitable zone of the repulsion region and attraction region. 'GF' component has not been considered for this case and the wind force 'WA' part is always towards the goal ($\hat{T}_d$). Eqn (36) proves that the modified next location of a grasshopper is defined based on its present location, the position of the goal, and the position of remaining grasshoppers. However, GOA updates the position of a search agent stationed on its present position, global best, and the location of other search agents. GOA requires every search agents to get performed in defining the later position of every search agent. For supervising the grade of exploitative and exploratory attitudes in GOA, the control parameter c should be reduced accordingly to the cycle of iterations. It is observed that inner 'c' has been used to reduce the search coverage towards the target grasshopper as varies to the iterations, and the outer c has been used to decreases the search coverage as the iteration counter increases. It is observed that the inside 'c' contributes to the decrease of attraction/repulsion forces among grasshoppers equal to the number of cycles, while the external 'c' reduces the exploration coverage around the objective as the iteration cycle increases.

C parameter has been upgraded with the following relation, and it should be inversely proportional to the executed iterations number (Saremi, Mirjalili, & Lewis, 2017).

$$C = C_{max} - l \frac{C_{max} - C_{min}}{L} \tag{37}$$

where c_{max}, c_{min} are the highest value and the lowest value of the factor 'c', respectively; 'l' and 'L' indicates the present iteration and entire number of iteration respectively.

In the final steps of optimization, though, grasshoppers will reach towards the goal as good as possible, which is important in exploitation.

Now, it should be calculated to the next new suitable location of a grasshopper is calculated by its present position, the final position and the position of remaining grasshoppers is calculated in eqn (36).

The computational flow chart of GOA is shown in the Figure 1. The algorithm steps of GO are as under:

1. Firstly, the candidate search approach shares its initial value haphazardly using its maximum and minimum values of uniform inflexible number choice within the space of the periphery of the control variables as per (2).

2. The GOA parameters have been given such that self number and the highest iterations.

3. The next position of the same grasshopper is calculated by its existing location, from target location and the position of new grasshoppers.

4. Generate new positions based on the finest respective of the preceding cycle.

5. Update the locations of the respective member to fulfill the limits, if essential.

6. Continue steps II–V until the breaking condition is achieved.

7. If the present number of repetition cycles reaches the predefined target cycles, the explore method is going to be stopped.

Figure 1. Flowchart of GOA

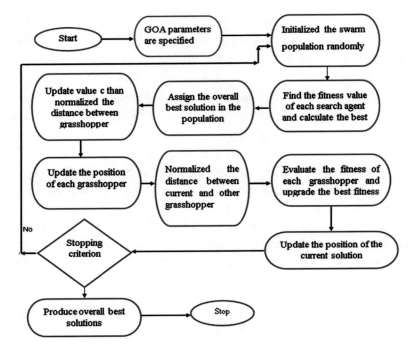

4. APPLICATION AND RESULTS

In current article, seven various cases have been considered. The proposed GO algorithm is implemented and extended with the MATLAB software. All cases of the programmes are conducted by MATLAB 2014 software on an Intel Core i5, processors 2.5 GHz with 4GB RAM and also employing parallel transforming to execute the algorithm for several runs simultaneously. A Dell makes a laptop with computer processor division Intel Core i5 is applied for every case study.

The suggested method has been tested to a modified test system which includes conventional thermal operated generators as well as wind generators units. To assess the feasibility of the GOA, two examples of power generations with IEEE 30-units and IEEE 57-units of MOOPF problems are applied. In response to assessing the performance of GO algorithm, the average, worst, best and standard deviation (SD) of the emission and production costs to get close to optimum results are used for assessment.

Various single and multi-target cases are analyzed to assess the execution of the newly developed suggested method in addition to the judgment for other approaches. To accept the robustness and performance of the presented GO approach for finding MO-OPF issue, regular IEEE 30-units and IEEE 57-units test systems are carefully studied. The total loads are modeled just as the permanent loads specified in the article. Then simulation results evaluated from GOA method with and without incorporating wind generation are compared with others algorithm available in the articles. The GO algorithm has been implemented to explain the OPF problem for different cases with dissimilar objective functions.

4.1 Test System 1: IEEE 30-Bus Test Power System

In order to express the performance, efficiency and robustness of the suggested GO algorithm is verified for solving IEEE 30-unit power system. In this initial assessment, five various studies have been considered with four single dissimilar objectives and one multi-objective with wind energy and without wind energy. This test system consists of 30 buses, 41 branches, six generators, nine reactive compensators and four transformers. There are two wind energy buses are considered in this present system i.e., 22 and 23 buses. The generator fuel cost coefficients with their restrictions, bus and line information are taken from (Ray, Zimmerman, & David, Matpower). The ranges of generator buses along with load connected buses are considered within 0.95 to 1.1 p.u, and 0.90 to 1.05 p.u., subsequently. The permissible ranges of the transformer to set taps are taken from 0.90 to 1.05 p.u., subsequently. The projected performance has been verified to explain the OPF type issue for various basics with various objective purposes. The results obtained after optimization for this newly developed GOA technique for all cases are examined with the established results of similar methods recorded in the current research. The GO method is implemented in the IEEE 30-bus power system to prove its performance. The objective functions that are tested in this article are the total emission and total cost of power generation individually and simultaneously of the units.

4.1.1 Minimization of Fuel Cost

Here, the IEEE 30-bus structure is considered for the first case judgment to find the effectiveness of the considered OPF issues considering the thermal and wind hybrid power plant. In this case, all generators generation costs characteristics are expressed as quadratic cost function. Further, IEEE 30-units system is rearranged carefully to agree on the wind generator inclusions at buses 22 and 23, respectively to test the proposed approach. The outcomes of the 1st case study are illustrated inside this part. Also, the power plant with wind power generation is also confirmed and established through the experimental results. The obtained dispatch outcomes of the GOA justification for the 30-unit assessment system (without and with wind power) are arranged in Table 1.

The generation costs in this scenario without wind power and with incorporating wind power are equal to 799.0000 $/hr and 795.6000 $/hr correspondingly. Table 2 displays the computation outcomes of the study. The outcomes obtained by GOA are validated with the help of results published by BSA, DE, PSO, GA, ABC and BBO (Chaib, Bouchekara, Mehasni, & Abido, 2016). The results show the superior characteristics of GOA. This validates the usefulness of the suggested approach to explain the

Table 1. Simulation results of various cost & emission minimization using GOA without as well as with considering wind over IEEE 30-bus combination

Control Variable	Cost Optimization Using GOA						Emission Optimization (ton/hr) Using GOA	
	Quadratic ($/hr)		Multi-Fuels ($/hr)		Valve-Point Effect ($/hr)			
	Conventional	Incorporating Wind	Conventional	Incorporating Wind	Conventional	Incorporating Wind	Conventional	Incorporating Wind
P_{T1}	177.10000	164.0000	139.9000	139.9000	200.0000	198.7000	63.9000	50.0000
P_{T2}	48.7000	45.6000	54.9000	54.9000	43.0000	22.8000	67.5000	46.6000
P_{T5}	21.3000	20.4000	23.5000	22.5000	18.6000	15.0000	50.0000	50.0000
P_{T8}	21.0000	13.4000	35.0000	19.5000	10.0000	10.0000	35.0000	35.0000
P_{T11}	11.9000	10.0000	18.6000	13.8000	10.0000	10.0000	30.0000	30.0000
P_{T13}	12.0000	12.0000	17.8000	13.3000	12.0000	12.0000	40.0000	40.0000
P_{w22}	----	13.8000	----	14.1000	----	12.9000	----	28.5000
P_{w23}	----	11.7000	----	12.2000	----	11.2000	----	16.4000
Vg_1	1.1000	1.1000	1.1000	1.0000	1.1000	1.1000	1.1000	1.0000
Vg_2	1.1000	1.1000	1.9000	1.0000	1.1000	1.1000	1.1000	1.0000
Vg_5	1.1000	1.1000	1.1000	1.0000	1.0000	1.0000	1.1000	1.0000
Vg_8	1.1000	1.1000	1.1000	1.0000	1.0000	1.1000	1.1000	1.1000
Vg_{11}	1.1000	1.1000	1.1000	1.1000	1.1000	1.1000	1.1000	1.0000
Vg_{13}	1.1000	1.1000	1.0000	1.0000	1.1000	1.1000	1.1000	1.1000
Vg_{22}	----	1.1000	----	1.0000	----	1.1000	----	1.1000
Vg_{23}	----	1.1000	----	1.0000	----	1.1000	----	1.1000
$T_{(6-9)}$	1.0000	1.0000	1.1000	1.0000	1.0000	1.0000	1.0000	1.0000
$T_{(6-10)}$	0.9000	1.0000	1.0000	1.0000	0.9000	0.9000	0.9000	1.0000
$T_{(4-12)}$	1.0000	1.0000	1.0000	1.0000	0.9000	0.9000	0.9000	1.0000
$T_{(28-27)}$	0.9000	1.0000	1.0000	1.0000	0.9000	0.9000	0.9000	1.0000
Q_{10}	5.0000	0.0000	1.5000	1.5000	3.6000	3.4000	4.6000	4.0000
Q_{12}	5.0000	2.8000	1.5000	0.0000	5.0000	2.8000	0.3000	0.7000
Q_{15}	5.0000	3.3000	2.1000	3.1000	3.3000	4.2000	5.0000	1.3000
Q_{17}	5.0000	5.0000	3.4000	0.0000	5.0000	5.0000	2.8000	1.4000
Q_{20}	4.3000	2.6000	5.0000	4.3000	5.0000	3.6000	4.9000	4.9000
Q_{21}	5.0000	0.9000	2.4000	3.9000	5.0000	2.8000	5.0000	1.6000
Q_{23}	2.7000	0.7000	2.3000	4.6000	2.7000	4.6000	2.8000	0.3000
Q_{24}	5.0000	4.0000	2.2000	4.1000	5.0000	3.9000	4.0000	2.7000
Q_{29}	2.3000	2.8000	3.5000	2.9000	2.4000	2.0000	2.8000	3.0000
Fuel cost($/hr)	799.0000	795.6000	646.0000	639.0000	830.0000	826.0000	944.0000	959.0000
Trans loss(MW)	8.6000	7.5000	6.5000	7.0000	10.2000	9.3000	3.0000	13.1000
Emission(ton/hr)	0.3700	0.3400	0.2800	0.2900	0.4000	0.4000	0.2000	0.2000

Table 2. Comparability table of the GOA with BSA, DE, GA, PSO, ABC and BBO for single objective of IEEE 30-bus system

	Best ($/hr)	Average ($/hr)	Median ($/hr)	Worst ($/hr)	SD
Quadratic Cost					
GOA with Wind	795.6000	795.7000	795.9000	796.1000	0.1200
GOA without Wind	799.0000	799.1000	799.2000	799.5000	0.1300
BSA	799.0760	799.2721	799.2448	799.6240	0.1357
DE	799.0376	799.3047	799.0458	801.5552	0.6624
PSO	800.9310	-	-	-	-
GA	800.1636	802.6876	802.2552	806.2791	1.7071
ABC	799.0541	799.6945	799.4613	802.6327	0.8145
BBO	799.1267	801.1927	801.1287	803.1429	1.0251
Cost with Multi-Fuels					
GOA with Wind	639.0000	639.3000	638.5000	638.8000	0.6000
GOA without Wind	646.0000	646.1000	646.1000	646.9000	0.7000
BSA	646.1504	647.5781	647.5572	649.0638	0.6668
DE	645.3627	646.7220	646.4604	650.7419	1.0607
PSO	647.2879	681.7314	654.3286	839.6854	62.5562
GA	649.9246	659.6545	658.2511	671.9717	5.9728
ABC	648.5069	652.1451	651.6767	657.9807	2.6969
BBO	647.1179	651.0801	651.0284	656.9323	2.5840
Cost With Valve-Point Effect					
GOA with Wind	826.0000	826.3000	826.8000	827.0000	0.8000
GOA without Wind	830.0000	830.0000	830.0000	831.9000	0.8000
BSA	830.7779	832.0811	832.1224	834.3303	0.8474
DE	830.4425	831.4997	830.5125	842.7195	3.0912
PSO	837.5082	-	-	-	-
GA	834.2424	840.9013	840.2634	854.9337	4.5089
ABC	831.5783	834.4691	834.1686	839.0831	1.9432
BBO	831.4581	835.8153	835.3208	842.5715	2.6118

OPF problem. From the tables, it is established that the present approach proved as better than the other existing approaches.

4.1.2 Minimization of Fuel Cost With Multi-Fuels

Multiple fuel sources, like coal, oil, and natural gas, have been utilized by several thermal generating plants to generate electricity. This case represents the improvement of fuel cost with multiple fuels by minimizing the fuel cost which includes minimizing the production cost formulated by a quadratic cost function in IEEE 30-bus system. However, as a substitute for the basic quadratic cost function, the cost curve is framed by piecewise quadratic cost functions because of considering the multi-fuels option. The best manage control random variable parameters for fuel expense reduction with the multi-fuel objective function of this present test study, as yielded through the anticipated GO approach, are presented in Table 1. The minimum cost reported for this system using GOA are 639.0000 $/hr with wind integration and 646.0000 $/hr without wind integration. The proposed GOA process gives the least generation schedule with minimum cost as 639.0000 $/hr, which may be observed as the best one solution. A comparative study of the operating expense of the system without and with wind based power using BSA, DE, PSO, GA, ABC and BBO (Chaib, Bouchekara, Mehasni, & Abido, 2016), techniques are noticeable in Table 2. Furthermore, it can be concluded that the response achieved from the recommended concept is superior to other procedures in the research.

4.1.3 Minimization of Fuel Cost With Valve-Point Effect

This case represents the minimization of total fuel cost of generation with valve-point loading effect of generators. The parameter magnitudes are uniform to those in Case 1. In this study, eqn (9) is used for the calculation. In this case study, the GOA considers the valve-point effect of existing fuel-cost equation of thermal generators. The minimum production cost reported so far for this system is 826.0000 $/hr when wind power added with the system. The convergence of GO algorithm is indicated in Figure 2. The outcomes are in Table 1 and Figure 2 exhibit the excellent performance of GOA in solving the OPF problem. Comparison analysis with other optimization methods like BSA, DE, PSO, GA, ABC and BBO (Chaib, Bouchekara, Mehasni, & Abido, 2016), was also reported and their outcomes are illustrated in Table 2. This demonstrated that the fuel cost of the GOA method is significantly superior to the other four methods. From the outcomes, it can be remarked that the projected algorithm dominates the other with respect to solution quality.

Figure 2. Convergence characteristic of total cost with valve-point effect of IEEE 30-bus system using GO algorithm with and without wind

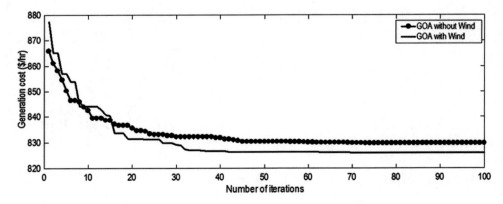

4.1.4 Emission Minimization

For this test system and last studies for the single objective, eqn (11) is considered for the calculation of emission minimization. Considering emission minimization another unique prime objective functions for this investigation power system network, obtained best possible values of the set of supervise suitable variables (as yielded with the GO approach) are listed in with Table 1 by the side of with those published in the literature like BSA, DE, GA, PSO, ABC and BBO. The resulting emission values in this case with incorporating wind power are 0.2000 ton/hr and 0.2100 ton/hr without wind power, correspondingly. The simulated outcomes are presented in Table 2 which demonstrates the detailed justifications of the minimum, mean and worst results of the anticipated GOA with the most currently published performance for OPF problems.

4.1.5 Cost and Emission Minimization

An ordinary MO optimization problem compositions of a numeral of objectives to be optimized concurrently and is connected with several of inequality and equality constraints. The wind and thermal mixture hybrid dispatch twofold problem is simulated for concurrent optimization of couple equations; fuel price along with emission with GO approach. The simulated data attained by the mentioned method and the results of the relating goals are arranged in Table 3. The obtaining fuel costs and polluting emission impacts with and without wind power, in this case, are 828.0000 $/hr, 835.0000 $/hr and 0.2300 ton/hr, 0.2400 ton/hr respectively. It is understandable that the algorithm proposed by this article can lower the overall operation expected generation cost and emission efficiency. From Table 3, we can study that the achievement of GOA is improved than all methods in both emission and fuel cost objectives.

Table 3. Simulation results of cost & emission for multi-objective OPF using GOA without as well as with considering wind over IEEE 30-bus combination

Cost and Emission Optimization								
Control Variable	**Conventional**	**Incorporating Wind**	**Control variable**	**Conventional**	**Incorporating Wind**	**Control Variable**	**Conventional**	**Incorporating Wind**
P_{T1}	112.9300	101.8300	Vg_8	1.0798	1.0824	Q_{15}	4.7800	5.0000
P_{T2}	59.0400	53.4100	Vg_{11}	1.1000	1.0996	Q_{17}	5.0000	2.7000
P_{T5}	27.5900	25.5400	Vg_{13}	1.1000	1.1000	Q_{20}	4.1000	1.7400
P_{T8}	35.0000	35.0000	Vg_{22}	----	1.0983	Q_{21}	5.0000	3.8500
P_{T11}	27.2200	21.9300	Vg_{23}	----	1.1000	Q_{23}	2.8900	1.7300
P_{T13}	26.6300	21.9100	$T_{(6-9)}$	1.0496	1.0064	Q_{24}	5.0000	3.8600
P_{w22}	----	15.3200	$T_{(6-10)}$	0.9000	0.9518	Q_{29}	2.3200	2.6900
P_{w23}	----	12.6900	$T_{(4-12)}$	0.9764	0.9787	Fuel Cost ($/hr)	835.0000	828.0000
Vg_1	1.1000	1.1000	$T_{(28-27)}$	0.9655	0.9708	Trans loss (MW)	5.0000	4.2000
Vg_2	1.0921	1.0921	Q_{10}	5.0000	4.8900	Emission (ton/hr)	0.2400	0.2300
Vg_5	1.0688	1.0687	Q_{12}	2.7800	5.0000			

4.2 Test System 2: IEEE 57-Bus

After that, for the second case consideration, a regular IEEE-57 bus method is taking into account for the next attempt combination. In order to demonstrate the robustness and efficiency of the projected approach in solving a bigger power system, IEEE 57-unit test system is examined as the next test system. The structure formations of 80 transmission lines, 7 generators (at the positions 1, 2, 3, 6, 8, 9, 12) and tap setting transformers in 15 branches are considered under load condition. There are 3 reactive control sources which are again placed at positions 18, 25 and 53. Bus one is preferred as the reference/swing bus. Bus 22 and 23 are considered for wind energy in this system the same as the previous case. The lowest and highest ranges of voltage data for all the units apart from the swing bus are considered from 0.90 to 1.10 p.u. Now, this is understood that here the tap changing ranges of total off-nominal value of tap changing transformers can be considered from 0.90 to 1.10 p.u. In this present example, three investigations with distinct purposes like decreasing the simple quadratic fuel price, quadratic fuel price along valve-point loading and later fuel price and emission are measured concurrently. Detailed data can be derived from (2014 OPF Problems, 2014). This area suggests the computation details on three evaluation systems for a single objective and one multi-objective which are performed to evaluate the success of the prospective method. In present simulation case, three individual objectives broadly fuel cost minimization, fuel cost with valve-point loading minimization and emission minimization; one bi-objective especially simultaneous minimization of emission along with fuel cost are considered to test the effectiveness of the recommended algorithm. In the following study to illustrate the application of the recommended approach, numerical results achieved with the IEEE 57-unit test system are shown in this part.

4.2.1 Quadratic Fuel Cost

In this assignment, the normal OPF without taking the multi-fuel and valve-point effect is proposed. In this section, the results of present studies conducted on an IEEE 57-units system to assess the credential of the GO algorithm are presented. The objective of the study is to optimize the overall fuel cost. Table 4 shows the data for the tests. The fuel cost minimization decreased to 5563.1000 $/hr in case of wind power in comparison to 6288.4000 $/hr in the case without wind power (Table 4). Therefore, the above simulation results display the usefulness of the projected method in handling economic with all practical constraints. To authenticate the results of the projected method on the IEEE 57-bus system, all suitable results were verified and analyzed with BSA, DE, GA, PSO, ABC and BBO (Chaib, Bouchekara, Mehasni, & Abido, 2016). The obtained results of the simulation of this comparison are listed in Table 5. Hence, the proposed GOA method provides the viable performance concerning the optimal answer and computation effort.

4.2.2 Quadratic Fuel Cost With Valve-Point Effect

In present study considers IEEE-57 units with valve-point effects in this addition. In the present discussion, the valve-loading effects are included in the cost function. This can be viewed from the Table 4, where the whole generation cost using GOA are 5784.0000 $/hr and 6274.8000 $/hr for wind integration and without wind integration respectively, which is less compared to the cost obtained using BSA, DE, PSO, GA, ABC and BBO (Chaib, Bouchekara, Mehasni, & Abido, 2016) methods respectively. The best

Table 4. Optimal arrangements of control parameters using GOA without and with considering wind for single goal of IEEE 57-bus combination

Control Variable	Cost Optimization Using GOA				Emission Optimization (ton/hr) Using GOA	
	Quadratic ($/hr)		Valve-point effect ($/hr)			
	Conventional	Incorporating Wind	Conventional	Incorporating Wind	Conventional	Incorporating Wind
P_{T1}	531.6800	493.1800	561.5500	500.7400	165.6900	170.9900
P_{T2}	82.2900	87.7800	84.7100	100.0000	100.0000	91.7900
P_{T3}	113.9300	97.0200	76.8100	93.4100	140.0000	140.0000
P_{T6}	100.0000	100.0000	100.0000	93.4200	100.0000	96.7500
P_{T8}	0.0000	61.8100	52.1500	54.0600	248.6200	245.5500
P_{T9}	68.5100	92.5600	28.3400	90.2000	100.0000	100.0000
P_{T12}	410.0000	252.7800	410.0000	301.4100	410.0000	304.8200
P_{w29}	----	90.0000	----	22.4700	----	76.0700
P_{w30}	----	21.6000	----	53.0200	----	53.0100
Vg_1	1.0419	1.0317	1.0580	1.0359	1.0307	0.9810
Vg_2	1.0212	0.9995	0.9680	0.9712	1.0291	1.0051
Vg_3	1.0569	1.0452	0.9671	0.9743	1.0335	1.0216
Vg_6	0.9400	0.9587	1.0146	0.9645	1.0168	1.0600
Vg_8	0.9495	0.9544	0.9601	1.0425	1.0047	0.9647
Vg_9	1.0099	0.9400	0.9827	1.0453	1.0127	0.9473
Vg_{12}	0.9821	1.0258	1.0078	0.9409	1.0087	1.0328
Vg_{29}	----	0.9469	----	1.0308	----	1.0585
Vg_{30}	----	0.9849	----	0.9539	----	1.0105
$T_{(4-18)}$	1.0290	0.9982	0.9268	1.0583	1.0275	1.0315
$T_{(4-18)}$	0.9262	1.0827	1.0482	0.9105	0.9912	0.9910
$T_{(21-20)}$	1.0178	1.1000	0.9641	1.0973	0.9796	0.9718
$T_{(24-25)}$	1.0744	0.9352	1.0758	0.9436	0.9986	1.0369
$T_{(24-25)}$	0.9269	0.9594	1.0690	1.0244	1.0361	1.0579
$T_{(24-26)}$	0.9818	0.9310	1.0628	1.0521	1.0375	0.9561
$T_{(7-29)}$	0.9269	0.9055	0.9635	1.1000	1.0267	1.0393
$T_{(34-32)}$	0.9425	1.0283	0.9603	1.0800	0.9992	0.9910
$T_{(11-41)}$	1.0262	1.0927	0.9084	1.0373	0.9920	0.9498
$T_{(15-45)}$	1.0929	0.9204	1.0129	0.9507	1.0031	1.0446
$T_{(14-46)}$	1.0593	1.0591	0.9138	0.9256	0.9261	0.9520
$T_{(10-51)}$	0.9048	1.0389	1.1000	0.9624	1.0178	0.9226
$T_{(13-49)}$	0.9786	0.9997	0.9556	0.9115	0.9643	0.9279
$T_{(11-43)}$	1.0045	0.9462	0.9146	0.9513	0.9691	1.0050
$T_{(40-56)}$	0.9836	1.0497	1.0990	1.0612	1.0437	0.9727
$T_{(39-57)}$	0.9111	0.9816	1.0183	0.9000	1.0098	0.9949

continues on following page

Multi-Objective Optimal Power Flow of Integrated Renewable Systems Using a Novel Evolutionary Algorithm

Table 4. Continued

Control Variable	Cost Optimization Using GOA				Emission Optimization (ton/hr) Using GOA	
	Quadratic ($/hr)		Valve-point effect ($/hr)			
	Conventional	Incorporating Wind	Conventional	Incorporating Wind	Conventional	Incorporating Wind
$T_{(9-55)}$	1.0274	0.9989	0.9146	0.9024	1.0196	1.0496
Q_{18}	13.0900	0.1814	4.0800	13.6300	10.5500	16.0600
Q_{25}	2.4500	0.0293	3.6900	2.4300	0.6100	2.5700
Q_{53}	3.7700	0.0309	7.6300	5.6100	5.2600	6.7700
Fuel Cost ($/hr)	6288.4000	5563.1000	6274.8000	5784.0000	9148.2000	8829.6000
Trans loss (MW)	56.6000	44.5000	62.8000	58.2000	13.5000	29.3000
Emission (ton/hr)	2.2400	1.6800	1.8300	1.8100	0.9800	0.7600

mean and worst values of generation cost obtained by GO method with and without considering wind energy are put in Table 5 and data confirmed with other recent methods. It can be tested that the obtained simulation from the projected method is improved than different algorithms published in the literature.

4.2.3 Emission Minimization

The standard IEEE 57-units test case is utilised to demonstrate the proposed approach. The total pollutant emission function for this case is given by eqn (11). The test outcomes achieved for optimal parameter settings of manage control parameters for emission minimization are presented in Table 4 represents that the GOA gives the most excellent resolution while optimizing fuel expense for the aforementioned OPF related problem. Considering Table 4, again it can also be examined such that entire emission is reduced to 0.7600 ton/hr from 0.9800 ton/hr for wind power and without wind power, respectively. The minimum, average and maximum values of emission calculated by GOA method in this simulation are carefully arranged in Table 5 and verified with other algorithms like BSA, DE, GA, PSO, ABC and BBO (Chaib, Bouchekara, Mehasni, & Abido, 2016) which are already well-established. It is observed that employing wind turbine generator can significantly save the overall pollutant emission for power production.

4.2.4 Cost and Emission Minimization

Lastly, the proposed GOA method has been simulated to minimize fuel price and poisoning emission objectives at the equivalent time. In view of this division, all the constraints concerning fuel price and poisoning emission are taken into consideration. Here, the OPF issue is designed as the multi-objective concern. The optimization function used here is eqn (17). The optimized control parameter for this setting obtained by GOA is presented in Table 6. The best compromise result by using GOA is given in Table 5. In this category, it is noticed that the fuel cost is decreased by as much as 2.1900% in comparison to 6563.4000 $/hr in case of with wind power. As much as 6.0500% also reduces the emission in comparison to 1.2300 ton/hr in case wind power. It can be checked that the newly recommended GOA technique is better considered to all recently accepted methods. It is recorded from the outcomes in Table 5 that the

Table 5. Comparability of the GOA with BSA, DE, GA, PSO, ABC and BBO for single objective for IEEE 57-bus system

	Best ($/hr)	**Average ($/hr)**	**Median ($/hr)**	**Worst ($/hr)**	**SD**
GOA with wind	5563.1000	5572.0000	5574.1000	5583.7000	1.0000
GOA without wind	6288.4000	6291.1000	6290.6000	6302.8000	1.1000
BSA	6411.0043	6411.7690	6411.2924	6414.9844	1.1107
DE	6410.1888	-	-	-	-
PSO	6748.6052	-	-	-	-
GA	6673.7958	-	-	-	-
ABC	6411.4506	6423.8702	6422.3992	6449.4900	7.9744
BBO	6418.5723	6450.9358	6439.3508	6639.2789	52.0784

Table 6. Simulation results of cost & emission minimization simultaneous using GOA without as well as with considering wind for IEEE 57-bus combination

Cost and Emission Optimization Using GOA								
Control Variable	**Conventional**	**Incorporating Wind**	**Control Variable**	**Conventional**	**Incorporating Wind**	**Control Variable**	**Conventional**	**Incorporating Wind**
P_{T1}	332.1400	346.5700	Vg_9	0.9615	0.9436	$T_{(14-46)}$	0.9132	1.0214
P_{T2}	100.0000	100.0000	Vg_{12}	1.0103	0.9573	$T_{(10-51)}$	1.0891	0.9316
P_{T3}	140.0000	90.2800	Vg_{29}	----	1.0433	$T_{(13-49)}$	0.9692	0.9293
P_{T6}	98.5200	100.0000	Vg_{30}	----	0.9400	$T_{(11-43)}$	0.9000	1.0791
P_{T8}	123.5400	83.2200	$T_{(4-18)}$	0.9000	1.0484	$T_{(40-56)}$	1.1000	0.9362
P_{T9}	100.0000	88.1200	$T_{(4-18)}$	1.0580	0.9492	$T_{(39-57)}$	1.0011	0.9566
P_{T12}	390.8800	359.8600	$T_{(21-20)}$	0.9582	1.0068	$T_{(9-55)}$	0.9274	1.0679
P_{w29}	----	70.5200	$T_{(24-25)}$	1.0772	1.0379	Q_{18}	5.0600	2.5700
P_{w30}	----	57.8700	$T_{(24-25)}$	1.0770	0.9467	Q_{25}	4.2600	2.3500
Vg_1	1.0494	1.0447	$T_{(24-26)}$	1.0826	0.9300	Q_{53}	8.0000	1.2800
Vg_2	0.9814	0.9687	$T_{(7-29)}$	0.9532	1.0990			
Vg_3	0.9725	1.0507	$T_{(34-32)}$	0.9400	1.0540	Fuel Cost ($/hr)	6563.4000	6419.6000
Vg_6	1.0143	1.0371	$T_{(11-41)}$	0.9491	0.9942	Trans loss (MW)	34.3000	43.4000
Vg_8	0.9576	0.9622	$T_{(15-45)}$	1.02000	0.9000	Emission (ton/hr)	1.2300	1.1500

results of emission and fuel cost from the GO method are least than those from the various algorithms. Altogether, it can guide to the conclusion that the suggested GOA is a very prospective approach for solving optimal results for the IEEE 57-unit system.

5. CONCLUSION

A new methodology proposes a multi-purpose GO algorithm to explain the multi-direction OPF difficulty in power structures that give attention to the fuel expense and emission as the conflicting objective function. This chapter introduces the GO approach for finding the OPF problem of a thermal-wind mixture power system. The wind unpredictability costs are also incorporated in the proposed model. Two assessments namely, IEEE 30-bus along with IEEE 57-bus assessment systems holding unlike objectives along with limitations are studied to judge the usefulness of this suggested approach. The regular IEEE 30-bus and 57-bus systems are investigated by the proposed algorithm. In this approach more wind energy penetrated which has straight contact with the environment throughout decreasing carbon discharges from the thermal power plant. The results obtained from the GOA approach for both cases i.e., with wind power and without wind power are investigated with those explored in the recent research. It is essential mentioning that when wind power included in the same system such a one the GOA presents improved responses than various acknowledged techniques like BSA, DE, PSO, GA, ABC and BBO. The suggested method has been successfully verified on two standard case studies. The GO method is successfully presented to search near-global or global best possible settings of the control parameters of the IEEE 30-bus and the IEEE 57-bus test systems. The model regulates the best possible generation level of the traditional units, at the same time curtailment of the predicted gap of wind power generation. Based on the estimated wind power, the GO algorithm is applied to answer the OPF to supply the outstanding power demand out of the usable thermal generation. It is accepted that the recommended GO approach is advantageous in presenting superiority explanations every time for non-concave with multi-objective OPF difficulty. Furthermore, this may be completed that the recommended GOA is extremely rising and inspiring approach for the wind power inclusion as well as future engineering optimization task.

6. FUTURE RESEARCH DIRECTIONS

In this research work, the proposed GOA method has successfully been used to solve OPF problem and found to be best in terms of minimum operating cost, minimum transmission loss and least execution time among various popular optimization method available in the literature. Therefore, the proposed algorithms may also be applied to other power system optimization problems like, ELD, DED, DEED, unit commitment, power system stabilizer etc. For ELD and OPF problem, the feasibility of the proposed methods may be verified by introducing more practical constraints like prohibited zone, valve-point loading, ramp rate limit and spinning reserve. The same study may be extended to large-scale interconnected four or more multi-area power system with integration for different renewable energy sources.

Furthermore, the framework of the GO technique presented in this article could be elongated for new types of evolutionary methods to explain dynamic economic dispatch, dynamic MO optimization and DEED problems in terms of environmental load and economic dispatch. In the prospect, the GOA suggests to suit an essential tool for finding difficult power system optimization problems in look for improved superiority results. Due to the risky and uncertain renewable energy investments, a similar method could be applied to the evaluation of other renewable energy generation. Thus, the proposed algorithm can act as a judgment supporting algorithm for power plant engineers in the operation and planning of power networks with wind penetration.

REFERENCES

Abarghooee, R. A., Golestaneh, F., Gooi, H. B., Lin, J., Bavafa, F., & Terzija, V. (2016). Corrective economic dispatch and operational cycles for probabilistic unit commitment with demand response and high wind power. *Applied Energy*, *182*, 634–651. doi:10.1016/j.apenergy.2016.07.117

Abido, M. A. (2002). Optimal power flow using tabu search algorithm. *Electric Power Components and Systems*, *30*(5), 469–483. doi:10.1080/15325000252888425

Adaryani, M. R., & Karami, A. (2013). Artificial bee colony algorithm for solving multi-objective optimal power flow problem. *Electrical Power and Energy Systems*, *53*, 219–230. doi:10.1016/j.ijepes.2013.04.021

Alham, M. H., Elshahed, M., Ibrahim, D. K., & Zahab, E. E. D. A. (2016). A dynamic economic emission dispatch considering wind power uncertainty incorporating energy storage system and demand side management. *Renewable Energy*, *96*, 800–811. doi:10.1016/j.renene.2016.05.012

Alsac, O., Bright, J., Prais, M., & Stott, B. (1990). Further developments in LP-based optimal power flow. *IEEE Transactions on Power Systems*, *5*(3), 697–711. doi:10.1109/59.65896

Alsac, O., & Stott, B. (1974). Optimal load flow with steady state security. *IEEE Transactions on Power Apparatus and Systems*, *93*(3), 745–751. doi:10.1109/TPAS.1974.293972

Amirsaman, A., Mahmoud, G., & Mehdi, E. A. (2013). Cost analysis of a power system using probabilistic optimal power flow with energy storage integration and wind generation. *International Journal of Electrical Power & Energy Systems*, *53*, 832–841. doi:10.1016/j.ijepes.2013.05.053

Bahman, B. F., Ebrahim, F., & Rasoul, A. A. (2013). An efficient scenario-based and fuzzy self-adaptive learning particle swarm optimization approach for dynamic economic emission dispatch considering load and wind power uncertainties. *Energy*, *50*, 232–244. doi:10.1016/j.energy.2012.11.017

Bai, L., Li, F., Cui, H., Jiang, T., Sun, H., & Zhu, J. (2016). Interval optimization based operating strategy for gas-electricity integrated energy systems considering demand response and wind uncertainty. *Applied Energy*, *167*, 270–279. doi:10.1016/j.apenergy.2015.10.119

Bai, W., & Lee, Y. (2016). Modified optimal power flow on storage devices and wind power integrated system. *Proc. IEEE International conference on power and energy society general meeting (PESGM)*, Boston, MA, July 17-21.

Bakirtzis, A. G., Biskas, P. N., Zoumas, C. E., & Petridis, V. (2002). Optimal power flow by enhanced genetic algorithm. *IEEE Transactions on Power Systems*, *17*(2), 229–236. doi:10.1109/TPWRS.2002.1007886

Basu, M. (2011). Multi-objective optimal power flow with FACTS devices. *Energy Conversion and Management*, *52*(2), 903–910. doi:10.1016/j.enconman.2010.08.017

Biswas, P. P., Suganthan, P. N., & Amaratunga, G. A. J. (2017). Optimal power flow solutions incorporating stochastic wind and solar power. *Energy Conversion and Management*, *148*, 1194–1207. doi:10.1016/j.enconman.2017.06.071

Bonou, A., Laurent, A., & Olsen, S. I. (2016). Life cycle assessment of onshore and offshore wind energy-from theory to application. *Applied Energy*, *180*, 327–337. doi:10.1016/j.apenergy.2016.07.058

Bukar, A. L., Tan, C. W., & Kwan, K. Y. (2019). Optimal sizing of an autonomous photovoltaic/wind/battery/diesel generator microgrid using grasshopper optimization algorithm. *Solar Energy, 2*(188), 685–696. doi:10.1016/j.solener.2019.06.050

Burchett, R. C., Happ, H. H., & Vierath, D. R. (1984). Quadratically convergent optimal power flow. *IEEE Transactions on Power Apparatus and Systems, 103*(11), 3267–3276. doi:10.1109/TPAS.1984.318568

Chaib, A. E., Bouchekara, H. R. E. H., Mehasni, R., & Abido, M. A. (2016). Optimal power flow with emission and non-smooth cost functions using backtracking search optimization algorithm. *International Journal of Electrical Power & Energy Systems, 81*, 64–77. doi:10.1016/j.ijepes.2016.02.004

Chang, Y. C., Lee, T. Y., Chen, C. L., & Jan, R. M. (2014). Optimal power flow of a wind-thermal generation system. *International Journal of Electrical Power & Energy Systems, 55*, 312–320. doi:10.1016/j.ijepes.2013.09.028

Chen, H., Bo, M. L., & Zhu, Y. (2014). Multi-hive bee foraging algorithm for multi-objective optimal power flow considering the cost, loss, and emission. *Electrical Power and Energy Systems, 60*, 203–220. doi:10.1016/j.ijepes.2014.02.017

Chen, Y., Wei, W., Liu, F., & Mei, S. (2016). Distributionally robust hydro-thermal-wind economic dispatch. *Applied Energy, 173*, 511–519. doi:10.1016/j.apenergy.2016.04.060

Council, G. W. E. (2012). Global wind energy outlook 2012. Retrieved November 2012 from https://gwec.net/publications/global-wind-energy-outlook/global-wind-energy-outlook-2012/

Dubey, H. M., Pandit, M., & Panigrahi, B. K. (2015). Hybrid flower pollination algorithm with time-varying fuzzy selection mechanism for wind integrated multi-objective dynamic economic dispatch. *Renewable Energy, 83*, 188–202. doi:10.1016/j.renene.2015.04.034

Ewees, A. A., Elaziz, M. A., & Houssein, E. H. (2018). Improved grasshopper optimization algorithm using opposition-based learning. *Expert Systems with Applications, 112*, 156–172. doi:10.1016/j.eswa.2018.06.023

Fathabadi, H. (2018). Utilizing solar and wind energy in plug-in hybrid electric vehicles. *Energy Conversion and Management, 156*, 317–328. doi:10.1016/j.enconman.2017.11.015

Ghasemi, M., Ghavidel, S., Ghanbarian, M. H., Gharibzadeh, M., & Vahed, A. Z. (2014). Multi-objective optimal power flow considering the cost, emission, voltage deviation and power losses using multi-objective modified imperialist competitive algorithm. *Energy, 78*, 1–14. doi:10.1016/j.energy.2014.10.007

Hu, Z., Zhang, M., Wang, X., Li, C., & Hu, M. (2016). Bi-level robust dynamic economic emission dispatchconsidering wind power uncertainty. *Electric Power Systems Research, 135*, 35–47. doi:10.1016/j.epsr.2016.03.010

HetzerJ, ., & David, C. Y., & BhattaraiK, . (2008). An economic dispatch model incorporating wind power. *IEEE Transactions on Energy Conversion, 23*(2), 603–611. doi:10.1109/TEC.2007.914171

Khalid, M., Aguilera, R. P., Savkin, A. V., & Agelidis, V. G. (2018). On maximizing profit of wind-battery supported power station based on wind power and energy price forecasting. *Applied Energy, 211*, 764–773. doi:10.1016/j.apenergy.2017.11.061

Krishnasamy, U., & Nanjundappan, D. (2016). Hybrid weighted probabilistic neural network and biogeography based optimization for dynamic economic dispatch of integrated multiple-fuel and wind power plants. *International Journal of Electrical Power & Energy Systems*, *77*, 385–394. doi:10.1016/j.ijepes.2015.11.022

Lai, L. L., Ma, J. T., Yokoyama, R., & Zhao, M. (1997). Improved genetic algorithm for optimal power flow under both normal and contingent operation states. *International Journal of Electrical Power & Energy Systems*, *19*(5), 287–292. doi:10.1016/S0142-0615(96)00051-8

Lau, E. T., Yang, Q., Taylor, G. A., Forbes, A. B., Wright, P. S., & Livina, V. N. (2016). Optimization of costs and carbon savings in relation to the economic dispatch problem as associated with power system operation. *Electric Power Systems Research*, *140*, 173–183. doi:10.1016/j.epsr.2016.06.025

Lee, J. C., Lin, W. M., Liao, G. C., & Tsao, T. P. (2011). Quantum genetic algorithm for dynamic economic dispatch with valve-point effects and including wind power system. *International Journal of Electrical Power & Energy Systems*, *33*(2), 189–197. doi:10.1016/j.ijepes.2010.08.014

Majid, B. W., & Louis, A., D. (2017). Multi-objective stochastic optimal power flow considering voltage stability and demand response with significant wind penetration. *IET Generation, Transmission, & Distribution*, *11*(14), 3499–3509. doi:10.1049/iet-gtd.2016.1994

Mandal, B., & Roy, P. K. (2014). Multi-objective optimal power flow using quasi-oppositional teaching learning based optimization. *Applied Soft Computing*, *21*, 590–606. doi:10.1016/j.asoc.2014.04.010

Mirjalili, S., & Lewis, A. (2016). The grasshopper optimization algorithm. *Advances in Engineering Software*, *95*, 51–67. doi:10.1016/j.advengsoft.2016.01.008

Mohammad, J. M., & Alireza, A. (2014). Hybrid imperialist competitive-sequential quadratic programming (HIC-SQP) algorithm for solving economic load dispatch with incorporating stochastic wind power: A comparative study on heuristic optimization techniques. *Energy Conversion and Management*, *84*, 30–40. doi:10.1016/j.enconman.2014.04.006

Momoh,, J. A., El-Hawary, M. E., & Adapa, R. (1999). A review of selected optimal power flow literature to 1993, Part II: Newton, linear programming and interior point methods. *IEEE Transactions on Power Systems*, *14*(1), 104–111.

Momoh, J. A., Adapa, R., & El-Hawary, M. E. (1999). A review of selected optimal power flow literature to 1993, Part I: Nonlinear and quadratic programming approach. *IEEE Transactions on Power Systems*, *14*(1), 96–104. doi:10.1109/59.744492

Momoh, J. A., & Zhu, J. Z. (1999). Improved interior point method for OPF problems. *IEEE Transactions on Power Systems*, *14*(3), 1114–1120. doi:10.1109/59.780938

Mondal, S., Bhattacharya, A., & Halder, D. S. (2013). Multi-objective economic emission load dispatch solution using gravitational search algorithm and considering wind power penetration. *International Journal of Electrical Power & Energy Systems*, *44*(1), 282–292. doi:10.1016/j.ijepes.2012.06.049

Monticelli, A., Pereira, M. V. F., & Granville, S. (1987). Security-constrained optimal power flow with post-contingency corrective rescheduling. *IEEE Transactions on Power Systems*, *2*(1), 175–180. doi:10.1109/TPWRS.1987.4335095

Morshed, J. M., Hmida, J. B., & Fekih, A. (2018). A probabilistic multi-objective approach for power flow optimization in hybrid wind-PV-PEV systems. *Applied Energy*, *211*, 1136–1149. doi:10.1016/j.apenergy.2017.11.101

Morteza, A., Masoud, R., & Mahmud, F. F. (2015). Probabilistic optimal power flow in correlated hybrid wind-PV power systems: A review and a new approach. *Renewable & Sustainable Energy Reviews*, *41*, 1437–1446. doi:10.1016/j.rser.2014.09.012

Mota-Palomino, R., & Quintana, V. H. (1986). Sparse reactive power rescheduling by a penalty-function linear programming technique. *IEEE Transactions on Power Systems*, *1*(3), 31–39. doi:10.1109/TP-WRS.1986.4334951

Nayak, M. R., Krishnanand, K. R., & Rout, P. K. (2011). *Modified differential evolution optimization algorithm for multi-constraint optimal power flow. In: 2011 international conference on energy, automation, and signal* (pp. 1–7). ICEAS. doi:10.1109/ICEAS.2011.6147113

Optis, M., & Perr-Sauer, J. (2019). The importance of atmospheric turbulence and stability in machine-learning models of wind farm power production. *Renewable & Sustainable Energy Reviews*, *112*, 27–41. doi:10.1016/j.rser.2019.05.031

2014 . Problems, O. P. F. (2014). IEEE PES Working Group on Modern Heuristic Optimization. Retrieved from https://www.uni-due.de/ieee-wgmho/competition2014

Quan, H., Srinivasan, D., Khambadkone, A. M., & Khosravi, A. (2015). A computational framework for uncertainty integration in stochastic unit commitment with intermittent renewable energy sources. *Applied Energy*, *152*, 71–82. doi:10.1016/j.apenergy.2015.04.103

Rahman, I., & Saleh, J. M. (2018). Hybrid Bio-Inspired Computational Intelligence Techniques for Solving Power System Optimization Problems: A Comprehensive Survey. *Applied Soft Computing*, *69*, 72–130. doi:10.1016/j.asoc.2018.04.051

Rarick, R., Simon, D., Villaseca, F. E., & Vyakaranam, B. (2009). Biogeography-based optimization and the solution of the power flow problem. Proceedings *IEEE international conference on systems, man, and cybernetics* (pp. 1003–1018). SMC.

Rasoul, A. A., Taher, N., Mohammad, A. B., & Mohsen, Z. (2014). Coordination of combined heat and power-hermal-wind photovoltaic units in economic load dispatch using chance constrained and jointly distributed random variables methods. *Energy*, *79*(C), 50–67.

Ray, D., Zimmerman, C. S., & David, G. (n.d.). Matpower retrieved from http://www.pserc.cornell.edu/matpower/#docsn.d

Reddy, S. S., & Bijwe, P. R. (2016). Day-ahead and real time optimal power flow considering renewable energy resources. *International Journal of Electrical Power & Energy Systems*, *82*, 400–408. doi:10.1016/j.ijepes.2016.03.033

Roa-Sepulveda, C. A., & Pavez-Lazo, B. J. (2003). A solution to the optimal power flow using simulated annealing. *International Journal of Electrical Power & Energy Systems*, *25*(1), 47–57. doi:10.1016/S0142-0615(02)00020-0

Roy, P. K., Ghoshal, S. P., & Thakur, S. S. (2010). Biogeography based optimization for multi constraint optimal power flow with emission and non-smooth cost function. *Expert Systems with Applications*, *37*(12), 8221–8228. doi:10.1016/j.eswa.2010.05.064

Saremi, S., Mirjalili, S., & Lewis, A. (2017). Grasshopper optimisation algorithm. *Theory and Application Advances in Engineering Software*, *105*, 30–47. doi:10.1016/j.advengsoft.2017.01.004

Saxena, A. (2019). A comprehensive study of chaos embedded bridging mechanisms and crossover operators for grasshopper optimisation algorithm. *Expert Systems with Applications*, *132*, 166–188. doi:10.1016/j.eswa.2019.04.043

Sayah, S., & Zehar, K. (2008). Modified differential evolution algorithm for optimal power flow with non-smooth cost functions. *Energy Conversion and Management*, *49*(11), 3036–3042. doi:10.1016/j.enconman.2008.06.014

Shabanzadeh, M., Sheikh-El-Eslami, M. K., & Haghifam, M. R. (2015). The design of a risk hedging tool for virtual power plants via robust optimization approach. *Applied Energy*, *155*, 766–777. doi:10.1016/j.apenergy.2015.06.059

Shoults, R., & Sun, D. (1982). Optimal power flow based on P–Q decomposition. *IEEE Transactions on Power Apparatus and Systems*, *101*(2), 397–405. doi:10.1109/TPAS.1982.317120

Sivasubramani, S., & Swarup, K. S. (2011). Multi-objective harmony search algorithm for optimal power flow problem. *Electrical Power Energy Systems*, *33*(3), 745–752. doi:10.1016/j.ijepes.2010.12.031

Sousa, T., Soares, J., Vale, Z. A., Morais, H., & Faria, P. (2011). *Simulated annealing metaheuristic to solve the optimal power flow. Proceedings 2011 IEEE power and energy society general meeting, 1-8*. doi:10.1109/PES.2011.6039543

Su, W., Wang, J., & Roh, J. (2014). Stochastic energy scheduling in microgrids with intermittent renewable energy resources. *IEEE Transactions on Smart Grid*, *5*(4), 1876–1883. doi:10.1109/TSG.2013.2280645

Tharwat, A., Houssein, E. H., Ahmed, M. M., Hassanien, A. E., & Gabel, T. (2017). MOGOA algorithm for constrained and unconstrained multi-objective optimization problems. *Applied Intelligence*, 1–16.

Ting, W., Qiang, Y., Zhejing, B., & Wenjun, Y. (●●●). (2103). Coordinated energy dispatching in microgrid with wind power generation and plug-in electric vehicles. *IEEE Transactions on Smart Grid*, *4*(3), 1453–1463.

Wei, H., Sasaki, H., Kubokawa, J., & Yokoyama, R. (1998). An interior point nonlinear programming for optimal power flow problems whit a novel structure data. *IEEE Transactions on Power Systems*, *13*(3), 870–877. doi:10.1109/59.708745

Yan, X., & Quantana, V. H. (1999). Improving an interior point based OPF by dynamic adjustments of step sizes and tolerances. *IEEE Transactions on Power Systems*, *14*(2), 709–717. doi:10.1109/59.761902

Yao, F., & Xu, Z. (2012). Quantum-inspired particle swarm optimization for power system operations considering wind power uncertainty and carbon tax in Australia. *IEEE Transactions on Industrial Informatics, 8*(4), 880–888. doi:10.1109/TII.2012.2210431

Yashen, L., Jeremiah, X. J., & Johanna, L. M. (2016). Emissions impacts of using energy storage for power system reserves. *Applied Energy, 168*, 444–456. doi:10.1016/j.apenergy.2016.01.061

Zhang, X., Miao, Q., Zhang, H., & Wang, L. (2018). A parameter-adaptive VMD method based on grasshopper optimization algorithm to analyze vibration signals from rotating machinery. *Mechanical Systems and Signal Processing, 108*, 58–72. doi:10.1016/j.ymssp.2017.11.029

Zhao, J. H., Wen, F., Dong, Z. Y., Xue, Y., & Wong, K. P. (2012). Optimal dispatch of electric vehicles and wind power using enhanced particle swarm optimization. *IEEE Transactions on Industrial Informatics, 8*(4), 889–899. doi:10.1109/TII.2012.2205398

Chapter 10
Genetic Algorithm–Influenced Top-N Recommender System to Alleviate the New User Cold Start Problem

Sharon Moses J.
Vellore Institute of Technology, India

Dhinesh Babu L. D.
Vellore Institute of Technology, India

Santhoshkumar Srinivasan
Vellore Institute of Technology, India

Nirmala M.
Vellore Institute of Technology, India

ABSTRACT

Most recommender systems are based on the familiar collaborative filtering algorithm to suggest items. Quite often, collaborative filtering algorithm fails in generating recommendations due to the lack of adequate user information resulting in new user cold start problem. Cold start problem is one of the prevailing issues in recommendation system where the system fails to render recommendation. To overcome the new user cold start issue, demographical information of the user is utilised as the user information source. Among the demographical information, the impact of user gender is less explored when compared with other information like age, profession, region, etc. In this chapter, genetic algorithm influenced gender-based top-n recommender algorithm is proposed to address the new user cold start problem. The algorithm utilises the evolution concepts of genetic algorithm to render top-n recommendations to a new user. The evaluation of the proposed algorithm using real world datasets proved that the algorithm has a better efficiency than the state-of-art approaches.

DOI: 10.4018/978-1-7998-3222-5.ch010

INTRODUCTION

Every day huge volumes of information are getting accumulated to cater to the needs of growing web users. In this scenario, for a common man traversing through this enormous pile of information and getting the needed information continues to be a complex task. In order to simplify the task of searching for the needed information from the web, researchers developed the recommender system. Generally, most of the recommender system uses collaborative filtering algorithm to predict recommendations for a user (Su & Khoshgoftaar, 2009) (Konstan & Riedl, 2003; Linden, Smith, & York, 2003; Harper & Konstan, 2016; Koschmider, Hornung, & Oberweis, 2011). Collaborative filtering (CF) algorithm utilizes the user information to find the neighbour with the highest similarity (Herlocker, J. A., & Riedl, 2000; Herlocker, Konstan, Borchers, & Riedl, 1999). The item ratings given by the neighbours are computed to render the list of recommendations to the user (Resnick, Iacovou, Suchak, Bergstrom, & Riedl, 1994). However, when a new user enters the system CF algorithm fails to process recommendations due to lack of information about the user resulting in new user cold start problem (Victor, Cornelis, Teredesai, & Cock, 2008; Son, 2016; Khusro, Ali, & Ullah, 2016). The new user cold start problem is defined as the inability of the system to render recommendations due to the unavailability of information about the user. Even though researchers came up with solutions to alleviate the persisting new user cold start problem, yet there is a huge room for improvement (Son, 2016; Chen, Wan, Chung, & Sun, 2013).

The existing solutions try to fetch the user-related information from other third-party sources or try to cluster the user to a specific group based on minimal user rating information. Other methodologies like asking a newly visited user to fill some survey forms or give ratings and even asking them to authenticate other social web platforms to get their information will annoy the user at a certain point. Also, it becomes the responsibility of recommendation systems to gain user trust and assist user so if a user starts to believe the system is wrong then it will be a total failure of the recommendation system's primary objective. Therefore, in this paper, a genetic algorithm influenced recommendation system acting on user gender and movie genre information is proposed to alleviate the cold start problem specifically in the movie recommendation system.

By employing the genetic evolution principles on genre and user gender, movies that interest the user is sorted out from the huge amount of information. After computing, when a new user enters the system based on the user gender, interesting as well as a unique item will be recommended to the user. Genetic algorithm is used widely in searching the best solution among the various possible solutions to a certain problem (Goldberg, 1989; Michalewicz, 2013; Ribeiro Filho, Treleaven, & Cesare, 1994). The effectiveness of the genetic algorithm in finding the optimal solution made researchers adapt genetic algorithm (GA) influenced procedures to solve the optimization problems belonging to various domains (Maulik & Bandyopadhyay, 2000; Leu, Yang, & Huang, 2000).

GA algorithm follows the principle of natural evolution to frame the advanced heuristic approach in order to find the optimal solution. The basic GA algorithm utilizes the selection, crossover and mutation process to find the best among all the feasible solution (Goldberg, 1989; Gen & Cheng, 1997). Rendering the user desired recommendations without any sort of user information results in the failure of the recommendation system in assisting the user. Therefore, the recommendation system needs to render best-fit recommendations to the new users resulting in optimal solution problems. Henceforth Selection and Crossover phase of the GA approach along with user gender and genre information is utilized to render optimal recommendations to the new user. This paper is constructed as follows section one tells about the cold start problem and section 2 details the similar works of recommender system utilizing gender and genre information along with the motivation behind using genre and gender information. Section 3 elaborates on the proposed hybrid approach, Section 4 details the discussion on evaluating the system and section 5 concludes the paper.

RELATED WORKS

Utilization of Gender and Genre Information in Recommendation System

Gender is normally categorized as one of the demographical information of the user and genre or category represents the specifications or contents of an item. In the movie recommender system, genre corresponds to the movie genre which deliberately determines the characteristic composition of a movie. The significance of demographical information particularly age and gender are analysed and it was concluded that demographical information has substantial importance in recommender systems (Beel, Langer, Nürnberger, & Genzmehr, 2013). In another work, it was stated that demographical information can be used along with the single value decomposition model to find the similarity among the users. (Pazzani, 1999). Some researchers proved that the CF algorithm can generate a more precise recommendation by utilizing the demographical information (Vozalis & Margaritis, 2004). Further, they used a single value decomposition (SVD) technique along with demographical information and found that the SVD along with the demographical information is more efficient than the CF algorithm (Vozalis & Margaritis, 2007). In some works, demographical information also utilized to enhance the accuracy of the CF algorithm (Moreno, Aida, David, Lucas, & Joan, 2013). Researchers Alan Said and others specifically pointed out that demographical information gender has a greater impact on the CF algorithm (Said, Plumbaum, De Luca, & Albayrak, 2011). Silvia and Analia addressed the cold start problem in CF algorithm-based travel agent by coming up with a hybrid approach comprising demographical information (SilviaN & Analía, 2009). Akram and Laila worked on the user age, gender and occupation information to address the cold start problem (Safoury & Salah, 2013). In their method, user demographic information will be correlated with the neighbouring user to find a similar neighbour. Based on the similar neighbour the recommendations are generated (Safoury & Salah, 2013). A user profiling based demographic recommendation system (DRS) was derived in (Al-Shamri, 2016). In this work, user profiling is combined with the CF algorithm to provide demographic based recommendations. Naime and Sasan used multi-criteria along with CF in their neuro-fuzzy based recommendation system (Kermany & Alizadeh, 2017). This work used a neuro-fuzzy system to identify the relationship between each criterion. To address the cold-start problem, this work used movie and user-based similarities. Iosif and others addressed the cold-start problem by combining community-created knowledge with a demographic-based recommendation system (Viktoratos, Tsadiras, & Bassiliades, 2018). These recommendations systems that use collaboration filtering along with other techniques like contextual information are called as context-aware recommendation systems. Recently, Shi and others have utilized the mobile phone usage information in their DRS to alleviate the cold-start problem (Shi, Chen, Xu, & Lyu, 2019). In order to profile the users for better recommendations, this method extracts different types of mobile phone usages along with demographic information. In most of the cases, demographical information is used along with the CF algorithm to address the cold-start problem (SilviaN & Analía, 2009; Safoury & Salah, 2013; Chen & He, 2009).

In recent years, the CF based recommendation systems have started using deep learning approaches in their works to provide better recommendations (Dacrema, Boglio, Cremonesi, & Jannach, 2019). After the successful implementation of neural networks in other domains (Srinivasan & LD, 2019; Srinivasan & LD, A Neuro-Fuzzy Approach to Detect Rumors in Online Social Networks, 2020), deep learning approaches have been started applied to recommendation systems as well (Dacrema, Boglio, Cremonesi, & Jannach, 2019). In Christakou, Vrettos, & Stafylopatis, (2007), movie ratings are predicted using multilayer perceptrons for movie, user and actors. Some of Other recommendation systems used neural networks techniques in their works for collaboration filtering (Ebesu, Shen, & Fang, 2018; Wang, Wang, & Yeung, 2015; Zhang, Cao, Zhu, Li, & Sun, 2018). But using neural networks in the recommendation system is not providing better results compared to classic machine learning methods (Dacrema, Boglio, Cremonesi, & Jannach, 2019). Also, user cold start problems may not have enormous data related to new users that neural networks require for better generalization.

In a factorized user genre matrix-based recommender algorithm, the movie genre is indirectly inferred to enhance the user profile (Manzato, 2012). Eric and Lenskiy in their work detailed the possibility of finding the movie genre based on the user rating by computing the Bernoulli model and genre correlation (Makita & Lenskiy, 2016). A hybrid recommender algorithm by used genre information to categorize the ratings, after the categorization, rating based correlation technique is employed to generate suggestions (Berkovsky, Kuflik, & Ricci, 2007). Also, the clustering of the genre is used in addressing the cold start problem. In this method, user-related information is crawled from social networking websites (You, Rosli, Ha, & Jo, 2013). Once the genre interest of the user is crawled from the social networking websites, clusterization is done for the user with other users based on their genre interest (You, Rosli, Ha, & Jo, 2013). Ashish and Pragya used modified matrix factorization for cross-category recommendations (Sahu & Dwivedi, 2018). User's information and latent factors are used for this transfer learning approach. Genre-based correlation techniques are introduced to overcome the cold start problem (Choi & Han, A content recommendation system based on category correlations, 2010; Choi, Ko, & Han, A movie recommendation algorithm based on genre correlations, 2012). Correlation of genre with movie rating information was used in CF algorithms for recommendations in some works (Hwang, Park, Hong, & Kim, 2016). Similarly, Ma and others used the combination of genre and tags for the recommendations (Ma, et al., 2016). In this approach latent semantic indexing, a statistical method for topic identification is used for item regularization. Recently, machine learning algorithms are applied to extract user preferences for better accuracy in recommendations. Yuan and Yan used K-means, a clustering algorithm, to extract item genre and other user preferences which helped to establish user ratings prediction models (Wang & Tang, 2019). Another method used support vector machine along with logistic regression for movie genre preference prediction (Wang & Zhang, 2018). These approaches improved the accuracy of the recommendation systems for test datasets. In one of the above mentioned genre-based recommendation system requires gaining access to the social networking site and weight distribution among the genre before clusterization also the system renders irrelevant recommendations when number of genre gets increased (You, Rosli, Ha, & Jo, 2013; Zhang, Sun, Zhu, & Fang, 2010).

$$Movie1\_Genre = (Genre1, Genre2, Genre3) \qquad (1)$$

$$Weightage(Movie1_{Genre}) = (0.6, 0.3, 0.1) \qquad (2)$$

Consider a movie that has a combination of genres as in equation (1), which states that the movie will have all the elements of the described genre. When the genres in the equation are given weight according to the above-mentioned genre correlation method then the first genre takes the highest value and the remaining value will be shared between the next two genres with respect to the maximum value of 1 as in equation (2). The weight cannot be distributed between genres based on the genre interest-based clustering method order (You, Rosli, Ha, & Jo, 2013). Because when the genre combination exceeds, each genre will get an irrelevant weight.

Genre combination represents that the movie will have a mixture of the genre so without proper understanding one cannot award weight based on the order of the genre. In content-based recommendation system, the movie genre is correlated with the user preferred genre to find out the most similar genre to the user (Choi & Han, A content recommendation system based on category correlations, 2010; Choi, Ko, & Han, A movie recommendation algorithm based on genre correlations, 2012). Once the user gives his/her preferred genre the system will start correlating to find a similar genre and will suggest the movies. Recommending the movie based on correlating the user's preferred genre will result in recommending user known item which will make the user ignore the rendered recommendations. From the above study, it is evident that the demographical information gender and category description like genre are utilized by the recommender algorithm to enhance the efficiency of the recommendations. Generally, information about the movie genre or any item characteristics is mostly given by the movie experts, critics or by the people who have the proper knowledge. So, it remains as one of the available reliable sources of information about the item. When a new user enters the system, it will be as easy as a mouse click to get the gender detail. Both the genre information and user gender are less exploited in addressing the cold start issue and in many cases, both are used as an adhesive agent to enhance the efficiency of recommendations. In the proposed GA based top-n recommendation algorithm, user gender and movie genre information are utilized to overcome the new user problem in the recommender system.

Existing GA Algorithm Based Recommendation System

Adaptation of a genetic algorithm-based approach is one among the less concentrated research area of recommendation system (Bobadilla J., Fernando, Antonio, & Abraham, 2013). Alahmadi and Zeng utilised a genetic algorithm to compute trust optimization in the online social network. Later based on the computed trust and friends are recommended to a new user (Alahmadi & Zeng, 2015). In another work, personalised balanced diet recommendation mechanism based on genetic fuzzy markup language and fuzzy sets are architectured (Lee, Wang, & Lan, 2015). It was concluded that the end results have increased efficiency when compared with type1 fuzzy sets. The Genetic algorithm is also used to compute the weight of a node in order to suggest friends in social networks (Silva, Tsang, Cavalcanti, & Tsang, 2010). Kim and Ahn used a genetic algorithm to find the relevant clusters and based on the relevant clusters' recommendations are generated to the user (Kim & Ahn, 2008). Gang lv and others developed a genetic algorithm-based recommendation system by building domain ontology and calculated weight for relational products using a genetic algorithm (Lv, Hu, & Chen, 2016). Recently, the gray wolf optimizer algorithm along with fuzzy c-mean clustering was used for movie rating prediction (Katarya & Verma, 2018). For a similar task, an artificial algae algorithm was used with fuzzy c-mean clustering in (Katarya & Verma, Effectual recommendations using artificial algae algorithm and fuzzy c-mean, 2017). Chai and others used a multi-objective immune algorithm to optimize the recommendation list (Chai, Li, Han, & Zhu, 2018). In this method, a singular value decomposition, machine learning method, is utilized to generate the recommendations from ratings. Similarly, few more works such as (Mohammadpour, Bidgoli, Enayatifar, & Javadi, 2019; Kaur & Ratnoo, 2019; Linda, Minz, & Bharadwaj, 2019) used genetic algorithms in recommender systems. Most of the existing methods incorporated genetic algorithms in addition to the other algorithms to render a recommendation. Even though authors Alahmadi and Zeng tried to address the new user problem, accessing social networking information of the users invokes security issues. Also, a first-time visitor will hesitate to input the details needed to compute the recommendation so the method will not produce any recommendations when the user is not willing to give his\her details. The top-n approach by Gang lv and others uses the genetic algorithm to find the similarity between each product. They also state that the top-n recommendations based on their approach can also be used to alleviate the cold start problem. The proposed approach by Gang lv and others uses a genetic algorithm only to calculate a similar coefficient. Just by considering the user has viewed the product one cannot conclude that the product will be liked by the user. When the system goes wrong and recommends the wrong product then the user might lose interest in the recommendation system. Whereas in the proposed approach, based on the user gender information and the item genre information top-n recommendation is rendered by utilizing the fitness, Selection and Crossover phases of the GA algorithm. The results prove that the proposed GA influenced algorithm outperforms the existing methodology in alleviating new user cold start problems.

Genetic Algorithm Based Top-N Recommender Approach

The natural evolution principle of the GA algorithm is utilized in various fields to address the optimal search problem. Genetic algorithm is a high-level evolutionary-based algorithm that effectively employs bio-inspired genetic operators such as mutations, crossover, and selection to attain an optimal solution for a search problem. In a genetic algorithm, initially, an n number of chromosomes are taken, and they are iteratively evaluated to find the best offspring producing chromosome. The evaluation process involves calculating fitness, selection, crossover, and computing mutation the processing loop continues until the arrival of the best solution. These natural evaluation principles of the GA algorithm are utilized along with the demographical information user gender and item characteristics movie genre to process top-n recommendation for a new user.

Like computing the fitness in the GA algorithm, the likeness of the movie genre with relation to a particular gender is computed and stored in the system. Consider that the system consists of user gender information and movie information along with user ratings. Based on the user gender information two movie lists are created separately for male users $(M_{List}(M))$ and female users as a list $(M_{List}(F))$. Each movie list has n number of movie genres and m number of movies along with its user ratings under each movie genre in the list. The list containing the total number of the genre in the system is represented as list G^L. The list G^L is given as input to find the best user interested movie based on the movie genre. After getting the input the fitness that is likeness of each genre is calculated for further computing. To calculate the likeness of genre $L(G)$, rating count set R_G, Positive score of the genre P_S are initialized.

$$R_G = [(R_G)^1, (R_G)^2, \ldots, (R_G)^5] \tag{3}$$

Algorithm 1. *Genre Likeness L(G) Computation*

```
GᴸThe genre list, m_G→Movie Genre
Initialize list R_G
R_G={ (R_G)¹,.., (R_G)⁵}
Initialize P_s=0
For i in length of  Gᴸ
    For  each m_G in length of M _list
       IF  Gᴸ(i)  == M _list(m_G)
          Get r value on m
          IF(r==5): Increase count (R_G)⁵
          Else if(r==4): Increase count (R_G)⁴
          Else if(r==3): Increase count (R_G)³
          Else if(r==2): Increase count (R_G)²
          Else if(r==1): Increase count (R_G)¹
          EndIF
       EndIF
    EndFor
    Append (R_G) ¹ᵗᵒ⁵ to R_G
      P_s =(R_G)⁵ + (R_G)⁴ + (R_G)³ /2
      L(G) = P_s/ N_U* G(i)_n(m)
    Append the L(G)  into Gᴸ(i)
EndFor
```

Each genre in the genre list G^L is compared with the m_G movie genre in the M_{List}. If both the genres are similar, then the movie rating given by the user is added to the rating count list R_G based on the corresponding rating count. In the proposed approach the five-star rating scale is considered so the rating count ranges from 1 to 5. The rating counters in the rating count list are depicted in equation (3). Likewise, for the total movies belonging to the specific genre and rating associated with the genre are counted and appended to the list R_G. After the successful iteration of the genre throughout the list, a positive score P_s is computed to find the likeness of the genre. In a five-star rating scale, each star represents the characteristics of the user rating. In this work, a rating of 4 and 5 is calculated as positive and the rating of 3 is calculated as a dilemma. Depending on this rating criterion the positive score of a genre and Positive score for the entire genres is calculated as in the equation (4).

$$P_S = \left(R_G\right)^5 + \left(R_G\right)^4 + \left(\left(R_G\right)^3 \Big/ 2\right) \tag{4}$$

$$L\left(G\right) = P_S \Big/ \left(N_U \times G_{n(m)}\right) \tag{5}$$

After getting the value of the positive score the likeness of the genre is computed by dividing the positive score with the product of the total number of users in the list and the total number of movies belonging to that particular genre as shown in equation (5). Finally, the likeness value of the specific genre is saved to the list G^L this is elaborated in the likeness computation algorithm. Also, for each gender genre likeness varies so for both the male and female users genre likeness is calculated separately using the genre likeness computation algorithm as $G^L(me)$ and $G^L(fe)$. After the computation of the $L(G)$ for all the genres in the list G^L, selection and crossover process are computed to find the user interested item.

In GA based on the fitness function best and worst individuals are classified, similar to the fitness function likeness is computed. Likeness defines the weight of the item to get recommended. Based on the likeness value, the recommender algorithm processes the selection and crossover stage to render recommendations. In the selection stage, each genre in the list is compared with each other based on the $L(G)$ value step by step procedure of the same is detailed in algorithm 2. If the genre has the maximum genre likeness among the genre in the list G^L then it gets to the top position likewise each and every genre in the list G^L is sorted. The computation of selecting the top genre is computed separately for both the genders as $G^L(me)$ and $G^L(fe)$. Top twenty genre T belongs to both the list are considered for the cross over the process.

Algorithm 2. *Genetic Algorithm based Top-N Recommender*

```
Initialize T=25, Ulike→User Like the item
Begin:
FOR each gender get the list of genres Gᴸ
IF Gᴸ is True:
    Calculate Genre likeness L(G):
    Return Gᴸ with the L(G)
EndIF
While Ulike=0:
  Selection:
  FOR each genre in the list Gᴸ
    Compare with Each other
    Sort the Genre based on the L(G)
    Select the Top T Genre
  EndFOR
CrossOver:
FOR each genre in list Gᴸ(me)
 FOR each genre in list Gᴸ(fe)
   IF genre of Gᴸ(me) in Gᴸ(fe)
      Append to list ∩(Gᴸ)
   EndIF
 EndFor
EndFor
FOR each genre in list Gᴸ(me) and Gᴸ(fe)
  FOR each genre in list ∩(Gᴸ)
     IF Gᴸ(me) not in  ∩(Gᴸ):Append to u(Gᴸ(me))
```

```
    EndIF
    IF G^L(fe) not in   ∩(G^L): Append to u(G^L(fe))
    EndIF
  EndFor
EndFor
IF user gender is male:
  Then recommend movies belong to list u(G^L(me))
Else: Recommend Movies belong to list u(G^L(fe))
End IF
Verify IF user response to the recommendation = true:
    Change ULike=1
Else:
   Assign T=Next 25
   Got To Selection
EndIF
```

Next to the selection process is a cross over, generally in GA cross over is carried out using more than one parent to produce offspring. Cross over operator is defined to carry out this operation. The proposed hybrid genetic algorithm uses intersection as the cross over operator to produce the needed unique offspring. The successful computation of the selection stage is followed by the cross over the process. In the selection stage, the top twenty-five genres for each gender are computed, now cross over operation is carried out to find the possible parent to produce the offspring. Whereas in the process of recommendation, after the selection stage the genre that has the possibility to get recommended is discovered.

$$\cap\left(G^L\right) = \left\{ G^L\left(me\left(i\right)\right) \cap G^L\left(fe\left(i\right)\right) \right\}_{i=0 to l} \tag{6}$$

Figure 1. Number of movies in each genre

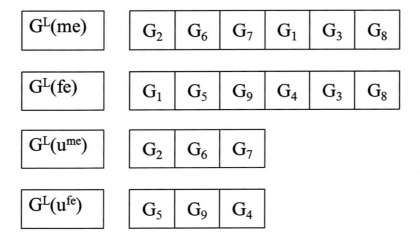

$$G^L\left(u^{me}\right) = G^L\left(me\right) not\ in \cap\left(G^L\right) \tag{7}$$

$$G^L\left(u^{fe}\right) = G^L\left(fe\right) not\ in \cap\left(G^L\right) \tag{8}$$

Each genre in the list G^L(me) and G^L(fe) is considered as the possible parent to produce the offspring. The cross over operation is applied between both the lists to get the offspring that is the unique genre list G^L(u). As depicted in the figure, let us consider genre list for males consist of genres {G_2, G_6, G_7, G_1, G_3, G_8} and the genre list of the female has the top genres as {G_1, G_5, G_9, G_4, G_3, G_8}. The intersection operation is applied to find a similar genre in both the top lists of male and female users. As depicted in the equation (6), the list $\cap$(G^L) constitutes the genre that is present in both the lists G^L(me) and G^L(fe). After the intersection operation, the remaining genre in the G^L(me) and G^L(fe) produces the new offspring G^L(u^{me}) and G^L(u^{fe}) are derived from the equation (7) and (8). Movies belong to list G^L(u^{me}) are recommended to the male user and the movies of G^L(u^{fe}) are suggested to the female user. If the user does not like the recommended movie, again the algorithm goes to the selection state to find the next twenty top genres. Usually, in top-n recommendation, total data will be gathered, and similarity will be rendered to get the recommendation list. By these traditional methods, the genres that are different from high likeness but sparse in nature will be left out. The proposed algorithm finds the unique genres that have a high likeness and recommends it to the user. The new user interests on the uniquely generated top-n recommendation, accuracy of the proposed approach and reliability of the system are discussed in the evaluation section.

Evaluating the Proposed Approach

The proposed recommender algorithm is evaluated using the movielens standard real-world dataset (Harper & Konstan, 2016). The recommended top fifteen movie genres for a new male and female user are tabulated in table 1. In the top fifteen genres of table 1, one can notice that after the top second genre the order of many genres gets scrambled across the table. This clearly determines that the preference of female users is not the same as that of the male users in watching the film. Finally, the system computes and different genres among the top fifteen and based on that different genre the films are suggested to the new user. Based on this, the different genres of the top fifteen are tabulated in table 2.

Once the different genres that exist in the top fifteen are rendered, based on the rendered genres the films are suggested to the user. Instead of generating recommendations from the total list, the developed algorithm suggests movies from genres that are unique in nature. The unique, genre mostly consists of movies that are sparse in nature, though these movies are liked by most of the users who watched it. Many users in the system did not view the suggested movies. By evaluating the movielens dataset based on the Top-N recommendation, it can be learned that 1739 male users out of 4331 and 749 female users out of 1709 have watched the movies. The user figure states that most of the users in the system did not view the recommended movies. In the 1739 male users, 984 users watched at least one movie of the recommended movies. 519 users viewed two movies and 199 out of 1739 male users have seen three movies of the suggested movies. Total of 37 male users watched all the recommended movies this is depicted in figure 2 where c1 points to users who viewed the entire movie, c2 and c3 corresponds

Table 1. Top fifteen genre for male and female users

S. No	Male Users	Female Users
1	Action, Adventure, Drama, Sci-Fi, War	Action, Adventure, Drama, Sci-Fi, War
2	Action, Adventure, Romance, Sci-Fi, War	Action, Adventure, Romance, Sci-Fi, War
3	Action, Adventure, Comedy, Sci-Fi	Comedy, Romance, War
4	Children's, Drama, Fantasy, Sci-Fi	Children's, Drama, Fantasy, Sci-Fi
5	Action, Sci-Fi, Thriller, War	Action, Adventure, Comedy, Sci-Fi
6	Film-Noir, Sci-Fi	Adventure, Comedy, Drama
7	Comedy Romance War	Adventure, Children's, Drama, Musical
8	Action, Adventure, Fantasy, Sci-Fi	Adventure, Animation, Film-Noir
9	Adventure, Comedy, Drama	Animation, Children's, Comedy, Musical, Romance
10	Drama, Mystery, Sci-Fi, Thriller	Action, Adventure, Fantasy, Sci-Fi
11	Adventure, Children's, Drama, Musical	Action, Adventure, Comedy, Romance
12	Sci-Fi, War	Adventure, Drama, Western
13	Adventure, Animation, Film-Noir	Comedy, Fantasy, Romance
14	Crime, Film-Noir, Mystery, Thriller	Crime, Film-Noir, Mystery, Thriller
15	Adventure, Drama, Western	Action, Adventure, Romance, War

Table 2. Different genres of the top fifteen

S. No	Male Users	Female Users
1.	Action, Sci-Fi, Thriller, War	Animation, Children's, Comedy, Musical, Romance
2.	Film-Noir, Sci-Fi	Action, Adventure, Comedy, Romance
3.	Drama, Mystery, Sci-Fi, Thriller	Comedy, Fantasy, Romance
4.	Sci-Fi, War	Action, Adventure, Romance, War

to three and two movies, c4 represents users who watched only one movie and c5 corresponds to total users present in the system.

In figure 2, female user's interest in viewing the recommended movies is depicted. Where each category points to the number of movies that users viewed. Category C8 corresponds to the user who viewed at least one of the recommended movies. C7 and C6 show the 370 female users who watched only 1 movie and 197 out of 749 saw at least 2 among the overall recommended movies, C5 stands for 102 users who viewed three movies. C4 and C3 represent the 50 users and 18 users who saw four and five movies respectively. C2 corresponds to the user who viewed 6 movies of the total recommended movie and C1 points to the user who viewed all the recommended movies as shown in figure 3.

Comparing both the male and female users' one can find the vast difference between the users who are interested in viewing the recommended movies. Generally, a number of male users in the system are more than that of female users, the earlier process of suggesting movies would have rendered movies based on the total user irrespective of the gender. Whereas the proposed algorithm analyses the user interest based on gender and tries to retrieve user personified movies that are unique in nature. From figure

Figure 2. Number of male users who watched the recommended movies

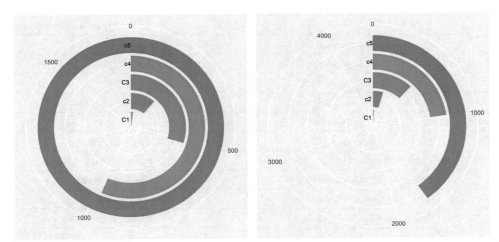

Figure 3. Number of female users who watched the recommended movies

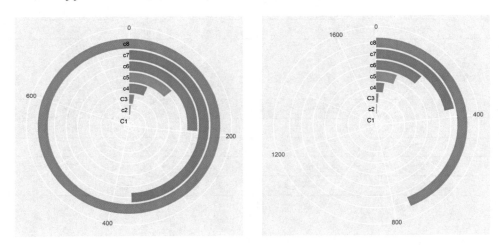

2 and 3, it is concluded that the majority of users does not view the recommended movies this shows the uniqueness of the recommendations. The various parameters involved in this study are elaborately discussed in tables 1, 2 and figures 2, 3. The visualized representations in figures 2 and 3 are clearly indicating the genre and gender are correlated features which combinedly can give good prediction accuracy to the machine learning models. In order to find the accuracy scores, Mean absolute error and Root mean square error accuracy measures of the proposed algorithm are calculated and compared with the Akram and Laila approach (Safoury & Salah, 2013).

Akram and Laila utilized the demographical information like age, gender, and occupation to address the cold start problem in recommendation system (Safoury & Salah, 2013). In our proposed hybrid approach, demographical information gender is computed along with the genre information to render recommendations. In figure 4 comparison graph is plotted where AL-G, AL-O, AL-A denotes different approaches of gender, occupation, and age by Akram and Laila. A1 and A2 represent the MAE and

Figure 4. MAE and RMSE score comparison

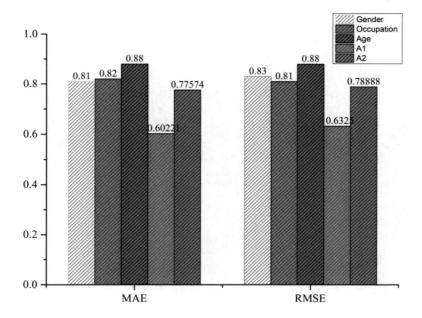

RMSE scores of the proposed approach for male and female users. Comparatively the proposed algorithm outperforms the Akram Laila approach as seen in figure 4.

$$Precision = \frac{Recommended\ movie \cap User\ liked}{total\ Movie\ recommended} \qquad (7)$$

$$Recall = \frac{User\ liked\ movie}{User\ liked\ and\ disliked \cap Recommended\ movie} \qquad (8)$$

$$F1Score = 2\left(\frac{Precision \times Recall}{Precision + Recall}\right) \qquad (9)$$

For further analysis of prediction accuracy precision, recall and F1 scores are evaluated. Precision stands for, the intersection of movies suggested and liked by the users to the movies that users viewed from the recommended list as depicted in the equation (7). Recall stands for the ratio between user liked movies among the recommended and the movie that is viewed by the user (8). F1 Score is the combined arithmetic mean of precision and recall as depicted in the equation (9).

In order to define the efficiency of the proposed GA based top-n recommender algorithm, the precision and recall rate are compared with the traditional as well as current approaches like Pearson correlation, cosine similarity, proximity impact popularity based similarity measure (Pip) (Ahn, 2008), Collaborative models on pre-prediction errors (uerror) (Kim, El-Saddik, & Jo, 2011), JSMD (Bobadilla, Francisco, &

Figure 5. Comparison of precision score @5

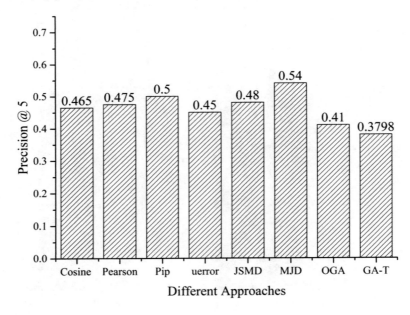

Figure 6. Comparison of Recall @5

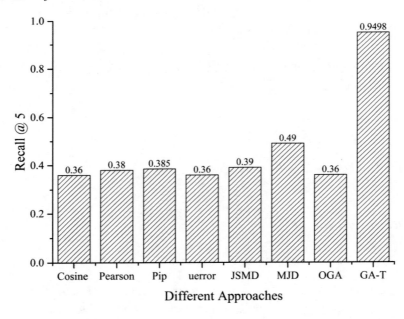

Jesus, A new collaborative filtering metric that improves the behavior of recommender systems, 2010), MJD (Bobadilla J., Fernando, Antonio, & JesúS, 2012) and OGA (Lv, Hu, & Chen, 2016). In figures 5 and 6, precision and recall score comparison between the proposed GA based top-n recommender algorithm (GA-T) and other algorithms are depicted for 5 recommendations. The precision rate of the proposed algorithm is low comparing the other algorithms whereas the recalls score of GA-T is high

Figure 7. Comparison of F1Score @5

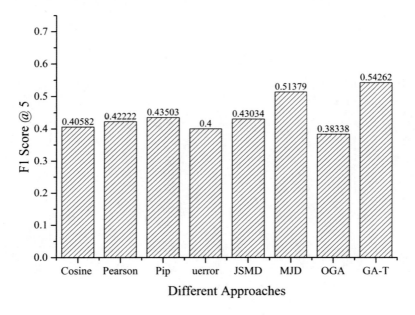

Figure 8. Comparison of Precision Score @10

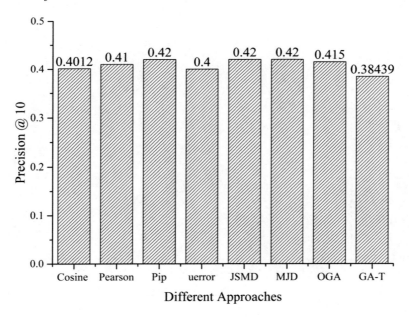

and remains standard. The low in precision rate is because most of the recommended items are new to the user since the items are new it cannot be considered as disliked or interested by the user. This caused a low precision score though most of the recommended items are liked by the user which is evident through the recall rate which is depicted in figure 6. For finding the mean between the precision and recall score the f1 score is computed and depicted in figure 7. The F1 score of the proposed algorithm

Figure 9. Comparison of Recall @10

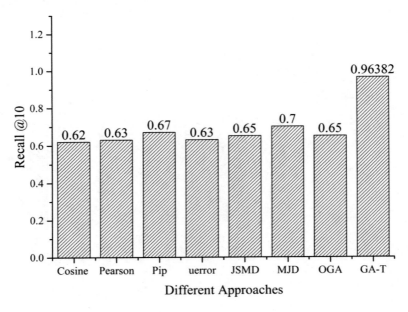

Figure 10. Comparison of F1Score @10

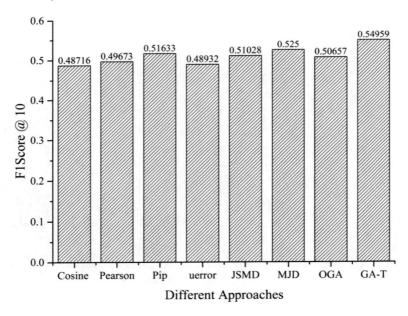

shows that the genetic algorithm-based top-n recommender approach is better than all the other approaches. For further evaluation, prediction measures are computed for ten recommendations. In that too, the precision is low and the recall score is much higher than all the other approaches this is depicted in figures 8 and 9. Also, the F1 score for a total of 10 recommendations depicted in figure 10 shows that the system outperforms all the other approaches. The evaluation of the system shows that many of the recommended items are new to the users as seen in figures 2 and 3. The comparison of our method with the demographical recommender in figure 4 proves that the proposed (GA-T) algorithm performs better then Akram and Laila's approach. Also, the prediction accuracy measures precision, recall and f1 score comparison depicted in figures 5-10 conclude that the GA-T algorithm has less precision but good recall rate and better overall f1 score.

DISCUSSION

Movie recommendation for new users has been an important research topic in the recommendation system domain. Utilizing the genre of the movie for this kind of recommendation is a proven idea for better results (You, Rosli, Ha, & Jo, 2013) (Choi, Ko, & Han, A movie recommendation algorithm based on genre correlations, 2012). Recently, genetic algorithms with other methods like fuzzy are utilized to provide genre-based recommendations (Katarya & Verma, 2018). In such methods, the genetic algorithms generate the relevant clusters for the users and these clusters are used in recommendations (Kim & Ahn, 2008).

Though such genre-based methods provide better overall results, these methods are handling both genders similarly for recommendations. But demographic information and gender play a vital role in movie recommendations (Said, Plumbaum, De Luca, & Albayrak, 2011). The proposed work effectively utilized this information to address the cold-start problem. The genetic algorithm used in this method is giving top-N recommendations by optimally utilizing gender and genre information. As shown in figure 4, the MAE and RMSE scores are lesser for the proposed approach compared to other approaches. These scores are calculated separately for both genders. It shows significant differences in MAE and RMSE scores for both genders. It also implies that gender plays a vital role while computing the movie recommendations. The top-N recommendations provided in this proposed work are based on genre and gender which have effectively addressed the cold start problem using the genetic algorithm.

CONCLUSION

The prevailing cold start problem of the Collaborative filtering algorithm reduces the accuracy of the recommender system and affects the user experience and trust in the system. In order to generate the CF algorithm-based recommendations, the system needs a history of user information. One cannot make the user to input loads of information at their first visit to the application. Considering this scenario, a hybrid recommender algorithm is proposed. Unlike other algorithms, the proposed genetic algorithm based top-n recommender algorithm recommends unique as well as user interested items. Since known items will make the user feel tired and skip off the recommendations the algorithm is entitled to render unique recommendations. Once gender information is garnered, based on computed genre list recommendations are rendered based on the genetic operators. Evaluation of the proposed algorithm shows that the system outperforms the other similar demographical recommendation systems. The low precision score with the traditional algorithm is due to the rendering of items that are unique and unknown to the user. Currently, the proposed algorithm is developed and evaluated only on the movie domain. In future, the same approach will be applied to various domains like music and books. The genetic algorithm based top-n recommendation approach will pave new channels towards the demographical and item properties combined recommendations research.

REFERENCES

Ahn, H. J. (2008). A new similarity measure for collaborative filtering to alleviate the new user cold-starting problem. *Information Sciences*, *178*(1), 37–51. doi:10.1016/j.ins.2007.07.024

Al-Shamri, M. Y. (2016). User profiling approaches for demographic recommender systems. *Knowledge-Based Systems*, *100*, 175–187. doi:10.1016/j.knosys.2016.03.006

Alahmadi, D. H., & Zeng, X.-J. (2015). Twitter-based recommender system to address cold-start: A genetic algorithm-based trust modelling and probabilistic sentiment analysis. *2015 IEEE 27th International Conference on Tools with Artificial Intelligence (ICTAI)*, (pp. 1045-1052).

Beel, J., Langer, S., Nürnberger, A., & Genzmehr, M. (2013). The impact of demographics (age and gender) and other user-characteristics on evaluating recommender systems. In *Research and Advanced Technology for Digital Libraries* (pp. 396–400). Springer. doi:10.1007/978-3-642-40501-3_45

Berkovsky, S., Kuflik, T., & Ricci, F. (2007). Distributed collaborative filtering with domain specialization. *Proceedings of the 2007 ACM conference on Recommender systems*. 10.1145/1297231.1297238

Bobadilla, J., Fernando, O., Antonio, H., & Abraham, G. (2013). Recommender systems survey. *Knowledge-Based Systems*, *46*, 109–132. doi:10.1016/j.knosys.2013.03.012

Bobadilla, J., Fernando, O., Antonio, H., & Jesú, S. B. (2012). A collaborative filtering approach to mitigate the new user cold start problem. *Knowledge-Based Systems*, *26*, 225–238. doi:10.1016/j.knosys.2011.07.021

Bobadilla, J., Francisco, S., & Jesus, B. (2010). A new collaborative filtering metric that improves the behavior of recommender systems. *Knowledge-Based Systems*, *23*(6), 520–528. doi:10.1016/j.knosys.2010.03.009

Chai, Z.-Y., Li, Y.-L., Han, Y.-M., & Zhu, S.-F. (2018). Recommendation System Based on Singular Value Decomposition and Multi-Objective Immune Optimization. *IEEE Access: Practical Innovations, Open Solutions*, *7*, 6060–6071. doi:10.1109/ACCESS.2018.2842257

Chen, C. C., Wan, Y.-H., Chung, M.-C., & Sun, Y.-C. (2013). An effective recommendation method for cold start new users using trust and distrust networks. *Information Sciences*, *224*, 19–36. doi:10.1016/j.ins.2012.10.037

Chen, T., & He, L. (2009). Collaborative filtering based on demographic attribute vector. *Proceedings ETP International Conference on Future Computer and Communication (pp. 225-229). IEEE.*

Choi, S.-M., & Han, Y.-S. (2010). A content recommendation system based on category correlations. Proceedings 2010 Fifth International Multi-conference on Computing in the Global Information Technology (pp. 66-70). IEEE.

Choi, S.-M., Ko, S.-K., & Han, Y.-S. (2012). A movie recommendation algorithm based on genre correlations. *Expert Systems with Applications, 39*(9), 8079–8085. doi:10.1016/j.eswa.2012.01.132

Deng, T., Fan, W., & Geerts, F. (2015). On recommendation problems beyond points of interest. *Information Systems, 48*, 64–88. doi:10.1016/j.is.2014.08.002

Gen, M., & Cheng, R. (1997). *Genetic algorithms and engineering design.* New York: John Wiley & Sons.

Goldberg, D. E. (1989). *Genetic algorithms in search, optimization, and machine learning, 1989.* Reading: Addison-Wesley.

Harper, F. M., & Konstan, J. A. (2016). The movielens datasets: History and context. [TiiS]. *ACM Transactions on Interactive Intelligent Systems, 5*(4), 19.

Herlocker, J., Konstan, J. A., Borchers, A., & Riedl, J. (1999). An algorithmic framework for performing collaborative filtering. *Proceedings of the 22nd annual international ACM SIGIR conference on Research and development in information retrieval.* 10.1145/312624.312682

Herlocker, J. L., Joseph, A. K., & Riedl, J. (2000). Explaining collaborative filtering recommendations. *Proceedings of the 2000 ACM conference on Computer supported cooperative work* (pp. 241-250). ACM.

Huang, Z., Chen, H., & Zeng, D. (2004). Applying associative retrieval techniques to alleviate the sparsity problem in collaborative filtering. [TOIS]. *ACM Transactions on Information Systems, 22*(1), 116–142. doi:10.1145/963770.963775

Hwang, T.-G., Park, C.-S., Hong, J.-H., & Kim, S. K. (2016). An algorithm for movie classification and recommendation using genre correlation. *Multimedia Tools and Applications, 75*(20), 12843–12858. doi:10.100711042-016-3526-8

Karypis, G. (2001). Evaluation of item-based top-n recommendation algorithms. *Proceedings of the 10th International Conference on Information and Knowledge Management* (pp. 247-254). ACM.

Katarya, R., & Verma, O. P. (2017). Effectual recommendations using artificial algae algorithm and fuzzy c-mean. *Swarm and Evolutionary Computation, 36*, 52–61. doi:10.1016/j.swevo.2017.04.004

Katarya, R., & Verma, O. P. (2018). Recommender system with grey wolf optimizer and FCM. *Neural Computing & Applications, 30*(5), 1679–1687. doi:10.100700521-016-2817-3

Kermany, N. R., & Alizadeh, S. H. (2017). A hybrid multi-criteria recommender system using ontology and neuro-fuzzy techniques. *Electronic Commerce Research and Applications, 21*, 50–64. doi:10.1016/j.elerap.2016.12.005

Khusro, S., Ali, Z., & Ullah, I. (2016). Recommender Systems: Issues, Challenges, and Research Opportunities. [ICISA]. *Information Science and Applications, 2016*, 1179–1189. doi:10.1007/978-981-10-0557-2_112

Kim, H.-N., El-Saddik, A., & Jo, G.-S. (2011). Collaborative error-reflected models for cold-start recommender systems. *Decision Support Systems, 51*(3), 519–531. doi:10.1016/j.dss.2011.02.015

Kim, K., & Ahn, H. (2008). A recommender system using GA K-means clustering in an online shopping market. *Expert Systems with Applications, 34*(2), 1200–1209. doi:10.1016/j.eswa.2006.12.025

Konstan, J. A., & Riedl, J. T. (2003). Recommender Systems for the Web. In *Visualizing the Semantic Web* (pp. 151-167). London, UK: Verlag Springer. doi:10.1007/978-1-4471-3737-5_10

Koschmider, A., Hornung, T., & Oberweis, A. (2011). Recommendation-based editor for business process modeling. *Data & Knowledge Engineering*, *70*(6), 483–503. doi:10.1016/j.datak.2011.02.002

Lee, C.-S., Wang, M.-H., & Lan, S.-T. (2015). Adaptive personalized diet linguistic recommendation mechanism based on type-2 fuzzy sets and genetic fuzzy markup language. *IEEE Transactions on Fuzzy Systems*, *23*(5), 1777–1802. doi:10.1109/TFUZZ.2014.2379256

Leu, S.-S., Yang, C.-H., & Huang, J.-C. (2000). Resource leveling in construction by genetic algorithm-based optimization and its decision support system application. *Automation in Construction*, *10*(1), 27–41. doi:10.1016/S0926-5805(99)00011-4

Linden, G., Smith, B., & York, J. (2003). Amazon. com recommendations: Item-to-item collaborative filtering. *IEEE Internet Computing*, *7*(1), 76–80. doi:10.1109/MIC.2003.1167344

Lv, G., Hu, C., & Chen, S. (2016). Research on recommender system based on ontology and genetic algorithm. *Neurocomputing*, *187*, 92–97. doi:10.1016/j.neucom.2015.09.113

Ma, T., Suo, X., Zhou, J., Tang, M., Guan, D., Tian, Y., ... Al-Rodhaan, M. (2016). Augmenting matrix factorization technique with the combination of tags and genres. *Physica A*, *461*, 101–116. doi:10.1016/j.physa.2016.05.021

Makita, E., & Lenskiy, A. (2016). A movie genre prediction based on Multivariate Bernoulli model and genre correlations. *arXiv preprint*.

Manzato, M. G. (2012). Discovering latent factors from movies genres for enhanced recommendation. *Proceedings of the sixth ACM conference on Recommender systems*. 10.1145/2365952.2366006

Matlab. (2015, December 22). *Combing Algorithm: Finding Unique Equaltiy between Vectors of Different Sizes Using Ranges*. (Mathworks) Retrieved July 28, 2016, from https://in.mathworks.com/matlabcentral/answers/261393-combing-algorithm-finding-unique-equaltiy-between-vectors-of-different-sizes-using-ranges

Maulik, U., & Bandyopadhyay, S. (2000). Genetic algorithm-based clustering technique. *Pattern Recognition*, *33*(9), 1455–1465. doi:10.1016/S0031-3203(99)00137-5

Michalewicz, Z. (2013). Genetic algorithms+ data structures= evolution programs. Springer Science & Business Media.

Moreno, A., Aida, V., David, I., Lucas, M., & Joan, B. (2013). Sigtur/e-destination: Ontology-based personalized recommendation of tourism and leisure activities. *Engineering Applications of Artificial Intelligence*, *26*(1), 633–651. doi:10.1016/j.engappai.2012.02.014

Papagelis, M., Plexousakis, D., & Kutsuras, T. (2005). Alleviating the sparsity problem of collaborative filtering using trust inferences. *Proceedings International Conference on Trust Management* (pp. 224-239). Springer. 10.1007/11429760_16

Pazzani, M. J. (1999). A framework for collaborative, content-based and demographic filtering. *Artificial Intelligence Review, 13*(5-6), 393–408. doi:10.1023/A:1006544522159

Polat, H., & Du, W. (2005). Privacy-preserving top-n recommendation on horizontally partitioned data. *Proceedings of the 2005 IEEE/WIC/ACM International Conference on Web Intelligence*, (pp. 725-731). 10.1109/WI.2005.117

Resnick, P., Iacovou, N., Suchak, M., Bergstrom, P., & Riedl, J. (1994). GroupLens: an open architecture for collaborative filtering of netnews. *Proceedings of the 1994 ACM conference on Computer supported cooperative work.* 10.1145/192844.192905

Ribeiro Filho, J. L., Treleaven, P. C., & Cesare, A. (1994). Genetic-algorithm programming environments. *Computer, 27*(6), 28–43. doi:10.1109/2.294850

Safoury, L., & Salah, A. (2013). Exploiting user demographic attributes for solving cold-start problem in recommender system. *Lecture notes on software engineering, 1*(3), 303.

Sahu, A. K., & Dwivedi, P. (2018). Matrix factorization in Cross-domain Recommendations Framework by Shared Users Latent Factors. *Procedia Computer Science, 143*, 387–394. doi:10.1016/j.procs.2018.10.410

Said, A., Plumbaum, T., De Luca, E. W., & Albayrak, S. (2011). A comparison of how demographic data affects recommendation. *User Modeling, Adaptation, and Personalization (UMAP)*, 7.

Shi, H., Chen, L., Xu, Z., & Lyu, D. (2019). Personalized location recommendation using mobile phone usage information. *Applied Intelligence, 49*(10), 1–14. doi:10.100710489-019-01477-6

Silva, N. B., Tsang, R., Cavalcanti, G. D., & Tsang, J. (2010). A graph-based friend recommendation system using genetic algorithm. *Proceedings 2010 IEEE Congress on Evolutionary Computation (CEC)* (pp. 1-7). IEEE.

Silvia, N. S., & Analía, A. (2009). Building an expert travel agent as a software agent. *Expert Systems with Applications, 36*(2), 1291–1299. doi:10.1016/j.eswa.2007.11.032

Son, L. H. (2016). Dealing with the new user cold-start problem in recommender systems: A comparative review. *Information Systems, 58*, 87–104. doi:10.1016/j.is.2014.10.001

Su, X., & Khoshgoftaar, T. M. (2009). A survey of collaborative filtering techniques. *Advances in Artificial Intelligence, 2009*(1), 4.

Victor, P., Cornelis, C., Teredesai, A. M., & Cock, M. D. (2008). Whom should I trust?: the impact of key figures on cold start recommendations. *Proceedings of the 2008 ACM symposium on Applied computing* (pp. 2014--2018). ACM. 10.1145/1363686.1364174

Viktoratos, I., Tsadiras, A., & Bassiliades, N. (2018). Combining community-based knowledge with association rule mining to alleviate the cold start problem in context-aware recommender systems. *Expert Systems with Applications, 101*, 78–90. doi:10.1016/j.eswa.2018.01.044

Vozalis, M., & Margaritis, K. G. (2004). Collaborative filtering enhanced by demographic correlation. *AIAI symposium on professional practice in AI, of the 18th world computer congress.*

Vozalis, M. G., & Margaritis, K. G. (2007). Using SVD and demographic data for the enhancement of generalized collaborative filtering. *Information Sciences*, *177*(15), 3017–3037. doi:10.1016/j.ins.2007.02.036

Wang, H., & Zhang, H. (2018). Movie genre preference prediction using machine learning for customer-based information. *2018 IEEE 8th Annual Computing and Communication Workshop and Conference (CCWC)*, 110-116.

Wang, Y., & Tang, Y. (2019). A Recommendation Algorithm Based on Item Genres Preference and GBRT. *Journal of Physics: Conference Series*, *1229*(1). doi:10.1088/1742-6596/150/1/012053

Wilson, D. C., Smyth, B., & Sullivan, D. O. (2003). Sparsity reduction in collaborative recommendation: A case-based approach. *International Journal of Pattern Recognition and Artificial Intelligence*, *17*(5), 863–884. doi:10.1142/S0218001403002678

You, T., Rosli, A. N., Ha, I., & Jo, G.-S. (2013). Clustering method based on genre interest for cold-start problem in movie recommendation. *Journal of Intelligent Information Systems*, *19*(1), 51–77.

Zhang, C., Sun, J., Zhu, X., & Fang, Y. (2010). Privacy and security for online social networks: Challenges and opportunities. *IEEE Network*, *24*(4), 13–18. doi:10.1109/MNET.2010.5510913

Chapter 11
Experimental Study on Boundary Constraints Handling in Particle Swarm Optimization

Shi Cheng

https://orcid.org/0000-0002-5129-995X

Shaanxi Normal University, China

Yuhui Shi

https://orcid.org/0000-0002-8840-723X

Southern University of Science and Technology, China

ABSTRACT

With an improper boundary constraints handling method, particles may get "stuck in" the boundary. Premature convergence means that an algorithm has lost its ability of exploration. Population diversity (PD) is an effective way to monitor an algorithm's ability for exploration and exploitation. Through the PD measurement, useful search information can be obtained. PSO with a different topology structure and different boundary constraints handling strategy will have a different impact on particles' exploration and exploitation ability. In this chapter, the phenomenon of particles gets "stuck in" the boundary in PSO and is experimentally studied and reported. The authors observe the position diversity time-changing curves of PSOs with different topologies and different boundary constraints handling techniques and analyze the impact of these strategies on the algorithm's ability of exploration and exploitation.

1. INTRODUCTION

Particle Swarm Optimization (PSO) was introduced by Eberhart and Kennedy in 1995 (Eberhart & Kennedy, 1995; Kennedy & Eberhart, 1995). It is a population-based stochastic algorithm modeled on social behaviors observed in flocking birds. A particle flies through the search space with a velocity that is dynamically adjusted according to its own and its companion's historical behaviors. Each particle's

DOI: 10.4018/978-1-7998-3222-5.ch011

position represents a solution to the problem. Particles tend to fly toward better and better search areas over the course of the search process (Eberhart & Shi, 2001).

Optimization, in general, is concerned with finding the "best available" solution(s) for a given problem. Optimization problems can be simply divided into unimodal problems and multimodal problems. As indicated by the name, a unimodal problem has only one optimum solution; on the contrary, a multimodal problem has several or numerous optimum solutions, of which many are local optimal solutions. Evolutionary optimization algorithms are generally difficult to find the global optimum solutions for multimodal problems due to the possible occurrence of premature convergence.

Most reported optimization methods are designed to avoid premature convergence in solving multimodal problems (Blackwell & Bentley, 2002). However, premature convergence also happens in solving unimodal problems when the algorithm has an improper boundary constraint handling method. For example, even for the simplest benchmark function—Sphere, or termed as a Parabolic problem, which has a convex curve in each dimension, particles may "stick in" the boundary and the applied PSO algorithm, therefore, cannot find the global optimum at the end of its search process. With regard to this, premature convergence needs to be addressed in both unimodal and multimodal problems. Avoiding premature convergence is important in problem optimization, i.e., an algorithm should have a balance between fast convergence speed and the ability of "jumping out" of local optima.

Particles fly in the search space. If particles can easily get clustered together in a short time, particles will lose their "search potential." Premature convergence means particles have a low possibility to explore new search areas. Although many methods were reported to be designed to avoid premature convergence (Chen & Montgomery, 2011), these methods did not incorporate an effective way to measure the degree of premature convergence, in other words, the measurement of particles' exploration/exploitation is still needed to be investigated. Shi and Eberhart gave several definitions of diversity measurement based on particles' positions (Shi & Eberhart, 2008; Shi & Eberhart, 2009). Through diversity measurements, useful exploration and/or exploitation search information can be obtained.

PSO is simple in concept and easy in implementation, however, there are still many issues that need to be considered (Kennedy, 2007). Boundary constraint handling is one of them (Xu and Rahmat-Samii, 2007; Helwig, *et al.*, 2013). In this chapter, different boundary constraints handling methods and their impacts are discussed. Position diversity will be measured and analyzed for PSO with different boundary constraints handle strategies and different topology structures.

This chapter is organized as follows. Section 2 reviews the basic PSO algorithm, four different topology structures, and definitions of population diversities. Section 3 describes several boundary constraints handling techniques, which include the classic strategy, deterministic strategy, and stochastic strategy. Experiments are conducted in Section 4 followed by analysis and discussion on the population diversity changing curves of PSOs with different boundary constraints handling methods and four kinds of topology structures. Finally, Section 6 concludes with some remarks and future research directions.

2. PARTICLE SWARM OPTIMIZATION

For the purpose of generality and clarity, m represents the number of particles and n the number of dimensions. Each particle is represented as x_{ij}, i represents the ith particle, $i=1,\ldots,m$, and j is the jth dimension, $j=1,\ldots,n$. The basic equations of the original PSO algorithm are as follow (Kennedy et al., 2001, Eberhart & Shi, 2007):

$$v_i \leftarrow wv_i + c_1 rand() \times (p_i - x_i) + c_2 Rand() \times (p_g - x_i)$$

$$x_i \leftarrow x_i + \upsilon_i$$

where w denotes the inertia weight and usually is less than 1, c_1 and c_2 are two positive acceleration constants, rand() and Rand()are two random functions to generate uniformly distributed random numbers in the range [0, 1], $x_i = (x_{i1}, x_{i2}, \cdots, x_{in})$ represents the ith particle's position, $v_i = (v_{i1}, v_{i2}, \cdots, v_{in})$ represents the ith particle's velocity υ_{ij} represents the velocity of the ith particle at the jth dimension, p_i refers to the best position found by the ith particle, and p_g refers to the position found by the member in its neighborhood that has the best fitness evaluation value so far.

2.1 Topology Structure

A particle updates its position in the search space at each iteration. The velocity update in Equation (1) consists of three parts, previous velocity, cognitive part, and social part. The cognitive part means that a particle learns from its own search experience, and correspondingly, the social part means that a particle can learn from other particles, or learn from the best in its neighbors in particular. Topology defines the neighborhood of a particle.

Particle swarm optimization algorithm has different kinds of topology structures, e.g., star, ring, four clusters, or Von Neumann structure. A particle in a PSO with a different structure has a different number of particles in its neighborhood with different scopes. Learning from a different neighbor means that a particle follows different neighborhood (or local) best, in other words, topology structure determines the connections among particles. Although it does not relate to the particle's cognitive part directly, topology can affect the algorithm's convergence speed and the ability to avoid premature convergence, i.e., the PSO algorithm's ability of exploration and exploitation.

A topology structure can be seen as the environment for particles (Bentley, 1999). Particles live in the environment and each particle competes to be the global/local best. If a particle is chosen to be the global or local best, its (position) information will affect other particles' positions, and this particle is considered as a leader in its neighborhood. The structure of PSO determines the environment for particles, the process of a particle competing to be a leader is like an animal struggling in its population.

In this chapter, the four most commonly used topology structures are considered. They are the star, ring, four clusters and Von Neumann structure, which are shown in Figure 1.

- **Star:** The star topology is shown in Figure 1 (a). Because all particles or nodes are connected, search information is shared in global scope, this topology is frequently termed as *global* or *all* topology. With this topology, the search information is shared in the whole swarm, and a particle with the best fitness value will be chosen to be the "leader." Other particles will follow this particle to find an optimum. This topology can be seen as a completive competition pattern. In this pattern, each particle competes with all others in the population and this requires N–1 total competitions for a single-species population of N particles.

- **Ring:** The ring topology is shown in Figure 1 (b). A particle is connected with two neighbors in this topology. A particle compares its fitness value with its left neighbor at first, and then the winner particle compares with the right neighbor. A particle with better fitness value in this small scope is determined by these two comparisons. This is like a small competition environment, each particle only competes with its two neighbors. This requires 2(N–1) times of total competition for a population of N particles.

- **Four Clusters:** The topology of four clusters is shown in Figure 1 (c). This topology can be seen as a species divided into four groups. Each group is a small star topology, which has a "leader" particle in this group, sharing its own search information. Besides that, each group has three link particles links to the other three groups. The link particles are used to exchange search information with the other three groups. For N particles, each group has $N/4$ particles, this needs N–4 times of competitions, plus with 12 times search information exchange. This requires N+8 times of total competition.

- **Von Neumann:** The Von Neumann topology is shown in Figure 1 (d). This topology is also named as *Square* (Mendes et al. 2004b) or ***NWES*** neighborhood (for North, East, West, and South) (Dorronsoro & Bouvry, 2011). In this topology, every particle has four neighbors that are wrapped on four sides, and the swarm is organized as a mesh. For N particles, this needs 4(N–1) times of total competition.

Figure 1. Four Topologies used in this chapter: (a) Star topology, where all particles or nodes share the search information in the whole swarm; (b) Ring topology, where every particle is connected to two neighbors; (c) Four clusters topology, where four fully connected subgroups are interconnected among themselves by linking particles; (d) Von Neumann topology, which is a lattice and where every particle has four neighbors that are wrapped on four sides.

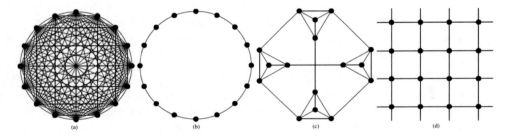

Topology determines the structure of particles' connections and the transmission of search information in the swarm. Star and ring are the two most commonly used structures. A PSO with a star structure, where all particles are connected to each other, has the smallest average distance in swarm, and on the contrary, a PSO with a local ring structure, where every particle is connected to two near particles, has the biggest average distance in swarm (Mendes et al., 2003; Mendes 2004a; Mendes et al. 2004b).

2.2 Population Diversity

An algorithm's ability to "exploration" and "exploitation" is an important factor to impact its optimization performance (Olorunda & Engelbrecht, 2008). Exploration means the ability of an optimization algorithm to explore different areas of the search space in order to have a high possibility to find a good optimum. Exploitation, on the other hand, means the ability for particles to concentrate the search around a promising region in order to refine a candidate solution. A good optimization algorithm should optimally balance the two conflicting objectives.

Population diversity of PSO measures the distribution of particles, and the diversity's changing curve is a way to monitor the degree of convergence / divergence of the PSO search process. In other words, the status of particles, whether it is in the state of exploration or exploitation, could be obtained from this measurement. Shi and Eberhart gave several definitions on diversity measurement based on particles' positions (Shi & Eberhart, 2008; Shi & Eberhart, 2009, Cheng et al, 2018). Position diversity is used to measure the distribution of particles' current positions. Cheng and Shi introduced the modified definitions of the diversity measurement based on L_1 norm (Cheng & Shi, 2011a; Cheng & Shi, 2011b; Cheng, 2013).

From diversity measurements, useful search information can be obtained. Position diversity measures the distribution of particles' current positions. One definition of position diversity, which is based on the L_1 norm, is as follows:

$$\overline{x}_j = \frac{1}{m} \sum_{i=1}^{m} x_{ij}$$

$$D_j^p = \frac{1}{m} \sum_{i=1}^{m} |x_{ij} - \overline{x}_j|$$

$$D^p = \sum_{j=1}^{n} w_j D_j^p$$

where $\overline{x}_j$ represents the pivot of particles' position in dimension j, and D_j^p measures particles position diversity based on L_1 norm for dimension j. Then we define $\overline{x} = [\overline{x}_1, \cdots, \overline{x}_j, \cdots, \overline{x}_n]$, $\overline{x}$ represents the mean of particles' current positions on each dimension, and $D^p = [D_1^p, \cdots, D_j^p, \cdots, D_n^p]$, which measures particles' position diversity for each dimension. D^p measures the whole swarm's population diversity.

Without loss of generality, every dimension is considered equally in this chapter. Setting all $w_j = \frac{1}{n}$, then the position diversity of the whole swarm can be defined as:

$$D^p = \sum_{j=1}^{n} \frac{1}{n} D_j^p = \frac{1}{n} \sum_{j=1}^{n} D_j^p$$

Position diversities, which are observed based on a dimension or on the whole swarm of particles, are experimented in Section 5 of the Chapter.

3. BOUNDARY CONSTRAINTS HANDLING

This section presents a brief survey of the main existing methods that deal with boundary constraints in the literature. Even PSO is simple and easy in implementation, there are still some issues need to be considered (Kennedy, 2007), and boundary constraints handling is one of the issues. There are different strategies to handle a particle's position when this particle exceeds its boundary limit.

3.1. "Stuck In" the Boundary

Algorithms are generally tested on the standard benchmark functions for the purpose of comparison. These functions have an optimum in the center of solution space (Yao et al., 1999). However, for real problems, we don't know the location of an optimum, and the optimum could be at any place in the solution space. With an improper boundary constraints handling strategy, a phenomenon of particles "stuck in" the boundary will occur.

A classic boundary constraint handling strategy resets a particle at a boundary in one dimension when this particle's position is exceeding the boundary in that dimension. If the fitness value of the particle at a boundary is better than that of other particles, all particles in its neighborhood in this dimension will move to the boundary. If particles could not find a position with better fitness value, all particles will "stick in" the boundary at this dimension.

A particle is difficult to "jump out" of boundary even we increase the total number of fitness evaluations or the maximum number of iterations, and this phenomenon occurs more frequently for high-dimensional problems.

3.2. Classical Strategy

The conventional boundary handling methods try to keep the particles inside the feasible search space S. Search information is obtained when particles fly in the search space. However, if a particle's position exceeds the boundary limit in one dimension at one iteration, that search information will be abandoned. Instead, a new position will be reset to the particle in that dimension. The classic strategy is to set the particle at boundary when it exceeds the boundary (Zhang et al., 2004). The equation of this strategy is as follows:

$$x_{i,j,G+1} = \begin{cases} X_{\max,j} & \textit{if } x_{i,j,G+1} > X_{\max,j} \\ X_{\min,j} & \textit{if } x_{i,j,G+1} < X_{\min,j} \\ x_{i,j,G+1} & \textit{otherwise} \end{cases}$$

where G is the number of the last iteration, and $G+1$ is the number of current iteration. This strategy resets particles in a particular point—the boundary, which constrains particles to fly in the search space limited by the boundary.

3.3. Deterministic Strategy

A deterministic method was reported in (Zielinski et al., 2009), which resets a boundary-violating position to the middle between the old position and the boundary. The equation is as follows:

$$
x_{i,j,G+1} = \begin{cases} \dfrac{1}{2}(x_{i,j,G} + X_{max,j}) & if \ x_{i,j,G+1} > X\,max,j \\ \dfrac{1}{2}(x_{i,j,G} + X_{min,j}) & if \ x_{i,j,G+1} < X_{min,j} \\ x_{i,j,G+1} & otherwise \end{cases}
$$

The position in last iteration is used in this strategy. Both classic strategy and this strategy reset a particle to a deterministic position.

3.4. Stochastic Strategy

Eberhart and Shi utilized a stochastic strategy to reset the particles when particles exceed the position boundary (Eberhart & Shi, 2007).

$$
x_{i,j,G+1} = \begin{cases} X_{max,j} - \left(\dfrac{1}{2} rand()(X_{max,j} - X_{min,j})\right) & if \ x_{i,j,G+1} > X_{max,j} \\ X_{min,j} + \left(\dfrac{1}{2} Rand()(X_{max,j} - X_{min,j})\right) & if \ x_{i,j,G+1} < X_{min,j} \\ x_{i,j,G+1} & otherwise \end{cases} \tag{6}
$$

where rand() and Rand() are two random functions to generate uniformly distributed random numbers in the range [0, 1].

By this strategy, particles will be reset within the half search space when particles exceed the boundary limit. This will increases the algorithm's exploration, that is, particles have higher possibilities to explore new search areas. However, it decreases the algorithm's ability to exploitation at the same time. A particle exceeding the boundary means the global or local optimum may be close to the boundary region. An algorithm should spend more iterations in this region. With the consideration of keeping the ability of exploitation, the resetting scope should be taken into account. For most benchmark functions, particles "fly in" a symmetric search space. With regards to this,

$$
X_{max,j} = \frac{1}{2}(X^{top,j} - X^{bottom,j}) = \frac{1}{2}X^{scope,j}
$$

and $X_{min,j} = -X_{max,j}$. The equation of resetting particle into a special area is as follows:

$$x_{i,j,G+1} = \begin{cases} X_{\max,j} \times (rand() \times c + 1 - c) & if \; x_{i,j,G+1} > X_{\max,j} \\ X_{\min,j} \times (Rand() \times c + 1 - c) & if \; x_{i,j,G+1} < X_{\min,j} \\ x_{i,j,G+1} & otherwise \end{cases} \tag{7}$$

where c is a parameter to control the resetting scope. When $c=1$, this strategy is the same as the equations (6), that is, particles reset within a half space. On the contrary, when $c=0$, this strategy is the same as the equation (4), i.e., it is the same as the classic strategy. The closer to 0 the c is, the more particles have a high possibility to be reset close to the boundary.

4. EXPERIMENTAL STUDY

Several performance measurements are utilized in the experiments below. The first is the best fitness value attained after a fixed number of iterations. In our case, we report the mean result found after the pre-determined maximum number of iterations. The second is the time t which indicates the times of particles stuck in the boundary. At the end of each run, we count the number of the particles, which has the best fitness value and which get stuck in boundary in at least one dimension. The number will be larger if a particle is stuck in boundary in more dimensions. All numbers will be summed after 50 runs. The summed number indicates the frequency of particles that may get stuck in boundary. Standard deviation values of the best fitness values are also utilized in this chapter, which gives the solution's distribution. These values give a measurement of goodness of the algorithm.

4.1. Benchmark Test Functions

The experiments have been conducted on testing the benchmark functions listed in Table 1. Without loss of generality, five standard unimodal and five multimodal test functions are selected (Liang et al., 2006; Yao et al., 1999).

All functions are run 50 times to ensure a reasonable statistical result necessary to compare the different approaches. Every tested function's optimal point in solution space S is shifted to a randomly generated point with different value in each dimension, and $S \subseteq \mathbb{R}^n$, $\mathbb{R}^n$ is a n-dimensional Euclidean space.

4.2. Velocity Constraints

In the experiments, all benchmark functions have $V_{\min} = -V_{\max}$, it means that $V_{\min}$ has the same magnitude but opposite direction. The velocity also has a constraint to limit particle's search step:

if $\upsilon_{ij} > V_{\max}$ then $\upsilon_{ij} = V_{\max}$

else if $\upsilon_{ij} < -V_{\max}$ then $\upsilon_{ij} = -V_{\max}$

Table 1. The benchmark functions used in our experimental study, where n is the dimension of each problem, $z=(x–0)$, $x=[x_1,x_2,...,x_n]$. o_i is an randomly generated number in problem's search space S, it is the same for each function at different run, but different for different function in each dimension. Global optimum $x^*=o$, f_{min} is the minimum value of the function, and $S \subseteq \mathbb{R}^n$.

Function	Test Function	S	f_{min}
Parabolic	$f_0(x) = \sum_{i=1}^{n} z_i^2 + bias_0$	$[-100, 100]^n$	-450.0
Schwefel's P2.22	$f_1(x) = \sum_{i=1}^{n}\lvert z_i \rvert + \prod_{i=1}^{n}\lvert z_i \rvert + bias_1$	$[-10, 10]^n$	-330.0
Schwefel's P1.2	$f_2(x) = \sum_{i=1}^{n}\left(\sum_{k=1}^{i} z_k\right)^2 + bias_2$	$[-100, 100]^n$	450.0
Step	$f_3(x) = \sum_{i=1}^{n}\left(\lvert z_i + 0.5 \rvert\right)^2 + bias_3$	$[-100, 100]^n$	330.0
Quadric Noise	$f_4(x) = \sum_{i=1}^{n} iz_i^4 + random[0,1) + bias_4$	$[-1.28, 1.28]^n$	-450.0
Griewank	$f_5(x) = \dfrac{1}{4000}\sum_{i=1}^{n} z_i^2 - \prod_{i=1}^{n}\cos\left(\dfrac{z_i}{\sqrt{i}}\right) + 1 + bias_5$	$[-600, 600]^n$	120.0
Rosenbrock	$f_6(x) = \sum_{i=1}^{n-1}\left[100\left(z_{i+1} - z_i^2\right)^2 + (z_i - 1)^2\right] + bias_6$	$[-10, 10]^n$	-330.0
Rastrigin	$f_7(\mathbf{x}) = \sum_{i=1}^{n}[z_i^2 - 10\cos(2\pi z_i) + 10] + bias_7$	$[-5.12, 5.12]^n$	450.0
Ackley	$f_8(x) = -20\exp\left(-0.2\sqrt{\dfrac{1}{n}\sum_{i=1}^{n} z_i^2}\right)$ $-\exp\left(\dfrac{1}{n}\sum_{i=1}^{n}\cos(2\pi z_i)\right) + 20 + e + bias_8$	$[-32, 32]^n$	180.0
Generalized Penalized	$f_9(x) = \dfrac{\pi}{n}\{10\sin^2(\pi y_1) + \sum_{i=1}^{n-1}(y_i - 1)^2$ $\times[1 + 10\sin^2(\pi y_{i+1})] + (y_n - 1)^2\} + \sum_{i=1}^{n} u(z_i,10,100,4) + bias_9$ $y_i = 1 + \dfrac{1}{4}(z_i + 1)$ $u(z_i,a,k,m) = \begin{cases} k(z_i - a)^m & z_i > a, \\ 0 & -a < z_i < a \\ k(-z_i - a)^m & z_i < -a \end{cases}$	$[-50, 50]^n$	330.0

4.3. Parameter Setting

In all experiments, each PSO has 32 particles, and parameters are set as in the standard PSO, $w=0.72984$, and $c_1=c_2=1.496172$ (Bratton & Kennedy, 2007). Each algorithm runs 50 times.

4.4. Experimental Results

4.4.1. Observation of "Stuck in" Boundary

By applying the classic strategy of boundary handling method, the position will be reset on the boundary if the position value exceeds the boundary of the search space. Table 2 gives the experimental results of applying this strategy. Each benchmark function will be tested with dimension 25, 50, and 100 to see whether similar observation can be obtained. The maximum number of iterations will be set to be 1000, 2000, 4000 corresponding to dimension 25, 50, and 100, respectively.

From the results, we can conclude that each algorithm has different possibilities of "being stuck in" boundary when it is applied to different problems. Problem dimension does not have a significant impact on the possibility of particles "being stuck in" the boundary at least for the benchmark functions with dimensions 25, 50, and 100 that we tested. Furthermore, generally speaking, the PSO with star structure is more like to be attracted to and then to be "stuck in" the boundary, and the PSO with ring structure is less like to be "stuck in" boundary.

If particles are "stuck in" the boundary, it is difficult for them to "jump out" of the local optima even we increase the maximum number of fitness evaluations. The fitness evaluation number of each function with dimension 100 in Table 2 is $32 \times 4000 = 128\,000$, we then increase this number to $32 \times 10000 = 320\,000$. The experimental results are given in Table 3. From Table 3, we can see that there is no significant improvement neither on the fitness value nor on the number of particles "stuck in" the boundary. This means that by only increasing the number of fitness evaluations cannot help particles "jump out" of boundary constraints. Some techniques should be utilized for particles to avoid converge to the boundary.

Table 4 gives the experimental results of the algorithm that ignores the boundary constraints. In the Table 4 and 5, only the PSO with star topology has the "t" column, while PSOs with other topologies do not have the "t" column because the "t" values are all zeros. For the same reason, other tables below do not have the "t" column. Particles take no strategy when particles meet the boundary. Some tested functions will get good fitness value with most of the obtained solutions being out of the search space. This may be good for particles flying in a periodic search space (Zhang et al., 2004). However, most problems have strict boundary constraints which this strategy does not fit for.

4.4.2. Comparison of PSOs With Different Boundary Constraint Handling Techniques

Table 5 shows the results of PSOs with the deterministic strategy. A particle takes a middle value of the former position and the boundary limit value when the particle meets the boundary constraint. PSOs with ring, four clusters, and Von Neumann structure can obtain good fitness values by utilizing this strategy. However, "struck in" boundary will still happen for PSO with star structure for most problems. This is because particles with star structure will progressively move to boundary. With this tendency, particles will get clustered together at the boundary and be difficult to "jump out." Therefore, the exploration ability decreases over the iterations.

Table 2. Results of the strategy that a particle "sticks in" boundary when it exceeds the boundary constraints. All algorithms are run for 50 times, the maximum number of iterations is 1000, 2000, and 4000 when the dimensions are 25, 50, and 100, respectively. Where "mean" indicates the average of the best fitness values for each run, "times" t indicates the number of particle with the best fitness value "stuck in" the boundary at a dimension. The percentage shows the frequency of particles "stuck in" the boundary of the search space.

Fun.		Star		Ring		Four Clusters		Von Neumann	
	n	Mean	Times t	Mean	t	Mean	t	Mean	t
f_0	25	4950.914	301 (24.08%)	-441.0717	2 (0.16%)	347.1880	72 (5.76%)	-64.9233	36 (2.88%)
	50	18512.65	681 (27.24%)	-391.2514	29 (1.16%)	1284.592	249 (9.96%)	467.7678	178 (7.12%)
	100	66154.79	1552 (31.04%)	**-269.469**	48 (0.96%)	7744.016	615 (12.3%)	4053.870	421 (8.42%)
f_1	25	-312.9603	159 (12.72%)	-329.9257	2 (0.16%)	-328.008	38 (3.04%)	-328.354	30 (2.4%)
	50	-265.9373	575 (23%)	-326.8749	80 (3.2%)	-314.148	242 (9.68%)	-323.725	158 (6.32%)
	100	-170.1893	1212 (24.24%)	**-299.1541**	395 (7.9%)	-254.349	791 (15.82%)	-273.921	630 (12.6%)
f_2	25	6556.133	223 (17.84%)	1418.165	55 (4.4%)	1551.690	82 (6.56%)	1151.919	68 (5.44%)
	50	59401.84	838 (33.52%)	20755.67	286 (11.44%)	18687.75	411 (16.44%)	16730.74	327 (13.08%)
	100	149100.1	1614 (32.28%)	119188.2	762 (15.24%)	97555.70	1049 (20.98%)	**93162.75**	778 (15.56%)
f_3	25	6483.32	284 (22.72%)	439.7	8 (0.64%)	1105.8	86 (6.88%)	876.56	53 (4.24%)
	50	19175.24	724 (28.96%)	476.58	29 (1.16%)	2697.68	238 (9.52%)	1604.98	166 (6.64%)
	100	70026.22	1449 (28.98%)	**859.12**	36 (0.72%)	7688.02	396 (7.92%)	7021.66	311 (6.22%)
f_4	25	-446.843	245 (19.6%)	-449.9543	24 (1.92%)	-449.836	61 (4.88%)	-449.901	33 (2.64%)
	50	-386.667	696 (27.84%)	-449.8241	44 (1.76%)	-447.068	157 (6.28%)	-448.661	91 (3.64%)
	100	49.74071	1606 (32.12%)	**-448.7530**	67 (1.34%)	-418.627	359 (7.18%)	-433.289	282 (5.64%)
f_5	25	169.2253	319 (25.52%)	120.4066	7 (0.56%)	128.1231	88 (7.04%)	123.0943	36 (2.88%)
	50	308.2321	739 (29.56%)	121.6709	49 (1.96%)	141.3122	270 (10.8%)	128.9908	187 (7.48%)
	100	676.8980	1415 (28.3%)	**122.7015**	66 (1.32%)	194.1575	591 (11.82%)	156.2124	428 (8.56%)

Table 2. Continued

Fun.	n	Star Mean	Times t	Ring Mean	t	Four Clusters Mean	t	Von Neumann Mean	t
f_6	25	102391.65	334 (26.72%)	-236.9387	25 (2%)	13681.40	107 (8.56%)	1472.597	76 (6.08%)
	50	1075433.7	870 (34.8%)	215.3156	118 (4.72%)	16784.12	368 (14.72%)	25350.40	287 (11.48%)
	100	3500148.0	1614 (32.28%)	**2311.019**	222 (4.44%)	167064.1	712 (14.24%)	123572.6	586 (11.72%)
f_7	25	529.9848	210 (16.8%)	503.0551	103 (8.24%)	500.5270	135 (10.8%)	497.6501	129 (10.32%)
	50	730.7713	445 (17.8%)	638.3773	196 (7.84%)	635.7780	281 (11.24%)	612.3373	253 (10.12%)
	100	1168.550	664 (13.28%)	968.5158	369 (7.38%)	957.5405	519 (10.38%)	**879.3672**	479 (9.58%)
f_8	25	192.2881	239 (19.12%)	181.1893	15 (1.2%)	186.4093	94 (7.52%)	184.0952	64 (5.12%)
	50	195.2231	420 (16.8%)	182.6727	69 (2.76%)	188.7666	267 (10.68%)	185.2521	183 (7.32%)
	100	199.0853	521 (10.42%)	191.6770	258 (5.16%)	191.9497	490 (9.8%)	**189.5658**	450 (9%)
f_9	25	7773207.1	250 (20%)	3567.791	15 (1.2%)	473424.72	76 (6.08%)	10931.296	54 (4.32%)
	50	163596583	749 (29.96%)	331.2763	172 (6.88%)	5365821.9	345 (13.8%)	2296129.5	291 (11.64%)
	100	1063146706	1765 (35.3%)	**5394.753**	394 (7.88%)	26421658	789 (15.78%)	6918596.1	646 (12.92%)

Table 3. Results of the strategy that a particle stays at boundary when it exceeds the boundary constraints. Algorithms have a large maximum number of fitness evaluations, i.e. 10000. The dimension n is 100.

Fun.	Star Mean	Times t	Ring Mean	t	Four Clusters Mean	t	Von Neumann Mean	t
f_0	67822.60	1540 (30.8%)	**-256.0704**	70 (1.4%)	7843.960	604 (12.08%)	2944.748	410 (8.2%)
f_1	-176.428	1225 (24.5%)	**-297.9756**	475 (9.5%)	-237.3498	874 (17.48%)	-279.874	603 (12.06%)
f_2	126974.8	1675 (33.5%)	**68200.22**	845 (16.9%)	71934.29	1099 (21.98%)	68816.78	1002 (20.04%)
f_3	71393.22	1528 (30.56%)	**931.7**	45 (0.9%)	10083.18	529 (10.58%)	6138.18	371 (7.42%)
f_4	143.0742	1599 (31.98%)	**-448.580**	49 (0.98%)	-400.9793	425 (8.5%)	-439.6080	284 (5.68%)
f_5	723.8275	1556 (31.12%)	123.6233	106 (2.12%)	189.9494	589 (11.96%)	154.8893	454 (9.08%)
f_6	3963368.9	1881 (37.62%)	**1690.535**	299 (5.98%)	229710.9	810 (16.2%)	68857.72	640 (12.8%)
f_7	1201.7850	722 (14.44%)	965.6807	413 (8.26%)	971.4570	550 (11%)	**912.0553**	552 (11.04%)
f_8	199.5501	545 (10.9%)	193.9069	312 (6.24%)	194.2383	526 (10.52%)	**190.3066**	532 (10.64%)
f_9	969621012	1874 (37.48%)	**73541.50**	487 (9.74%)	42652667	979 (19.58%)	14202759	808 (16.16%)

Table 4. Results of the strategy that a particles ignores the boundary when it exceeds the boundary constraints. All algorithms are run for 50 times, where "mean" and σ indicate the average and standard deviation of the best fitness values for each run. n is 100, and maximum iteration number is 4 000.

Fun.	Star			Ring		Four Clusters		Von Neumann	
	Mean	σ	t	Mean	σ	Mean	σ	Mean	σ
f_0	-449.6162	1.727025	0 (0%)	-449.9999	1.20E-06	**-449.9999**	6.47E-09	-449.9999	8.77E-07
f_1	-327.3012	6.104924	1 (0.02%)	-329.9900	0.025155	-329.9998	0.000425	**-329.9998**	0.000224
f_2	**35458.463**	9998.671	396 (7.92%)	116972.62	23299.66	66411.144	14308.29	71154.160	14523.52
f_3	3343.06	2330.047	39 (0.78%)	**334.28**	3.376625	353.92	39.25701	363.56	65.76508
f_4	-449.0495	2.311998	191 (3.82%)	-449.6915	0.055767	-449.8339	0.038184	**-449.8358**	0.039501
f_5	120.4391	0.890941	1 (0.02%)	**120.0007**	0.003132	120.0176	0.056479	120.0205	0.037423
f_6	-87.33991	69.15844	216 (4.32%)	-15.65356	67.65250	**-107.9635**	54.60742	-92.00367	58.01067
f_7	1058.2517	125.6292	412 (8.24%)	988.66426	63.58231	945.39263	74.93225	**892.9344**	65.63141
f_8	199.47550	1.349835	395 (7.9%)	199.26132	3.396034	194.99493	7.570846	**184.6948**	5.632849
f_9	**331.5831**	0.911304	117 (2.34%)	336.1132	2.149815	332.4632	1.849387	332.10723	1.336155

Table 5. Results of PSO with a deterministic boundary constraint strategy. Particles will be reset to the middle between old position and boundary when particle's position exceeds the boundary.n is 100, and iteration number is 4 000.

Fun.	Star			Ring		Four Clusters		Von Neumann	
	Mean	σ	t	Mean	σ	Mean	σ	Mean	σ
f_0	18125.68	12771.54	523 (10.46%)	**-449.9999**	3.15E-06	-409.4909	127.3536	-420.4673	155.7340
f_1	-267.2679	26.3105	368 (7.36%)	-324.0182	9.402653	-315.4557	15.36290	**-324.0810**	8.879355
f_2	63749.30	23677.19	11 (0.22%)	95768.66	21022.066	61791.362	17080.59	**58886.36**	14324.72
f_3	27628.66	14213.33	103 (2.06%)	**343.04**	25.91521	1378.16	1385.743	719.52	691.3372
f_4	-300.7705	173.088	0 (0%)	**-449.7622**	0.074653	-449.0363	1.945231	-449.3194	2.434300
f_5	271.0433	114.9603	508 (10.16%)	**120.0399**	0.192983	122.2650	5.086505	120.83178	1.275821
f_6	627095.6	1084062.7	657 (13.14%)	**-46.8004**	74.09709	360.9332	1304.484	66.08107	462.4078
f_7	1104.514	120.0267	20 (0.4%)	944.5443	70.81612	944.4611	87.02924	**839.2663**	68.15615
f_8	198.1596	2.591173	67 (1.34%)	**183.1589**	3.415466	185.4077	4.043386	183.4269	1.466134
f_9	88647933	232053019	333 (6.66%)	333.7982	1.770645	339.5574	51.57181	**331.4686**	1.385780

With a stochastic strategy, a particle will be reset to a random position when the particle meets the boundary. Table 6 gives the result of PSOs with the stochastic strategy, that is, a particle is reset to be within the upper half space when the particle meets the upper bound, and correspondingly, a particle is reset to be within the lower half space when the particle meets the lower bound. Compared with the classic strategy and the deterministic strategy, this strategy improves the result of PSO with the star structure, but it does not get better optimization performance for PSOs with other structures in this chapter.

Table 6. Results of the strategy that a particle is randomly re-initialized within the half search space when the particle meets the boundary constraints. n is 100, and maximum iteration number is 4 000.

Fun.	Star		Ring		Four Clusters		Von Neumann	
	Mean	σ	Mean	σ	Mean	σ	Mean	σ
f_0	15106.480	5401.915	6395.5801	1164.004	6456.2857	1471.815	**5777.2014**	1252.942
f_1	-204.55407	27.57007	-283.72265	5.047291	-282.5310	7.374081	**-286.1511**	5.525085
f_2	90226.816	38529.56	128790.177	28617.91	**86885.81**	31845.28	89231.033	33283.20
f_3	16437.02	4735.015	7593.56	1181.772	6954.9	1147.187	**6874.76**	1237.944
f_4	-442.9050	5.455450	-447.7014	0.651993	-447.9193	0.610410	-448.1605	0.490777
f_5	266.77115	36.43274	186.8523	12.45620	180.9738	10.21838	**178.7420**	11.10882
f_6	68586.660	68055.93	16834.993	6821.930	13083.356	6063.868	**12442.671**	4804.749
f_7	903.1275	69.44400	928.1833	51.27520	870.4047	72.80328	**823.6537**	59.78453
f_8	193.9104	1.330059	190.0964	0.488740	190.1364	0.627680	189.6701	0.616846
f_9	1834.0033	8708.160	2073.1476	3587.605	489.12695	220.7106	**406.0229**	121.9164

In Table 6, particles are reset within half space when particles meet the boundary. This increases an algorithm's the ability of exploration, and it decreases the ability of exploitation. A particle being close to the boundary may mean that the optimal area may be near the boundary, the resetting area should be restricted. Table 7 gives the result of resetting area limited to $[0.9V_{max}, V_{max}]$ when a particle meets the upper bound, and $[V_{min}, 0.9V_{min}]$ when a particle meets the lower bound. This strategy can obtain better results.

In both the Table 6 and 7, the resetting area does not change during the whole search process. Intuitively, at the beginning of search process, we want a large ability of exploration and small ability of exploitation to be able to search more areas of the search space (Shi & Eberhart, 1998; Shi & Eberhart, 1999). Correspondingly, at the end of search process, the exploitation ability should be more favored to find an optimum in "good" areas. With regards to this, the resetting search space should be dynamically changed in the search process. Table 8 gives the results of the strategy that the resetting space linearly decreases in the search process.

By examining the experimental results, it is clear that different boundary constraints handling techniques have different impacts on particles' diversity changing and optimization performance. The deterministic strategy fits for PSOs with ring, four clusters and Von Neumann structure. Resetting particles randomly in a small area fits for all the four topologies utilized in this chapter. Using this strategy, the PSO with star structure will have a good balance between ability of exploration and exploitation, which get the best performance than other strategies.

Table 7. Results of strategy that a particle is randomly re-initialized within a limited search space when the particle meets the boundary constraints. n is 100, and the maximum iteration number is 4 000.

Fun.	Star		Ring		Four Clusters		Von Neumann	
	Mean	σ	Mean	σ	Mean	σ	Mean	σ
f_0	-421.0384	106.7571	-446.7030	1.301631	**-448.6723**	0.544163	-448.2624	0.800959
f_1	-315.9906	14.73397	-329.2227	0.155278	-329.1543	2.610519	**-329.4232**	0.520195
f_2	**35799.38**	13401.02	99311.642	17424.32	56011.555	11425.04	56913.228	10526.66
f_3	2592.84	2381.520	**351.12**	6.556340	359.58	45.46123	368.96	77.62009
f_4	-449.5926	0.901977	-449.7613	0.055156	**-449.8691**	0.029105	-449.8604	0.034106
f_5	121.8713	3.279144	120.9374	0.090210	**120.5187**	0.120787	120.6400	0.102622
f_6	271.2483	757.2085	111.6548	176.7045	23.60728	144.9963	**1.658537**	120.5905
f_7	1059.5079	86.42771	971.4921	74.61998	930.1978	105.0998	**838.0115**	57.72716
f_8	197.5319	3.148760	183.0840	3.434429	182.9285	2.463089	**182.3226**	0.544321
f_9	331.9493	1.019762	334.1176	1.364879	332.1842	1.408311	**331.2558**	0.917983

Table 8. Results of the strategy that particles are randomly re-initialized in a linearly decreased search space when particles meet the boundary constraints. n is 100, and the maximum iteration number is 4000.

Fun.	Star		Ring		Four Clusters		Von Neumann	
	Mean	σ	Mean	σ	Mean	σ	Mean	σ
f_0	1702.3219	2184.3429	**-408.3616**	10.80574	-399.17565	53.23343	-404.6038	49.48885
f_1	-264.9917	22.439393	-327.3860	0.269110	-326.7792	2.130535	**-327.5687**	0.721141
f_2	**53393.692**	19574.620	90638.595	19706.681	59016.266	16850.516	57652.796	17353.163
f_3	5143.02	3071.211	**420.66**	17.44890	495.92	152.5970	484.9	180.2659
f_4	-448.64071	1.947832	-449.5890	0.082450	-449.7233	0.075943	**-449.7304**	0.075108
f_5	143.2678	16.39704	**121.3696**	0.0904944	121.4365	0.420780	121.3901	0.284098
f_6	9488.6354	18895.481	695.27241	429.34077	461.98764	413.84524	**341.3105**	246.16785
f_7	932.30625	74.40180	929.71921	60.000384	894.04412	61.824412	**835.0238**	47.61768
f_8	193.20420	2.508372	**183.1691**	0.417221	184.14282	1.085659	183.6688	0.974338
f_9	335.42590	1.713722	338.85667	3.039058	335.04291	1.578953	**334.1127**	1.2826316

5. POPULATION DIVERSITY ANALYSIS AND DISCUSSION

Without loss of generality and for the purpose of simplicity and clarity, the results for one function from five unimodal benchmark functions and one function from five multimodal functions will be displayed because others will be similar.

There are several definitions on the measurement of population diversities (Shi & Eberhart, 2008; Shi & Eberhart, 2009, Cheng & Shi, 2011b). The dimension-wised population diversity based on the L_1 norm is utilized in this chapter.

Figure 2. Position diversity changing curves for PSO solving parabolic function f_0 with different strategies: (a) classic, (b) cross, (c) deterministic, (d) stochastic, (e) limit, (f) linear.

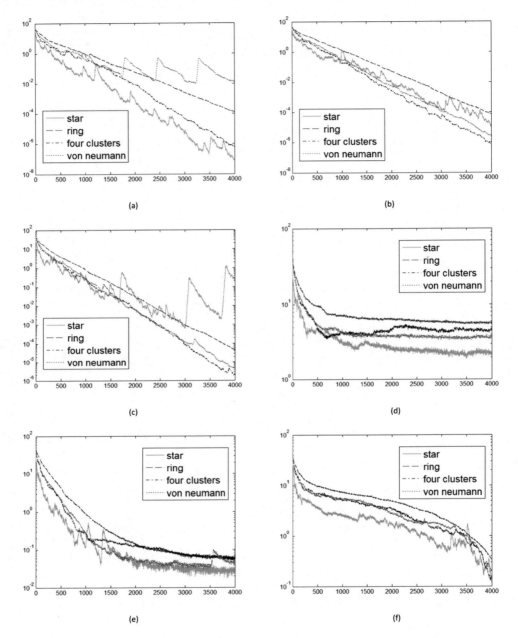

5.1. Position Diversity Monitoring

Figure 2, and 3 display the position diversity changing curves when PSO is applied to solve benchmark functions. Figure 2 displays the curves for the unimodal function f_0, and Figure 3 displays for multimodal function f_5. In both figures, (a) is for functions f_0 and f_5 with a classic boundary handling technique, (b)

Figure 3. Position diversity changing curves for PSO solving multimodal function f_5 with different strategies: (a) classic, (b) cross, (c) deterministic, (d) stochastic, (e) limit, (f) linear.

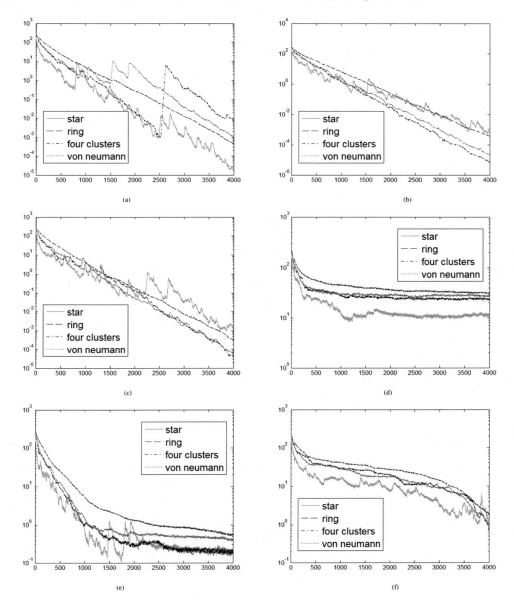

is for functions f_0 and f_5 with particles ignoring the boundary, (c) is for functions f_0 and f_5 with particles close to boundary gradually, (d) is for functions f_0 and f_5 with particles resetting in half search space, (e) is for functions f_0 and f_5 with limited resetting space at a small range near boundary, (f) is for functions f_0 and f_5 with a linearly decreased resetting scope, respectively.

Figures 2, and 3, displayed the position diversity changing curves of particles with four kinds of topologies. Some conclusion can be made that PSO with star topology has the most rapid position diversity decreasing curve, and PSO with ring topology can keep its diversity in the large number of iterations, generally. PSO with four clusters and Von Neumann also keep their diversity well in the search process, and the curves of diversity changing are smooth in most times.

The impact of different boundary constraint handling strategy on the position diversity also can be seen from these two figures. The values of position diversity changing will be very small when we utilize classic or deterministic strategies, and on the contrary, the position diversity will be kept at a "large" value when we utilize a stochastic strategy. The different position diversity changing curves indicate that particles will get clustered to a small region when we utilize a classic or deterministic strategy, and particles will be distributed in the large region when we utilize a stochastic strategy.

The changing curves of position diversity reveal the algorithm's ability of exploration and / or exploitation. The position diversity of PSO with a stochastic strategy will keep a "large" value, which indicates that with this strategy, PSO will have a good exploration ability.

5.2. Position Diversity Comparison

Different topology structures and boundary constraint handling methods will have different impacts on PSO algorithms' convergence. Figure 4 and below give some comparison among PSOs with different structures. There are four curves in each figure, which are the minimum, middle, and maximum dimensional position diversity, and position diversity as a whole. It should be noted that the dimension that has the minimum, middle, or maximum value is not fixed and may change over iterations. In other words, if the dimension i has the minimum value at iteration k, and it may be the dimension j that has the minimum value at iteration $k+1$. The figures only display position diversity's minimum, middle and maximum values at each iteration.

Figure 4 and 5 display the position diversity changing curves of a PSO with the classic boundary constraints handling method to solve unimodal function f_0 and multimodal function f_5, respectively. Four subfigures display the PSO with star, ring, four clusters, and Von Neumann topology, respectively. As can be seen from the figures, the dimensional minimum value of position diversity is quickly getting zero for PSO with star, four clusters, and Von Neumann topology, while the dimensional minimum value of position diversity will exist during the whole search process for the PSO with ring topology.

Compared with other topologies, the position diversity of PSO with star structure can get to the smallest value at the early iteration numbers, which means particles have clustered together in a small region, and any particle generally has the smallest distance to other particles. On the contrary, the position diversity of PSO with ring structure has the largest value, which means particles are distributed in a large region, and any particle generally has the largest distance to other particles.

Figure 6 and 7 display the position diversity curve of PSO with the strategy that a particle ignores the boundary constraints when the particle's position exceeds the limit. Figure 6 is for f_0, and Figure 7 is for f_5. Particles can keep their search "potential" with this strategy, the position diversity decreases in the whole search space, and not getting to zero at the end of each run.

Figures 8 and 9 display the position diversity changing curves of PSO with a deterministic boundary handling strategy on unimodal function f_0 and multimodal function f_5. PSO with star topology is easily "stuck in" the boundary with this strategy, and the minimum of position diversity quickly became zero in Figure 8 (a) and Figure 9 (a). PSO with the other three topologies has some ability to "jump out" of local optima. Figure 8 (c) and Figure9 (c) display the diversity changing curves of PSO with four clusters structure. Figure 8 (d) and Figure9 (d) display the diversity changing curves of PSO with the Von Neumann structure. From Figure 8 (c), (d) and Fig 9 (c), (d), we can observe dramatically "up and

Figure 4. Comparison of PSO population diversities for solving unimodal function f_0 with classic boundary constraints handling techniques: (a) star, (b) ring, (c) four clusters, (d) Von Neumann.

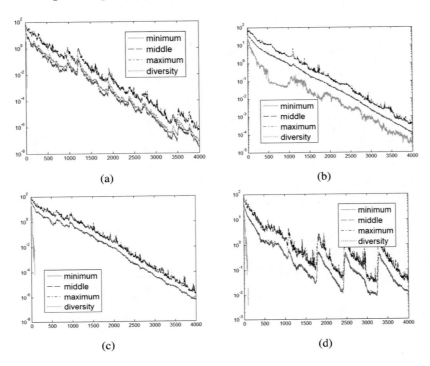

Figure 5. Comparison of PSO population diversities for solving multimodal function f_5 with classic boundary constraints handling techniques: (a) star, (b) ring, (c) four clusters, (d) Von Neumann.

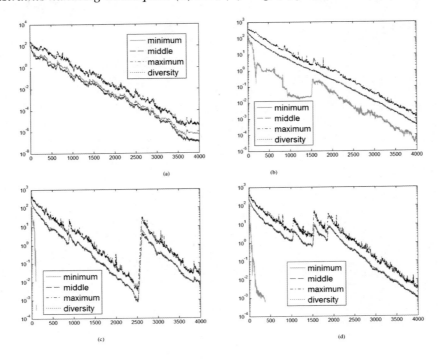

Figure 6. Comparison of PSO population diversities for solving unimodal function f_0 with exceeding boundary constraints handling techniques: (a) star, (b) ring, (c) four clusters, (d) Von Neumann.

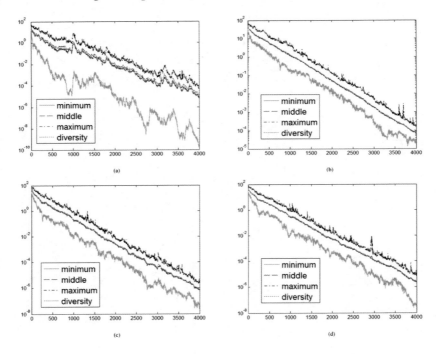

Figure 8. Comparison of PSO population diversities for solving unimodal function f_0 with deterministic boundary constraints handling techniques: (a) star, (b) ring, (c) four clusters, (d) Von Neumann.

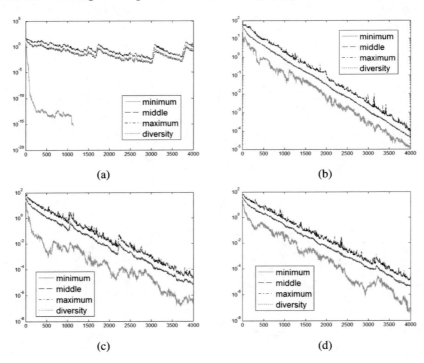

Figure 9. Comparison of PSO population diversities for solving multimodal function f_5 with deterministic boundary constraints handling techniques: (a) star, (b) ring, (c) four clusters, (d) Von Neumann.

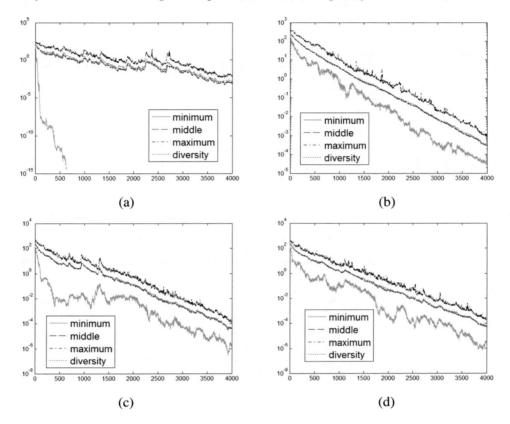

down" changes of the position diversity curve, which may mean that as a whole, the search process is convergent but there are divergent process embedded in the convergent process.

Figures 10 and 11 display the position diversity changing curves of PSO with a stochastic boundary constraint handling technique to solve unimodal function f_0 and multimodal function f_5, respectively. By utilizing a half search space resetting technique, the values of position diversities are larger than that of PSOs with other strategies, which means that particle search in a larger region, i.e., the ability of exploration can be kept with this strategy. However, the ability of exploitation will be decreased when particles are getting close to the boundary. In general, a distance between any pair of particles is larger than that in PSOs with other boundary constraint handling techniques at the same iterations.

Figures 12 and 13 display the position diversity changing curves of PSO with a linearly decreased resetting space to solve unimodal function f_0 and multimodal function f_5, respectively. Four subfigures are displayed for PSO with a star, ring, four clusters, and Von Neumann topology, respectively. Like in other figures, the position diversities for PSO with star topology have the smallest value, and position diversities for PSO with ring topology have the largest value.

Figures 14 and 15 display the position diversity changing curves of PSO with a small resetting area to solve unimodal function f_0 and multimodal function f_5, respectively. PSO with this strategy can have a good balance between exploration and exploitation. From the figures, we can see that the minimum

Figure 10. Comparison of PSO population diversities for solving unimodal function f_0 with stochastic boundary constraints handling techniques that randomly reset particles in half search space: (a) star, (b) ring, (c) four clusters, (d) Von Neumann.

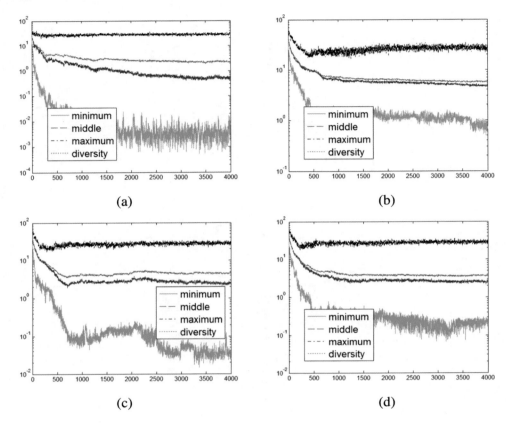

position diversity is kept to a small value but not to zero in the whole search process. This means that particles can exploit some specific areas, and at the same time, particles will not be clustered together in this area. Particles can "jump out" of the local optima with this strategy, and the experimental results also show that PSO with this strategy can get a good performance.

From Figures 4 to 15 we can see that PSO with star topology can achieve the smallest value of position diversity, and PSO with ring topology has the largest value at the same iteration. PSO with four clusters and Von Neumann nearly have the same diversity curve in our experiments. In summary, the PSO with star topology has the greatest ability to exploit the small area at the same iteration, and in contrast, the PSO with ring topology has the greatest ability to explore new search areas.

The search "potential" of particles is important to an algorithm's performance. Particles "fly" in a limited area. To ensure the performance of algorithms, not only the center of the search area but also the areas close to the boundary should be searched carefully. Some strategies should be utilized for the reason that if we take no action, particles can easily cross the boundary limit, and not return to the "limited" search area. It is a frequently used method that resets a particle's position when the particle meets the boundary. This method also has some drawbacks. Resetting a particle's position in a specific location will decrease the particle's search "potential", and the ability of exploration and exploitation

Figure 11. Comparison of PSO population diversities for solving multimodal function f_5 with stochastic boundary constraints handling techniques that randomly reset particles in half search space: (a) star, (b) ring, (c) four clusters, (d) Von Neumann.

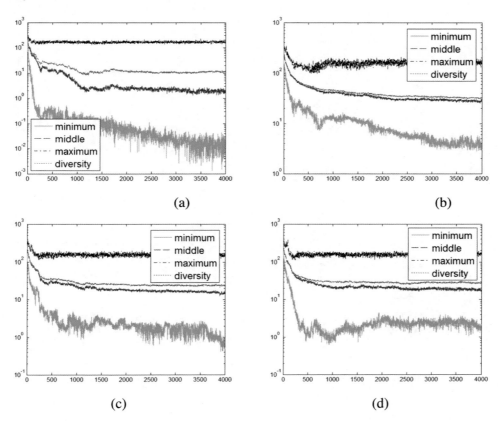

will also be affected; on the other hand, resetting particles on a large area will decrease the algorithm's ability of exploitation, and particles will have difficulties to exploit the solution areas near the boundary.

From experimental results of applying a deterministic strategy and three variants of stochastic strategy, we can observe that the deterministic strategy usually can obtain better optimization performance for PSO with ring, four clusters, or Von Neumann structure than PSO with other strategies at least for the ten benchmark functions and three boundary constraints handling strategies we experimented in this chapter. A random re-initialization strategy fits for PSO with a star, four clusters, and Von Neumann structures, and the space of re-initialization also should be considered. This conclusion is also verified on the population diversity observation.

Figures 8 and 9 display the position changing curves of PSO with a deterministic strategy. It can be seen that particles in PSO with star topology are easily get clustered together. Some dimensional position diversities are quickly becoming zero, which may mean all particles stay in the same position and lose the search "potential" in these dimensions. All particles with four clusters and Von Neumann are also clustered together to the same position in some dimensions, i.e., the minimum position diversity becomes zero after several iterations.

Figure 12. Comparison of PSO population diversities for solving unimodal function f_0 with stochastic boundary constraints handling techniques that randomly reset particles in a small and close to boundary search space: (a) star, (b) ring, (c) four clusters, (d) Von Neumann.

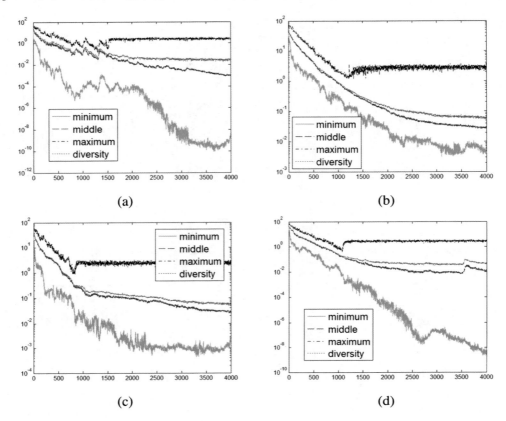

(a) (b)

(c) (d)

PSO with a random resetting strategy can avoid the above problem. Figure 10~15 displayed the position diversity curves of PSO with a stochastic strategy to handle boundary constraints. Particles can keep their position diversities with this strategy. Considering about algorithm's ability of exploitation, resetting particles in a small or decreased region can generally get better performance.

PSO with different topology will have different convergence speed. PSO with star structure has the fastest convergence speed, PSO with ring structure has the slowest speed, PSO with four clusters or Von Neumann structure is in the middle of them. Keeping a particle's search "potential" and having a good balance of exploration and exploitation is important in the search process. Different boundary constraints handling strategy needs to be considered when we determine the PSO's topology because a proper strategy can give an improvement on the algorithm's performance.

Figure 13. Comparison of PSO population diversities for solving multimodal function f_5 with stochastic boundary constraints handling techniques that randomly reset particles in a small and close to boundary search space: (a) star, (b) ring, (c) four clusters, (d) Von Neumann.

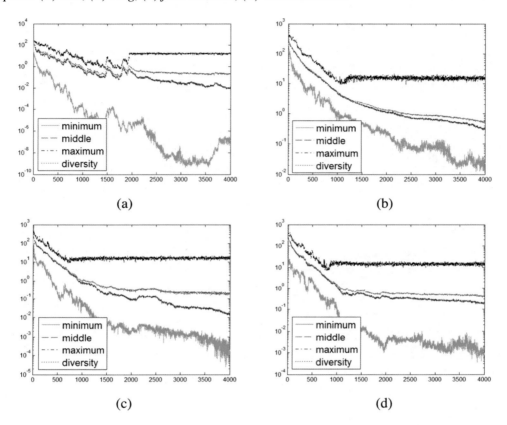

(a) (b)

(c) (d)

6. CONCLUSION

An algorithm's ability of exploration and exploitation is important in the optimization process. With good exploration ability, an algorithm can explore more areas in the search space, and find some potential regions that "good enough" solutions may exist. On the other hand, an algorithm with the ability of exploitation can finely search the potentially good regions, and find the optimum ultimately. An algorithm should have a good balance between exploration and exploitation during the search process.

In this chapter, we have reviewed the different strategies to handle particles exceeding the position boundary constraint. Position diversity changing curves were utilized to study variants of the algorithm's ability of the exploration and/or exploitation. The position diversity changing curves of different variants of PSO were compared. From the position diversity measurement, the impacts of different boundary constraint handling strategies on the optimization performance were studied. Boundary constraints handling can affect particles' search "potential". The classic method resets particles on the boundary when particles exceed the boundary limit, which may mislead particles to the wrong search area, and cause particles "stuck in" the boundary.

Figure 14. Comparison of PSO population diversities for solving unimodal function f_0 with stochastic boundary constraints handling techniques that randomly reset particles in a linearly decreased search space: (a) star, (b) ring, (c) four clusters, (d) Von Neumann.

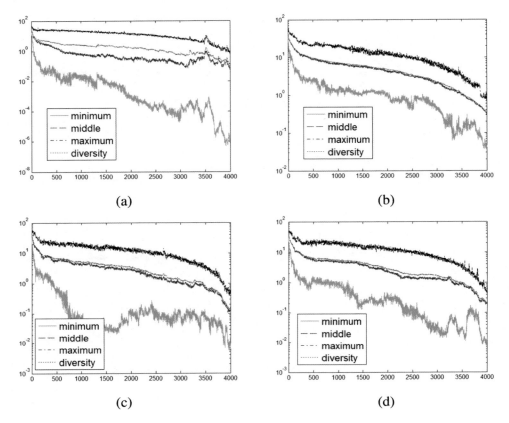

The position diversities of PSO with a star, ring, four clusters, and Von Neumann topology experimented in this chapter. PSO with different topology will have different convergence. From the diversity measurement, the convergence speed and the ability of "jumping out" of local optima could be observed and/or analyzed. A deterministic boundary handling technique may improve the search results of PSO with a ring, four clusters, or Von Neumann topology, but not star topology. Premature convergence still occurs in PSO with star topology. The stochastic method can avoid premature convergence, and resetting particles in a small or decreased region will keep PSO's ability of exploitation and therefore have a better performance.

Besides the boundary constraints handling techniques discussed in this chapter, there are many other methods, such as "invisible boundaries", "damping boundaries", etc. (Huang & Mohan, 2005; Xu & Rahmat-Samii, 2007). These methods will have a different impact on the optimization performance of PSO algorithms. As the same as the boundary constraints handling methods discussed in this chapter, these methods also can be analyzed by position diversity changing curves during the search process. The proper boundary constraint handling method should be considered together with the topology.

As indicated by the "no free lunch theory", there is no algorithm that is better than the other one on average for all problems (Wolpert & Macready, 1997). Different variants of PSO fit for different kinds of

Figure 15. Comparison of PSO population diversities for solving multimodal function f_5 with stochastic boundary constraints handling techniques that randomly reset particles in a linearly decreased search space: (a) star, (b) ring, (c) four clusters, (d) Von Neumann.

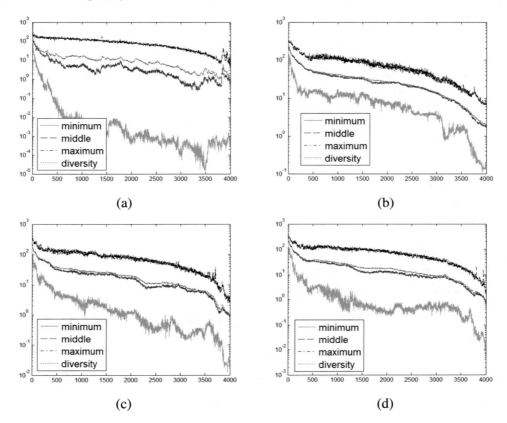

(a)　　　　　　　　　　　　　(b)

(c)　　　　　　　　　　　　　(d)

problems. The comparison between different variants of PSOs and their population diversities should be studied when they are applied to solve different problems. The impact of parameters tuning on population diversity for solving different problems is also needed to be researched.

In addition to the position diversity, there are velocity diversity and cognitive diversity defined in PSO algorithms (Shi & Eberhart, 2008; Shi & Eberhart, 2009), which are unique to PSO algorithms. Experimental study on boundary constraints handling strategy based on velocity diversity and cognitive diversity should also be conducted to gain a better understanding of PSO algorithms. The above are our future research work.

ACKNOWLEDGMENT

This work was supported by National Natural Science Foundation of China (Grant Nos. 61806119, 61672334, 61761136008, and 61773103), and Natural Science Basic Research Plan In Shaanxi Province of China (Grant No. 2019JM-320).

REFERENCES

Bentley, P. J. (1999). *Evolutionary Design by Computers*. Morgan Kaufmann Publishers.

Blackwell, T. M., & Bentley, P. (2002). Don't push me! collision-avoiding swarms. *Proceedings of the Fourth Congress on Evolutionary Computation (CEC 2002)*, (pp. 1691-1696).

Bratton, D., & Kennedy, J. (2007). Defining a standard for particle swarm optimization. *Proceedings of the 2007 IEEE Swarm Intelligence Symposium*, (pp. 120-127). 10.1109/SIS.2007.368035

Chen, S., & Montgomery, J. (2011). A simple strategy to maintain diversity and reduce crowding in particle swarm optimization. *Proceedings of the 13th annual conference companion on Genetic and evolutionary computation (GECCO 2011)*, (pp. 811-812). 10.1145/2001858.2002101

Cheng, S. (2013). *Population Diversity in Particle Swarm Optimization: Definition, Observation, Control, and Application*. (Doctoral dissertation), University of Liverpool, UK.

Cheng, S., Lu, H., Lei, X., & Shi, Y. (2018). A Quarter Century of Particle Swarm Optimization. *Complex & Intelligent Systems*, *4*(3), 227–239. doi:10.100740747-018-0071-2

Cheng, S., & Shi, Y. (2011a). Diversity control in particle swarm optimization. *Proceedings of the 2011 IEEE Swarm Intelligence Symposium*, (pp. 110-118).

Cheng, S., & Shi, Y. (2011b): Normalized population diversity in particle swarm optimization. *Proceedings of the 2nd International Conference on Swarm Intelligence. Lecture Notes in Computer Science*, *6728*, (pp. 38-45). 10.1007/978-3-642-21515-5_5

Dorronsoro, B., & Bouvry, P. (2011). Improving classical and decentralized differential evolution with new mutation operator and population topologies. *IEEE Transactions on Evolutionary Computation*, *15*(1), 67–98. doi:10.1109/TEVC.2010.2081369

Eberhart, R., & Kennedy, J. (1995). A new optimizer using particle swarm theory. *Proceedings of the Sixth International Symposium on Micro Machine and Human Science*, (pp. 39-43). 10.1109/MHS.1995.494215

Eberhart, R., & Shi, Y. (2001). Particle swarm optimization: Developments, applications, and resources. *Proceedings of the 2001 Congress on Evolutionary Computation (CEC2001)*, (pp. 81-86). 10.1109/CEC.2001.934374

Eberhart, R., & Shi, Y. (2007). *Computational Intelligence: Concepts to Implementations*. Morgan Kaufmann. doi:10.1016/B978-155860759-0/50002-0

Helwig, S., Branke, J., & Mostaghim, S. (2013). Experimental Analysis of Bound Handling Techniques in Particle Swarm Optimization. *IEEE Transactions on Evolutionary Computation*, *17*(2), 259–271. doi:10.1109/TEVC.2012.2189404

Huang, T., & Mohan, A. (2005). A hybrid boundary condition for robust particle swarm optimization. *IEEE Antennas and Wireless Propagation Letters*, *4*, 112–117. doi:10.1109/LAWP.2005.846166

Kennedy, J. (2007). Some issues and practices for particle swarms. *Proceedings of the 2007 IEEE Swarm Intelligence Symposium (SIS 2007)*, (pp. 162-169). 10.1109/SIS.2007.368041

Kennedy, J., & Eberhart, R. (1995). Particle swarm optimization. *Proceedings of IEEE International Conference on Neural Networks*, (pp. 1942-1948). 10.1109/ICNN.1995.488968

Kennedy, J., Eberhart, R., & Shi, Y. (2001). *Swarm Intelligence*. Morgan Kaufmann Publisher.

Liang, J., Qin, A., Suganthan, P., & Baskar, S. (2006). Comprehensive learning particle swarm optimizer for global optimization of multimodal functions. *IEEE Transactions on Evolutionary Computation, 10*(3), 281–295. doi:10.1109/TEVC.2005.857610

Mendes, R. (2004a). *Population Topologies and Their Influence in Particle Swarm Performance*. (Doctoral dissertation), University of Minho, Portugal.

Mendes, R., Kennedy, J., & Neves, J. (2003). Avoiding the pitfalls of local optima: How topologies can save the day. *Proceedings of the 12th Conference Intelligent Systems Application to Power Systems (ISAP 2003)*. IEEE Computer Society.

Mendes, R., Kennedy, J., & Neves, J. (2004b). The fully informed particle warm: Simpler, maybe better. *IEEE Transactions on Evolutionary Computation, 8*(3), 204–210. doi:10.1109/TEVC.2004.826074

Olorunda, O., & Engelbrecht, A. P. (2008) Measuring exploration/exploitation in particle swarms using swarm diversity. *Proceedings of the 2008 Congress on Evolutionary Computation(CEC 2008)*, (pp. 1128-1134). 10.1109/CEC.2008.4630938

Shi, Y., & Eberhart, R. (1998). Parameter selection in particle swarm optimization. In Evolutionary Programming VII, Lecture Notes in Computer Science, 1447, 591-600. Berlin, Germany: Springer. doi:10.1007/BFb0040810

Shi, Y., & Eberhart, R. (1999). Empirical study of particle swarm optimization. *Proceedings of the 1999 Congress on Evolutionary Computation (CEC 1999)*, (pp. 1945-1950). 10.1109/CEC.1999.785511

Shi, Y., & Eberhart, R. (2008). Population diversity of particle swarms. *Proceedings of the 2008 Congress on Evolutionary Computation (CEC 2008)*, (pp. 1063-1067). 10.1109/CEC.2008.4630928

Shi, Y., & Eberhart, R. (2009). Monitoring of particle swarm optimization. *Frontiers of Computer Science, 3*(1), 31–37. doi:10.100711704-009-0008-4

Wolpert, D., & Macready, W. (1997). No free lunch theorems for optimization. *IEEE Transactions on Evolutionary Computation, 1*(1), 67–82. doi:10.1109/4235.585893

Xu, S., & Rahmat-Samii, Y. (2007). Boundary conditions in particle swarm optimization revisited. *IEEE Transactions on Antennas and Propagation, 55*(3), 760–765. doi:10.1109/TAP.2007.891562

Yao, X., Liu, Y., & Lin, G. (1999). Evolutionary programming made faster. *IEEE Transactions on Evolutionary Computation, 3*(2), 82–102. doi:10.1109/4235.771163

Zhang, W., Xie, X. F., & Bi, D. C. (2004). Handling boundary constraints for numerical optimization by particle swarm flying in periodic search space. *Proceedings of the 2004 Congress on Evolutionary Computation (CEC 2004)*, (pp. 2307-2311). 10.1109/CEC.2004.1331185

Zielinski, K., Weitkemper, P., Laur, R., & Kammeyer, K. D. (2009). Optimization of power allocation for interference cancellation with particle swarm optimization. *IEEE Transactions on Evolutionary Computation*, *13*(1), 128–150. doi:10.1109/TEVC.2008.920672

KEY TERMS AND DEFINITIONS

Boundary Constraints Handling: In particle swarm optimization algorithm, particles may "stick in" the boundary. The boundary constraints handling strategies are some methods to handle the particles (or individuals) cross the search boundary, i.e., to handle the phenomenon that solutions out of the predefined search space.

Exploitation: The exploitation ability means that an algorithm focuses on the refinement of found promising areas.

Exploration: The exploration ability means that an algorithm can explore more search place to increase the possibility that the algorithm can find good enough solutions.

Particle Swarm Optimizer/Optimization: Particle Swarm Optimizer/Optimization, which is one of the evolutionary computation techniques, was invented by Eberhart and Kennedy in 1995. It is a population-based stochastic algorithm modeled on the social behaviors observed in flocking birds. Each particle, which represents a solution, flies through the search space with a velocity that is dynamically adjusted according to its own and its companion's historical behaviors.

Population Diversity: Population diversity is a measure of individuals' search information in population-based algorithms. From the distribution of individuals and change of this distribution information, the algorithm's status of exploration or exploitation can be obtained.

Position Diversity: Position diversity measures distribution of particles' current positions, therefore, can reflect particles' dynamics. Position diversity gives the current position distribution information of particles, whether the particles are going to diverge or converge could be reflected from this measurement.

Premature Convergence: Premature convergence is a phenomenon that occurs in population-based algorithms. Premature convergence occurs when all individuals in population-based algorithms are trapped in local optima.

Chapter 12
Contour Gradient Optimization

Zhou Wu
ChongQing University, China

Shi Cheng
https://orcid.org/0000-0002-5129-995X
Shaanxi Normal University, China

Yuhui Shi
https://orcid.org/0000-0002-8840-723X
Southern University of Science and Technology, China

ABSTRACT

Inspired by local cooperation in the real world, a new evolutionary algorithm, Contour Gradient Optimization algorithm (CGO), is proposed for solving optimization problems. CGO is a new type of population-based algorithm that emulates the cooperation among neighbors. Each individual in CGO evolves in its neighborhood environment to find a better region. Each individual moves with a velocity measured by the field of its nearest individuals. The field includes the attractive forces from its better neighbor in the higher contour level and the repulsive force from its worse neighbor in the lower contour level. In this chapter, CGO is compared with six different widely used optimization algorithms, and comparative analysis shows that CGO is better than these algorithms in respect of accuracy and effectiveness.

1. INTRODUCTION

Optimization is the process of finding the most promising solution for a given problem. It requires maximizing or minimizing a desired objective function globally in a multi-dimensional search space. Optimization has already been one of the most important topics in science and engineering research. In research areas such as machine learning, artificial intelligence, and complex systems, plenty of instances can be regarded as optimization problems. Generally, a continuous optimization problem can be defined as $\min f(x), x \in \mathcal{R}^D$, where D is the number of the decision variables.

DOI: 10.4018/978-1-7998-3222-5.ch012

Conventional optimization techniques, such as gradient-based methods, can be successfully applied in some relatively less complicated applications. But they are easily getting trapped in local optima for many multimodal problems in the real world. The stochastic algorithms that have been proposed for globally solving optimization problems can be divided into two major types. The first type is based on the local search strategy such as the simulated annealing algorithm (SA). SA (Kirkpatrick, Gelatt, & Vecchi, 1983) was firstly derived from the analogy of the heating and cooling process of materials. Many variants of SA algorithms were subsequently proposed to improve the performance of SA (Ingber, 1996; Wu & Chow, 2007). The second type is based on the global search strategy such as Genetic Algorithm (GA) (Vose, 1999; Kumar & Rockett, 1998; Maruyama & Lgarashi, 2008), Evolution Strategy (ES) (Beyer, 2001), Differential Evolution (DE) (Storn & Price, 1997; Kim, Chong, & Park, *et al.* 2007; Lampinen & Storn, 2004), Particle Swarm Optimization (PSO) (Eberhart & Kennedy, 1995; Kennedy & Eberhart, 1995; Shi, & Eberhart, 1998; Eberhart & Shi, 2001), and Self-Organizing Migrating Algorithm (SOMA) (Zelinka, 2004). The second type, also called Evolutionary Algorithms (EAs), has become increasingly popular for solving highly complicated optimization problems. Recently, there are other newly developed optimization algorithms using neural networks (Huhse, Villmann, & Merz *et al.*, 2002; Milano, Koumoutsakos, & Schmidhuber, 2004). An algorithm called self-organizing potential field network (SOPFN) is proposed with significant performance improvement on the multimodal problems (Xu & Chow, 2010). SOPFN combines the self-organizing map (SOM) (Kohonen, 1997) and vector potential field algorithm (VPF) (Masoud & Masoud 2000; Khatib, 1986) to model the search space as a self-organizing potential field. Compared with local search methods, global search methods are not easily getting trapped in the local optima. But the global search algorithms need much more computation time to find the optimum, as they costly explore the whole search space. For example, the original PSO (Eberhart & Kennedy, 1995; Kennedy & Eberhart, 1995) is proposed to evolve each agent using the successful histories cooperatively. In the original PSO, each member called a particle adapts its position towards its own historical best position and the best position found so far by its companion.

Researchers have taken efforts on hybridizing local search methods into EAs, as the local search methods can accelerate the convergence speed to the global optimum when starting from promising solutions. These hybrid evolutionary algorithms are inspired by the local phenomenon that individuals are mostly affected by the local environment rather than the global environment (Wu, & Chow, 2013). In the so-called local PSO (LPSO) (Shi, & Eberhart, 1998; Eberhart & Shi, 2001), each particle is influenced by the best performing neighbor. In (Mendes, Kennedy & Neves, 2004; Li, Dong & Liu, 2010; Beegom & Rajasree, 2019), the authors proposed some improved PSO algorithms,which can solve some special functions better than traditional PSO.Some other hybrid evolutionary algorithms called memetic algorithms (MAs) are proposed to combine the local search with evolutionary algorithms (Molina, Lozano, & Sánchez, *et al.*, 2011; Zhong, Liu, & Xue, *et al.*, 2004), super-fit memetic differential evolution (SFMDE)(Caponio, Neri & Tirronen, 2009), Besides the benefit of accelerating convergence, another benefit of hybridization is overcoming the drawback "two steps forward, one step back" (Van den Bergh & Engelbrecht, 2004). "Two steps forward, one step back" problem means that certain components of the solution may have drifted away from the optimum when majority of the components may have moved towards the optimum in the evolvement. Van den Bergh, *et al.* states that the "two steps forward, one step back" phenomenon can cause the difficulty of global optimization (Van den Bergh & Engelbrecht, 2004). For instance, this problem is likely experienced by the original PSO, because it complies with the principle of fully learning from the best solution that may be a local optimum. The memetic PSOs can overcome this drawback and deliver promising results but at the expense of convergence rate (Van den Bergh & Engelbrecht, 2004; Liang, Qin, & Suganthan, *et al.*, 2006).

The aforementioned PSOs suffer certain deficiencies when employing local information. First, these PSOs have not considered the gradient information, which may be useful to guide the evolving direction. This chapter proposes a new evolutionary algorithm utilizing the local cooperation information with certain gradient-like properties. Leaning from the neighbors can decrease the chance of "one step back" because the neighbors are creditable with many components close to each other. Second, in these PSOs, each particle learns from its neighbors only by approaching the neighbors' historical successful solutions. This approach seems like a kind of positive learning effect, but they seldom model the behavior that neighboring individuals always share their memories of failure in the local environment. In fact, one individual may learn from the failed neighbors not to experience the same failures again with a negative learning effect. The failures (i.e. the worst solution found so far) have been modeled with repelling forces on particles (Leontitsis, Kontogiorgos, & Pagge, 2006). This chapter models both the positive and negative effects as the neighborhood field, in which the attractive pole is the current position of the superior neighbor, and the repulsive pole is the current position of the inferior neighbor. Based on the above motivations, a new neighborhood field model (NFM) is proposed to learn from the neighbors, including the superior and inferior neighbors. Then a simple but effective optimization algorithm is proposed as a Contour Gradient Optimization algorithm (CGO). The scope of this chapter is to discuss how local information can deliver a global algorithm with a fast convergence rate.

The contributions of this chapter are in three aspects. First, we model the behavior of "learning from the betters" as the neighborhood field, which provides an effective way to find the global optimum. Second, attributing to the characteristics of the neighborhood field, the proposed CGO algorithm can obtain comparably good results in terms of convergence rate, accuracy, and effectiveness. Our proposed CGO has exhibited excellent ability in optimizing high-dimensional multimodal problems. Third, this chapter introduces a new search mechanism using a sorting approach. The sorting of the population is called contouring, in which the resultant neighbors can approximate a descent direction. The proposed approach does not really construct the contour map like (Lin, Zhang, & Lan, 2008) to sample uniformly large grid networks, but employs the neighborhood field with descend directions for optimization. As the structure of CGO is simple, it is an effective and computationally efficient algorithm for globally solving optimization problems.

The chapter is organized as follows. Section 2 introduces the background to optimization algorithms. Section 3 presents the methodology and implementation of CGO. Section 4 shows the simulation comparison results of algorithms on the benchmark functions. Section 5 analyzes the searching behavior of CGO and evaluates the set of parameters. Conclusions are given in Section 6.

2. BACKGROUND

Cooperative learning has played an important role in many kinds of computational intelligence researches. One of the earliest research works is Kohonen's self-organizing map (SOM) (Kohonen, 1997), which combines cooperative learning with competitive learning. In SOM, training procedures not only apply to the best winning neuron in the competition but also involve other neighbors around the winner. Inspired by SOM, many optimization algorithms with a self-organizing property are proposed, such as SOMA (Zelinka, 2004) and SOPFN (Xu & Chow, 2010) evaluated in this paper. The details of SOM, SOMA, and SOPFN can be referred to their corresponding original papers. As the proposed algorithm utilizes the local cooperation inspired by potential field model (PFM), the concept of PFM will be briefly presented in this section. The popular algorithms PSO and DE will also be introduced, because they are evaluated in the later comparative study.

2.1 Potential Field Model

Potential Field Model (PFM) is widely used in the context of robots' collision avoidance (Khatib, 1986). The concept of potential field has been schematically described in (Khatib 1986) as "The manipulator moves in a field of forces. The target position is an attractive pole as the positive effect, and obstacles are repulsive surfaces for the manipulators as the negative effect." Considering the collision avoidance problem of a robot x with a single obstacle O and a target x_d, the control of the robot with respect to the target and obstacle can be achieved by the artificial potential energy

$$U_{pf}\left(x\right) = U_{x_d}\left(x\right) + U_O\left(x\right), \tag{1}$$

where U_{pf} is the potential energy, U_{x_d} and U_O are the energy caused by the target and the obstacle respectively. The potential field is expressed as the gradient of the energy

Figure 1. The potential field model: a robot is driven by the attractive force from the target and the repulsive force from the obstacle. F is the overall force driving on the robot, which is composed of the target's attractive force from and the obstacle's repulsive force.

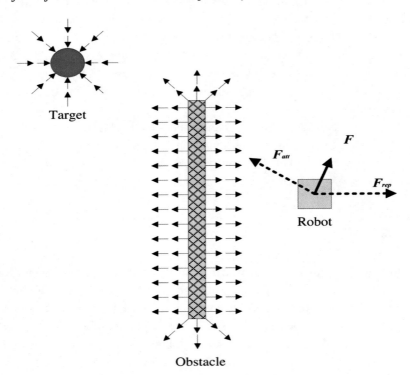

$$F = F_{att} + F_{rep},$$

$$F_{att} = -\nabla[U_{x_d}(x)], \tag{2}$$

$$F_{rep} = -\nabla[U_O(x)],$$

where F is the overall force driven on the robot. F_{att} is the attractive force generated by the target x_d, and F_{rep} is the repulsive force generated by the obstacle O. In PFM the targets have the force to attract the robot, and the obstacles have the force to repulse the robot as shown in Figure 1. It is obvious that the overall force on the robot is composed of attractive and repulsive forces.

2.2 Particle Swarm Optimization

Particle Swarm Optimization (PSO) (Eberhart & Kennedy, 1995; Kennedy & Eberhart, 1995) is a population-based algorithm inspired by the social behavior of flocks. The population is called a swarm and an individual is called a particle. In PSO, a particle moves with an adaptive velocity by the cooperation with other particles. When a specific particle finds the best solution, other particles are informed and move towards the position. Every particle has two features, position, and velocity. The position and velocity vectors of the ith particle are denoted as

$$x_i = \left[x_{i,1}, x_{i,2}, ..., x_{i,D}\right] \text{ and } v_i = \left[v_{i,1}, v_{i,2}, ..., v_{i,D}\right].$$

Let

$$xp_i = \left[xp_{i,1}, xp_{i,2}, ..., xp_{i,D}\right]$$

be the best position of the ith particle, and

$$x_g = \left[x_{g,1}, x_{g,2}, ..., x_{g,D}\right]$$

be the best position in the population. Then the new position and velocity of the ith particle are updated by

$$v_i = \omega v_i + c_1 * rand * (xp_i - x_i) + c_2 * rand * (x_g - x_i), \tag{3}$$

$$x_i = x_i + v_i. \tag{4}$$

where ω is the momentum of velocity called inertia weight, c_1 and c_2 are positive constants called learning rates, and *rand* is a random vector uniformly distributed in the range of [0, 1]. The local PSO (Shi & Eberhart, 1998; Eberhart & Shi, 2001) is different from the original PSO in the mutation step, where each particle does not learn from the global best individual, but from its neighbors as

$$v_i = \omega v_i + c_1 * rand * (xp_i - x_i) + c_2 * rand * (x_{lbest} - x_i),$$ (5)

where x_{lbest} is the best position of its best performing neighbor. The other parameters and updating rules are the same as those of the original PSO.

2.3 Differential Evolution

Differential Evolution (DE) (Storn & Price, 1997) is a population-based stochastic optimization algorithm. It uses the difference between two randomly chosen parameter vectors to perturb an existing vector. Compared with PSO, the major difference of DE is that it mutates and recombines the population to produce a population of trial vectors. For each parameter vector denoted as

$$x_i = \left[x_{i,1}, x_{i,2}, ..., x_{i,D} \right],$$

its corresponding trial vector

$$u_i = \left[u_{i,1}, u_{i,2}, ..., u_{i,D} \right]$$

is computed as

$$v_i = x_{r0} + F(x_{r1} - x_{r2}),$$ (6)

$$u_{i,j} = \begin{cases} v_{i,j}, & if\ rand \leq Cr\ or\ j = k \\ x_{i,j}, & otherwise \end{cases}, j = 1, 2, ...D$$ (7)

where x_{r0}, x_{r1}, x_{r2} are three random distinct individuals in the population, $F \in [0,1]$ is a mutation factor that controls the evolving step, and v_i is the mutant vector. The trial vector u_i is generated by recombining x_i and v_i as in Equation 7. Cr is a crossover probability and $rand \in [0,1]$ is a random number. k is a random component for acceptance of the mutant vector, so that the trial vector is different from the tart vector x_i in at least one component. After mutation and crossover, the next generation of the ith vector is selected by

$$x_i = \begin{cases} u_i, & if\ f(x_i) \leq f(u_i) \\ x_i, & otherwise \end{cases}$$ (8)

where $f(x_i)$ is the objective function to be minimized. Note that only the better vector between the trial vector and the target parameter vector will be accepted in the next generation.

3. CONTOUR GRADIENT OPTIMIZATION

3.1 Neighborhood Field Model

Inspired by the potential field model, the contour gradient optimization algorithm (CGO) is proposed based on our newly derived neighborhood field model (NFM). As agents in some real-world networks are likely connected with their neighbors rather than other distant agents, the cooperation of neighboring agents may have significant effects on modeling optimization algorithms. In the NFM, the behaves of each individual x_i like a robot; the superior neighbors behave like targets; the inferior neighbors behave like obstacles. The following equation illustrates the field of an individual x_i with one superior neighbor and one inferior neighbor:

$$F = \Phi(xc_i - x_i) - \Phi(xr_i - x_i), \tag{9}$$

where F is the overall force driving on the x_i, xc_i is the superior neighbor as a target, xr_i is the inferior neighbor as an obstacle, and $\Phi(\bullet)$ is a kind of dynamical force function related with the vector difference. In Equation 9, the first component of the right-hand side represents the attractive force generated from xc_i and the second component represents the repulsive force generated from xr_i.

For instance, in minimizing the objective function $f(x_1, x_2) = 8 - x_1^2 - x_2^2$ with each component constrained in [-2, 2], the global optimum value is 0 at positions (-2, -2), (-2, 2), (2, -2), (2, 2). Figure 2 (a) shows the contour map of this function, Figure 2 (b) shows the neighborhood field of the individual "X". In this example, a population of 70 individuals is randomly initialized in the search space. The contours have sorted the population into 7 levels shown in Figure 2 (a). The individuals in the low level are fitter than those in the higher level. The individuals "X1", "X2", "X3", "X4", "X5" and "X7" are called "contour neighbors" in this chapter, which are all the nearest individuals to "X" in each level. In Figure 2 (b) we highlight "X" and its corresponding contour neighbors. As described above, these

Figure 2. An example to illustrate the neighborhood field. (a) The initial individuals' distribution. They are contoured in seven levels. The contour neighbors of X are X_1, X_3, X_4, X_5, X_6, X_7 (b) Differential fields from contour neighbors. The directions of vectors are denoted as arrows. The dashed arrow is the gradient.

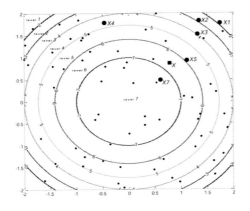

(a)

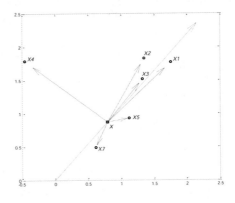

(b)

contour neighbors "*X1*", "*X2*", "*X3*", "*X4*", "*X5*" are better than "*X*", and the neighborhood field of these better individuals are denoted in the solid arrows shown in Figure 2 (b). It can be noticed that most of field lie in a similar direction with the gradient denoted as the dashed arrow. Furthermore, "*X7*" is worse than "*X*", and the inverse neighborhood field generated by "*X7*" also lies in a similar direction with the gradient. The above example illustrates the mechanism of the NFM scheme, which complies with the behavior of "learning from the better and the worse ones" rather than the behavior of "learning from the best". These better and worse individuals are the specified contouring neighbors that generate the neighborhood field. Under the NFM scheme, "*X*" will be evolved when moving towards "*X1*", "*X2*", "*X3*", "*X4*" and "*X5*", and moving away from "*X7*". Therefore, the NFM scheme includes two kinds of behaviors: "learning from the better neighbors" positively and "learning from the worse neighbors" negatively. In this example, when using the NFM, "*X*" will apparently be moving towards the global optimum (2, 2). In addition, individuals in different regions will possibly search towards different optimal solutions, which can maintain the diversity of population. The CGO we proposed is mainly based on the NFM, which models the cooperation between contour neighbors.

3.2 Contour Gradient Optimization Algorithm

Before introducing CGO, we first give the notations in CGO. To minimize a D dimensional function $f(x)$, a population of *NP* individuals cooperatively evolves for searching the global optimum. These individuals are ranked by their fitness values from the best to the worst and sorted into *M* levels evenly. For the ith individual x_i, its level is denoted as $L(x_i)$. The contour neighbors in the kth level is denoted as $C_k(x_i)$, which is defined as the nearest one among all individuals in the kth level.

$$C_k(x_i) = \arg \min_{L(x_j)=k} \|x_j - x_i\|, k = 1, 2, ..., M. \tag{10}$$

where • means the Euclidean distance in the search space.

In CGO, the sorting of individuals emulates contouring the search space. The sorting is called contouring operation in CGO. The details of CGO algorithm are as follows:

1. Initialization: randomize the initial *NP* individuals in the search space.
2. Contouring: rank all individuals by their function values in ascend order, and sort them into *M* even levels. For each individual x_i, recognize the superior contour neighbor xc_i in the level $L(x_i)-1$, and the inferior contour neighbor xr_i in the level $L(x_i)+1$ according to Equation 10. If x_i is in the first level, xc_i is defined as x_i. If x_i is in the last level, xr_i is defined as x_i.
3. Crossover: perturb each individual x_i as follows

$$u_i = x_i + \alpha * s_c * r * \left(xc_i - x_i\right) - \alpha * s_r * r * \left(xr_i - x_i\right), \tag{11}$$

where r is a random vector uniformly distributed in [0, 1], α is the learning rates, s_c and s_r are two D dimensional random binary vectors calculated as

$$\begin{cases} s_c = rand \leq Cr, & s_{c,d_c} = 1 \\ s_r = rand \leq Cr, & s_{r,d_r} = 1 \end{cases} \tag{12}$$

where *rand* is a random vector uniformly distributed in [0, 1], *Cr* is a constant in [0, 1] called the cross-over probability. d_c and d_r are two random integers in [1, *D*]. To ensure s_c and s_r are nonzero vector, the d_cth component of s_c and the d_rth component of s_r are specified as one.

4.   Selection: in the next generation each individual will be updated as the better one between x_i and u_i as

$$x_i = \begin{cases} u_i, & iff\left(u_i\right) \leq f\left(x_i\right) \\ x_i, & otherwise \end{cases} \tag{13}$$

5.   Update the best solution in the current population. Go to step 2 until the stopping criteria are satisfied.

CGO mainly includes two operators, namely contouring operator and crossover operator. In contouring operation, the method firstly ranks all individuals by their fitness values in descending order. In a simple way, the population can be ranked by their function values in ascending order for minimization problems. These individuals are then sorted into *M* classes called contour levels according to the ranking. Each level includes the same number of individuals. The sorting procedure has emulated contouring the search space, which constructs the contours in the search space.

The crossover operation can perturb each individual towards the superior regions. The *i*th individual x_i moves towards the superior contour neighbor in the lower level $L(x_i)-1$, and away from the inferior contour neighbor in the higher level $L(x_i)+1$. In the crossover, x_i is not perturbed in full *D* dimensions, but only updated in a few dimensions selected randomly. Therefore, the contour neighbor can motivate x_i to search the superior regions without causing the "two steps forward, and one step back". After the crossover, some dimensions in the new solution u_i may be out of the constrained search space, so we use a repairing method to reinitialize these dimensions randomly before selection. In CGO, two contour neighbors are chosen in a local environment, and differential vector between them can approximate descending directions of the fitness function if the neighbors are close enough to the target individual. Although the approximation is not accurate on all the *D* dimensions, the deterministic differential vectors are obviously more accurate and efficient than random vectors.

In the selection step, for each individual the new solution is compared with the original solution; the better one will be selected into the next generation. As a result, the new updated individuals tend to concentrate in superior regions. The crossover and selection can ensure the contours to centrically distribute in the fitter region. When the number of iterations increases, the fitness values become increasingly close to the global optimum, so the *M* levels are distributed increasingly close. The stopping criteria could be that the found best fitness value meets the predefined accuracy level, or the overall number of iterations meets the predefined maximum number (as used in this chapter).

The pseudo-code of CGO is presented as Figure 3. We can analyze CGO's computation complexity from its pseudo-code. Compared with PSO and DE, CGO is undoubtedly more time demanding because it has additional computation of finding the contour neighbors. To find the superior and inferior contour neighbors for each individual, CGO needs to calculate x_i's distances away from individuals in the closest level. So the computation complexity is $O(D*N*N/M)$, while DE and PSO have the computation complexity of $O(D*N)$. When the contour size N/M is usually a constant, CGO's computation complexity becomes the same as PSO and DE. Especially when $M=N$, CGO's computation time is equivalent with that of DE, because there is no need to find the neighbor in this case. The proposed CGO is a stochastic population-based algorithm. The mechanism of CGO is derived directly according to our newly proposed neighborhood field.

Figure 3. Pseudo-code for CGO algorithm

1: Initialize the population randomly $\{x_i \mid i = 1,2,...NP\}$
2: Evaluate the fitness for each individual
3: Set $\alpha = 1.5$; $Cr = 0.1$; $M = 10$; $G = 1$
4: **While** *the stopping criterion is not satisfied*
5: Sort out all particles by their fitness to m levels
6: Compute each particle's contour level $L(x_i) \in [1, m]$
9: Generate s_c and s_r;
7: Find the superior contour neighbor xc_i and the inferior contour neighbor xr_i for each particle
8:   **For** $i = 1$ to NP
9:     Generate s_c and s_r;
10:     $u_i = x_i + \alpha s_c \cdot rand \cdot (xc_i - x_i) - \alpha s_r \cdot rand \cdot (xr_i - x_i)$
11:     **If** $f(u_i) \leq f(x_i)$
12:       $x_i = u_i$;
13:     **End If**
14:   **End For**
15:   $G = G + 1$
16: **End While**

Compared with DE, the main difference of CGO is their selection of differential vectors. DE chooses differential vectors randomly among the whole population, but CGO chooses several deterministic differential vectors in a local environment. DE calculates the differential vector of two individuals selected randomly. In DE, the dynamics between the random individuals cannot ensure target individuals with fine-moves at each generation. The dynamics in CGO can be clearly classified as positive and negative after contouring all individuals. It is worth noting that CGO has a better chance of making such a fine-move compared with DE.

Compared with PSO, CGO is different in many aspects. First, their basic inspirations are different. CGO is a global algorithm of using local information, i.e., the neighborhood field, while the original PSO is using global information. PSO has a blackboard to record the successful memories of all particles. CGO does not require the blackboard because it only utilizes the information in the current generation. Second, each particle in PSO is updated towards historical best positions positively. But apart from positive influences, each individual in CGO is also influenced by the inferior neighbor negatively. Third, each particle in the original PSO is updated in all dimensions, but in CGO individuals are updated in randomly chosen dimensions.

4. SIMULATION RESULTS

To demonstrate the ability of CGO, there are sixteen benchmark functions are used as objective functions to test CGO and other algorithms such as PSO, CLPSO, CPSO-S_K, SOMA, SOPFN, and DE. These benchmark functions are widely used real-parameter functions for providing a rigorous test on different optimization algorithms (Suganthan, Hansen, & Liang *et al.*, 2005). We test these algorithms on the benchmarks with 30 dimensions and 100 dimensions. We run the seven algorithms 30 times for each function. For the stopping criterion of each run, the maximal fitness evaluation times (FEs) is set to be 300000 for the 30-Dimensianal case and 1000000 for the 100-Dimensional case. Then we analyze the mean and standard deviation of 30 runs. When an algorithm can obtain its mean result close to the global optimum with a low standard deviation, it can be regarded as having a good performance. Among the 30 runs of each algorithm, a run is said to be successful when obtaining a result close to the global optimum within the given threshold $1e^{-6}$. For an algorithm, a great number of successful runs implies that the algorithm has a larger chance to find the global optimum.

The simulations of the evaluated algorithms are conducted on MATLAB 2007. The parameters of the algorithms are set as in Table 1. In PSO, the population size *NP* is set to 30, the inertia weight ω is set to 0.72, and the learning rates c_1, c_2 are set to 1.49 (Eberhart & Shi, 2000). In CLPSO, the population size, the inertia weight and the learning rate are the same as PSO, and the refreshing gap *m* is set to 7. In CPSO-S_K, the population size, the inertia weight and the learning rate are the same as PSO, and the split factor *K* is set to 5. In SOMA, the population size is set to 30, the number of migration *k* is set to 13, step Δ is set to 0.11, and the mutation rate *PRT* is set to 0.1. In DE, the population size is set to 30, the evolving rate *F* is set to 0.7, and the crossover rate *Cr* is 0.1. In SOPFN, the network size is set to 5×5, step Δ and migrate number *k* are set to 1 and 3 respectively. The learning rates α_1, α_2 are set to 0.3, and the radius σ is set to 3. In CGO, the population size is set to 30, the number of contour levels *M* is set to 10 and the learning rate α is set to 1.5, which are obtained in the following section of parameter evaluations.

Table 1. Parameters of the evaluated algorithms

Algorithms	Parameters
PSO	$NP. =30$, $\omega =0.72$, $c_1=1.49$, $c_2=1.49$
CLPSO	$NP =30$, $\omega=0.72$, $c_1=1.49$, $c_2=1.49$, $m=7$
CPSO-S_K	$NP=30$, $\omega=0.72$, $c_1=1.49$, $c_2=19$, $K=5$
SOMA	$NP=30$, $k=13$, $\Delta=0.11$, $PRT=0.1$
DE	$NP=30$, $F=0.7$, $Cr=0.1$
SOPFN	$NP=5×5$, $k=3$, $\Delta=1$, $\alpha_1=0.3$, $\alpha_2=0.3$, $\sigma=3$
CGO	$NP=30$, $M=10$, $\alpha=1.5$, $Cr=0.1$

Among the sixteen benchmark functions, the first 4 functions are unimodal and the others are multimodal. According to their properties, these functions can be divided into four groups: shifted unimodal problems, shifted unrotated multimodal problems, shifted rotated multimodal problems, and composition problems. All the sixteen benchmarks are shifted by random vectors to make them asymmetric in the search space. We generated two random vectors in [0, 1] in 30 and 100 dimensions. For each function, its global optimum is shifted linearly in each dimension of search space. All functions have their optima, their initialization spaces and their thresholds as shown in Table 2. The benchmark functions are listed as the following.

Group A: shifted unimomdal functions.

1. Shifted Sphere function

$$f_1(x) = \sum_{i=1}^{D} z_i^{2}, z = x - o.$$

2. Shifted 4th De Jong function

$$f_2(x) = \sum_{i=1}^{D} i z_i^{4}, z = x - o.$$

3. Shifted Schwefel' function

$$f_3(x) = \sum_{i=1}^{D} \left(\sum_{j=1}^{i} z_j \right)^2, z = x - o.$$

4. Shifted Rosenbrock's function

$$f_4(x) = \sum_{i=1}^{D-1} \left(100 \left(z_i^2 - z_{i+1} \right)^2 - \left(z_i - 1 \right)^2 \right), z = x - o + 1.$$

Group B: shifted unrotated multimodal functions.

5. Shifted Ackley's function

$$f_5(x) = 20 + e - 20 \exp\left(-0.2 \sqrt{\frac{1}{D} \sum_{i=1}^{D} z_i^2} \right) - \exp\left(\frac{1}{D} \sum_{i=1}^{D} \cos\left(2\pi z_i\right) \right), z = x - o.$$

6. Shifted Griewank's function

$$f_6(x) = \sum_{i=1}^{D} \frac{z_i^2}{4000} - \prod_{i=1}^{D} \cos\left(\frac{z_i}{\sqrt{i}} \right) + 1, z = x - o.$$

7. Shifted Stretched V sine wave function

$$f_7(x) = \sum_{i=1}^{D-1} \left(z_i^2 + z_{i+1}^2 \right)^{0.25} \left[1 + \sin^2 \left(50 \left(z_i^2 + z_{i+1}^2 \right)^{0.1} \right) \right], z = x - o.$$

8. Shifted Rastrigin's function

$$f_8(x) = \sum_{i=1}^{D} \left(z_i^2 - 10\cos(2\pi z_i) + 10 \right), z = x - o.$$

9. Shifted Schaffer's function

$$f_9(x) = \sum_{i=1}^{D-1} \left(0.5 + \frac{\sin^2 \sqrt{z_i^2 + z_{i+1}^2} - 0.5}{\left(1 + 0.001 \left(z_i^2 + z_{i+1}^2 \right)^2 \right)^2} \right), z = x - o.$$

Table 2. Information of the sixteen functions

f_i	Optimal Solution	Minimum	Searching Space	Threshold
1	o_1	0	$[-5.12,5.11]^D$	10^{-6}
2	o_2	0	$[-5.12,5.11]^D$	10^{-6}
3	o_3	0	$[-5.12,5.11]^D$	10^{-6}
4	o_4	0	$[-2.048,2.047]^D$	10^{-6}
5	o_5	0	$[-30,30]^D$	10^{-6}
6	o_6	0	$[-600,600]^D$	10^{-6}
7	o_7	0	$[-10,10]^D$	10^{-6}
8	o_8	0	$[-5.12,5.11]^D$	10^{-6}
9	o_9	0	$[-2.048,2.047]^D$	10^{-6}
10	o_{10}	0	$[-30,30]^D$	10^{-6}
11	o_{11}	0	$[-600,600]^D$	10^{-6}
12	o_{12}	0	$[-10,10]^D$	10^{-6}
13	o_{13}	0	$[-5.12,5.11]^D$	10^{-6}
14	o_{14}	0	$[-2.048,2.047]^D$	10^{-6}
15	o_{15}	0	$[-5,5]^D$	10^{-6}
16	o_{16}	0	$[-5,5]^D$	10^{-6}

Note: o_i, $i=1,...,16$ is the bias vector in the definition of f_i

Group C: *shifted rotated multimodal functions.* We have rotated the above five multimodal function to make them inseparable using the method in (Liang, Suganthan, & Deb, 2005; Salomon, 1996). (o is the vector of shifting values; M is the matrix for rotation.)

10. Shifted Rotated Ackley's function

$$f_{10}(x) = 20 + e - 20\exp\left(-0.2\sqrt{\frac{1}{D}\sum_{i=1}^{D} z_i^2}\right) - \exp\left(\frac{1}{D}\sum_{i=1}^{D}\cos\left(2\pi z_i\right)\right), z = (x - o) * M.$$

11. Shifted Rotated Griewank's function

$$f_{11}(x) = \sum_{i=1}^{D}\frac{z_i^2}{4000} - \prod_{i=1}^{D}\cos(\frac{z_i}{\sqrt{i}}) + 1, z = (x - o) * M.$$

12. Shifted Rotated Stretched V sine wave function:

$$f_{12}(x) = \sum_{i=1}^{D-1}\left(z_i^2 + z_{i+1}^2\right)^{0.25}\left(1 + \sin^2\left(50\left(z_i^2 + z_{i+1}^2\right)^{0.1}\right)\right), z = (x - o) * M.$$

13. Shifted Rotated Rastrigin's function:

$$f_{13}(x) = \sum_{i=1}^{D}\left(z_i^2 - 10\cos(2\pi z_i) + 10\right), z = (x - o) * M.$$

14. Shifted Rotated Schaffer's function:

$$f_{14}(x) = \sum_{i=1}^{D-1}\left(0.5 + \frac{\sin^2\sqrt{z_i^2 + z_{i+1}^2} - 0.5}{\left(1 + 0.001\left(z_i^2 + z_{i+1}^2\right)^2\right)^2}\right), z = (x - o) * M.$$

Group D: *Composition Problems.* Composition functions are constructed by using some basic benchmark functions to form more asymmetric problems with a randomly located global optimum and several randomly located deep local optima. The following two functions belong to this type (Liang, Suganthan, & Deb, 2005).

15. Composite Function 1 (CF1): CF1 is chosen as f_{15} in the benchmark set. It is composed using ten sphere functions. The global optimum is easy to find once the global basin is found.
16. Composite Function 5 (CF5): CF5 is a hybrid composition function with more complex landscape than CF1, as it is constructed with different basic functions. CF5 is constructed with ten functions: two rotated Rastrigin's functions, two rotated Weierstrass functions, two rotated Griewank's functions, two rotated Ackley's functions, and two sphere functions.

4.1 Results of 30-D Functions

The means and standard deviations of 30 runs on each function are listed in Table 3. The best performer on each function has been highlighted in bold. For the unimodal problems, PSO undoubtedly deliver the best performance, especially for f_5. But for the multimodal and hybrid problems, CGO achieves better results than PSO on all twelve functions. Compared with CPSO, CGO surpass CPSO on the eleven functions

$$f_4, f_5, f_6, f_8, f_9, f_{10}, f_{11}, f_{13}, f_{14}, f_{15}, f_{16}.$$

Note that CGO is able to deliver significant improvement on the multimodal functions $f_6, f_8, f_9, f_{10}, f_{11}$. Compared with SOMA, CGO obtains better results on all functions. For CLPSO and SOPFN, CGO shows more suitable when solving rotated multimodal functions f_9, f_{10}, f_{11}. CGO shows better than DE on function f_9 while obtaining comparative performance on others. From this perspective of accuracy, CGO shows its global converging ability, especially when solving the multimodal problems.

Table 4 shows the results of non-parametric Wilcoxon's test at a confidence level of 5% between CGO and the other six studied algorithms (García, Molina, & Lozano, *et al.*, 2009). In Table IV, "+" means the compared algorithm is significantly better than CGO, and "−" means the compared algorithm is significantly worse than CGO. "~" indicates that the difference between CGO and the compared algorithm is not statistically significant. For the unimodal function f_3, f_4, CGO is significantly better than SOMA, SOPFN, and DE. For the multimodal problems, CGO is significantly better than PSO, CPSO, CLPSO, SOMA and SOPFN. Compared with DE, CGO delivers significantly better performance on $f_3, f_4, f_8, f_9, f_{11}, f_{14}$. From the Wilcoxon's test results, CGO owns better performance on most functions statistically

Figure 4 shows the convergence graphs of the evaluated algorithms at different FEs. Figure 4 (a), (b), (c), (d) illustrate the convergence performance on unimodal functions. Among these algorithms, PSO converges to the global optimum with the fastest speed, as it has the smallest computations complexity. Figure 4 (e), (f), (g), (h), (i) demonstrate the convergence performance on the unrotated multimodal functions. DE and CGO evidently surpass others on these multimodal functions, because they can obtain the most accurate results with the fastest convergence speed. DE is the best performer in (e), (f), (g), (h), while CGO is the best performer in (i). Figure 4 (j), (k), (l) show the convergence performance on the rotated multimodal functions. It can be noticed that CGO can converge to the global optimum with the fastest speed.

Table 5 lists the number of successful runs out of 30 runs and the mean fitness evaluation times (FEs) over the successful runs. The effectiveness of algorithms can be reflected by these average numbers. The average successful number of CGO is larger than other algorithms, which implies CGO could exhibit the most effective performance among these algorithms. From Table 5, we can also analyze the numbers of functions that can be solved by the seven algorithms. This numbers of PSO, CPSO-S_K, CLPSO, SOMA, SOPFN, DE, and CGO, are 8, 9, 7, 10, 8, 10 and 10, respectively. The mean computing time is also given in the table. It can be noticed that CGO has the competitive convergence speed, especially for rotated functions. From this perspective, we can find that CGO is an effective algorithm on the comprehensive test set.

Table 3. Means and standard deviations of each algorithm in 30-D cases (30 runs)

Alg.	Func.			
	Group A	**Group A**	**Group A**	**Group A**
	1	2	3	4
PSO	**0±0**	**0±0**	**3.42e-30±2.47e-30**	2.26e-01±1.01e+00
CPSO	**0±0**	**0±0**	1.29e-29±4.20e-30	3.99e-01±1.22e-00
CLPSO	**0±0**	**0±0**	4.88e-03±1.80e-03	7.72e-03±9.20e-01
SOMA	8.05e-32±3.30e-31	1.25e-56±4.92e-56	6.09e-01±4.86e-01	1.30e+01±2.32e+01
SOPFN	**0±0**	**0±0**	2.60e+01±8.18e+00	8.79e-02±1.03e-01
DE	**0±0**	**0±0**	3.94e-04±2.16e-04	5.08e+00±4.09e+00
CGO	**0±0**	**0±0**	4.22e-05±2.31e-05	**6.37e-03±9.72e-03**
	Group B	**Group B**	**Group B**	**Group B**
	5	6	7	8
PSO	7.73e-01±8.63e-01	1.77e-02±1.93e-02	1.12e+01±5.41e+00	4.50e+01±1.09e+01
CPSO	1.30e-14±4.21e-15	4.27e-02±3.74e-02	**0±0**	2.35e+00±1.34e+00
CLPSO	4.97e-15±1.77e-15	3.43e-12±7.06e-12	**0±0**	**0±0**
SOMA	8.76e-15±6.51e-15	7.55e-03±1.39e-02	2.51e-02±8.89e-02	2.32e+00±1.62e+00
SOPFN	2.24e-14±3.97e-15	7.16e-03±1.08e-02	**0±0**	4.74e-15±1.08e-14
DE	**4.03e-15±1.22e-15**	**0±0**	**0±0**	3.32e-01±5.44e-01
CGO	6.99e-15±6.49e-16	**0±0**	**0±0**	**0±0**
	Group B	**Group C**	**Group C**	**Group C**
	9	10	11	12
PSO	1.28e+00±2.52e-01	2.68e+00±4.81e-01	1.89e-02±1.74e-02	2.60e+01±7.34e+00
CPSO	7.44e-01±3.36e-01	3.14e+00±6.53e+00	3.58e-02±3.23e-02	2.79e+01±8.46e+00
CLPSO	1.81e-01±2.10e-01	2.40e-01±5.29e-01	1.51e-06±3.89e-06	1.85e+01±4.04e+00
SOMA	2.90e-01±2.87e-01	6.71e-01±8.76e-01	2.54e-02±3.15e-02	1.51e+01±4.35e+00
SOPFN	7.25e-01±2.84e-01	1.47e+01±7.35e+00	2.54e-02±3.15e-12	4.49e+01±3.66e+00
DE	3.90e-02±1.00e-01	**4.86e-15±1.74e-15**	3.99e-05±9.83e-05	**1.50e+01±2.16e+00**
CGO	**1.33e-04±7.28e-04**	6.28e-15±1.53e-15	**1.60e-08±8.36e-08**	2.62e+01±3.82e+00
	Group C	**Group C**	**Group D**	**Group D**
	13	14	15	16
PSO	6.38e+01±2.62e+01	1.41e+00±2.78e-01	1.76e+02±7.93e+01	1.80e+02±1.03e+02
CPSO	6.74e+01±2.08e+01	1.26e+00±3.29e-01	1.76e+02±1.07e+02	1.86e+02±2.44e+02
CLPSO	5.36e+01±1.06e+01	8.33e-01±2.18e-01	6.19e+01±3.58e+01	9.12e+01±2.61e+01
SOMA	6.16e+01±9.57e+00	1.35e+00±3.43e-01	8.33e+01±9.50e+01	5.21e+01±4.64e+01
SOPFN	1.14e+02±1.64e+01	1.19e+00±2.15e-01	4.30e-01±1.80e+00	6.05e+01±8.18e+00
DE	**3.24e+01±5.61e+01**	1.03e+00±1.45e-01	**1.54e-01±7.44e-01**	**1.47e+01±5.38e+00**
CGO	5.34e+01±9.87e+00	**7.03e-01±1.88e-01**	5.98e-01±2.09e+00	3.23e+01±1.17e+01

Table 4. Statistical analysis results of Wilcoxon's test in 30-D case. Note: "−" means the compared algorithm is significantly worse than CGO; "+" means the compared algorithm is significantly better than CGO; "~"means the algorithm is not significantly different with CGO.

Alg.	Func.															
	1	2	3	4	5	6	7	8	9	10	11	12	13	14	15	16
PSO	~	~	+	−	−	−	−	−	−	−	−	~	−	−	−	−
CPSO	~	~	+	−	−	−	~	−	−	−	−	−	−	−	−	−
CLPSO	~	~	−	−	~	−	~	~	−	−	−	+	~	−	−	−
SOMA	~	~	−	−	−	−	−	−	−	−	−	+	−	−	−	−
SOPFN	~	~	−	−	−	−	~	−	−	−	−	−	−	−	~	−
DE	~	~	−	−	+	~	~	−	−	~	−	+	+	−	~	+

4.2 Results of 100-D Functions

Table 6 lists the mean and standard deviation results of 100-D cases. In Tab. 6 the best performer on each function is marked in bold. For the unimodal functions, the results are similar to 30-D cases that CGO is able to solve f_1, f_2, but unable to solve f_3, f_4. For the unrotated multimodal functions, CGO and DE can solve three functions f_5, f_6, f_7 with better performance than the other algorithms. For the rotated multimodal functions, CGO outperforms others when solving f_{10}, f_{12}. But for the composite functions f_{15}, f_{16}, DE exhibits better performance than CGO. The results indicate that CGO can deliver competitive performance in terms of accuracy on the comprehensive set.

Table 7 illustrates the number of successful runs in 30 runs. The numbers of functions successfully solved by PSO, CPSO-S_K, CLPSO, SOMA, SOPFN, DE and CGO, are 5, 6, 7, 3, 8, 8, and 8, respectively. This indicates that CGO is one of the most effective algorithms when solving these types of 100-D problems. The average of successful runs for CGO is the largest among all other algorithms. Moreover, the mean computing time is also given in the table. It can be noticed that CGO has the competitive convergence speed, especially for 100-D rotated functions.

Table 8 shows the results of Wilconxon's test at the confidence level of 5% between CGO and other algorithms. For the unimodal functions f_1, f_2, CGO is statistically insignificant with PSO, SOMA and SOPFN. However, for multimodal functions $f_5, f_6, ..., f_{14}$ CGO is significantly better than PSO, CPSO, CLPSO, SOMA, SOPFN and DE.

For the 100-D case, in the respects of accuracy and effectiveness, CGO can deliver competitive performance, which is the same as the 30-D case. In (Wolpert & Macready, 1997), it states that an algorithm may not solve all different classes of problems with good performance. From the results of 30-D and 100-D cases, we find that CGO is suitable to solve the complicated multimodal problems in high dimensional space.

Figure 4. The convergence graphs on 30-D functions. (a) f_1; (b) f_2; (c) f_3; (d) f_4; (e) f_5; (f) f_6; (g) f_7; (h) f_8; (i) f_9; (j) f_{10}; (k) f_{11}; (l) f_{15}.

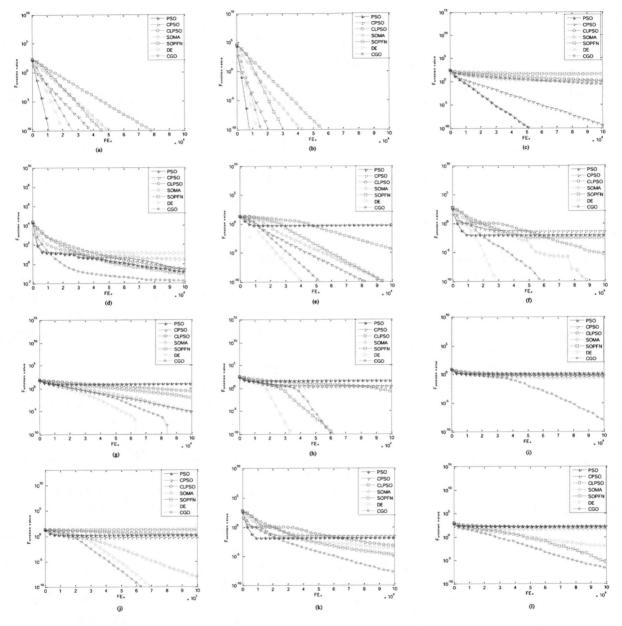

5. ANALYSIS OF CGO

5.1 CGO's Searching Behavior

In order to visualize the impacts of these dynamics, we design an experiment to simulate the evolving process of CGO. We utilize CGO to optimize the two-dimensional Ackley's function and Rastrigin's function without shift and rotation. The population size is set to 8, and the contour level is set to 2, and the learning rate is 1.5. The population is divided into two levels, namely the superior group and the inferior group. In other words, all individuals are assigned into the superior group and inferior group. The differential vectors between the nearest pair of individuals in these two classes are used in neighborhood field to motivate the evolving process.

For the 2-D Ackley's function, we plot distributions of all individuals in the 50th iteration, 100th iteration, 150th iterations and 200th iteration in Figure 5 (a). In each subplot, we denote the superior individual with big dots, and denote the inferior individuals with small dots. The global optimum is (0, 0) denoted in a star in Figure 5 (a). In each pairs of contour neighbors, the inferior individual moves towards its superior neighbors, and the superior one moves away from its inferior neighbor. In the 50th iteration, the individuals are evolved and distributed in $[-1e^{-5}, 1e^{-5}]$, where the contours can be expressed. In the 100th iteration, the individuals mainly express the contours in the space $[-1e^{-8}, 1e^{-8}]$. In the 150th iteration, the individuals can mainly express the contours in a smaller space $[-1e^{-10}, 1e^{-10}]$. In the 200th iteration, all individual converges to the optimum and expresses the contours' distribution around the optimum. We randomly choose an individual in the population, and plot its evolving trace in Figure 5 (b). The initial individual denoted as pentagram can converge to the global optimum based on the neighborhood field. It can jump directly from a low contour level area to a high contour level area in a large step regardless to the local optima in the nearby area.

For 2-D Rastrigin's function, the same conclusion can be drawn. Along with the increment of iterations individuals can converge to the global optimum step by step, and can express contours in different scales. Figure 6 (a) shows the distribution of all individuals in the 50th iteration, 100th iteration, 150th iterations and 200th iteration. In the 50th iteration, the individuals roughly express the contours in the scale $[-1,1]$. In the 100th iteration, the individuals are distributed in a smaller scale $[-1e^{-3}, 1e^{3}]$. In the 150th iteration, the individuals can only express the contours in a smaller scale $[-1e^{-5}, 1e^{5}]$. In the 200th iteration, all individuals converge to the global optimum, which are distributed in the scale $[-1e^{-7}, 1e^{7}]$. Figure 6 (b) shows the evolving trace of a random individual, which simulates the same behavior property as the Ackley's function.

5.2 Parameter Evaluations

First, we study the effect of using different number of contour level M. In CGO, M determines the number of contour neighbors that involve in updating. We test CGO in several functions with different M values. The population size is set 30, and the learning rate is 1.5. We test CGO at cases of $M = 3, 6, 10, 15$, and the number of individuals in each level (contour size) N/M is then 10, 5, 3, and 2 respectively. We have calculated the means and standard deviations of 30 runs on all 30-D test functions. Only the results on $f_1, f_5, f_6, f_7, f_8, f_9, f_{10}$ and f_{11} are different, so we only listed them in Table 9. The best results are marked in bold for each function. For f_1 and f_7, CGO with these different M values can all converge to the global optimum. For f_8, only the contour size less than 10 can ensure CGO's convergence. For f_5, f_9, f_{10} and f_{11},

Table 5. Success runs and function evaluations in 30-D case (30 runs)

	No. of Successful Runs							FEs Over Successful Runs						
	PSO	CPSO	CLPSO	SOMA	SOPFN	DE	CGO	PSO	CPSO	CLPSO	SOMA	SOPFN	DE	CGO
1	30	30	30	30	30	30	30	**7.56e+3**	2.40e+4	5.24e+4	3.38e+4	3.20e+4	1.37e+4	2.46e+4
2	30	30	30	30	30	30	30	**5.80e+3**	1.40e+4	4.06e+4	2.97e+4	2.24e+4	9.3e+3	1.89e+4
3	30	30	0	0	0	0	0	**3.42e+4**	6.97e+4	NA	NA	NA	NA	NA
4	6	0	0	0	0	0	0	**2.43e+5**	NA	NA	NA	NA	NA	NA
5	15	30	30	30	30	30	30	**1.46e+4**	5.17e+4	1.20e+5	6.28e+4	6.66e+4	2.73e+4	4.96e+4
6	9	1	30	17	12	30	30	**1.05e+4**	1.95e+5	1.14e+5	5.39e+4	6.44e+4	2.22e+4	5.04e+4
7	0	30	30	20	30	30	30	NA	1.13e+5	2.31e+5	1.09e+5	1.56e+5	**6.02e+4**	1.14e+5
8	0	2	30	2	30	21	30	NA	7.84e+4	1.43e+5	5.36e+4	4.85e+4	**2.69e+4**	5.06e+4
9	0	0	0	6	0	8	29	NA	NA	NA	6.18e+4	NA	2.23e+5	**6.05e+4**
10	10	15	0	24	0	30	30	**1.58e+4**	5.34e+4	NA	9.23e+4	NA	5.61e+4	7.29e+4
11	4	3	22	5	29	21	30	**1.19e+4**	3.69e+4	2.29e+5	1.71e+5	1.45e+5	1.85e+5	9.03e+4
12	0	0	0	0	0	0	0	NA	NA	NA	NA	NA	NA	NA
13	0	0	0	0	0	0	0	NA	NA	NA	NA	NA	NA	NA
14	0	0	0	0	0	0	0	NA	NA	NA	NA	NA	NA	NA
15	0	0	0	14	23	20	21	NA	NA	NA	1.15e+4	1.01e+5	1.84e+5	**7.5e+4**
16	0	0	0	0	0	0	0	NA	NA	NA	NA	NA	NA	NA
Avg.	8.37	10.69	12.62	11.13	13.38	15.62	18.13							

Table 6. Means and standard deviations of each evaluated algorithm in 100-D cases (30 runs)

Alg.	Func.			
	Group A	**Group A**	**Group B**	**Group B**
	1	2	3	4
PSO	2.06e-19±1.13e-18	6.14e-49±2.61e-48	1.43e-01±1.62e-01	1.73e+01±3.67e+01
CPSO	1.59e-31±3.45e-31	2.02e-59±8.63e-59	**7.63e-03±6.78e-03**	6.21e+01±3.64e+01
CLPSO	**0±0**	2.45e-34±4.28e-34	2.75e+02±3.88e+01	7.00e+01±5.11e+01
SOMA	1.82e-06±8.11e-06	2.59e-01±9.16e-01	1.74e+02±2.44e+01	3.37e+02±1.11e+02
SOPFN	**0±0**	1.09e-45±3.45e-45	7.73e+02±7.00e+01	**1.66e-01±1.43e-01**
DE	**0±0**	**0±0**	4.50e+02±3.90e+01	9.06e+01±1.98e+00
CGO	1.59e-30±3.27e-30	4.12e-61±1.00e-60	2.87e+02±2.38e+01	5.34e+01±7.21e+02
	Group B	**Group B**	**Group B**	**Group C**
	5	6	7	8
PSO	1.90e+01±1.26e+00	7.83e-01±1.11e-01	2.45e+02±1.37e+01	6.13e+02±1.03e+02
CPSO	1.58e-03±3.24e+00	5.91e-03±9.81e-03	5.65e+01±1.33e+01	2.00e+02±3.59e+01
CLPSO	2.17e-14±1.71e-15	2.96e-17±1.62e-16	1.37e-03±5.80e-03	1.82e+02±1.35e+01
SOMA	5.36e+00±1.49e+00	6.85e-01±7.54e-01	3.88e+01±7.88e+00	9.55e+01±1.71e+01
SOPFN	1.50e-13±7.25e-15	6.10e-04±2.64e-03	4.97e-10±2.72e-09	**5.00e-13±1.25e-13**
DE	**2.17e-14±1.43e-15**	**0±0**	**0±0**	3.15e+01±6.64e-01
CGO	3.53e14±6.39e-14	**0±0**	**0±0**	6.50e+00±2.17e+00
	Group C	**Group C**	**Group C**	**Group C**
	9	10	11	12
PSO	8.79e+00±1.21e-01	1.94e+01±8.60e-01	9.14e-02±1.71e-01	2.64e+02±1.51e+01
CPSO	7.24e+00±6.30e-01	9.21e+00±8.68e-01	3.28e-03±6.96e-03	2.00e+02±2.00e+01
CLPSO	1.05e+01±6.43e-01	3.70e-02±1.12e-01	1.59e-10±4.80e-10	1.47e+02±1.67e+01
SOMA	6.20e+00±1.11e+00	6.49e+00±1.27e+00	3.10e-01±3.75e-01	2.14e+02±1.53e+01
SOPFN	6.63e+00±5.06e-01	2.06e+01±7.01e-02	1.24e-05±2.71e-05	3.05e+02±5.72e-05
DE	1.37e+01±6.64e-01	5.75e+00±6.75e+00	**0±0**	1.32e+02±1.78e+01
CGO	**2.83e+00±1.05e+00**	**5.75e-04±2.21e-03**	7.36e-16±3.18e-15	**1.33e+01±3.07e+00**
	Group C	**Group C**	**Group D**	**Group D**
	13	14	15	16
PSO	8.20e+02±1.34e+02	9.12e+00±1.35e+00	7.87e+02±1.47e+02	7.73e+02±1.13e+02
CPSO	**4.48e+02±6.21e+01**	8.10e+00±8.77e-01	2.75e+02±2.94e+02	1.97e+02±1.41e+02
CLPSO	7.04e+02±3.56e+01	1.50e+01±7.97e-01	6.09e+02±3.20e+02	4.27e+02±2.76e+02
SOMA	6.08e+02±3.78e+01	**7.89e+00±9.24e-01**	2.42e+02±3.75e+02	1.89e+02±2.53e+02
SOPFN	1.18e+03±4.92e+01	8.46e+00±5.79e-01	1.93e-08±1.03e-07	5.21e+01±4.91e+00
DE	7.98e+02±2.47e+01	2.31e+01±8.92e-01	**1.70e-12±-9.34e-12**	**2.87e+01±1.58e+00**
CGO	7.21e+02±3.77e+01	1.10e+01±5.64e-01	5.12e+01±9.80e+01	8.58e+01±7.55e+01

Table 7. Success runs of function evaluations the evaluated algorithms in 100-D case (30 runs)

	No. of Successful Runs							FEs Over Successful Runs						
	PSO	CPSO	CLPSO	SOMA	SOPFN	DE	CGO	PSO	CPSO	CLPSO	SOMA	SOPFN	DE	CGO
1	30	30	30	28	30	30	30	1.15e+5	8.35e+4	1.96e+5	5.60e+5	2.15e+5	**7.95e+4**	1.83e+5
2	30	30	30	4	30	30	30	8.51e+4	6.98e+4	1.80e+5	5.82e+5	1.71e+5	**6.77e+4**	1.73e+5
3	0	0	0	0	0	0	0	NA	NA	NA	NA	NA	NA	NA
4	1	0	0	0	0	0	0	8.84e+5	NA	NA	NA	NA	NA	NA
5	0	7	30	0	30	30	30	NA	1.58e+5	3.79e+5	NA	4.03e+5	**1.45e+5**	3.25e+5
6	1	19	30	3	25	30	30	1.38e+5	1.08e+5	2.66e+5	7.77e+5	3.18e+5	1.01e+5	**9.37e+4**
7	0	0	28	0	30	30	30	NA	NA	7.35e+05	NA	9.03e+5	**3.44e+5**	7.15e+5
8	0	0	0	0	30	0	0	NA	NA	NA	NA	3.16e+5	NA	NA
9	0	0	0	0	0	0	0	NA	NA	NA	NA	NA	NA	NA
10	0	0	10	0	0	10	25	NA	NA	8.06e+5	NA	NA	7.03e+5	**6.55e+5**
11	10	22	30	0	3	30	30	2.02e+5	**1.20e+5**	3.82e+5	NA	9.17e+5	1.92e+5	7.99e+5
12	0	0	0	0	0	0	0	NA	NA	NA	NA	NA	NA	NA
13	0	0	0	0	0	0	0	NA	NA	NA	NA	NA	NA	NA
14	0	0	0	0	0	0	0	NA	NA	NA	NA	NA	NA	NA
15	0	0	0	0	30	30	20	NA	NA	NA	NA	4.74e+5	1.26e+5	**1.09e+5**
16	0	0	0	0	0	0	0	NA	NA	NA	NA	NA	NA	NA
Avg.	4.5	6.75	11.75	2.19	13	13.75	14.06							

Table 8. Statistical analysis results of Wilcoxon's test in 100-D cases. Note: "−" means the compared algorithm is significantly worse than CGO; "+" means the compared algorithm is significantly better than CGO; "~"means the algorithm is not significantly different with CGO.

Alg.	Func.															
	1	**2**	**3**	**4**	**5**	**6**	**7**	**8**	**9**	**10**	**11**	**12**	**13**	**14**	**15**	**16**
PSO	−	~	+	+	−	−	−	−	−	−	−	−	−	+	−	−
CPSO	~	~	+	−	−	−	−	−	−	−	−	−	+	+	−	−
CLPSO	−	−	+	−	+	−	−	−	−	−	−	−	~	−	−	−
SOMA	~	−	+	−	−	−	−	−	−	−	−	−	+	+	−	−
SOPFN	+	~	−	+	−	−	−	+	−	−	−	−	−	+	+	+
DE	+	+	−	−	+	~	~	−	−	−	+	−	−	−	+	+

Figure 5. The individuals' distribution in CGO for 2-D Ackley's function in the evaluated iterations. (a) The population's distribution in 2-D space at the 50st iteration (upper left), the 100th iteration (upper right), the 150th iteration (bottom left) and the 200th iteration (bottom right). (b) An individual's evolving process in CGO for 2-D Ackley's function. The line is one solution's trace, and the background is the contour map of the objective function.

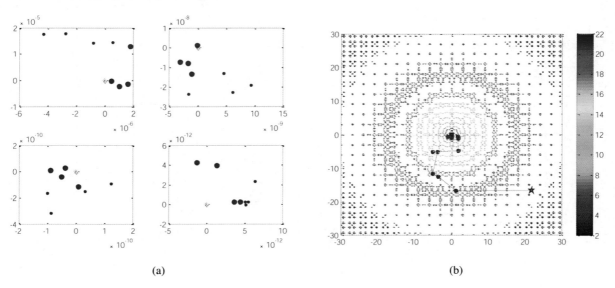

(a)   (b)

small contour sizes (less than 5) in CGO delivers better results than the large contour size. In all, CGO with a small contour size N/M performs relatively high accuracy. A proper contour size is usually set less than 5 (the optimal contour size is 3 as used in our experiments).

Figure 7 shows the median performance of CGO on these functions with different M values. For most unimodal and unrotated multimodal functions shown in Figure 9 (a), (b), (c), (d) and (e), M values have few effects on their convergence. This indicates that the contour level number M is robust enough in CGO. For rotated functions, $M=15$ is more accurate than other M values. Thus, we can conclude that CGO requires a larger M when handling these kinds of complex rotated functions.

Figure 6. The individuals' distribution in CGO for 2-D Rastrigin's function in the evaluated iterations. (a) The population's distribution in 2-D space at the 50st iteration (upper left), the 100th iteration (upper right), the 150th iteration (bottom left) and the 200th iteration (bottom right). (b) An individual's evolving process in CGO for 2-D Rastrigin's function. The line is one solution's trace, and the background is the contour map of the objective function.

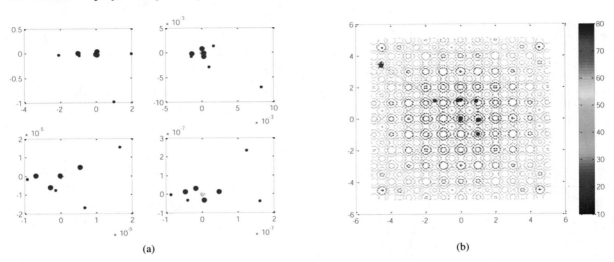

(a)　　　　　　　　　　　　　　　　(b)

Table 9. The mean and standard deviation results in different N/M values

Func.	N/M			
	10	5	3	2
f_1	**0±0**	**0±0**	**0±0**	**0±0**
f_5	7.11e-15±9.33e-16	6.63e-15±1.23e-15	**5.80e-15±1.74e-15**	6.51e-15±1.34e-15
f_6	3.11e-14±9.04e-04	1.64e-04±6.19e-04	2.99e-14±1.64e-13	**0±0**
f_7	**0±0**	**0±0**	**0±0**	**0±0**
f_8	3.21e-02±1.54e-01	**0±0**	**0±0**	**0±0**
f_9	8.26e-02±1.28e-01	1.83e-07±6.68e-07	6.25e-15±3.10e-15	**4.87e-15±2.67e-15**
f_{10}	2.83e-01±7.65e-01	2.08e-07±6.95e-07	**7.58e-15±2.03e-15**	9.83e-15±9.82e-15
f_{11}	1.99e-03±4.03e-03	5.12e-07±1.38e-07	**2.20e-15±1.20e-07**	4.56e-14±2.50e-14

Second, we also evaluate the effect of learning rate α. In the following simulation, the population size is 30 and the contour level is set to 10. We test CGO on 30-D functions $f_1, f_5, f_6, f_7, f_8, f_9, f_{10}$ and f_{11}. In this experiment, learning rate is set as 0.7, 1.0, 1.3, 1.4, 1.5, 1.6, 1.7, and 2.0 respectively. The test is conducted 30 times for each function. The mean and standard deviation results of the 30 runs are listed in Table 10. For the functions f_1, f_5, f_6, f_7, f_8, CGO with different rates $1.0 \leq \alpha \leq 2.0$ can all converge to the global optimum. This indicates that this parameter is not sensitive in CGO. Among all these functions, $1.4 \leq \alpha \leq 1.6$ is able to deliver slightly better results than other settings. CGO is effective with regard to different learning rates. When the learning rate is small as 0.7, CGO still can converge on the functions

Figure 7. The convergence graph of CGO with different contour levels on 30-D functions. In these subplots, the horizontal coordinate represents the FEs, and the vertical coordinate represents the function values.

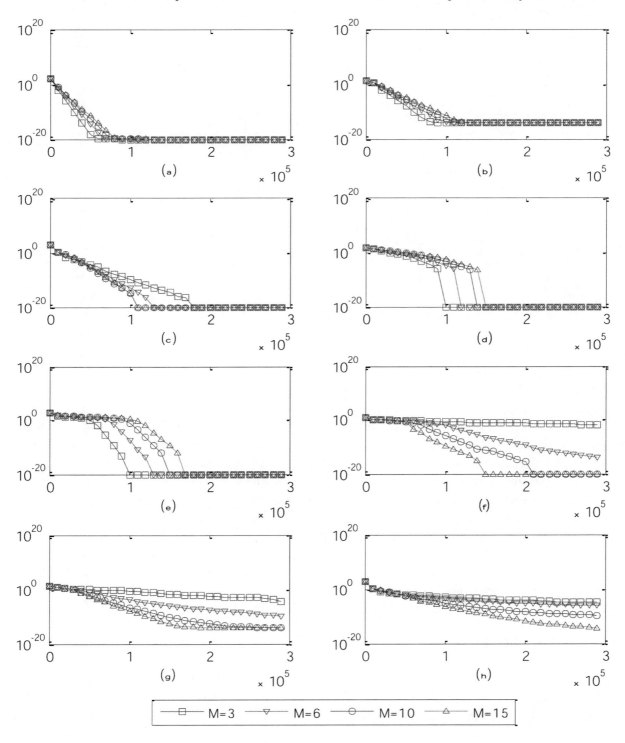

Table 10. The mean and standard deviation performance of CGO in different rate α

α Func.	0.7	1.0	1.3	1.4
f_1	0±0	**0±0**	**0±0**	**0±0**
f_5	9.12e-15±2.59e-15	6.39e-15±1.45e-15	6.28e-15±1.53e-15	6.39e-15±1.45e-15
f_6	2.96e-17±8.21e-17	7.40e-18±4.05e-17	9.11e-08±4.99e-07	**0±0**
f_7	1.17e-03±2.68e-03	**0±0**	**0±0**	**0±0**
f_8	1.04e-03±1.32e+00	**0±0**	**0±0**	**0±0**
f_9	1.65e-02±5.05e-02	**1.11e-17±6.08e-17**	1.40e-15±4.42e-15	1.52e-15±8.35e-15
f_{10}	3.32e-01±6.13e-01	2.31e-10±1.27e-09	8.05e-15±2.27e-15	7.70e-15±2.30e-15
f_{11}	3.81e-07±2.09e-06	6.30e-10±3.38e-10	2.87e-10±1.57e-10	9.65e-10±5.26e-10
	1.5	1.6	1.7	2.0
f_1	**0±0**	**0±0**	**0±0**	**0±0**
f_5	**5.80e-15±1.74e-15**	6.63e-15±1.23e-15	6.51e-15±1.35e-15	6.75e-15±1.08e-15
f_6	2.99e-14±1.64e-13	**0±0**	**0±0**	9.49e-15±5.20e14
f_7	**0±0**	**0±0**	**0±0**	**0±0**
f_8	**0±0**	**0±0**	**0±0**	**0±0**
f_9	6.25e-15±3.10e-15	9.95e-15±6.03e-15	4.87e-03±2.67e-02	5.19e-03±2.84e-02
f_{10}	**7.58e-15±2.03e-15**	9.00e-15±6.03e-15	9.83e-15±9.82e-15	2.29e-13±8.24e-13
f_{11}	**2.20e-11±1.20e-11**	2.04e-10±7.87-10	4.56e-06±2.50e-05	1.32e-03±3.45e-03

f_1, f_3, f_4, f_7 and f_9. Considering $1.0 \leq α \leq 2.0$, CGOs with different learning rate have almost the same convergence speed. (the optimal learning setting is 1.5 as used in our experiments).

In this chapter, we do not study the effect of crossover probability Cr in CGO, because the same parameter Cr existed in DE has already been evaluated in many previous literatures (Ronkkonen, Kukkonen, & Price, 2005; Zhang & Sanderson, 2009). The first reasonable attempt of choosing Cr can be 0.1, and a Cr value of 0.9 may be a good initial choice if the problem is near unimodal. It is worth pointing out that Ronkkonen (Ronkkonen, Kukkonen, & Price, 2005) suggested that Cr should lie in the range of [0, 0.2] if the function is separable, and lie in the range of [0.8, 1] when the function is non-separable. Despite above guidelines, a self-adaptive technique for Cr is recently proposed in (Zhang & Sanderson, 2009). In order to provide a fair comparative analysis, we prefer to have a fixed parameter for all algorithms. Extending the CGO with self-adaptive parameters will be a future work to enhance the performance, which is out of scope of this chapter.

6. CONCLUSION

A new population-based algorithm CGO has been developed to solve optimization problems globally. The newly proposed algorithm employs local information to form a new type of search mechanism. We tested the CGO algorithm on sixteen demanding benchmark problems. The results of simulation show that CGO is able to surpass other global search algorithms under comprehensive evaluations in the respect of accuracy and effectiveness. This is a significant improvement because via local information CGO can perform global optimization efficiently.

CGO uses a fundamentally different approach, i.e. neighborhood field. It models the principle "learning from the neighbors" instead of the popular principle "learning from the best". The concept of neighboring cooperation emulates the practical situations that neighbors, both the better and worse ones, are more realistic objects for learning. They are less noisy compared with the best individual. This concept is proved useful for performing global optimization. In CGO, every individual is influenced by the positive dynamic from the superior neighbor and the negative dynamic from the inferior neighbor. These dynamics are more or less on the gradient of the search space. The propagation process emulates the process of contouring the multi-dimensional search space. The contouring process is new in optimization and can find the global optimum or close optimum in a less computationally way.

Apart from the optimization algorithm described in this study, it is believed that the contour searching mechanism may have other potential applications in machine learning. Further work of the CGO algorithm will include extending CGO to time-variant optimization, multi-objective optimization and discrete optimization.

ACKNOWLEDGMENT

The authors' work was supported by National Natural Science Foundation of China under grant No. 61803054.

REFERENCES

Beegom, A. S. A., & Rajasree, M. S. (2019). A discrete PSO algorithm for task scheduling in cloud computing systems. *Evolutionary Intelligence*, *12*(2), 227–239. doi:10.100712065-019-00216-7

Beyer, H. G. (2001). *The Theory of Evolutionary Strategies*. Berlin, Germany: Springer-Verlag. doi:10.1007/978-3-662-04378-3

Caponio, A., Neri, F., & Tirronen, V. (2009). Super-fit control adaptation in memetic differential evolution frameworks. *Soft Computing*, *13*(8–9), 811–831. doi:10.100700500-008-0357-1

Eberhart, R., & Kennedy, J. (1995). A new optimizer using particle swarm theory. *Proceedings of the Sixth International Symposium on Micro Machine and Human Science*, (pp. 39-43). 10.1109/MHS.1995.494215

Eberhart, R., & Shi, Y. (2000). Comparing inertia weights and constriction factors in particle swarm optimization. *Proceedings of the 2000 IEEE Congress on Evolutionary Computation (CEC2000)*, (pp. 84-89). 10.1109/CEC.2000.870279

Eberhart, R., & Shi, Y. (2001). Particle swarm optimization: developments, applications, and resources. *Proceedings of the 2001 IEEE Congress on Evolutionary Computation (CEC2001)*, (pp. 81-86). 10.1109/CEC.2001.934374

García, S., Molina, D., Lozano, M., & Herrera, F. (2009). A Study on the Use of Non-Parametric Tests for Analyzing the Evolutionary Algorithms' Behavior: A Case Study on the CEC'2005 Special Session on Real Parameter Optimization. *Journal of Heuristics*, *6*(15), 617–644.

Huhse, J., Villmann, T., Merz, P., & Zell, A. (2002). Evolution strategy with neighborhood attraction using a neural gas approach. *Proceedings of the Parallel Problem Solving from Nature - PPSN VII* (LNCS 2439, pp. 391-400). 10.1007/3-540-45712-7_38

Ingber, L. (1996). Adaptive simulated annealing (ASA): Lessons learned. *Control and Cybernetics*, *25*, 33–54.

Kennedy, J., & Eberhart, R. (1995) Particle swarm optimization. *Proceedings of IEEE International Conference on Neural Networks*, (pp.1942-1948). 10.1109/ICNN.1995.488968

Khatib, O. (1986). Real-time obstacle avoidance for manipulators and mobile robots. *The International Journal of Robotics Research*, *5*(1), 90–98. doi:10.1177/027836498600500106

Kim, H. K., Chong, J. K., Park, K. Y., & Lowther, D. A. (2007). Differential evolution strategy for constrained global optimization and application to practical engineering problems. *IEEE Transactions on Magnetics*, *43*(4), 1565–1568. doi:10.1109/TMAG.2006.892100

Kirkpatrick, S., Gelatt, C. D., & Vecchi, M. P. (1983). Optimization by simulated annealing. *Science*, *220*(4598), 671–680. doi:10.1126cience.220.4598.671 PMID:17813860

Kohonen, T. (1997). *Self-Organizing Maps*. Berlin, Germany: Springer-Verlag. doi:10.1007/978-3-642-97966-8

Kumar, R., & Rockett, P. (1998). Multiobjective genetic algorithm partitioning for hierarchical learning of high-dimensional pattern spaces: A learning-follows-decomposition strategy. *IEEE Transactions on Neural Networks*, *9*(5), 822–830. doi:10.1109/72.712155 PMID:18255769

Lampinen, J., & Storn, R. (2004). Differential evolution. In G. Onwubolu, & B. V. Babu (Eds.), *New Optimization Techniques in Engineering* (pp. 123–166). Germany: Springer-Verlag. doi:10.1007/978-3-540-39930-8_6

Leontitsis, A., Kontogiorgos, D., & Pagge, J. (2006). Repel the swarm to the optimum! *Applied Mathematics and Computation*, *173*(1), 265–272. doi:10.1016/j.amc.2005.04.004Liang, J. J., Qin, A. K., Suganthan, P. N., & Baskar, S. (2006). Comprehensive learning particle swarm optimizer for global optimization of multimodal functions. *IEEE Transactions on Evolutionary Computation*, *10*(3), 281–295. doi:10.1109/TEVC.2005.857610

Li, Y., Dong, X., & Liu, J. (2010). An Improved PSO for Continuous Optimization. Proceedings Advances in Swarm Intelligence (ICSI 2010), (pp. 86-93).

Liang, J., Suganthan, P. N., & Deb, K. (2005). Novel composition test functions for numerical global optimization. *Proceedings of the 2005 IEEE Swarm Intelligence Symposium (SIS2005)*, (pp. 68-75). 10.1109/SIS.2005.1501604

Lin, Y., Zhang, J., & Lan, L. (2008). A contour method in population-based stochastic algorithms. *Proceedings of the 2008 IEEE Congress on Evolutionary Computation (CEC2008)*, (pp. 2388-2395). IEEE.

Maruyama, T., & Lgarashi, H. (2008). An effective robust optimization based on genetic algorithm. *IEEE Transactions on Magnetics, 44*(6), 990–993. doi:10.1109/TMAG.2007.916696

Masoud, S. A., & Masoud, A. A. (2000). Constrained motion control using vector potential fields. *IEEE Transactions on Systems, Man, and Cybernetics. Part A, Systems and Humans, 30*(3), 251–272. doi:10.1109/3468.844352

Mendes, R., Kennedy, J., & Neves, J. (2004). The fully informed particle swarm: Simpler, maybe better. *IEEE Transactions on Evolutionary Computation, 8*(3), 204–210. doi:10.1109/TEVC.2004.826074

Milano, M., Koumoutsakos, P., & Schmidhuber, J. (2004). Self-organizing nets for optimization. *IEEE Transactions on Neural Networks, 15*(3), 758–765. doi:10.1109/TNN.2004.826132 PMID:15384562

Molina, D., Lozano, M., Sánchez, A., & Herrera, F. (2011). Memetic algorithms based on local search chains for large scale continuous optimisation problems: MA-SSW-Chains. *Soft Computing, 15*(11), 2201–2220. doi:10.100700500-010-0647-2

Ronkkonen, J., Kukkonen, S., & Price, K. V. (2005). Real-parameter optimization with differential evolution. *Proceedings of the 2005 IEEE Congress on Evolutionary Computation (CEC2005)*, (pp. 506-513). 10.1109/CEC.2005.1554725

Salomon, R. (1996). Reevaluating genetic algorithm performance under coordinated rotation of benchmark functions. *Bio Systems, 39*, 263–278. doi:10.1016/0303-2647(96)01621-8 PMID:8894127

Shi, Y., & Eberhart, R. (1998). A modified particle swarm optimizer. *Proceedings of the 1998 IEEE Congress on Evolutionary Computation (CEC1998)*, (pp. 69-73). 10.1109/ICEC.1998.699146

Storn, R., & Price, K. (1997). Differential Evolution - A Simple and Efficient Heuristic for Global Optimization over Continuous Space. *Journal of Global Optimization, 11*(4), 341–359. doi:10.1023/A:1008202821328

Suganthan, P. N., Hansen, N., Liang, J. J., Deb, K., Chen, Y. P., Auger, A., & Tiwari, S. (2005). *Problem definitions and evaluation criteria for the cec2005 special session on real parameter optimization. Technical report*. Nanyang Technological University.

Van den Bergh, F., & Engelbrecht, A. P. (2004). A cooperative approach to particle swarm optimization. *IEEE Transactions on Evolutionary Computation, 8*(3), 225–239. doi:10.1109/TEVC.2004.826069

Vose, M. D. (1999). *Simple Genetic Algorithm: Foundation and Theory*. Cambridge, MA: MIT Press.

Wolpert, D. H., & Macready, W. G. (1997). No free lunch theorems for optimization. *IEEE Transactions on Evolutionary Computation, 1*(1), 67–82. doi:10.1109/4235.585893

Wu, S., & Chow, T. W. S. (2007). Self-organizing and self-evolving neurons: A new neural network for optimization. *IEEE Transactions on Neural Networks, 18*(2), 385–396. doi:10.1109/TNN.2006.887556 PMID:17385627

Wu, Z., & Chow, T. W. S. (2013). Neighborhood field for cooperative optimization. *Soft Computing, 17*(5), 819–834. doi:10.100700500-012-0955-9

Xu, L., & Chow, T. W. S. (2010). Self-organizing potential field network: A new optimization algorithm. *IEEE Transactions on Neural Networks*, *21*(9), 1482–1495. doi:10.1109/TNN.2010.2047264 PMID:20570771

Zelinka, I. (2004). SOMA-self-organizing migrating algorithm. In G. Onwubolu, & B. V. Babu (Eds.), *New Optimization Techniques in Engineering* (pp. 167–217). Germany: Springer-Verlag. doi:10.1007/978-3-540-39930-8_7

Zhang, J., & Sanderson, A. C. (2009). JADE: Adaptive Differential Evolution With Optional External Archive. *IEEE Transactions on Evolutionary Computation*, *13*(5), 945–958. doi:10.1109/TEVC.2009.2014613

Zhong, W., Liu, J., Xue, M., & Jiao, L. (2004). A multiagent genetic algorithm for global numerical optimization. *IEEE Transactions on Systems, Man, and Cybernetics. Part B, Cybernetics*, *34*(2), 1128–1141. doi:10.1109/TSMCB.2003.821456 PMID:15376858

Chapter 13
An Analysis of Fireworks Algorithm Solving Problems With Shifts in the Decision Space and Objective Space

Shi Cheng
ⓘ https://orcid.org/0000-0002-5129-995X
Shaanxi Normal University, China

Junfeng Chen
ⓘ https://orcid.org/0000-0002-3642-007X
Hohai University, China

Quande Qin
Shenzhen University, China

Yuhui Shi
ⓘ https://orcid.org/0000-0002-8840-723X
Southern University of Science and Technology, China

ABSTRACT

Fireworks algorithms for solving problems with the optima shifts in the decision space and/or objective space are analyzed. The standard benchmark problems have several weaknesses in the research of swarm intelligence algorithms for solving single-objective problems. The optimum shift in decision space and/or objective space will increase the difficulty of problem-solving. Modular arithmetic mapping is utilized in the original fireworks algorithm to handle solutions out of the search range. The solutions are implicitly guided to the center of search range for problems with symmetrical search range via this strategy. The optimization performance of the fireworks algorithm on shift functions may be affected by this strategy. Four kinds of mapping strategies are compared with different problems. The fireworks algorithms with mapping to the boundary or mapping to a limited stochastic region obtain good performance on problems with the optimum shift.

DOI: 10.4018/978-1-7998-3222-5.ch013

1. INTRODUCTION

An optimization problem in $\mathcal{R}^n$, or simply an optimization problem, is a mapping $f : \mathcal{R}^n \to \mathcal{R}^k$, where $\mathcal{R}^n$ is termed as decision space (Adra, Dodd, & Griffin, *et al.*, 2009) (or parameter space (Jin & Send-hoff, 2009), problem space), and $\mathcal{R}^k$ is termed as objective space (Sundaram, 1996). Swarm intelligence is based on a population of individuals (Kennedy, Eberhart, & Shi, 2001). In swarm intelligence, an algorithm maintains and successively improves a collection of potential solutions until some stopping condition is met. The solutions are initialized randomly in the search space. The search information is propagated through the interaction among solutions. With solutions' converging and/or diverging behaviors, solutions are guided toward the better and better areas.

In swarm intelligence algorithms, there is a population of solutions that exist at the same time. The premature convergence may happen due to solutions getting clustered together too fast. The population diversity is a measure of exploration and exploitation status. Based on the population diversity changing measurement, the state of exploration and exploitation can be obtained. The population diversity definition is the first step to give an accurate observation of the search state. Many studies of population diversity in evolutionary computation algorithms and swarm intelligence have been developed (Burke, Gustafson, & Kendall, 2002; Cheng, & Shi, 2011; Cheng, Shi, & Qin, 2011; Cheng, 2013; Cheng, Shi, & Qin, 2013; Mauldin, 1984; Shi, & Eberhart, 2008; Shi, & Eberhart, 2009).

The concept of developmental swarm intelligence algorithms was proposed in Shi (2014). The developmental swarm intelligence algorithm should have two kinds of ability: capability learning and capacity developing. The Capacity Developing focuses on moving the algorithm's search to the area(s) where higher searching potential may be possessed, while the capability learning focuses on its actual searching from the current solution for single-point based optimization algorithms and from the current population for population-based swarm intelligence algorithms (Cheng, & Shi, 2019).

The capacity developing is top-level learning or macro-level learning. The capacity developing could be the learning ability of an algorithm to adaptively change its parameters, structures, and/or its learning potential according to the search states on the problem to be solved. In other words, the capacity developing is the search strength possessed by an algorithm. Capability learning is a bottom-level learning or micro-level learning. The capability learning is the ability for an algorithm to find a better solution(s) from the current solution(s) with the learning capacity it is possessing (Shi, 2014).

The Fireworks algorithm (FWA) (Tan, & Zhu, 2010; Tan, Yu, & Zheng, *et al.*, 2013) and brain storm optimization (BSO) (Cheng, Shi, & Qin, *et al.*, 2014; Shi, 2011a; Shi, 2011b; Cheng, Qin, & Chen, *et al.*, 2016;) algorithm are two good examples of developmental swarm intelligence (DSI) algorithms. The "good enough" optimum could be obtained through solutions' diverging and converging in the search space. In the FWA algorithm, mimicking the fireworks exploration, the new solutions are generated by the exploration of existed solutions. While in BSO algorithm, the solutions are clustered into several categories, and new solutions are generated by the mutation of clusters or existed solutions. The capacity developing, i.e., the adaptation in search, is another common feature in these two algorithms.

Swarm intelligence is based on a population of individuals. In swarm intelligence, an algorithm maintains and successively improves a collection of potential solutions until some stopping condition is met. The solutions are initialized randomly in the search space, and are guided toward the better and better areas through the interaction among solutions. Mathematically, the updating process of population of individuals over iterations can be viewed as a mapping process from one population of individuals to another population of individuals from one iteration to the next iteration, which can be represented as $P_{t+1} = f(P_t)$, where P_t is the population of individuals at the iteration t, $f()$ is the mapping function.

As a general principle, the expected fitness of a solution returned should be improved as the search method is given more computational resources in time and/or space. More desirable, in any single run, the quality of the solution returned by the method should be improved monotonically - that is, the quality of the solution at time $t+1$ should be no worse than the quality at time t, i.e., *fitness*$(t+1) \leq$ *fitness*(t) for minimum problems (Cheng, Shi, & Qin, *et al.*, 2013; Ficici, 2005).

The ability of capacity developing of FWA means that FWA could dynamically change its search ability on different problems. This ability is shown on the adaptation of the parameters in the new solution generation. In the fireworks algorithm, the parameters to control the number and range of new solutions are adaptively determined by the fitness of fireworks. The capability learning ability of FWA means that the obtained solutions are getting better and better iteratively.

In this chapter, the fireworks algorithms for solving problems with the optima shifts in the decision space and/or objective space are analyzed. This chapter is organized as follows: Section 2 reviews the basic fireworks algorithm. Section 3 introduces and analyzes four kinds of mapping strategies. Section 4 defines two kinds of population diversities in fireworks and sparks, respectively. Experiments are conducted in Section 5 followed by the discussion on the firework diversity and spark diversity changing curves in Section 6. Finally, Section 7 concludes with some remarks and future research directions.

2. FIREWORKS ALGORITHM

Fireworks algorithm (FWA) is a swarm intelligence optimization method that mimics the explosion process of fireworks (Tan, & Zhu, 2010; Tan, Yu, & Zheng, *et al.*, 2013; Tan, 2015; Zheng, Janecek, & Tan, 2013). The basic framework of fireworks algorithm is given in Figure 1 (Tan, 2015). The procedure of fireworks algorithm is given in Algorithm 1. There are four operators/strategies in FWA, which are explosion operator, mutation operator, mapping strategy, and selection strategy, respectively.

Algorithm 1. *The procedure of fireworks algorithm*

```
1   Initialize n locations;
2   While have not found "good enough" solution or not reached the pre-deter-
mined maximum number of iterations do
3       Set off fireworks at n locations;
4       Generate sparks through explosion operator;
5       Generate sparks through mutation operator;
6       Obtain the locations of sparks;
7       Map the locations into feasible search space;
8       Evaluate the quality of the locations;
9       Select n locations as new fireworks;
```

Figure 1. The framework of fireworks algorithm

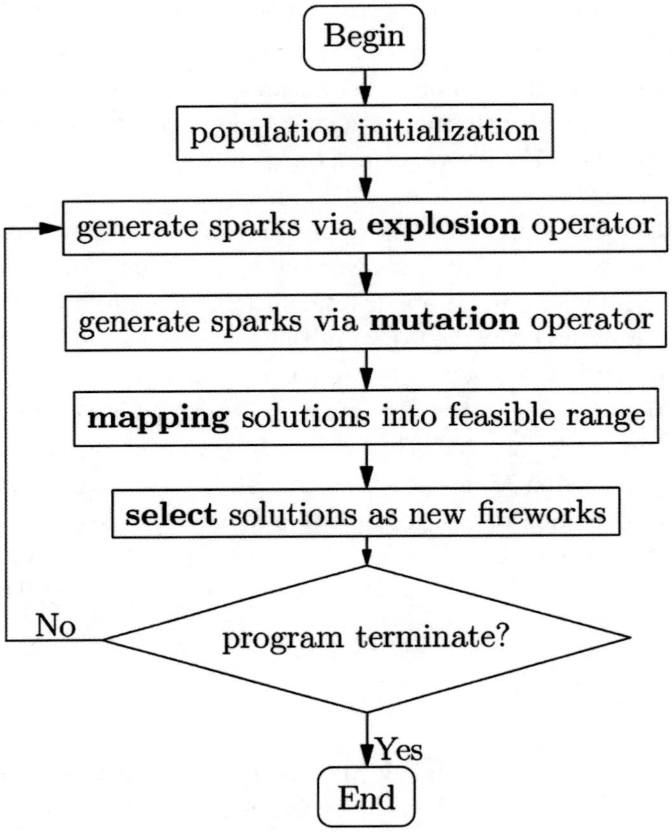

2.1 Explosion Operator

In explosion operator, the number of sparks and amplitude of explosion are calculated for each firework.

2.1.1 Number of Sparks

Based on the concept that more sparks should be generated from a firework with good fitness value, the number of sparks generated by firework i is defined as follows:

$$s_i = m \times \frac{y_{\max} - f(x_i) + \varepsilon}{\sum\limits_{i=1}^{n}(y_{\max} - f(x_i)) + \varepsilon} \tag{1}$$

where m is a parameter that controlling the total number of sparks generated by the n fireworks, $y_{\max}$ is the maximum (worst for minimum problem) fitness value among the n fireworks, $y_{\max} = \max(f(x_i))$, $i=1,2,\dots,n$, and ε, which is a tiny constant number, is utilized to avoid zero-division-error.

To keep the population diversity of fireworks, sparks should be generated from all fireworks. To avoid that many sparks are generated from one firework, the greatest lower bound $a \bullet m$ and the least upper bound $b \bullet m$ are set to sparks number s_i (Tan, & Zhu, 2010; Tan, 2015):

$$
\hat{s}_i = \begin{cases} round(a \cdot m) & if \ s_i < a \cdot m \\ round(b \cdot m) & if \ s_i > b \cdot m \\ round(s_i) & otherwise. \end{cases} \tag{2}
$$

where a and b are constant parameters, and $a<b<1$.

2.1.2 Amplitude of Explosion

For a firework with good fitness value, the sparks are generated close to the firework. This could enhance the exploitation ability of the algorithm. While for a firework with a bad fitness value, the sparks are generated far from the firework. This is aimed to enhance the exploration ability of the algorithm.

$$
A_i = \hat{A} \times \frac{f(x_i) - y_{\min} + \varepsilon}{\sum_{i=1}^{n}(f(x_i) - y_{\min}) + \varepsilon} \tag{3}
$$

where $\hat{A}$ is the maximum explosion amplitude, and $y_{\min}$ is the minimum (best for the minimum problem) fitness value among the n fireworks, $y_{\min}=\min(f(\mathbf{x}_i))$, $i=1,2,...,n$.

2.2 Mutation Operator

The Gaussian mutation is utilized to generate new sparks from a firework. For a firework i, randomly select z dimensions,

$$
x_i^k = x_i^k \times \mathcal{N}(1,1), \forall k \in z \tag{4}
$$

The Gaussian operator could help solutions "jumping out" of the local optima.

2.3 Mapping Strategy

In the explosion operator and mutation operator, a new solution may be generated out of search space. Then the mapping strategy is utilized to set the solution into the feasible search range. The mapping by modular arithmetic is used in the original fireworks algorithm (Tan, & Zhu, 2010). The mapping equation is shown in equation (5).

$$
x_i^k = x_{\min}^k + \left| x_i^k \right| \mathrm{mod} \left(x_{\max}^k - x_{\min}^k \right) \tag{5}
$$

The solution could be reset to the feasible search range via this strategy.

2.4 Selection Strategy

At the beginning of each explosion generation, n locations are selected for the fireworks explosion. The current best location $x^\star$, corresponding to the objective value $f(x^\star)$ that is best among current locations, is always kept for the next explosion generation. The other $n–1$ locations are selected based on the distance among a solution and other solutions. The distance between a solution x_i and other solutions is defined in Equation (6):

$$R(x_i) = \sum_{j \in K} d(x_x, x_j) = \sum_{j \in K} \left\| x_x, x_j \right\| \tag{6}$$

The selection probability of a location x_i is defined as follows:

$$p(x_i) = \frac{R(x_i)}{\sum_{j \in K} R(x_j)} \tag{7}$$

3. MAPPING STRATEGIES IN FIREWORKS ALGORITHM

3.1 Mapping by Modular Arithmetic

The mapping by modular arithmetic is used in the original fireworks algorithm (Tan, & Zhu, 2010). The solution could be reset to the feasible search range via this strategy. However, in most cases, the distance between a solution, which exceeds the feasible search space, and the search boundary is very close. In other words, the value of $\left| x_i^k - x_{\max}^k \right|$ for x_i^k is larger than $x_{\max}^k$, or $\left| x_{\min}^k - x_i^k \right|$ for x_i^k is smaller than $x_{\min}^k$, is very tiny when solution x_i^k exceeds the feasible search space.

Moreover, for most optimization problems, the search space is symmetrical, i.e., $-x_{\min}^k = x_{\max}^k$, and the center of search range is 0. We define that $x_{\max}^k = -x_{\min}^k = x_{half}^k$, and the distance between solution and boundary is Δx_i^k, $0 < \Delta x_i^k < x_{half}^k$. Then we have solution

$$x_{i,up}^k = x_{\max}^k + \Delta x_i^k = x_{half}^k + \Delta x_i^k$$

for $x_{i,up}^k$ exceeding the upper bound $x_{\max}^k$, and solution

$$x_{i,low}^k = x_{\min}^k - \Delta x_i^k = -x_{half}^k - \Delta x_i^k$$

for $x_{i,low}^k$ exceeding the lower bound $x_{\min}^k$. For the first case, $x_{i,up}^k = x_{half}^k + \Delta x_i^k$, then

$$x_{i,up}^k = x_{min}^k + \left| x_i^k \right| \bmod \left(x_{max}^k - x_{min}^k \right)$$

$$= -x_{half}^k + \left| x_{half}^k + \Delta x_i^k \right| \bmod 2x_{half}^k$$

$$= -x_{half}^k + x_{half}^k + \Delta x_i^k$$

$$= \Delta x_i^k$$

For the second case, $x_{i,low}^k = -x_{half}^k - \Delta x_i^k$, then

$$x_{i,low}^k = x_{min}^k + \left| x_i^k \right| \bmod \left(x_{max}^k - x_{min}^k \right)$$

$$= -x_{half}^k + \left| -x_{half}^k - \Delta x_i^k \right| \bmod 2x_{half}^k$$

$$= -x_{half}^k + x_{half}^k + \Delta x_i^k$$

$$= \Delta x_i^k$$

From the analysis, mapping by modular arithmetic strategy always set the solution to a position value Δx_i^k when the distance Δx_i^k is less than half of the search range x_{half}^k. The closer to 0 the Δx_i^k is, the closer the solution will be reset to the center of the search range.

For problem with symmetrical search space, $\left| x_i^k \right|$ is less than $x_{max}^k - x_{min}^k$ when $\Delta x_i^k < x_{half}^k$. The result of $\left| x_i^k \right| \bmod \left(x_{max}^k - x_{min}^k \right)$ is $\left| x_i^k \right|$. This conclusion is not accurate for problems with asymmetrical search space. The value of $\left| x_i^k \right|$ may be larger than $x_{max}^k - x_{min}^k$ even $\Delta x_i^k < x_{half}^k$. The result of $\left| x_i^k \right| \bmod \left(x_{max}^k - x_{min}^k \right)$ is affected by the initialized value of x_{max}^k or x_{min}^k.

The problems with asymmetrical search space are rare in the standard benchmark functions; and it can be shifted to problems with symmetrical search space by adding or subtracting a certain value. For the problems with asymmetrical search space, it is difficult to analyze the result of mapping by modular arithmetic strategy. The sign of x_{max}^k, and x_{min}^k, and the relation between x_{max}^k, x_{min}^k and x_{half}^k should be considered in the investigation. For example, the $\Delta x_i^k = 2$, in the following three scenarios:

1. for $x_{max}^k = 40, x_{min}^k = 0$,

$$x_i^k = 0 + \left| -2 \right| \bmod (40 - 0) = 2$$

The new solution x_i^k is close to the lower bound x_{min}^k.

2. for $x_{max}^k = 30, x_{min}^k = -10$,

$$x_i^k = -10 + \left| -12 \right| \bmod (30 - (-10)) = 2$$

The new solution x_i^k is in the lower range of search space.

3.   for $x^k_{\max} = 120, x^k_{\min} = 80$,

$$x_i^k = 80 + \left| 78 \right| \bmod (120 - 80) = 118$$

The new solution x_i^k is in the upper range of search space, and it is close to the upper bound $x^k_{\max}$.

To overwhelm the implicit guiding to the center of the search space, random mapping in the whole search range is proposed to replace mapping by modular arithmetic strategy in Zheng, Janecek, & Tan (2013). The equation of random mapping in the whole search range is given in equation (8)

$$x_i^k = x^k_{\min} + r_1 \times \left(x^k_{\max} - x^k_{\min} \right) \tag{8}$$

where r_1 is a uniformly distributed random numbers in the range [0,1). This strategy could avoid implicit guiding to the center; however, the search tendency is also abandoned.

3.2 Mapping to the Boundary

The conventional boundary handling methods try to keep the solutions inside the feasible search space *S*. Search information is obtained only when solutions stay in the search space. If a solution exceeds the boundary limit in one dimension at one iteration, that search information will be abandoned. Instead, a new solution will replace the previous solution in that dimension. The classic strategy is to set the solution at boundary when it exceeds the boundary (Zhang, Xie, & Bi, 2004). The equation of this strategy is as follows:

$$x_i^k = \begin{cases} x^k_{\min} & x_i^k < x^k_{\min} \\ x^k_{\max} & x_i^k > x^k_{\max} \\ x_i^k & otherwise. \end{cases} \tag{9}$$

This strategy resets solutions in a particular point—the boundary, which constrains solutions to stay in the search space limited by the boundary.

3.3 Mapping to Stochastic Region

The stochastic strategy can also be used to reset the solutions into a feasible range when solutions exceed the search boundary (Cheng, 2013; Cheng, Shi, & Qin, 2011; Eberhart, & Shi, 2007). The equation is shown in equation (10),

$$x_i^k = \begin{cases} x_{min}^k + r_1 \times \dfrac{1}{2}(x_{max}^k - x_{min}^k) & x_i^k < x_{min}^k \\ x_{max}^k - r_2 \times \dfrac{1}{2}(x_{max}^k - x_{min}^k) & x_i^k > x_{max}^k \\ x_i^k & otherwise. \end{cases} \qquad (10)$$

where r_1 and r_2 are two uniformly distributed random numbers in the range $[0,1)$. The $\dfrac{1}{2}(x_{max}^k - x_{min}^k) = x_{half}^k$ is half of the search range on dimension k. By this strategy, solutions will be reset within the half search space when solutions exceed the boundary limit. This will increases the algorithm's exploration, that is, solutions have higher possibilities to explore new search areas. However, it decreases the algorithm's ability of exploitation at the same time.

3.4 Mapping to Limited Stochastic Region

A solution exceeding the boundary may mean that the global or local optimum may be close to the boundary region. An algorithm should spend more iterations in this region. With the consideration of keeping the ability of exploitation, the resetting scope should be taken into account. The equation of resetting solution into a special area is as follows:

$$x_i^k = \begin{cases} x_{min}^k + r_1 \times c \times \dfrac{1}{2}(x_{max}^k - x_{min}^k) & x_i^k < x_{min}^k \\ x_{max}^k - r_2 \times c \times \dfrac{1}{2}(x_{max}^k - x_{min}^k) & x_i^k > x_{max}^k \\ x_i^k & otherwise. \end{cases} \qquad (11)$$

where c is a parameter to control the resetting scope. When $c=1$, this strategy is the same as the equations (10), that is, solutions are reset within a half space. On the contrary, when $c=0$, this strategy is the same as the equation (9), i.e., it is the same as the classic strategy. The closer to 0 the c is, the more particles have a high possibility to be reset close to the boundary.

4. POPULATION DIVERSITY

In a fireworks optimization algorithm, the population diversity should be measured on the two groups of individuals at the same time. The first group is the population of fireworks, which contains n individuals. The second group is the population of sparks, which contains m individuals.

4.1 Population Diversity in Fireworks

The fireworks are the "seeds" of new solutions. Population diversity in fireworks, or firework diversity, is a measurement of fireworks' distribution. The definition of the firework diversity, which is dimension-wise and based on the L_1 norm, is given below.

$$\overline{x}^k = \frac{1}{n}\sum_{i=1}^{n} x_i^k$$

$$div^k = \frac{1}{n}\sum_{i=1}^{n} \left| x_i^k - \overline{x}^k \right|$$

$$div_f = \sum_{k=1}^{D} w^k Div^k$$

where $\overline{x}^k$ represents the pivot of fireworks in dimension k, and Div^k measures firework diversity for dimension k. Then we define

$$\overline{x} = \left[\overline{x}^1, \ldots, \overline{x}^k, \ldots, \overline{x}^D \right],$$

$\overline{x}$ represents the mean of current fireworks on each dimension, and

$$div = \left[div^1, \ldots, div^k, \ldots, div^D \right],$$

which measures firework diversity for each dimension. w^k is a weight for dimension k. div_f measures the whole firework group's population diversity.

4.2 Population Diversity in Sparks

The sparks are generated via the operations on the fireworks. The distribution of sparks shows the algorithm's exploration or exploitation ability. The definition of the spark diversity is as follows:

$$\overline{x}^k = \frac{1}{m}\sum_{i=1}^{m} x_i^k$$

$$div^k = \frac{1}{m}\sum_{i=1}^{m} \left| x_i^k - \overline{x}^k \right|$$

$$div_s = \sum_{k=1}^{D} w^k Div^k$$

where $\bar{x}^k$ represents the pivot of sparks in dimension k, and div^k measures spark diversity for dimension k. Then we define

$$\bar{x} = \left[\bar{x}^1, \ldots, \bar{x}^k, \ldots, \bar{x}^D \right],$$

$\bar{x}$ represents the mean of current sparks on each dimension, and

$$div = \left[div^1, \ldots, div^k, \ldots, div^D \right],$$

which measures spark diversity for each dimension. div_s measures the whole spark group's population diversity.

Without loss of generality, every dimension is considered equally. Setting all weights $w^k = \dfrac{1}{D}$, then the dimension-wise population diversity in fireworks and sparks can be rewritten as:

$$div = \sum_{k=1}^{D} \frac{1}{D} div^k = \frac{1}{D} \sum_{k=1}^{D} div^k$$

5. EXPERIMENTAL STUDY

5.1 Benchmark Functions

The experiments have been conducted to test the fireworks algorithm with different mapping strategies on the benchmark functions listed in Table 1. Considering the generality, twelve standard benchmark functions are selected, which include six unimodal functions and six multimodal functions (Liang, Qin, & Suganthan, *et al.*, 2006; Yao, Liu, & Lin, 1999). All functions are run 50 times to ensure a reasonable statistical result. There are 5000 iterations for 100 dimensional problems, and 20000 iterations for 200 in every run. For problems with the shifted search space, randomly shifting of the location of the optimum is utilized in each dimension for every run.

In all experiments, the parameters of fireworks algorithm are set as follows: n=5, m=50, a=0.04, b=0.8, $\hat{A} = 40$, and $\hat{m} = 5$ (Tan, & Zhu, 2010).

Table 1. The benchmark functions used in an experimental study, where D is the dimension of each problem, $z=(x-o)$, $x=[x_1, x_2, ..., x_D]$, o_i is a randomly generated number in problem's search space S and it is different in each dimension, global optimum $x^*=o$, f_{min} is the minimum value of the function, and $S \subseteq \mathcal{R}^D$.

Name	Function	S	f_{min}
Parabolic	$f_0(x) = \sum_{i=1}^{D} z_i^2 + bias_0$	$[-100, 100]^D$	-450.0
Schwefel's P2.22	$f_1(x) = \sum_{i=1}^{D} |z_i| + \prod_{i=1}^{D} |z_i| + bias_1$	$[-10, 10]^D$	-330.0
Schwefel's P1.2	$f_2(x) = \sum_{i=1}^{D} \left(\sum_{k=1}^{i} z_k \right)^2 + bias_2$	$[-100, 100]^D$	450.0
Step	$f_3(x) = \sum_{i=1}^{D} \left(\lfloor z_i + 0.5 \rfloor \right)^2 + bias_3$	$[-100, 100]^D$	330.0
Quartic Noise	$f_4(x) = \sum_{i=1}^{D} i z_i^4 + random[0,1) + bias_4$	$[-1.28, 1.28]^D$	-450.0
Zakharov	$f_5(x) = \sum_{i=1}^{D} x_i^2 + \left(\sum_{i=1}^{D} 0.5 i x_i \right)^2 + \left(\sum_{i=1}^{D} 0.5 i x_i \right)^4 + bias_5$	$[-100, 100]^D$	120.0
Rosenbrock	$f_6(x) = \sum_{i=1}^{D-1} \left[100(z_{i+1} - z_i^2)^2 + (z_i - 1)^2 \right] + bias_6$	$[-10, 10]^D$	180.0
Rastrigin	$f_7(x) = \sum_{i=1}^{D} \left[z_i^2 - 10\cos(2\pi z_i) + 10 \right] + bias_7$	$[-5.12, 5.12]^D$	-330.0
Noncontinuous Rastrigin	$f_8(x) = \sum_{i=1}^{D} \left[y_i^2 - 10\cos(2\pi y_i) + 10 \right] + bias_8$ $y_i = \begin{cases} z_i & |z_i| < \frac{1}{2} \\ \dfrac{round(2z_i)}{2} & |z_i| \geq \frac{1}{2} \end{cases}$	$[-5.12, 5.12]^D$	450.0
Ackley	$f_9(x) = -20\exp\left(-0.2\sqrt{\frac{1}{D}\sum_{i=1}^{D} z_i^2} \right) - \exp\left(\frac{1}{D}\sum_{i=1}^{D}\cos(2\pi z_i) \right) + 20 + e + bias_9$	$[-32, 32]^D$	180.0

continues on following page

Table 1. Continued

Name	Function	S	f_{min}
Griewank	$f_{10}(x) = \dfrac{1}{4000} \sum\limits_{i=1}^{D} z_i^2 - \prod\limits_{i=1}^{D} \cos\left(\dfrac{z_i}{\sqrt{i}}\right) + 1 + bias_{10}$	$[-600, 600]^D$	120.0
Generalized Penalized	$f_{11}(x) = \dfrac{\pi}{D}$ $\left\{ 10\sin^2(\pi y_1) + \sum\limits_{i=1}^{D-1}(y_i - 1)^2 \times \left[1 + 10\sin^2(\pi y_{i+1})\right] + (y_D - 1)^2 \right\}$ $+ \sum\limits_{i=1}^{D} u(z_i, 10, 100, 4) + bias_{11}$ $y_i = 1 + \dfrac{1}{4}(z_i + 1) \qquad u(z_i, a, k, m) = \begin{cases} k(z_i - a)^m & z_i > a, \\ 0 & -a < z_i < a \\ k(-z_i - a)^m & z_i < -a \end{cases}$	$[-50, 50]^D$	330.0

5.2 Experimental Results on 100 Dimensional Problems

Several performance measurements are utilized in the experiments below. The best, median, worst, and mean fitness values are attained after a fixed number of iterations. Standard deviation values of the best fitness values are also utilized, which gives the solution's distribution. These values give a measurement of goodness of the algorithm.

5.2.1 Optima Shifted in Objective Space

In this experimental test, the fitness values of all functions are shifted, *i.e.*, the optima are shifted in the objective space. Except Rosenbrock f_6 which has the optimum 1 in each dimension, all optima for other optimized problems are zero, and in the center of each dimension. Tables 2 give results of fireworks algorithm with variants of mapping strategies on problems with 100 dimensions. Almost for all functions, exclude Zakharov f_5 and Rosenbrock f_6, a solution close to the global optima could be found. This indicates the good global search ability of FWA algorithm on unshifted problems or problems only shifted in objective space.

The function value of the best solution found by an algorithm in a run is denoted by $f(x_{best})$. The error of this run is denoted as $error = f(x_{best}) - f(x^*)$. Figure 2 shows the mean error convergence curves of the fireworks algorithm with variants of mapping strategies on problems with 100 dimensions. In Figure 2, the optimal solutions of all problems are not shifted in the decision space, *i.e.*, the optimal solutions are in the original position.

Table 2. Results of fireworks algorithm solving unimodal and multimodal benchmark functions with 100 dimensions. All algorithms are run for 50 times, where "best", "median", "worst", and "mean" indicate the best, median, worst, and mean of the best fitness values for all runs, respectively.

Func.	f_{min}	Strategy	Best	Median	Worst	Mean	Std. Dev.
f_0	-450.0	module	-449.3444	-448.9598	-448.0658	-448.9147	0.277065
		boundary	-449.3933	-448.8824	-448.1283	-448.8809	0.269637
		half	**-449.4268**	-449.0027	-448.3215	**-448.9606**	0.222348
		limit	-449.3760	-448.9099	-448.1133	-448.8917	0.240857
f_1	-330.0	module	**-328.4559**	-324.0381	-322.4086	**-324.2528**	1.248930
		boundary	-326.6667	-324.1527	-320.7364	-324.2165	1.120473
		half	-326.8668	-324.2639	-321.2152	-324.2125	1.125782
		limit	-326.2929	-323.6833	-321.2341	-323.7082	1.081387
f_2	450.0	module	466.7780	546.6010	714.5826	**552.9967**	64.1812
		boundary	463.4458	575.6690	794.2512	578.5310	76.4414
		half	460.5627	538.5312	745.8827	555.7664	70.3049
		limit	**456.9129**	547.6564	874.6852	563.8786	82.8116
f_3	330.0	module	**330**	336	345	335.96	4.35871
		boundary	**330**	335	347	334.6	3.74699
		half	**330**	336	349	335.72	4.29902
		limit	**330**	334	343	**334.38**	3.34598
f_4	-450.0	module	-449.2060	-448.2023	-445.1228	-447.7778	0.982955
		boundary	**-449.9999**	-449.9049	-449.5053	**-449.8794**	0.106480
		half	-449.5537	-449.07995	-448.5039	-449.0770	0.203279
		limit	-449.9862	-449.8835	-449.7018	-449.8774	0.065388
f_5	120.0	module	154.4391	810.4756	2991.5770	951.9720	628.2422
		boundary	**148.8349**	790.9108	4181.2270	1018.600	719.174
		half	190.5590	756.5600	2577.424	**908.3718**	577.2972
		limit	162.5348	679.6599	4990.6583	945.4303	815.660
f_6	180.0	module	295.9601	323.2955	342.7281	323.6606	9.85196
		boundary	305.3805	325.0340	362.4316	325.9969	10.7647
		half	**203.5266**	322.2850	346.0957	318.8226	19.6244
		limit	243.9741	320.6150	348.5671	**318.8161**	15.2322
f_7	-330.0	module	-329.3937	-313.2504	-279.8374	**-311.3391**	12.6960
		boundary	-329.3313	-305.3798	-279.3557	-305.8558	12.8952
		half	-327.1825	-309.3691	-281.2410	-307.2591	12.8290
		limit	**-329.8486**	-312.1943	-279.7763	-310.4771	11.5374
f_8	450.0	module	456.4441	479.1351	511.2062	480.6478	12.7667
		boundary	**451.4516**	476.0076	500.5704	**475.8197**	13.2851
		half	457.5641	475.5994	514.1108	477.5237	12.2246
		limit	454.4522	478.2005	506.8727	478.0259	11.8877

continues on following page

Table 2. Continued

Func.	f_{min}	Strategy	Best	Median	Worst	Mean	Std. Dev.
f_9	180.0	module	180.3149	180.9512	182.1143	180.9825	0.398409
		boundary	180.3529	180.9668	182.0348	181.0494	0.437793
		half	180.2285	181.1495	182.3711	181.1747	0.531463
		limit	**180.0838**	180.9081	181.9618	**180.9706**	0.410570
f_{10}	120.0	module	120.0206	120.0358	120.1574	120.0411	0.022477
		boundary	120.0129	120.0374	120.0664	**120.0365**	0.013280
		half	120.0105	120.0356	120.1430	120.0372	0.019784
		limit	**120.0038**	120.0345	120.0955	120.0367	0.016191
f_{11}	330.0	module	330.0000	330.0000	330.0000	330.0000	2.784E-08
		boundary	330.0000	330.0000	330.0000	330.0000	5.460E-08
		half	330.0000	330.0000	330.0000	330.0000	4.942E-08
		limit	330.0000	330.0000	330.0000	330.0000	5.511E-08

Table 3. Results of fireworks algorithm solving unimodal and multimodal benchmark functions with 100 dimensions. All algorithms are run for 50 times, where "best", "median", "worst", and "mean" indicate the best, median, worst, and mean of the best fitness values for all runs, respectively.

Func.	f_{min}	Strategy	Best	Median	Worst	Mean	Std. Dev.
f_0	-450.0	module	123.38703	443.5230	1024.782	471.1070	207.9864
		boundary	**-446.2835**	279.5694	645.2740	257.7740	195.3318
		half	15.00762	325.4885	740.7109	328.8860	154.7432
		limit	-27.8817	247.1299	626.7375	**238.2201**	157.8467
f_1	-330.0	module	-297.4991	-279.6044	-239.9893	-278.3370	12.97823
		boundary	**-328.0924**	-310.2071	-284.0640	**-309.9837**	9.525181
		half	-313.2956	-307.4991	-295.1823	-307.0945	3.801982
		limit	-319.1543	-309.5740	-281.7188	-307.7595	7.662498
f_2	450.0	module	190329.82	231705.97	310290.72	235824.79	26547.04
		boundary	**167252.70**	228470.79	290612.78	228660.62	27511.23
		half	178236.02	221880.83	275190.32	**223549.86**	22957.08
		limit	167518.92	227517.45	272639.00	227843.97	24968.41
f_3	330.0	module	1186	1717	2286	1714.72	286.861
		boundary	849	1118	1887	1141.56	211.747
		half	895	1467	3066	1508.5	347.288
		limit	**806**	1091	1509	**1108.88**	157.111
f_4	-450.0	module	-132.4733	-41.7221	516.0298	-21.7028	95.46532
		boundary	**-176.7556**	-170.7187	-162.4072	**-170.3907**	3.404519
		half	-143.7480	-110.7060	3.395777	-106.3327	25.8994
		limit	-170.9285	-150.3782	-112.2938	-150.4278	10.6696

continues on following page

Table 3. Continued

Func.	f_{min}	Strategy	Best	Median	Worst	Mean	Std. Dev.
f_5	120.0	module	**233004.90**	281065.51	303928.92	278050.29	13639.96
		boundary	236792.74	278681.803	307744.19	278568.44	12960.83
		half	243372.02	280375.01	306615.69	278327.38	12064.30
		limit	234127.21	281461.05	304418.64	**277011.29**	14991.12
f_6	180.0	module	4944.945	6932.558	14801.02	7923.657	2561.422
		boundary	**1877.569**	3057.027	7633.572	**3433.112**	1279.323
		half	3172.771	5496.0507	13117.97	6138.764	2313.946
		limit	2605.176	3963.499	7196.590	4036.601	1124.613
f_7	-330.0	module	-178.2166	-125.5192	-68.2343	-121.5790	24.4702
		boundary	-175.1720	-129.2962	-95.6616	-131.1400	19.2129
		half	-184.2904	-126.8511	-71.6192	-129.8883	23.9738
		limit	**-187.1445**	-132.5406	-82.3374	**-133.4027**	20.7342
f_8	450.0	module	595.4057	643.4495	702.5768	642.4688	20.6502
		boundary	601.8870	636.1157	699.7248	633.6486	20.2862
		half	590.4379	634.3766	694.2829	633.9112	24.9922
		limit	**567.0588**	622.7443	710.5508	**627.0450**	30.0756
f_9	180.0	module	186.2686	187.7935	190.8406	187.9336	0.943194
		boundary	185.0179	185.8210	186.9406	**185.8798**	0.444148
		half	185.7822	187.1204	188.7718	187.1224	0.712018
		limit	**184.8649**	185.9802	187.4313	186.0757	0.522148
f_{10}	120.0	module	126.8078	130.9325	137.7229	131.6190	2.623525
		boundary	**124.4869**	126.9145	132.5153	127.1530	1.688852
		half	125.6894	130.0155	134.8119	129.9716	2.033134
		limit	124.5314	127.0915	131.5167	**127.0913**	1.574195
f_{11}	330.0	module	338.2957	344.8616	384.4356	346.0932	6.868677
		boundary	335.6560	339.3348	349.1999	339.3016	2.212450
		half	337.1561	341.4568	348.4833	341.4121	2.710028
		limit	**334.8988**	338.4259	344.13725	**338.4819**	2.049914

5.2.2 Optima Shifted in Whole Decision Space

For each problem, both the optimal solution in decision space and fitness value in the objective space are shifted in this experimental test. All the optimal solutions are shifted at a random position in each dimension. The shifted range for new optimal solution is the whole decision space, *i.e.*, the new optimal solution x_i^* is a random value in the range $\left[x_i^{lower}, x_i^{upper} \right]$. The x_i^{lower} and x_i^{upper} are the lower and upper search bound for optimized problem at the ith dimension, respectively. Tables 3 give results of fireworks algorithm with variants of mapping strategies on problems with 100 dimensions. The optimal results

Figure 2. The average performance of the fireworks algorithm solving unimodal and multimodal problems. The optima of each problem are only shifted in objective space; and the dimension of each problem is 100.

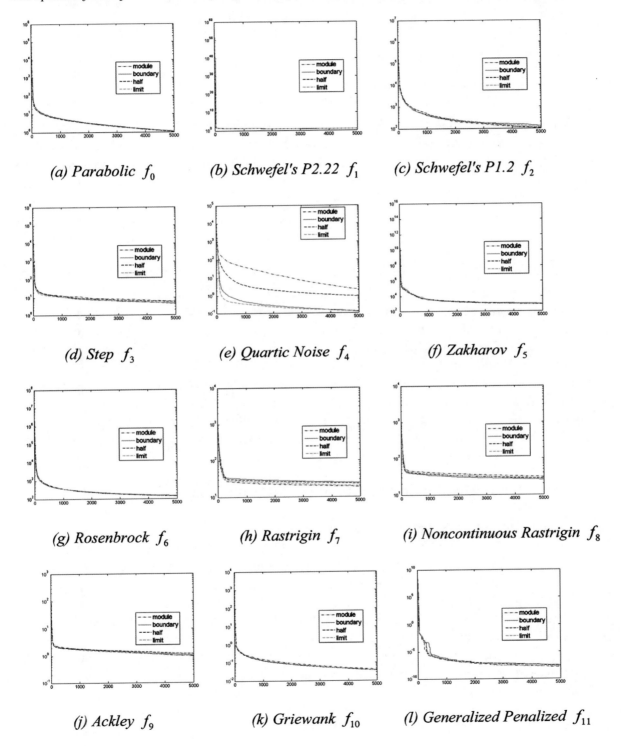

(a) Parabolic f_0 *(b) Schwefel's P2.22* f_1 *(c) Schwefel's P1.2* f_2

(d) Step f_3 *(e) Quartic Noise* f_4 *(f) Zakharov* f_5

(g) Rosenbrock f_6 *(h) Rastrigin* f_7 *(i) Noncontinuous Rastrigin* f_8

(j) Ackley f_9 *(k) Griewank* f_{10} *(l) Generalized Penalized* f_{11}

found on problems with shift in decision space are significantly worse than the problems with original solutions. This indicates that the shift in decision space could affect the algorithm's search performance.

Figure 3 shows the convergence curves of fireworks algorithm with variants of mapping strategies on problems with 100 dimensions. In the Figure 3, the optimal solutions of all problems are shifted to random positions of the whole decision space.

5.2.3 Optima Shifted in Half Decision Space

To test the impact of different shifted ranges, the optimal solutions are shifted in the half search range. All the optimal solutions are shifted at a random position in each dimension. The shifted range for new optimal solution is the half decision space, *i.e.*, the new optimal solution x_i^* is a random value in the range

$$\left[x_i^{lower} + x_i^{quarter}, x_i^{upper} - x_i^{quarter} \right].$$

The x_i^{lower} and x_i^{upper} are the lower and upper search bound for optimized problem at the ith dimension, respectively. The $x_i^{quarter}$ is a quarter of search range in the ith dimension.

In this experiments, the optimal solutions are shifted away the original positions, but the shift range for each dimension is only half of search dimension. Tables 4 give results of fireworks algorithm with variants of mapping strategies on problems with 100 dimensions. The optimal results found on problems with shift in small range are better than the problems with a large shifted range. This indicates that the shifted range in decision space could also affect the algorithm's search performance. In general, the larger the shifted range is in the decision space, the harder the optimized problem is.

Figure 4 shows the convergence curves of fireworks algorithm with variants of mapping strategies on problems with 100 dimensions. In the Figure 4, the optimal solutions of all problems are shifted to random positions, which is in a half search range of each dimension.

5.3 Experimental Results on 200 Dimensional Problems

5.3.1 Optima Shifted in Objective Space

The dimension of each problem is increased to 200 in this experiment. The best fitness value of each problem is shifted in the objective space. Tables 5 give results of fireworks algorithm with variants of mapping strategies on problems with 200 dimensions. Similar to the results on the problems with 100 dimensions, almost for all functions, exclude Zakharov f_5 and Rosenbrock f_6, a solution close to the global optima could be found.

Figure 5 shows the convergence curves of fireworks algorithm with variants of mapping strategies on problems with 200 dimensions. In the Figure 5, the optimal solutions of all problems are not shifted in the decision space.

Figure 3. The average performance of the fireworks algorithm solving unimodal and multimodal problems. The optima of each problem are shifted in both decision and objective space; and the dimension of each problem is 100.

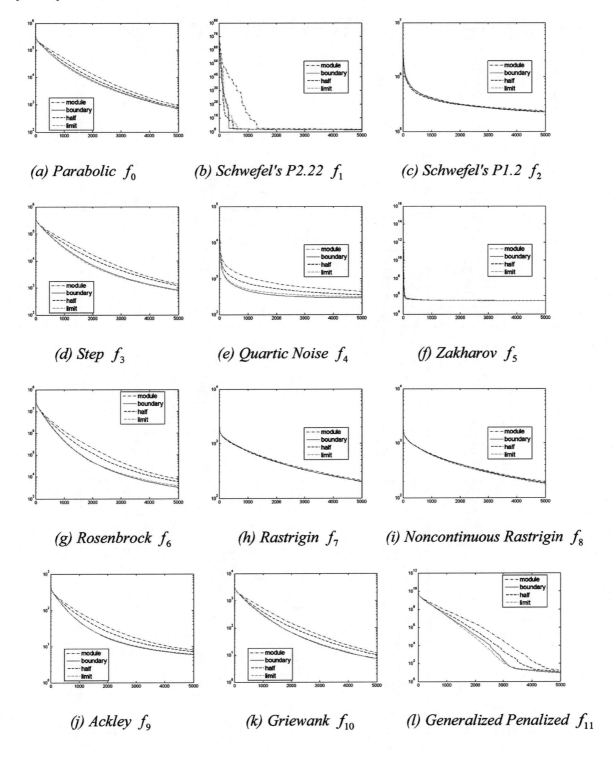

(a) Parabolic f_0

(b) Schwefel's P2.22 f_1

(c) Schwefel's P1.2 f_2

(d) Step f_3

(e) Quartic Noise f_4

(f) Zakharov f_5

(g) Rosenbrock f_6

(h) Rastrigin f_7

(i) Noncontinuous Rastrigin f_8

(j) Ackley f_9

(k) Griewank f_{10}

(l) Generalized Penalized f_{11}

Table 4. Results of fireworks algorithm solving unimodal and multimodal benchmark functions with 100 dimensions. All algorithms are run for 50 times, where "best", "median", "worst", and "mean" indicate the best, median, worst, and mean of the best fitness values for all runs, respectively.

Func.	f_{min}	Strategy	Best	Median	Worst	Mean	Std. Dev.
f_0	-450.0	module	**-185.2914**	14.124529	357.49391	22.65004	112.39337
		boundary	-170.9602	3.1493202	370.92748	29.78895	120.7512
		half	-158.6821	-12.79981	397.20201	6.803467	106.20981
		limit	-155.5196	-6.377236	292.4456	**1.292926**	103.8833
f_1	-330.0	module	-314.4221	-308.9646	-301.6953	-308.3745	2.783527
		boundary	**-326.1371**	-311.2448	-298.5137	**-310.9007**	5.826472
		half	-314.9783	-309.1535	-302.59113	-309.1055	3.336730
		limit	-318.4399	-308.2525	-290.3827	-307.7114	5.4887411
f_2	450.0	module	47557.582	63642.825	85357.492	63686.660	8761.1986
		boundary	**47057.204**	63779.287	106367.379	64493.506	10147.306
		half	47479.674	62648.683	88905.105	63061.961	8241.791
		limit	50431.186	60840.592	89216.749	**62422.461**	8719.6751
f_3	330.0	module	751	949	1300	965.62	139.2567
		boundary	738	918	1320	921.56	109.4660
		half	**629**	896	1293	**901.24**	117.3573
		limit	734	914	1132	924.6	100.3035
f_4	-450.0	module	-433.4983	-417.1620	-386.0282	-416.452	11.51628
		boundary	**-445.3929**	-444.3586	-443.2284	**-444.3283**	0.537208
		half	-440.9928	-435.9998	-422.3887	-435.4715	3.449639
		limit	-444.3015	-442.3910	-440.3623	-442.4090	0.758719
f_5	120.0	module	82793.752	90584.970	100624.392	91183.738	4211.676
		boundary	**82713.117**	90566.392	103864.368	**90552.685**	4347.262
		half	82826.388	90321.555	99659.297	90573.473	3713.694
		limit	84033.593	90897.924	102699.253	91193.423	4259.793
f_6	180.0	module	1248.1614	1823.0720	3437.7023	1925.9554	527.1532
		boundary	1154.8582	1762.7420	3785.1613	1866.3426	558.5631
		half	1141.6439	1656.6525	4073.5192	**1793.1689**	540.0707
		limit	**1131.7994**	1830.8568	4144.4995	1989.3950	639.3603
f_7	-330.0	module	-219.1855	-192.3446	-152.0295	-191.5501	15.12473
		boundary	-227.9418	-193.4013	-156.2992	-195.1035	14.73017
		half	**-228.7098**	-197.8581	-166.2823	-198.7240	13.74228
		limit	-223.1445	-192.7464	-146.8072	-191.8345	14.74619
f_8	450.0	module	542.0665	564.9106	598.6952	**567.1226**	13.16895
		boundary	**542.0561**	573.9182	606.0742	574.0390	15.47853
		half	542.3951	568.8122	603.5879	568.1229	12.79338
		limit	544.1801	570.7855	604.5505	572.7924	16.63077

continues on following page

Table 4. Continued

Func.	f_{min}	Strategy	Best	Median	Worst	Mean	Std. Dev.
f_9	180.0	module	184.5027	185.2573	186.7207	**185.3615**	0.521935
		boundary	184.7380	185.4617	186.6033	185.5006	0.460228
		half	184.7292	185.4794	186.64792	185.4792	0.398503
		limit	**184.4612**	185.3615	186.5080	185.4033	0.435109
f_{10}	120.0	module	123.4223	125.0873	127.7308	125.2388	1.160101
		boundary	123.6241	124.8859	128.4585	**124.9565**	0.932499
		half	123.7914	124.8900	126.5411	124.9768	0.670491
		limit	**123.2259**	125.0623	127.1870	125.1186	0.739124
f_{11}	330.0	module	334.3172	337.1139	341.8405	337.2946	1.544227
		boundary	**334.2016**	336.9861	343.3512	337.2948	1.616435
		half	334.2971	337.1736	341.5528	337.1456	1.557392
		limit	335.2080	337.07096	342.2122	**337.1267**	1.314208

Table 5. Results of fireworks algorithm solving unimodal and multimodal benchmark functions with 200 dimensions. All algorithms are run for 50 times, where "best", "median", "worst", and "mean" indicate the best, median, worst, and mean of the best fitness values for all runs, respectively.

Func.	f_{min}	Strategy	Best	Median	Worst	Mean	Std. Dev.
f_0	-450.0	module	**-449.2836**	-447.9331	-447.2188	-447.9011	0.351210
		boundary	-448.5346	-448.0384	-447.0821	**-447.9858**	0.306007
		half	-448.7739	-447.9997	-447.1211	-447.9708	0.295745
		limit	-449.0540	-447.8710	-447.3707	-447.9279	0.331783
f_1	-330.0	module	**-327.3319**	-317.4173	-312.2510	-317.3661	2.563841
		boundary	-323.1203	-317.9470	-311.9309	**-318.1197**	2.165784
		half	-325.3018	-317.6230	-310.5166	-317.9416	2.884145
		limit	-321.8501	-317.1449	-311.0070	-317.2362	1.922750
f_2	450.0	module	**496.5504**	729.0643	1369.7020	**766.9991**	176.0479
		boundary	557.2692	796.3215	1311.5603	835.1774	176.7223
		half	518.0539	793.2134	2028.4127	842.6432	248.2963
		limit	531.0513	835.5607	1609.3941	843.3504	191.1417
f_3	330.0	module	**330**	338	354	339.88	7.146019
		boundary	**330**	338	366	340.94	8.331650
		half	**330**	338	359	**339.36**	7.024983
		limit	**330**	338	357	339.6	6.702238
f_4	-450.0	module	-447.4834	-442.8298	-370.4542	-437.4525	13.96694
		boundary	-449.9728	-449.5250	-448.4757	-449.4665	0.360087
		half	-448.4886	-447.5657	-446.2801	-447.5325	0.492155
		limit	**-449.9761**	-449.7147	-449.1239	**-449.6729**	0.180545

continues on following page

Table 5. Continued

Func.	f_{min}	Strategy	Best	Median	Worst	Mean	Std. Dev.
f_5	120.0	module	525.5551	2708.646	6734.9040	2722.429	1474.514
		boundary	338.8051	3055.294	14271.281	3566.716	2933.513
		half	**171.0216**	2378.5118	8330.3818	**2696.532**	1838.365
		limit	285.0780	2554.061	17667.789	3332.777	3026.411
f_6	180.0	module	436.1458	467.1124	493.9468	466.4139	15.05203
		boundary	433.7179	467.3060	501.9691	**465.5784**	14.18886
		half	**424.7823**	467.2277	495.5025	467.7276	13.68348
		limit	438.4786	469.0342	501.8399	469.0162	13.59741
f_7	-330.0	module	-326.8973	-289.4301	-222.7455	-283.8403	26.5466
		boundary	-328.1163	-288.2729	-206.3530	**-287.4119**	28.7910
		half	**-328.4341**	-289.5011	-203.8046	-287.0577	27.1837
		limit	-326.9404	-283.1533	-236.4542	-285.4177	24.7744
f_8	450.0	module	462.7835	504.1687	558.7536	505.8180	23.4710
		boundary	460.6350	501.0622	565.1147	501.9267	26.0457
		half	**460.2330**	495.4389	549.2493	**496.4361**	21.9924
		limit	462.9024	497.0098	557.4533	501.3018	25.0063
f_9	180.0	module	180.5112	181.0231	181.8271	181.0744	0.376529
		boundary	**180.3096**	180.9057	182.0348	181.0780	0.449329
		half	180.4998	180.9239	182.4185	181.0551	0.438899
		limit	180.4222	180.9975	181.5995	**180.9861**	0.337914
f_{10}	120.0	module	**120.0139**	120.0424	120.0638	120.0427	0.010187
		boundary	120.0155	120.0412	120.0665	120.0401	0.010327
		half	120.0152	120.0398	120.0607	**120.0400**	0.010177
		limit	120.0177	120.0419	120.0653	120.0413	0.010468
f_{11}	330.0	module	330	330.0000	330.0000	330.0000	2.757E-09
		boundary	330	330.0000	330.0000	330.0000	1.386E-09
		half	330	330.0000	330.0000	330.0000	2.938E-09
		limit	330	330.0000	330.0000	330.0000	1.615E-09

5.3.2 Optima Shifted in Decision Space

The optimal solutions in the decision space are shifted to random positions and the best fitness values are also shifted in the objective space. The shifted range in the decision space is the whole dimension. Tables 6 give results of fireworks algorithm with variants of mapping strategies on problems with 200 dimensions. All optimized results are significantly affected by the shift in the decision space. Even the function evaluation times are doubled in this experiment, the results obtained on the problems with 200 dimensions are worse than the problems with 100 dimensions under the same optimal solutions shift conditions.

Figure 4. The average performance of the fireworks algorithm solving unimodal and multimodal problems. The optima of each problem are shifted in both decision and objective space; and the dimension of each problem is 100.

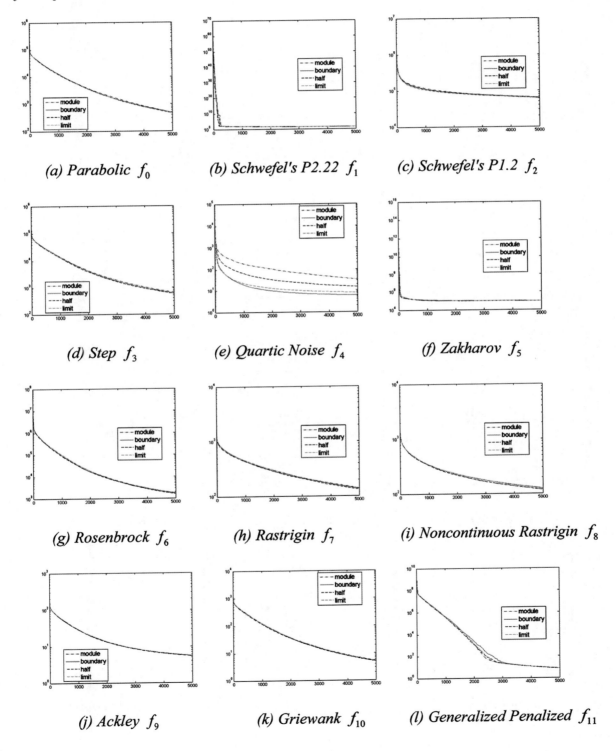

(a) Parabolic f_0

(b) Schwefel's P2.22 f_1

(c) Schwefel's P1.2 f_2

(d) Step f_3

(e) Quartic Noise f_4

(f) Zakharov f_5

(g) Rosenbrock f_6

(h) Rastrigin f_7

(i) Noncontinuous Rastrigin f_8

(j) Ackley f_9

(k) Griewank f_{10}

(l) Generalized Penalized f_{11}

Figure 5. The average performance of the fireworks algorithm solving unimodal and multimodal problems. The optima of each problem are only shifted in objective space; and the dimension of each problem is 200.

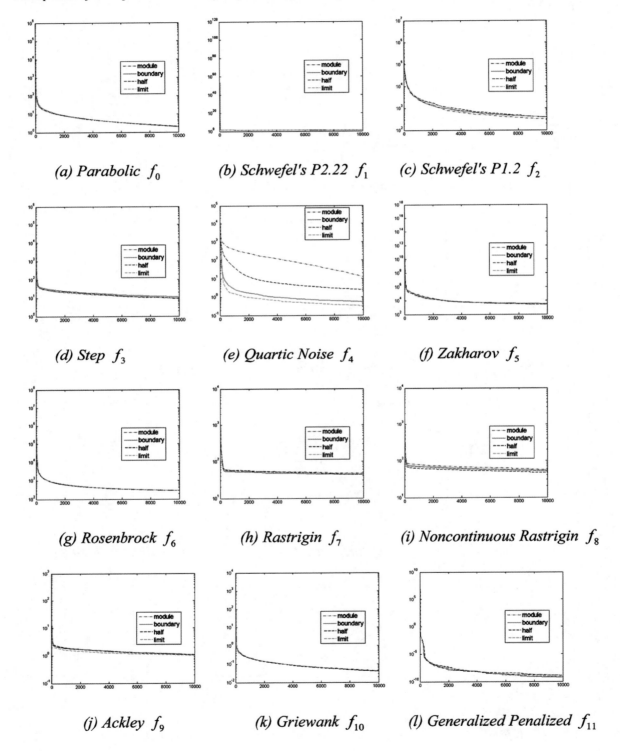

(a) Parabolic f_0

(b) Schwefel's P2.22 f_1

(c) Schwefel's P1.2 f_2

(d) Step f_3

(e) Quartic Noise f_4

(f) Zakharov f_5

(g) Rosenbrock f_6

(h) Rastrigin f_7

(i) Noncontinuous Rastrigin f_8

(j) Ackley f_9

(k) Griewank f_{10}

(l) Generalized Penalized f_{11}

Table 6. Results of fireworks algorithm solving unimodal and multimodal benchmark functions with 200 dimensions. All algorithms are run for 50 times, where "best", "median", "worst", and "mean" indicate the best, median, worst, and mean of the best fitness values for all runs, respectively.

Func.	f_{min}	Strategy	Best	Median	Worst	Mean	Std. Dev.
f_0	-450.0	module	2633.5281	4541.9890	7896.2774	4736.1439	1068.09
		boundary	**1177.1030**	1842.7156	3370.1812	1926.8348	412.118
		half	2411.7845	3206.3989	5305.3913	3337.2975	653.833
		limit	1198.8100	1927.2931	3376.7372	**1979.7717**	441.416
f_1	-330.0	module	-314.6008	-304.5344	-292.4016	-303.8969	4.87418
		boundary	**-318.7313**	-304.6878	-288.6522	-304.7134	4.89172
		half	-318.0285	-304.7728	-290.8962	**-304.8829**	5.19988
		limit	-315.1103	-304.2532	-290.7561	-303.7305	4.68894
f_2	450.0	module	557411.97	721239.96	953638.32	725740.38	68419.2
		boundary	**525312.99**	714435.56	803750.03	**696277.02**	58846.4
		half	587178.84	726235.39	864398.05	722311.60	61986.5
		limit	568161.72	696164.80	855042.67	705439.46	63807.4
f_3	330.0	module	3868	5473	8067	5429.58	1027.13
		boundary	2205	3186	4097	**3189.02**	376.496
		half	3165	4552	6975	4510.46	782.330
		limit	**2162**	3293	4657	3250.88	416.908
f_4	-450.0	module	2241.3121	2839.0026	4211.7633	2910.9279	435.221
		boundary	**1156.3118**	1231.4673	1344.8921	**1236.2261**	35.7139
		half	1769.0354	2056.5928	2516.4782	2086.4998	89.8391
		limit	1341.5657	1481.8088	1615.5291	1480.9908	70.2946
f_5	120.0	module	**707100.23**	748014.08	797751.58	**749491.89**	19327.1
		boundary	717639.56	754655.29	824502.04	754097.57	22249.4
		half	708950.02	750832.970	812571.581	751447.45	8664.82
		limit	719123.12	758264.90	805581.84	758901.82	19770.6
f_6	180.0	module	15345.225	22013.788	39844.803	23815.367	6221.89
		boundary	**4958.8938**	8831.6828	16359.1349	**8926.5821**	1923.07
		half	9335.0608	15917.656	29292.100	16094.783	4194.44
		limit	6752.6277	9136.7606	13969.7060	9394.9959	1657.57
f_7	-330.0	module	233.7510	336.5764	436.6258	338.4481	50.2967
		boundary	176.9333	270.6839	378.2411	**274.6178**	49.7996
		half	205.1035	313.4778	424.9427	309.3778	55.1056
		limit	**153.9582**	298.8610	408.2567	292.5787	46.6232
f_8	450.0	module	953.2389	1062.5557	1193.8228	1070.1834	58.7348
		boundary	**896.6237**	1048.3495	1215.6763	**1051.9569**	57.2677
		half	955.6467	1050.5059	1170.9600	1055.7335	56.9554
		limit	939.6675	1071.7209	1213.1681	1060.4554	60.8931

continues on following page

Table 5. Continued

Func.	f_{min}	Strategy	Best	Median	Worst	Mean	Std. Dev.
f_9	180.0	module	189.3461	191.0274	193.5268	191.04263	0.97840
		boundary	**186.3560**	187.5791	188.8159	**187.6379**	0.54196
		half	187.7469	189.4291	190.8975	189.3868	0.69846
		limit	186.3658	187.76619	189.1711	187.7668	0.58992
f_{10}	120.0	module	164.0023	184.5372	212.4104	187.6732	11.8809
		boundary	136.4422	141.0826	149.9158	141.4925	3.10751
		half	147.7439	160.3801	180.6264	161.4745	7.38680
		limit	**136.3016**	142.3075	158.0976	142.4169	3.91170
f_{11}	330.0	module	369.0072	1310.812	26983.41	2975.131	4716.50
		boundary	**342.5246**	351.9261	366.2908	352.2404	5.25540
		half	351.9593	376.7778	1273.1508	440.3222	181.216
		limit	344.2784	351.0091	367.6420	**351.6486**	4.58822

Figure 6 shows the convergence curves of the fireworks algorithm with variants of mapping strategies on problems with 200 dimensions. In Figure 6, the optimal solutions of all problems are shifted to random positions of the whole decision space.

5.4 Experimental Results Discussion

From the experimental results on the problems with different dimensions, the problems with different shifted space (objective space and/or decision space), and the problem with different shifted search range (the whole dimension or the half dimension), several conclusions could be made as follows:

- The optima shift in objective space has tiny or no effect on the difficulty of the optimization problem. The fireworks algorithms could find the equivalent solutions on problems with or without optima shift in the objective space.
- The optimization problems are getting harder when the optima are shifted in the decision space, i.e., the optima are more difficult to obtain when the optima are different in each dimension and/or not located in the center of search space.
- The difficulty of shifted optimization problems is affected by the dimension of problems. The difficulty is significantly increased when the number of problems' dimensionality is increased. The performance of the algorithm on optima shift problems is getting worse when the number of dimensions increases. For optima shifted problems with a doubled number of dimensions (from 100 dimensions to 200 dimensions), even doubled the number of iterations, the performance is not linearly improved.
- The difficulty of optimization problems is affected by the shift range in decision space. The problems are getting harder when the optima are shifted in a large space. It is more difficult to obtain optima when the optima are shifted far away to the center of the search space.

Figure 6. The average performance of the fireworks algorithm solving unimodal and multimodal problems. The optima of each problem are shifted in both decision and objective space; and the dimension of each problem is 200.

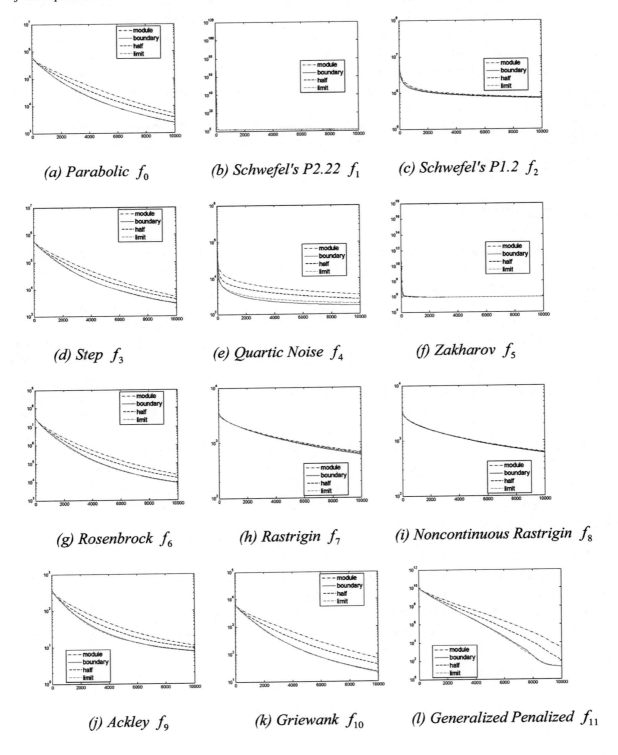

(a) Parabolic f_0 *(b) Schwefel's P2.22 f_1* *(c) Schwefel's P1.2 f_2*

(d) Step f_3 *(e) Quartic Noise f_4* *(f) Zakharov f_5*

(g) Rosenbrock f_6 *(h) Rastrigin f_7* *(i) Noncontinuous Rastrigin f_8*

(j) Ackley f_9 *(k) Griewank f_{10}* *(l) Generalized Penalized f_{11}*

6. POPULATION DIVERSITY DISCUSSION

The population diversities measurements on the fireworks group and sparks group are given in figures 7, 8, 9, and 10. The Figure 7 and Figure 8 are curves of population diversities changing for FWA solving the unimodal problem f_2, while the Figure 9 and Figure 10 are curves of population diversities changing for FWA solving the multimodal problem f_6. For problems f_2 and f_6, the firework diversity and spark diversity are vibrated during the whole search process, and the firework diversity vibrated in a large range than the spark diversity. In all figures, there is no significant difference among FWA algorithms with different mapping strategies.

The population diversities are vibrated in the different search ranges. The range of firework diversity may be related to the setting of ε value. The range of spark diversity may be related to the step size of new solution generation.

7. CONCLUSION

The fireworks algorithms for solving problems with the optima shift in the decision space and/or objective space were analyzed in this chapter. The benchmark problems have several weaknesses in the original research of swarm intelligence algorithms for solving single-objective problems. The optimum is in the center of the search range, and is the same at each dimension of the search space. The optimum shift in decision space and/or objective space could increase the difficulty of problem-solving.

The solutions are implicitly guided to the center of the search range for problems with symmetrical search range via mapping by modular arithmetic strategy. The optimization performance of the fireworks algorithm on the shift functions may be affected by this strategy. Four kinds of mapping strategies, which include mapping by modular arithmetic, mapping to the boundary, mapping to stochastic region, and mapping to limited stochastic region, were compared on problems with different dimensions and different optimum shift range. From the experimental results, the fireworks algorithms with mapping to the boundary, or mapping to the limited stochastic region had a good performance on problems with the optimum shift. This is probably because the search tendency is kept in these two strategies.

The definitions of population diversities measurement were also proposed in this chapter, from observation on population diversity changes, the useful information of fireworks algorithm solving different kinds of problems could be obtained.

In this chapter, population diversities were monitored on FWA for solving single-objective problems. Multi-objective problems have different goals of the optimization, it does not find one single solution, but many. The concept of convergence has different meanings between single and multiple objective problems (Jin & Sendhoff, 2009). Population diversity is also important when applying FWA to solve multi-objective problems (Adra, & Fleming, 2011; Cheng, Shi, & Qin, 2012). Defining population diversity for multi-objective fireworks algorithms and monitoring its change during the search process is our future research work.

Figure 7. The population diversities of the fireworks algorithm solving the shifted unimodal problem f_2. The fitness value of the problem is only shifted in objective space, and the dimension of the problem is 200.

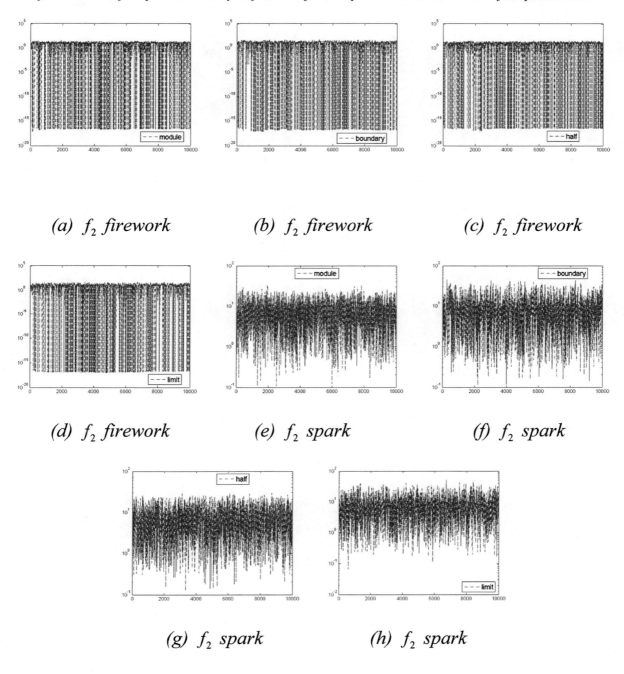

(a) f_2 firework

(b) f_2 firework

(c) f_2 firework

(d) f_2 firework

(e) f_2 spark

(f) f_2 spark

(g) f_2 spark

(h) f_2 spark

Figure 8. The population diversities of the fireworks algorithm solving shifted the unimodal problem f_2. The optima of the problem are shifted in both decision and objective space, and the dimension of the problem is 200.

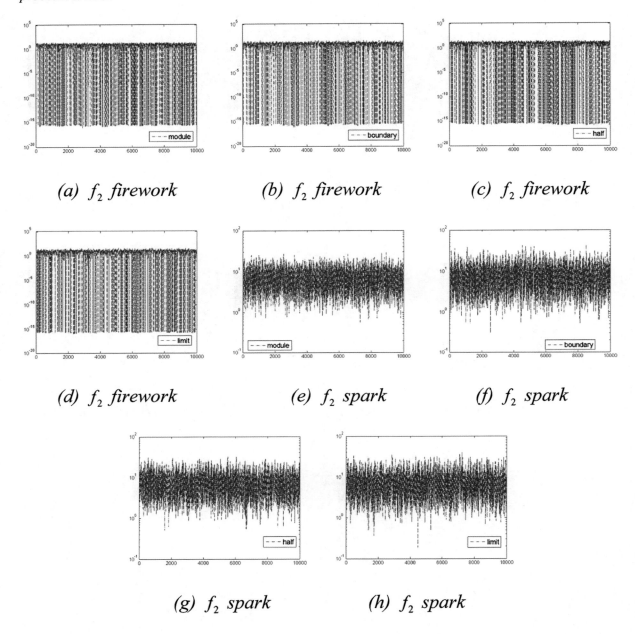

(a) f_2 firework

(b) f_2 firework

(c) f_2 firework

(d) f_2 firework

(e) f_2 spark

(f) f_2 spark

(g) f_2 spark

(h) f_2 spark

Figure 9. The population diversities of the fireworks algorithm solving shifted multimodal problem f_6. The fitness value of the problem is only shifted in objective space; and the dimension of the problem is 200.

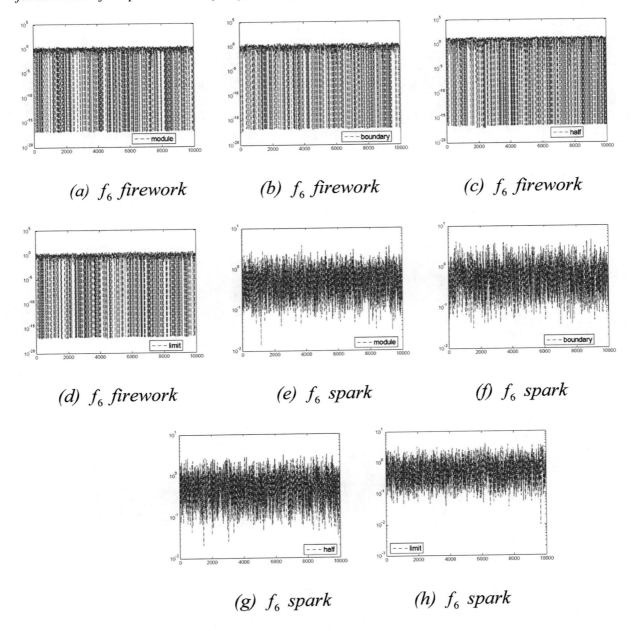

(a) f_6 firework *(b) f_6 firework* *(c) f_6 firework*

(d) f_6 firework *(e) f_6 spark* *(f) f_6 spark*

(g) f_6 spark *(h) f_6 spark*

Figure 10. The population diversities of the fireworks algorithm solving shifted the multimodal problem f_6. The optima of the problem are shifted in both decision and objective space, and the dimension of the problem is 200.

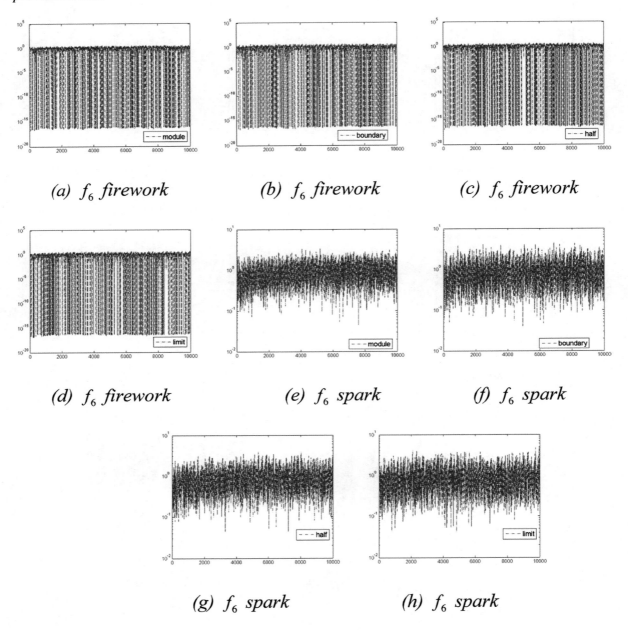

(a) f_6 firework

(b) f_6 firework

(c) f_6 firework

(d) f_6 firework

(e) f_6 spark

(f) f_6 spark

(g) f_6 spark

(h) f_6 spark

ACKNOWLEDGMENT

This work was supported by National Natural Science Foundation of China (Grant Nos. 61806119, 61672334, 61761136008, and 61773103), and Natural Science Basic Research Plan In Shaanxi Province of China (Grant No. 2019JM-320).

REFERENCES

Adra, S. F., Dodd, T. J., Griffin, I. A., & Fleming, P. J. (2009). Convergence acceleration operator for multiobjective optimization. *IEEE Transactions on Evolutionary Computation*, *12*(4), 825–847. doi:10.1109/TEVC.2008.2011743

Adra, S. F., & Fleming, P. J. (2011). Diversity management in evolutionary many-objective optimization. *IEEE Transactions on Evolutionary Computation*, *15*(2), 183–195. doi:10.1109/TEVC.2010.2058117

Burke, E. K., Gustafson, S., & Kendall, G. (2002). A survey and analysis of diversity measures in genetic programming. *Proceedings of the Genetic and Evolutionary Computation Conference (GECCO 2002)*, (pp. 716-723). San Francisco, CA: Morgan Kaufmann.

Cheng, S. (2013). *Population diversity in particle swarm optimization: Definition, observation, control, and application.* (Ph.D. dissertation), University of Liverpool, UK.

Cheng, S., Qin, Q., Chen, J., & Shi, Y. (2016). Brain storm optimization algorithm: A review. *Artificial Intelligence Review*, *46*(4), 445–458. doi:10.100710462-016-9471-0

Cheng, S., & Shi, Y. (2011). Diversity control in particle swarm optimization. *Proceedings of 2011 IEEE Symposium on Swarm Intelligence (SIS 2011)*, (pp. 110-118).

Cheng, S., & Shi, Y. (2019). Brain Storm Optimization Algorithms: Concepts, Principles, and Applications, 23. Adaptation, Learning, and Optimization. Springer International Publishing AG. doi:10.1007/978-3-030-15070-9

Cheng, S., Shi, Y., & Qin, Q. (2011). Experimental study on boundary constraints handling in particle swarm optimization: From population diversity perspective. [IJSIR]. *International Journal of Swarm Intelligence Research*, *2*(3), 43–69. doi:10.4018/jsir.2011070104

Cheng, S., Shi, Y., & Qin, Q. (2012). Population diversity of particle swarm optimizer solving single and multi-objective problems [IJSIR]. *International Journal of Swarm Intelligence Research*, *3*(4), 23–60. doi:10.4018/jsir.2012100102

Cheng, S., Shi, Y., & Qin, Q. (2013). A study of normalized population diversity in particle swarm optimization. [IJSIR]. *International Journal of Swarm Intelligence Research*, *4*(1), 1–34. doi:10.4018/jsir.2013010101

Cheng, S., Shi, Y., Qin, Q., & Gao, S. (2013). Solution clustering analysis in brain storm optimization algorithm. *Proceedings of The 2013 IEEE Symposium on Swarm Intelligence, (SIS 2013)*, (pp. 111-118). Singapore: IEEE. 10.1109/SIS.2013.6615167

Cheng, S., Shi, Y., Qin, Q., Zhang, Q., & Bai, R. (2014). Population diversity maintenance in brain storm optimization algorithm. *Journal of Artificial Intelligence and Soft Computing Research*, *4*(2), 83–97. doi:10.1515/jaiscr-2015-0001

Eberhart, R., & Shi, Y. (2007). *Computational Intelligence: Concepts to Implementations*. Morgan Kaufmann. doi:10.1016/B978-155860759-0/50002-0

Ficici, S. G. (2005). Monotonic solution concepts in coevolution. *Proceedings Genetic and Evolutionary Computation Conference (GECCO 2005)*, (pp. 499-506).

Jin, Y., & Sendhoff, B. (2009). A systems approach to evolutionary multiobjective structural optimization and beyond. *IEEE Computational Intelligence Magazine*, *4*(3), 62–76. doi:10.1109/MCI.2009.933094

Kennedy, J., Eberhart, R., & Shi, Y. (2001). *Swarm Intelligence*. Morgan Kaufmann.

Liang, J. J., Qin, A. K., Suganthan, P. N., & Baskar, S. (2006). Comprehensive learning particle swarm optimizer for global optimization of multimodal functions. *IEEE Transactions on Evolutionary Computation*, *10*(3), 281–295. doi:10.1109/TEVC.2005.857610

Mauldin, M. L. (1984). Maintaining diversity in genetic search. *Proceedings of the National Conference on Artificial Intelligence (AAAI 1984)*, (pp. 247-250).

Shi, Y. (2011a). Brain storm optimization algorithm. In Y. Tan, Y. Shi, Y. Chai, & G. Wang (Eds.), Advances in Swarm Intelligence, ser. Lecture Notes in Computer Science, 6728 (pp. 303-309). Berlin, Germany: Springer. doi:10.1007/978-3-642-21515-5_36

Shi, Y. (2011b). An optimization algorithm based on brainstorming process [IJSIR]. *International Journal of Swarm Intelligence Research*, *2*(4), 35–62. doi:10.4018/ijsir.2011100103

Shi, Y. (2014). Developmental swarm intelligence: Developmental learning perspective of swarm intelligence algorithms [IJSIR]. *International Journal of Swarm Intelligence Research*, *5*(1), 36–54. doi:10.4018/ijsir.2014010102

Shi, Y., & Eberhart, R. (2008). Population diversity of particle swarms, *Proceedings of the 2008 Congress on Evolutionary Computation (CEC 2008)*, (pp. 1063-1067). 10.1109/CEC.2008.4630928

Shi, Y., & Eberhart, R. (2009). Monitoring of particle swarm optimization. *Frontiers of Computer Science*, *3*(1), 31–37. doi:10.100711704-009-0008-4

Sundaram, R. K. (1996). *A First Course in Optimization Theory*. Cambridge University Press. doi:10.1017/CBO9780511804526

Tan, Y. (2015). *Fireworks Algorithm: A Novel Swarm Intelligence Optimization Method*. Springer. doi:10.1007/978-3-662-46353-6

Tan, Y., Yu, C., Zheng, S., & Ding, K. (2013). Introduction to fireworks algorithm. [IJSIR] *International Journal of Swarm Intelligence Research*, *4*(4), 39–70. doi:10.4018/ijsir.2013100103

Tan, Y., & Zhu, Y. (2010) Fireworks algorithm for optimization, in Advances in Swarm Intelligence, ser. Lecture Notes in Computer Science, Y. Tan, Y. Shi, and K. C. Tan, Eds. Springer Berlin Heidelberg, 6145, (pp. 355-364). doi:10.1007/978-3-642-13495-1_44

Yao, X., Liu, Y., & Lin, G. (1999). Evolutionary programming made faster. *IEEE Transactions on Evolutionary Computation*, *3*(2), 82–102. doi:10.1109/4235.771163

Zhang, W., Xie, X.-F., & Bi, D.-C. (2004). Handling boundary constraints for numerical optimization by particle swarm flying in periodic search space. *Proceedings of the 2004 Congress on Evolutionary Computation*, (pp. 2307-2311). 10.1109/CEC.2004.1331185

Zheng, S., Janecek, A., & Tan, Y. (2013). Enhanced fireworks algorithm. *Proceedings of 2013 IEEE Congress on Evolutionary Computation, (CEC 2013)*, (pp. 2069-2077). Cancun, Mexico: IEEE. 10.1109/CEC.2013.6557813

Chapter 14
Population Diversity of Particle Swarm Optimization Algorithm on Solving Single and Multi-Objective Problems

Shi Cheng

https://orcid.org/0000-0002-5129-995X

Shaanxi Normal University, China

Yuhui Shi

https://orcid.org/0000-0002-8840-723X

Southern University of Science and Technology, China

Quande Qin

Shenzhen University, China

ABSTRACT

Premature convergence occurs in swarm intelligence algorithms searching for optima. A swarm intelligence algorithm has two kinds of abilities: the exploration of new possibilities and the exploitation of old certainties. The exploration ability means that an algorithm can explore more search places to increase the possibility that the algorithm can find good enough solutions. In contrast, the exploitation ability means that an algorithm focuses on the refinement of found promising areas. An algorithm should have a balance between exploration and exploitation, that is, the allocation of computational resources should be optimized to ensure that an algorithm can find good enough solutions effectively. The diversity measures the distribution of individuals' information. From the observation of the distribution and diversity change, the degree of exploration and exploitation can be obtained.

DOI: 10.4018/978-1-7998-3222-5.ch014

1. INTRODUCTION

Optimization, in general, is concerned with finding "best available" solution(s) for a given problem within the allowable time. In mathematical terms, an optimization problem in $\mathcal{R}^n$, or simply an optimization problem, is a mapping $f : \mathcal{R}^n \to \mathcal{R}^k$, where $\mathcal{R}^n$ is termed as decision space (Adra, Dodd, & Griffin, *et al.*, 2009),parameter space (Jin & Sendhoff, 2009), or problem space (Weise, Zapf, & Chiong, *et al.*, 2009)), and $\mathcal{R}^k$ is termed as objective space (Sundaram, 1996). Optimization problems can be divided into two categories depending on the value of k. When $k=1$, this kind of problem is called Single Objective Optimization (SOO), and when $k>1$, this is called Multi-Objective Optimization (or Many Objective Optimization, MOO).

Particle Swarm Optimizer/Optimization (PSO), which is one of the evolutionary computation techniques, was invented by Eberhart and Kennedy in 1995 (Eberhart & Kennedy, 1995; Kennedy & Eberhart, 1995). It is a population-based stochastic algorithm modeled on the social behaviors observed in flocking birds. Each particle, which represents a solution, flies through the search space with a velocity that is dynamically adjusted according to its own and its companion's historical behaviors. The particles tend to fly toward better search areas over the course of the search process (Eberhart & Shi, 2001; Hu, Shi, & Eberhart, 2004, Cheng et al. 2018).

Premature convergence occurs when all individuals in population-based algorithms are trapped in local optima. In this situation, the exploration of an algorithm is greatly reduced, i.e., the algorithm is searching in a narrow space. For continuous optimization problems, there are infinite numbers of potential solutions. Even with consideration of computational precision, there still have a great number of feasible solutions. The computational resources allocation should be optimized, i.e., maintaining an appropriate balance between exploration and exploitation is a primary factor.

Different problems have different properties. The single objective problem could be divided into the unimodal problem and multi-modal problem. As the name indicated, a unimodal problem has only one optimum solution, on the contrary, a multi-modal problem has several or number of optimum solutions, of which many are local optimal solutions. Optimization algorithms are difficult to find the global optimum solutions because generally it is hard to balance between fast converge speed and the ability of "jumping out" of local optimum. In other words, we need to avoid premature in the search process.

Different computational resource allocation methods should be taken when dealing with different problems. A good algorithm should balance its exploration and exploitation ability during its search process. The concept of exploration and exploitation was firstly introduced in organization science (March, 1991; Gupta, Smith, & Shalley, 2006). The exploration ability means an algorithm can explore more search place, to increase the possibility that the algorithm can find a "good enough" solution(s). In contrast, the exploitation ability means that an algorithm focuses on the refinement of found promising areas.

The population diversity (De Jong, 1975; Mauldin, 1984; Olorunda & Engelbrecht, 2008; Corriveau, Guilbault, & Tahan, *et al.*, 2012) is a measure of individuals' search information. From the distribution of individuals and change of this distribution information, we can obtain the algorithm's status of exploration or exploitation. An important issue in multiobjective is the fitness metric in solutions. The Pareto domination is frequently used in current research to compare between two solutions. The Pareto domination has many strengths, such as easy to understand, computational efficiency, however, it has some drawbacks:

1. It only can be used to compare two single solutions, for several groups of solutions, the Pareto domination is difficult to measure which group is better than others.
2. For multiobjective problems with a large number of objectives, almost every solution is Pareto nondominated (Ishibuchi, Tsukamoto, & Nojima, 2008). The Pareto domination is not appropriate for the multiobjective problem with a large number of objectives.

In this chapter, we will analyze and discuss the population diversity of particle swarm optimizer for solving single and multi-objective problems. For multiobjective problems, the population diversity is observed on both the particles and the solutions in the archive. The population of particles measures the distribution of the positions, while the population of solutions can be used to measure the goodness of a set of solutions. This metric may guide the search in multiobjective problems with numerous objectives. Adaptive optimization algorithms can be designed through controlling balance between exploration and exploitation.

The rest of the chapter is organized as follows: the basic PSO algorithm and the multiobjective optimization are reviewed in Section 2. In Section 3, several definitions of dimension-wise PSO diversities, which based on L_1 norm, are given on single objective optimization and multiobjective optimization. The Section 4 gives the experiments on diversity monitoring for some single and multi-objective benchmark functions. The analysis and discussion of population diversities for single and multi-objective optimization are given in Section 5. Finally, Section 6 concludes with some remarks and future research directions.

2. PRELIMINARIES

2.1. Particle Swarm Optimizer

Particle swarm optimization emulates the swarm behavior and the individuals represent points in the n-dimensional search space. A particle represents a potential solution. Each particle is associated with two vectors, i.e., the velocity vector and the position vector. The position x_{ij} and velocity v_{ij} represent the position and velocity of ith particle at jth dimension, respectively. For the purpose of generality and clarity, m represents the number of particles and n the number of dimensions. The i represents the ith particle, $i=1,\ldots,m$, and j is the jth dimension, $j=1,\ldots,n$ (Cheng, 2013).

The canonical PSO algorithm is simple in concept and easy in implementation. The velocity and position update equations are as follow (Shi & Eberhart, 1998; Kennedy, Eberhart, & Shi, 2001; Eberhart & Shi, 2007):

$$v_i(t+1) \leftarrow w_i v_i(t) + c_1 rand()(p_i - x_i(t)) + c_2 Rand()(p_g - x_i(t)) \tag{1}$$

$$x_i(t+1) \leftarrow x_i(t) + v_i(t+1) \tag{2}$$

where w denotes the inertia weight and usually is less than 1 (Shi & Eberhart, 1998; Shi & Eberhart, 2011; Cheng, Shi, & Qin, et al., 2012), c_1 and c_2 are two positive acceleration constants, $rand()$ and $Rand()$ are two random functions to generate uniformly distributed random numbers in the range [0,1) and are different for each dimension and each particle, $x_i = [x_{i1}, \cdots, x_{ij}, \cdots, x_{in}]$ represents the ith particle's position, $v_i = [v_{i1}, \cdots, v_{ij}, \cdots, v_{in}]$ represents the ith particle's velocity, $p_i = [p_{i1}, \cdots, p_{ij}, \cdots, p_{in}]$ is termed as personal best, which refers to the best position found by the ith particle, and $p_g = [p_{g1}, \cdots, p_{gj}, \cdots, p_{gn}]$ is termed as local best, which refers to the position found by the members in the ith particle's neighborhood that has the best fitness value so far.

The basic procedure of PSO is given as Algorithm 1.

Algorithm 1. *The basic procedure of particle swarm optimization*

```
1: Initialize velocity and position randomly for each particle in every dimen-
sion.
2: While not found the "good enough" solution or not reached the maximum num-
ber of iterations do
3:       Calculate each particle's fitness value
4:     Compare fitness value between that of current position and that of the
best position in history (personal best, termed as pbest). For each particle,
if the fitness value of current position is better than pbest, then update
pbest to be the current position.
5:       Select the particle which has the best fitness value among current par-
ticle's neighborhood, this particle is called the neighborhood best (termed as
nbest). If current particle's neighborhood includes all particles then this
neighborhood best is the global best (termed as gbest), otherwise, it is local
best (termed as lbest).
6:       for each particle do
7:             Update particle's velocity and position according to the equation
(1) and (2), respectively.
8:       end for
9: end while
```

2.2. Multiobjective Optimization

Multiobjective Optimization refers to optimization problems that involve two or more objectives. Usually for multiobjective optimization problems, a set of solutions is sought instead of one. A general *multiobjective optimization problem* can be described as a vector function f that maps a tuple of n parameters (decision variables) to a tuple of k objectives. Without loss of generality, minimization is assumed throughout this chapter.

minimize $f(x) = (f_1(x), f_2(x), \dots, f_k(x))$

subject to $x = (x_1, \dots, x_p, \dots, x_n) \in X$

$y = (y_1, \dots, y_p, \dots, y_k) \in Y$

where x_i is a decision variable, x is called the *decision vector*, X is the *decision space*; y_j is an objective, y is the *objective vector*, and Y is the *objective space*, and $f\colon X \rightarrow Y$ consists of k real-valued objective functions.

Let $u = (u_1,\ldots,u_k)$, $\upsilon = (\upsilon_1,\ldots,\upsilon_k) \in Y$, be two vectors, u is said to dominate υ (denoted as $u \preceq \upsilon$), if $u_i \leq \upsilon_i$, $\forall i = 1,\ldots,k$, and $u \neq \upsilon$. A point $x^* \in X$ is called Pareto optimal if there is no $x \in X$ such that $f(x)$ dominates $f(x^*)$. The set of all the Pareto optimal points is called the *Pareto set* (denoted as **PS**). The set of all the Pareto objective vectors, $PF = \{f(x) \in X \mid x \in PS\}$, is called the *Pareto front* (denoted as **PF**).

In a multiobjective optimization problem, we aim to find the set of optimal solutions known as the Pareto optimal set. Pareto optimality is defined with respect to the concept of nondominated points in the objective space.

3. POPULATION DIVERSITY

Premature convergence occurs in population-based algorithms. Holland has introduced a well-known phenomenon of "hitchhiking" in population genetics (Holland, 2000). In population-based algorithms, all individuals search for optima at the same time. If, compared with other individuals, some newly searched solution gives extremely good fitness value; all other individuals may converge rapidly toward it. It is difficult to handle premature convergence. Once individuals "get stuck" in local optima, the exploration of the algorithm is greatly reduced, i.e., solutions lose their diversity in decision space.

Another kind of premature convergence occurs due to improper setting of boundary constraints (Cheng, Shi, & Qin, 2011). A classic boundary constraint handling strategy resets a particle at boundary in one dimension when this particle's position is exceeding the boundary in that dimension. If the fitness value of the particle at boundary is better than that of other particles, all particles in its neighborhood in this dimension will move to the boundary. If particles could not find a position with better fitness value, all particles will "stick in" the boundary at this dimension. A particle is difficult to "jump out" of boundary even we increase the total number of fitness evaluations or the maximum number of iterations, and this phenomenon occurs with higher possibility for high-dimensional problems.

The most important factor affecting an optimization algorithm's performance is its ability of "exploration" or "exploitation". Exploration means the ability of a search algorithm to explore different areas of the decision space in order to have high probability of finding good optimum. Exploitation, on the other hand, means the ability to concentrate the search around a found promising region in order to refine a candidate solution. A good optimization algorithm optimally balances these conflicted objectives. Within the PSO, these objectives are addressed by the velocity update equation.

Many strategies have been proposed to adjust an algorithm's exploration and exploitation ability. Velocity clamp was firstly used to adjust the ability between exploration and exploitation (Eberhart, Dobbins, & Simpson, 1996). Like the equation (3), current velocity will be equal to maximum velocity or minus maximum velocity if velocity is greater than the maximum velocity or less than the minus maximum velocity, respectively. Adding an inertia weight is more effective than velocity clamp because it not only increases the probability for an algorithm to converge, but have a way to control the whole searching process of an algorithm (Shi & Eberhart, 1998). There are many adaptive strategies to tune algorithms' parameters during the search (Cheng, Shi, & Qin, 2012a; Cheng, Shi, & Qin, et al., 2012). The properties of population diversity in single objective optimization have been discussed in many papers (Cheng, Shi, & Qin, 2012c; Corriveau, Guilbault, & Tahan, et al., 2012). The properties of population in multiobjective optimization and the difference between population diversity in SOP and MOP are still needed to be analyzed and discussed.

$$v_{ij} = \begin{cases} V_{max} & v_{ij} > V_{max} \\ v_{ij} & -V_{max} \leq v_{ij} \leq V_{max} \\ -V_{max} & v_{ij} < -V_{max} \end{cases} \tag{3}$$

3.1 Diversity in Single Objective Optimization

Population diversity of PSO is useful for measuring and dynamically adjusting an algorithm's ability of exploration or exploitation accordingly. Shi and Eberhart gave three definitions on population diversity, which are position diversity, velocity diversity, and cognitive diversity (Shi & Eberhart, 2008; Shi & Eberhart, 2009). Position, velocity, and cognitive diversity are used to measure the distribution of particles' current positions, current velocities, and *pbests* (the best position found so far for each particles), respectively. Cheng and Shi introduced the modified definitions of the three diversity measures based on L_1 norm (Cheng & Shi, 2011a; Cheng & Shi, 2011b).

3.1.1. Position Diversity

Position diversity measures distribution of particles' current positions, therefore, can reflect particles' dynamics. Position diversity gives the current position distribution information of particles, whether the particles are going to diverge or converge could be reflected from this measurement. From diversity measurements, useful search information can be obtained. Definition of dimension-wise position diversity, which is based on the L_1 distance, is as follows

$$\bar{x}_j = \frac{1}{m} \sum_{i=1}^{m} x_{ij}$$

$$D_j^p = \frac{1}{m} \sum_{i=1}^{m} |x_{ij} - \bar{x}_j|$$

$$D^p = \sum_{j=1}^{n} w_j D_j^p$$

where $\bar{x}_j$ represents the pivot of particles' position in dimension j, and D_j^p measures particles position diversity based on L_1 norm for dimension j. $\bar{x} = [\bar{x}_1, \cdots, \bar{x}_j, \cdots, \bar{x}_n]$, represents the mean of particles' current positions for all dimensions, and $D^p = [D_1^p, \cdots, D_j^p, \cdots, D_n^p]$, measures particles' position diversity based on L_1 norm for all dimensions. D^p measures the whole swarm's population diversity.

3.1.2. Velocity Diversity

Velocity diversity, which represents diversity of particles' "moving potential", measures the distribution of particles' current velocities. In other words, velocity diversity measures the "activity" information of particles. Based on the measurement of velocity diversity, particle's tendency of expansion or convergence could be revealed. The dimension-wise velocity diversity based on L_1 distance is defined as follows

$$\overline{v}_j = \frac{1}{m} \sum_{i=1}^{m} v_{ij}$$

$$D^v = \frac{1}{m} \sum_{i=1}^{m} \left| v_{ij} - \overline{v}_j \right|$$

$$D^v = \sum_{j=1}^{n} w_j D_j^v$$

where $\overline{v}_j$ represents the pivot of particles' velocity in dimension j, and D_j^v measures particles velocity diversity based on L_1 norm for dimension j. $\overline{v} = [\overline{v}_1, \cdots, \overline{v}_j, \cdots, \overline{v}_n]$, represents the mean of particles' current velocities for all dimensions, and $D^v = [D_1^v, \cdots, D_j^v, \cdots, D_n^v]$, measures velocity diversity of all particles for all dimensions. D^v represents the whole swarm velocity diversity based on L_1 norm.

3.1.3. Cognitive Diversity

Cognitive diversity, which represents distribution of particles' "moving target", measures the distribution of historical best positions for all particles. The measurement definition of cognitive diversity is the same as that of the position diversity except that it utilizes each particle's current personal best position instead of current position. The definition of dimension-wise PSO cognitive diversity is as follows

$$\overline{p}_j = \frac{1}{m} \sum_{i=1}^{m} p_{ij}$$

$$D_j^c = \frac{1}{m} \sum_{i=1}^{m} \left| p_{ij} - \overline{p}_j \right|$$

$$D^c = \sum_{j=1}^{n} w_j D_j^c$$

where $\overline{p}_j$ represents the pivot of particles' previous best position in dimension j, and D_j^v measures particles cognitive diversity based on L_1 norm for dimension j. $\overline{p} = [\overline{p}_1, \cdots, \overline{p}_j, \cdots, \overline{p}_n]$ represents the average of all particles' personal best position in history (*pbest*) for all dimensions; $D^c = [D_1^p, \cdots, D_j^p, \cdots, D_n^p]$ represents the particles' cognitive diversity for all dimensions based on L_1 norm. D^c measures the whole swarm's cognitive diversity.

Without loss of generality, every dimension is considered equally in this chapter. Setting all weights $w_j = \dfrac{1}{n}$, then the position diversity, velocity diversity, and cognitive diversity of the whole swarm can be rewritten as:

$$D^p = \sum_{j=1}^{n} \frac{1}{n} D_j^p = \frac{1}{n} \sum_{j=1}^{n} D_j^p$$

$$D^v = \sum_{j=1}^{n} \frac{1}{n} D_j^v = \frac{1}{n} \sum_{j=1}^{n} D_j^v$$

$$D^c = \sum_{j=1}^{n} \frac{1}{n} D_j^c = \frac{1}{n} \sum_{j=1}^{n} D_j^c .$$

3.1.4. Change of Position Diversity and Cognitive Diversity

The position diversity and cognitive diversity measure the distribution of particles' current position and previous best position. From the change of position diversity and cognitive diversity, the algorithm's status of exploration and exploitation may be obtained. The change of position diversity and cognitive diversity are defined as follow:

$$C^p = D^p(t+1) - D^p(t)$$

$$C^c = D^c(t+1) - D^c(t)$$

where C^p is the change of position diversity, and C^c is the change of cognitive diversity.

From the changing of position diversity and cognitive diversity, the speed of swarm convergence or divergence can be observed. The changing of position diversity and cognitive diversity can be divided into four cases:

1. position diversity increasing, cognitive diversity increasing, i.e., position diversity and cognitive diversity getting increased at the same time.
2. position diversity decreasing, cognitive diversity decreasing, i.e., position diversity and cognitive diversity getting decreased at the same time.
3. position diversity increasing, cognitive diversity decreasing.
4. position diversity decreasing, cognitive diversity increasing.

For the first two cases, if the position diversity and cognitive diversity increase at the same time, the swarm is diverging, i.e., the algorithm is in the exploration status, and on the contrary, if the position diversity and cognitive diversity decrease at the same time, the swarm is converging, i.e., the algorithm is in the exploitation status. The last two cases reflect more complicated situations.

3.1.5. Ratio of Position Diversity to Cognitive Diversity

Cognitive diversity represents the distribution of all current moving targets found by particles. From the relationship of position diversity and cognitive diversity, particles' dynamical movement can be observed.

The ratio of position diversity to cognitive diversity is defined as follows:

$$R = \frac{Position\ Diversity}{Cognitive\ Diversity} = \frac{D^p}{D^c}$$

The ratio of position diversity to cognitive diversity indicates the movement of particles. If the value large than 1, the particles are searching in a relatively larger space, and the previous best solutions are in a relatively smaller space. On the contrast, if the value is less than 1, the particles' search is in a relatively smaller space. Different strategies should be utilized under these different situations to maintain an appropriate balance between exploration and exploitation.

3.2. Diversity in Multiobjective Optimization

Optimization has different meanings between single objective optimization and multiobjective optimization (Jin & Sendhoff, 2009). For MOO, optimization means to find not a single, but a lot, maybe infinite solutions. The population diversity is also important in multiobjective optimization (Zhang & Mühlenbein, 2004; Zhou, Zhang, & Jin, 2009). Unlike in single objective optimization, the diversity in multiobjective optimization not only concerns the convergence in decision space, but also the convergence in objective space. There are many discussions of population diversity in multiobjective optimization, such as convergence acceleration (Adra, Dodd, & Griffin, *et al.*, 2009), diversity management (Adra & Fleming 2011), and diversity improvement (Ishibuchi, Tsukamoto, & Nojima, 2010).

3.2.1 Population Diversity of Particles

For the single objective optimization, each individual represents a potential solution. The individual with the best fitness value is the best solution for the problem to be solved. For the multiobjective optimization, if an individual corresponds to a nondominated solution, this solution may be chosen to be put into an additional archive. All nondominated solutions are stored in the archive.

The population diversity should be measured on current solutions and the found nondominated solutions, i.e., the distribution of particles and distribution of solutions in the archive should both be observed. The measurement of distribution of particles is the same as that for PSO solving single objective problems. The position diversity, velocity diversity, and cognitive diversity should be measured. These diversity definitions and equations are the same as that for PSO for single objective optimization.

3.2.2. Population Diversity of Solutions

Unlike the single objective optimization, the multiobjective problems has many or infinite solutions (Bosman & Thierens, 2003). The optimization goal of an MOP consists of three objectives:

1. The distance of the resulting nondominated solutions to the true optimal Pareto front should be minimized;
2. A good (in most cases uniform) distribution of the obtained solutions is desirable;
3. The spread of the obtained nondominated solutions should be maximized, i.e., for each objective a wide range of values should be covered by the nondominated solutions.

The number of solutions in the archive may be different from that of particles. For the purpose of generality and clarity, h represents the number of solutions, n represents the number of problem dimensions, and k is the number of objectives. The u represents the uth solution, $u=1,\ldots,h$, υ is the vth objective, $\upsilon=1,\ldots,k$, and j is the jth dimension, $j=1,..,n$. Two kinds of population diversity should be measured for solutions, diversity in solution space and diversity in objective space. Convergence in objective space is not preferred. All objectives should have a uniform distribution in the Pareto front.

3.2.3 Population Diversity of Pareto Set

Population diversity of Pareto set measures distribution of nondominated solutions in the search space, therefore, it can reflect solutions' dynamics. Definition of diversity of Pareto set, which is based on the L_1 norm, is as follows

$$\overline{s}_j = \frac{1}{h}\sum_{u=1}^{h} s_{uj}$$

$$D_j^s = \frac{1}{h}\sum_{u=1}^{h} \left| s_{uj} - \overline{s}_j \right|$$

$$D^s = \frac{1}{n}\sum_{j=1}^{n} D_j^s$$

where $\overline{s}_j$ is the center of solutions on dimension j, $\overline{s} = [\overline{s}_1, \cdots, \overline{s}_j, \cdots, \overline{s}_n]$ represents the average of all solutions on each dimension. The parameter h is the number of solutions in the archive, h and number of particles m can be different. The vector $D^s = [D_1^s, \cdots, D_j^s, \cdots, D_n^s]$ represents the diversity of Pareto set for all dimensions based on L_1 norm. D^s measures the diversity of solutions in Pareto set.

3.2.4. Population Diversity of Pareto Front

Population diversity of Pareto Front measures distribution of fitness value in the objective space, therefore, it can reflect goodness of solutions. Definition of diversity of Pareto front, which is based on the L_1 norm, is as follows

$$\bar{f}_v = \frac{1}{h} \sum_{u=1}^{h} f_{uv}$$

$$D_v^f = \frac{1}{h} \sum_{u=1}^{h} \left| f_{uv} - \bar{f}_v \right|$$

$$D^f = \frac{1}{k} \sum_{v=1}^{k} D_v^f$$

where $\bar{f}_v$ is the center of solutions on objective v, $\bar{f} = [\bar{f}_1, \cdots, \bar{f}_v, \cdots, \bar{f}_k]$ represents the average of all fitness values for all objectives; $D^f = [D_1^f, \cdots, D_v^f, \cdots, D_k^f]$ represents the diversity of Pareto front for each objective based on L_1 norm. D^f measures the diversity of fitness values in Pareto front.

The diversity measurement can be utilized to metrics the solutions of multiobjective optimization. One of the main differences between SOPs and MOPs is that MOPs constitute a multidimensional objective space. In addition, a set of solutions representing the tradeoff among the different objectives rather than an unique optimal solution is sought in Multiobjective optimization (MOO). How to measure the goodness of solutions and the performance of algorithms is important in MOO (Cheng, Shi, & Qin, 2012b). The defined diversity metrics have several properties: (Deb, & Jain, 2002)

1. **Comparability:** For the benchmark functions, the target (or desired) metric value (calculated for an ideally converged and diversified set of points) can be calculated. For the real world problems, the metric values can be compared.
2. **Monotonicity:** The metric should provide a monotonic increase or decrease in its value, as the solution gets improved or deteriorated slightly. This will also help in evaluating the extent of superiority of one approximation set over another.
3. **Scalability:** The metric should be scalable to any number of objectives. The Multiobjective optimization contains only two or three objectives, while the many objective optimization contains more than four objectives. The Pareto domination is utilized in these optimizations, however, there has been reported that almost every solution is Pareto nondominated in the problems with more than ten objectives (Ishibuchi, Tsukamoto, & Nojima, 2010). For the large scale multiobjective problems, especially a problem with large number of objectives, the Pareto domination may not be appropriated to metric the goodness of solutions. In this situation, we need to consider the scalability of metrics. Although the scalability is not discuss a lot in current research, and it is not an absolutely necessary property, but if followed, it will certainly be convenient for evaluating scalability issues of Multi-Objective Evolutionary Algorithms (MOEAs) in terms of number of objectives.

4. **Computational Efficiency:** The metric should be computationally inexpensive, although this is not a stringent condition to be followed. In swarm intelligence algorithms, many iterations are taken to search the optima. Consider the number of iterations, a fast metric can accelerate the search speed.

4. EXPERIMENTAL STUDY

4.1. Benchmark Test Functions

Wolpert and Macerady have proved that under certain assumptions no algorithm is better than other one on average for all problems (Wolpert & Macready, 1997). Consider the generalization, eleven single objective and six multiobjective benchmark functions were used in our experimental studies (Yao, Liu, & Lin, 1999; Liang, Qin, & Suganthan, *et al.*, 2006; Zhang, Zhou, & Zhao, *et al.*, 2009). The aim of the experiment is not to compare the ability nor the efficacy of PSO algorithm with different parameter setting or structure, e.g., global star or local ring, but to measure the exploration and exploitation information when PSOs are running.

4.1.1. Single Objective Problems

The experiments have been conducted to test single objective benchmark functions listed in Table 1. Without loss of generality, five standard unimodal and six multimodal test functions are selected (Yao, Liu, & Lin, 1999; Liang, Qin, & Suganthan, *et al.*, 2006). All functions are run for 50 times to have statistical meaning for comparison among different approaches. Randomly shifting of the location of optimum is utilized in each dimension for each run.

4.1.2. Multiobjective Problems

There are six unconstrained (bound constrained) problem (Zhang, Zhou, & Zhao, *et al.*, 2009) in the experimental study, each problem has two objectives to be minimized. The unconstrained problem 1, 2, 3, 4, and 7 have a continuous Pareto front, the unconstrained problem 5 has a discrete Pareto front.

1. Unconstrained problem 1 (UCP1)

$$f_1 = x_1 + \frac{2}{|J_1|} \sum_{j \in J_1} \left[x_j - \sin\left(6\pi x_1 + \frac{j\pi}{n}\right) \right]^2$$

$$f_2 = 1 - \sqrt{x_1} + \frac{2}{|J_2|} \sum_{j \in J_2} \left[x_j - \sin\left(6\pi x_1 + \frac{j\pi}{n}\right) \right]^2$$

Table 1. The benchmark functions used in our experimental study, where n is the dimension of each problem, z=(x–o), x= [x_1,x_2,...,x_n], o_i is an randomly generated number in problem's search space S and it is different in each dimension, global optimum x^*=o, n=100, f_{min} is the minimum value of the function, and $S \subseteq \mathcal{R}^n$.

Function	Test Function	S	f_{min}
Parabolic	$f_0(x) = \sum_{i=1}^{n} z_i^2 + bias_0$	$[-100, 100]^n$	-450.0
Schwefel's P2.22	$f_1(x) = \sum_{i=1}^{n} \lvert z_i \rvert + \prod_{i=1}^{n} \lvert z_i \rvert + bias_1$	$[-10, 10]^n$	-330.0
Schwefel's P1.2	$f_2(x) = \sum_{i=1}^{n} \left(\sum_{k=1}^{i} z_k \right)^2 + bias_2$	$[-100, 100]^n$	450.0
Step	$f_3(x) = \sum_{i=1}^{n} \left(\lfloor z_i + 0.5 \rfloor \right)^2 + bias_3$	$[-100, 100]^n$	330.0
Quartic Noise	$f_4(x) = \sum_{i=1}^{n} i z_i^4 + random[0,1) + bias_4$	$[-1.28, 1.28]^n$	-450.0
Rosenbrock	$f_5(x) = \sum_{i=1}^{n-1} [100(z_{i+1} - z_i^2)^2 + (z_i - 1)^2] + bias_5$	$[-10, 10]^n$	180.0
Rastrigin	$f_6(x) = \sum_{i=1}^{n} [z_i^2 - 10\cos(2\pi z_i) + 10] + bias_6$	$[-5.12, 5.12]^n$	-330.0
Noncontinuous Rastrigin	$f_7(x) = \sum_{i=1}^{n} [y_i^2 - 10\cos(2\pi y_i) + 10] + bias_7$ $y_i = \begin{cases} z_i & \lvert z_i \rvert < \frac{1}{2} \\ \frac{round(2z_i)}{2} & \lvert z_i \rvert \geq \frac{1}{2} \end{cases}$	$[-5.12, 5.12]^n$	450.0
Ackley	$f_8(x) = -20\exp\left(-0.2\sqrt{\frac{1}{n}\sum_{i=1}^{n} z_i^2}\right)$ $-\exp\left(\frac{1}{n}\sum_{i=1}^{n}\cos(2\pi z_i)\right) + 20 + e + bias_8$	$[-32, 32]^n$	180.0
Griewank	$f_9(x) = \frac{1}{4000}\sum_{i=1}^{n} z_i^2 - \prod_{i=1}^{n}\cos\left(\frac{z_i}{\sqrt{i}}\right) + 1 + bias_9$	$[-600, 600]^n$	120.0

continues on following page

Table 1. Continued

Function	Test Function	S	f_{min}
Generalized Penalized	$f_{10}(x) = \dfrac{\pi}{n}$ $\left\{10\sin^2(\pi y_1) + \sum_{i=1}^{n-1}(y_i - 1)^2 \times [1 + 10\sin^2(\pi y_{i+1})] + (y_n - 1)^2\right\}$ $+ \sum_{i=1}^{n} u(z_i, 10, 100, 4) + bias_{10}$ $y_i = 1 + \dfrac{1}{4}(z_i + 1)$ $u(z_i, a, k, m) = \begin{cases} k(z_i - a)^m & z_i > a, \\ 0 & -a < z_i < a \\ k(-z_i - a)^m & z_i < -a \end{cases}$	$[-50, 50]^n$	330.0

where

$J_1 = \{j \mid j \text{ is odd and } 2 \leq j \leq n\}$

and

$J_2 = \{j \mid j \text{ is even and } 2 \leq j \leq n\}.$

The search space is $[0,1] \times [-1,1]^{n-1}$. The Pareto front is

$$f_2 = 1 - \sqrt{f_1}, 0 \leq f_1 \leq 1.$$

The Pareto set is

$$x_j = \sin\left(6\pi x_1 + \frac{j\pi}{n}\right), j = 2, \cdots, n, 0 \leq x_1 \leq 1.$$

2.   Unconstrained problem 2 (UCP2)

$$f_1 = x_1 + \frac{2}{|J_1|}\sum_{j \in J_1} y_j^2$$

$$f_2 = 1 - \sqrt{x_1} + \frac{2}{|J_2|}\sum_{j \in J_2} y_j^2$$

where

$$J_1 = \{j| \; j \text{ is odd and } 2 \le j \le n\}$$

and

$$J_2 = \{j| \; j \text{ is even and } 2 \le j \le n\},$$

and

$$y_i = \begin{cases} x_j - \left[0.3x_1^2 \cos\left(24\pi x_1 + \dfrac{4j\pi}{n}\right) + 0.6x_1\right] \cos\left(6\pi x_1 + \dfrac{j\pi}{n}\right) & j \in J_1 \\ x_j - \left[0.3x_1^2 \cos\left(24\pi x_1 + \dfrac{4j\pi}{n}\right) + 0.6x_1\right] \sin\left(6\pi x_1 + \dfrac{j\pi}{n}\right) & j \in J_2 \end{cases}$$

The search space is $[0,1]\times[-1,1]^{n-1}$. The Pareto front is

$$f_2 = 1 - \sqrt{f_1}, 0 \le f_1 \le 1.$$

The Pareto set is

$$x_j = \begin{cases} \left\{0.3x_1^2 \cos\left(24\pi x_1 + \dfrac{4j\pi}{n}\right) + 0.6x_1\right\} \cos\left(6\pi x_1 + \dfrac{j\pi}{n}\right) & j \in J_1 \\ \left\{0.3x_1^2 \cos\left(24\pi x_1 + \dfrac{4j\pi}{n}\right) + 0.6x_1\right\} \sin\left(6\pi x_1 + \dfrac{j\pi}{n}\right) & j \in J_2 \end{cases}$$

$$0 \le x_1 \le 1$$

3. Unconstrained problem 3 (UCP3)

$$f_1 = x_1 + \frac{2}{|J_1|}\left(4\sum_{j \in J_1} y_j^2 - 2\prod_{j \in J_1} \cos\left(\frac{20y_j\pi}{\sqrt{j}}\right) + 2\right)$$

$$f_2 = 1 - \sqrt{x_1} + \frac{2}{|J_2|}\left(4\sum_{j \in J_2} y_j^2 - 2\prod_{j \in J_2} \cos\left(\frac{20y_j\pi}{\sqrt{j}}\right) + 2\right)$$

where

$$J_1 = \{j|\ j \text{ is odd and } 2 \leq j \leq n\},$$

$$J_2 = \{j|\ j \text{ is even and } 2 \leq j \leq n\},$$

and

$$y_i = x_j - x_1^{0.5\left(1.0+\frac{3(j-2)}{n-2}\right)}, j = 2,\cdots,n.$$

The search space is $[0,1]^n$. The Pareto front is

$$f_2 = 1 - \sqrt{f_1}, 0 \leq f_1 \leq 1.$$

The Pareto set is

$$x_j = x_1^{0.5\left(1.0+\frac{3(j-2)}{n-2}\right)}, j = 2,\cdots,n.0 \leq x_1 \leq 1.$$

4. Unconstrained problem 4 (UCP4)

$$f_1 = x_1 + \frac{2}{|J_1|}\sum_{j\in J_1} h(y_j)$$

$$f_2 = 1 - x_1^2 + \frac{2}{|J_2|}\sum_{j\in J_2} h(y_j)$$

where

$$J_1 = \{j|\ j \text{ is odd and } 2 \leq j \leq n\},$$

and

$$J_2 = \{j|\ j \text{ is even and } 2 \leq j \leq n\}.$$

$$y_i = x_j - \sin\left(6\pi x_1 + \frac{j\pi}{n}\right), j = 2,\cdots,n.$$

and

$$h(t) = \frac{|t|}{1 + e^{2|t|}}.$$

The search space is $[0,1] \times [-2,2]^{n-1}$. The Pareto front is

$$f_2 = 1 - f_1^2, 0 \le f_1 \le 1.$$

The Pareto set is

$$x_j = \sin\left(6\pi x_1 + \frac{j\pi}{n}\right), j = 2, \cdots, n, 0 \le x_1 \le 1.$$

5. Unconstrained problem 5 (UCP5)

$$f_1 = x_1 + \left(\frac{1}{2N} + \varepsilon\right)\left|\sin(2N\pi x_1)\right| + \frac{2}{|J_1|}\sum_{j \in J_1} h(y_j)$$

$$f_2 = 1 - x_1 + \left(\frac{1}{2N} + \varepsilon\right)\left|\sin(2N\pi x_1)\right| + \frac{2}{|J_2|}\sum_{j \in J_2} h(y_j)$$

where

$$J_1 = \{j| j \text{ is odd and } 2 \le j \le n\},$$

$$J_2 = \{j| j \text{ is even and } 2 \le j \le n\}.$$

N is an integer, $\varepsilon > 0$, $N = 10$, $\varepsilon = 0.1$ in the parameter setting.

$$y_j = x_j - \sin\left(6\pi x_1 + \frac{j\pi}{n}\right), j = 2, \cdots, n.$$

and

$$h(t) = 2t^2 - \cos(4\pi t) + 1$$

The search space is $[0,1] \times [-1,1]^{n-1}$. The Pareto front has $2N+1$ Pareto optimal solutions:

$$\left(\frac{i}{2N}, 1 - \frac{i}{2N}\right) \text{ for } i = 0, 1, \cdots, 2N.$$

328

6. Unconstrained problem 7 (UCP7)

$$f_1 = \sqrt[5]{x_1} + \frac{2}{|J_1|} \sum_{j \in J_1} y_j^2$$

$$f_2 = 1 - \sqrt[5]{x_1} + \frac{2}{|J_2|} \sum_{j \in J_2} y_j^2$$

where

$$J_1 = \{j | j \text{ is odd and } 2 \leq j \leq n\},$$

$$J_2 = \{j | j \text{ is even and } 2 \leq j \leq n\}$$

and

$$y_j = x_j - \sin\left(6\pi x_1 + \frac{j\pi}{n}\right), j = 2, \cdots, n.$$

The search space is $[0,1] \times [-1,1]^{n-1}$. The Pareto front is

$$f_2 = 1 - \sqrt{f_1}, 0 \leq f_1 \leq 1.$$

The Pareto set is

$$x_j = \sin\left(6\pi x_1 + \frac{j\pi}{n}\right), j = 2, \cdots, n, 0 \leq x_1 \leq 1.$$

4.2. Parameter Setting

4.2.1 Single Objective Optimization

In all experiments of PSO solving single objective problems, PSO has 50 particles. All functions are run 50 times to have statistical meaning for comparison among different approaches.

The parameter setting is the same as that of the standard PSO. In all experiments, PSO has 50 particles, $c_1 = c_2 = 1.496172$, and the inertia weight $w = 0.72984$ (Clerc & Kennedy, 2002; Bratton & Kennedy, 2007). For each algorithm, the maximum number of iterations is 5000 for 100 dimensional problems in every run. There is also a limitation in velocity to control the search step size. The setting could prevent particles from crossing the search boundary. The *maximum velocity* is set as follows:

maximum velocity $= 0.2\times$(position upper bound $-$ position lower bound).

4.2.2. Multiobjective Optimization

In all experiments of PSO solving multiobjective problems, PSO has 250 particles. The maximum number h of solutions in archive is 100. The maximum number of iterations is 2000 for 10 dimensional problems in every run. Other parameters are the same as that of the standard PSO.

4.3. Boundary Constraints Handling

Many strategies have been proposed to handle the boundary constraints. However, with an improper boundary constraints handling method, particles may get "stuck in" the boundary (Cheng, Shi, & Qin, 2011). The classical boundary constraints handling method is as follows:

$$x_{i,j}(t+1) = \begin{cases} X_{max,j} & if\ x_{i,j}(t+1) > X_{max,j} \\ X_{min,j} & if\ x_{i,j}(t+1) < X_{min,j} \\ x_{i,j}(t+1) & otherwise \end{cases} \tag{4}$$

where t is the index number of the last iteration, and $t+1$ is the index number of current iteration. This strategy resets particles in a particular point-the boundary, which constrains particles to fly in the search space limited by boundary.

In the single objective optimization, for PSO with star structure, a stochastic boundary constraints handling method was utilized in this experiment. The equation (5) gives a method that particles are reset into a special area (Cheng, Shi, & Qin, 2011)

$$x_{i,j}(t+1) = \begin{cases} X_{max,j} \times (rand() \times c + 1 - c) & if\ x_{i,j}(t+1) > X_{max,j} \\ X_{min,j} \times (Rand() \times c + 1 - c) & if\ x_{i,j}(t+1) < X_{min,j} \\ x_{i,j}(t+1) & otherwise \end{cases} \tag{5}$$

where c is a parameter to control the resetting scope. When $c=1$, particles are reset within a half search space. On the contrary, when $c=0$, this strategy is the same as the equation (4), i.e., particles are reset to be on the boundary. The closer to 0 the c is, the more particles have a high possibility to be reset close to the boundary.

In our experiment, the c is set to 0.1. A particle will be close to the boundary when position is beyond the boundary. This will increase the exploitation ability of algorithm searching the solution close to the boundary.

A deterministic method, which resets a boundary-violating position to the middle between old position and the boundary (Zielinski, Weitkemper, & Laur, *et al.*, 2009), was utilized for PSO with local ring structure. The equation is as follows:

$$x_{i,j,G+1} = \begin{cases} \frac{1}{2}(x_{i,j,G} + X_{\max,j}) & \text{if } x_{i,j,G+1} > X\max, j \\ \frac{1}{2}(x_{i,j,G} + X_{\min,j}) & \text{if } x_{i,j,G+1} < X_{\min,j} \\ x_{i,j,G+1} & \text{otherwise} \end{cases} \tag{6}$$

The position in last iteration is used in this strategy. Both classic strategy and this strategy reset a particle to a deterministic position.

For the multiobjective particle swarm optimizer, the equation (4) is utilized to handle the boundary constraints.

4.4. Experimental Results

The result of PSO solving single objective problems is given in Table 2. The bold numbers indicate the better solutions. Five measures of performance are reported. The first is the best fitness value attained after a fixed number of iterations. In our case, we report the best result found after 5000 iterations. The following measures are the median value, worst value, mean value, and the standard deviation of the best fitness values for all runs. It is possible that an algorithm will rapidly reach a relatively good result while becoming trapped into a local optimum. These values reflect the algorithm's reliability and robustness.

From the result in Table 2, we can conduct that for seven functions $f_0, f_1, f_3, f_4, f_8, f_9$, and f_{10} good optimization results can be obtained, while for the other four functions f_2, f_5, f_6, and f_7, obtained results are not very good. This is because of the properties of the functions, some functions will become significantly difficult when the dimension increases.

Figure 1 shows a single-run results of PSO solving multiobjective problems. The multiobjective problems will become difficult with the increasing of objective's number and problem's dimension.

5. ANALYSIS AND DISCUSSION

5.1. Diversity in Single Objective Optimization

Different functions have different properties. Considered the number of local optima, the benchmark functions can be categorized as unimodal function and multimodal function. The benchmark functions also can be divided as separable functions and non-separable functions based on the inter-dependence among dimensions. Due to the limit of space, four representative benchmark functions in Table 3 are chosen to analyze different normalized population diversities.

5.1.1. Definition of Population Diversity

Figure 2 and 3 show the population diversities on particle swarm optimizer solving single objective problems. Figure 2 is PSO with star structure, and Figure 3 is PSO with ring structure. The diversity measures show the distribution of particles' positions, velocities, and cognitive positions. The PSO with ring structure has more smooth curve than the PSO with star structure.

Table 2. Results of PSO with global star and local ring structure for solving benchmark functions. All algorithms are run for 50 times, where "Best", "Median", "Worst", and "Mean" indicate the best, median, worst, and mean of the best fitness values for all runs, respectively.

	F_{min}	Best	Median	Worst	Mean	Std. Dev.
Result		**PSO With Global Star Structure**				
f_0	-450.0	-449.9999	-449.9045	-421.1076	-448.4784	5.01505
f_1	-330.0	-329.9999	-329.9993	328.3578	-316.8113	92.1670
f_2	450.0	**4538.646**	8024.012	23007.12	**9129.964**	3939.06
f_3	330.0	359	566	2220	635.6	314.235
f_4	-450.0	**-449.9691**	-449.9432	-449.1378	**-449.9251**	0.11416
f_5	180.0	272.4658	516.5409	1498.878	599.9292	246.224
f_6	-330.0	**63.6766**	320.3105	630.1263	312.8142	103.560
f_7	450.0	**610.0011**	802.0023	1059.000	**803.5421**	97.1025
f_8	180.0	182.4990	197.7353	199.8314	192.0871	7.48450
f_9	120.0	120.0809	120.2979	122.4966	120.3902	0.38224
f_{10}	330.0	330.0116	330.8841	333.4218	330.9681	0.67871
Result		**PSO With Local Ring Structure**				
f_0	-450.0	**-449.9999**	-449.9999	-449.9999	**-449.9999**	3.62E-10
f_1	-330.0	**-329.9999**	-329.9999	-329.0500	**-329.9771**	0.13457
f_2	450.0	30211.37	40847.52	54352.03	41051.55	5739.44
f_3	330.0	**330**	331	337	**331.3**	1.5
f_4	-450.0	-449.9165	-449.8565	-449.8119	-449.8604	0.02441
f_5	180.0	**269.4788**	368.9582	442.3104	**360.0133**	41.4152
f_6	-330.0	73.2817	325.6967	441.0884	**309.8727**	74.7981
f_7	450.0	836.0000	1034.000	1182.250	1022.319	86.6742
f_8	180.0	**180.0000**	181.9515	199.5519	**183.8464**	5.75737
f_9	120.0	**120.0000**	120.0000	120.5880	**120.0117**	0.08232
f_{10}	330.0	**330.0033**	330.7748	332.7372	**330.9090**	0.61122

5.1.2. Change of Position Diversity and Cognitive Diversity

Figure 4 and 5 show the population diversity change on PSO solving the four single objective problems. The diversities measure the distribution of particles, and the convergence or divergence information can be obtained from the change of diversities. From the figures, some conclusions could be made that the diversity changes very quickly at the beginning of search which indicates that the particle swarm has a good global search ability. Particles then get clustered in a small region quickly. The convergence speed should be controlled during the search, the fast convergence may cause premature convergence.

Figure 1. The solution of particle swarm optimizer solving multiobjective UCP problems

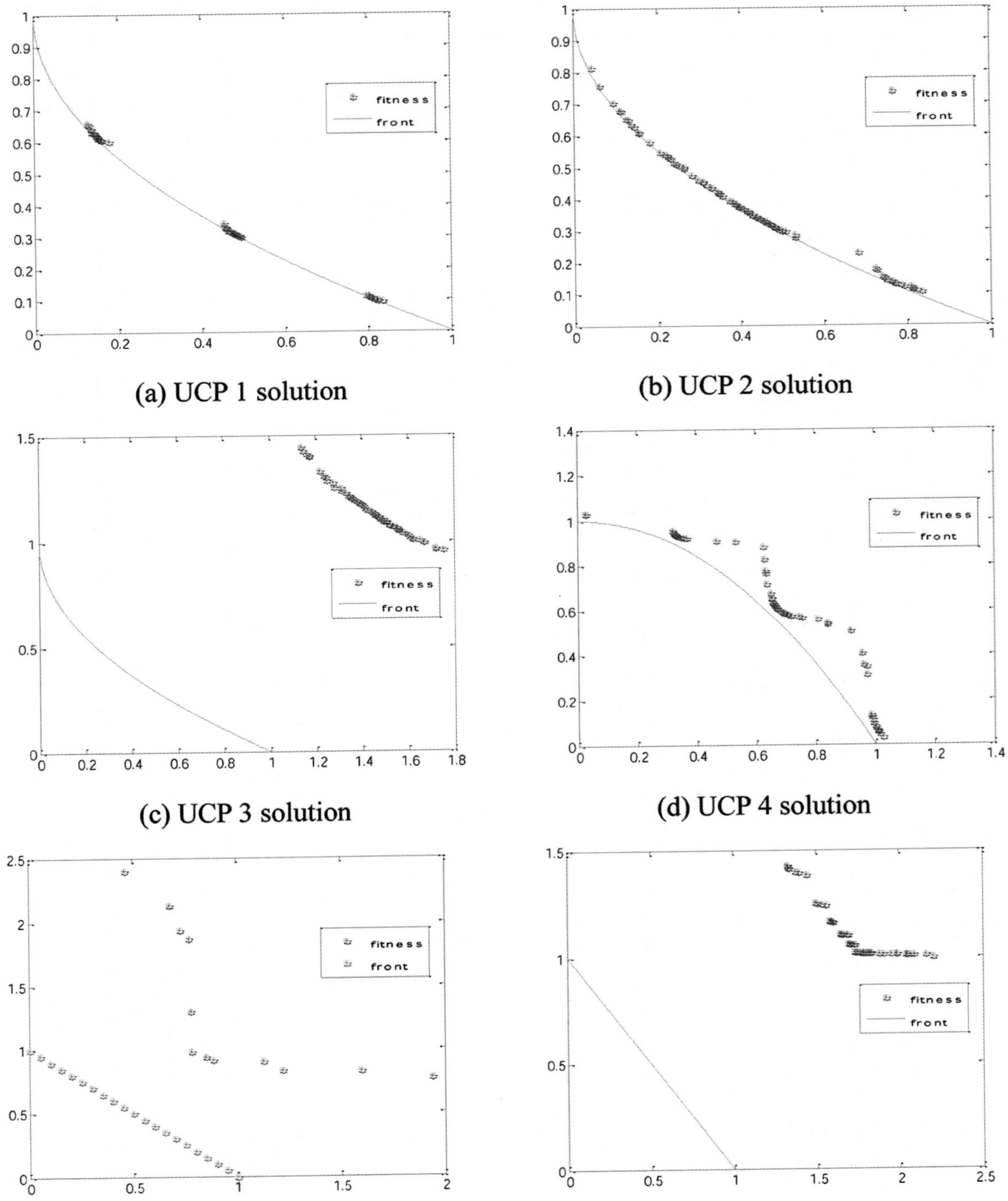

(a) UCP 1 solution

(b) UCP 2 solution

(c) UCP 3 solution

(d) UCP 4 solution

(e) UCP 5 solution

(f) UCP 7 solution

Table 3. Some representative benchmark functions

Parabolic	f_0	unimode	separable
Schwefel's P1.2	f_2	unimode	non-separable
Rosenbrock	f_5	multimode	non-separable
Ackley	f_8	multimode	separable

Figure 2. Population diversities observation on particle swarm optimizer with star structure solving single objective problems

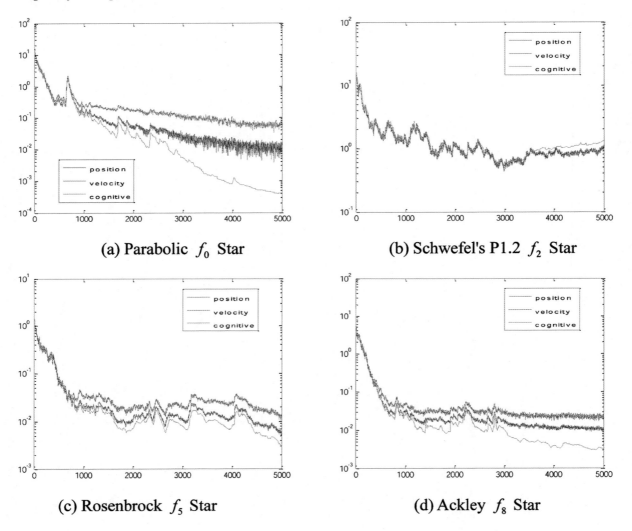

(a) Parabolic f_0 Star

(b) Schwefel's P1.2 f_2 Star

(c) Rosenbrock f_5 Star

(d) Ackley f_8 Star

Figure 3. Population diversities observation on particle swarm optimizer with ring structure solving single objective problems

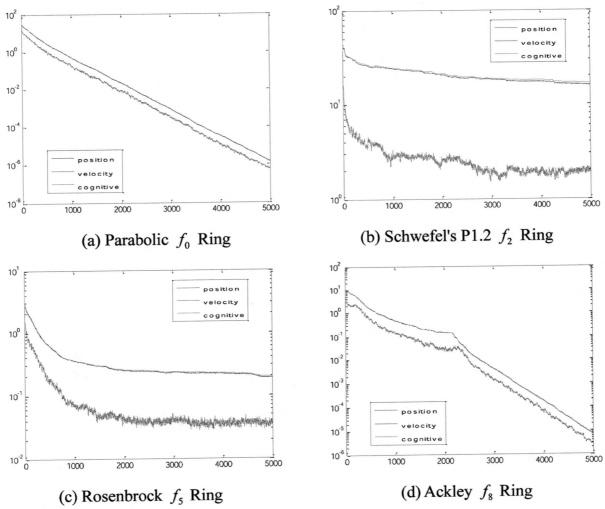

(a) Parabolic f_0 Ring

(b) Schwefel's P1.2 f_2 Ring

(c) Rosenbrock f_5 Ring

(d) Ackley f_8 Ring

5.1.3. Ratio of Position Diversity to Cognitive Diversity

Figure 6 shows the ratio of position diversity to cognitive diversity on PSO solving single objective problems. Particle swarm optimizer with star or ring structure has different properties. The particle swarm optimizer with star structure has a strong vibration in the ratio of position diversity to cognitive diversity. The particle swarm optimizer with ring structure has a smooth curve in the ratio of position diversity to cognitive diversity.

The ratio of position diversity and cognitive diversity show the comparison between the "search space" and "cognitive space." In PSO with star structure, a particle follows the global best, the position will change rapidly. In PSO with ring structure, the ratio is very stable. From Figure 3 and 6, the Parabolic f_0 and Ackley f_8 problems have good search results, and the diversities are decreased to a tiny value. We

Figure 4. Population diversity change observation on PSO with star structure solving single objective problems

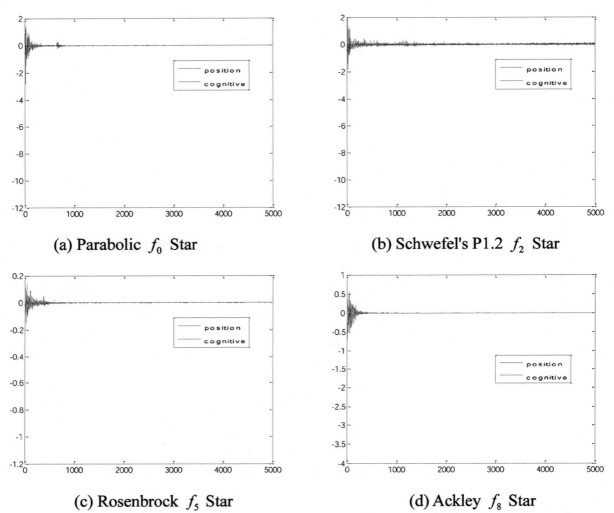

(a) Parabolic f_0 Star

(b) Schwefel's P1.2 f_2 Star

(c) Rosenbrock f_5 Star

(d) Ackley f_8 Star

can conclude that in PSO with ring structure, the problems may get good results if its position diversity and cognitive diversity decrease to tiny value within a stable ratio.

5.2. Diversity in Multiobjective Optimization

Figure 7 displays the population diversities of PSO solving multiobjective problems. In Figure 7 (a), (c) and (e), the diversity curves in particles and solutions are very similar, on the contrast, diversity of positions and solutions have different changing curves in other figures.

The multiobjective particle swarm optimization algorithms (MOPSOs) have a fast convergence in solving MOPs (Domínguez & Pulido, 2011). The particles are very quickly converged to the solutions, corresponding to the population diversities; the diversities nearly have a straight line after few iterations.

Figure 5. Population diversity change observation on PSO with ring structure solving single objective problems

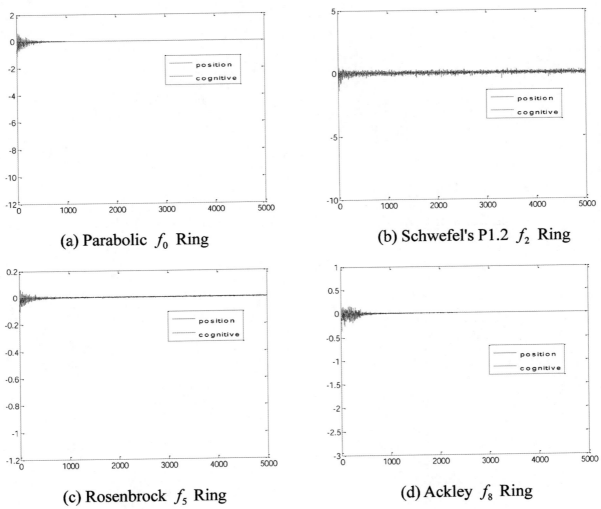

5.3. Discussions

Particle swarm has a different diversity changing in single and multiobjective problems. For single-objective problems, we only consider the diversity in solution space, however, for multiobjective problems; the diversity in the objective space is also needed to be concerned.

For single-objective problems, the diversity which decreases fast and may cause premature convergence, in contrast, the diversity which decreases slowly may cause the algorithm searching ineffectively. The algorithm should have a proper decreasing diversity, and the diversity may also need to be enhanced during the search.

For multiobjective problems, a diversified target should be kept, i.e., the particles or solutions should not converge into a small region. Maintaining population diversity in the search process is important for multiobjective optimization algorithms. More specifically, we want the searching results to be uniformly

Figure 6. The ratio of position diversity to cognitive diversity on PSO solving single objective problems

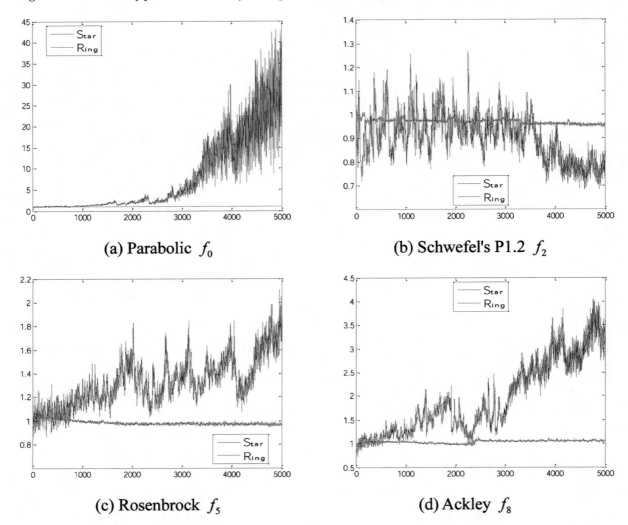

(a) Parabolic f_0

(b) Schwefel's P1.2 f_2

(c) Rosenbrock f_5

(d) Ackley f_8

distributed, and the fitness of solutions to be close to the real Pareto front. This indicates that diversity should be maintained on a proper level during the search. This is a problem-dependent setting for different problems having different shapes of Pareto front and a different number of solutions on Pareto front.

6. CONCLUSION

This chapter discussed an analysis of the population diversity of particle swarm optimizer solving single and multi-objective problems. The performance of a search algorithm is determined by its two kinds of abilities: the exploration of new possibilities and exploitation of old certainties. These two abilities should be balanced during the search process to obtain a good performance, i.e., the computational resources should be reallocated at the algorithm running time.

Figure 7. Population diversities observation on PSO solving multiobjective UCP problems

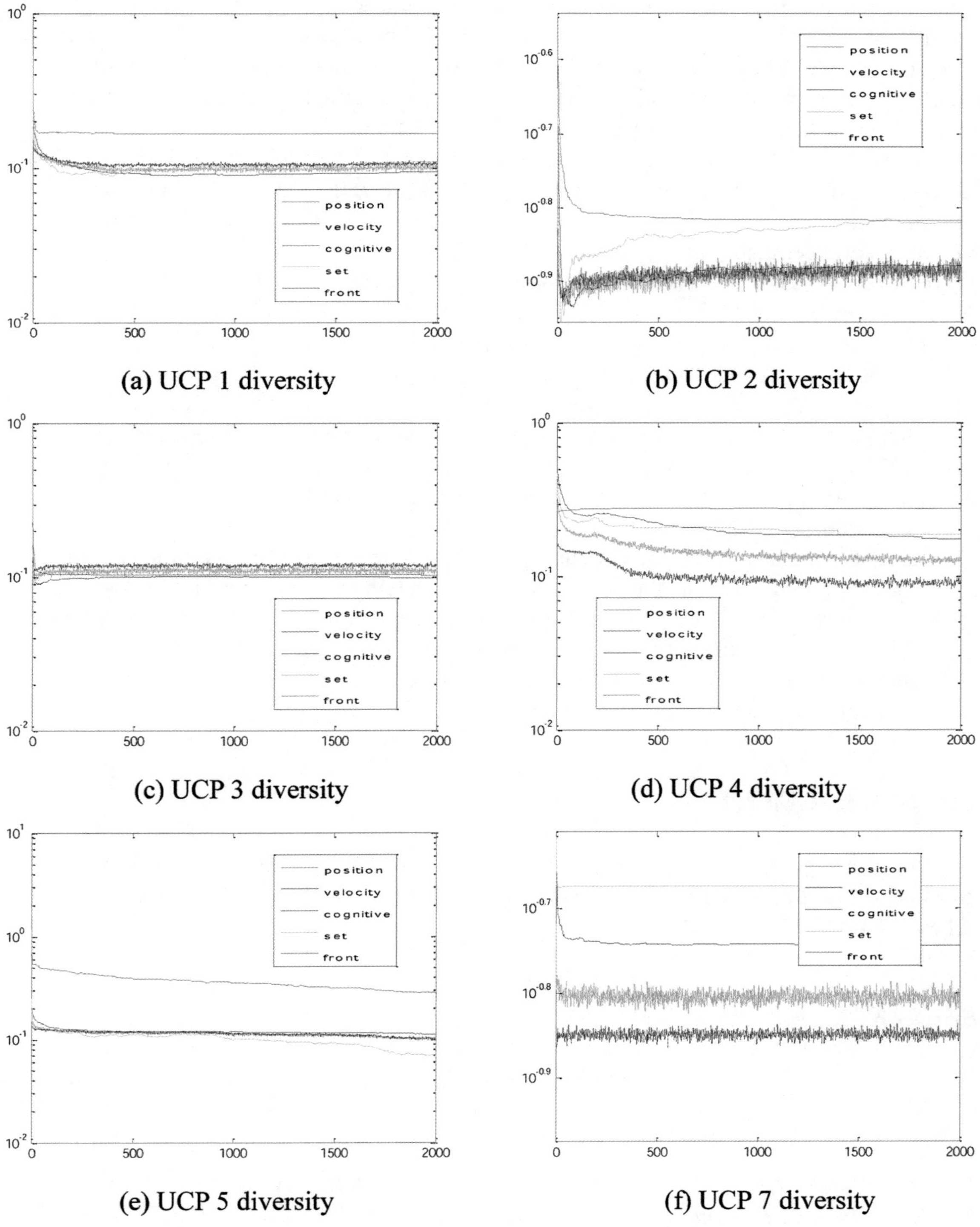

(a) UCP 1 diversity

(b) UCP 2 diversity

(c) UCP 3 diversity

(d) UCP 4 diversity

(e) UCP 5 diversity

(f) UCP 7 diversity

For single-objective optimization, the population diversity measures the distribution of particles, while for multiobjective optimization; the distribution of nondominated solutions also should be measured. From the observation of distribution and diversity change, the degree of exploration and exploitation can be obtained. In this chapter, we have analyzed the population diversity of particle swarm optimizer solving single objective and multiobjective problems. Adaptive optimization algorithms can be designed by controlling the balance between exploration and exploitation.

For multiobjective optimization, different problems have different kinds of diversity changing curves. The properties of the problem, such as "hardness", the number of local minima, continue or discrete Pareto front, all affect the performances of optimization algorithms. Through the information, the problems can be solved effectively.

Particles on the state of "expansion" or "converge" can be determined by the diversity measurement. From the population diversity, the diversity changing of PSO variants on different types of functions can be compared and analyzed. The particles' dynamical search state, the "hardness" of function, the number of local optima, and other information can be obtained. With the information, the performance of an optimization algorithm can be improved by adjusting population diversity dynamically during the PSO search process. The different topology structure of particles and the dimensional dependence of problems also affect the search process and performance of search algorithms. Seeking the influence of PSO topology structure and dimensional dependence on population diversity is the research that needs to be explored further.

The idea of population diversity measuring can also be applied to other evolutionary algorithms, e.g., genetic algorithm, differential evolution because evolutionary algorithms have the same concepts of current population solutions and search steps. The performance of evolutionary algorithms can be improved by taking advantage of the measurement of population diversity. Dynamically adjusting the population diversity controls an algorithm's ability of exploration or exploitation; hence, the algorithm could have a higher possibility to reach optimum.

ACKNOWLEDGMENT

This work was supported by National Natural Science Foundation of China (Grant Nos. 61806119, 61672334, 61761136008, and 61773103), and Natural Science Basic Research Plan In Shaanxi Province of China (Grant No. 2019JM-320).

REFERENCES

Adra, S. F., Dodd, T. J., Griffin, I. A., & Fleming, P. J. (2009). Convergence acceleration operator for multiobjective optimization. *IEEE Transactions on Evolutionary Computation, 12*(4), 825–847. doi:10.1109/TEVC.2008.2011743

Adra, S. F., & Fleming, P. J. (2011). Diversity management in evolutionary many-objective optimization. *IEEE Transactions on Evolutionary Computation, 15*(2), 183–195. doi:10.1109/TEVC.2010.2058117

Bosman, P. A. N., & Thierens, D. (2003). The balance between proximity and diversity in multiobjective evolutionary algorithms. *IEEE Transactions on Evolutionary Computation, 7*(2), 174–188. doi:10.1109/TEVC.2003.810761

Bratton, D., & Kennedy, J. (2007). Defining a standard for particle swarm optimization. *Proceedings of the 2007 IEEE Swarm Intelligence Symposium (SIS 2007),* (pp. 120-127). 10.1109/SIS.2007.368035

Cheng, S. (2013). *Population Diversity in Particle Swarm Optimization: Definition, Observation, Control, and Application.* (Doctoral dissertation), University of Liverpool, UK.

Cheng, S., Lu, H., Lei, X., & Shi, Y. (2018). A Quarter Century of Particle Swarm Optimization. *Complex & Intelligent Systems, 4*(3), 227–239. doi:10.100740747-018-0071-2

Cheng, S., & Shi, Y. (2011a). Diversity control in particle swarm optimization. *Proceedings of 2011 IEEE Symposium on Swarm Intelligence (SIS 2011),* (pp. 110-118).

Cheng, S., & Shi, Y. (2011b). Normalized population diversity in particle swarm optimization. In Y. Tan, Y. Shi, Y. Chai, & G. Wang (Eds.), Advances in Swarm Intelligence, (LNCS 6728, pp. 38-45). Berlin, Germany: Springer. doi:10.1007/978-3-642-21515-5_5

Cheng, S., Shi, Y., & Qin, Q. (2011). Experimental study on boundary constraints handling in particle swarm optimization: From population diversity perspective. [IJSIR]. *International Journal of Swarm Intelligence Research, 2*(3), 43–69. doi:10.4018/jsir.2011070104

Cheng, S., Shi, Y., & Qin, Q. (2012a). Dynamical exploitation space reduction in particle swarm optimization for solving large scale problems. *Proceedings of 2012 IEEE Congress on Evolutionary Computation, (CEC 2012),* (pp. 3030-3037), Brisbane, Australia. IEEE. 10.1109/CEC.2012.6252937

Cheng, S., Shi, Y., & Qin, Q. (2012b). On the performance metrics of multiobjective optimization. In Y. Tan, Y. Shi, & Z. Ji, (Eds.), Advances in Swarm Intelligence, volume 7331 of LNCS, pp. 504-512. Berlin, Germany: Springer. doi:10.1007/978-3-642-30976-2_61

Cheng, S., Shi, Y., & Qin, Q. (2012c). Population diversity based study on search information propagation in particle swarm optimization. *Proceedings of 2012 IEEE Congress on Evolutionary Computation, (CEC 2012),* (pp. 1272-1279), Brisbane, Australia. IEEE. 10.1109/CEC.2012.6256502

Cheng, S., Shi, Y., Qin, Q., & Ting, T. O. (2012) Population diversity based inertia weight adaptation in particle swarm optimization. *Proceedings of The Fifth International Conference on Advanced Computational Intelligence, (ICACI 2012),* (pp.395-403). 10.1109/ICACI.2012.6463194

Clerc, M., & Kennedy, J. (2002). The particle swarm—Explosion, stability, and convergence in a multidimensional complex space. *IEEE Transactions on Evolutionary Computation, 6*(1), 58–73. doi:10.1109/4235.985692

Corriveau, G., Guilbault, R., Tahan, A., & Sabourin, R. (2012). Review and Study of Genotypic Diversity Measures for Real-Coded Representations. *IEEE Transactions on Evolutionary Computation, 16*(5), 695–710. doi:10.1109/TEVC.2011.2170075

De Jong, K. A. (1975). An analysis of the behavior of a class of genetic adaptive systems. (Doctoral dissertation), University of Michigan, Michigan.

Deb, K., & Jain, S. (2002). Running performance metrics for evolutionary multi-objective optimization. Technical Report 2002004, Kanpur Genetic Algorithms Laboratory (KanGAL), Indian Institute of Technology Kanpur.

Domínguez, J. S. H., & Pulido, G. T. (2011). A comparison on the search of particle swarm optimization and differential evolution on multi-objective optimization. *Proceedings of the 2011 Congress on Evolutionary Computation (CEC2011)*, (pp. 1978-1985). 10.1109/CEC.2011.5949858

Eberhart, R., & Kennedy, J. (1995). A new optimizer using particle swarm theory. *Proceedings of the Sixth International Symposium on Micro Machine and Human Science*, (pp. 39-43). 10.1109/MHS.1995.494215

Eberhart, R., & Shi, Y. (2001). Particle swarm optimization: Developments, applications, and resources. *Proceedings of the 2001 Congress on Evolutionary Computation (CEC2001)*, (pp. 81-86). 10.1109/CEC.2001.934374

Eberhart, R., & Shi, Y. (2007). *Computational Intelligence: Concepts to Implementations*. Morgan Kaufmann. doi:10.1016/B978-155860759-0/50002-0

Eberhart, R. C., Dobbins, R. W., & Simpson, P. K. (1996). *Computational Intelligence PC Tools*. Academic Press Professional.

Gupta, A. K., Smith, K. G., & Shalley, C. E. (2006). The interplay between exploration and exploitation. *Academy of Management Journal*, 49(4), 693–706. doi:10.5465/amj.2006.22083026

Holland, J. H. (2000). Building blocks, cohort genetic algorithms, and hyperplane-defined functions. *Evolutionary Computation*, 8(4), 373–391. doi:10.1162/106365600568220 PMID:11130921

Hu, X., Shi, Y., & Eberhart, R. (2004) Recent advances in particle swarm. *Proceedings of the 2004 Congress on Evolutionary Computation (CEC2004)*, (pp. 90-97). Academic Press.

Ishibuchi, H., Tsukamoto, N., & Nojima, Y. (2008). Evolutionary Many-Objective Optimization: A Short Review. *Proceedings of the 2008 Congress on Evolutionary Computation (CEC2004)*, (pp. 2419-2426). 10.1109/CEC.2008.4631121

Ishibuchi, H., Tsukamoto, N., & Nojima, Y. (2010). Diversity improvement by non-geometric binary crossover in evolutionary multiobjective optimization. *IEEE Transactions on Evolutionary Computation*, 14(6), 985–998. doi:10.1109/TEVC.2010.2043365

Jin, Y., & Sendhoff, B. (2009). A systems approach to evolutionary multiobjective structural optimization and beyond. *IEEE Computational Intelligence Magazine*, 4(3), 62–76. doi:10.1109/MCI.2009.933094

Kennedy, J., & Eberhart, R. (1995). Particle swarm optimization. *Proceedings of IEEE International Conference on Neural Networks*, (pp.1942-1948). 10.1109/ICNN.1995.488968

Kennedy, J., Eberhart, R., & Shi, Y. (2001). Swarm Intelligence. Morgan Kaufmann.

Liang, J. J., Qin, A. K., Suganthan, P. N., & Baskar, S. (2006). Comprehensive learning particle swarm optimizer for global optimization of multimodal functions. *IEEE Transactions on Evolutionary Computation*, 10(3), 281–295. doi:10.1109/TEVC.2005.857610

March, J. G. (1991). Exploration and exploitation in organizational learning. *Organization Science, 2*(1), 71–87. doi:10.1287/orsc.2.1.71

Mauldin, M. L. (1984). Maintaining diversity in genetic search. *Proceedings of the National Conference on Artificial Intelligence (AAAI 1984).* (pp. 247-250). Academic Press.

Olorunda, O., & Engelbrecht, A. P. (2008). Measuring exploration/exploitation in particle swarms using swarm diversity. *Proceedings of the 2008 Congress on Evolutionary Computation(CEC 2008).* (pp. 1128-1134). 10.1109/CEC.2008.4630938

Shi, Y., & Eberhart, R. (1998). A modified particle swarm optimizer. *Proceedings of the 1998 Congress on Evolutionary Computation (CEC1998),* (pp. 69-73). 10.1109/ICEC.1998.699146

Shi, Y., & Eberhart, R. (1999). Empirical study of particle swarm optimization. *Proceedings of the 1999 Congress on Evolutionary Computation (CEC 1999),* (pp. 1945-1950). 10.1109/CEC.1999.785511

Shi, Y., & Eberhart, R. (2001). Fuzzy adaptive particle swarm optimization. *Proceedings of the 2001 Congress on Evolutionary Computation (CEC2001),* (pp.101-106). 10.1109/CEC.2001.934377

Shi, Y., & Eberhart, R. (2008). Population diversity of particle swarms. *Proceedings of the 2008 Congress on Evolutionary Computation (CEC 2008),* (pp. 1063-1067). 10.1109/CEC.2008.4630928

Shi, Y., & Eberhart, R. (2009). Monitoring of particle swarm optimization. *Frontiers of Computer Science, 3*(1), 31–37. doi:10.100711704-009-0008-4

Sundaram, R. K. (1996). *A First Course in Optimization Theory.* Cambridge University Press. doi:10.1017/CBO9780511804526

Weise, T., Zapf, M., Chiong, R., & Nebro, A. J. (2009). Why is optimization difficult? In Nature-Inspired Algorithms for Optimisation, Vol. 193 of Studies in Computational Intelligence, pp. 1-50. Berlin, Germany: Springer. doi:10.1007/978-3-642-00267-0_1

Wolpert, D., & Macready, W. (1997). No free lunch theorems for optimization. *IEEE Transactions on Evolutionary Computation, 1*(1), 67–82. doi:10.1109/4235.585893

Yao, X., Liu, Y., & Lin, G. (1999). Evolutionary programming made faster. *IEEE Transactions on Evolutionary Computation, 3*(2), 82–102. doi:10.1109/4235.771163

Zhang, Q., & Mühlenbein, H. (2004). On the convergence of a class of estimation of distribution algorithms. *IEEE Transactions on Evolutionary Computation, 8*(2), 127–136. doi:10.1109/TEVC.2003.820663

Zhang, Q., Zhou, A., Zhao, S., Suganthan, P. N., Liu, W., & Tiwari, S. (2009). Multiobjective optimization Test Instances for the CEC 2009 Special Session and Competition, Technical Report CES-487, University of Essex.

Zhou, A., Zhang, Q., & Jin, Y. (2009). Approximating the set of Pareto-optimal solutions in both the decision and objective spaces by an estimation of distribution algorithm. *IEEE Transactions on Evolutionary Computation, 13*(5), 1167–1189. doi:10.1109/TEVC.2009.2021467

Zielinski, K., Weitkemper, P., Laur, R., & Kammeyer, K. D. (2009). Optimization of power allocation for interference cancellation with particle swarm optimization. *IEEE Transactions on Evolutionary Computation, 13*(1), 128–150. doi:10.1109/TEVC.2008.920672

KEY TERMS AND DEFINITIONS:

Cognitive Diversity: Cognitive diversity, which represents distribution of particles' "moving target", measures the distribution of historical best positions for all particles. The measurement definition of cognitive diversity is the same as that of the position diversity except that it utilizes each particle's current personal best position instead of current position.

Exploitation: The exploitation ability means that an algorithm focuses on the refinement of found promising areas.

Exploration: The exploration ability means that an algorithm can explore more search place to increase the possibility that the algorithm can find good enough solutions.

Particle Swarm Optimizer/Optimization: Particle Swarm Optimizer/Optimization, which is one of the evolutionary computation techniques, was invented by Eberhart and Kennedy in 1995. It is a population-based stochastic algorithm modeled on the social behaviors observed in flocking birds. Each particle, which represents a solution, flies through the search space with a velocity that is dynamically adjusted according to its own and its companion's historical behaviors.

Population Diversity: Population diversity is a measure of individuals' search information in population-based algorithms. From the distribution of individuals and change of this distribution information, the algorithm's status of exploration or exploitation can be obtained.

Position Diversity: Position diversity measures distribution of particles' current positions, therefore, can reflect particles' dynamics. Position diversity gives the current position distribution information of particles, whether the particles are going to diverge or converge could be reflected from this measurement.

Premature Convergence: Premature convergence is a phenomenon that occurs in population-based algorithms. Premature convergence occurs when all individuals in population-based algorithms are trapped in local optima.

Velocity Diversity: Velocity diversity, which represents diversity of particles' "moving potential", measures the distribution of particles' current velocities. In other words, velocity diversity measures the "activity" information of particles.

Chapter 15
A Study of Normalized Population Diversity in Particle Swarm Optimization

Shi Cheng
https://orcid.org/0000-0002-5129-995X
Shaanxi Normal University, China

Yuhui Shi
https://orcid.org/0000-0002-8840-723X
Southern University of Science and Technology, China

Quande Qin
Shenzhen University, China

ABSTRACT

The values and velocities of a Particle swarm optimization (PSO) algorithm can be recorded as a series of matrix and its population diversity can be considered as an observation of the distribution of matrix elements. Each dimension is measured separately in the dimension-wise diversity. On the contrary, the element-wise diversity measures all dimensions together. In this chapter, the PSO algorithm is first represented in the matrix format. Then, based on the analysis of the relationship between pairs of vectors in the PSO solution matrix, different normalization strategies are utilized for dimension-wise and element-wise population diversity, respectively. Experiments on benchmark functions are conducted. Based on the simulation results of 10 benchmark functions (including unimodal/multimodal function, separable/non-separable function), the properties of normalized population diversities are analyzed and discussed.

DOI: 10.4018/978-1-7998-3222-5.ch015

1. INTRODUCTION

Swarm intelligence is a collection of nature-inspired searching techniques. Particle Swarm Optimization (PSO), which is one of the swarm intelligence algorithms, was introduced by Eberhart and Kennedy in 1995 (Eberhart & Kennedy, 1995; Kennedy & Eberhart, 1995). It is a population-based stochastic algorithm modeled on the social behaviors observed in flocking birds. Each particle, which represents a solution, flies through the search space with a velocity that is dynamically adjusted according to its own and its companion's historical behaviors. The particles tend to fly toward better search areas over the course of the search process (Eberhart & Shi, 2001; Eberhart & Shi, 2007).

Optimization, in general, is concerned with finding the "best available" solution(s) for a given problem, and the problem may have several or numerous optimum solutions, of which many are local optima. Evolutionary optimization algorithms are generally difficult to find the global optimum solutions for multimodal problems due to the possible occurrence of premature convergence.

Particles fly in the search space. If particles can easily get clustered together in a short time, these particles will lose their "search potential." Population premature convergence around a local optimum is a common problem for population-based algorithms. It is a result of individuals congregating within a small region of the search space. An algorithm's search ability of exploration is decreased when premature convergence occurs, and particles will have a low possibility to explore new search areas. Normally, diversity, which is lost due to particles getting clustered together, is not easy to be recovered. An algorithm may lose its search efficacy due to premature convergence. As a population becomes converged, the algorithm will spend most of the iterations to search in a small region.

Diversity has been defined to measure the search process of an evolutionary algorithm. Generally, it is not to measure whether the algorithm finds a "good enough" solution or not, but to measure the distribution of individuals in the population (current solutions). Leung et al. used Markov chain analysis to measure the degree of population diversity in the premature convergent process of genetic algorithms (Leung, Gao, & Xu, 1997). Olorunda and Engelbrecht utilized swarm diversity to measure the state of exploration or exploitation during particles searching (Olorunda, & Engelbrecht, 2008). Shi and Eberhart introduced three different definitions of population diversity to measure the PSO search process (Shi, & Eberhart, 2008; Shi, & Eberhart, 2009). Cheng and Shi utilized these three kinds of population diversities on different subjects, which includes the population diversity control (Cheng, & Shi, 2011a), search space boundary constraints handle (Cheng, Shi, & Qin, 2011a), promoting diversity to solve multimodal problems (Cheng, Shi, & Qin, 2011b), search information propagation analysis (Cheng, Shi, & Qin, 2012b), and dynamical exploitation space reduction for solving large scale problems (Cheng, Shi, & Qin, 2012a).

Compared with other evolutionary algorithms, e.g., genetic algorithm, PSO has more search information, that includes not only the solution (position) but also the velocity and the previous best solution (cognitive). Population diversities, which include position diversity, velocity diversity, and cognitive diversity, are utilized to measure the information, respectively. There are several definitions on the measurement of population diversities (Shi, & Eberhart, 2008; Shi, & Eberhart, 2009; Cheng, & Shi, 2011b).

Because different problems have different dynamic ranges, the dynamic ranges of these defined diversities generally will be different. As a consequence, the diversity observation on one problem will be different from that on another problem. Therefore it is necessary to have normalized diversity definitions.

The rest of the chapter is organized as follows. The basic PSO algorithm and the importance of diversity are reviewed in Section 2. In Section 3, definitions and categories of population diversities are given, three kinds of population diversity: position diversity, velocity diversity, and cognitive diversity are reviewed and analyzed. In Section 4, fundamental concepts of matrix computation, normalization of position diversity, velocity diversity, and cognitive diversity are given for separable problems and non-separable problems, respectively. In Section 5, experiments on measuring population diversity are tested on benchmark functions. In Section 6, simulation results are analyzed and discussed to illustrate the effectiveness and usefulness of the proposed normalized diversity definitions. Finally, conclusions are given in Section 7 together with some remarks and future research directions.

2. PARTICLE SWARM OPTIMIZATION

The canonical particle swarm optimization algorithm is simple in concept and easy in implementation (Shi, & Eberhart, 1998; Shi, & Eberhart, 1999; Kennedy, Eberhart, & Shi, 2001; Eberhart, & Shi, 2007; Fang, Sun, & Ding, *et al.*, 2010; Cheng et al. 2018). For the purpose of generality and clarity, m represents the number of particles and n the number of dimensions. Each particle's position is represented as x_{ij}, i represents the ith particle, $i=1,\ldots,m$, and j is the jth dimension, $j=1,\ldots,n$. The basic equations are as follow:

$$v_i \leftarrow wv_i + c_1 rand()(p_i - x_i) + c_2 Rand()(p_g - x_i)$$

$$x_i \leftarrow x_i + v_i$$

where w denotes the inertia weight and usually is less than 1, c_1 and c_2 are two positive acceleration constants, rand() and Rand() are two random functions to generate uniformly distributed random numbers in the range [0, 1], x_i represents the ith particle's position, v_i represents the ith particle's velocity, p_i is termed as personal best, which refers to the best position found by the ith particle, and p_g is termed as local best, which refers to the position found by the members in the ith particle's neighborhood that has the best fitness value so far.

The equations above can also be written in matrix form as follow

$$V = wV + c_1 rand()(P - X) + c_2 Rand()(N - X)$$

$$X = X + V$$

where rand() and Rand() are different for each matrix element, and

$$X = \begin{bmatrix} x_1 \\ x_2 \\ \vdots \\ x_m \end{bmatrix} = \begin{bmatrix} x_{11} & x_{12} & \cdots & x_{1n} \\ x_{21} & x_{22} & \cdots & x_{2n} \\ \vdots & & x_{ij} & \vdots \\ x_{m1} & x_{m2} & \cdots & x_{mn} \end{bmatrix}$$

$$
V = \begin{bmatrix} v_1 \\ v_2 \\ \vdots \\ v_m \end{bmatrix} = \begin{bmatrix} v_{11} & v_{12} & \cdots & v_{1n} \\ v_{21} & v_{22} & \cdots & v_{2n} \\ \vdots & & v_{ij} & \vdots \\ v_{m1} & v_{m2} & \cdots & v_{mn} \end{bmatrix}
$$

$$
P = \begin{bmatrix} p_1 \\ p_2 \\ \cdots \\ p_m \end{bmatrix} = \begin{bmatrix} p_{11} & p_{12} & \cdots & p_{1n} \\ p_{21} & p_{22} & \cdots & p_{2n} \\ \vdots & & p_{ij} & \vdots \\ p_{m1} & p_{m2} & \cdots & p_{mn} \end{bmatrix}
$$

$$
N = \begin{bmatrix} p_1^* \\ p_2^* \\ \cdots \\ p_m^* \end{bmatrix} = \begin{bmatrix} p_{11}^* & p_{12}^* & \cdots & p_{1n}^* \\ p_{21}^* & p_{22}^* & \cdots & p_{2n}^* \\ \vdots & & p_{ij}^* & \vdots \\ p_{m1}^* & p_{m2}^* & \cdots & p_{mn}^* \end{bmatrix}
$$

The above four matrix are termed as position matrix X, velocity matrix V, cognitive (personal best) matrix P, and social (neighboring best) matrix N, which is a simplified personal matrix with only one particle's best position which is either the global best position in global star structure or a particle's personal best in this neighborhood in other structures, e.g., local ring.

In this chapter, the two most commonly used topology structures are considered (Eberhart, & Kennedy, 1995; Kennedy, & Mendes, 2002; Mendes, 2004). They are the global star, and local ring structure, which are shown in Figure 1.

Figure 1. Topologies used in the chapter are presented in the following order: (a) Star topology, where all particles or nodes share the search information in the whole swarm; (b) Ring topology, where every particle is connected to two neighbors. Each swarm has 16 particles.

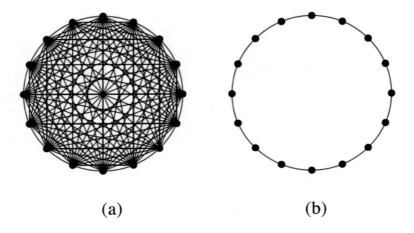

(a)   (b)

Random variables are frequently utilized in swarm optimization algorithms. The search step size is not determined in the optimization, i.e., the size is a random number, and different in each iteration. This approach belongs to an interesting class of algorithms that are known as randomized algorithms. A randomized algorithm does not guarantee an exact result but instead provides a high probability guarantee that it will return the correct answer or one close to it. The result(s) of optimization may be different in each run, but the algorithm has a high probability to find a "good enough" solution(s).

The basic process of PSO is shown in Algorithm 1. A particle updates its velocity according to equation (1), and updates its position according to equation (2). The $c_1 rand()(p_i - x_i)$ part can be seen as cognitive behaviors, while $c_2 Rand()(p_g - x_i)$ part can be seen as social behaviors.

In particle swarm optimization, a particle not only learns from its own experience, but it also learns from its companions. It indicates that a particle's 'moving position' is determined by its own experience and the neighbors' experience (Cheng, Shi, & Qin, 2011a).

Shi and Eberhart gave three definitions of population diversity, which are position diversity, velocity diversity and cognitive diversity (Shi, & Eberhart, 2009). According to the PSO matrix representation, diversity is a measurement of the variance of different elements in each dimension or in the whole matrix. Position diversity is used to measure the distribution of particles' current positions, that is, it concerns elements in the matrix X. Velocity diversity is used to measure the distribution of swarm's current velocity, that is, it concerns elements in the matrix V. Cognitive diversity measures the distribution of best positions for each particle finds so far, that is, it concerns elements in the matrix P. Which diversity definition to be utilized to measure the diversity of swarm is determined by the property of particle swarm algorithms and the problems to be solved.

Algorithm 1. *The basic process of particle swarm optimization*

```
1: Initialize velocity and position randomly for each particle in every dimen-
sion.
2: While not find the "good enough" solution or not reach the maximum number
of iterations do
3:      Calculate each particle's fitness value
4:      Compare fitness value between that of the current position and that of
the best position in history (personal best, termed as pbest). For each par-
ticle, if the fitness value of the current position is better than pbest, then
update pbest to be the current position.
5:      Select the particle which has the best fitness value among current par-
ticle's neighborhood, this particle is called the neighborhood best (termed
as nbest). If the current particle's neighborhood includes all particles then
this neighborhood best is the global best (termed as gbest), otherwise, it is
local best (termed as lbest).
6:      for each particle do
7:          Update particle's velocity and position according to the equation
(1) and (2), respectively.
8:      end for
9: end while
```

3. POPULATION DIVERSITY

The most important factor affecting an optimization algorithm's performance is its ability of "exploration" and "exploitation." Exploration means the ability of a search algorithm to explore different areas of the search space in order to have a high probability to find good promising solutions. Exploitation, on the other hand, means the ability to concentrate the search around a promising region in order to refine a candidate solution. A good optimization algorithm should optimally balance the two conflicting objectives.

Population diversity of PSO is useful for measuring and dynamically adjusting the algorithm's ability of exploration or exploitation accordingly. Shi and Eberhart gave three definitions of population diversity, which are position diversity, velocity diversity, and cognitive diversity (Shi, & Eberhart, 2008; Shi, & Eberhart, 2009). Position, velocity, and cognitive diversity are used to measure the distribution of particles' current positions, current velocities, and *pbest*s (the best position found so far for each particle), respectively. The position diversity and cognitive diversity can be seen as the "average distance" of particle's current positions or personal best positions, and the velocity diversity also can be seen as the "average value" of current velocities. This distance between each particle and their positions/velocities center can be measured by Euclidean distance (L_2 distance) or L_1 distance (Shi, & Eberhart, 2008; Shi, & Eberhart, 2009).

Cheng and Shi introduced the modified definitions of the three diversity measures based on L_1 distance (Cheng, & Shi, 2011a; Cheng, & Shi, 2011b; Cheng, Shi, & Qin, 2011a; Cheng, Shi, & Qin, 2011b). In this chapter, L_1 distance are utilized to measure the distance between each particle and their positions/velocities center.

The definition of population diversity can be dimension-wise or element-wise. In the dimension-wise population diversity, each dimension, such as vector x_i in position X, is measured independently. On the contrary, in the element-wise population diversity, all dimensions are combined together to calculate the center of particles.

From diversity measurements, useful information can be obtained. The detailed definitions of PSO population diversities can refer to (Cheng, & Shi, 2011a, Cheng, & Shi, 2011b; Cheng, Shi, & Qin, 2011a; Cheng, Shi, & Qin, 2011b):

3.1. Position Diversity

Position diversity measures the distribution of particles' current positions, therefore, can reflect particles' dynamics. Position diversity gives the current position distribution information of particles.

3.1.1. Dimension-Wise Diversity

Definition of dimension-wise position diversity, which is based on the L_1 distance, is as follows

$$\overline{x}_j = \frac{1}{m} \sum_{i=1}^{m} x_{ij}$$

$$D_j^p = \frac{1}{m} \sum_{i=1}^{m} \left| x_{ij} - \overline{x}_j \right|$$

$$D^p = \sum_{j=1}^{n} w_j D_j^p$$

where $\overline{x}_j$ represents the pivot of particles' position in dimension j, and $D_j^{\ p}$ measures particles position diversity based on L_1 norm for dimension j. Then we define $\overline{x} = [\overline{x}_1, \cdots, \overline{x}_j, \cdots, \overline{x}_n]$, $\overline{x}$ represents the mean of particles' current positions on each dimension. $D^p = [D_1^p, \cdots, D_j^p, \cdots, D_n^p]$, which measures particles' position diversity based on L_1 norm for each dimension. D^p measures the whole swarm's population diversity.

Without loss of generality, every dimension is considered equally in this chapter. Setting all weights $w_j = \frac{1}{n}$, then the dimension-wise position diversity can be rewritten as:

$$D^p = \sum_{j=1}^{n} \frac{1}{n} D_j^p = \frac{1}{n} \sum_{j=1}^{n} D_j^p$$

3.1.2. Element-Wise Diversity

The definition of element-wise PSO position diversity is as follows

$$\overline{x} = \frac{1}{n \times m} \sum_{i=1}^{m} \sum_{j=1}^{n} x_{ij}$$

$$D_E^p = \frac{1}{n \times m} \sum_{i=1}^{m} \sum_{j=1}^{n} \left| x_{ij} - \overline{x} \right|$$

3.2. Velocity Diversity

Velocity diversity, which represents the diversity of particles' "moving potential", measures the distribution of particles' current velocities. In other words, velocity diversity measures the "activity" information of particles. Based on the measurement of velocity diversity, particle's tendency of expansion or convergence could be revealed.

3.2.1. Dimension-Wise Diversity

The dimension-wise velocity diversity based on L_1 distance is defined as follows

$$\overline{v}_j = \frac{1}{m}\sum_{i=1}^{m} v_{ij}$$

$$D_j^v = \frac{1}{m}\sum_{i=1}^{m} \left| v_{ij} - \overline{v}_j \right|$$

$$D^v = \sum_{j=1}^{n} w_j D_j^v$$

where $\overline{v}_j$ represents the pivot of particles' velocity in dimension j, and $D_j^{\ v}$ measures particles velocity diversity based on L_1 norm for dimension j. Then we define $\overline{v} = [\overline{v}_1, \cdots, \overline{v}_j, \cdots, \overline{v}_n]$, $\overline{v}$ represents the mean of particles' current velocities on each dimension; and $D^v = [D_1^v, \cdots, D_j^v, \cdots, D_n^v]$, D^{υ} measures velocity diversity of all particles on each dimension. D^{υ} represents the whole swarm's velocity diversity.

Without loss of generality, every dimension is considered equally in this chapter. Setting all weights $w_j = \frac{1}{n}$, then the dimension-wise velocity diversity can be rewritten as:

$$D^v = \sum_{j=1}^{n} \frac{1}{n} D_j^v = \frac{1}{n}\sum_{j=1}^{n} D_j^v$$

3.2.2. Element-Wise Diversity

The definition of element-wise PSO velocity diversity is as follows

$$\overline{v} = \frac{1}{n \times m}\sum_{i=1}^{m}\sum_{j=1}^{n} v_{ij}$$

$$D_E^v = \frac{1}{n \times m}\sum_{i=1}^{m}\sum_{j=1}^{n} \left| v_{ij} - \overline{v} \right|$$

3.3. Cognitive Diversity

Cognitive diversity, which represents the distribution of particles' "moving target", measures the distribution of historical best positions for all particles. The measurement definition of cognitive diversity is the same as that of the position diversity except that it utilizes each particle's current personal best position instead of the current position.

3.3.1. Dimension-Wise Diversity

The definition of dimension-wise PSO cognitive diversity is as follows

$$\bar{p}_j = \frac{1}{m} \sum_{i=1}^{m} p_{ij}$$

$$D_j^c = \frac{1}{m} \sum_{i=1}^{m} \left| p_{ij} - \bar{p}_j \right|$$

$$D^c = \sum_{j=1}^{n} w_j D_j^c$$

where $\bar{p}_j$ represents the pivot of particles' previous best position in dimension j, and D_j^v measures particles cognitive diversity based on L_1 norm for dimension j. Then we define $\bar{p} = [\bar{p}_1, \cdots, \bar{p}_j, \cdots, \bar{p}_n]$ and $\bar{p}$ represents the average of all particles' personal best position in history (*pbest*) on each dimension; $D^c = [D_1^p, \cdots, D_j^p, \cdots, D_n^p]$, which represents the particles' cognitive diversity for each dimension based on L_1 norm. D^c measures the whole swarm's cognitive diversity.

Without loss of generality, every dimension is considered equally in this chapter. Setting all weights $w_j = \frac{1}{n}$, then the dimension-wise cognitive diversity can be rewritten as:

$$D^c = \sum_{j=1}^{n} \frac{1}{n} D_j^c = \frac{1}{n} \sum_{j=1}^{n} D_j^c$$

3.3.2. Element-Wise Diversity

The definition of element-wise PSO cognitive diversity is as follows

$$\bar{p} = \frac{1}{n \times m} \sum_{i=1}^{m} \sum_{j=1}^{n} p_{ij}$$

$$D_E^c = \frac{1}{n \times m} \sum_{i=1}^{m} \sum_{j=1}^{n} \left| p_{ij} - \bar{p} \right|$$

The population diversity measurement can be based on each dimension or the whole swarm. In the particle swarm optimization, each vector x_i, where $x_i = [x_{i1}, \cdots, x_{in}]$ in position matrix X, is a solution of the problem. Different vector x_i is measured independently in dimension-wise population diversity, while for element-wise diversity, all vectors are combined together to find the center of particles. For a dimension-wise diversity, it is independent to evaluate the contribution of each x_{ij} to measure the diversity; while for element-wise diversity, it is not independent. Therefore, for dimension-wise diversity, it is preferred to normalize population diversity with vector norm, while for element-wise diversity, it is preferred to normalize diversity with matrix norm.

4. NORMALIZED POPULATION DIVERSITY

4.1. Vector Norm and Matrix Norm

A vector norm is a map function $f : \mathcal{R}^n \rightarrow \mathcal{R}$. The *p-norms*, which is a useful class of vector norms are defined by

$$\left\| x \right\|_p = \left(\left| x_1 \right|^p + \cdots + \left| x_n \right|^p \right)^{\frac{1}{p}} p \geq 1.$$

The L_1 and L_∞ norms can be utilized to normalize the population diversity, the definitions are as follow:

$$\left\| x \right\|_1 = \left| x_1 \right| + \cdots + \left| x_n \right|.$$

$$\left\| x \right\|_\infty = \max_{1 \leq i \leq n} \left| x_i \right|$$

All norms on $\mathcal{R}^n$ are equivalent (Golub, & Van Loan, 1996), i.e., if $\left\| \cdot \right\|_\alpha$ and $\left\| \cdot \right\|_\beta$ are norms on $\mathcal{R}^n$, there exist positive constants, c_1 and c_2 such that $c_1 \left\| x \right\|_\alpha \leq \left\| x \right\|_\beta \cdots \leq c_2 \left\| x \right\|_\alpha$, Vector norm have the property that:

$$\left\| x \right\| \geq \left\| x \right\|_2 \cdots \geq \left\| x \right\|_\infty$$

A matrix norm is a map function $f : \mathcal{R}^{m \times n} \rightarrow \mathcal{R}$, the definition of a matrix norm should be equivalent to the definition of a vector norm. For a matrix A, the most frequently used matrix norm is the *p*-norms:

$$\left\| A \right\|_p = \sup_{x \neq 0} \frac{\left\| A x \right\|_p}{\left\| x \right\|_p}$$

and the matrix norm have the properties that:

$$\max_{i,j} \left| a_{ij} \right| \leq \left\| A \right\|_2 \leq \sqrt{mn} \, \max_{i,j} \left| a_{ij} \right|$$

$$\left\| A \right\|_1 = \max_{1 \leq j \leq n} \sum_{i=1}^{m} \left| a_{ij} \right|$$

$$\left\| A \right\|_\infty = \max_{1 \leq i \leq m} \sum_{j=1}^{n} \left| a_{ij} \right|$$

By applying matrix norms in PSO, the meaning of matrix norm is as follows:

- For each dimension, calculating the sum of absolute position value for every particle, the maximum is the matrix norm L_1 for the position matrix.
- For every particle, finding the sum of absolute position value in each dimension, the maximum is the matrix norm L_∞ for the position matrix.

The distinction between matrix L_1 norm and matrix L_∞ norm is the perspectives taken on the position matrix. Matrix L_1 norm measures the largest value on the dimension, while matrix L_∞ norm measures the largest value on particles.

Considered the property whether vectors are dependent on each other or not, vector norms are preferred to be applied to normalize dimension-wise population diversity and matrix L_∞ norms are preferred to be used for element-wise population diversity.

4.2. Position Diversity

Position diversity measures the distribution of particles' current position. The swarm is going to diverge into a wider search space or converge in a small area that can be obtained from this measurement. Position diversity concerns the elements in the position matrix.

4.2.1. Dimension-Wise Diversity

For dimension-wise diversity, each vector in the position matrix is independent. Vector norms are preferred to normalize the position, and three methods are as follows. These normalizations are based on the vector L_1 norm, or L_∞ norm, or maximum value of position:

$$x_{ij}^{nor} = \frac{x_{ij}}{\left\| x \right\|_1} = \frac{x_{ij}}{\sum_{j=1}^{n} \left| x_{ij} \right|},$$

or

$$x_{ij}^{nor} = \frac{x_{ij}}{\|x\|_\infty} = \frac{x_{ij}}{\max|x_{ij}|},$$

or

$$x_{ij}^{nor} = \frac{x_{ij}}{X_{\max}}$$

Considered the inequality (8), normalized position based on other vector norms is always larger than position based on L_1 norm and smaller than position based on L_∞ norm.

Normalized dimension-wise position diversities are calculated as follow:

$$\bar{x}_j^{nor} = \frac{1}{m}\sum_{i=1}^{m} x_{ij}^{nor}$$

$$D_j^p = \frac{1}{m}\sum_{i=1}^{m}\left|x_{ij}^{nor} - \bar{x}_j^{nor}\right|$$

$$D^p = \frac{1}{n}\sum_{j=1}^{n} D_j^p$$

where $D^p = [D_1^p, \cdots, D_n^p]$ are the diversities on each dimension, and D^p is the normalized position diversity for particles.

4.2.2. Element-Wise Diversity

For element-wise diversity, a vector in a position matrix is relative to other vector or vectors. This connection should be considered in diversity measurement. Three methods are preferred to normalize the position of each particle $\max|x_{ij}|$ in the matrix X, matrix L_∞ norm for X, or the maximum value of the position. The normalized position is as follows:

$$x_{ij}^{nor} = \frac{x_{ij}}{\max|x_{ij}|},$$

or

$$x_{ij}^{nor} = \frac{x_{ij}}{\|X\|_{\infty}} = \frac{x_{ij}}{\max\limits_{1 \leq i \leq m} \sum\limits_{j=1}^{n} |x_{ij}|},$$

or

$$x_{ij}^{nor} = \frac{x_{ij}}{X_{\max}}$$

After normalized the position, normalized element-wise position diversity is calculated as follows:

$$\bar{x}^{nor} = \frac{1}{m \times n} \sum_{i=1}^{m} \sum_{j=1}^{n} x_{ij}^{nor}$$

$$D^p = \frac{1}{m \times n} \sum_{i=1}^{m} \sum_{j=1}^{n} \left| x_{ij}^{nor} - \bar{x}^{nor} \right|$$

where D^p is the normalized position diversity for particles at this running step.

4.3. Velocity Diversity

Velocity diversity, which gives the tendency information of particles, measures the distribution of particles' current velocity. In other words, velocity diversity measures the "activity" information of particles. Based on the measurement of velocity diversity, particle's tendency of expansion or convergence could be obtained.

4.3.1. Dimension-Wise Diversity

A vector in the velocity matrix is independent to measure the dimension-wise diversity. Vector norm L_1, or L_{∞}, or the maximum value of velocity is applied to normalize velocity:

$$v_{ij}^{nor} = \frac{v_{ij}}{\|v\|_1} = \frac{v_{ij}}{\sum\limits_{j=1}^{n} |v_{ij}|},$$

or

$$v_{ij}^{nor} = \frac{v_{ij}}{\|v\|_{\infty}} = \frac{v_{ij}}{\max |v_{ij}|},$$

or

$$v_{ij}^{nor} = \frac{v_{ij}}{V_{max}}$$

Normalized dimension-wise velocity diversities are calculated as follow:

$$\overline{v}_j^{nor} = \frac{1}{m} \sum_{i=1}^{m} v_{ij}^{nor}$$

$$D_j^v = \frac{1}{m} \sum_{i=1}^{m} \left| v_{ij}^{nor} - \overline{v}_j^{nor} \right|$$

$$D^v = \frac{1}{n} \sum_{j=1}^{n} D_j^v$$

where $D^v = [D_1^v, \cdots, D_n^v]$ are the diversities on each dimension, and D^v is the normalized velocity diversity for particles.

4.3.2. Element-Wise Diversity

In the measurement of element-wise diversity, vectors is not independent in velocity matrix. Three operators: $\max |v_{ij}|$ in velocity matrix, or matrix L_∞ norm of V, or maximum value of velocity is applied to normalize the velocity.

$$v_{ij}^{nor} = \frac{v_{ij}}{\max \left| v_{ij} \right|},$$

or

$$v_{ij}^{nor} = \frac{v_{ij}}{\left\| V \right\|_\infty} = \frac{v_{ij}}{\max\limits_{1 \leq i \leq m} \sum\limits_{j=1}^{n} \left| v_{ij} \right|},$$

or

$$v_{ij}^{nor} = \frac{v_{ij}}{V_{max}}$$

Normalized element-wise velocity diversity is calculated as follows:

$$\bar{v}^{nor} = \frac{1}{m \times n} \sum_{i=1}^{m} \sum_{j=1}^{n} v_{ij}^{nor}$$

$$D^v = \frac{1}{m \times n} \sum_{i=1}^{m} \sum_{j=1}^{n} \left| v_{ij}^{nor} - \bar{v}^{nor} \right|$$

where D^v is the normalized velocity diversity for particles at this running step.

4.4. Cognitive Diversity

Cognitive diversity represents the target distribution of all particles found currently. The measurement of cognitive diversity is as same as position diversity except using each particle's current personal best position instead of the current position. Therefore, the analysis of position diversity is also effective for cognitive diversity.

4.4.1. Dimension-Wise Diversity

The normalized cognitive positions are as follow:

$$p_{ij}^{nor} = \frac{p_{ij}}{\|p\|_1} = \frac{p_{ij}}{\sum_{j=1}^{n} |p_{ij}|},$$

or

$$p_{ij}^{nor} = \frac{p_{ij}}{\|p\|_\infty} = \frac{p_{ij}}{\max |p_{ij}|},$$

or

$$p_{ij}^{nor} = \frac{p_{ij}}{X_{max}}$$

Normalized dimension-wise cognitive diversities are calculated as follow:

$$\bar{p}_j^{nor} = \frac{1}{m} \sum_{i=1}^{m} v_{ij}^{nor}$$

$$D_j^c = \frac{1}{m} \sum_{i=1}^{m} \left| v_{ij}^{nor} - \bar{v}_j^{nor} \right|$$

$$D^c = \frac{1}{n} \sum_{j=1}^{n} D_j^v$$

where $D^c = [D_1^c, \cdots, D_n^c]$ are the diversities on each dimension, and D^c is the normalized cognitive diversity for particles.

4.4.2. Element-wise Diversity

Like the definition of position diversity, the normalized personal best positions are as follow:

$$p_{ij}^{nor} = \frac{p_{ij}}{\max \left| p_{ij} \right|},$$

or

$$p_{ij}^{nor} = \frac{p_{ij}}{\|P\|_{\infty}} = \frac{p_{ij}}{\max\limits_{1 \leq i \leq m} \sum\limits_{j=1}^{n} \left| p_{ij} \right|},$$

or

$$p_{ij}^{nor} = \frac{p_{ij}}{X_{\max}}$$

Normalized element-wise cognitive diversity is calculated as follows:

$$\bar{p}^{nor} = \frac{1}{m \times n} \sum_{i=1}^{m} \sum_{j=1}^{n} p_{ij}^{nor}$$

$$D^c = \frac{1}{m \times n} \sum_{i=1}^{m} \sum_{j=1}^{n} \left| p_{ij}^{nor} - \bar{p}^{nor} \right|$$

where D^c is the normalized cognitive diversity for particles at this iterative step.

5. EXPERIMENTAL STUDIES

5.1. Benchmark Test Functions

The experiments have been conducted to test the benchmark functions listed in Table 1. Without loss of generality, five standard unimodal and six multimodal test functions are selected (Yao, Liu, & Lin, 1999; Liang, Qin, & Suganthan, *et al.*, 2006). All functions are run for 50 times to have statistical meaning for comparison among different approaches. Randomly shifting of the location of optimum is utilized in each dimension for each run.

5.2. Parameter Setting

The parameter setting is the same as the standard PSO. In all experiments, PSO has 50 particles, $c_1=c_2=1.496172$, and the inertia weight $w=0.72984$ (Clerc, & Kennedy 2002; Bratton, & Kennedy, 2007). For each algorithm, the maximum number of iteration is 5000 for 100-dimensional problems in every run. There is also a limitation in velocity to control the search step size. The setting could prevent the particles from crossing the search boundary. The *maximum velocity* is set as follows:

maximum velocity = 0.2×(position upper bound – position lower bound).

5.3. Boundary Constraints Handling

With improper boundary constraint handling method, particles may get "stuck in" the boundary (Cheng, Shi, & Qin, 2011a). The classical boundary constraints handling method is as follows:

$$x_{i,j}(t+1) = \begin{cases} X_{\max,j} & if \; x_{i,j}(t+1) > X_{\max,j} \\ X_{\min,j} & if \; x_{i,j}(t+1) < X_{\min,j} \\ x_{i,j}(t+1) & otherwise \end{cases}$$

where t is the index number of the last iteration, and $t+1$ is the index number of the current iteration. This strategy resets particles in a particular point—the boundary, which constrains particles to fly in the search space limited by the boundary.

For PSO with star structure, a stochastic boundary constraint handling method was utilized in this chapter. The equation (11) gives a method that particles are reset into a special area.

$$x_{i,j}(t+1) = \begin{cases} X_{\max,j} \times (rand() \times c + 1 - c) & if \; x_{i,j}(t+1) > X_{\max,j} \\ X_{\min,j} \times (Rand() \times c + 1 - c) & if \; x_{i,j}(t+1) < X_{\min,j} \\ x_{i,j}(t+1) & otherwise \end{cases}$$

Table 1. The benchmark functions used in our experimental study, where n is the dimension of each problem, z=(x–o), x= [x_1,x_2,...,x_n], o_i is an randomly generated number in problem's search space S and it is different in each dimension, global optimum x^*=o, n=100, f_{min} is the minimum value of the function, and $S \subseteq \mathcal{R}^n$.

Function	Test Function	S	f_{min}
Parabolic	$f_0(x) = \sum_{i=1}^{n} z_i^2 + bias_0$	$[-100, 100]^n$	-450.0
Schwefel's P2.22	$f_1(x) = \sum_{i=1}^{n} |z_i| + \prod_{i=1}^{n} |z_i| + bias_1$	$[-10, 10]^n$	-330.0
Schwefel's P1.2	$f_2(x) = \sum_{i=1}^{n} \left(\sum_{k=1}^{i} z_k \right)^2 + bias_2$	$[-100, 100]^n$	450.0
Step	$f_3(x) = \sum_{i=1}^{n} \left(\lfloor z_i + 0.5 \rfloor \right)^2 + bias_3$	$[-100, 100]^n$	330.0
Quartic Noise	$f_4(x) = \sum_{i=1}^{n} i z_i^4 + random[0,1) + bias_4$	$[-1.28, 1.28]^n$	-450.0
Rosenbrock	$f_5(x) = \sum_{i=1}^{n-1} \left[100(z_{i+1} - z_i^2)^2 + (z_i - 1)^2 \right] + bias_5$	$[-10, 10]^n$	180.0
Rastrigin	$f_6(x) = \sum_{i=1}^{n} \left[z_i^2 - 10\cos(2\pi z_i) + 10 \right] + bias_6$	$[-5.12, 5.12]^n$	-330.0
Noncontinuous Rastrigin	$f_7(x) = \sum_{i=1}^{n} \left[y_i^2 - 10\cos(2\pi y_i) + 10 \right] + bias_7$ $$y_i = \begin{cases} z_i & |z_i| < \frac{1}{2} \\ \dfrac{round(2z_i)}{2} & |z_i| \geq \frac{1}{2} \end{cases}$$	$[-5.12, 5.12]^n$	450.0
Ackley	$f_8(x) = -20\exp\left(-0.2\sqrt{\frac{1}{n}\sum_{i=1}^{n} z_i^2} \right)$ $- \exp\left(\frac{1}{n}\sum_{i=1}^{n} \cos(2\pi z_i) \right) + 20 + e + bias_8$	$[-32, 32]^n$	180.0
Griewank	$f_9(x) = \frac{1}{4000}\sum_{i=1}^{n} z_i^2 - \prod_{i=1}^{n} \cos\left(\frac{z_i}{\sqrt{i}} \right) + 1 + bias_9$	$[-600, 600]^n$	120.0

Table 1. Continued

Function	Test Function	S	f_{min}
Generalized Penalized	$f_{10}(x) = \dfrac{\pi}{n}$ $\left\{ 10\sin^2(\pi y_1) + \sum_{i=1}^{n-1}(y_i-1)^2 \times [1+10\sin^2(\pi y_{i+1})] + (y_n-1)^2 \right\}$ $+\sum_{i=1}^{n} u(z_i,10,100,4) + bias_{10}$ $y_i = 1 + \dfrac{1}{4}(z_i+1)$ $u(z_i,a,k,m) = \begin{cases} k(z_i-a)^m & z_i > a, \\ 0 & -a < z_i < a \\ k(-z_i-a)^m & z_i < -a \end{cases}$	$[-50, 50]^n$	330.0

where c is a parameter to control the resetting scope. When $c=1$, particles are reset within a half search space. On the contrary, when $c=0$, this strategy is the same as the equation (10), i.e., particles are reset to be on the boundary. The closer to 0 the c is, the more particles have a high possibility to be reset close to the boundary.

In our experiment, the c is set to 0.1. A particle will be close to the boundary when the position is beyond the boundary. This will increase the exploitation ability of algorithm searching the solution close to the boundary.

A deterministic method, which resets a boundary-violating position to the middle between the old position and the boundary (Zielinski, Weitkemper, & Laur, *et al.*, 2009), was utilized for PSO with a local ring structure. The equation is as follows:

$$x_{i,j,G+1} = \begin{cases} \dfrac{1}{2}(x_{i,j,G} + X_{max,j}) & if\ x_{i,j,G+1} > X\,max,j \\ \dfrac{1}{2}(x_{i,j,G} + X_{min,j}) & if\ x_{i,j,G+1} < X_{min,j} \\ x_{i,j,G+1} & otherwise \end{cases}$$

The position in last iteration is used in this strategy. Both classic strategy and this strategy reset a particle to a deterministic position.

5.4. Experimental Results

Table 2 is the results of variants of PSO solving unimodal and multimodal benchmark functions, respectively. The bold numbers indicate the better solutions. Five measures of performance are reported. The first is the best fitness value attained after a fixed number of iterations. In our case, we report the best result found after 5000 iterations. The following measures are the median value, worst value, mean

Table 2. Results of PSO with global star and local ring structure for solving benchmark functions. All algorithms are run for 50 times, where "Best", "Median", "Worst", and "Mean" indicate the best, median, worst, and mean of the best fitness values for all runs, respectively.

	F_{min}	Best	Median	Worst	Mean	Std. Dev.
Result		**PSO With Global Star Structure**				
f_0	-450.0	**-449.9999**	-449.6854	-442.6770	-449.1768	1.33996
f_1	-330.0	-329.9877	-329.2344	-304.9446	-326.7997	5.72326
f_2	450.0	3818.890	8427.7940	19023.334	9030.511	3068.57
f_3	330.0	363	583	2004	754.44	385.978
f_4	-450.0	**-449.9706**	-449.9444	-449.7928	-449.9363	0.03416
f_5	180.0	**267.7406**	462.5463	1304.6580	485.0325	164.280
f_6	-330.0	**46.2115**	208.2699	363.4809	**203.8959**	64.8012
f_7	450.0	**642.0642**	801.0000	1038.0011	**803.5064**	96.4137
f_8	180.0	183.1818	185.8173	199.6355	187.5995	5.10715
f_9	120.0	120.0169	120.2609	122.0702	120.3948	0.39427
f_{10}	330.0	330.6340	332.1802	334.3695	332.2510	1.01614
Result		**PSO With Local Ring Structure**				
f_0	-450.0	-449.9999	-449.9999	-449.9999	**-449.9999**	4.49E-10
f_1	-330.0	**-329.9999**	-329.9999	-318.1378	**-329.5631**	1.70413
f_2	450.0	26269.130	39541.160	52074.665	38807.785	5966.04
f_3	330.0	**330**	331	339	**331.46**	2.00209
f_4	-450.0	-449.9061	-449.8677	-449.7951	-449.8652	0.02438
f_5	180.0	308.5254	386.3057	524.9256	**396.6181**	48.9784
f_6	-330.0	97.8392	226.0655	413.9907	225.8784	61.4603
f_7	450.0	869.4427	1051.2509	1200.5000	1053.3454	69.4105
f_8	180.0	**180.0000**	181.9460	182.8799	**181.8619**	0.54818
f_9	120.0	**120.0000**	120.0000	120.0000	**120.0000**	6.35E-09
f_{10}	330.0	330.0017	330.5103	331.8971	330.6488	0.48609

value, and the standard deviation of the best fitness values for all runs. It is possible that an algorithm will rapidly reach a relatively good result while becoming trapped into a local optimum. These values reflect the algorithm's reliability and robustness.

From the result in Table 2, we can conduct that for seven functions $f_0, f_1, f_3, f_4, f_8, f_9$, and f_{10} good optimization results were obtained, while for the other four functions f_2, f_5, f_6, and f_7, the results obtained are not very good. This is because of the property of functions, some functions will become significantly difficult to solve when the dimension increases. The PSO with global star structure is better than PSO with local ring structure on some functions, and on others, the PSO with local ring structure is better.

Table 3. Some representative benchmark functions

Parabolic	f_0	unimode	separable
Schwefel's P1.2	f_2	unimode	non-separable
Rosenbrock	f_5	multimode	non-separable
Ackley	f_8	multimode	separable

6. DIVERSITY ANALYSIS AND DISCUSSION

Different functions have different properties. Considered the number of local optima, the benchmark functions can be categorized as unimodal function and multimodal function. The benchmark functions also can be divided as separable functions and non-separable functions based on the inter-dependence among dimensions. Due to the limit of space, four representative benchmark functions in table 3 are chosen to analyze the different normalized population diversity.

6.1. Population Diversity Definition

Figures 2, 3, 4, and 5 display the population diversity changing while PSO solving unimodal f_0, f_2, and multimodal function f_5, f_8, respectively. In the diversity figures, the horizontal coordinates are the number of iterations, and the vertical coordinates indicate the value of population diversities.

Figure 2 displays the population diversity changing while PSO solving unimodal Parabolic function f_0. The Parabolic function is a separable problem, i.e., each dimension is independent.

Compared with other problems, the "hardness" of this problem will not significantly increase when the problem getting large scale. The curve of population diversities changing is very smooth in this problem.

Figure 3 displays the population diversity changing while PSO solving unimodal Schwefel's P1.2 function f_2. Schwefel's P1.2 function is a non-separable problem, i.e., each dimension is dependent on others. This problem will significantly get "hard" when the problem becomes a large scale. The curve of population diversities changing has many vibrating, and the normalized diversity only has a slight decreasing. This indicates that particles cannot locate some good regions, most of search is spent on the exploration state. The conclusion can be drawn that the Schwefel's P1.2 function f_2 is more difficult to solve than Parabolic function f_0, and the result may be far from the optimum.

Figure 4 displays the population diversity changing while PSO solving multimodal Rosenbrock function f_5. The Rosenbrock function is also a non-separable problem. This problem also will significantly get "hard" when the problem becomes a large scale. The curve of population diversities changing has many vibrating, and the normalized diversity only has a slight decreasing. The curve of population diversities is similar to a function f_2.

Figure 5 displays the population diversity changing while PSO solving multimodal Ackley function f_8. The Ackley function is a separable problem (Tang, Li, & Suganthan, *et al.*, 2010). The particles are easily "stuck in" the local optima. The "hardness" of this problem increases when the problem getting large scale.

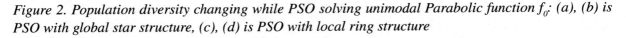

Figure 2. Population diversity changing while PSO solving unimodal Parabolic function f_0: (a), (b) is PSO with global star structure, (c), (d) is PSO with local ring structure

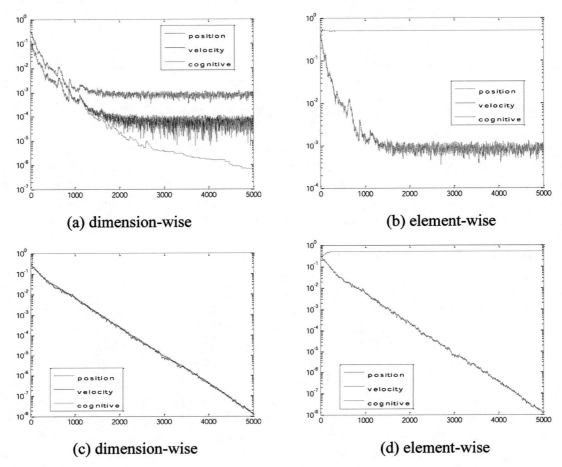

From the observation of population diversities in these figures, there are some conclusions that can be drawn as follows.

- The population diversities defined in this chapter can be divided into three categories: position diversity, velocity diversity, and cognitive diversity. These diversity definitions measure the distribution of particle positions, velocities, and cognitive positions, respectively.

- For position diversity and cognitive diversity, the value of diversities can be seen as the "average distance" among particles. A large value indicates that the particles are distributed in a large area, on the contrary, a small value indicates that the particles are get clustered in a small region.

- For velocity diversity, the value of diversity measures the "search potential" of the particles. A large value indicates that the particles are exploring the search space, it has highly possible to "jump out" of the local optima. On the contrary, a small value indicates that the particles are exploiting the potential regions.

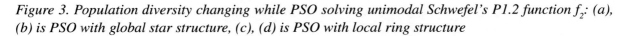

Figure 3. Population diversity changing while PSO solving unimodal Schwefel's P1.2 function f_2: (a), (b) is PSO with global star structure, (c), (d) is PSO with local ring structure

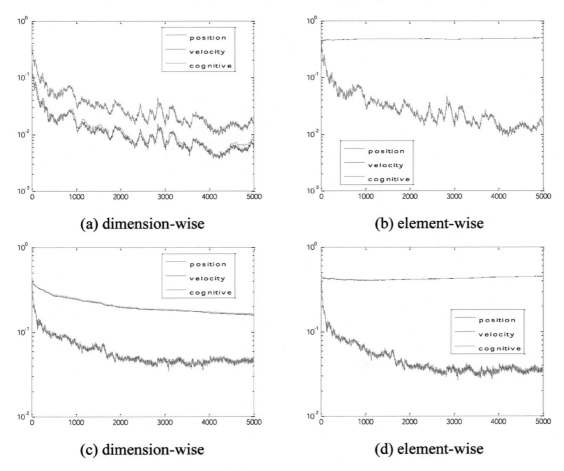

- The population diversities decrease after iterations in the search process. This indicates that particles are distributed in the large area, and get converged after iterations. This gives a simulation of the particle search process, particles spread in the search space at first, then get converged into local optima through the propagation of search information (Cheng, Shi, & Qin, 2012b).

- For dimension-wise population diversity, the changing curves of position, velocity, and cognitive diversity are very similar. These three definitions of population diversity are dependent on each other in the canonical particle swarm optimization algorithm. Cognitive diversity can be seen as a simplified version of the position diversity. The position diversity has more vibrating than cognitive diversity. The changing of velocity diversity affects the value of position diversity. With a large value of velocity diversity, particles search in a large region, the particles are distributed in this region, which will lead to a large value of position diversity. On the contrary, with a small value of velocity, the particle's position has a small movement, all particles stay in a small region, this will lead to a small value of position diversity.

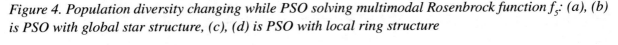

Figure 4. Population diversity changing while PSO solving multimodal Rosenbrock function f_5: (a), (b) is PSO with global star structure, (c), (d) is PSO with local ring structure

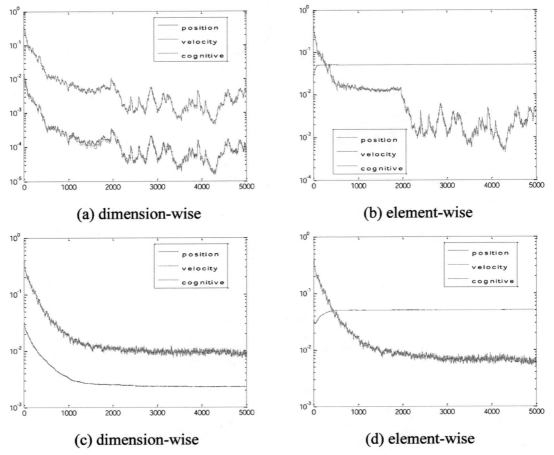

- Without additional diversity maintaining strategy (Jin, & Sendhoff, 2004; Cheng, Shi, & Qin, 2011b; Cheng, Shi, & Qin, 2012a), such as inserting randomly generated individuals, niching, re-initialization, or reformulating the fitness function considering the age of individuals, the population diversities usually will decrease in the whole search process. This indicates that the canonical particle swarm optimization algorithm is difficult to "jump out" of local optima. This is a trade-off in the search process. It is difficult to recognize local optima during the search, and an improper additional strategy may lead to algorithm ineffectiveness.

- For element-wise population diversity, there is no decreasing for position diversity and cognitive diversity. This definition combines all dimensions altogether. For a problem with different optimal values in different dimensions, this kind of definition may confuse about the difference in dimensions (Cheng, & Shi, 2011a).

- The definitions of diversity measurement give some useful information during particles search process. Position diversity and velocity diversity always have a continuous vibrate, this may confirm that particles "fly" from one side of optimum to another side on each dimension continually (Spears, Green, & Spears, 2010).

Figure 5. Population diversity changing while PSO solving multimodal Ackley function f_8: (a), (b) is PSO with global star structure, (c), (d) is PSO with local ring structure

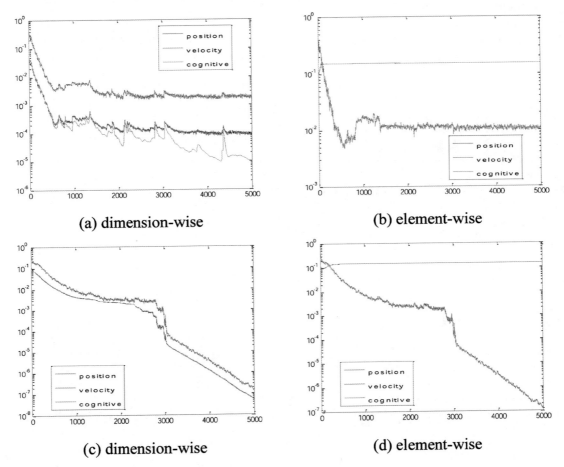

(a) dimension-wise   (b) element-wise

(c) dimension-wise   (d) element-wise

6.2. Normalized Population Diversity Comparison

Figures 6, 7, 8, and 9 display the curves of different normalized population diversities when PSO solving unimodal function f_0, and f_2, respectively.

Figure 6 displays the population diversities of PSO with global star structure, and Figure 7 displays the population diversities of PSO with a local ring structure. The population diversity of PSO with star structure decreases faster than PSO with a ring structure at the beginning of the search. However, the PSO with ring structure can reach a smaller value than PSO with a star structure. This indicates that the PSO with ring structure has a better exploitation ability.

Figure 8 displays the population diversities of PSO with global star structure, and Figure 9 displays the population diversities of PSO with local ring structure. This problem is difficult to solve, the result is not good. The population diversity doesn't have a significant decreasing during the search process.

Figures 10, 11, 12, and 13 display the curves of different normalized population diversity when PSO solving multimodal function f_5, and f_8, respectively.

Figure 6. Comparison of different normalization of PSO population diversity: PSO with global star structure on unimodal Parabolic function f_0, (a), (c), and (e) are dimension-wise diversity, (b), (d), and (f) are element-wise diversity

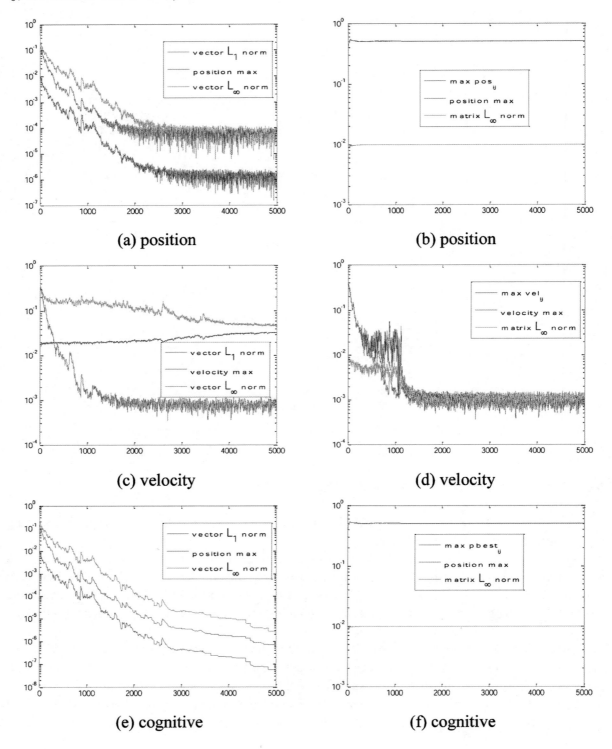

(a) position   (b) position

(c) velocity   (d) velocity

(e) cognitive   (f) cognitive

Figure 7. Comparison of different normalization of PSO population diversity: PSO with local ring structure on unimodal Parabolic function f_0, (a), (c), and (e) are dimension-wise diversity, (b), (d), and (f) are element-wise diversity

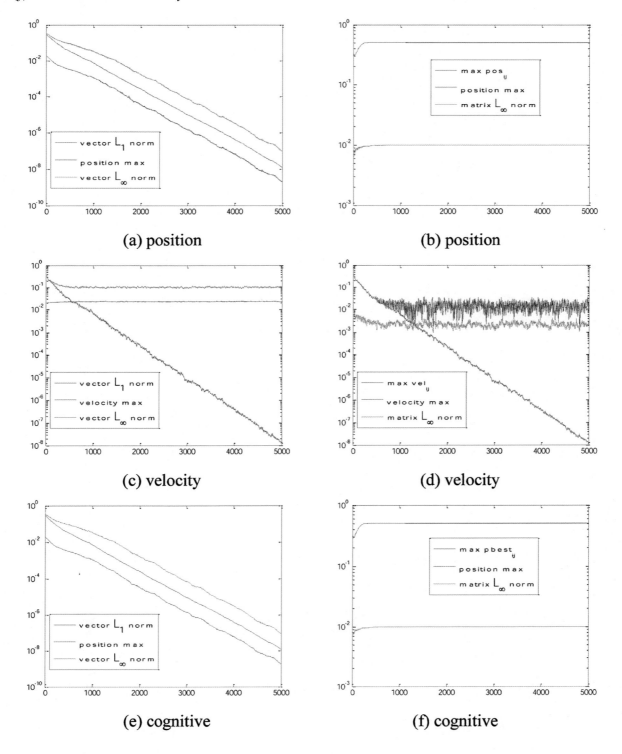

(a) position

(b) position

(c) velocity

(d) velocity

(e) cognitive

(f) cognitive

Figure 8. Comparison of different normalization of PSO population diversity: PSO with global star structure on unimodal Schwefel's P1.2 function f_2, (a), (c), and (e) are dimension-wise diversity, (b), (d), and (f) are element-wise diversity

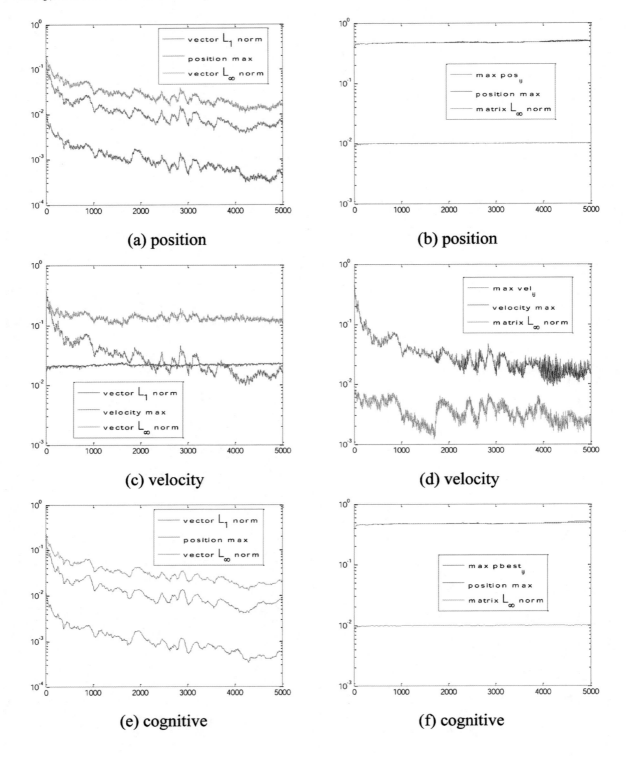

(a) position
(b) position
(c) velocity
(d) velocity
(e) cognitive
(f) cognitive

Figure 9. Comparison of different normalization of PSO population diversity: PSO with local ring structure on unimodal Schwefel's P1.2 function f_2, (a), (c) and, (e) are dimension-wise diversity, (b), (d), and (f) are element-wise diversity

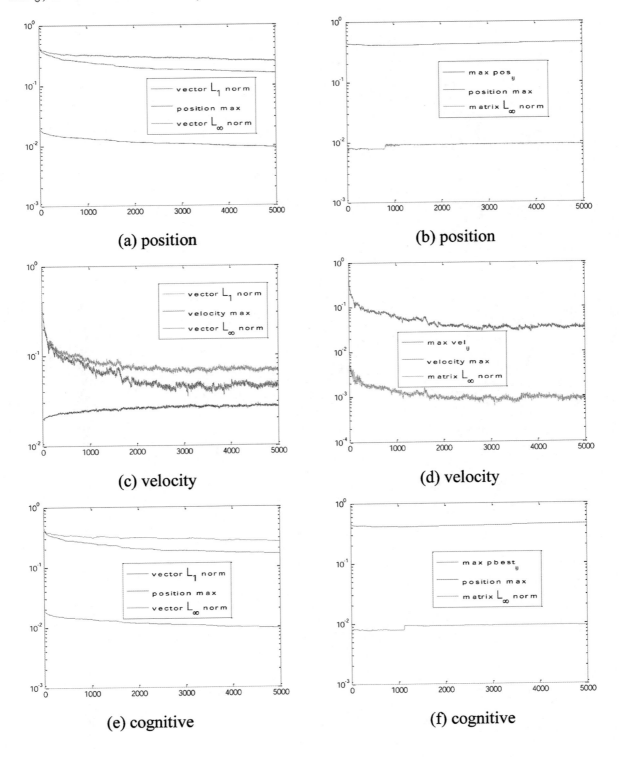

(a) position   (b) position

(c) velocity   (d) velocity

(e) cognitive   (f) cognitive

Figure 10. Comparison of different normalization of PSO population diversity: PSO with global star structure on multimodal Rosenbrock function f_5, (a), (c), and (e) are dimension-wise diversity, (b), (d), and (f) are element-wise diversity

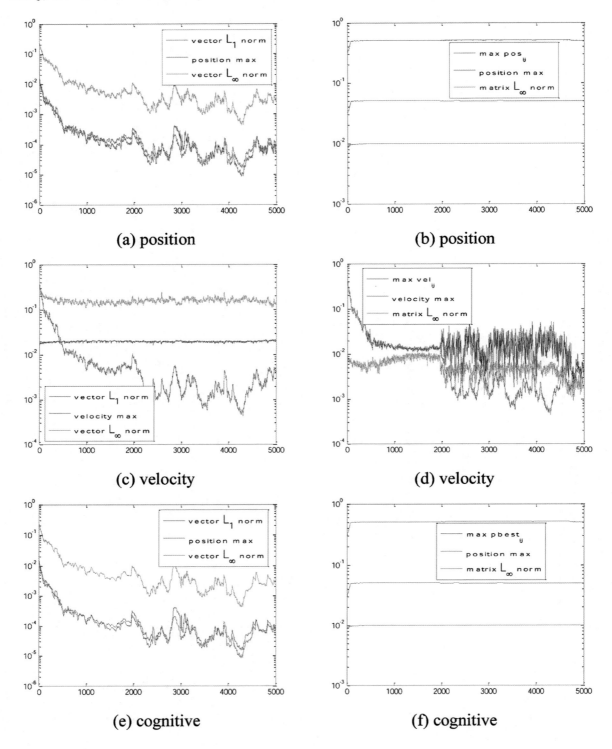

(a) position

(b) position

(c) velocity

(d) velocity

(e) cognitive

(f) cognitive

Figure 11. Comparison of different normalization of PSO population diversity: PSO with local ring structure on multimodal Rosenbrock function f_5, (a), (c), and (e) are dimension-wise diversity, (b), (d), and (f) are element-wise diversity

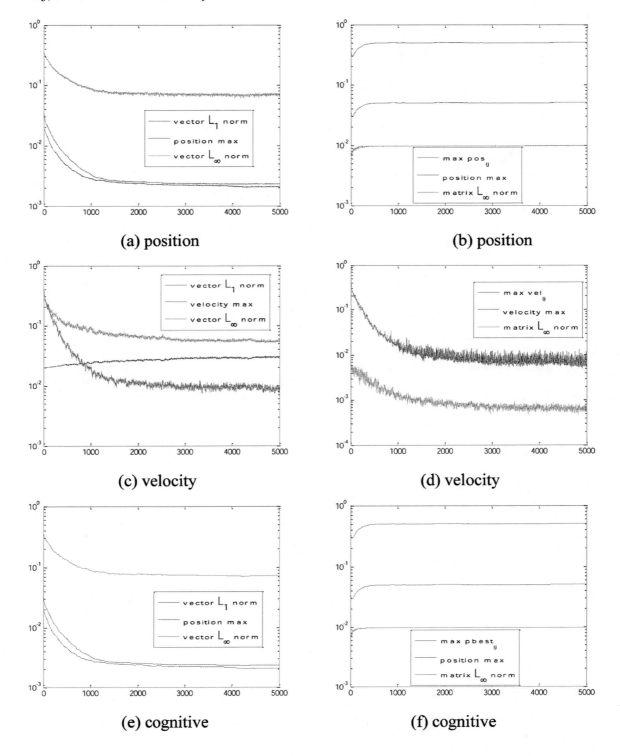

(a) position

(b) position

(c) velocity

(d) velocity

(e) cognitive

(f) cognitive

Figure 12. Comparison of different normalization of PSO population diversity: PSO with global star structure on multimodal Ackley function f_g, (a), (c), and (e) are dimension-wise diversity, (b), (d), and (f) are element-wise diversity

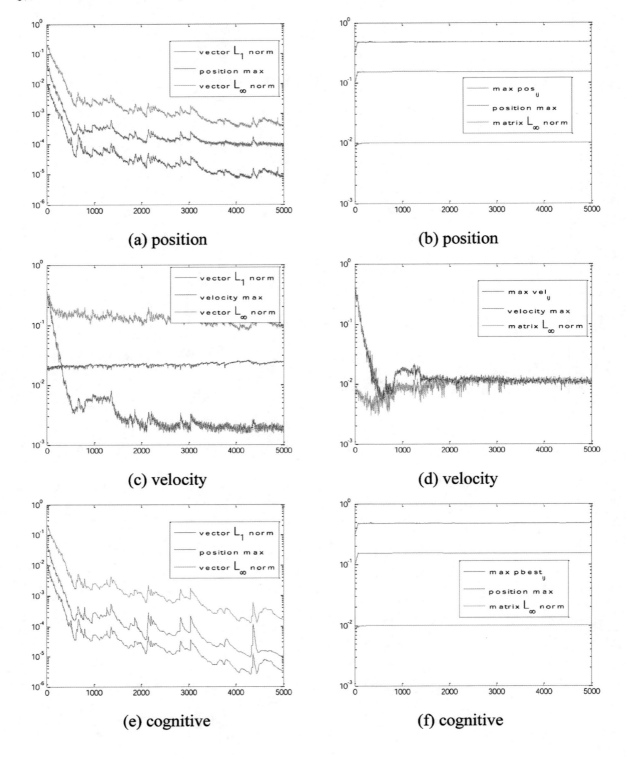

(a) position

(b) position

(c) velocity

(d) velocity

(e) cognitive

(f) cognitive

Figure 13. Comparison of different normalization of PSO population diversity: PSO with local ring structure on multimodal Ackley function f_8, (a), (c) and, (e) are dimension-wise diversity, (b), (d), and (f) are element-wise diversity

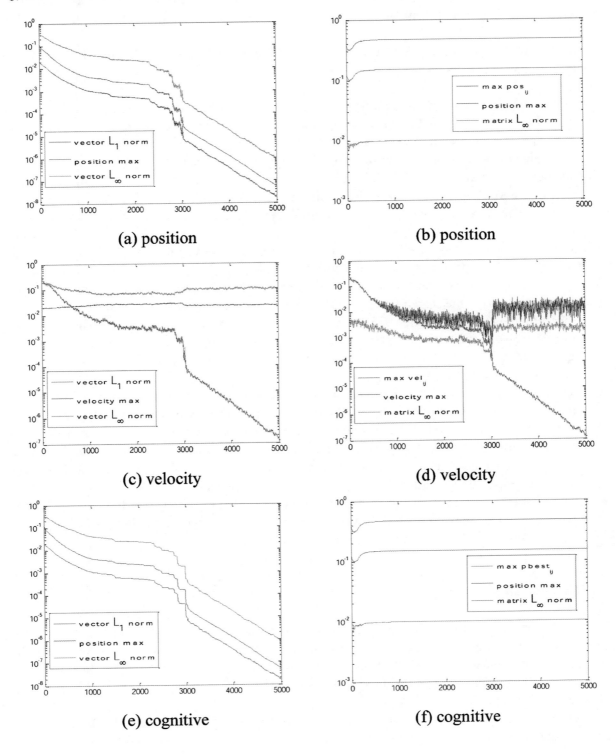

(a) position   (b) position

(c) velocity   (d) velocity

(e) cognitive   (f) cognitive

Figures 10 and 12 display the population diversities of PSO with global star structure when PSO solving multimodal function f_5 and f_8, respectively. Figures 11 and 13 display the population diversities of PSO with local ring structure when PSO solving multimodal function f_5 and f_8, respectively. The population diversities of PSO with global star structure have more vibrating than the PSO with the local ring structure.

From the observation of different normalized population diversities in these figures, there are some conclusions that can be drawn as follows.

- In general, the curves of different normalized population diversities are very similar. Even with the different strategies to normalize the population diversities, the tendency of population diversities changing is the same.
- The value of vector L_1 norm is always larger than the value of vector L_∞ norm, and in most cases, the position maximum is larger than the value of vector L_∞ norm, and smaller than the value of vector L_1 norm. This leads the value of normalized diversity based on vector L_∞ norm to have the largest value, and normally, the value of vector L_1 norm based normalized diversity has the smallest value.
- Particles have large "average" velocities at the beginning of the search. The velocity will decrease to a small value after iterations. The sum of velocity values may be smaller than the velocity maximum in some benchmark functions. For velocity diversity, the velocity maximum is a constant value during the search process, and velocity maximum based velocity diversity has more vibrating than other strategies based velocity diversities. The velocity maximum based velocity diversity gives more accurate information on "average" velocity changing behavior. Other strategies based velocity diversity gives a ratio between "average" velocity and current largest velocity value (or sum of current velocity values).
- There is a significant decreasing in dimension-wise population diversities. The dimension-wise population diversities also have more vibrating than element-wise population diversities. For dimension-wise population diversities, the measurement is based on every single dimension, and particles are observed as "flying" around the center of each dimension. On the contrary, for element-wise population diversities, the measurement is based on whole dimensions, and particles are observed as "flying" around the center of the whole dimension.
- The detailed information of the particles' movement can be obtained from the dimension-wise population diversities. The element-wise diversities give a "dynamic equilibrium" of particles, which gives a dynamic search range during optimization.

7. CONCLUSION

This chapter proposed an analysis of population diversity based on the category of dimension-wise and element-wise diversities. Each dimension is measured separately in the dimension-wise diversity, on the contrary, the element-wise diversity measures all dimensions together. In other words, each vector of position matrix is independent in the dimension-wise diversity measurement, and in the element-wise diversity observation, the vectors are considered together. Considered the property whether vectors are dependent on each other or not, vector norms are preferred to normalize dimension-wise population diversity and matrix L_∞ norm is preferred to be used for element-wise population diversity.

Particles on the state of "expansion" or "convergence" can be determined by this diversity measurement. From the normalized population diversity, the diversity changing of PSO variants on different types of functions can be compared and analyzed. The particles' dynamical search state, the "hardness" of function, the number of local optima, and other information can be obtained. With this information, the performance of the optimization algorithm can be improved by adjusting population diversity dynamically during the PSO search process. Particles with different topology structures also have different vector dependence in position or velocity matrix. Seeking the influence of PSO topology structure and vector partial dependence analysis is the research that needs to be explored further.

The idea of normalized population diversity measurement can also be applied to other evolutionary algorithms, e.g., genetic algorithm, differential evolution for evolutionary algorithms have the same concepts of current population solutions and search step. The performance of evolutionary algorithms can be improved by taking advantage of utilizing the measurement of population diversity. Dynamically adjusting the population diversity controls the algorithm's ability of exploration or exploitation, hence, the algorithm has a large possibility to reach optimum.

ACKNOWLEDGMENT

This work was supported by National Natural Science Foundation of China (Grant Nos. 61806119, 61672334, 61761136008, and 61773103), and Natural Science Basic Research Plan In Shaanxi Province of China (Grant No. 2019JM-320).

REFERENCES

Bratton, D., & Kennedy, J. (2007). Defining a standard for particle swarm optimization. *Proceedings of the 2007 IEEE Swarm Intelligence Symposium (SIS 2007)*, (pp. 120-127). 10.1109/SIS.2007.368035

Cheng, S., Lu, H., Lei, X., & Shi, Y. (2018). A Quarter Century of Particle Swarm Optimization. *Complex & Intelligent Systems*, 4(3), 227–239. doi:10.100740747-018-0071-2

Cheng, S., & Shi, Y. (2011a). Diversity control in particle swarm optimization. *Proceedings of 2011 IEEE Symposium on Swarm Intelligence (SIS 2011)*, (pp. 110-118).

Cheng, S., & Shi, Y. (2011b). Normalized population diversity in particle swarm optimization. In Y. Tan, Y. Shi, Y. Chai, & G. Wang (Eds.), Advances in Swarm Intelligence, (LNCS 6728, pp. 38-45). Berlin, Germany: Springer. doi:10.1007/978-3-642-21515-5_5

Cheng, S., Shi, Y., & Qin, Q. (2011a). Experimental study on boundary constraints handling in particle swarm optimization: From population diversity perspective. [IJSIR]. *International Journal of Swarm Intelligence Research*, 2(3), 43–69. doi:10.4018/jsir.2011070104

Cheng, S., Shi, Y., & Qin, Q. (2011b). Promoting diversity in particle swarm optimization to solve multimodal problems. In B.-L. Lu, L. Zhang, & J. Kwok (Eds.), Neural Information Processing, (LNCS 7063, pp. 228-237). Berlin, Germany: Springer. doi:10.1007/978-3-642-24958-7_27

Cheng, S., Shi, Y., & Qin, Q. (2012a). Dynamical exploitation space reduction in particle swarm optimization for solving large scale problems. *Proceedings of 2012 IEEE Congress on Evolutionary Computation, (CEC 2012)*, (pp. 3030-3037), Brisbane, Australia. IEEE. 10.1109/CEC.2012.6252937

Cheng, S., Shi, Y., & Qin, Q. (2012b). Population diversity based study on search information propagation in particle swarm optimization. *Proceedings of 2012 IEEE Congress on Evolutionary Computation, (CEC 2012)*, (pp. 1272-1279), Brisbane, Australia. IEEE. 10.1109/CEC.2012.6256502

Clerc, M., & Kennedy, J. (2002). The particle swarm—Explosion, stability, and convergence in a multidimensional complex space. *IEEE Transactions on Evolutionary Computation*, 6(1), 58–73. doi:10.1109/4235.985692

Eberhart, R., & Kennedy, J. (1995). A new optimizer using particle swarm theory. *Proceedings of the Sixth International Symposium on Micro Machine and Human Science*, (pp. 39-43). 10.1109/MHS.1995.494215

Eberhart, R., & Shi, Y. (2001). Particle swarm optimization: Developments, applications, and resources. *Proceedings of the 2001 Congress on Evolutionary Computation (CEC2001)*, (pp. 81-86). 10.1109/CEC.2001.934374

Eberhart, R., & Shi, Y. (2007). *Computational Intelligence: Concepts to Implementations*. Morgan Kaufmann. doi:10.1016/B978-155860759-0/50002-0

Fang, W., Sun, J., Ding, Y., Wu, X., & Xu, W. (2010). A Review of Quantum-behaved Particle Swarm Optimization. *IETE Technical Review*, 27(4), 336–348. doi:10.4103/0256-4602.64601

Golub, G. H., & Van Loan, C. F. (1996). *Matrix Computations* (3rd ed.). The Johns Hopkins University Press.

Jin, Y., & Sendhoff, B. (2004). Constructing dynamic optimization test problems using the multi-objective optimization concept. In G. R. Raidl, S. Cagnoni, J. Branke, D. W. Corne, R. Drechsler, Y. Jin, C. G. Johnson, P. Machado, E. Marchiori, F. Rothlauf, G. D. Smith, & G. Squillero (Eds.), Applications of Evolutionary Computing, (LNCS 3005, pp. 525-536). Berlin, Germany: Springer. doi:10.1007/978-3-540-24653-4_53

Kennedy, J., & Eberhart, R. (1995). Particle swarm optimization. *Proceedings of IEEE International Conference on Neural Networks*, (pp. 1942-1948). 10.1109/ICNN.1995.488968

Kennedy, J., Eberhart, R., & Shi, Y. (2001). Swarm Intelligence. Morgan Kaufmann.

Kennedy, J., & Mendes, R. (2002). Population structure and particle swarm performance. *Proceedings of The Fourth Congress on Evolutionary Computation (CEC 2002)*, (pp. 1671-1676). Academic Press.

Leung, Y., Gao, Y., & Xu, Z.-B. (1997). Degree of population diversity—A perspective on premature convergence in genetic algorithms and its Markov chain analysis. *IEEE Transactions on Neural Networks*, 8(5), 1165–1176. doi:10.1109/72.623217 PMID:18255718

Liang, J. J., Qin, A. K., Suganthan, P. N., & Baskar, S. (2006). Comprehensive learning particle swarm optimizer for global optimization of multimodal functions. *IEEE Transactions on Evolutionary Computation*, 10(3), 281–295. doi:10.1109/TEVC.2005.857610

Mendes, R. (2004). Population Topologies and Their Influence in Particle Swarm Performance. (Unpublished doctoral dissertation), University of Minho, Portugal.

Olorunda, O., & Engelbrecht, A. P. (2008). Measuring exploration/exploitation in particle swarms using swarm diversity. *Proceedings of the 2008 Congress on Evolutionary Computation (CEC 2008)*, (pp. 1128-1134). 10.1109/CEC.2008.4630938

Shi, Y., & Eberhart, R. (1998). A modified particle swarm optimizer. *Proceedings of the 1998 Congress on Evolutionary Computation (CEC1998)*, (pp. 69-73). 10.1109/ICEC.1998.699146

Shi, Y., & Eberhart, R. (1999). Empirical study of particle swarm optimization. *Proceedings of the 1999 Congress on Evolutionary Computation (CEC 1999)*. (pp. 1945-1950) 10.1109/CEC.1999.785511

Shi, Y., & Eberhart, R. (2008). Population diversity of particle swarms. *Proceedings of the 2008 Congress on Evolutionary Computation (CEC 2008)*. (pp. 1063-1067) 10.1109/CEC.2008.4630928

Shi, Y., & Eberhart, R. (2009). Monitoring of particle swarm optimization. *Frontiers of Computer Science, 3*(1), 31–37. doi:10.100711704-009-0008-4

Spears, W. M., Green, D. T., & Spears, D. F. (2010). Biases in particle swarm optimization. [IJSIR]. *International Journal of Swarm Intelligence Research, 1*(2), 34–57. doi:10.4018/jsir.2010040103

Tang, K., Li, X., Suganthan, P. N., Yang, Z., & Weise, T. (2010). Benchmark Functions for the CEC'2010 Special Session and Competition on Large-Scale Global Optimization. Technical report, 1-23.

Yao, X., Liu, Y., & Lin, G. (1999). Evolutionary programming made faster. *IEEE Transactions on Evolutionary Computation, 3*(2), 82–102. doi:10.1109/4235.771163

Zielinski, K., Weitkemper, P., Laur, R., & Kammeyer, K. D. (2009). Optimization of power allocation for interference cancellation with particle swarm optimization. *IEEE Transactions on Evolutionary Computation, 13*(1), 128–150. doi:10.1109/TEVC.2008.920672

Chapter 16
Multi–Objective Short–Term Hydro–Thermal Scheduling Using Meta–Heuristic Approaches

Moumita Pradhan
Dr. B. C. Roy Engineering College, India

Provas Kumar Roy
(iD) https://orcid.org/0000-0002-3433-5808
Kalyani Government Engineering College, India

Tandra Pal
National Institute of Technology, Durgapur, India

ABSTRACT

Every day humans face new challenges to survive in this world. It is a big challenge to utilize hydro and thermal generating unit properly. Researchers are trying to explore new techniques to improve scheduling of generating units. Environmental matter is a big issue to modern society. This chapter suggests a well-organized and effective approach using concept of grey wolf optimization (GWO) to deal with nonlinear, multi-objective, short-term, hydro-thermal scheduling (MOHTS) problem. Moreover, authors have incorporated oppositional based learning (OBL) to enhance characteristics of GWO to achieve solution more consistently and accurately. To explore authenticity of our proposed algorithms, GWO and OGWO (oppositional based GWO) are applied to multi-chain cascade of 4-hydro and 3-thermal test system. Effective constraints like valve-point loading, water discharge, water storage, etc., are considered here. Statistical comparisons with other enlisted heuristic methods are done. The projected methods solve MOHTS problem quickly and efficiently.

DOI: 10.4018/978-1-7998-3222-5.ch016

1. INTRODUCTION

Multi-objective short-term hydrothermal scheduling (MOHTS) is a vital organizing task in operation of the power system. Usually, hydro-thermal power system scheduling is more complex than thermal system scheduling. The bordering manufacture price of hydroelectric plants is insignificant, but one of the important problems is usage of available water. The cost of thermal generation is increased if they are present alone in the power system. However, the presence of large number of hydroelectric plants with a set of constraints coupled in proper time periods to maximize power generation from hydroelectric plants may decrease the cost. Economic load dispatch (ELD) is an optimization approach in the thermal power system which try to schedule power generation according to the load demand from the power plant. Conventionally, the hydrothermal power systems are worked in such a way that the total fuel cost is reduced with optimal power generation by both hydro and thermal power plant.

In our research work, we want to schedule the power generating units in such a way that's why manufacturing cost is minimized. Load demand is circulated among generating units in ELD (Wood & Wollenberg, 1994; Happ, 1997; Chowdhury & Rahman, 1990; Liu & Cai, 2005) problem which will satisfy generation limit, prohibited operating zone, ramp rate, etc., considering transmission loss at every time interval such that the over-all cost is minimum. Fossil fuel produces various pollutants, like nitrogen oxides, carbon dioxide, sulfur oxides, etc., into the atmosphere at the time of generation of electricity from thermal power plant. The power companies have to assured standards concerning about the emission levels of pollutants for the strict government guidelines on ecological protection. As a responsible citizen, we must try to clean the air from different poisonous gasses. By European Clean Air Act Amendments of 1990 and similar acts by Japanese governments and others, show their concern by the management rules (Yalcinoz, Altun & Hasan, 2002). The awareness due to the increasing anxiety over contaminants, society bothers apposite and safe electric power must get in low price but in lower level of pollution. Newly, ELD problem has been incorporated by emission dispatch (CEED) problem (Roy, Ghoshal & Thakur, 2010a; Roy, Ghoshal & Thakur, 2010b; Zhang, Luh & Zhang, 1999); where many researchers consider emission as an additional constraint or second objective function with minimize the cost economy. For the instance of short-term hydro-thermal load managing, it is typically expected that the water volume entrances essential to encounter the load necessities and load demand are recognized through certainty. The several restrictions that cannot be disrupted HTS is a complicated decision-making process. Water discharge rate, hydraulic continuity restriction, lower and upper bounds of the reservoir volumes, water spillage, effective capacity limits of hydro plant etc., constraints makes the HTS problem as a complex optimization problem whose viable solution space is enormous.

Numerous optimization algorithms for mathematics are applied to the hydrothermal scheduling problem (Zhang, Luh & Zhang, 1999; Al-Agtash, 2001). Several classical methods, such as decomposition approach (DA) (Pereira & Pinto, 1983), dynamic programming (DP) (Yang & Chen, 1989), linear programming (LP) (Mohan, Kuppusamy & Khan, 1992), non-linear programming (Gul et al., 2019) and progressive optimality algorithm (Turgeon, 1981) have been deployed to solve the HTS problem. DP faces dimensionality problem in multi-dimensional search space. Other algorithms also have different kinds of obstacles like fall into local optima instead of the global optima in multi-dimensional search space, low convergence rate etc.

To overcome the face trouble and time consuming problem with various constraints some of the significant soft computing approaches such as simulated annealing (Wong &Wong, 1994), evolutionary programming (Yang, Yang & Huang, 1996), genetic algorithm (Orero & Irving, 1998; Ramirez & Ontae,

2006; Gil, Bustos & Rudnick, 2003), evolutionary strategy (Werner & Verstege, 1999), fuzzy satisfying evolutionary programming (Basu, 2004), teaching learning based optimization (TLBO) (Roy, 2013), quasi oppositional TLBO (Roy, Sur & Pradhan, 2013), Quasi-oppositional gravitational search algorithm (Roy & Paul,2015), fuzzy decision-making methodology (Dhillon, Parti & Kothari, 2002), neural network (Liang, Villaseca & Renovich, 1992), artificial neural network (Liang & Hsu,1994; Shahidehpour, Fujisawa & Maeda, 1990), immune algorithm (IA) (Yong, Sunan & Wanxing, 2002; Wang, Han, Liu, Dong & Jiao, 2002; Kim, 2002), back-propagation neural network (Kulkarni, Kothari & Kothari, 2000), multi-objective evolutionary algorithms (Abido, 2003), differential evolution (DE) (Mandal & Chakraborty, 2009), modified DE (MDE) (Shu et al., 2019), hybrid multi-objective cultural algorithm (Lu, Zhou, Qin, Wang & Zhang, 2011), quantum-behaved particle swarm optimization (QPSO) (Songfeng, Chengfu & Zhengding, 2010), time-varying acceleration coefficients particle swarm optimization (TVAC-PSO) (Patwal et al., 2018) are employed. MOHTS is boosted by mutation and neighborhood characteristic in multi-objective quantum-behaved particle swarm optimization for economic environmental hydrothermal energy system scheduling (Feng, Niu, & Cheng, 2017). Remarkable outcomes were obtained by using those techniques for generating near optimal solutions. Dasgupta *et al.* implemented sine cosine algorithm on the wind based HTS system (Dasgupta *et al.* 2020) to provide less generation cost and the bus voltages, power flow through transmission line remain within the operating range with the variation of load. Chen *et al.* established a non-dominated sorting modified gravitational search algorithm (Chen et al., 2017) to solve combined economic emission dispatch provblem where contribution of renewable sources was shown by reducing the impact of emission on environment while fulfilling the energy demand. Recently, Zhang et al. (Zhang, et al. 2018) proposed multi-objective based improved particle swarm optimization to solve hydro-thermal-wind coordination scheduling integrated with large-scale electric vehicles. Very recently, Chen et al, developed probability interval optimization model (Chen et al., 2017) to solve HTS problem incorporating wind energy. Ant lion optimization technique was invented by Dubey et al. for solving HTS-wind scheduling problem during a day for 24-hour interval (Dubey et al., 2016). In this optimization technique, composite ranking index was used to handle equality and inequality constraints for optimal solution. Two new efficient optimization algorithms namely, bee colony optimization (BCO) (Zhou et al., 2016) and krill herd algorithm (KHA) (Roy et al., 2018) were successfully applied to solve HTS problem. Yin et al., proposed whale optimization algorithm (WOA) (Yin et al., 2019) to solve hydro-photovoltaic-wind power generation problem, where both cost and emission were minimized simultaneously. Market price and uncertainty-based load demand are handled by robust optimal stochastic strategy (Heris et al., 2018). Panda *et al.* successfully incorporated STATCOM in HTS system using hydro, thermal and wind units to increase the power generation efficiency and reduce the voltage fluctuation applying bacteria foraging algorithm (Panda et al., 2017).

However, the weaknesses of those methodologies are that the optimality of the solution cannot be guaranteed and even it does not give any touch about how far away these produced possible solutions are from the optimal solution. Moreover, most of the aforementioned methodologies mostly suffer from hasty convergence, slow convergence rate within refined search area, and input parameters dependence. win

To get success from these disadvantages, an innovative optimization procedure named grey wolf optimization (GWO) is employed to resolve multi-objective HTS problem. Furthermore, the speed of the GWO algorithm is improved incorporating oppositional based learning (OBL) with the original GWO. The presentation of the proposed GWO and OGWO are compared with other famous population-based optimization methods existing in literature. Finally, strength of the projected GWO and OGWO are authenticated by numerical scrutiny. Efficient nature of GWO forces the researchers to develop its modified version like binary grey wolf optimization (Emary, Zawbaa & Hassanien, 2016), chaotic GWO (Kohali & Arora, 2018) etc.

The novelty of this chapter are as mentioned below:

1.   A novel optimization technique named GWO has been implemented to analyse HTS problems. Moreover, to enhance the convergence spped further, OBL concept is integrated with GWO.
2.   In this chapter, attention is given to successfully implement GWO and OGWO in HTS problem. Firstly, the authors have focused on cost optimization of HTS. Secondly, emission minimization has been carried out. Finally, both cost and emission are simultaneously minimized using weighted sum approach. weighted sum approach is used to bring both cost and emission in same priority level.

This research paper has been systematized like: Section 2 offers mathematical representation of the problem; the strategy of grey wolf optimization strategy (GWO) is shortened in section 3; in section 4 GWO is applied for multi-objective hydro-thermal scheduling problem; section 5 deals with oppositional based GWO (OGWO) by incorporating the concept of oppositional based learning. Simulation results of the multi-objective hydrothermal scheduling is configureured and the enlisted in section 6; and section 7 represents conclusion of this paper. Finally, future scope of work is furnished in section 8.

2. MATHEMATICAL REPRESENTATION OF THE PROBLEM

To achieve minimum production cost in multi-objective hydrothermal scheduling problem for the short range scheduling (1 week or 1 day) comprises the hour – by- hour arrangement of total generation in the system for the specified time period. The load, net head, the reservoir inflows, unit availabilities for scheduling each interval are presumed to be same for each interval of the hydro plant where spillover of water, water travel time, and evaporation are neglected. Thermal constraints like ramp rate, load power balance, real power generation limit and prohibited operating zones are also included. The fuel cost of the hydro generating units is ignored when measure up to the thermal units. The mentioned problem is predictable to reduce thermal fuel cost to use the maximum availability of hydro resource. For MOHTS, environmental awareness is considered with the cost minimization of the HTS.

2.1 Objective Function

Reduction of cost is prime objective of the HTS. With T number of thermal units and H hydro units over t time subintervals is numerically described as follows:

$$\text{Minimize FC} = \sum_{i=1}^{T} \sum_{t=1}^{TTI} F_{it}\left(Pg_{it}\right) = \sum_{i=1}^{T} \sum_{t=1}^{TTI} \left(a_i Pg_{it}^2 + b_i Pg_{it} + c_i\right) \tag{1}$$

The effect of valve-point loading effect may be reflected with multi-valve turbines by addition of the sinusoidal effect to the quadratic cost function.

Hence, the mathematical equation (1) is rewrite as like below:

$$\text{Minimize } FC = \sum_{i=1}^{T} \sum_{t=1}^{TTI} \left(a_i Pg_{it}^2 + b_i Pg_{it} + c_i + \left| d_i \times \sin\{ e_i \times (Pg_i^{\min} - Pg_{it}) \} \right| \right) \tag{2}$$

where a_i, b_i, c_i, d_i, and e_i are the cost coefficient of the ith generating unit; Pg_{it} and $Pg_i^{\min}$ are the operating power and minimum active power of the ith generating unit, respectively.

The quantity of emission is not imitated in the mentioned cost calculation part. The emission production can be articulated as a summation of an exponential and a quadratic function (Abido, 2003; Lu et al. 2011; Mandal & Chakraborty, 2009; Kulkarni, Kothari & Kothari, 2000).

Representation of the numerical equation of the emission scheduling is described by (3).

$$EM(Pg_{it}) = \sum_{i=1}^{T} \sum_{t=1}^{TTI} [\alpha_i (Pg_{it}^2) + \beta_i Pg_{it} + \gamma_i + \eta_i \exp(\delta_i Pg_{it})] \tag{3}$$

where β_i, α_i, γ_i, η_i, and δ_i are the emission coefficient of the ith generating unit; Pg_{it} is the operating power of the ith generating unit, respectively.

To check the algorithm's superiority and advantages under multi-objective environment, both emission and cost are simultaneously optimized in this article. In this research work, the multi-objective HTS problem is handled by changing fitness function into a single objective function using penalty factor approach.

$$\text{Minimize } FCE = \sum_{i=1}^{T} \sum_{t=1}^{TTI} [FC_{it}(Pg_{it}^2) + h \times EM(Pg_{it})], \tag{4}$$

where h represents the penalty factor.

2.2 Active Power Balance

Demand and supply is a very important issue in all aspect of real world existence. Entire power generation from thermal and hydro unit essentially equal to the sum of power demand and loss of power at that particular time, here that time represents by t.

Hence, active power balance can be represented by:

$$\sum_{i=1}^{T} Pg_{it} + \sum_{j=1}^{H} P_{hjt} = DT_t + L_t \tag{5}$$

2.3 Hydropower Generation Characteristics

Typically in short-term scheduling, water head is acknowledged constant in case of enormous volume reservoirs. The generated power from hydro unit is a function of reservoir storage volume, water discharge rate etc., which can be described as below:

$$P_{hjt} = C_{1j}(V_{hjt}^2) + C_{2j}(Q_{hjt}^2) + C_{3j}(V_{hjt})(Q_{hjt}) + C_{4j}(V_{hjt}) + C_{5j}(Q_{hjt}) + C_{6j} \tag{6}$$

2.4 Constraints for the Hydro and Thermal Power Generation Unit

2.4.1 Power Generation Limit

At the time of power generation from generating units irrespective of hydro or thermal unit, must lie in between a specific range.

2.4.1.1 Hydro Generator Constraint

The generating limits of jth hydro unit lies in between its superior and inferior bounds.

$$P_{hj}^{min} \le P_{hjt} \le P_{hj}^{max} \tag{7}$$

2.4.1.2 Thermal Generator Constraint

Thermal generators have the upper and lower operational limit bounds so that it lies in between given boundaries:

$$Pg_i^{min} \le Pg_{it} \le Pg_i^{max} \tag{8}$$

2.5 Hydro and Thermal System Constraints

2.5.1 Hydro Generating Unit

2.5.1.1 Capacity Constraint of the Reservoir

The water storage level for j^{th} reservoir should present in between the maximum and minimum capacity of the reservoir limits.

$$V_{hj}^{min} \le V_{hjt} \le V_{hj}^{max} \tag{9}$$

2.5.1.2 Hydro Plant Discharge Rate Constraints

The physical restriction of the water discharge rate of turbines presents in between its two (minimum and maximum) operating limits, as expressed below:

$$Q_{hj}^{min} \le Q_{hjt} \le Q_{hj}^{max} \tag{10}$$

$$Q_{hjt} = Q_{hj}^{min} + rand\left(Q_{hj}^{max} - Q_{hj}^{min}\right) \tag{11}$$

2.5.1.3 Coupling Constraint

Midterm scheduling process sets the terminal reservoir volumes V_{hj}^0 and V_{hj}^t are formerly. Coupling constraints represents the amount of total accessible water is entirely used.

$$V_{hj}^{ini} = V_{hj}^0 \tag{12}$$

$$V_{hj}^{fin} = V_{hj}^t \tag{13}$$

2.5.1.4 Water Dynamic Balance

Water dynamic balance constraint is measured by the water transportation delay between reservoirs. Net inflow, net outflow during the present time intermission, storage during earlier intermission, flow balance calculation of the with the storage, is measured by (14).

$$V_{hjt} = V_{hj,t-1} + I_{hjt} - Q_{hjt} - S_{hjt} + \sum_{w=1}^{Up}\left(Q_{hw,t-\tau_{wj}} + S_{hw,t-\tau_{wj}}\right) \tag{14}$$

2.5.1.5 Spillage

The maximum discharge limits form the reservoir through the turbine exceeds and spillage takes place. During time t water spilled from the reservoir is expressed as below:

If $Q_{hjt} > x_{hjt}$

$$V_{hjt} = Q_{hjt} - x_{hjt} \tag{15}$$

Else

$$V_{hjt} = 0 \tag{16}$$

2.5.2 Thermal Generator Constraints

2.5.2.1 Ramp Rate Limits

Electric services are essential to find the optimum schedules for time variation. In practical the unit output cannot be accustomed immediately when load changes. Due to implementation of shaft bearing and other factors the operating range is controlled by ramp-rate. DR_{it} and UR_{it} represent down and upper operating limit. Ramp rate limits can be described as:

$$\max\left(Pg_i^{min}, Pg_{it}^0 - DR_{it}\right) \le Pg_{it} \le \min\left(Pg_i^{max}, Pg_{it}^0 + UR_{it}\right) \tag{17}$$

2.5.2.2 Prohibited Operating Zones

Due to steam valve, thermal generating units are not capable to operate in specified operating zone. This is known as prohibited operating zone and can be expressed in (18).

$$Pg_i^{\min} \leq Pg_{it} \leq Pg_{i,poz_{y-1}}^{l}$$

$$Pg_{i,poz_{y-1}}^{u} \leq Pg_{it} \leq Pg_{i,poz_y}^{l} \tag{18}$$

$$Pg_{i,y}^{u} \leq Pg_{it} \leq Pg_i^{\max}$$

Above equations are applicable, if number of prohibited zone is more than 2.

If y=1, then

$$Pg_i^{\min} \leq Pg_{it} \leq Pg_{i,poz_y}^{l} \tag{19}$$

$$Pg_{i,poz_y}^{u} \leq Pg_{it} \leq Pg_i^{\max}$$

3. GREY WOLF OPTIMIZATION

Nature gives us immense inspiration to develop solution approaches for different kinds of problem. Based on the hunting approach and leadership hierarchy of the grey wolf individuals, GWO algorithm is proposed by Mirjalili et al. in 2014 (Mirjalili, Mirjalili, & Lewis, 2014). The grey wolf normally lives in pack (generally 5- 12 individuals). Grey wolfs can be categorized into four definite groups, like alpha, beta, delta and omega (Mirjalili, Mirjalili, & Lewis, 2014; Muro, Escobedo et al., 2011) on the basis of the behaviour and responsibilities. To look for a prey, a particular number of grey wolves move in a multi-dimensional search space. The grey wolf moves to the superior location to get the prey. The aim of this algorithm is reaching to the prey in optimal manner. The effort of each wolf is prejudiced by three processes namely,

1. Searching and encircling prey (exploration)
2. Hunting
3. Attacking prey(exploitation)

3.1 Searching and Encircling Prey

Different types of searching agents like alpha, beta, delta grey wolves deviate from each grey wolf for searching the prey. This express the exploration capability of the metaheuristic optimization algorithm.

After searching prey, the grey wolves try to encircle the prey. This concept can be expressed by the following equation proposed by (Mirjalili, Mirjalili, & Lewis, 2014):

$$\vec{EB} = \left| \vec{G} \cdot \vec{P}(n) - \vec{S}(n) \right| \tag{20}$$

$$\vec{S}(n+1) = \vec{P}(n) - \vec{H} \cdot \vec{EB} \tag{21}$$

$\vec{G}, \vec{H}$ can be expressed as below:

$$\vec{G} = 2\vec{y} \tag{22}$$

$$\vec{H} = 2 \times \vec{g} \times \vec{z} - \vec{g} \tag{23}$$

3.2 Hunting

Hunting characteristic is supervised by alpha wolf and other wolves (beta and delta wolf). We assume that the alpha, beta, and delta wolf provide the best, the second best and the third best outcomes consequently. Mathematically mimic the hunting behavior of grey wolves are represented by:

$$\vec{EB}_\alpha = \left| \vec{G}_\alpha \cdot \vec{P}_\alpha(n) - \vec{S}_\alpha(n) \right| \tag{24}$$

$$\vec{S}_1 = \vec{S}_\alpha(n) - \vec{H}_1 \cdot \left(\vec{E}_\alpha \right) \tag{25}$$

$$\vec{EB}_\beta = \left| \vec{G}_\beta \cdot \vec{P}_\beta(n) - \vec{S}_\beta(n) \right| \tag{26}$$

$$\vec{S}_2 = \vec{S}_\beta(n) - \vec{H}_2 \cdot \left(\vec{E}_\beta \right) \tag{27}$$

$$\vec{EB}_\gamma = \left| \vec{G}_\gamma \cdot \vec{P}_\gamma(n) - \vec{S}_\gamma(n) \right| \tag{28}$$

$$\vec{S}_3 = \vec{S}_\gamma(n) - \vec{H}_3 \cdot \left(\vec{E}_\gamma \right) \tag{29}$$

$$\vec{S}(n+1) = \frac{\vec{S}_1 + \vec{S}_2 + \vec{S}_3}{3} \tag{30}$$

Using the above values, position of the grey wolves is modified.

3.3. Attacking Prey (Exploitation)

We decrease the value of g in the above equations to modify the position of search agent. The prey stops moving then the grey wolves attack the prey.

4. APPLICATION OF GWO FOR MOHTS

In GWO search agents or grey wolves move through a multidimensional search space for searching a prey. Here, the position of search agents is measured as dissimilar location variables and distances of search agents and prey is the fitness value of the objective function. Three candidate solutions i.e. eqs. (25, 27, 29) are measured among which (25) is considered the best solution. This optimization methodology of the projected explanation for resolving the MOHTS is defined here.

Step 1: Input data is taken for HTS problem considering emission.
Step 2: Initial and final iteration number is declared.
Step 3: Different constraints for GWO is incorporated.
Step 4: By the equation (11) the rate of water discharge for hydro generators are randomly scheduled for each time interval but last hour discharge is calculated by difference of its boundary values. Infeasible solutions are discarded and other feasible solutions are repeatedly generated.
Step 5: Water discharge helps to calculate the volume of each reservoir at each hour using (14). The infeasible solutions are discarded others are accepted. Compute the hydro generation schedule of all the hydro generation plants over the scheduled time spans using (6).
Step 6: Equation (5) evaluate the power generation in all the intervals to create the initial population. The ith population string for the initial position of the ith search agent or i^{th} grey wolf represents by Pi.

$$Pi = \begin{bmatrix} QD_{h11,k}, & QD_{h21,k}, & \cdots & QD_{hH1,k}, & Pg_{11,k}, & Pg_{21,k}, & \cdots & Pg_{N1,k} \\ QD_{h12,k}, & QD_{h22,k}, & \cdots & QD_{hH2,k}, & Pg_{12,k}, & Pg_{22,k}, & \cdots & Pg_{N2,k} \\ \vdots & \vdots & \vdots & \vdots & \vdots & \vdots & \vdots & \vdots \\ QD_{h1DT,k}, & QD_{h2DT,k}, & \cdots & QD_{hHDT,k}, & Pg_{1DT,k}, & Pg_{2DT,k}, & \cdots & Pg_{NDT,k} \end{bmatrix} \quad (31)$$

The initial population string can be represented by P. Depending on the population size, the initial population string is represented as $P=[P_1,P_2,...,P_k...,P_p]$.

Step 7: The fitness value for the initial position of grey wolves of the population set is evaluated by (1-4).
Step 8: Using equations (20-29), calculation is done for the mentioned 3 processes like searching prey, hunting and attacking prey.
Step 9: Using equation (30), location of the grey wolves are updated. The modified position of each search agent or grey wolf indicates a solution incorporates the water discharge rate for (TTI-1) time span and (T-1) number of thermal generators. Then check whether equality constraints are satisfied

or not. If any values exceed the maximum level, then the maximum value is considered. Likewise, if the value is less than the minimum level, it is made equal to minimum value.

Step 10: The water discharge rate for last (TTI) time interval and thermal generation for last (T) thermal plant is also modernized. The infeasible solutions are discarded others are accepted.

Step 11: Updated distance of search agents and prey (fitness value of each currently generated feasible solution) are calculated.

Step 12: Go to step 4 until the predefined number of iterations are done or no significant updated position is recognized from search agent and prey.

Step 13: Print the best solution set (alpha wolf) from the population.

5. OPPOSITIONAL BASED LEARNING

Opposition based learning (OBL) tries to accelerate convergence speed as an optimization tool. Tizhoosh (Tizhoosh, 2005) introduces this concept for improvement in solution. Here, current population and opposite population are created for the similar generation to get improved candidate solution of a given problem. This idea applies on various metaheuristics to increase the convergence speed. Let consider real number $W(W \in w1, w2)$. The opposite number W^0 can be expressed as:

$$W^0 = w2 + w1 - W \tag{32}$$

This follow the concept of the image of the mirror. Most of the cases, opposition based learning concept can improve performance of any evolutionary algorithm.

5.1 Oppositional Grey Wolf Optimization (OGWO)

In our research work, oppositional based idea is incorporated to GWO algorithm to improvement in the performance of the GWO. Jumping rate is present with our complex and multi-dimensional problem.

5.1.1 Brief Description of the OGWO

OGWO is the optimization tool for resolving different kinds of mathematical problem. This metaheuristic algorithm efficiently gives superior results. The steps of OGWO are as under:

Step 1: In the search space randomly initialize the position of search agents. Iteration numbers and population size (number of wolves) are initiated.

Step 2: Calculation of fitness value of each search agent is done.

Step 3: Using opposite points, opposite population is produced and the fitness of every individual population is calculated.

Step 4: From the combined section of current and its opposite population fittest solutions are selected. Sorting is made from current and opposite population considering fitness value.

Step 5: The best(α), the second best (β) and the third best (δ) solutions are recognized for the different kinds of grey wolves (α, β and δ) respectively.

Step 6: Using (24-30) modify the positions of the search agents.

Step 7: The opposite population is fashioned using jumping rate from the current population.
Step 8: From the combination of present and its opposite population, fittest solution is suggested.
Step 9: Until reaching to the maximum iteration, step 5 to step 9 is repeated.
Step 10: Finally, best solution comparing with others is considered as output.

The Flow chart of the short-term hydro-thermal scheduling using GWO and OGWO are listed in Figure 1.

6. SIMULATION RESULTS

Our research work deals with multi-chain cascade of 4-hydro and 3-thermal units (Basu, 2004) to prove efficiency of our research work. A newly developed meta-heuristic approach named GWO and incorporation of oppositional concept to GWO gives us very efficient and effective result to solve different kind of problems. Our proposed GWO and OGWO are applied for multi-objective HTS. Here, one hour time interval is scheduled for every 24 hours for the model. Both single and multi-objective case studies give very acceptable results. Multi-objective HTS problem is solved by GWO and OGWO on Matlab 7.5 with 2.0 GHz speed and 1 GB RAM.

As the presentation of any meta-heuristics methods mostly depends on its input parameters, the projected methods are applied on the Test system (multi chain cascade 4-hydro and 3-thermal power system) for cost minimization for different combination of input parameters of these algorithms before selecting their optimal input parameters. It is observed from simulation study that the least fitness value is gained with $\vec{b} = 0.6$ and jumping rate (j) of 0.3. Thus, these values of input parameters are chosen as input parameters to perform the entire simulation study. 100 is set as maximum iteration number and population size is fixed to 50 for multi-objective HTS problem.

Our GWO and OGWO has been applied on descriptive test system with different cases to acquire the simulation results for 24 h on hourly basis considering all the reservoirs starting to fill up at the rainy season.

6.1 Case 1 (Cost Minimization)

Our proposed methods give the better performance in cost optimization. To check the performance of the probable GWO and OGWO algorithms, they are applied to the mentioned test system. The optimal discharges and hydro generation during 24-hour time horizon for cost minimization using GWO is exhibited in Figures 2 and 3, respectively. The optimal hourly thermal generation and thermal cost and emission acquired by the projected GWO and OGWO algorithms are established in Tables 1 and 2. The optimal discharges and hydro generation achieved by OGWO approach in 24-hour time span are illustrated in Figures 4 and 5, respectively. For legitimacy, these results are also compared with existing methods like differential evolution (Mandal & Chakraborty, 2009), cultural algorithm (Lu, Zhou, Qin, Wang, & Zhang, 2011), SOHPSO_TVAC (Mandal et al. 2012), MHDE (Lakshminarasimman, 2008), IQPSO (Sun et al. 2010), CSA (Swain et al., 2011), PSO (Yu et al., 2007), QADEVT (Lu et al., 2010), MDE (Lakshminarasimman, 2006), IPSO (Hota et al., 2009) and the comparative outputs are shown in the Table 3.

Figure 1. Flow chart of the short term hydro thermal scheduling using GWO and OGWO

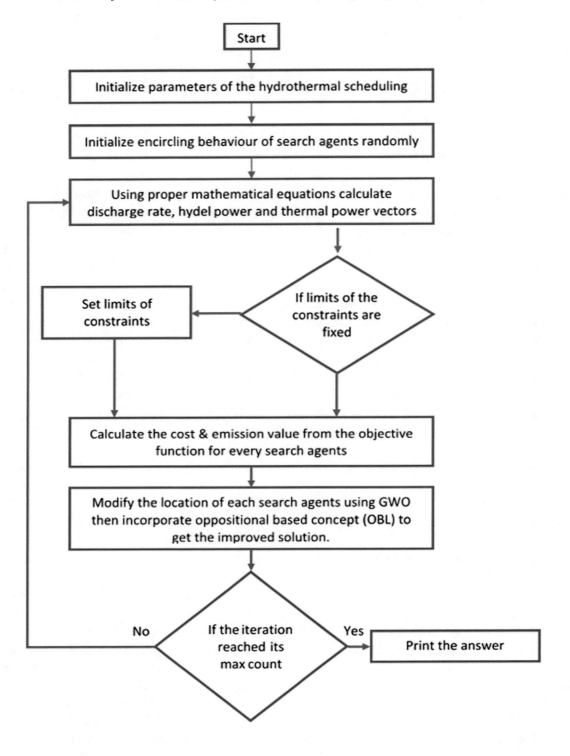

Figure 2. Optimal discharges (×10⁴ m³) during 24 hours for cost minimization using GWO

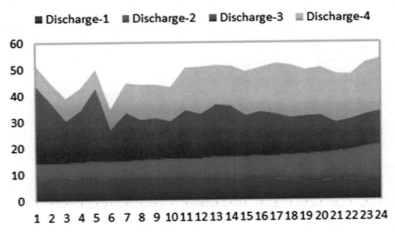

Figure 3. Hydro generation (MW) during 24 hours for cost minimization using GWO

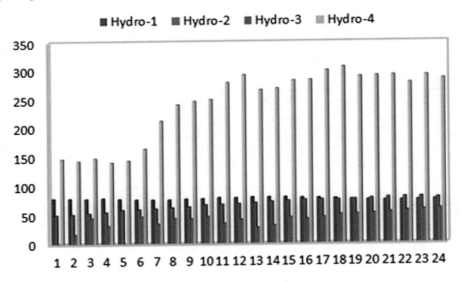

The performance of the OGWO shows efficient outcomes comparing with the other algorithms present in the literature. It may also be noted that each iteration of the OGWO method requires less time as compared to original GWO and other approaches. As a result, the CPU time for simulation of the OGWO method is 28 sec., whereas GWO method is 36 sec, DE method is 72.96 sec, SOHPSO_TVAC method is 112 sec, CSA approach is 109.12 sec, PSO approach is 123.52 sec. MDE approach is 125 sec, IPSO approach is 43.66 sec. From the literature, we have got idea that our proposed methods are getter. Among OGWO and GWO approaches, performance of OGWO is better.

Water volume of the four hydro-plants during 24-hour time horizon obtained using the proposed method is illustrated in Figure 6. The convergence property of the hydrothermal scheduling for the fitness function is given in Figure 7. For both GWO and OGWO, the fitness function converges efficiently to the optimum value without any unexpected oscillations. Answers effectively converges to the optimality without any unexpected interference.

Table 1. Optimal thermal generation, cost and emission during 24 h for cost minimization using GWO algorithm

Hour	Thermal Generation (MW)			Hydro Generation (MW)	Cost ($)	Emission (lb)
	G_1	G_2	G_3			
1	103.25	142.31	229.52	274.93	711.02	549.73
2	32.99	138.58	319.28	289.14	973.42	1132.51
3	21.76	125.87	229.54	322.84	711.19	549.84
4	171.03	123.83	50.01	305.13	258.83	33.31
5	36.03	125.53	229.69	278.75	712.65	550.61
6	102.67	211.04	139.79	346.50	473.04	190.87
7	41.88	295.76	229.53	382.84	711.08	549.78
8	156.36	292.02	139.75	421.86	472.82	190.78
9	132.11	209.21	319.27	429.413	973.45	1132.39
10	21.89	298.63	319.29	440.19	973.49	1132.56
11	103.66	216.71	319.31	460.32	973.66	1132.70
12	139.52	210.88	319.29	480.31	973.46	1132.54
13	142.33	294.77	229.50	443.41	711.08	549.65
14	57.28	292.05	229.52	451.1494	711.02	549.75
15	95.80	294.20	139.74	480.27	472.87	190.75
16	136.84	125.05	319.29	478.84	973.47	1132.54
17	22.28	209.72	319.32	498.68	973.85	1132.85
18	172.98	209.77	229.51	507.74	711.06	549.68
19	138.87	210.18	229.54	491.41	711.23	549.86
20	31.32	294.97	229.52	494.20	711.05	549.76
21	101.27	171.05	139.75	497.9	472.81	190.79
22	22.49	210.36	139.77	487.39	472.88	190.82
23	96.42	200.34	50.00	503.241	258.77	33.31
24	23.87	49.37	229.58	497.18	711.62	550.06
Cost ($/day)					42587	
Emission (lb/day)					23668	

6.2 Case 2 (Emission Minimization)

In order to explore the superiority of the proposed GWO and OGWO algorithms, the presence of the emission is also considered and the simulation result with emission optimization is enlisted in Tables 4-5. The optimal discharges and hydro generation during 24-hour time horizon for emission minimization using GWO are exhibited in Figures 8 and 9, respectively. The optimal discharges and hydro generation achieved by OGWO approach in 24-hour time span for emission minimization are illustrated in Figures 10 and 11, respectively. Table 6 compares statistical results and simulation time obtained using OGWO and GWO approaches and the other optimization techniques like DE (Mandal et al., 2009), CA (Lu et

Table 2. Optimal thermal generation, cost and emission during 24 h for cost minimization using OGWO algorithm

Hour	Thermal Generation (MW)			Hydro Generation (MW)	Cost ($)	Emission (lb)
	G_1	G_2	G_3			
1	107.18	40.48	322.16	280.17	1624.79	1229.62
2	175.00	206.95	140.10	257.94	1764.85	630.30
3	175.00	124.97	139.65	260.38	1526.09	448.34
4	35.03	126.83	230.60	257.54	1438.47	683.49
5	28.75	124.97	230.22	286.06	1367.52	682.96
6	175.00	180.27	139.60	305.13	1830.90	556.32
7	95.15	294.30	139.95	420.61	1755.97	852.97
8	20.99	211.79	319.91	457.32	1806.99	1468.72
9	174.67	125.97	319.29	470.07	2036.38	1391.05
10	175.00	209.92	227.92	467.16	1996.38	988.97
11	175.00	212.31	229.05	483.64	2014.01	1002.12
12	175.00	280.22	231.44	463.34	2297.30	1279.67
13	103.57	293.45	232.86	480.12	2011.17	1230.99
14	101.04	127.63	318.08	483.25	1798.35	1259.68
15	175.00	209.92	140.28	484.80	1756.33	639.76
16	175.00	209.92	230.15	444.93	1995.79	1000.48
17	99.12	210.21	226.42	514.24	1754.71	855.54
18	174.72	212.24	229.69	503.35	2013.79	1004.49
19	104.09	215.02	231.32	519.57	1804.83	899.94
20	175.00	126.28	231.82	516.91	1798.29	821.48
21	175.00	124.97	140.08	469.95	1528.63	449.58
22	31.44	124.97	228.07	475.51	1388.69	669.96
23	20.90	124.97	228.08	476.05	1300.28	678.31
24	102.28	124.97	135.50	437.25	1283.32	312.66
Cost ($/day)					42587	
Emission (lb/day)					23668	

al., 2011), SOHPSO_TVAC (Mandal et al. 2012), PSO (Yu et al., 2007), QADEVT (Lu et al., 2010), IQPSO (Sun et al. 2010) methods. The results of Table 6 further establish the superiority of OGWO over GWO, DE (Mandal et al., 2009), CA (Lu et al., 2011), SOHPSO_TVAC (Mandal et al. 2012), PSO (Yu et al., 2007), QADEVT (Lu et al., 2010), IQPSO (Sun et al. 2010) in terms of minimum fitness value and computational time. This table also exhibits the comparison among best, mean and worst emission. It may be concluded that the proposed OGWO give satisfactory and superior statistical results compared to others. Water volume of the four hydro-plants during 24-hour time horizon obtained via the proposed method for this case is illustrated in Figure 12. The behavior for the emission optimization can be observed in the Figure 13 which shows the variation of the emission with iteration numbers for the proposed OGWO and GWO approaches.

Figure 4. Optimal discharges (×10⁴ m³) during 24 hours for cost minimization using OGWO

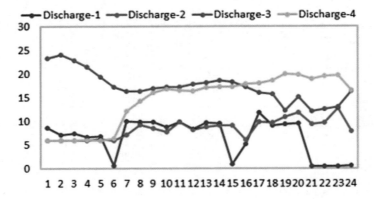

Figure 5. hydro generation (MW) during 24 hours for cost minimization using OGWO

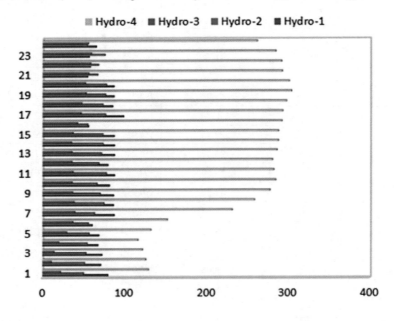

Figure 6. Volume (m³) during 24 hours for cost minimization using OGWO

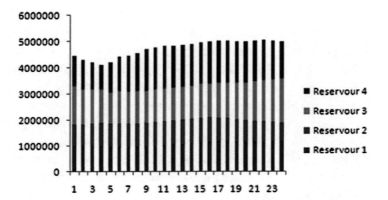

Table 3. Comparison of optimal costs obtained by different algorithms

Algorithms	Best Cost ($/day)	Worst Cost ($/day)	Mean Cost ($/day)	Computational Time (S)
DE (Mandal et al., 2009)	43500.0000	-	-	72.96
CA (Lu et al., 2011)	43278.0000	-	-	-
SOHPSO_TVAC (Mandal et al. 2012)	41983	-	-	112
MHDE (Lakshminarasimman, 2008)	42337	-	-	-
IQPSO (Sun et al. 2010)	42359.00	-	-	-
CSA (Swain et al., 2011)	42440.574	-	-	109.12
PSO (Yu et al., 2007)	42,474	-	-	123.52
QADEVT (Lu et al., 2010)	42,587	-	-	-
MDE (Lakshminarasimman, 2006)	42611	-	-	125
IPSO (Hota et al., 2009)	44321.236	-	-	43.66
GWO	42587	42906	42713	36
OGWO	41894	41906	41897	28

NA (or -) means the related result is not available in the respective reference

Figure 7. Cost convergence using OGWO and GWO

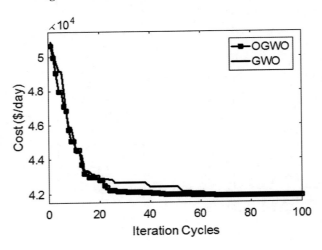

6.3 Case 3 (Combined Cost and Emission Minimization)

Finally, in our research work, objectives like cost and emission are concurrently minimized our proposed algorithms. Here, proposed GWO and OGWO are established in terms of solution quality considering cost and emission concurrently. The simulation results with CEED optimization for GWO and OGWO are enlisted in Tables 7-8. The optimal discharges and hydro generation during 24-hour time horizon for combined cost and emission minimization using GWO are exhibited in Figures 14 and 15, respectively. The optimal discharges and hydro generation achieved by OGWO approach in 24-hour time span for combined cost and emission minimization are illustrated in Figures 16 and 17, respectively. Table

Table 4. Optimal thermal generation, cost and emission during 24 h for cost minimization using GWO algorithm

Hour	Thermal Generation (MW)			Hydro Generation (MW)	Cost ($)	Emission (lb)
	G_1	G_2	G_3			
1	173.72	185.74	115.61	262.67	523.88	158.58
2	174.80	189.53	126.51	284.99	512.57	165.86
3	154.85	159.91	62.41	276.85	573.29	113.35
4	131.01	127.97	85.88	305.82	528.44	71.60
5	118.53	110.80	161.93	367.41	457.33	55.23
6	170.10	180.65	102.74	325.34	538.57	148.63
7	174.99	230.01	162.17	380.22	690.38	270.14
8	174.87	221.66	191.61	456.52	629.68	243.59
9	174.87	293.06	192.65	389.27	743.07	566.85
10	174.98	261.92	202.92	446.95	803.62	391.98
11	174.88	262.80	202.00	465.36	803.50	395.49
12	174.97	276.76	217.96	485.52	775.44	466.74
13	174.98	254.71	236.91	491.75	797.43	360.19
14	175.00	231.75	172.11	456.91	701.15	275.58
15	174.99	226.21	128.54	447.41	665.31	258.44
16	174.94	251.36	154.87	448.55	790.22	346.41
17	174.83	230.52	145.97	479.36	693.94	271.90
18	174.87	257.89	179.50	495.27	801.87	374.27
19	174.96	233.47	170.17	493.61	711.91	281.34
20	174.99	228.11	152.72	483.94	677.20	263.83
21	152.69	156.94	102.46	494.23	574.46	108.72
22	136.82	135.84	99.95	496.42	551.41	80.66
23	135.28	133.45	78.04	492.05	545.41	77.90
24	120.56	113.56	68.70	490.65	471.06	57.70
Total Cost ($/day)					48693	
Emission (lb/day)					16428	

9 exemplifies the results in terms of thermal generation, cost, emission and simulation time obtained using various discussed algorithms. It is evidently seen that the proposed OGWO and GWO methods yield satisfactory outcome in terms of fuel cost and the amount of emission. Furthermore, to judge the superiority, the results of the proposed are compared with the results obtained by other popular methods like differential evolution (Mandal & Chakraborty, 2009), fuzzy satisfying evolutionary programming

Table 5. Optimal thermal generation, cost and emission during 24 h for emission minimization using OGWO algorithm

Hour	Thermal Generation (MW)			Hydro Generation (MW)	Cost ($)	Emission (lb)
	G_1	G_2	G_3			
1	162.01	162.28	123.31	302.39	1892.72	440.38
2	173.76	197.83	133.27	275.14	1827.01	581.72
3	156.81	145.88	83.80	313.50	1782.63	318.86
4	137.48	140.86	91.90	279.76	1735.99	285.97
5	143.05	160.61	124.95	241.40	1862.62	402.40
6	174.25	190.24	125.37	310.14	1879.03	541.74
7	174.90	227.74	146.57	400.78	1975.44	715.77
8	171.96	251.81	188.39	397.85	2379.43	946.35
9	174.86	272.30	206.60	436.24	2377.51	1120.50
10	174.38	273.84	198.09	433.69	2387.53	1088.46
11	173.71	270.69	187.35	468.25	2386.53	1027.20
12	174.62	273.38	198.00	504.00	2387.78	1086.58
13	172.90	262.56	188.16	486.39	2394.27	992.47
14	173.18	233.73	162.37	460.73	2160.61	783.25
15	174.86	227.25	156.12	451.77	2057.03	744.02
16	172.38	248.92	168.24	470.46	2285.47	858.77
17	174.24	227.86	167.88	480.01	2152.29	784.68
18	173.91	253.88	182.00	510.21	2363.92	934.11
19	171.83	233.06	162.73	502.38	2161.94	778.69
20	174.75	219.58	153.26	502.41	1966.91	708.90
21	158.29	163.41	112.97	475.33	1926.38	410.49
22	138.32	156.04	96.24	469.40	1854.69	323.40
23	137.36	143.42	94.13	475.09	1762.12	294.10
24	126.28	118.57	86.17	468.99	1537.38	225.00
Cost ($/day)					49497	
Emission (lb/day)					16394	

(Basu, 2004), quantum-behaved particle swarm optimization (Songfeng, Chengfu & Zhengding, 2010), cultural algorithm (Lu, Zhou, Qin, Wang, &Zhang, 2011), SOHPSO_TVAC (Mandal et al. 2012), MHDE (Lakshminarasimman, 2008), PSO (Yu et al., 2007), QADEVT (Lu et al., 2010) and IQPSO (Sun et al. 2010) and the comparative results are illustrated in Table 9. The results clearly exhibit that the proposed OGWO method not only minimizes the cost and emission but also effectively reduce the computational time as compared to other discussed algorithms including original GWO approach. The water storage of the four hydro-plants during 24-hour time horizon obtained using the proposed OGWO method for this case is illustrated in Figure 18.

Table 6. Comparison of optimal emission obtained by different algorithms

Algorithms	Best Cost ($/day)	Worst Cost ($/day)	Mean Cost ($/day)	Computational Time (S)
DE (Mandal et al., 2009)	18257.0000	-	-	72.74
CA (Lu et al., 2011)	17019.0000	-	-	NA
SOHPSO_TVAC (Mandal et al. 2012)	16803	-	-	112.56
PSO (Yu et al., 2007)	16928	-	-	124.66
QADEVT (Lu et al., 2010)	17535	-	-	-
IQPSO (Sun et al. 2010)	17767	-	-	-
GWO	16428	16513	16453	36
OGWO	16394	16398	16395	29

NA means the related result is not available in the respective reference

Figure 8. Optimal discharges (×10⁴ m³) during 24 hours for emission minimization using GWO

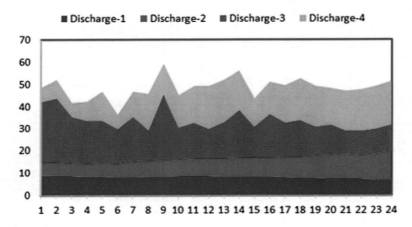

Figure 9. Hydro generation (MW) during 24 hours for emission minimization using GWO

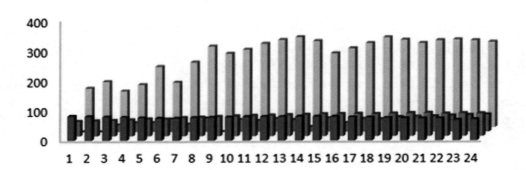

Figure 10. Optimal discharges (×10⁴ m³) during 24 hours for emission minimization using OGWO

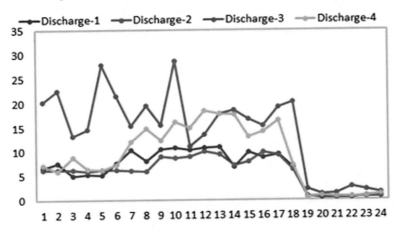

Figure 11. Hydro generation (MW) during 24 hours for emission minimization using OGWO

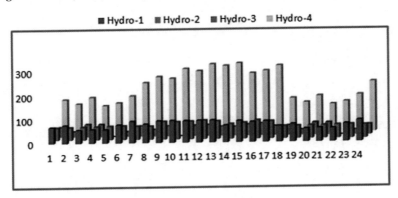

Figure 12. Volume (m³) during 24 hours for emission minimization using OGWO

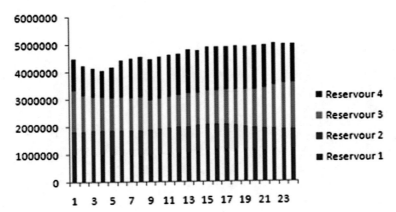

Figure 13. Emission convergence using OGWO and GWO

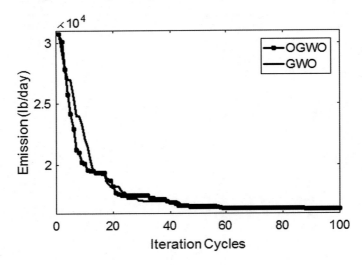

Figure 14. The optimal discharges (×10⁴ m³) during 24 hours for CEED using GWO

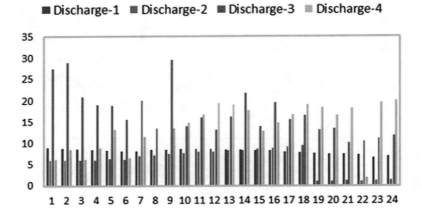

Figure 15. Hydrop generation (MW) during 24 hours for CEED using GWO

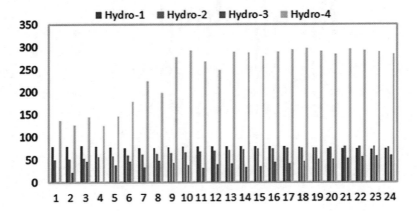

Table 7. Optimal thermal generation, cost and emission during 24 h for combined cost and emission minimization using GWO

Hour	Thermal Generation (MW)			Hydro Generation (MW)	Cost ($)	Emission (lb)
	G₁	G₂	G₃			
1	141.48	203.99	129.61	264.48	475.57	191.64
2	162.56	200.62	127.67	277.63	475.30	189.20
3	114.83	121.14	141.19	323.02	484.65	194.38
4	127.23	124.72	92.92	258.51	473.75	190.19
5	98.08	128.27	164.90	318.87	535.51	150.77
6	170.66	128.85	153.99	361.30	475.32	189.19
7	166.81	248.46	151.90	395.03	473.013	190.66
8	173.78	220.22	194.14	385.10	724.60	556.95
9	174.83	223.36	262.40	460.86	724.99	557.16
10	175.00	290.35	174.46	474.45	476.99	192.06
11	17310	251.05	215.53	446.34	711.05	549.69
12	174.57	296.05	199.06	436.82	835.69	619.50
13	174.73	222.78	269.10	481.15	728.89	559.24
14	126.94	291.18	160.72	472.05	473.42	190.99
15	174.34	211.23	144.17	468.75	619.07	239.47
16	141.96	289.20	150.02	488.91	474.47	191.30
17	168.57	210.28	172.47	490.29	777.12	329.43
18	173.93	226.59	211.75	497.08	740.54	513.60
19	173.36	261.87	143.37	494.46	478.08	192.39
20	173.39	210.58	171.84	487.71	767.29	319.63
21	127.72	139.91	144.45	502.85	473.87	190.11
22	102.70	124.06	145.86	500.86	505.39	170.38
23	99.42	122.77	124.57	498.73	519.11	161.68
24	102.70	128.24	71.89	496.39	453.05	54.51
Cost ($/day)					44204	
Emission (lb/day)					16910	

7. CONCLUSION

We want make welfare of our society. That's why we are concentrate to utilize natural resources properly. Human civilization cannot survive without power, so proper utilization of electric power is very essential. We have chosen multi-objective HTS problem where power generation is scheduled in the proper way utilizing sources of the power plants. Cost and emission both the fitness function are minimized using our proposed approaches. Here, hydro and thermal generation both are considered to deliver dynamic load. We have successfully applied GWO to solve multi-objective HTS and OGWO is used to accelerate the result. Using our approaches, we are getting better results comparing with other existing results.

Table 8. Optimal thermal generation, cost and emission during 24 h for combined cost and emission minimization using OGWO

Hour	Thermal Generation (MW)			Hydro Generation (MW)	Cost ($)	Emission (lb)
	G_1	G_2	G_3			
1	175.00	155.65	139.62	279.73	1768.89	501.47
2	174.89	206.75	139.94	258.41	1764.38	628.94
3	174.83	125.02	139.84	260.33	1527.22	448.50
4	128.53	124.99	139.30	257.19	1468.77	353.70
5	123.05	124.94	139.60	282.41	1430.68	346.85
6	174.94	185.04	139.73	300.28	1826.26	568.50
7	174.94	210.01	142.16	422.90	1775.18	645.29
8	174.85	211.91	173.36	449.89	2041.42	754.12
9	175.00	216.93	228.24	469.83	2060.32	1012.48
10	174.94	210.115	228.54	466.40	1995.69	992.60
11	174.93	219.55	229.33	476.19	2079.80	1026.39
12	175.00	280.014	229.67	465.31	2280.55	1269.46
13	174.93	224.95	228.51	481.62	2130.33	1040.01
14	174.94	214.68	149.88	490.51	1891.14	683.05
15	174.97	209.98	140.42	484.62	1758.39	640.28
16	174.95	210.06	218.54	456.44	2035.56	942.34
17	175.00	214.53	140.47	520.01	1801.25	654.55
18	174.99	212.12	228.96	503.92	2012.64	1001.09
19	174.85	214.85	153.28	527.01	1923.49	694.10
20	175.00	210.34	146.92	517.74	1823.028	660.65
21	174.93	124.90	140.41	469.77	1531.31	450.22
22	124.42	125.09	139.28	471.21	1443.11	348.00
23	111.48	125.06	139.70	473.76	1340.54	333.44
24	102.75	124.87	139.58	432.82	1264.03	324.30
Cost ($/day)				42974		
Emission (lb/day)				16320		

8. FUTURE SCOPE OF WORK

Though, the projected procedures create acceptable outcomes, still there are numerous features unclut-tered for investigation in the precise area to recover the power system economy that may be measured as an forthcoming development of the current work. Some of the upcoming works are as underneath:

- Although the probable methods have the ability to explore nearby the globally optimal explana-tion, yet these algorithms may further be modified to construct possible global optimal explana-tions in sensible time.

Figure 16. Optimal discharges (×10⁴ m³) during 24 hours for CEED using OGWO

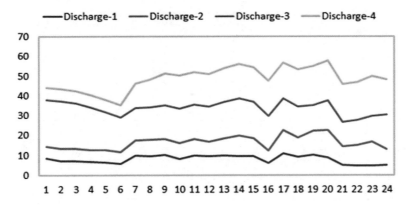

Figure 17. Hydro generation (MW) during 24 hours CEED using OGWO

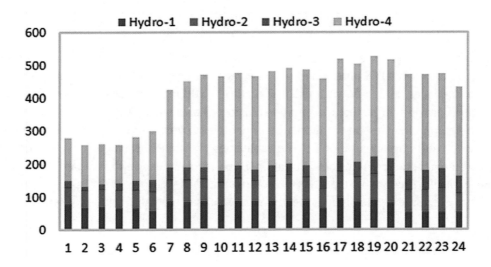

Figure 18. Volume (m³) during 24 hours for CEED using OGWO

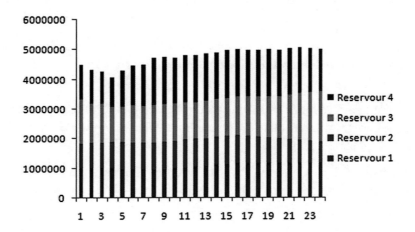

Table 9. Comparison of optimal costs obtained by different algorithms

Algorithms	Cost ($/day)	Emission (lb/day)	Computational Time (S)
DE (Mandal et al., 2009)	44914.0000	19615.0000	74.97
EP (Basu, 2004)	47906.0000	26234.0000	4582
QPSO (Songfeng et al., 2010)	44122.0000	18102.0000	-
CA (Lu et al., 2011)	44344.0000	17408.0000	-
SOHPSO_TVAC (Mandal et al. 2012)	43045	17003	120
(Lakshminarasimman, 2008)	43198	20385	-
PSO (Yu et al., 2007)	43280	17899	132.45
QADEVT (Lu et al., 2010)	43395	18324	-
IQPSO (Sun et al. 2010)	44259	18229	-
GWO	44204	16910	36
OGWO	42974	16320	30

- In this article, two advance optimization methods have been deliberated and applied for the effective outcomes of MOHTS problem of power system. However, these algorithms propose progressive consequences compared with existing methods, additional enhancement of these algorithms with hybridization will be the upcoming extension of present work.
- Developing apprehension on the reduction of ecological possessions for power generation has led to the search and implementation of renewable energy sources-based power generation. In future, wind turbine generator, solar photo voltaic, will be incorporated in the research.
- Moreover, as the predictable methods are demonstrated as well-organized optimization techniques for the projected areas, they may be recommended as talented algorithms for other problem also.

REFERENCES

Abido, M. A. (2003). Environmental/economic power dispatch using multi-objective evolutionary algorithms. *IEEE Transactions on Power Systems*, *18*(4), 1529–1537. doi:10.1109/TPWRS.2003.818693

Al-Agtash, S. (2001). Hydrothermal scheduling by augmented Lagrangian: Consideration of transmission constraints and pumped-storage units. *IEEE Transactions on Power Systems*, *16*(4), 750–756. doi:10.1109/59.962422

Basu, M. (2004). An interactive fuzzy satisfying method based on evolutionary programming technique for multi-objective short-term hydrothermal scheduling. *Electric Power Systems Research*, *69*(2-3), 277–285. doi:10.1016/j.epsr.2003.10.003

Chen, F., Zhou, J., Wang, C., Li, C., & Lu, P. (2017). A modified gravitational search algorithm based on a non-dominated sorting genetic approach for hydro-thermal-wind economic emission dispatching. *Energy*, *121*, 276-291.

Chowdhury, B. H., & Rahman, S. (1990). A review of recent advances in economic dispatch. *IEEE Transactions on Power Systems*, *5*(4), 1248–1257. doi:10.1109/59.99376

Dasgupta, K., Roy, P., & Mukherjee, V. (2020). Power flow based hydro-thermal-wind scheduling of hybrid power system using sine cosine algorithm. *Electric Power Systems Research*, 178.

Dhillon, J. S., Parti, S. C., & Kothari, D. P. (2002). Fuzzy decision-making in stochastic multi objective short-term hydrothermal scheduling. *IEE Proceedings. Generation, Transmission and Distribution*, *149*, 191–200.

Dubey, H., Pandit, M., & Panjigrahi, B. (2016). Hydro-thermal-wind scheduling employing novel ant lion optimization technique with composite ranking index. *Renewable Energy*, *99*, 18–34. doi:10.1016/j. renene.2016.06.039

Emary, E., Zawabaa, H. M., & Hassanien, A. E. (2016). Binary grey wolf optimization approaches for feature selection. *Neurocomputing*, *172*, 371–381. doi:10.1016/j.neucom.2015.06.083

Feng, Z.-K., Niu, W. J., & Cheng, C. T. (2017, July). Multi-objective quantum-behaved particle swarm optimization for economic environmental hydrothermal energy system scheduling. *Energy*, *131*(15), 165–178. doi:10.1016/j.energy.2017.05.013

Gil, E., Bustos, J., & Rudnick, H. (2003). Short-term hydrothermal generation scheduling model using a genetic algorithm. *IEEE Transactions on Power Systems*, *18*(4), 1256–1264. doi:10.1109/TP-WRS.2003.819877

Gul, E., Kang, C., & Wang, J. (2019). Multi-objective short-term integration of hydrothermal operation with wind and solar power using nonlinear programming. *Energy Procedia*, *158*, 6274–6281. doi:10.1016/j. egypro.2019.01.447

Happ, H. H. (1977). Optimal power dispatch – a comprehensive survey. *IEEE Transactions on Power Apparatus and Systems*, *96*(3), 841–854. doi:10.1109/T-PAS.1977.32397

Heris, M. Z., Ivatloo, B. M., & Asadi, S. (2018). Robust stochastic optimal short-term generation scheduling of hydrothermal systems in deregulated environment. *Journal of Energy Systems (JES)*, *2*(4), 168-179.

Hota, P. K., Barisal, A. K., & Chakrabarti, R. (2009). An improved PSO technique for short-term optimal hydrothermal scheduling. *Electric Power Systems Research*, *79*(7), 1047–1053. doi:10.1016/j. epsr.2009.01.001

Kim, D. H. (2002). Parameter tuning of fuzzy neural networks by immune algorithm, fuzzy system. *Proceedings of the 2002 IEEE International Conference*, *1*, 408–413. IEEE.

Kohali, M., & Arora, S. (2018). Chaotic grey wolf optimization algorithm for constrained optimization problems. *Journal of Computational Design and Engineering*, *5*(4), 458–472. doi:10.1016/j. jcde.2017.02.005

Kulkarni, P. S., Kothari, A. G., & Kothari, D. P. (2000). Combined economic and emission dispatch using improved back-propagation neural network. *Electric Power Components and Systems*, *28*, 31–44.

Lakshminarasimman, L., & Subramanian, S. (2006). Short-term scheduling of hydrothermal power system with cascaded reservoirs by using modified differential evolution. *IEE Proceedings. Generation, Transmission, and Distribution*, *153*(6), 693–700. doi:10.1049/ip-gtd:20050407

Lakshminarasimman, L., & Subramanian, S. (2008). A modified hybrid differential evolution for short-term scheduling of hydrothermal power systems with cascaded reservoirs. *Energy Conversion and Management*, *49*(10), 2513–2521. doi:10.1016/j.enconman.2008.05.021

Liang, R. H., & Hsu, Y. Y. (1994). Scheduling of hydroelectric generations using artificial neural networks. *IEEE Proceedings C on Generation, Transmission, and Distribution*, *141*(5), 452–458. 10.1049/ip-gtd:19941156

Liang, Z. J., Villaseca, F. E., & Renovich, F. (1992). Neural networks for generation scheduling in power systems. *Proceedings of the 1992 International Joint Conference on Neural Networks*, 2, 233–238.

Liu, D., & Cai, Y. (2005). Taguchi method for solving the economic dispatch problem with non smooth cost functions. *IEEE Transactions on Power Systems*, *20*(4), 2006–2014. doi:10.1109/TPWRS.2005.857939

Lu, S., Sun, C., & Lu, Z. (2010). An improved quantum-behaved particle swarm optimization method for short-term combined economic emission hydrothermal scheduling. *Energy Conversion and Management*, *51*(3), 561–571. doi:10.1016/j.enconman.2009.10.024

Lu, Y., Zhou, J., Qin, H., Wang, Y., & Zhang, Y. (2011). A hybrid multi-objective cultural algorithm for short-term environmental/economic hydrothermal scheduling. *Energy Conversion and Management*, *52*(5), 2121–2134. doi:10.1016/j.enconman.2010.12.003

Mandal, K. K., & Chakraborty, N. (2009). Short-term combined economic emission scheduling of hydrothermal power systems with cascaded reservoirs using differential evolution. *Energy Conversion and Management*, *50*(1), 97–104. doi:10.1016/j.enconman.2008.08.022

Mandal, K. K., & Chakraborty, N. (2012). Daily combined economic emission scheduling of hydrothermal systems with cascaded reservoirs using self-organizing hierarchical particle swarm optimization technique. *Expert Systems with Applications*, *39*(3), 3438–3445. doi:10.1016/j.eswa.2011.09.032

Mirjalili, S., Mirjalili, S. M., & Lewis, A. (2014). Grey wolf optimizer. *Advances in Engineering Software*, *69*, 46–61. doi:10.1016/j.advengsoft.2013.12.007

Mohan, M. R., Kuppusamy, K., & Khan, M. A. (1992). Optimal short-term hydro-thermal scheduling using decomposition approach and linear programming method. *International Journal of Electrical Power & Energy Systems*, *14*(1), 39–44. doi:10.1016/0142-0615(92)90007-V

Muro, C., Escobedo, R., Spector, L., & Coppinger, R. (2011). Wolf-pack (Canis lupus) hunting strategies emerge from simple rules in computational simulations. *BehavProcess*, *88*(3), 192–197. doi:10.1016/j.beproc.2011.09.006 PMID:21963347

Orero, S.O., & Irving, M. R. (1998). A genetic algorithm modeling framework and solution technique for short-term optimal hydrothermal scheduling. *IEEE Transaction on PWRS*. 13.

Panda, A., Tripathy, M., Barisal, A., & Prakash, T. (2017). A modified bacteria foraging based optimal power flow framework for Hydro-Thermal-Wind generation system in the presence of STATCOM. *Energy*, *124*, 720–740. doi:10.1016/j.energy.2017.02.090

Patwal, R., Narang, N., & Garg, H. (2018). A novel TVAC-PSO based mutation strategies algorithm for generation scheduling of pumped storage hydrothermal system incorporating solar units. *Energy*, *142*, 822–837. doi:10.1016/j.energy.2017.10.052

Pereira, M., & Pinto, L. (1983). Application of decomposition techniques to the mid and short-term scheduling of hydrothermal Systems. *IEEE Transactions on Power Apparatus and Systems*, *102*(11), 3611–3618. doi:10.1109/TPAS.1983.317709

Ramirez, M., & Ontae, P. E. (2006). The short-term hydrothermal coordination via genetic algorithms. *Electric Power Components and Systems*, *34*(1), 1–19. doi:10.1080/15325000691001584

Roy, P. K. (2013). Teaching learning based optimization for short-term hydrothermal scheduling problem considering valve point effect and prohibited discharge constraint. *Electrical Power and Energy Systems*, *53*, 10–19. doi:10.1016/j.ijepes.2013.03.024

Roy, P. K., Ghoshal, S. P., & Thakur, S. S. (2010). Biogeography based optimization for multi-constraint optimal power flow with emission and non-smooth cost function. *Expert Systems with Applications*, *37*(12), 8221–8228. doi:10.1016/j.eswa.2010.05.064

Roy, P. K., Ghoshal, S. P., & Thakur, S. S. (2010a). Combined economic and emission dispatch problems using biogeography-based optimization. *Electrical Engineering*, *92*(4-5), 173–184. doi:10.100700202-010-0173-3

Roy, P. K., & Paul, C. (2015). Quasi-oppositional gravitational search algorithm applied to short-term hydrothermal scheduling problems. *InderScience*, *5*(6), 165. doi:10.1504/IJPEC.2015.069437

Roy, P. K., Sur, A., & Pradhan, D. (2013). Optimal short-term hydro-thermal scheduling using quasi-oppositional teaching learning based optimization. *Engineering Applications of Artificial Intelligence*. doi:10.1016/j.engappai.2013.08.002

Shahidehpour, M., Fujisawa, Y., & Maeda, Y. (1990). Multi-stage generation scheduling by neural networks. *Proceedings of the Workshop on Applications of Artificial Neural Network Methodology in Power Systems Engineering,* pp. 66–70. Clemson, SC.

Shu, S., Mo, L., & Wang, Y. (2019). Peak shaving strategy of wind-solar-hydro hybrid Generation System Based on Modified Differential Evolution Algorithm. *Energy Procedia*, *158*, 3500–3505. doi:10.1016/j.egypro.2019.01.920

Songfeng, L., Chengfu, S., & Zhengding, L. (2010). An improved quantum-behaved particle swarm optimization method for short-term combined economic emission hydrothermal scheduling. School of Computer Science and Technology, Huazhong University of Science and Technology, Wuhan 430074, China. *Energy Conversion and Management*, *51*, 561–571. doi:10.1016/j.enconman.2009.10.024

Sun, C., & Lu, S. (2010). Short-term combined economic emission hydrothermal scheduling using improved quantum-behaved particle swarm optimization. *Expert Systems with Applications, 37*(6), 4232–4421. doi:10.1016/j.eswa.2009.11.079

Sun, C., & Lu, S. (2011). Quadratic approximation based differential evolution with valuable trade off approach for bi-objective short-term hydrothermal scheduling. *Expert Systems with Applications, 38*(11), 13950–13960.

Swain, R. K., Barisal, A. K., Hota, P. K., & Chakrabarti, R. (2011). Short-term hydrothermal scheduling using clonal selection algorithm. *Electrical Power and Energy Systems, 33*(3), 647–656. doi:10.1016/j.ijepes.2010.11.016

Tizhoosh, H. R. (2005). Opposition-based learning: a new scheme for machine intelligence. In *Computational intelligence for modelling, controland automation, 2005 and international conference on intelligent agents, web technologies, and internet commerce* (Vol. 1, pp. 695–701). IEEE. doi:10.1109/CIMCA.2005.1631345

Turgeon, A. (1981). Optimal short-term hydro scheduling from the principle of progressive optimality. *Water Resources Research, 17*(3), 481–486. doi:10.1029/WR017i003p00481

Wang, D. F., Han, N., Liu, Z., & Dong, S. M., & Jiao. (2002). Modelling the circulating fluidized bed boiler using RBF-NN based on immune genetic algorithm. *Proceedings of the First International Conference on Machine Learning and Cybernetics*, 2121–2125. 10.1109/ICMLC.2002.1175413

Werner, T. G., & Verstege, J. F. (1999). An evolutionary strategy for short-term operation planning of hydro-thermal power systems. *IEEE Transactions on Power Systems, 14*(4), 1362–1368. doi:10.1109/59.801897

Wong, K. P., & Wong, Y. W. (1994). Short-term hydrothermal scheduling part 1: Simulated annealing approach. *IEE Proceedings. Generation, Transmission, and Distribution, 141*(5), 497–501. doi:10.1049/ip-gtd:19941350

Wood, A. J., & Wollenberg, B. F. (1994). *Power generation, operation, and control*. New York: John Wiley & Sons.

Yalcinoz, T., Altun, H., & Hasan, U. (2002). Environmentally constrained economic dispatch via neural networks. IEEE *6th AFRICON Conference in Africa*, 923–928. George, South Africa. 10.1109/AFRCON.2002.1160037

Yang, J. S., & Chen, N. (1989). Short-term hydrothermal coordination using multi-pass dynamic programming. *IEEE Transactions on Power Systems, 4*(3), 1050–1056. doi:10.1109/59.32598

Yang, P. C., Yang, H. T., & Huang, C. L. (1996). Scheduling short-term hydrothermal generation using evolutionary programming techniques. *IEE Proceedings. Generation, Transmission, and Distribution, 143*(4), 371–376. doi:10.1049/ip-gtd:19960463

Yin, X., Cheng, L., Wang, X., Lu, J., & Qin, H. (2019). Optimization for hydro-photovoltaic-wind power Generation System Based on Modified Version of Multi-Objective Whale Optimization Algorithm. *Energy Procedia, 158*, 6208–6216. doi:10.1016/j.egypro.2019.01.480

Yong, Y., Sun'an, W., & Wanxing, S. (2002). Short-term load forecasting using artificial immune network. *Power con 2002 International Conference on Power System Technology Proceedings*, 4, 2322–2325. 10.1109/ICPST.2002.1047199

Yu, B., Yuan, X., & Wang, J. (2007). Short-term hydro-thermal scheduling using particle swarm optimization method. *Energy Conversion and Management*, 48(7), 1902–1908. doi:10.1016/j.enconman.2007.01.034

Zhang, D., Luh, P. B., & Zhang, Y. (1999). A bundle method for hydrothermal scheduling. *IEEE Transactions on Power Systems*, 14(4), 1355–1361. doi:10.1109/59.801896

KEY TERMS AND DEFINITIONS

T: Summation of the thermal units.

RES: Aggregation of reservoirs for hydro unit.

H: Total number of hydro unit.

TTI: Accumulated time intervals.

t: Time schedule.

FC: Aggregation of the burning cost of the thermal unit.

FCE: Aggregation of fuel cost considering emission.

FC_{it}: Sum of overall fuel costs of the ith thermal generator at t time.

a_i, b_i, c_i, d_i, e_i: Fuel cost coefficients for i^{th} thermal generator.

$\alpha_i, \beta_i, \gamma_i, \eta_i, \delta_i$: Coefficients for the emission of the ith thermal generator.

$C_{1j}, C_{2j}, C_{3j}, C_{4j}, C_{5j}, C_{6j}$: Power generation coefficients of the jth hydro generator.

Pg_{it}: Power generation of the ith thermal generator at time t.

P_{hjt}: Power generation at time t for the jth hydro generator.

$WD_{r,t}$: At time t, water discharge rate of the rth hydro generator.

h_i: Price penalty factor.

D_t: At time t aggregation of power demand.

Lt: Total power loss at t time.

$Q_{hj}^{\min}, Q_{hj}^{\max}$: Maximum and minimum water discharge rate.

Q_{hjt}: Water discharge rate of the jth hydro reservoir for time t interval.

I_{hjt}: Inflow of the jth hydro reservoir.

x_{hjt}: Discharge rate of turbine at t time for the jth hydro reservoir.

V_{hjt}: Reservoir volume of the jth hydro plant at t time.

V_{hj}^0: Previous volume of the jth hydro reservoir.

V_{hj}^{ini}: j^{th} hydro reservoir's initial storage volume.

$VOL_{hj}^{\max}, VOL_{hj}^{\min}$: The smallest and the extreme volume of the jth hydro reservoir.

VOL_{hj}^{fin}: Final volume of jth hydro reservoir.

UP: Upstream hydro plants immediately upstairs the hydro reservoir.

Ψ: From wth to j^{th} reservoir's water transport delay.

$\vec{E}$: Encircling behaviour representation for grey wolf.

$\vec{G}, \vec{H}$: Coefficient vectors for GWO algorithm.

n: Current iteration number for GWO algorithm.

$P(n)$: Position vector of the prey.

$\vec{S}(n)$: Position vector of grey wolf or search agents.

$\vec{y}, \vec{z}$: Vectors of random in range[0,1].

$\vec{g}$: Vector of GWO.

P: Population size.

P_i: i[th] population for the hydrothermal scheduling.

poz: Number of prohibited operating zones.

$Pg^l_{i,poz_{y-1}}$: Prohibited operating zone's lower limit for i^{th} thermal unit.

$Pg^u_{i,poz_{y-1}}$: Upper prohibited operating zone limit for i^{th} thermal generator.

Pg^0_{it} : Previous hour's power output of ith thermal unit.

$Pg^{\min}_i$: Minimum value of the power output of ith thermal unit.

$Pg^{\max}_i$: Maximum power output of thermal unit i.

Chapter 17
Mobile Anchor–Assisted Localization Using Invasive Weed Optimization Algorithm

Vaishali Raghavendra Kulkarni
M. S. Ramaiah University of Applied Sciences, India

Veena Desai
https://orcid.org/0000-0002-6964-1135
KLS Gogte Institute of Technology, India

Akash Sikarwar
M. S. Ramaiah University of Applied Sciences, India

Raghavendra V. Kulkarni
M. S. Ramaiah University of Applied Sciences, India

ABSTRACT

Sensor localization in wireless sensor networks has been addressed using mobile anchor (MA) and a metaheuristic algorithm. The path of a MA plays an important role in localizing maximum number of sensor nodes. The random and circle path planning methods have been presented. Each method has been evaluated for number of localized nodes, accuracy, and computing time in localization. The localization has been performed using trilateration method and two metaheuristic stochastic algorithms, namely invasive weed optimization (IWO) and cultural algorithm (CA). Experimental results indicate that the IWO-based localization outperforms the trilateration method and the CA-based localization in terms of accuracy but with higher computing time. However, the computing speed of trilateration localization is faster than the IWO- and CA-based localization. In the path-planning algorithms, the results show that the circular path planning algorithm localizes more nodes than the random path.

DOI: 10.4018/978-1-7998-3222-5.ch017

1. INTRODUCTION

A wireless sensor network (WSN) is a collection of thousands of small sensor nodes used for several monitoring and tracking applications. Applications of WSNs include traffic surveillance, environmental monitoring, military and health applications and wildfire detection (Mohamed et al., 2018). The location of a sensor is a geographically meaningful information in a WSN. The data generated in a WSN node is useful only if the location of the node is known. For example, emergency services in disasters, such as fire, landslide or accidents can be made available if the geographical coordinates of accidents are known. Some routing protocols use the location information as an important decision parameter. Localization is a process aimed to determine the location of the sensor nodes in WSNs (Paul and Sato, 2017). In many WSNs, localization is performed using special sensor nodes referred as beacons or anchors that are aware of their geographical location. The nodes that are not aware of their location are referred to as unknown, dumb or target nodes. The installation of global positioning system (GPS) adds to the cost and size of the hardware on tiny sensors. Therefore, it is not practical to load all the sensor nodes with GPS hardware, but use as small number of beacons as possible in WSN localization. The use of a minimum number of beacons is a critical issue in sensor localization. The most commonly used alternative to static beacons is to use a GPS-equipped mobile anchor (MA) that travels in the WSN. The MA broadcasts its current position to localize the dumb nodes in its communication range. The coordinates broadcasted by an MA are referred as anchor points (Erdemir et al., 2018). A WSN with static unknown nodes and a MA is depicted in Figure 1. Localization process takes place in two phases. In the first phase, a dumb node checks whether it is in the vicinity of an MA and records the anchor points and measures the distance from itself and the anchor points. In the second phase, the anchor points and distance measurement values are used to determine the locations. For the distance measurement, several metrics, such as received signal strength indication (RSSI), angle of arrival, time of arrival, time difference of arrival or communication range method have been presented in previous research (Alrajeh et al., 2013). The different geometric methods, such as trilateration, multilateration, triangulation, bounding box, distance vector hop routing etc. are used for location estimation. The localization process can be centralized or distributed, range-based or range-free, anchor-based or anchor-free.

Use of mobility for the sensor nodes in WSN plays an important role. Mobile WSNs (MWSNs) are useful in tracking movement in applications such as traffic surveillance, animal habitat, package tracking etc. (Mohamed et al., 2017). Localization is more challenging in MWSN than static. There is a need of dynamic navigation in MWSNs as the sensors frequently change their positions. Unlike in static WSNs, there is a need for frequent localization in MWSNs, which consumes more time and energy. Usually, centralized localization is not preferred in MWSNs because it takes more time and involves communication overhead.

In a static WSN, the localization process is performed only once, immediately after the deployment. Whereas, in an MWSN, the continuously travelling nodes require frequent localization. Mobility results in extra time and energy utilization. The communication may be unreliable due to ad hoc network. If the sink node is travelling at different locations, it is also necessary that the number of anchors should be available for localization process. In traditional routing protocols for WSNs, the routing tables are fixed, and they get refreshed after a certain amount of time. In case of a mobile WSN, the routing tables get outdated very fast and new entries in routing tables must be stored frequently. This increases the time, energy and cost of localization. The frequent localization requires higher capacity of batteries with more lifetime (Chelouah et al., 2018).

Figure 1. MA and unknown nodes in WSN

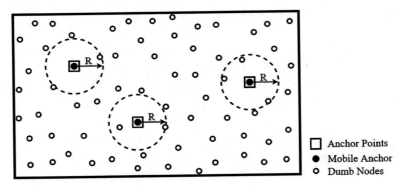

In many monitoring applications of WSNs, MAs (robots equipped with GPS) have been used. The advantages of using this type of MA is that it can improve the number of localized nodes by covering different areas in the network (Alomari et al., 2018). Unlike other sensor nodes, energy and resource constraints are less intensive in MAs. The main objective of using an MA is to maximize the number of localized nodes. This requires determining an optimal path for an MA for maximum coverage of a search field. The design of a path of an MA must be such that each dumb node is in the vicinity of three or more anchor points at minimum distance. The communication between the dumb node and the anchor point must be as less as possible to reduce time and energy consumption. The most fundamental form of the movement of an MA is in a random fashion. The MAs have been categorized based on individual/group MAs, static/dynamic etc. (Han et al., 2016). Two such path-planning schemes, namely random and circle have been analysed for their localization coverage in this chapter. After receiving the anchor locations and the distance metrics, the dumb nodes are localized by a conventional trilateration method. Localization using trilateration method is simple, deterministic, geometric method. However, the distance measurement between anchor points and the dumb node is inaccurate due to environmental noise, resulting in erroneous location estimation. This problem has been addressed with the application of metaheuristic algorithms based on swarm intelligence (SI) (V. R. Kulkarni et al., 2016).

In stochastic optimization-based localization, an invasive weed optimization (IWO) algorithm has been proposed. Weed is the plant that grows enormously by adopting to the changes in the environment. Weed improves its fitness against the crisis in the environment and shows more robustness. The IWO algorithm is inspired by the randomness and robust behaviour of weed plants. The results of IWO-based localization have been compared with the localization using the cultural algorithm (CA). The CA is based on the culture evolution in society. The culture is stored as a set of population space and belief space components representing the experiences of the individuals. The CA has been applied in many optimization problems with real value parameters. A MA assisted multistage localization using geometry-based trilateration and metaheuristic algorithms is the main objective of this chapter. The main contributions of this study are:

1. A distributed sensor localization using MA, geometric method and metaheuristic algorithms have been presented.

2. Two path planning methods, namely random and circular have been used for building an itinerary of an MA. The results of path planning methods have been compared in terms of number of localized nodes.

3. The dumb nodes have been localized using the conventional deterministic trilateration method and the two metaheuristic algorithms, the IWO algorithm and the CA.

4. The simulation results of localization using trilateration and IWO-based localization have been presented for comparing accuracy of location estimation and computing time.

The remainder of this chapter has been organized as follows: Previous research in sensor localization and the path planning methods for MAs have been surveyed in Section 2. An overview of the path planning methods for an MA in multistage localization has been presented in section 3. The localization using trilateration and IWO algorithm has been presented in Section 4. The IWO algorithm and the CA have been outlined in Section 5 and Section 6, respectively. The simulation results have been presented in Section 7. Finally, concluding remarks and suggestions for future research have been given in Section 8.

2. RELATED WORK

The different algorithms for localization have been presented in the past literature based on characteristics, such as range-free or range-based, centralized/distributed, conventional/stochastic, static/mobile etc. Sensor localization in an MWSN is different from that in a static WSN in terms of the operation. Mobile node localization has been presented in three steps: Coordination, distance measurement and location calculation (Amundson et al., 2009). Localization algorithms have been designed for both the centralized and distributed manner. The performance of centralized algorithms has been superior to that in the distributed approach, with drawbacks of communication overhead, energy computation and more delay. The centralized localization algorithms are not scalable. Distributed algorithms use anchors' location information or their neighbors' location to localize themselves. This approach is simple and less costly compared to centralized algorithm. But the location estimation in this approach is not accurate as there is no global map of the entire network as in case of the centralized method. Distributed algorithm is more suitable for large scale WSNs.

Another way of classification of localization algorithms for mobile WSNs is given in (Lopatka et al., 2016). Localization algorithms are classified based on the occurrence of an event and time. Examples, such as monitoring the flow of a river passing through thick forest have been discussed. These examples of time-based algorithms present the localization process in a periodic manner. The crucial factor in MWSN localization include path planning or movement strategy of a MA or for a group of MAs that addresses the impact of obstacles and other environmental hurdles. A power-based algorithm has been proposed in (Sohail Jabbar et al., 2018), where the beacons broadcast their maximum power level. A mobile node receives maximum power by three e neighboring beacons and acknowledges them. The beacons then reduce their power level and retransmits their locations. The threshold of power level is decided by the moving node. The results of this work illustrate that there has been considerable improvement in the accuracy of location estimation and number of localized nodes. The localization coverage has been better in this approach, but there is a burden of calculation of power level on mobile node to determine the number of beacons in its vicinity.

Localization using a group of MAs results in minimum delay and less energy consumption in comparison with that a single MA. In (Liu Xiao et al., 2008), a five-anchor localization (FAL) has been presented. The FAL method has been implemented using a group-based MA model without any distance or angle information, but with geometric calculations. Minimum delay and energy requirements are the advantages of using group-based MA.

Static path planning scheme is advantageous if the unknown nodes are located in a uniform manner. However, the path used by the MA can be too long and can result in a long delay. This has inspired the researchers to come up with dynamic path planning strategies for MAs. The dynamic path planning strategies have an advantage of detecting the presence of obstacle and to change the itinerary accordingly. Graph-based algorithms, such as breadth first search, greedy and backtracking concepts have been used for designing effective path planning for MAs. The main objective of dynamic path planning methods is to design an efficient path based on the density of unknown nodes (Yi-lun Yang et al., 2013).

The localization problem for mobile sensors has been addressed as an optimization problem in the past research using paradigms of computational intelligence (CI) (Kulkarni et al., 2019). Localization using particle swarm intelligence (PSO) algorithm, artificial bee colony algorithm and firefly algorithm have been examples of intelligent algorithms to improve the localization accuracy of sensors in WSN (Kulkarni et al., 2016). The localization process has been optimized using iterative metaheuristic algorithms based on swarm intelligence (SI) and evolutionary computing to obtain efficient solutions.

The fuzzy logic-based on approximate reasoning is yet another CI paradigm used in localization (Chiang et al., 2009). In this study, a fuzzy membership function has been defined using RSS values, distance measurement between the localizable mobile node and the anchor positions, the direction of movement and the previously stored locations. The locations of a mobile node have been estimated using weighted centroid algorithm. This fuzzy-based localization algorithm has been tested on indoor environment with T-mote sky wireless sensor nodes using ZigBee protocol and computer simulations. There has been significant improvement in accuracy using this approach, compared to the conventional method.

For localizing a dumb node using beacon positions, it is necessary that the beacons should be non-collinear. The collinearity of beacons leads to flip ambiguity problem, resulting incorrect localization. The PSO algorithm has been used solve the flip ambiguity problem and to achieve a precise localization in (Li et al., 2015). The localization has been performed using a modified version of the PSO algorithm, where the initialization of particles is in a bounding box area. Consider an unknown node U with three beacon nodes A_1, A_2 and A_3 with communication range $2r$. Thus, the initial search space is in overlapping portion of three squares. This modification has shown better results in computing time than the original PSO. The flip ambiguity problem has been addressed using a threshold value to detect the near-collinear beacons. If the unknown node is within the near-collinear beacons, it is not included in that localization phase.

A modified version of cuckoo search algorithm (CSA) has been presented in (Cheng et al., 2016). In this study, the CSA has been modified in its step size for reaching to the global solution at a faster speed. The insignificant search and the early local convergence in the CSA have been avoided by calculating mutation probability. The results of the modified CSA have been compared with the PSO algorithm by varying anchor and unknown sensor nodes density and communication radius. The simulation results in the research indicate that the modified CSA performs better than the original CSA and the PSO algorithm in reducing the mean localization error. Another advantage shown in this work is restricting the population in a certain range to avoid unnecessary search. This feature has been related to reduce energy consumption in sensor nodes of WSN. Another example of application of metaheuristic algorithm in sensor localization is use of distance vector (DV) routing with genetic algorithm (GA) in (Peng et al., 2015). In this study, the GA has been applied in range-free localization for improvement in accuracy and computing speed. The results indicate that there has been considerable improvement in DV routing, with the application of GA.

In summary, metaheuristic optimization algorithms in SI, and other paradigms of CI have been popularly used in addressing the challenges in sensor localization. Use of the IWO algorithm and mobile path planning in sensor localization is yet another step in the direction of improving localization process.

3. PATH PLANNING ALGORITHM FOR AN MA

The path planning methods for an MA have been classified based on a single MA or a group of MAs. The MA can overcome the limitations present in the static anchor nodes. The path planning algorithms can be classified based on two factors. In the first type, the network conditions and parameters are not considered, and the movement trajectory is static. In the second type, the MA algorithms are customized for specific WSN localization. Two static path-planning algorithms have been used in this study. Each algorithm uses a single MA for localization of multiple static dumb nodes.

1. Circular movement path
2. Random movement path

3.1. Circular Path Method

In this method, a path for an MA is a set of concentric circles in a monitoring area. The MA starts it journey at the midpoint of a mission field. The MA moves with the speed S and travels in a circular manner, as depicted in Figure 2. After completion of one circle, the MA moves to the next concentric circle. The process of moving in circle is repeated till the boundary of the space is reached. Let (x,y) be the coordinates of the MA, as given in (1).

$$x = 0.5 \times x_{max} \qquad (1)$$

$$y = 0.5 \times y_{max}$$

The MA moves in the circular manner with the increment in new (x,y) direction using (2).

$$x = r \cos \theta + x_1 \qquad (2)$$

$$y = r \sin \theta + y_1$$

Here, (x_1,y_1) refers to the initial position of the MA, and r represents the radius. The value of r is changed by a fixed increment denoted by α. The value of α is given in (3).

$$\alpha = 2C \qquad (3)$$

Figure 2. Concentric circular path for MA

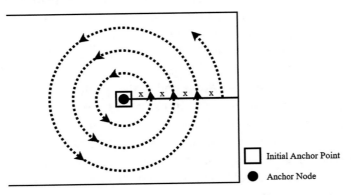

The term C denotes the communication range of an MA. To form the different circles, the value of θ is changed from 0 to 360 degrees with the increment value β as given in (4).

$$\beta = \frac{r_1}{r} \tag{4}$$

The term r_1 is a constant for the arc of the incremental circular path. The MA waits at each anchor point represented as

$$\left(a_{1x}, a_{1y}\right), \left(a_{2x}, a_{2y}\right), \dots \left(a_{nx}, a_{ny}\right).$$

The coordinates (a_{ix}, a_{iy}) help the surrounding dumb nodes in localization using trilateration as given in the following section. The nodes that are at the border of the mission space remain un-localized. These nodes are localized by using coordinates of the already settled nodes.

3.2. Random Path

In the past literature multiple path planning algorithms have been proposed for mobile WSNs. In a random path-based algorithm, a mobility model for a MA can be classified as follows:

1. Random Walk (RW)
2. Random Waypoint (RWP)
3. Random Direction (RD)

The RW model uses a random direction and speed for the trajectory of a MA. The speed of the movement is determined by the limits $[V_1, V_2]$ with the direction in the range $[0, 2\pi]$. The movement in this model is based on fixed interval of time. After the expiry of the time slice, the new direction and the limits for speed are calculated. This model depicts sudden changes in the mobility movement of MA, because if the MA is crossing the boundaries of the mission space, the movement of the MA is changed to a new direction. A range-based localization using RSSI, with the help of a moving aerial robotic beacon with GPS or a multidimensional scaling-based mobile beacon localization has been presented in (Caballero et al., 2008) and (Kim et al., 2006), respectively.

In the RWP method, the movement of an MA is kept on hold for some time. The MA determines its speed limit and direction as discussed in random walk method, travels to a certain destination position and waits in that position for a pause time. At the end of the fixed time slot, it changes in a new direction in the range 0 to 180 degrees and repeats the process. The RW and RWP model have drawback of forming clusters of anchor points at a specified area in the field. This can be overcome using RD model. In the RD model, the MA selects a random direction and a speed, but it is forced to reach the boundary region for a given period of time. After reaching the boundary, the MA waits for a fixed interval of time and then repeats the process. This model has been used in this research. The movement of a MA using RD model has been depicted in Figure 3.

Figure 3. MA using RD path

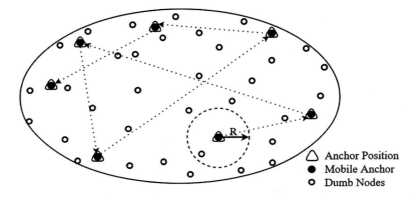

4. LOCALIZATION PROCESS

Localization process is applied in a MWSN with static nodes represented as $s_1, s_2, \ldots, s_m$. Each s_i sensor is at a position (x, y). The term $i = 1, 2, \ldots, m$ and m represent the total number of sensor nodes in a two-dimensional field. An MA is termed as M is moving in the network at different anchor points represented as $m_1, m_2, \ldots$ Each anchor point is given by its (x, y) position. The localization is performed in three steps as given below:

1. The three anchor points in the vicinity of a static dumb node are determined. It is necessary that the anchor points need to be non-collinear. If the centre point of all the three anchors is on the same line, then it can lead to infinite solutions, causing an error. Another assumption in this study is that there are no obstacles in the range of the dumb nodes and anchor points.
2. The distance d between the dumb node and the three anchor points is measured using RSS.
3. The geometric and SI-based localization algorithms are applied to compute locations.

The localization algorithms have been used in this study are given in the following subsections.

Figure 4. Localization using trilateration

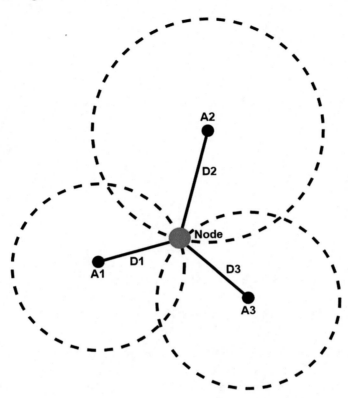

4.1 Localization Using Trilateration Method

In this method, a dumb node along with the distance values between them uses three anchor locations as depicted in Figure 4. Consider the coordinates of three anchors as follows: $A(x_a, y_a)$, $B(x_b, y_b)$ and $C(x_c, y_c)$ with distance values d_1, d_2 and d_3 respectively. The locations of a dumb node are given as (x, y). Then the distance measurement can be given by the equations (5) (Oguejiofor O.S et al., 2013).

$$d_1 = \sqrt{\left(x_a - x\right)^2 + \left(y_a - y\right)^2}$$

$$d_2 = \sqrt{\left(x_b - x\right)^2 + \left(y_b - y\right)^2}$$

$$d_3 = \sqrt{\left(x_c - x\right)^2 + \left(y_c - y\right)^2} \tag{5}$$

Consider two temporary variables T_1 and T_2 expressed as given in (6).

$$T_1 = 0.5\left(\left(d_2^2 - d_3^2\right) - \left(x_b^2 - x_c^2\right) - \left(y_b^2 - y_c^2\right)\right)$$

$$T_2 = 0.5\left(\left(d_2^2 - d_1^2\right) - \left(x_b^2 - x_a^2\right) - \left(y_b^2 - y_a^2\right)\right) \qquad (6)$$

By solving T_1 and T_2, the values of x and y is determined as given in (7).

$$y = \frac{T_1\left(x_c - x_b\right) - T_2\left(x_a - x_b\right)}{\left(y_a - y_b\right)\left(x_c - x_b\right) - \left(y_c - y_b\right)\left(x_a - x_b\right)}$$

$$x = \frac{T_1 - y\left(y_c - y_b\right)}{x_c - x_b} \qquad (7)$$

The (x,y) coordinate represents the estimated location of a dumb node.

4.2 Localization Using the IWO Algorithm

The weed plant adapts the environmental condition in nature and grows fast by optimizing the available space. The useful features of weed are: Adaptability, randomness and robustness against the climatic conditions. These features have inspired the development of the IWO algorithm. The IWO algorithm is based on this optimizing behavior of colonies of weed plants (Misaghi et al., 2019). The steps used in IWO-based localization are as follows:

- **Distance Estimation**: The dumb node s estimates the distance d_i using (8). The distance is calculated by the difference in the RSSI values in the sender and the receiver.

$$d_i = \sqrt{\left(a_{ix} - s_{ix}\right)^2 + \left(a_{iy} - s_{iy}\right)^2} + e \qquad (8)$$

Here the term $\left(\hat{s}_{ix}, \hat{s}_{iy}\right)$ represent the location of the dumb static node and (a_{ix}, a_{iy}) refer to the ith position of anchor point, and (s_{ix}, s_{iy}) is the position of the dumb node to be localized. The environmental noise is represented by the term e as a Gaussian distribution as expressed in (9).

$$e = \alpha\left(\frac{p}{100}\right)(-1)^\beta \qquad (9)$$

Where, α is a uniformly distributed random number in the range [0, 1]. The term β is a random number assumed as 0 or 1. The term p denotes the percentage of the noise in the atmosphere. This value is assumed as constant.

- **Identification of Anchors**: Each dumb static node records the three non-collinear anchor points. If the d_i is within the communication range of an anchor, then the node is considered to be localizable.
- **Fitness/Objective Function**: The node to be localized stores the three anchor points. The IWO algorithm is executed by each node for localization. The IWO algorithm uses a fitness function as given in (10). The terms (s_x, s_y) represent the random weed position in each iteration. The IWO algorithm is used here to optimize the value of the error E_i to zero. The values of $(\hat{s}_{ix}, \hat{s}_{iy})$ are changed in every iteration, such that the term E is minimized. The IWO algorithm performs exploration and exploitation operations to get the values of $(\hat{s}_{ix}, \hat{s}_{iy})$ for which the term error is zero or near to zero. The threshold value of a zero is assumed as 0.0001 is this study. The optimized variables are the values of $(\hat{s}_{ix}, \hat{s}_{iy})$.

$$E_i = \frac{1}{3} \sum_{i=1}^{3} \left(\sqrt{\left(a_{ix} - \hat{s}_x\right)^2 + \left(a_{iy} - \hat{s}_y\right)^2} - \hat{d}_i^2 \right) \tag{10}$$

- **Localization Error:** After completion of all the iterations, the mean square error E_r is calculated using the actual locations (s_{ix}, s_{iy}) used in the simulation and the locations estimated by the IWO algorithm, denoted as $(\hat{s}_{ix}, \hat{s}_{iy})$. The E_r is given by the (11). The term L denoted number of localized nodes in one trial.

$$E_r = \frac{1}{L} \sqrt{\left(s_{ix} - \hat{s}_{ix}\right)^2 + \left(s_{iy} - \hat{s}_{iy}\right)^2} \tag{11}$$

The details of the IWO algorithm are given in the following section.

5. INVASIVE WEED OPTIMISATION

The IWO algorithm has been invented by the scientists Mehrabian and Lucas in 2006. The colonies of invasive weeds in agriculture have been used as base in this algorithm. The algorithm is simple, robust and with minimum number of parameters. These features make it attractive in various optimization applications. Some of the examples of IWO-based optimization include, design and operation of PID controller, training in neural network, data clustering, job scheduling, pattern recognition etc. (Sang et al., 2018). The main components of IWO are:

1. Population of weeds: At the initial stage, the seeds are assigned to random locations.
2. Evaluation of fitness: The fitness is evaluated for each weed plant in every cycle and compared with the remaining plants.
3. Reproduction: Weed produce seeds based on their fitness. The weed with maximum seeds is considered as the best fitness, termed as w_{max}. The weed with lowest number of seeds is considered as

a plant with worst fitness and it is denoted by the term w_{min}. The number of seeds produced by the weed plant is as expressed in (12).

$$s = w_{min} + \left(w_{max} - w_{min}\right) \times \frac{f - f_w}{f_b - f_w} \tag{12}$$

The fitness of the weed is denoted by f, the best and worst fitness in the entire population is denoted by the terms f_b and f_w respectively. In the reproduction step, the plants with minimum and maximum fitness are allowed to produce seeds. This strategy is different than the other evolutionary algorithms, where the solutions with poor fitness are discarded. The number of seeds are increased in every iteration of the algorithm.

4.   Spatial Dispersal: In this stage, the generation of the new plants is around the parent weed. The spatial dispersal leads to the local search around each plant. The plant seeds are randomly spread out around the parent weeds according to a normal distribution with mean μ equal to zero and variance equals to σ^2. The standard deviation of the seed dispersion is denoted by the term σ. The value of σ is reduced in each iteration k. The σ for each generation is as given in (13).

$$\sigma_c = \frac{\left(k_{max} - k\right)^n}{\left(k_{max}\right)^n} \left(\sigma_i - \sigma_f\right) + \sigma_f \tag{13}$$

Here, k_{max} is the maximum number of iterations. The term γ_k is the standard deviation at the current iteration and n is the nonlinear modulation index. The terms σ_c, σ_i and σ_f denote the current, initial and final variance respectively. The value of σ_c determines the exploration ability of the weeds. In this stage, the plants with more fitness are gathered together and the unfit plants are discarded.

5.   Complete Exclusion: After, k_{max} iterations, an elimination mechanism is adopted. The seeds and their parents are ranked together and only those with better fitness can survive and become reproductive. The plants with poor fitness are thus eliminated to balance the maximum population. The solution to the optimization problem is represented by the plant with a highest fitness.

6. CULTURAL ALGORITHM

The CA is metaheuristic algorithm including both the characteristics of EC and SI paradigms. The CA is an extended version of the GA. The CA is based on culture evolution in the society. The culture in the society is described by the beliefs, moral, customs, knowledge and habits of the individuals. The culture in the people has considerable impact on the society. The culture plays an inspiration to interact with an environment and this is known as cultural ecology. The CA use a repository of the knowledge database contributed by each individual in the society. The solution to a given problem is represented by the stored culture database in a knowledge repository. If the solutions is useful, then it is passed to the next generation with a positive feedback, else it is discarded. The culture gets refined in the successive iterations and provides better quality solutions. Every new generation of individuals get to exploit these solutions to solve the given problem (Kuo et al., 2013).

There are two levels in the CA, namely, cultural level and the population level. The cultural level represents the belief or knowledge space. The population level refers to the set of individuals that are in search of the solution.

Each individual represents the candidate solution. The quality of these individuals is tested by the fitness function. The cultural level is also known as belief space or knowledge database. Both these levels are connected by communication protocol. The influence function is used to create a new offspring using the updated useful culture in the belief space.

CA Dynamics

Main components of CA are:

1. **Population**: It is a set of individual solutions used in n-dimensional space.
2. **Belief Space**: The belief space comprises of situational knowledge termed as S, normative knowledge as N or both, represented as $S|N(S,N)$. The value of S is represented as in (14).

$$S = (E_1, E_2, E_e, A_F(e)) \tag{14}$$

The terms $(E_1, E_2, \ldots, E_e)$ represent the exemplar individuals in the history of evolution. The number of best exemplars in S is termed as e. The belief space operator $A_F(e)$ is applied to generate the best exemplar individuals in the S. The best individual is selected by normative knowledge that belongs to the desirable value where an individual behavior is acceptable. The normative knowledge is represented as given in (15).

$$N = I_j, L_j, U_j, A_N \tag{15}$$

where $j=1,2,3,\ldots,N$ and each I_j is a real number representing the interval for variable j. The value of I_j consists of four parameters as expressed in (16).

$$I_j = [L_j, U_j] = x| L_j \leq x \leq U_j \tag{16}$$

The value of the performance by each parameter is termed as L_j in the bound I_j to U_j in the given domain. The other knowledge component of belief space are spatial knowledge and temporal knowledge. The spatial knowledge represents knowledge about the topography of search space. The temporal knowledge belongs to the history of the search space.

3. **Update and Influence Function**: The update function is used to select a best individual s. Update function refines the belief space as expressed in (17).

$$s^{t+1} = f(x) = \begin{cases} x_b^t, & f(x_b^t) < f(s^t) \\ s, & Otherwise \end{cases} \qquad (17)$$

The term x_b^t represents the best individual at a time t. The influence function is used to create an offspring. There are different strategies for influence function. The roulette wheel method has been used in this study. The creation of the influence function is such that, individuals are kept away from the undesirable behavior. The steps in the CA are as given in Figure 5.

7. NUMERIC SIMULATIONS AND RESULTS

The simulation for localization process has been carried out on MATLAB 12.0. The simulation consists of different itinerary for MA to travel in a two-dimensional WSN field. The parameter setting for path planning and localization algorithms have been mentioned in the following subsection.

7.1 Parameter Setup for Path Planning Models

The details of parameters used in the random and the circle mobility models have been given in Table 1. The setting of parameters for the IWO algorithm and the CA has been given in Table 2.

The parameter setup for trilateration localization is as given in Table 3.

The number of localizable nodes using circle and RD method have been given in Table 4. MA using random and circle path planning methods. The term L denotes localizable dumb node with three anchor points. The results in the Table 4 indicate that the circle-based MA has been able to localize more number of nodes than the random algorithm.

The simulation results of the MA using RD and Circle have been depicted in Figure 6 and 7 respectively.

The anchor points obtained in each model are stored in a vector (a_{ix}, a_{iy}), where $i=1,2,3$ for each dumb node s. The anchor points have been checked for collinearity problem. The collinear anchor points have been discarded. The dumb node that gets localized in one trial at positions (s_x, s_y) has been considered as a beacon for further localization. The IWO-based localization is applied for each localizable node to optimize the localization error. The results of IWO-based localization have been represented in Table 6. The terms E and T represent the localization error and the computing time respectively.

The results of IWO-based localization have been compared with the localization using trilateration. The analysis of results has been shown in Table 6. The results indicate that the localization using the IWO and the CA is more accurate than the trilateration technique. Thus, the use of SI-based algorithm optimizes the localization error and improves the accuracy. The IWO-based localization is showing better performance than the CA but with more delay. The CA is more suitable for quick localization. The simulation results of the initial deployment for 20 beacons with communication range of 30m has been shown in Figure 8. Some of the dumb nodes are localized and they serve as beacons for remaining nodes as shown in Figure 9. The complete localized network in multiple iterations of IWO has been shown in Figure 10.

Figure 5. Flowchart for cultural algorithm

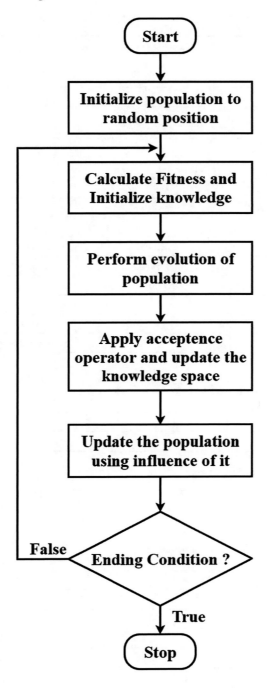

Table 1. Parameter Setup in Mobility Model and Circle Mobility Model

Random Model			Circle Model		
Description	**Term**	**Value**	**Description**	**Term**	**Value**
Initial Position	(x_0, y_0)	Random values	Initial Position	$(m_x, m_y)P_1$	(50,50)
Hop Distance	h_i	1	Range of MA	R	5m
Direction	*Theta*	random	Radius	r	Increments of $2 \times R$

Table 2. Parameter setup in IWO and CA localization

IWO			CA		
Description	**Term**	**Value**	**Description**	**Term**	**Value**
Initial Variance	υ_i	100	Population		100
Final Variance	υ_f	0.001	Acceptance Ratio	A_R	0.035
Maximum seeds	w_{max}	15	Accepted Individuals	$A_R \cdot P_1$	
Minimum seeds	w_{min}	1	Random Constant	α	0.3
The nonlinear modulation index	n	3	Random Constant	β	0.5
Maximum Iterations	k_{max}	100	Maximum Iterations	k_{max}	100

Table 3. Parameter setup in trilateration and localization field

Description	**Term**	**Value**
Static Nodes	s_{id}	100
Communication Range	R	30m
Noise Level	p	1%
Sensor Field	(x_{min}, x_{max})	(0,100)

Table 4. Results of RD and circle path methods

Trial No.	L	
	RD	**Circle**
1	36	**42**
2	35	**40**
3	29	**43**
4	37	**42**
5	39	**45**

Figure 6. Results of RD path for MA

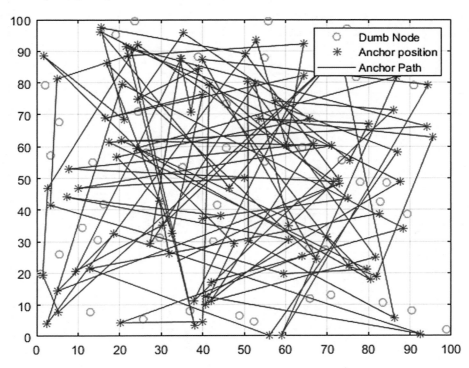

Figure 7. Results of circle path for MA

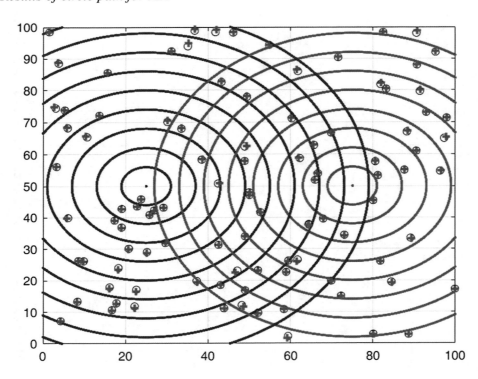

Table 5. Statistics of localization using IWO

Trial	L	E	T
1	42	0.144	140
2	40	0.112	120
3	43	0.213	112
4	42	0.236	98
5	45	0.320	160

Table 6. Comparison of localization using IWO, CA and trilateration

Trial	L	E			T		
		IWO	CA	Trilateration	IWO	CA	Trilateration
1	42	**0.144**	0.213	0.723	1.15	1.24	**1.01**
2	40	**0.112**	0.312	0.657	5.20	3.45	**1.21**
3	43	**0.113**	0.152	0.763	8.50	2.98	**1.51**
4	42	**0.136**	0.112	1.456	9.56	3.13	**1.31**
5	45	**0.320**	0.212	5.123	5.134	4.13	**0.98**

Figure 8. Initial deployment

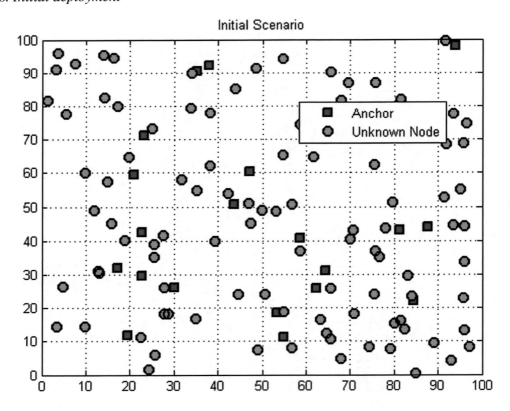

Figure 9. Results of intermediate stage of localization

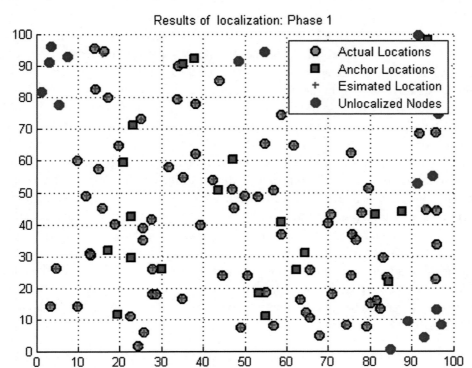

Figure 10. Results of final localization

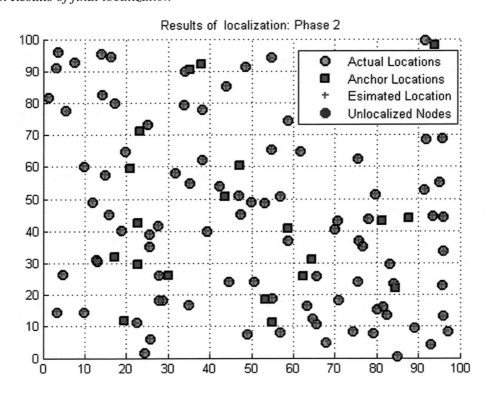

8. CONCLUSION

An MA assisted distributed sensor localization algorithm has been presented in this chapter. The main objective is to select a best path for a MA. The merit of the best path is decided by the number of localizable nodes. The random and circle path planning methods for MAs have been presented. The anchor positions broadcasted by the MA on the best path are referred as anchor points. The simulation results have shown that circle path results in localization of a greater number of nodes than the random model.

The distance between anchor points and the dumb nodes and positions of the MA is used as input in two population-based algorithms, namely the IWO algorithm and the CA. An objective function that optimizes the location estimation has been used in the metaheuristic algorithms. The results of metaheuristic-based localization have been compared with the results of trilateration. The mean localization error in both the IWO and trilateration-based localization has been computed along with computing time. The IWO-based localization is found superior than trilateration. The localization accuracy obtained using the CA has been superior to the IWO algorithm. In future, authors plan to combine the features of other SI-based algorithms for optimizing the localization. The localization presented in this study assumes that there are no obstacles and anchor points are non-collinear. Identifying the collinearity and obstacles using stochastic algorithms can be another direction of this study. Several other challenges in localization such as security, energy consumption, and path optimization can be the areas of optimization using SI algorithms.

REFERENCES

Alomari, A., Comeau, F., Phillips, W., & Aslam, N. (2018). New path planning model for mobile anchor-assisted localization in wireless sensor networks. *Wireless Networks, 24*(7), 2589–2607. doi:10.100711276-017-1493-2

Alrajeh, N. A., Bashir, M., & Shams, B. (2013). Localization techniques in wireless sensor networks. *International Journal of Distributed Sensor Networks, 9*(6). doi:10.1155/2013/304628

Amundson, I., & Koutsoukos, X. D. (2009). A survey on localization for mobile wireless sensor networks. Proceedings of Mobile Entity Localization and Tracking in GPS-less Environments (pp. 235–254). Berlin, Germany: Springer. doi:10.1007/978-3-642-04385-7_16

Jabbar, S., Asif Habib, M., Minhas, A. A., Ahmad, M., Ashraf, R., Khalid, S., & Han, K. (2018). Analysis of factors affecting energy aware routing in wireless sensor network. *Wireless Communications and Mobile Computing*.

Caballero, F., Merino, L., Maza, I., & Ollero, A. (2008). A particle filtering method for wireless sensor network localization with an aerial robot beacon. *Proceedings of IEEE International Conference on Robotics and Automation*, (pp. 596-601). 10.1109/ROBOT.2008.4543271

Chelouah, L., Semchedine, F., & Bouallouche-Medjkoune, L. (2018). Localization protocols for mobile wireless sensor networks: A survey. *Computers & Electrical Engineering, 71*, 733–751. doi:10.1016/j.compeleceng.2017.03.024

Cheng, J., & Xia, L. (2016). An effective cuckoo search algorithm for node localization in wireless sensor network. *Sensors (Basel), 16*(9), 1390. doi:10.339016091390 PMID:27589756

Chiang, S. Y., & Wang, J. L. (2009). Localization in Wireless Sensor Networks by Fuzzy Logic System. In J. D. Velásquez, S. A. Ríos, R. J. Howlett, & L. C. Jain (Eds.), Lecture Notes in Computer Science: Vol. 5712. *Knowledge-Based and Intelligent Information and Engineering Systems. KES 2009*. Berlin, Germany: Springer. doi:10.1007/978-3-642-04592-9_89

Erdemir, E., & Tuncer, T. E. (2018). Path planning for mobile anchor based wireless sensor network localization: Static and dynamic schemes. *Ad Hoc Networks, 77*, 1–10. doi:10.1016/j.adhoc.2018.04.005

Han, G., Jiang, J., Zhang, C., Duong, T. Q., Guizani, M., & Karagiannidis, G. K. (2016). A survey on mobile anchor node assisted localization in wireless sensor networks. *IEEE Communications Surveys and Tutorials, 18*(3), 2220–2243. doi:10.1109/COMST.2016.2544751

Kim, S., Lee, I., Cho, D., & Lee, J. (2006). Dynamic localization of a mobile robot with active beacon sensors. *IFAC Proceedings Volumes, 39*(16), (pp. 921-925).

Kulkarni, V. R., & Desai, V. (2019). Computational intelligence for localization of mobile wireless sensor networks. *Proceedings of Computational Intelligence: Theories, Applications, and Future Directions* (Vol. II, pp. 449–463). Springer Singapore. doi:10.1007/978-981-13-1135-2_34

Kulkarni, V. R., Desai, V., & Kulkarni, R. V. (2016). Multistage localization in wireless sensor networks using artificial bee colony algorithm. *Proceedings of the IEEE Symposium Series on Computational Intelligence (SSCI)*, (pp. 1-8). 10.1109/SSCI.2016.7850273

Kuo, H., & Lin, C. (2013). Cultural evolution algorithm for global optimizations and its applications. *Journal of Applied Research and Technology, 11*(4), 510–522. doi:10.1016/S1665-6423(13)71558-X

Li, D., & Wen, X. (2015). An improved PSO algorithm for distributed localization in wireless sensor networks. *International Journal of Distributed Sensor Networks, 11*(7). doi:10.1155/2015/970272

Lopatka, K., Kotus, J., & Czyzewski, A. (2016). Detection, classification and localization of acoustic events in the presence of background noise for acoustic surveillance of hazardous situations. *Multimedia Tools and Applications, 75*(17), 10407–10439. doi:10.100711042-015-3105-4

Misaghi, M., & Yaghoobi, M. (2019). Improved invasive weed optimization algorithm (IWO) based on chaos theory for optimal design of PID controller. *Journal of Computational Design and Engineering, 6*(3), 284–295. doi:10.1016/j.jcde.2019.01.001

Mohamed, R. E., Saleh, A. I., Abdelrazzak, M., & Samra, A. S. (2018). Survey on wireless sensor network applications and energy efficient routing protocols. *Wireless Personal Communications, 101*(2), 1019–1055. doi:10.100711277-018-5747-9

Mohamed, S. M., Hamza, H. S., & Saroit, I. A. (2017). Coverage in mobile wireless sensor networks (M-WSN): A survey. *Computer Communications, 110*, 133–150. doi:10.1016/j.comcom.2017.06.010

Oguejiofor, O. S., Aniedu, A. N., Ejiofor, H. C., Okolibe, A. U. (2013). Trilateration Based localization Algorithm for Wireless Sensor Network. *International Journal of Science and Modern Engineering (IJISME)*, 2319-6386.

Paul, A. K., & Sato, T. (2017). Localization in wireless sensor networks: A survey on algorithms, measurement techniques, applications and challenges. *Journal of Sensor and Actuator Networks*, 6(4), 24. doi:10.3390/jsan6040024

Sang, H. Y., Duan, P. Y., & Li, J. Q. (2018). An effective invasive weed optimization algorithm for scheduling semiconductor final testing problem. *Swarm and Evolutionary Computation*, *38*, 42–53. doi:10.1016/j.swevo.2017.05.007

Xiao, L., Wang, J., & Yun, W. (2008). A novel localization algorithm based on received signal strength for mobile wireless sensor networks. *Proceedings of International Conference on Microwave and Millimeter Wave Technology*, Vol. 1, (pp. 92-95).

Yang, Y., & Zhang, L. (2013). Dynamic path planning of mobile beacon for localization in wireless sensor network. *Proceedings of International Conference on Wireless Communications and Signal Processing*, (pp. 1-5).

Compilation of References

2014 . Problems, O. P. F. (2014). IEEE PES Working Group on Modern Heuristic Optimization. Retrieved from https://www.uni-due.de/ieee-wgmho/competition2014

Abarghooee, R. A., Golestaneh, F., Gooi, H. B., Lin, J., Bavafa, F., & Terzija, V. (2016). Corrective economic dispatch and operational cycles for probabilistic unit commitment with demand response and high wind power. *Applied Energy*, *182*, 634–651. doi:10.1016/j.apenergy.2016.07.117

Abd-Alsabour, N., & Ramakrishnan, S. (2016). *Hybrid metaheuristics for classification problems*. Pattern Recognition-Analysis and Applications. doi:10.5772/65253

Abeyrathna, K. D., & Jeenanunta, C. (2019). Hybrid particle swarm optimization with genetic algorithm to train artificial neural networks for short-term load forecasting. [IJSIR]. *International Journal of Swarm Intelligence Research*, *10*(1), 1–14. doi:10.4018/IJSIR.2019010101

Abido, M. A. (2002). Optimal power flow using tabu search algorithm. *Electric Power Components and Systems*, *30*(5), 469–483. doi:10.1080/15325000252888425

Abido, M. A. (2003). Environmental/economic power dispatch using multi-objective evolutionary algorithms. *IEEE Transactions on Power Systems*, *18*(4), 1529–1537. doi:10.1109/TPWRS.2003.818693

Abshouri, A. A., & Bakhtiary, A. (2012). A New Clustering Method Based on Firefly and KHM. *Journal of Communication and Computer*, *9*, 387–391.

Acampora, G., Ishibuchi, H. H., & Vitiello, A. (2014). A comparison of multi-objective evolutionary algorithms for the ontology meta-matching problem. *Proceedings IEEE Congress on Evolutionary Computation (CEC 2014)*, (pp. 413-420). Beijing, China. 10.1109/CEC.2014.6900544

Acampora, G., Kaymak, U., Loia, V., & Vitiello, A. (2013). Applying NSGA-II for solving the Ontology Alignment Problem. *Proceedings 2013 IEEE International Conference on Systems, Man, and Cybernetics (SMC 2013)*, (pp. 1098-1103). Manchester, UK: IEEE. 10.1109/SMC.2013.191

Acampora, G., Loia, V., Salerno, S., & Vitiello, A. (2012). A hybrid evolutionary approach for solving the ontology alignment problem. *International Journal of Intelligent Systems*, *27*(3), 189–216. doi:10.1002/int.20517

Adaryani, M. R., & Karami, A. (2013). Artificial bee colony algorithm for solving multi-objective optimal power flow problem. *Electrical Power and Energy Systems*, *53*, 219–230. doi:10.1016/j.ijepes.2013.04.021

Adra, S. F., Dodd, T. J., Griffin, I. A., & Fleming, P. J. (2009). Convergence acceleration operator for multiobjective optimization. *IEEE Transactions on Evolutionary Computation*, *12*(4), 825–847. doi:10.1109/TEVC.2008.2011743

Adra, S. F., & Fleming, P. J. (2011). Diversity management in evolutionary many-objective optimization. *IEEE Transactions on Evolutionary Computation*, *15*(2), 183–195. doi:10.1109/TEVC.2010.2058117

Ahn, H. J. (2008). A new similarity measure for collaborative filtering to alleviate the new user cold-starting problem. *Information Sciences*, *178*(1), 37–51. doi:10.1016/j.ins.2007.07.024

Aizpurua, A., Harper, S., & Vigo, M. (2016). Exploring the relationship between web accessibility and user experience. *International Journal of Human-Computer Studies*, *91*, 13–23. doi:10.1016/j.ijhcs.2016.03.008

Al-Agtash, S. (2001). Hydrothermal scheduling by augmented Lagrangian: Consideration of transmission constraints and pumped-storage units. *IEEE Transactions on Power Systems*, *16*(4), 750–756. doi:10.1109/59.962422

Alahmadi, D. H., & Zeng, X.-J. (2015). Twitter-based recommender system to address cold-start: A genetic algorithm-based trust modelling and probabilistic sentiment analysis. *2015 IEEE 27th International Conference on Tools with Artificial Intelligence (ICTAI)*, (pp. 1045-1052).

Alaoui, A., & Elberrichi, Z. (2018). Feature Subset Selection Using Ant Colony Optimization for a Decision Trees Classification of Medical Data. *International Journal of Information Retrieval Research*, *8*(4), 39–50. doi:10.4018/IJIRR.2018100103

Alfimtsev, A., Sakulin, S., & Levanov, A. (2016). Formalization of Expert Knowledge About the Usability of Web Pages Based on User Criteria Aggregation [IJSI]. *International Journal of Software Innovation*, *4*(3), 38–50. doi:10.4018/IJSI.2016070103

Alham, M. H., Elshahed, M., Ibrahim, D. H., Din, E. E., & Zahab, A. E. (2016). A dynamic economic emission dispatch considering wind power uncertainty incorporating energy storage system and demand side management. *Renewable Energy*, *96*, 800–811. doi:10.1016/j.renene.2016.05.012

Ali, A., & Majhi, S. (2006). Design of optimum PID controller by bacterial foraging strategy. *Proceedings 2006 IEEE International Conference on Industrial Technology*, 601-605. 10.1109/ICIT.2006.372205

Almugren, N., & Alshamlan, H. (2019). A Survey on Hybrid Feature Selection Methods in Microarray Gene Expression Data for Cancer Classification. *IEEE Access: Practical Innovations, Open Solutions*, *7*, 78533–78548. doi:10.1109/ACCESS.2019.2922987

Alomari, A., Comeau, F., Phillips, W., & Aslam, N. (2018). New path planning model for mobile anchor-assisted localization in wireless sensor networks. *Wireless Networks*, *24*(7), 2589–2607. doi:10.100711276-017-1493-2

Alomari, O. A., Khader, A. T., Al-Betar, M. A., & Awadallah, M. A. (2018). A novel gene selection method using modified MRMR and hybrid bat-inspired algorithm with β-hill climbing. *Applied Intelligence*, *48*(11), 4429–4447. doi:10.100710489-018-1207-1

Alor, A., Mota, D., Olmos-Sánchez, K., & Rodas-Osollo, J. (2019). An Order-Picking Model Associated With Hospital Components and Solved by a Firefly Algorithm. In *Handbook of Research on Metaheuristics for Order Picking Optimization in Warehouses to Smart Cities* (pp. 173–188). Hershey, PA: IGI Global. doi:10.4018/978-1-5225-8131-4.ch009

Alrajeh, N. A., Bashir, M., & Shams, B. (2013). Localization techniques in wireless sensor networks. *International Journal of Distributed Sensor Networks*, *9*(6). doi:10.1155/2013/304628

Alsac, O., Bright, J., Prais, M., & Stott, B. (1990). Further developments in LP-based optimal power flow. *IEEE Transactions on Power Systems*, *5*(3), 697–711. doi:10.1109/59.65896

Alsac, O., & Stott, B. (1974). Optimal load flow with steady state security. *IEEE Transactions on Power Apparatus and Systems*, *93*(3), 745–751. doi:10.1109/TPAS.1974.293972

Alshamlan, H. M., Badr, G. H., & Alohali, Y. A. (2015). Genetic Bee Colony (GBC) algorithm: A new gene selection method for microarray cancer classification. *Computational Biology and Chemistry*, *56*, 49–60. doi:10.1016/j.compbiolchem.2015.03.001 PMID:25880524

Al-Shamri, M. Y. (2016). User profiling approaches for demographic recommender systems. *Knowledge-Based Systems*, *100*, 175–187. doi:10.1016/j.knosys.2016.03.006

Al-Sumait, J. S., AL-Othman, A. K., & Sykulski, J. K. (2007). Application of pattern search method to power system valve-point economic load dispatch. *Electr. Power Energy Syst*, *29*(10), 720–730. doi:10.1016/j.ijepes.2007.06.016

Amundson, I., & Koutsoukos, X. D. (2009). A survey on localization for mobile wireless sensor networks. Proceedings of Mobile Entity Localization and Tracking in GPS-less Environments (pp. 235–254). Berlin, Germany: Springer. doi:10.1007/978-3-642-04385-7_16

Ang, J. C., Mirzal, A., Haron, H., & Hamed, H. N. A. (2015). Supervised, unsupervised, and semi-supervised feature selection: A review on gene selection. *IEEE/ACM Transactions on Computational Biology and Bioinformatics*, *13*(5), 971–989. doi:10.1109/TCBB.2015.2478454 PMID:26390495

Arabali, A., Ghofrani, M., & Amoli, M. E. (2013). Cost analysis of a power system using probabilistic optimal power flow with energy storage integration and wind generation. *Electrical Power and Energy Systems*, *53*, 832–841. doi:10.1016/j.ijepes.2013.05.053

Arora, P., Boyne, D., Slater, J. J., Gupta, A., Brenner, D. R., & Drudzel, M. J. (2019). Bayesian Networks for Risk Prediction Using Real-World Data: A Tool for Precision Medicine. Elsevier, 439- 445.

Asadieh, B., & Afshar, A. (2019). Optimization of Water-Supply and Hydropower Reservoir Operation Using the Charged System Search Algorithm. *Hydrology*, *6*(1), 5. doi:10.3390/hydrology6010005

Asar, A. U., Hassnain, S. R. U., & Khan, A. (2007). Short-Term Load Forecasting Using Particle Swarm Optimization Based ANN Approach. *Proceedings 2007 International Joint Conference on Neural Networks*, 1476–1481. (IEEE). 10.1109/IJCNN.2007.4371176

Ashish, T., Kapil, S., & Manju, B. (2018). Parallel bat algorithm-based clustering using mapreduce. In *Networking Communication and Data Knowledge Engineering* (pp. 73–82). Singapore: Springer. doi:10.1007/978-981-10-4600-1_7

Askari, M. B., & Ahsaee, M. G. (2018). Bayesian network structure learning based on cuckoo search algorithm. *Proceedings 2018 6th Iranian Joint Congress on Fuzzy and Intelligent Systems (CFIS)*, pp. 127-130. IEEE. Kerman, Iran.

Australian Bureau of Meteorology. Last accessed 2012. [Online]. Available at http://www.bom.gov.au

Babicki, S., Arndt, D., Marcu, A., Liang, Y., Grant, J. R., Maciejewski, A., & Wishart, D. S. (2016). Heatmapper: Web-enabled heat mapping for all. *Nucleic Acids Research*, *44*(W1), W147–W153. doi:10.1093/nar/gkw419 PMID:27190236

Bai, L., Li, F., Cui, H., Jiang, T., Sun, H., & Zhu, J. (2016). Interval optimization based operating strategy for gas-electricity integrated energy systems considering demand response and wind uncertainty. *Applied Energy*, *167*, 270–279. doi:10.1016/j.apenergy.2015.10.119

Bailly, G., Lecolinet, E., & Nigay, L. (2016). Visual Menu Techniques [CSUR]. *ACM Computing Surveys*, *49*(4), 60. doi:10.1145/3002171

Bailly, G., Oulasvirta, A., Kötzing, T., & Hoppe, S. (2013). Menuoptimizer: Interactive optimization of menu systems. *Proceedings of the 26th annual ACM symposium on User interface software and technology*, 331-342. ACM.

Bai, W., & Lee, Y. (2016) Modified Optimal Power Flow on Storage Devices and Wind Power Integrated System. *Proceedings IEEE International Conference on Power and Energy Society General Meeting(PESGM)*, Boston, USA. IEEE.

Bai, W., & Lee, Y. (2016).Modified optimal power flow on storage devices and wind power integrated system. *Proc. IEEE International conference on power and energy society general meeting (PESGM)*, Boston, MA, July 17-21.

Bakirtzis, A. G., Biskas, P. N., Zoumas, C. E., & Petridis, V. (2002). Optimal power flow by enhanced genetic algorithm. *IEEE Transactions on Power Systems, 17*(2), 229–236. doi:10.1109/TPWRS.2002.1007886

Bala, J., Huang, J., Vafaie, H., DeJong, K., & Wechsler, H. (1995, August). Hybrid learning using genetic algorithms and decision trees for pattern classification. In IJCAI (1) (pp. 719-724).

Baliarsingh, S. K., Vipsita, S., Muhammad, K., & Bakshi, S. (2019). Analysis of high-dimensional biomedical data using an evolutionary multi-objective emperor penguin optimizer. *Swarm and Evolutionary Computation, 48*, 262–273. doi:10.1016/j.swevo.2019.04.010

Basu, M. (2004). An interactive fuzzy satisfying method based on evolutionary programming technique for multi-objective short-term hydrothermal scheduling. *Electric Power Systems Research, 69*(2-3), 277–285. doi:10.1016/j.epsr.2003.10.003

Basu, M. (2011). Multi-objective optimal power flow with FACTS devices. *Energy Conversion and Management, 52*(2), 903–910. doi:10.1016/j.enconman.2010.08.017

Beegom, A. S. A., & Rajasree, M. S. (2019). A discrete PSO algorithm for task scheduling in cloud computing systems. *Evolutionary Intelligence, 12*(2), 227–239. doi:10.100712065-019-00216-7

Beel, J., Langer, S., Nürnberger, A., & Genzmehr, M. (2013). The impact of demographics (age and gender) and other user-characteristics on evaluating recommender systems. In *Research and Advanced Technology for Digital Libraries* (pp. 396–400). Springer. doi:10.1007/978-3-642-40501-3_45

Begum, S., Chakraborty, S., Banerjee, A., Das, S., Sarkar, R., & Chakraborty, D. (2018). Gene selection for diagnosis of cancer in microarray data using memetic algorithm. In *Intelligent Engineering Informatics* (pp. 441–449). Singapore: Springer. doi:10.1007/978-981-10-7566-7_43

Bentley, P. J. (1999). *Evolutionary Design by Computers*. Morgan Kaufmann Publishers.

Berkovsky, S., Kuflik, T., & Ricci, F. (2007). Distributed collaborative filtering with domain specialization. *Proceedings of the 2007 ACM conference on Recommender systems.* 10.1145/1297231.1297238

Beyer, H. G. (2001). *The Theory of Evolutionary Strategies*. Berlin, Germany: Springer-Verlag. doi:10.1007/978-3-662-04378-3

Bhattacharya, A., & Chattopadhyay, P. K. (2010). Hybrid differential evolution with biogeography-based optimization for solution of economic load dispatch. *IEEE Transactions on Power Systems, 25*(4), 1955–1964. doi:10.1109/TPWRS.2010.2043270

Bidi, N., & Elberrichi, Z. (2018). Best Features Selection for Biomedical Data Classification Using Seven Spot Ladybird Optimization Algorithm. [IJAMC]. *International Journal of Applied Metaheuristic Computing, 9*(3), 75–87. doi:10.4018/IJAMC.2018070104

Bilchev, G., & Parmee, I. C. (1995). The Ant Colony Metaphor for Searching Continuous Design Spaces. *Selected Papers from AISB Workshop on Evolutionary Computing*, pp. 25-39. Berlin, Germany: Springer.

Biswas, P. P., Suganthan, P. N., & Amaratunga, G. A. J. (2017). Optimal power flow solutions incorporating stochastic wind and solar power. *Energy Conversion and Management, 148*, 1194–1207. doi:10.1016/j.enconman.2017.06.071

Blackwell, T. M., & Bentley, P. (2002). Don't push me! collision-avoiding swarms. *Proceedings of the Fourth Congress on Evolutionary Computation (CEC 2002)*, (pp. 1691-1696).

Blum, C., & Roli, A. (2003). Metaheuristics in combinatorial optimization: Overview and conceptual comparison. *ACM Computing Surveys*, *35*(3), 268–308. doi:10.1145/937503.937505

Bobadilla, J., Fernando, O., Antonio, H., & Abraham, G. (2013). Recommender systems survey. *Knowledge-Based Systems*, *46*, 109–132. doi:10.1016/j.knosys.2013.03.012

Bobadilla, J., Fernando, O., Antonio, H., & Jesú, S. B. (2012). A collaborative filtering approach to mitigate the new user cold start problem. *Knowledge-Based Systems*, *26*, 225–238. doi:10.1016/j.knosys.2011.07.021

Bobadilla, J., Francisco, S., & Jesus, B. (2010). A new collaborative filtering metric that improves the behavior of recommender systems. *Knowledge-Based Systems*, *23*(6), 520–528. doi:10.1016/j.knosys.2010.03.009

Bock, J., & Hettenhausen, J. (2012). Discrete particle swarm optimisation for ontology alignment. *Information Sciences*, *192*, 152–173. doi:10.1016/j.ins.2010.08.013

Bonou, A., Laurent, A., & Olsen, S. I. (2016). Life cycle assessment of onshore and offshore wind energy-from theory to application. *Applied Energy*, *180*, 327–337. doi:10.1016/j.apenergy.2016.07.058

Bosman, P. A. N., & Thierens, D. (2003). The balance between proximity and diversity in multiobjective evolutionary algorithms. *IEEE Transactions on Evolutionary Computation*, *7*(2), 174–188. doi:10.1109/TEVC.2003.810761

Bouckaert, R. R. (1995). *Bayesian belief networks: from construction to inference*. The Netherlands: Utrecht University.

Bratton, D., & Kennedy, J. (2007). Defining a standard for particle swarm optimization. *Proceedings of the 2007 IEEE Swarm Intelligence Symposium*, (pp. 120-127). 10.1109/SIS.2007.368035

Bresson, X., Esedoglu, S., Vandergheynst, P., Thiran, J. P., & Osher, S. (2007). Fast global minimization of the active contour/snake model. *Journal of Mathematical Imaging and Vision*, *28*(2), 151–167. doi:10.100710851-007-0002-0

Brezočnik, L., Fister, I. Jr, & Podgorelec, V. (2018). Swarm intelligence algorithms for feature selection: A review. *Applied Sciences (Basel, Switzerland)*, *8*(9), 1521. doi:10.3390/app8091521

Bukar, A. L., Tan, C. W., & Kwan, K. Y. (2019). Optimal sizing of an autonomous photovoltaic/wind/battery/diesel generator microgrid using grasshopper optimization algorithm. *Solar Energy*, *2*(188), 685–696. doi:10.1016/j.solener.2019.06.050

Burchett, R. C., Happ, H. H., & Vierath, D. R. (1984). Quadratically convergent optimal power flow. *IEEE Transactions on Power Apparatus and Systems*, *103*(11), 3267–3276. doi:10.1109/TPAS.1984.318568

Burke, E. K., Gustafson, S., & Kendall, G. (2002). A survey and analysis of diversity measures in genetic programming. *Proceedings of the Genetic and Evolutionary Computation Conference (GECCO 2002)*, (pp. 716-723). San Francisco, CA: Morgan Kaufmann.

Caballero, F., Merino, L., Maza, I., & Ollero, A. (2008). A particle filtering method for wireless sensor network localization with an aerial robot beacon. *Proceedings of IEEE International Conference on Robotics and Automation*, (pp. 596-601). 10.1109/ROBOT.2008.4543271

Cai, Z., Niu, J., & Yang, X. (2018, May). A Multi Measure Improved Firefly Algorithm. *Proceedings 2018 2nd IEEE Advanced Information Management, Communicates, Electronic, and Automation Control Conference (IMCEC)* (pp. 20-26). IEEE.

Campos, L. M. (2006). A Scoring Function for Learning Bayesian Networks based on Mutual Information and Conditional Independence Tests. *Journal of Machine Learning Research*, (7), 2149–2187.

Caponio, A., Neri, F., & Tirronen, V. (2009). Super-fit control adaptation in memetic differential evolution frameworks. *Soft Computing*, *13*(8–9), 811–831. doi:10.100700500-008-0357-1

Chaib, A. E., Bouchekara, H. R. E. H., Mehasni, R., & Abido, M. A. (2016). Optimal power flow with emission and non-smooth cost functions using backtracking search optimization algorithm. *International Journal of Electrical Power & Energy Systems*, *81*, 64–77. doi:10.1016/j.ijepes.2016.02.004

Chai, Z.-Y., Li, Y.-L., Han, Y.-M., & Zhu, S.-F. (2018). Recommendation System Based on Singular Value Decomposition and Multi-Objective Immune Optimization. *IEEE Access: Practical Innovations, Open Solutions*, *7*, 6060–6071. doi:10.1109/ACCESS.2018.2842257

Chakraborty, A., & Kar, A. K. (2017). Swarm intelligence: A review of algorithms. Nature-Inspired Computing and Optimization, 475-494. Springer International Publishing.

Chakravorty, J., Shah, S., & Nagraja, H. M. (2018). ANN and ANFIS for Short Term Load Forecasting. *Engineering, Technology, & Applied Scientific Research*, *8*(2), 2818–2820.

Chang, Y. C., Lee, T. Y., Chen, C. L., & Jan, R. M. (2014). Optimal power flow of a wind-thermal generation system. *International Journal of Electrical Power & Energy Systems*, *55*, 312–320. doi:10.1016/j.ijepes.2013.09.028

Chelouah, L., Semchedine, F., & Bouallouche-Medjkoune, L. (2018). Localization protocols for mobile wireless sensor networks: A survey. *Computers & Electrical Engineering*, *71*, 733–751. doi:10.1016/j.compeleceng.2017.03.024

Chen, F., Zhou, J., Wang, C., Li, C., & Lu, P. (2017). A modified gravitational search algorithm based on a non-dominated sorting genetic approach for hydro-thermal-wind economic emission dispatching. *Energy,* 121, 276-291.

Chen, T., & He, L. (2009). Collaborative filtering based on demographic attribute vector. *Proceedings ETP International Conference on Future Computer and Communication (pp. 225-229). IEEE.*

Chen, Y. B., & Chen, O. T. (2009). Image Segmentation Method Using Thresholds Automatically Determined from Picture Contents, *Journal on Image and Video Processing*, EURASIP.

Chen, C. C., Wan, Y.-H., Chung, M.-C., & Sun, Y.-C. (2013). An effective recommendation method for cold start new users using trust and distrust networks. *Information Sciences*, *224*, 19–36. doi:10.1016/j.ins.2012.10.037

Chen, C., Wang, F., Zhou, B., Chan, K. W., Cao, Y., & Tan, Y. (2015). An interval optimization-based day-ahead scheduling scheme for renewable energy management in smart distribution systems. *Energy Conversion and Management*, *106*, 584–596. doi:10.1016/j.enconman.2015.10.014

Cheng, S. (2013). *Population Diversity in Particle Swarm Optimization: Definition, Observation, Control, and Application.* (Doctoral dissertation), University of Liverpool, UK.

Cheng, S. (2013). *Population diversity in particle swarm optimization: Definition, observation, control, and application.* (Ph.D. dissertation), University of Liverpool, UK.

Cheng, S., & Shi, Y. (2011b): Normalized population diversity in particle swarm optimization. *Proceedings of the 2nd International Conference on Swarm Intelligence. Lecture Notes in Computer Science, 6728,* (pp. 38-45). 10.1007/978-3-642-21515-5_5

Cheng, S., & Shi, Y. (2019). Brain Storm Optimization Algorithms: Concepts, Principles, and Applications, 23. Adaptation, Learning, and Optimization. Springer International Publishing AG. doi:10.1007/978-3-030-15070-9

Cheng, S., Shi, Y., & Qin, Q. (2011b). Promoting diversity in particle swarm optimization to solve multimodal problems. In B.-L. Lu, L. Zhang, & J. Kwok (Eds.), Neural Information Processing, (LNCS 7063, pp. 228-237). Berlin, Germany: Springer. doi:10.1007/978-3-642-24958-7_27

Cheng, S., Shi, Y., & Qin, Q. (2012b). On the performance metrics of multiobjective optimization. In Y. Tan, Y. Shi, & Z. Ji, (Eds.), Advances in Swarm Intelligence, volume 7331 of LNCS, pp. 504-512. Berlin, Germany: Springer. doi:10.1007/978-3-642-30976-2_61

Cheng, J., & Xia, L. (2016). An effective cuckoo search algorithm for node localization in wireless sensor network. *Sensors (Basel)*, *16*(9), 1390. doi:10.339016091390 PMID:27589756

Cheng, S., Lu, H., Lei, X., & Shi, Y. (2018). A Quarter Century of Particle Swarm Optimization. *Complex & Intelligent Systems*, *4*(3), 227–239. doi:10.100740747-018-0071-2

Cheng, S., Qin, Q., Chen, J., & Shi, Y. (2016). Brain storm optimization algorithm: A review. *Artificial Intelligence Review*, *46*(4), 445–458. doi:10.100710462-016-9471-0

Cheng, S., & Shi, Y. (2011). Diversity control in particle swarm optimization. *Proceedings of 2011 IEEE Symposium on Swarm Intelligence (SIS 2011)*, (pp. 110-118).

Cheng, S., & Shi, Y. (2011a). Diversity control in particle swarm optimization. *Proceedings of the 2011 IEEE Swarm Intelligence Symposium*, (pp. 110-118).

Cheng, S., Shi, Y., & Qin, Q. (2011). Experimental study on boundary constraints handling in particle swarm optimization: From population diversity perspective. [IJSIR]. *International Journal of Swarm Intelligence Research*, *2*(3), 43–69. doi:10.4018/jsir.2011070104

Cheng, S., Shi, Y., & Qin, Q. (2012). Population diversity of particle swarm optimizer solving single and multi-objective problems [IJSIR]. *International Journal of Swarm Intelligence Research*, *3*(4), 23–60. doi:10.4018/jsir.2012100102

Cheng, S., Shi, Y., & Qin, Q. (2012a). Dynamical exploitation space reduction in particle swarm optimization for solving large scale problems. *Proceedings of 2012 IEEE Congress on Evolutionary Computation, (CEC 2012)*, (pp. 3030-3037), Brisbane, Australia. IEEE. 10.1109/CEC.2012.6252937

Cheng, S., Shi, Y., & Qin, Q. (2012c). Population diversity based study on search information propagation in particle swarm optimization. *Proceedings of 2012 IEEE Congress on Evolutionary Computation, (CEC 2012)*, (pp. 1272-1279), Brisbane, Australia. IEEE. 10.1109/CEC.2012.6256502

Cheng, S., Shi, Y., & Qin, Q. (2013). A study of normalized population diversity in particle swarm optimization. [IJSIR]. *International Journal of Swarm Intelligence Research*, *4*(1), 1–34. doi:10.4018/jsir.2013010101

Cheng, S., Shi, Y., Qin, Q., & Gao, S. (2013). Solution clustering analysis in brain storm optimization algorithm. *Proceedings of The 2013 IEEE Symposium on Swarm Intelligence, (SIS 2013)*, (pp. 111-118). Singapore: IEEE. 10.1109/SIS.2013.6615167

Cheng, S., Shi, Y., Qin, Q., & Ting, T. O. (2012) Population diversity based inertia weight adaptation in particle swarm optimization. *Proceedings of The Fifth International Conference on Advanced Computational Intelligence, (ICACI 2012)*, (pp.395-403). 10.1109/ICACI.2012.6463194

Cheng, S., Shi, Y., Qin, Q., Zhang, Q., & Bai, R. (2014). Population diversity maintenance in brain storm optimization algorithm. *Journal of Artificial Intelligence and Soft Computing Research*, *4*(2), 83–97. doi:10.1515/jaiscr-2015-0001

Chen, H., Bo, M. L., & Zhu, Y. (2014). Multi-hive bee foraging algorithm for multi-objective optimal power flow considering the cost, loss, and emission. *Electrical Power and Energy Systems*, *60*, 203–220. doi:10.1016/j.ijepes.2014.02.017

Chen, K. H., Wang, K. J., Tsai, M. L., Wang, K. M., Adrian, A. M., Cheng, W. C., ... Chang, K. S. (2014). Gene selection for cancer identification: A decision tree model empowered by particle swarm optimization algorithm. *BMC Bioinformatics*, *15*(1), 49. doi:10.1186/1471-2105-15-49 PMID:24555567

Chen, L., & Aihara, K. (1995). Chaotic simulated annealing by a neural network model with transient chaos. *Neural Networks*, *8*(6), 915–930. doi:10.1016/0893-6080(95)00033-V

Chen, S., & Montgomery, J. (2011). A simple strategy to maintain diversity and reduce crowding in particle swarm optimization. *Proceedings of the 13th annual conference companion on Genetic and evolutionary computation (GECCO 2011)*, (pp. 811-812). 10.1145/2001858.2002101

Chen, Y., Wei, W., Liu, F., & Mei, S. (2016). Distributionally robust hydro-thermal-wind economic dispatch. *Applied Energy*, *173*, 511–519. doi:10.1016/j.apenergy.2016.04.060

Chiang, S. Y., & Wang, J. L. (2009). Localization in Wireless Sensor Networks by Fuzzy Logic System. In J. D. Velásquez, S. A. Ríos, R. J. Howlett, & L. C. Jain (Eds.), Lecture Notes in Computer Science: Vol. 5712. *Knowledge-Based and Intelligent Information and Engineering Systems. KES 2009*. Berlin, Germany: Springer. doi:10.1007/978-3-642-04592-9_89

Chickering, D. (1996). *Learning Bayesian Networks is NP-Complete*. Springer-Verlag. doi:10.1007/978-1-4612-2404-4_12

Choi, S.-M., & Han, Y.-S. (2010). A content recommendation system based on category correlations. Proceedings 2010 Fifth International Multi-conference on Computing in the Global Information Technology (pp. 66-70). IEEE.

Choi, S.-M., Ko, S.-K., & Han, Y.-S. (2012). A movie recommendation algorithm based on genre correlations. *Expert Systems with Applications*, *39*(9), 8079–8085. doi:10.1016/j.eswa.2012.01.132

Chowdhury, B. H., & Rahman, S. (1990). A review of recent advances in economic dispatch. *IEEE Transactions on Power Systems*, *5*(4), 1248–1257. doi:10.1109/59.99376

Chuang, L. Y., Chang, H. W., Tu, C. J., & Yang, C. H. (2008). Improved binary PSO for feature selection using gene expression data. *Computational Biology and Chemistry*, *32*(1), 29–38. doi:10.1016/j.compbiolchem.2007.09.005 PMID:18023261

Chung, J., Hong, S., Kim, Y., Kang, S. J., & Kim, C. (2019). Layout placement optimization methods using repeated user interface sequence patterns for client applications. *Information Visualization*, *18*(3), 357–370. doi:10.1177/1473871618825334

Chung, S. H., & Chan, H. K. (2012). A two-level genetic algorithm to determine production frequencies for economic lost scheduling problem. *IEEE Transactions on Industrial Electronics*, *59*(1), 611–619. doi:10.1109/TIE.2011.2130498

Clerc, M., & Kennedy, J. (2002). The particle swarm-explosion, stability, and convergence in a multidimensional complex space. *IEEE Transactions on* Evolutionary Computation, *6*(1), 58–73.

Clerc, M., & Kennedy, J. (2002). The particle swarm—Explosion, stability, and convergence in a multidimensional complex space. *IEEE Transactions on Evolutionary Computation*, *6*(1), 58–73. doi:10.1109/4235.985692

Cooper, G. (2000). A Bayesian Method for Causal Modeling and Discovery Under Selection. *Proceedings of the Sixteenth conference on Uncertainty in artificial intelligence* (pp. 98-106). California: Morgan Kaufmann.

Cooper, G. F., & Yoo, C. (1999). Causal Discovery from a Mixture of Experimental and Observational Data. *Proceedings of the Fifteenth conference on Uncertainty in artificial intelligence* (pp. 116-125). California: Morgan Kaufmann.

Cooper, G. F., & Herskovits, E. (1992). A Bayesian method for the induction of probabilistic networks from data. *Machine Learning*, *9*(4), 309–347. doi:10.1007/BF00994110

Corne, D. W., Jerram, N. R., Knowles, J. D., & Oates, M. J. (2001) PESA-II: Region-based selection in evolutionary multiobjective optimization, *Proceedings of the 3rd Annual Conference on Genetic and Evolutionary Computation*. San Francisco, CA: Morgan Kaufmann, (pp. 283-290).

Corriveau, G., Guilbault, R., Tahan, A., & Sabourin, R. (2012). Review and Study of Genotypic Diversity Measures for Real-Coded Representations. *IEEE Transactions on Evolutionary Computation*, *16*(5), 695–710. doi:10.1109/TEVC.2011.2170075

Council, G. W. E. (2012). Global wind energy outlook 2012. Retrieved November 2012 from https://gwec.net/publications/global-wind-energy-outlook/global-wind-energy-outlook-2012/

Cowie, J., Oteniya, L., & Coles, R. (2007). *Particle Swarm Optimisation for learning Bayesian Networks*. Engineering and Physical Sciences Research Council.

Danilov, N., Shulga, T., Frolova, N., Melnikova, N., Vagarina, N., & Pchelintseva, E. (2016). Software Usability Evaluation Based on the User Pinpoint Activity Heat Map. In *Software Engineering Perspectives and Application in Intelligent Systems*, (pp. 217–225). Cham, Switzerland: Springer. doi:10.1007/978-3-319-33622-0_20

Das, G. S. (2017). Forecasting the energy demand of Turkey with a NN based on an improved particle swarm optimization. *Neural Computing & Applications*, *28*(S1), 539–549. doi:10.100700521-016-2367-8

Dasgupta, K., Roy, P., & Mukherjee, V. (2020). Power flow based hydro-thermal-wind scheduling of hybrid power system using sine cosine algorithm. *Electric Power Systems Research*, 178.

Dashtban, M., & Balafar, M. (2017). Gene selection for microarray cancer classification using a new evolutionary method employing artificial intelligence concepts. *Genomics*, *109*(2), 91–107. doi:10.1016/j.ygeno.2017.01.004 PMID:28159597

Das, K., Mishra, D., & Shaw, K. (2016). A metaheuristic optimization framework for informative gene selection. *Informatics in Medicine Unlocked*, *4*, 10–20. doi:10.1016/j.imu.2016.09.003

De Jong, K. A. (1975). An analysis of the behavior of a class of genetic adaptive systems. (Doctoral dissertation), University of Michigan, Michigan.

Deb, K., & Jain, S. (2002). Running performance metrics for evolutionary multi-objective optimization. Technical Report 2002004, Kanpur Genetic Algorithms Laboratory (KanGAL), Indian Institute of Technology Kanpur.

Deb, K., Pratap, A., Agarwal, S., & Meyarivan, T. (2002). A fast and elitist multiobjective genetic algorithm: NSGA-II. *IEEE Transactions on Evolutionary Computation*, *6*(2), 182–197. doi:10.1109/4235.996017

Deepthi, P. S., & Thampi, S. M. (2016). A metaheuristic approach for simultaneous gene selection and clustering of microarray data. In *Intelligent Systems, Technologies, and Applications* (pp. 449–461). Cham, Switzerland: Springer. doi:10.1007/978-3-319-23258-4_39

Deng, T., Fan, W., & Geerts, F. (2015). On recommendation problems beyond points of interest. *Information Systems*, *48*, 64–88. doi:10.1016/j.is.2014.08.002

Dhillon, J. S., Parti, S. C., & Kothari, D. P. (2002). Fuzzy decision-making in stochastic multi objective short-term hydrothermal scheduling. *IEE Proceedings. Generation, Transmission and Distribution*, *149*, 191–200.

Diego-Mas, J. A., Garzon-Leal, D., Poveda-Bautista, R., & Alcaide-Marzal, J. (2019). User-interfaces layout optimization using eye-tracking, mouse movements and genetic algorithms. *Applied Ergonomics*, *78*, 197–209. doi:10.1016/j.apergo.2019.03.004 PMID:31046951

Dif (b), N., & Elberrichi, Z. (2018). A Multi-Verse Optimizer Approach for Instance Selection and Optimizing 1-NN Algorithm. *International Journal of Strategic Information Technology and Applications (IJSITA), 9*(2), 35-49.

Dif, N., & Elberrichi, Z. (2017, December). Microarray Data Feature Selection and Classification Using an Enhanced Multi-Verse Optimizer and Support Vector Machine. In 3rd International Conference on Networking and Advanced Systems. Academic Press.

Dif, N., Walid Attaoui, M., & Elberrichi, Z. (2018, December). Gene Selection for Microarray Data Classification Using Hybrid Meta-Heuristics. *Proceedings International Symposium on Modelling and Implementation of Complex Systems* (pp. 119-132). Cham, Switzerland: Springer.

Dif, N., & Elberrichi, Z. (2019). An Enhanced Recursive Firefly Algorithm for Informative Gene Selection. [IJSIR]. *International Journal of Swarm Intelligence Research, 10*(2), 21–33. doi:10.4018/IJSIR.2019040102

Dikbas, S., Arici, T., & Altunbasak, Y. (2007). Chrominance Edge preserving Grayscale Transformation with approximate First Principal Component for Colour Edge Detection. *Proceedings of IEEE Conference of Image Processing (ICIP'07)*, 9, pp. 497-500. IEEE.

Dingli, A., & Cassar, S. (2014). An intelligent framework for website usability. *Advances in Human-Computer Interaction, 2014*, 5. doi:10.1155/2014/479286

Djan-Sampson, P. O., & Sahin, F. (2004). Structural Learning; of Bayesian Networks from Complete Data using the Scatter Search Documents. *Proceedings IEEE International Conference on Systems, Man, and Cybernetics.* 10.1109/ICSMC.2004.1400904

Domínguez, J. S. H., & Pulido, G. T. (2011). A comparison on the search of particle swarm optimization and differential evolution on multi-objective optimization. *Proceedings of the 2011 Congress on Evolutionary Computation (CEC2011)*, (pp. 1978-1985). 10.1109/CEC.2011.5949858

Dorigo, M., & Stutzle, T. (2004). Ant Colony Optimization. Cambridge: The MIT Press.

Dorigo, M., Maniezzo, V., & Colorni, A. (1996). Ant system: optimization by a colony of cooperating agents. *IEEE Transactions on* Systems, Man, and Cybernetics, Part B: Cybernetics, *26*(1), 29–41.

Dorigo, M., Maniezzo, V., & Colorni, A. (1996). Ant system: Optimization by a colony of cooperating agents. *IEEE Transactions on Systems, Man, and Cybernetics. Part B, Cybernetics, 26*(1), 29–41. doi:10.1109/3477.484436 PMID:18263004

Dorronsoro, B., & Bouvry, P. (2011). Improving classical and decentralized differential evolution with new mutation operator and population topologies. *IEEE Transactions on Evolutionary Computation, 15*(1), 67–98. doi:10.1109/TEVC.2010.2081369

Dragisic, Z., Ivanova, V., Lambrix, P., Faria, D., Jimenez-Ruiz, E., & Pesquita, C. (2016). User validation in ontology alignment. *Proceedings 15th International Semantic Web Conference 2016*. Kobe, Japan. Berlin, Germany: Springer. (pp. 200-217). 10.1007/978-3-319-46523-4_13

Dubey, H. M., Pandit, M., & Panigrahi, B. K. (2015). Hybrid flower pollination algorithm with time-varying fuzzy selection mechanism for wind integrated multi-objective dynamic economic dispatch. *Renewable Energy, 83*, 188–202. doi:10.1016/j.renene.2015.04.034

Dubey, H., Pandit, M., & Panjigrahi, B. (2016). Hydro-thermal-wind scheduling employing novel ant lion optimization technique with composite ranking index. *Renewable Energy, 99*, 18–34. doi:10.1016/j.renene.2016.06.039

Dubey, H., Panigrahi, B. K., & Pandit, M. (2014). Bio-inspired optimisation for economic load dispatch: A review. *International Journal of Bio-Inspired Compu., 6*(1), 7–21. doi:10.1504/IJBIC.2014.059967

Eberhart, R., & Kennedy, J. (1995, October). A new optimizer using particle swarm theory. *MHS'95. Proceedings of the Sixth International Symposium on Micro Machine and Human Science* (pp. 39-43). IEEE. 10.1109/MHS.1995.494215

Eberhart, R. C., Dobbins, R. W., & Simpson, P. K. (1996). *Computational Intelligence PC Tools*. Academic Press Professional.

Eberhart, R., & Shi, Y. (2000). Comparing inertia weights and constriction factors in particle swarm optimization. *Proceedings of the 2000 IEEE Congress on Evolutionary Computation (CEC2000)*, (pp. 84-89). 10.1109/CEC.2000.870279

Eberhart, R., & Shi, Y. (2001). Particle swarm optimization: Developments, applications, and resources. *Proceedings of the 2001 Congress on Evolutionary Computation (CEC2001)*, (pp. 81-86). 10.1109/CEC.2001.934374

Eberhart, R., & Shi, Y. (2007). *Computational Intelligence: Concepts to Implementations*. Morgan Kaufmann. doi:10.1016/B978-155860759-0/50002-0

Eladawy, H. M., Mohamed, A. E., & Salem, S. A. (2018). A New Algorithm for Repairing Web-Locators using Optimization Techniques. *Proceedings 2018 13th International Conference on Computer Engineering and Systems (ICCES)*, 327-331.

Elazim, S. A., & Ali, E. S. (2016). Optimal power system stabilizers design via cuckoo search algorithm. *International Journal of Electrical Power & Energy Systems*, 75, 99–107. doi:10.1016/j.ijepes.2015.08.018

Emary, E., Zawabaa, H. M., & Hassanien, A. E. (2016). Binary grey wolf optimization approaches for feature selection. *Neurocomputing*, 172, 371–381. doi:10.1016/j.neucom.2015.06.083

Emary, E., Zawbaa, H. M., Ghany, K. K. A., Hassanien, A. E., & Pârv, B. (2015, September). Firefly optimization algorithm for feature selection. *Proceedings of the 7th Balkan Conference on Informatics Conference* (p. 26). ACM.

Erdemir, E., & Tuncer, T. E. (2018). Path planning for mobile anchor based wireless sensor network localization: Static and dynamic schemes. *Ad Hoc Networks*, 77, 1–10. doi:10.1016/j.adhoc.2018.04.005

Ero_glu Y, & S. U. Seçkiner. (2013). Wind farm layout optimization using particle filtering approach. *Renew Energy*, 58, pp. 95-107.

Ewees, A. A., Elaziz, M. A., & Houssein, E. H. (2018). Improved grasshopper optimization algorithm using opposition-based learning. *Expert Systems with Applications*, 112, 156–172. doi:10.1016/j.eswa.2018.06.023

Falaghi, H., & Haghifam, M.-R. (2007). ACO based algorithm for distributed generation sources allocation and sizing in distribution systems. Power Tech, Lausanne. doi:10.1109/PCT.2007.4538377

Falconer, M. S., & Noy, F. N. (2011). Schema Matching and Mapping, Data-Centric Systems and Applications. Berlin, Germany: Springer.

Fang, W., Sun, J., Ding, Y., Wu, X., & Xu, W. (2010). A Review of Quantum-behaved Particle Swarm Optimization. *IETE Technical Review*, 27(4), 336–348. doi:10.4103/0256-4602.64601

Fan, X., & Malone, C. Y. (2014). *Tightening Bounds for Bayesian Network Structure Learning*. Association for the Advancement of Artificial Intelligence.

Faria, D., Martins, C., Nanavaty, A., Oliveiraand, D., Balasubramani, B. S., Taheri, A., . . . Cruz, I. F. (2015). AML results for OAEI 2015. *Proceedings 10th International Workshop on Ontology Matching*, (pp. 116-123). Bethlehem, PA. Academic Press.

Faris (b), H., Aljarah, I., Al-Betar, M. A., & Mirjalili, S. (2018). Grey wolf optimizer: a review of recent variants and applications. *Neural computing and applications*, 30(2), 413-435.

Faris, H., Aljarah, I., & Mirjalili, S. (2016). Training feedforward neural networks using multi-verse optimizer for binary classification problems. *Applied Intelligence*, *45*(2), 322–332. doi:10.100710489-016-0767-1

Faris, H., Hassonah, M. A., Ala'M, A. Z., Mirjalili, S., & Aljarah, I. (2018). A multi-verse optimizer approach for feature selection and optimizing SVM parameters based on a robust system architecture. *Neural Computing & Applications*, *30*(8), 2355–2369. doi:10.100700521-016-2818-2

Farooq, H., & Siddique, M. T. (2014). A Comparative Study on User Interfaces of Interactive Genetic Algorithm. *Procedia Computer Science*, *32*, 45–52. doi:10.1016/j.procs.2014.05.396

Faruqi, S. H., Alaeddini, A., Jaramillo, C. A., Potter, J. S., & Pugh, M. J. (2018). Mining patterns of comorbidity evolution in patients with multiple chronic conditions using unsupervised multi-level temporal Bayesian network. *PLoS One*, *13*(7), 1–22. doi:10.1371/journal.pone.0199768 PMID:30001371

Fast, A. S. (2010). *Learning the Structure of Bayesian Networks with Constraint Satisfaction.* Massachusetts: (PHD Thesis), Department of Computer Science, University of Massachusetts, February 2010.

Fathabadi, H. (2018). Utilizing solar and wind energy in plug-in hybrid electric vehicles. *Energy Conversion and Management*, *156*, 317–328. doi:10.1016/j.enconman.2017.11.015

Feit, A. M., Bachynskyi, M., & Sridhar, S. (2015). Towards multi-objective optimization for ui design. In *CHI 2015 Workshop on Principles, Techniques, and Perspectives on Optimization and HCI*.

Feng, Z.-K., Niu, W. J., & Cheng, C. T. (2017, July). Multi-objective quantum-behaved particle swarm optimization for economic environmental hydrothermal energy system scheduling. *Energy*, *131*(15), 165–178. doi:10.1016/j.energy.2017.05.013

Ficici, S. G. (2005). Monotonic solution concepts in coevolution. *Proceedings Genetic and Evolutionary Computation Conference (GECCO 2005)*, (pp. 499-506).

Firouzi, B. B., Farjah, E., & Abarghooee, R. A. (2013). An efficient scenario-based and fuzzy self-adaptive learning particle swarm optimization approach for dynamic economic emission dispatch considering load and wind power uncertainties. *Energy*, *50*(1), 232–244. doi:10.1016/j.energy.2012.11.017

Fister, I., Jr., Fister, D., & Yang, X. S. (2013). A hybrid bat algorithm. *arXiv preprint arXiv:1303.6310*.

Fong, S., Deb, S., Yang, X. S., & Zhuang, Y. (2014). Towards Enhancement of Performance of K-Means Clustering Using Nature-Inspired Optimization Algorithms. *The Scientific World Journal*, *2014*, 1–16. doi:10.1155/2014/564829 PMID:25202730

Fortier, N., Sheppard, J., & Pillai, K. G. (2013). Abductive Inference using Overlapping Swarm Intelligence. *Proceedings 2013 IEEE Symposium on Swarm Intelligence (SIS), pp. 263-270. IEEE.*.

Friedman, M. (1937). The use of ranks to avoid the assumption of normality implicit in the analysis of variance. *Journal of the American Statistical Association*, *32*(200), 675–701. doi:10.1080/01621459.1937.10503522

Friedman, N., Murphy, K., & Russell, S. (1998). Learning the structure of dynamic probabilistic networks. *Proceedings 14th Conference on Uncertainty in Artificial Intelligence (UAI-98)*, 139-147. San Francisco, CA: Morgan Kaufmann.

Frigui, H., & Krishnapuram, R. (1999). A Robust Competitive Clustering Algorithm with Applications. *Computer Vision Journal. IEEE Transactions on Pattern Analysis and Machine Intelligence*, *21*(5), 450–465. doi:10.1109/34.765656

Fu, Y., Zheng, Z., Gao, X., Yang, Y., Lv, P., Wang, Z., & Zhao, W. (2018). Application of Modified BFA for Fault Location in Distribution Networks. In *2nd IEEE Conference on Energy Internet and Energy System Integration (EI2)*, 1-6.

Gadekallu, T. R., & Khare, N. (2017). Cuckoo search optimized reduction and fuzzy logic classifier for heart disease and diabetes prediction. [IJFSA]. *International Journal of Fuzzy System Applications, 6*(2), 25–42. doi:10.4018/IJFSA.2017040102

Gandomi, A. H., Yang, X. S., Talatahari, S., & Alavi, A. H. (2013). Firefly algorithm with chaos. *Communications in Nonlinear Science and Numerical Simulation, 18*(1), 89–98. doi:10.1016/j.cnsns.2012.06.009

Gandomi, A. H., Yang, X.-S., Marand, S. T., & Alavi, A. H. (2013). *Metaheuristic applications in structures and infra-structures*. USA: Elsevier.

Gao, T., & Wei, D. (2018). Parallel Bayesian Network Structure Learning. *35th International Conference on Machine Learning*. PMLR 80, 1685-1694. Stockholm, Sweden.

García, S., Molina, D., Lozano, M., & Herrera, F. (2009). A Study on the Use of Non-Parametric Tests for Analyzing the Evolutionary Algorithms' Behavior: A Case Study on the CEC'2005 Special Session on Real Parameter Optimization. *Journal of Heuristics, 6*(15), 617–644.

Gen, M., & Cheng, R. (1997). *Genetic algorithms and engineering design*. New York: John Wiley & Sons.

Ghasemi, M., Ghavidel, S., Ghanbarian, M. H., Gharibzadeh, M., & Vahed, A. Z. (2014). Multi-objective optimal power flow considering the cost, emission, voltage deviation and power losses using multi-objective modified imperialist competitive algorithm. *Energy, 78*, 1–14. doi:10.1016/j.energy.2014.10.007

Gil, E., Bustos, J., & Rudnick, H. (2003). Short-term hydrothermal generation scheduling model using a genetic algorithm. *IEEE Transactions on Power Systems, 18*(4), 1256–1264. doi:10.1109/TPWRS.2003.819877

Gillispie, S. B., & Pearlman, M. D. (2001). Enumerating Markov Equivalence Classes of Acyclic Digraph Models. *Proceedings of the Seventeenth conference on Uncertainty in artificial intelligence* (pp. 171-177). California: Morgan Kaufmann.

Giuliani, D. (2017). A Grayscale Segmentation Approach using the Firefly Algorithm and the Gaussian Mixture Model. International Journal of Swarm Intelligence Research, 9(1). IGI Global.

Giuliani, D. (2018). Colour Image Segmentation based on Principal Component Analysis with application of Firefly Algorithm and Gaussian Mixture Model. *International Journal of Image Processing, 12*(4).

Goldberg, D. E. (1989). *Genetic Algorithms in Search, Optimization and Machine Learning*. Reading: Addison-Wesley Longman.

Goldberg, D. E. (1989). *Genetic algorithms in search, optimization, and machine learning, 1989*. Reading: Addison-Wesley.

Golshan, M. E. H., & Arefifar, S. A. (2006). Distributed generation, reactive sources and network-configuration planning for power and energy-loss reduction. *IEEE Proceedings-Generation, Transmission, and Distribution 153*(2), pp. 127-136. IEEE.

Golub, G. H., & Van Loan, C. F. (1996). *Matrix Computations* (3rd ed.). The Johns Hopkins University Press.

Gonzalez, R. C., & Wood, R. E. (2007). *Digital Image Processing* (3rd ed.). Prentice Hall.

Gould, S., Fulton, R., & Koller, D. (2009). Decomposing a scene into geometric and semantically consistent regions. *Proceedings, ICCV*. Academic Press.

Greiner, D., Winter, G., & Emperador, J. M. (2006). Enhancing the multiobjective optimum design of structural trusses with evolutionary algorithms using DENSEA. *Proceedings 44th AIAA (American Institute of Aeronautics and Astronautics) Aerospace Sciences Meeting and Exhibit*. Reno, Nevada. Berlin, Germany: Springer. (pp. 1474). 10.2514/6.2006-1474

Gu, C., Lim, J. J., Arbelaez, P., & Malik, J. (2009). Recognition using regions. *Proceedings CVPR 2009*. Academic Press.

Guckenheimer, J., & Holmes, P. J. (2013). *Nonlinear oscillations, dynamical systems, and bifurcations of vector fields* (Vol. 42). Springer Science & Business Media.

Gul, E., Kang, C., & Wang, J. (2019). Multi-objective short-term integration of hydrothermal operation with wind and solar power using nonlinear programming. *Energy Procedia, 158*, 6274–6281. doi:10.1016/j.egypro.2019.01.447

Gulic, M., Vrdoljak, B., & Banek, M. (2016). CroMatcher: An ontology matching system based on automated weighted aggregation and iterative final alignment. *Journal of Web Semantics, 41*, 50–71. doi:10.1016/j.websem.2016.09.001

Gupta, A. K., Smith, K. G., & Shalley, C. E. (2006). The interplay between exploration and exploitation. *Academy of Management Journal, 49*(4), 693–706. doi:10.5465/amj.2006.22083026

Gu, S., Cheng, R., & Jin, Y. (2018). Feature selection for high-dimensional classification using a competitive swarm optimizer. *Soft Computing, 22*(3), 811–822. doi:10.100700500-016-2385-6

Hancer, E., Xue, B., & Zhang, M. (2018). Differential evolution for filter feature selection based on information theory and feature ranking. *Knowledge-Based Systems, 140*, 103–119. doi:10.1016/j.knosys.2017.10.028

Han, G., Jiang, J., Zhang, C., Duong, T. Q., Guizani, M., & Karagiannidis, G. K. (2016). A survey on mobile anchor node assisted localization in wireless sensor networks. *IEEE Communications Surveys and Tutorials, 18*(3), 2220–2243. doi:10.1109/COMST.2016.2544751

Happ, H. H. (1977). Optimal power dispatch – a comprehensive survey. *IEEE Transactions on Power Apparatus and Systems, 96*(3), 841–854. doi:10.1109/T-PAS.1977.32397

Haralick, R. M., & Shapiro, L. G. (1985). Image Segmentation Techniques. *Computer Vision Graphics and Image Processing, 29*(1), 100–132. doi:10.1016/S0734-189X(85)90153-7

Harper, F. M., & Konstan, J. A. (2016). The movielens datasets: History and context. [TiiS]. *ACM Transactions on Interactive Intelligent Systems, 5*(4), 19.

Harrington, C. A., Rosenow, C., & Retief, J. (2000). Monitoring gene expression using DNA microarrays. *Current Opinion in Microbiology, 3*(3), 285–291. doi:10.1016/S1369-5274(00)00091-6 PMID:10851158

Hazra, S., Roy, P. K., & Sinha, A. (2015). An Efficient Evolutionary algorithm applied to Economic load dispatch problem. IEEE Computer, Communication, Control and Information Technology-C3IT. pp. 1-6. doi:10.1109/C3IT.2015.7060129

Hazra, S., Pal, T., & Roy, P. K. (2019). Renewable Energy Based Economic Emission Load Dispatch Using Grasshopper Optimization Algorithm. *International Journal of Swarm Intelligence Research, 10*(1), 38–57. doi:10.4018/IJSIR.2019010103

Hazra, S., & Roy, P. (2015). Economic Load Dispatch considering non-smooth cost functions using Predator Prey Optimization. *Intelligent Computing and Applications-SPRINGER., 343*, 67–78. doi:10.1007/978-81-322-2268-2_8

He, C.-C., & Gao, X.-G. (2018, July 25-27). Structure Learning of Bayesian Networks Based On the LARS-MMPC Ordering Search Method. Wuhan, China: *Chinese Control Conference* 10.23919/ChiCC.2018.8483049

Heckerman, D., Geiger, D., & Chickering, D. M. (1995). Learning Bayesian networks: The combination of knowledge and statistical data. *Machine Learning, 20*(3), 197–243. doi:10.1007/BF00994016

Helwig, S., Branke, J., & Mostaghim, S. (2013). Experimental Analysis of Bound Handling Techniques in Particle Swarm Optimization. *IEEE Transactions on Evolutionary Computation, 17*(2), 259–271. doi:10.1109/TEVC.2012.2189404

Heng, E. T., Srinivasan, D., & Liew, A. (1998). Short term load forecasting using genetic algorithm and neural networks. *Proceedings of EMPD'98 1998 International Conference on Energy Management and Power Delivery, 2*, 576–581 (IEEE). 10.1109/EMPD.1998.702749

Herbert, M., & Pantofaru, C. (2005). *A comparison of segmentation algorithms, Report of Robotic Institute*. Pittsburgh, PA: Carnegie Mellon University.

Heris, M. Z., Ivatloo, B. M., & Asadi, S. (2018). Robust stochastic optimal short-term generation scheduling of hydro-thermal systems in deregulated environment. *Journal of Energy Systems (JES), 2*(4), 168-179.

Herlocker, J. L., Joseph, A. K., & Riedl, J. (2000). Explaining collaborative filtering recommendations. *Proceedings of the 2000 ACM conference on Computer supported cooperative work* (pp. 241-250). ACM.

Herlocker, J., Konstan, J. A., Borchers, A., & Riedl, J. (1999). An algorithmic framework for performing collaborative filtering. *Proceedings of the 22nd annual international ACM SIGIR conference on Research and development in information retrieval*. 10.1145/312624.312682

Hesar, A. S. (2013). Structure Learning of Bayesian Belief Networks Using Simulated Annealing Algorithm. *Middle East Journal of Scientific Research, 18*, 1343–1348.

Hetzer, J., Yu, D. C., & Bhattrarai, K. (2008). An economic dispatch model incorporating wind power. *IEEE Transactions on Energy Conversion, 23*(2), 603–611. doi:10.1109/TEC.2007.914171

Hippert, H. S., Pedreira, C. E., & Souza, R. C. (2001). Neural networks for short-term load forecasting: A review and evaluation. *IEEE Transactions on Power Systems, 16*(1), 44–55. doi:10.1109/59.910780

Holland, J. H. (1992). *Adaptation in natural and artificial systems: an introductory analysis with applications to biology, control, and artificial intelligence*. MIT Press. doi:10.7551/mitpress/1090.001.0001

Holland, J. H. (2000). Building blocks, cohort genetic algorithms, and hyperplane-defined functions. *Evolutionary Computation, 8*(4), 373–391. doi:10.1162/106365600568220 PMID:11130921

Holm, S. (1979). A simple sequentially rejective multiple test procedure. *Scandinavian Journal of Statistics*, 65–70.

Hota, P. K., Barisal, A. K., & Chakrabarti, R. (2009). An improved PSO technique for short-term optimal hydrothermal scheduling. *Electric Power Systems Research, 79*(7), 1047–1053. doi:10.1016/j.epsr.2009.01.001

Hu, X., Shi, Y., & Eberhart, R. (2004) Recent advances in particle swarm. *Proceedings of the 2004 Congress on Evolutionary Computation (CEC2004)*, (pp. 90-97). Academic Press.

Huang, T., & Mohan, A. (2005). A hybrid boundary condition for robust particle swarm optimization. *IEEE Antennas and Wireless Propagation Letters, 4*, 112–117. doi:10.1109/LAWP.2005.846166

Huang, Z., Chen, H., & Zeng, D. (2004). Applying associative retrieval techniques to alleviate the sparsity problem in collaborative filtering. [TOIS]. *ACM Transactions on Information Systems, 22*(1), 116–142. doi:10.1145/963770.963775

Huhse, J., Villmann, T., Merz, P., & Zell, A. (2002). Evolution strategy with neighborhood attraction using a neural gas approach. *Proceedings of the Parallel Problem Solving from Nature - PPSN VII* (LNCS 2439, pp. 391-400). 10.1007/3-540-45712-7_38

Hu, Z., Zhang, M., Wang, X., Li, C., & Hu, M. (2016). Bi-level robust dynamic economic emission dispatch considering wind power uncertainty. *Electric Power Systems Research, 135*, 35–47. doi:10.1016/j.epsr.2016.03.010

Hwang, T.-G., Park, C.-S., Hong, J.-H., & Kim, S. K. (2016). An algorithm for movie classification and recommendation using genre correlation. *Multimedia Tools and Applications, 75*(20), 12843–12858. doi:10.100711042-016-3526-8

Ingber, L. (1996). Adaptive simulated annealing (ASA): Lessons learned. *Control and Cybernetics*, *25*, 33–54.

Inza, I., Larrañaga, P., Blanco, R., & Cerrolaza, A. J. (2004). Filter versus wrapper gene selection approaches in DNA microarray domains. *Artificial Intelligence in Medicine*, *31*(2), 91–103. doi:10.1016/j.artmed.2004.01.007 PMID:15219288

Ishibuchi, H., Tsukamoto, N., & Nojima, Y. (2008). Evolutionary Many-Objective Optimization: A Short Review. *Proceedings of the 2008 Congress on Evolutionary Computation (CEC2004)*, (pp. 2419-2426). 10.1109/CEC.2008.4631121

Ishibuchi, H., Tsukamoto, N., & Nojima, Y. (2010). Diversity improvement by non-geometric binary crossover in evolutionary multiobjective optimization. *IEEE Transactions on Evolutionary Computation*, *14*(6), 985–998. doi:10.1109/TEVC.2010.2043365

Jabbar, S., Asif Habib, M., Minhas, A. A., Ahmad, M., Ashraf, R., Khalid, S., & Han, K. (2018). Analysis of factors affecting energy aware routing in wireless sensor network. *Wireless Communications and Mobile Computing*.

Jaddi, N. S., Abdullah, S., & Hamdan, A. R. (2015). Multi-population cooperative bat algorithm-based optimization of artificial neural network model. *Information Sciences*, *294*, 628–644. doi:10.1016/j.ins.2014.08.050

Jain, A. K., Murry, M. N., & Flynn, P. J. (1999). Data Clustering a review. *ACM Computing Surveys*, *31*(3).

Jangir, P., Parmar, S. A., Trivedi, I. N., & Bhesdadiya, R. H. (2017). A novel hybrid particle swarm optimizer with multi verse optimizer for global numerical optimization and optimal reactive power dispatch problem. *Engineering Science and Technology, an International Journal*, *20*(2), 570-586.

Jaskirat, K., Sunil, A., & Renu, V. (2012). A comparative analysis of thresholding and edge detection segmentation techniques. *International Journal of Computers and Applications*, *39*.

Jayabarathi, T., Raghunathan, T., & Gandomi, A. H. (2018). The bat algorithm, variants and some practical engineering applications: a review. In *Nature-Inspired Algorithms and Applied Optimization* (pp. 313–330). Cham: Springer. doi:10.1007/978-3-319-67669-2_14

Jean-Mary, Y. R., Shironoshita, E. P., & Kabuka, M. R. (2009). Ontology matching with semantic verification. *Journal of Web Semantics*, *7*(3), 235–251. doi:10.1016/j.websem.2009.04.001 PMID:20186256

Jeenanunta, C., & Abeyrathna, K. D. (2016). The study of artificial neural network parameters for electricity forecasting. *Proceedings International Conference on Applied Statistics*, pp. 105–111. Phuket, Thailand, July 13-15. Academic Press.

Jeenanunta, C., & Abeyrathna, K. D. (2019). Neural network with genetic algorithm for forecasting short-term electricity load demand. *International Journal of Energy Technology and Policy*, *15*(2/3), 337–350. doi:10.1504/IJETP.2019.098957

Jeenanunta, C., Abeyrathna, K. D., Dilhani, M. H. M. R. S., Hnin, S. W., & Phyo, P. P. (2018). Time series outlier detection for short-term electricity load demand forecasting. [ISJET]. *International Scientific Journal of Engineering and Technology*, *2*(1), 37–50.

Jeenanunta, C., & Abeyrathn, K. D. (2017). Combine particle swarm optimization with artificial neural networks for short-term load forecasting. [ISJET]. *International Scientific Journal of Engineering and Technology*, *1*, 25–30.

Ji, J., Wei, H., & Liu, C. (December 2012). An artificial bee colony algorithm for learning Bayesian networks. *Springer-Verlag Berlin Heidelberg*.

Jiang, L., Kong, G., & Li, C. (2019). Wrapper Framework for Test-Cost-Sensitive Feature Selection. *IEEE Transactions on Systems, Man, and Cybernetics. Systems*, 1–10. doi:10.1109/TSMC.2019.2904662

Jimenez-Ruiz, E., Grau, B. C., & Cross, V. (2016). LogMap family participation in the OAEI 2016. *Proceedings 11th International Workshop on Ontology Matching*, (pp. 185-189). Kobe, Japan.

Jin, Y., & Sendhoff, B. (2004). Constructing dynamic optimization test problems using the multi-objective optimization concept. In G. R. Raidl, S. Cagnoni, J. Branke, D. W. Corne, R. Drechsler, Y. Jin, C. G. Johnson, P. Machado, E. Marchiori, F. Rothlauf, G. D. Smith, & G. Squillero (Eds.), Applications of Evolutionary Computing, (LNCS 3005, pp. 525-536). Berlin, Germany: Springer. doi:10.1007/978-3-540-24653-4_53

Jin, X., Mu, Y., Jia, H., Wu, J., Xu, X., & Yu, X. (2016). Optimal day-ahead scheduling of integrated urban energy systems. *Applied Energy*, *180*, 1–13. doi:10.1016/j.apenergy.2016.07.071

Jin, Y., & Sendhoff, B. (2009). A systems approach to evolutionary multiobjective structural optimization and beyond. *IEEE Computational Intelligence Magazine*, *4*(3), 62–76. doi:10.1109/MCI.2009.933094

Kar, A. K. (2016). Bio inspired computing–A review of algorithms and scope of applications. *Expert Systems with Applications*, *59*, 20–32. doi:10.1016/j.eswa.2016.04.018

Karaboga, D. (2005). *An idea based on honey bee swarm for numerical optimization, Technical Report*. Computer Engineering Department, Engineering Faculty, Erciyes University.

Karaboga, D., & Basturk, B. (2007). A powerful and efficient algorithm for numerical function optimization: Artificial bee colony (ABC) algorithm. *Journal of Global Optimization*, *39*(3), 459–471. doi:10.100710898-007-9149-x

Karaboga, D., Gorkemli, B., Orzturk, C., & Karaboga, N. (2014). A comprehensive survey: Artificial Bee Colony algorithm and applications. *Artificial Intelligence Review*, *42*(1), 21–57. doi:10.100710462-012-9328-0

Kareem, S. W., & Okur, M. C. (2019). Bayesian Network Structure Learning Based On Pigeon Inspired Optimization. *International Journal of Advanced Trends in Computer Science and Engineering, 8*(1.2), 131-137.

Kareem, S., & Okur, M. C. (2017). Evaluation Of Bayesian Network Structure Learning. *Proceedings 2nd International Mediterranean Science and Engineering Congress (IMSEC 2017)* (pp. 1313-1319). Adana, Turkey: Çukurova University.

Kareem, S., & Okur, M. C. (2018). *Bayesian Network Structure Learning Using Hybrid Bee Optimization and Greedy Search. Adana*, Turkey: Çukurova University.

Karypis, G. (2001). Evaluation of item-based top-n recommendation algorithms. *Proceedings of the 10th International Conference on Information and Knowledge Management* (pp. 247-254). ACM.

Katarya, R., & Verma, O. P. (2017). Effectual recommendations using artificial algae algorithm and fuzzy c-mean. *Swarm and Evolutionary Computation*, *36*, 52–61. doi:10.1016/j.swevo.2017.04.004

Katarya, R., & Verma, O. P. (2018). Recommender system with grey wolf optimizer and FCM. *Neural Computing & Applications*, *30*(5), 1679–1687. doi:10.100700521-016-2817-3

Kaur, K., & Singh, H. (2016). Click analytics: What clicks on webpage indicates? In *2016 2nd International Conference on Next Generation Computing Technologies (NGCT)*, 608-614.

Kaveh, A., & Behnam, A. F. (2013). Charged system search algorithm for the optimum cost design of reinforced concrete cantilever retaining walls. *Arabian Journal for Science and Engineering*, *38*(3), 563–570. doi:10.100713369-012-0332-0

Kaveh, A., & Talatahari, S. (2010). A novel heuristic optimization method: Charged system search. *Acta Mechanica*, *213*(3), 267–289. doi:10.100700707-009-0270-4

Kaveh, A., & Talatahari, S. (2012). Charged system search for optimal design of frame structures. *Applied Soft Computing*, *12*(1), 382–393. doi:10.1016/j.asoc.2011.08.034

Kennedy, J. (1997). The particle swarm: social adaptation of knowledge. *Proceedings IEEE International Conference on Evolutionary Computation, 1997.* (pp. 303-308). IEEE. 10.1109/ICEC.1997.592326

Kennedy, J., & Mendes, R. (2002). Population structure and particle swarm performance. *Proceedings of The Fourth Congress on Evolutionary Computation (CEC 2002)*, (pp. 1671-1676). Academic Press.

Kennedy, J., Eberhart, R., & Shi, Y. (2001). Swarm Intelligence. Morgan Kaufmann.

Kennedy, J. (2007). Some issues and practices for particle swarms. *Proceedings of the 2007 IEEE Swarm Intelligence Symposium (SIS 2007)*, (pp. 162-169). 10.1109/SIS.2007.368041

Kennedy, J., & Eberhart, R. (1995). Particle Swarm Optimization. *Proceedings of the IEEE International Conference on Neural Networks*, 4, pp. 1942–1948. 10.1109/ICNN.1995.488968

Kennedy, J., Eberhart, R., & Shi, Y. (2001). *Swarm intelligence.* Academic Press.

Kennedy, J., Eberhart, R., & Shi, Y. (2001). *Swarm Intelligence.* Morgan Kaufmann Publisher.

Kermany, N. R., & Alizadeh, S. H. (2017). A hybrid multi-criteria recommender system using ontology and neuro-fuzzy techniques. *Electronic Commerce Research and Applications*, 21, 50–64. doi:10.1016/j.elerap.2016.12.005

Khalid, M., Aguilera, R. P., Savkin, A. V., & Agelidis, V. G. (2018). On maximizing profit of wind-battery supported power station based on wind power and energy price forecasting. *Applied Energy*, 211, 764–773. doi:10.1016/j.apenergy.2017.11.061

Khanteymoori, A., Olayee, M. H., Abbaszadeh, O., & Valian, M. (2018). A novel method for Bayesian networks structure learning based on Breeding Swarm algorithm. *Soft Computing*, 9.

Khatib, O. (1986). Real-time obstacle avoidance for manipulators and mobile robots. *The International Journal of Robotics Research*, 5(1), 90–98. doi:10.1177/027836498600500106

Khusro, S., Ali, Z., & Ullah, I. (2016). Recommender Systems: Issues, Challenges, and Research Opportunities. [ICISA]. *Information Science and Applications*, 2016, 1179–1189. doi:10.1007/978-981-10-0557-2_112

Kim, S., Lee, I., Cho, D., & Lee, J. (2006). Dynamic localization of a mobile robot with active beacon sensors. *IFAC Proceedings Volumes, 39*(16), (pp. 921-925).

Kim, D. H. (2002). Parameter tuning of fuzzy neural networks by immune algorithm, fuzzy system. *Proceedings of the 2002 IEEE International Conference*, 1, 408–413. IEEE.

Kim, H. K., Chong, J. K., Park, K. Y., & Lowther, D. A. (2007). Differential evolution strategy for constrained global optimization and application to practical engineering problems. *IEEE Transactions on Magnetics*, 43(4), 1565–1568. doi:10.1109/TMAG.2006.892100

Kim, H.-N., El-Saddik, A., & Jo, G.-S. (2011). Collaborative error-reflected models for cold-start recommender systems. *Decision Support Systems*, 51(3), 519–531. doi:10.1016/j.dss.2011.02.015

Kim, K., & Ahn, H. (2008). A recommender system using GA K-means clustering in an online shopping market. *Expert Systems with Applications*, 34(2), 1200–1209. doi:10.1016/j.eswa.2006.12.025

Kirkpatrick, S., Gelatt, C. D., & Vecchi, M. P. (1983). Optimization by simulated annealing. *Science*, 220(4598), 671–680. doi:10.1126cience.220.4598.671 PMID:17813860

Koguma, Y., & Aiyoshi, E. (2010). Stability analysis in consideration of random numbers for particle swarm optimization dynamics: The best parameter for sustainable search. *IEEJ Transactions on Electronics, Information Systems*, 130, 29–38.

Kohali, M., & Arora, S. (2018). Chaotic grey wolf optimization algorithm for constrained optimization problems. *Journal of Computational Design and Engineering*, 5(4), 458–472. doi:10.1016/j.jcde.2017.02.005

Kohonen, T. (1997). *Self-Organizing Maps.* Berlin, Germany: Springer-Verlag. doi:10.1007/978-3-642-97966-8

Konstan, J. A., & Riedl, J. T. (2003). Recommender Systems for the Web. In Visualizing the Semantic Web (pp. 151-167). London, UK: Verlag Springer. doi:10.1007/978-1-4471-3737-5_10

Koschmider, A., Hornung, T., & Oberweis, A. (2011). Recommendation-based editor for business process modeling. *Data & Knowledge Engineering, 70*(6), 483–503. doi:10.1016/j.datak.2011.02.002

Koski, T., & Noble, J. M. (2009). *Bayesian Networks-An Introduction.* Wiley series in probability and statistics.

Krishnanand, K. N., & Ghose, D. (2008). Theoretical foundations for rendezvous of glowworm-inspired agent swarms at multiple locations. *Robotics and Autonomous Systems, 56*(7), 549–569. doi:10.1016/j.robot.2007.11.003

Krishnasamy, U., & Nanjundappan, D. (2016). Hybrid weighted probabilistic neural network and biogeography-based optimization for dynamic economic dispatch of integrated multiple-fuel and wind power plants. *Electrical Power and Energy Systems, 77*, 385–394. doi:10.1016/j.ijepes.2015.11.022

Kulkarni, A. J., Krishasamy, G., & Abraham, A. (2017). *Cohort Intelligence: A Socio-inspired Optimization Method.* Springer. doi:10.1007/978-3-319-44254-9

Kulkarni, P. S., Kothari, A. G., & Kothari, D. P. (2000). Combined economic and emission dispatch using improved back-propagation neural network. *Electric Power Components and Systems, 28*, 31–44.

Kulkarni, V. R., & Desai, V. (2019). Computational intelligence for localization of mobile wireless sensor networks. *Proceedings of Computational Intelligence: Theories, Applications, and Future Directions* (Vol. II, pp. 449–463). Springer Singapore. doi:10.1007/978-981-13-1135-2_34

Kulkarni, V. R., Desai, V., & Kulkarni, R. V. (2016). Multistage localization in wireless sensor networks using artificial bee colony algorithm. *Proceedings of the IEEE Symposium Series on Computational Intelligence (SSCI)*, (pp. 1-8). 10.1109/SSCI.2016.7850273

Kumar, R., & Rockett, P. (1998). Multiobjective genetic algorithm partitioning for hierarchical learning of high-dimensional pattern spaces: A learning-follows-decomposition strategy. *IEEE Transactions on Neural Networks, 9*(5), 822–830. doi:10.1109/72.712155 PMID:18255769

Kuo, H., & Lin, C. (2013). Cultural evolution algorithm for global optimizations and its applications. *Journal of Applied Research and Technology, 11*(4), 510–522. doi:10.1016/S1665-6423(13)71558-X

Labati, R. D., Donida, R., Piuri, V., & Scotti, F. (2011). All-IDB: The acute lymphoblastic leukemia image database for image processing. Proceedings 2011 18th IEEE International Conference on Image Processing (pp. 2045-2048). IEEE.

Lai, L. L., Ma, J. T., Yokoyama, R., & Zhao, M. (1997). Improved genetic algorithm for optimal power flow under both normal and contingent operation states. *International Journal of Electrical Power & Energy Systems, 19*(5), 287–292. doi:10.1016/S0142-0615(96)00051-8

Lakshminarasimman, L., & Subramanian, S. (2006). Short-term scheduling of hydrothermal power system with cascaded reservoirs by using modified differential evolution. *IEE Proceedings. Generation, Transmission, and Distribution, 153*(6), 693–700. doi:10.1049/ip-gtd:20050407

Lakshminarasimman, L., & Subramanian, S. (2008). A modified hybrid differential evolution for short-term scheduling of hydrothermal power systems with cascaded reservoirs. *Energy Conversion and Management, 49*(10), 2513–2521. doi:10.1016/j.enconman.2008.05.021

Lampinen, J., & Storn, R. (2004). Differential evolution. In G. Onwubolu, & B. V. Babu (Eds.), *New Optimization Techniques in Engineering* (pp. 123–166). Germany: Springer-Verlag. doi:10.1007/978-3-540-39930-8_6

Larraiiaga, P., & Poza, M. (1996). Structure Learning of Bayesian Networks by Genetic Algorithms. Berlin, Germany: Springer-Verlag.

Lau, E. T., Yang, Q., Taylor, G. A., Forbes, A. B., Wright, P. S., & Livina, V. N. (2016). Optimization of costs and carbon savings in relation to the economic dispatch problem as associated with power system operation. *Electric Power Systems Research*, *140*, 173–183. doi:10.1016/j.epsr.2016.06.025

Lee, C.-S., Wang, M.-H., & Lan, S.-T. (2015). Adaptive personalized diet linguistic recommendation mechanism based on type-2 fuzzy sets and genetic fuzzy markup language. *IEEE Transactions on Fuzzy Systems*, *23*(5), 1777–1802. doi:10.1109/TFUZZ.2014.2379256

Lee, J. C., Lin, W. M., Liao, G. C., & Tsao, T. P. (2011). Quantum genetic algorithm for dynamic economic dispatch with valve-point effects and including wind power system. *International Journal of Electrical Power & Energy Systems*, *33*(2), 189–197. doi:10.1016/j.ijepes.2010.08.014

Leontitsis, A., Kontogiorgos, D., & Pagge, J. (2006). Repel the swarm to the optimum! *Applied Mathematics and Computation*, *173*(1), 265–272. doi:10.1016/j.amc.2005.04.004Liang, J. J., Qin, A. K., Suganthan, P. N., & Baskar, S. (2006). Comprehensive learning particle swarm optimizer for global optimization of multimodal functions. *IEEE Transactions on Evolutionary Computation*, *10*(3), 281–295. doi:10.1109/TEVC.2005.857610

Leung, Y., Gao, Y., & Xu, Z.-B. (1997). Degree of population diversity—A perspective on premature convergence in genetic algorithms and its Markov chain analysis. *IEEE Transactions on Neural Networks*, *8*(5), 1165–1176. doi:10.1109/72.623217 PMID:18255718

Leu, S.-S., Yang, C.-H., & Huang, J.-C. (2000). Resource leveling in construction by genetic algorithm-based optimization and its decision support system application. *Automation in Construction*, *10*(1), 27–41. doi:10.1016/S0926-5805(99)00011-4

Li, J., & Chen, J. (2014). A Hybrid Optimization Algorithm for Bayesian Network Structure Learning Based on Database. *Journal of Computers, 9.*

Li, Y., Dong, X., & Liu, J. (2010). An Improved PSO for Continuous Optimization. Proceedings Advances in Swarm Intelligence (ICSI 2010), (pp. 86-93).

Liang, J. J., Qu, B. Y., Suganthan, P. N., & Hernández-Díaz, A. G. (2013). Problem definitions and evaluation criteria for the CEC 2013 special session on real-parameter optimization. Computational Intelligence Laboratory, Zhengzhou University, China, and Nanyang Technological University, Singapore, Technical Report, 201212.

Liang, R. H., & Hsu, Y. Y. (1994). Scheduling of hydroelectric generations using artificial neural networks. *IEEE Proceedings C on Generation, Transmission, and Distribution*, *141*(5), 452–458. 10.1049/ip-gtd:19941156

Liang, J., Qin, A., Suganthan, P., & Baskar, S. (2006). Comprehensive learning particle swarm optimizer for global optimization of multimodal functions. *IEEE Transactions on Evolutionary Computation*, *10*(3), 281–295. doi:10.1109/TEVC.2005.857610

Liang, J., Suganthan, P. N., & Deb, K. (2005). Novel composition test functions for numerical global optimization. *Proceedings of the 2005 IEEE Swarm Intelligence Symposium (SIS2005)*, (pp. 68-75). 10.1109/SIS.2005.1501604

Liang, Z. J., Villaseca, F. E., & Renovich, F. (1992). Neural networks for generation scheduling in power systems. *Proceedings of the 1992 International Joint Conference on Neural Networks*, *2*, 233–238.

Li, D., & Wen, X. (2015). An improved PSO algorithm for distributed localization in wireless sensor networks. *International Journal of Distributed Sensor Networks*, *11*(7). doi:10.1155/2015/970272

Linden, G., Smith, B., & York, J. (2003). Amazon. com recommendations: Item-to-item collaborative filtering. *IEEE Internet Computing*, *7*(1), 76–80. doi:10.1109/MIC.2003.1167344

Lindsay, B. G. (1995). *Mixture Models: Theory, Geometry, and Applications*. NFS-CBMS Regional Conference Series in Probability and Statistics.

Lin, X. N., Ke, S. H., Li, Z. T., Weng, H. L., & Han, X. H. (2010). A fault diagnosis method of power systems based on improved objective function and genetic algorithm-tabu search. *IEEE Transactions on Power Delivery*, *25*(3), 1268–1274. doi:10.1109/TPWRD.2010.2044590

Lin, Y. C., Yeh, C. H., & Wei, C. C. (2013). How will the use of graphics affect visual aesthetics? A user-centered approach for web page design. *International Journal of Human-Computer Studies*, *71*(3), 217–227. doi:10.1016/j.ijhcs.2012.10.013

Lin, Y., Zhang, J., & Lan, L. (2008). A contour method in population-based stochastic algorithms. *Proceedings of the 2008 IEEE Congress on Evolutionary Computation (CEC2008)*, (pp. 2388-2395). IEEE.

Li, S., & Wang, B. (2017). *A Method for Hybrid Bayesian Network Structure Learning from Massive Data Using MapReduce*. IEEE. doi:10.1109/BigDataSecurity.2017.42

Liu, D., & Cai, Y. (2005). Taguchi method for solving the economic dispatch problem with non smooth cost functions. *IEEE Transactions on Power Systems*, *20*(4), 2006–2014. doi:10.1109/TPWRS.2005.857939

Liu, X., & Xu, W. (2010). Minimum emission dispatch constrained by stochastic wind power availability and cost. *IEEE Transactions on Power Systems*, *25*(3), 1705–1713. doi:10.1109/TPWRS.2010.2042085

Longo, L., & Dondio, P. (2015). On the relationship between perception of usability and subjective mental workload of web interfaces. *Proceedings IEEE International Conference on Web Intelligence and Intelligent Agent Technology*, *1*, 345-352. 10.1109/WI-IAT.2015.157

Lopatka, K., Kotus, J., & Czyzewski, A. (2016). Detection, classification and localization of acoustic events in the presence of background noise for acoustic surveillance of hazardous situations. *Multimedia Tools and Applications*, *75*(17), 10407–10439. doi:10.100711042-015-3105-4

Lučić, P., & Teodorović, D. (2003). Computing with bees: Attacking complex transportation engineering problems. *International Journal of Artificial Intelligence Tools*, *12*(3), 375–394. doi:10.1142/S0218213003001289

Lu, S., Sun, C., & Lu, Z. (2010). An improved quantum-behaved particle swarm optimization method for short-term combined economic emission hydrothermal scheduling. *Energy Conversion and Management*, *51*(3), 561–571. doi:10.1016/j.enconman.2009.10.024

Lu, Y., Zhou, J., Qin, H., Wang, Y., & Zhang, Y. (2011). A hybrid multi-objective cultural algorithm for short-term environmental/economic hydrothermal scheduling. *Energy Conversion and Management*, *52*(5), 2121–2134. doi:10.1016/j.enconman.2010.12.003

Lv, G., Hu, C., & Chen, S. (2016). Research on recommender system based on ontology and genetic algorithm. *Neurocomputing*, *187*, 92–97. doi:10.1016/j.neucom.2015.09.113

Mahmoud, T. M., & Marshall, S. (2008). Edge-Detected Guided Morphological Filter for Image Sharpening, *Journal on Image and Video Processing*, EURASIP.

Majid, B. W., & Louis, A., D. (2017). Multi-objective stochastic optimal power flow considering voltage stability and demand response with significant wind penetration. *IET Generation, Transmission, & Distribution, 11*(14), 3499–3509. doi:10.1049/iet-gtd.2016.1994

Makita, E., & Lenskiy, A. (2016). A movie genre prediction based on Multivariate Bernoulli model and genre correlations. *arXiv preprint.*

Mandal, S. (2018). Elephant swarm water search algorithm for global optimization. Indian Academy of Sciences.

Mandal, B., & Roy, P. K. (2014). Multi-objective optimal power flow using quasi-oppositional teaching learning based optimization. *Applied Soft Computing, 21*, 590–606. doi:10.1016/j.asoc.2014.04.010

Mandal, K. K., & Chakraborty, N. (2008). Effect of control parameters on differential evolution based combined economic emission dispatch with valve-point loading and transmission loss. *Int. J. Emerg. Electric Power Syst., 9*(4), 1–18. doi:10.2202/1553-779X.1918

Mandal, K. K., & Chakraborty, N. (2009). Short-term combined economic emission scheduling of hydrothermal power systems with cascaded reservoirs using differential evolution. *Energy Conversion and Management, 50*(1), 97–104. doi:10.1016/j.enconman.2008.08.022

Mandal, K. K., & Chakraborty, N. (2012). Daily combined economic emission scheduling of hydrothermal systems with cascaded reservoirs using self-organizing hierarchical particle swarm optimization technique. *Expert Systems with Applications, 39*(3), 3438–3445. doi:10.1016/j.eswa.2011.09.032

Manzato, M. G. (2012). Discovering latent factors from movies genres for enhanced recommendation. *Proceedings of the sixth ACM conference on Recommender systems.* 10.1145/2365952.2366006

March, J. G. (1991). Exploration and exploitation in organizational learning. *Organization Science, 2*(1), 71–87. doi:10.1287/orsc.2.1.71

Margaritis, D. (2003). *Learning Bayesian Network Model Structure from Data.* Pittsburgh, PA. Available as Technical Report: Carnegie-Mellon University.

Martinez-Gil, J., Alba, E., & Montes, J. F. A. (2008). Optimizing ontology alignments by using genetic algorithms. *Proceedings of the First International Conference on Nature Inspired Reasoning for the Semantic Web*, (pp. 1-15). Berlin, Germany.

Maruyama, T., & Lgarashi, H. (2008). An effective robust optimization based on genetic algorithm. *IEEE Transactions on Magnetics, 44*(6), 990–993. doi:10.1109/TMAG.2007.916696

Masoud, S. A., & Masoud, A. A. (2000). Constrained motion control using vector potential fields. *IEEE Transactions on Systems, Man, and Cybernetics. Part A, Systems and Humans, 30*(3), 251–272. doi:10.1109/3468.844352

Masson, D., Demeure, A., & Calvary, G. (2010). Magellan, an evolutionary system to foster user interface design creativity. *Proceedings of the 2nd ACM SIGCHI symposium on Engineering interactive computing systems*, 87-92. 10.1145/1822018.1822032

Masters, G. M. (2004). *Renewable and Efficient Electric Power Systems.* New York: Wiley. doi:10.1002/0471668826

Ma, T., Suo, X., Zhou, J., Tang, M., Guan, D., Tian, Y., ... Al-Rodhaan, M. (2016). Augmenting matrix factorization technique with the combination of tags and genres. *Physica A, 461*, 101–116. doi:10.1016/j.physa.2016.05.021

Matlab. (2015, December 22). *Combing Algorithm: Finding Unique Equaltiy between Vectors of Different Sizes Using Ranges*. (Mathworks) Retrieved July 28, 2016, from https://in.mathworks.com/matlabcentral/answers/261393-combing-algorithm-finding-unique-equaltiy-between-vectors-of-different-sizes-using-ranges

Mauldin, M. L. (1984). Maintaining diversity in genetic search. *Proceedings of the National Conference on Artificial Intelligence (AAAI 1984)*. (pp. 247-250). Academic Press.

Mauldin, M. L. (1984). Maintaining diversity in genetic search. *Proceedings of the National Conference on Artificial Intelligence (AAAI 1984)*, (pp. 247-250).

Maulik, U., & Bandyopadhyay, S. (2000). Genetic algorithm-based clustering technique. *Pattern Recognition*, *33*(9), 1455–1465. doi:10.1016/S0031-3203(99)00137-5

Mazen, F., AbulSeoud, R. A., & Gody, A. M. (2016). Genetic algorithm and firefly algorithm in a hybrid approach for breast cancer diagnosis. [IJCTT]. *International Journal of Computer Trends and Technology*, *32*(2), 62–68. doi:10.14445/22312803/IJCTT-V32P111

McLachlan, G. J., & Basford, K. E. (1988). Mixture Models: Inference and Applications to Clustering. New York: Marcel Dekker.

Mendes, R. (2004). Population Topologies and Their Influence in Particle Swarm Performance. (Unpublished doctoral dissertation), University of Minho, Portugal.

Mendes, R. (2004a). *Population Topologies and Their Influence in Particle Swarm Performance*. (Doctoral dissertation), University of Minho, Portugal.

Mendes, R., Kennedy, J., & Neves, J. (2003). Avoiding the pitfalls of local optima: How topologies can save the day. *Proceedings of the 12th Conference Intelligent Systems Application to Power Systems (ISAP 2003)*. IEEE Computer Society.

Mendes, R., Kennedy, J., & Neves, J. (2004b). The fully informed particle warm: Simpler, maybe better. *IEEE Transactions on Evolutionary Computation*, *8*(3), 204–210. doi:10.1109/TEVC.2004.826074

Menges, R., Tamimi, H., Kumar, C., Walber, T., Schaefer, C., & Staab, S. (2018). Enhanced representation of web pages for usability analysis with eye tracking. *Proceedings of the 2018 ACM Symposium on Eye Tracking Research & Applications*, 18. 10.1145/3204493.3214308

Meng, K., Wang, H. G., Dong, Z. Y., & Wong, K. P. (2010). Quantum-inspired particle swarm optimization for valve-point economic load dispatch. *IEEE Transactions on Power Systems*, *25*(1), 215–222. doi:10.1109/TPWRS.2009.2030359

Michalewicz, Z. (2013). Genetic algorithms+ data structures= evolution programs. Springer Science & Business Media.

Miikkulainen, R., Iscoe, N., Shagrin, A., Cordell, R., Nazari, S., Schoolland, C., ... Lamba, G. (2017). Conversion rate optimization through evolutionary computation. *Proceedings of the Genetic and Evolutionary Computation Conference*, 1193-1199. ACM. 10.1145/3071178.3071312

Milano, M., Koumoutsakos, P., & Schmidhuber, J. (2004). Self-organizing nets for optimization. *IEEE Transactions on Neural Networks*, *15*(3), 758–765. doi:10.1109/TNN.2004.826132 PMID:15384562

Min, F., & Xu, J. (2016). Semi-greedy heuristics for feature selection with test cost constraints. *Granular Computing*, *1*(3), 199–211. doi:10.100741066-016-0017-2

Minkowski, H. (1989). Volumen und oberfläche. *In Ausgewählte Arbeiten zur Zahlentheorie und zur Geometrie*. 146-192. Springer Vienna.

Mirjalili, S., & Lewis, A. (2016). The grasshopper optimization algorithm. *Advances in Engineering Software, 95,* 51–67. doi:10.1016/j.advengsoft.2016.01.008

Mirjalili, S., Mirjalili, S. M., & Hatamlou, A. (2016). Multi-verse optimizer: A nature-inspired algorithm for global optimization. *Neural Computing & Applications, 27*(2), 495–513. doi:10.100700521-015-1870-7

Mirjalili, S., Mirjalili, S. M., & Lewis, A. (2014). A grey wolf optimizer. *Advances in Engineering Software, 69,* 46–61. doi:10.1016/j.advengsoft.2013.12.007

Misaghi, M., & Yaghoobi, M. (2019). Improved invasive weed optimization algorithm (IWO) based on chaos theory for optimal design of PID controller. *Journal of Computational Design and Engineering, 6*(3), 284–295. doi:10.1016/j.jcde.2019.01.001

Mishra, S., & Patra, S. K. (2008). Short term load forecasting using neural network trained with genetic algorithm & particle swarm optimization. *Proceedings 2008 First International Conference on Emerging Trends in Engineering and Technology,* 606–611 (IEEE). 10.1109/ICETET.2008.94

Mohamed, A. M., Ali, M. E., & Abdulrahman, I. A. (2017, September). Swarm intelligence-based optimization of grid-dependent hybrid renewable energy system. *Renewable & Sustainable Energy Reviews, 77,* 515–524. doi:10.1016/j.rser.2017.04.048

Mohamed, R. E., Saleh, A. I., Abdelrazzak, M., & Samra, A. S. (2018). Survey on wireless sensor network applications and energy efficient routing protocols. *Wireless Personal Communications, 101*(2), 1019–1055. doi:10.100711277-018-5747-9

Mohamed, S. M., Hamza, H. S., & Saroit, I. A. (2017). Coverage in mobile wireless sensor networks (M-WSN): A survey. *Computer Communications, 110,* 133–150. doi:10.1016/j.comcom.2017.06.010

Mohammad, J. M., & Alireza, A. (2014). Hybrid imperialist competitive-sequential quadratic programming (HIC-SQP) algorithm for solving economic load dispatch with incorporating stochastic wind power: A comparative study on heuristic optimization techniques. *Energy Conversion and Management, 84,* 30–40. doi:10.1016/j.enconman.2014.04.006

Mohan, M. R., Kuppusamy, K., & Khan, M. A. (1992). Optimal short-term hydro-thermal scheduling using decomposition approach and linear programming method. *International Journal of Electrical Power & Energy Systems, 14*(1), 39–44. doi:10.1016/0142-0615(92)90007-V

Molina, D., Lozano, M., Sánchez, A., & Herrera, F. (2011). Memetic algorithms based on local search chains for large scale continuous optimisation problems: MA-SSW-Chains. *Soft Computing, 15*(11), 2201–2220. doi:10.100700500-010-0647-2

Momoh,, J. A., El-Hawary, M. E., & Adapa, R. (1999). A review of selected optimal power flow literature to 1993, Part II: Newton, linear programming and interior point methods. *IEEE Transactions on Power Systems, 14*(1), 104–111.

Momoh, J. A., Adapa, R., & El-Hawary, M. E. (1999). A review of selected optimal power flow literature to 1993, Part I: Non-linear and quadratic programming approach. *IEEE Transactions on Power Systems, 14*(1), 96–104. doi:10.1109/59.744492

Momoh, J. A., & Zhu, J. Z. (1999). Improved interior point method for OPF problems. *IEEE Transactions on Power Systems, 14*(3), 1114–1120. doi:10.1109/59.780938

Mondal, S., Bhattacharya, A., & Dey, S. H. (2013). Multi-objective economic emission load dispatch solution using gravitational search algorithm and considering wind power penetration. *Electrical Power and Energy Systems, 44*(1), 282–292. doi:10.1016/j.ijepes.2012.06.049

Monticelli, A., Pereira, M. V. F., & Granville, S. (1987). Security-constrained optimal power flow with post-contingency corrective rescheduling. *IEEE Transactions on Power Systems, 2*(1), 175–180. doi:10.1109/TPWRS.1987.4335095

Moreno, A., Aida, V., David, I., Lucas, M., & Joan, B. (2013). Sigtur/e-destination: Ontology-based personalized recommendation of tourism and leisure activities. *Engineering Applications of Artificial Intelligence, 26*(1), 633–651. doi:10.1016/j.engappai.2012.02.014

Morshed, J. M., Hmida, J. B., & Fekih, A. (2018). A probabilistic multi-objective approach for power flow optimization in hybrid wind-PV-PEV systems. *Applied Energy, 211*, 1136–1149. doi:10.1016/j.apenergy.2017.11.101

Morteza, A., Masoud, R., & Mahmud, F. F. (2015). Probabilistic optimal power flow in correlated hybrid wind-PV power systems: A review and a new approach. *Renewable & Sustainable Energy Reviews, 41*, 1437–1446. doi:10.1016/j.rser.2014.09.012

Mota-Palomino, R., & Quintana, V. H. (1986). Sparse reactive power rescheduling by a penalty-function linear programming technique. *IEEE Transactions on Power Systems, 1*(3), 31–39. doi:10.1109/TPWRS.1986.4334951

Muro, C., Escobedo, R., Spector, L., & Coppinger, R. (2011). Wolf-pack (Canis lupus) hunting strategies emerge from simple rules in computational simulations. *BehavProcess, 88*(3), 192–197. doi:10.1016/j.beproc.2011.09.006 PMID:21963347

Nagarajan, R., Scutari, M., & Lèbre, S. (2013). *Bayesian Networks in R with Applications in Systems Biology*. New York: Springer. doi:10.1007/978-1-4614-6446-4

Nara, S., Davis, P., & Totsuji, H. (1993). Memory search using complex dynamics in a recurrent neural network model. *Neural Networks, 6*(7), 963–973. doi:10.1016/S0893-6080(09)80006-3

Nayak, M. R., Krishnanand, K. R., & Rout, P. K. (2011). *Modified differential evolution optimization algorithm for multi-constraint optimal power flow. In: 2011 international conference on energy, automation, and signal* (pp. 1–7). ICEAS. doi:10.1109/ICEAS.2011.6147113

Nguyen, T. T. A., & Conrad, S. (2015). Ontology Matching using multiple similarity measures. *Proceedings 7th International Joint Conference on Knowledge Discovery, Knowledge Engineering and Knowledge Management (IC3K 2015),* (pp. 603-611). Lisbon, Portugal: IEEE.

Nihar, R. N., Bikram, K. M., & Amiya, K. R. (2013). A Time Efficient Clustering Algorithm for Gray Scale Image Segmentation. *International Journal of Computer Vision and Image Processing, 3*(1), 22–32. doi:10.4018/ijcvip.2013010102

Nikhil, R. P., & Sankar, K. P. (1993). A Review on Image Segmentation Techniques. *Pattern Recognition, 26*(29).

Niknam, T., Golestaneh, F., & Shafiei, M. (2013). Probabilistic energy management of a renewable microgrid with hydrogen storage using self-adaptive charge search algorithm. *Energy, 49*, 252–267. doi:10.1016/j.energy.2012.09.055

Nikolić, M., & Teodorović, D. (2013). Empirical study of the Bee Colony Optimization (BCO) algorithm. *Expert Systems with Applications, 40*(11), 4609–4620. doi:10.1016/j.eswa.2013.01.063

Noessner, J., Niepert, M., Meilicke, C., & Stuckenschmidt, H. (2010) Leveraging terminological structure for object reconciliation. *Proceedings 7th Extended Semantic Web Conference,* (pp. 334-348). Heraklion, Greece: Springer.

Oguejiofor, O. S., Aniedu, A. N., Ejiofor, H. C., Okolibe, A. U. (2013). Trilateration Based localization Algorithm for Wireless Sensor Network. *International Journal of Science and Modern Engineering (IJISME),* 2319-6386.

Olorunda, O., & Engelbrecht, A. P. (2008) Measuring exploration/exploitation in particle swarms using swarm diversity. *Proceedings of the 2008 Congress on Evolutionary Computation(CEC 2008),* (pp. 1128-1134). 10.1109/CEC.2008.4630938

Optis, M., & Perr-Sauer, J. (2019). The importance of atmospheric turbulence and stability in machine-learning models of wind farm power production. *Renewable & Sustainable Energy Reviews, 112*, 27–41. doi:10.1016/j.rser.2019.05.031

Orero, S.O., & Irving, M. R. (1998). A genetic algorithm modeling framework and solution technique for short-term optimal hydrothermal scheduling. *IEEE Transaction on PWRS.* 13.

Orphanou, K., Thierens, D., & Bosman, P. A. (2018). *Learning Bayesian Network Structures with GOMEA.* kyoto. Japan: ACM.

Osman, I. H., & Laporte, G. (1996). Metaheuristics: A bibliography. *Annals of Operations Research, 63*(5), 511–623. doi:10.1007/BF02125421

Osuna-Enciso, V., Cuevas, E., & Sossa, H. (2013). *A Comparison of Nature Inspired Algorithms for Multi-Threshold Image Segmentation, 40*(4), pp. 1213-1219.

Osuna-Enciso, V. (2014). *Bioinspired metaheuristics for image segmentation* (Vol. 13, p. 2). Electronic Letters on Computer Vision and Analysis.

Panda, A., Tripathy, M., Barisal, A., & Prakash, T. (2017). A modified bacteria foraging based optimal power flow framework for Hydro-Thermal-Wind generation system in the presence of STATCOM. *Energy, 124,* 720–740. doi:10.1016/j.energy.2017.02.090

Pandey, A. C., Rajpoot, D. S., & Saraswat, M. (2017). Twitter sentiment analysis using hybrid cuckoo search method. *Information Processing & Management, 53*(4), 764–779. doi:10.1016/j.ipm.2017.02.004

Papagelis, M., Plexousakis, D., & Kutsuras, T. (2005). Alleviating the sparsity problem of collaborative filtering using trust inferences. *Proceedings International Conference on Trust Management* (pp. 224-239). Springer. 10.1007/11429760_16

Park, S. (2007). *Webpage design optimization using genetic algorithm driven CSS.* (Doctoral dissertation), Iowa State University.

Parpinelli, R. S., & Lopes, H. S. (2011). New inspirations in swarm intelligence: A survey. *International Journal of Bio-inspired Computation, 3*(1), 1–16. doi:10.1504/IJBIC.2011.038700

Passino, K. M. (2002). Biomimicry of bacterial foraging for distributed optimization and control. *IEEE Control Systems Magazine, 22*(3), 52–67. doi:10.1109/MCS.2002.1004010

Passino, K. M. (2010). Bacterial foraging optimization [IJSIR]. *International Journal of Swarm Intelligence Research, 1*(1), 1–16. doi:10.4018/jsir.2010010101

Patwal, R., Narang, N., & Garg, H. (2018). A novel TVAC-PSO based mutation strategies algorithm for generation scheduling of pumped storage hydrothermal system incorporating solar units. *Energy, 142,* 822–837. doi:10.1016/j.energy.2017.10.052

Paul, A. K., & Sato, T. (2017). Localization in wireless sensor networks: A survey on algorithms, measurement techniques, applications and challenges. *Journal of Sensor and Actuator Networks, 6*(4), 24. doi:10.3390/jsan6040024

Paz, F., Diaz, E., Paz, F. A., & Moquillaza, A. (2019). Application of the Usability Metrics of the ISO 9126 Standard in the E-Commerce Domain: A Case Study. *Proceedings International Conference on Intelligent Human Systems Integration, 352-356.* 10.1007/978-3-030-11051-2_54

Pazzani, M. J. (1999). A framework for collaborative, content-based and demographic filtering. *Artificial Intelligence Review, 13*(5-6), 393–408. doi:10.1023/A:1006544522159

Pe'er, D., Regev, A., Elidan, G., & Friedman, N. (2001.). Inferring Subnetworks from Perturbed Expression Profiles. *Ninth International Conference on Intelligent Systems for Molecular Biology (ISMB).* Copenhagen, Denmark. Academic Press.

Compilation of References

Pecora, L. M., Carroll, T. L., Johnson, G. A., Mar, D. J., & Heagy, J. F. (1997). Fundamentals of synchronization in chaotic systems, concepts, and applications. *Chaos (Woodbury, N.Y.)*, *7*(4), 520–543. doi:10.1063/1.166278 PMID:12779679

Pereira, M., & Pinto, L. (1983). Application of decomposition techniques to the mid and short-term scheduling of hydrothermal Systems. *IEEE Transactions on Power Apparatus and Systems*, *102*(11), 3611–3618. doi:10.1109/TPAS.1983.317709

Pham, D. T., Ghanbarzadeh, A., Koc, E., Otri, S., Rahim, S., & Zaidi, M. (2006). The Bees Algorithm: A Novel Tool for Complex Optimisation Problems. *Proceedings of IPROMS 2006 Conference*. 10.1016/B978-008045157-2/50081-X

Piotrowski, A. P., & Napiorkowski, J. J. (2018). Some metaheuristics should be simplified. *Information Sciences*, *427*, 32–62. doi:10.1016/j.ins.2017.10.039

Polat, H., & Du, W. (2005). Privacy-preserving top-n recommendation on horizontally partitioned data. *Proceedings of the 2005 IEEE/WIC/ACM International Conference on Web Intelligence*, (pp. 725-731). 10.1109/WI.2005.117

Pourret, O., & Naim, P. (2008). Bayesian networks: a practical guide to applications. UK: John Wiley & Sons, The Atrium, Southern Gate, Chichester, West Sussex PO19 8SQ. doi:10.1002/9780470994559

Prasad, Y., & Biswas, K. K. (2015, March). Gene selection in microarray datasets using progressively refined PSO scheme. *Proceedings Twenty-Ninth AAAI Conference on Artificial Intelligence*. Academic Press.

Precup, R. E., David, R. C., Petriu, E. M., Preitl, S., & Radac, M. B. (2012). Fuzzy control systems with reduced parametric sensitivity based on simulated annealing. *IEEE Transactions on Industrial Electronics*, *59*(8), 3049–3061. doi:10.1109/TIE.2011.2130493

Quan, H., Srinivasan, D., Khambadkone, A. M., & Khosravi, A. (2015). A computational framework for uncertainty integration in stochastic unit commitment with intermittent renewable energy sources. *Applied Energy*, *152*, 71–82. doi:10.1016/j.apenergy.2015.04.103

Qu, B. Y., Liang, J. J., Zhu, Y. S., Wang, Z. Y., & Suganthan, P. N. (2017). Economic emission dispatch problems with stochastic wind power using summation based multi-objective evolutionary algorithm. *Information Sciences*, *351*, 48–66. doi:10.1016/j.ins.2016.01.081

Quiroz, J. C., Louis, S. J., Shankar, A., & Dascalu, S. M. (2007). Interactive genetic algorithms for user interface design. *Proceedings 2007 IEEE Congress on Evolutionary Computation, 1366-1373*. IEEE. 10.1109/CEC.2007.4424630

Rahman, I., & Saleh, J. M. (2018). Hybrid Bio-Inspired Computational Intelligence Techniques for Solving Power System Optimization Problems: A Comprehensive Survey. *Applied Soft Computing*, *69*, 72–130. doi:10.1016/j.asoc.2018.04.051

Rahnamayan, S., Tizhoosh, H. R., & Salama, M. M. A. (2007). Quasi oppositional differential evolution. *Proceedings of IEEE Congress on Evolu. Comput.* pp. 2229–36. 10.1109/CEC.2007.4424748

Rajakumar, R., Dhavachelvan, P., & Vengattaraman, T. (2016). A survey on nature inspired meta-heuristic algorithms with its domain specifications. *Proceedings Communication and Electronics Systems (ICCES)*, 1-6.

Rajasekar, N., Kumar, N. K., & Venugopalan, R. (2013). Bacterial foraging algorithm based solar PV parameter estimation. *Solar Energy*, *97*, 255–265. doi:10.1016/j.solener.2013.08.019

Rajini, N. H. (2019). Image Segmentation for Diabetic Retinopathy Using Modified Bacterial Foraging Optimization Algorithm. *Indian Journal of Public Health Research & Development*, *10*(7), 1313–1319. doi:10.5958/0976-5506.2019.01769.8

Ramirez, M., & Ontae, P. E. (2006). The short-term hydrothermal coordination via genetic algorithms. *Electric Power Components and Systems*, *34*(1), 1–19. doi:10.1080/15325000691001584

Rana, M., & Koprinska, I. (2016). Forecasting electricity load with advanced wavelet neural networks. *Neurocomputing*, *182*, 118–132. doi:10.1016/j.neucom.2015.12.004

Rarick, R., Simon, D., Villaseca, F. E., & Vyakaranam, B. (2009). Biogeography-based optimization and the solution of the power flow problem. Proceedings *IEEE international conference on systems, man, and cybernetics* (pp. 1003–1018). SMC.

Rasoul, A. A., Taher, N., Mohammad, A. B., & Mohsen, Z. (2014). Coordination of combined heat and power-hermal-wind photovoltaic units in economic load dispatch using chance constrained and jointly distributed random variables methods. *Energy*, *79*(C), 50–67.

Rath, A., Samantaray, S., & Swain, P. C. (2019). Optimization of the Cropping Pattern Using Cuckoo Search Technique. In *Smart Techniques for a Smarter Planet* (pp. 19–35). Cham, Switzerland: Springer. doi:10.1007/978-3-030-03131-2_2

Ray, D., Zimmerman, C. S., & David, G. (n.d.). Matpower retrieved from http://www.pserc.cornell.edu/matpower/#docsn.d

Reddy, T. G., & Kare, N. (2016). FFBAT-optimized rule based fuzzy logic classifier for diabetes. International Journal of Engineering Research in Africa Trans Tech Publications, 137-152.

Reddy, S. S., & Bijwe, P. R. (2016). Day-ahead and real time optimal power flow considering renewable energy resources. *International Journal of Electrical Power & Energy Systems*, *82*, 400–408. doi:10.1016/j.ijepes.2016.03.033

Resnick, P., Iacovou, N., Suchak, M., Bergstrom, P., & Riedl, J. (1994). GroupLens: an open architecture for collaborative filtering of netnews. *Proceedings of the 1994 ACM conference on Computer supported cooperative work*. 10.1145/192844.192905

Rezaie,, H., & Kazemi-Rahbar,, M. H., Vahidi, B., & Rastegar, H. (2018). Solution of combined economic and emission dispatch problem using a novel chaotic improved harmony search algorithm. *Journal of Computational Design and Engg.*, *6*(3), 447–467.

Ribeiro Filho, J. L., Treleaven, P. C., & Cesare, A. (1994). Genetic-algorithm programming environments. *Computer*, *27*(6), 28–43. doi:10.1109/2.294850

Ridler, T. W., & Calvard, S. (1978). Picture thresholding using an iterative selection method. *IEEE Transactions on Systems, Man, and Cybernetics*, *8*(8), 630–632. doi:10.1109/TSMC.1978.4310039

Roa-Sepulveda, C. A., & Pavez-Lazo, B. J. (2003). A solution to the optimal power flow using simulated annealing. *International Journal of Electrical Power & Energy Systems*, *25*(1), 47–57. doi:10.1016/S0142-0615(02)00020-0

Robinson, R. (1977). Counting Unlabeled Acyclic Digraphs. Springer- Verlag, 622.

Roffo, G., Melzi, S., Castellani, U., & Vinciarelli, A. (2017). Infinite latent feature selection: A probabilistic latent graph-based ranking approach. *Proceedings of the IEEE International Conference on Computer Vision* (pp. 1398-1406). 10.1109/ICCV.2017.156

Rojas-Delgado, J., Trujillo-Rasúa, R., & Bello, R. (2019). A continuation approach for training Artificial Neural Networks with meta-heuristics. *Pattern Recognition Letters*, *125*, 373–380. doi:10.1016/j.patrec.2019.05.017

Romano, D., Raemaekers, S., & Pinzger, M. (2014). Refactoring fat interfaces using a genetic algorithm. *Proceedings International Conference on Software Maintenance and Evolution (ICSME)*, 351-360. 10.1109/ICSME.2014.57

Ronkkonen, J., Kukkonen, S., & Price, K. V. (2005). Real-parameter optimization with differential evolution. *Proceedings of the 2005 IEEE Congress on Evolutionary Computation (CEC2005)*, (pp. 506-513). 10.1109/CEC.2005.1554725

Rothlauf, F. (2011). Design of Modern Heuristics Principles and Application. Springer.

Roy, P. K., Ghoshal, S. P., & Thakur, S. S. (2010). Combined economic and emission dispatch problems using biogeography-based optimization. *Electrical Engineering, 92,* pp. 4-5, 173-184.

Roy, P. K. (2013). Teaching learning based optimization for short-term hydrothermal scheduling problem considering valve point effect and prohibited discharge constraint. *Electrical Power and Energy Systems, 53,* 10–19. doi:10.1016/j.ijepes.2013.03.024

Roy, P. K., Ghoshal, S. P., & Thakur, S. S. (2010). Biogeography based optimization for multi constraint optimal power flow with emission and non-smooth cost function. *Expert Systems with Applications, 37*(12), 8221–8228. doi:10.1016/j.eswa.2010.05.064

Roy, P. K., Ghoshal, S. P., & Thakur, S. S. (2010a). Combined economic and emission dispatch problems using biogeography-based optimization. *Electrical Engineering, 92*(4-5), 173–184. doi:10.100700202-010-0173-3

Roy, P. K., & Paul, C. (2015). Quasi-oppositional gravitational search algorithm applied to short-term hydrothermal scheduling problems. *InderScience, 5*(6), 165. doi:10.1504/IJPEC.2015.069437

Roy, P. K., Sur, A., & Pradhan, D. (2013). Optimal short-term hydro-thermal scheduling using quasi-oppositional teaching learning based optimization. *Engineering Applications of Artificial Intelligence.* doi:10.1016/j.engappai.2013.08.002

Russ, J. C., & Neal, F. B. (2015). *The image processing handbook* (7th ed.). Boca Raton, FL: CRC Press.

Safoury, L., & Salah, A. (2013). Exploiting user demographic attributes for solving cold-start problem in recommender system. *Lecture notes on software engineering, 1*(3), 303.

Sahu, A. K., & Dwivedi, P. (2018). Matrix factorization in Cross-domain Recommendations Framework by Shared Users Latent Factors. *Procedia Computer Science, 143,* 387–394. doi:10.1016/j.procs.2018.10.410

Said, A., Plumbaum, T., De Luca, E. W., & Albayrak, S. (2011). A comparison of how demographic data affects recommendation. *User Modeling, Adaptation, and Personalization (UMAP), 7.*

Sakulin S. A., & Alfimtsev, A. N. (2017). Data fusion based on the fuzzy integral: Model, methods, and applications. *Data Fusion: Methods, Applications, and Research,* 1-64.

Sakulin, S., Alfimtsev, A., Solovyev, D., & Sokolov, D. (2018). Web page interface optimization based on nature-inspired algorithms [IJSIR]. *International Journal of Swarm Intelligence Research, 9*(2), 28–46. doi:10.4018/IJSIR.2018040103

Sakulin, S., Alfimtsev, A., Tipsin, E., Devyatkov, V., & Sokolov, D. (2019). User Interface Distribution Method Based on Pi-Calculus [IJDST]. *International Journal of Distributed Systems and Technologies, 10*(3), 1–20. doi:10.4018/IJDST.2019070101

Salama, K. M., & Freitas, A. A. (2012). ABC-Miner: An Ant-Based Bayesian Classification Algorithm.

Salem, P. (2017). User Interface Optimization using Genetic Programming with an Application to Landing Pages. *Proceedings of the ACM on Human-Computer Interaction, 1*(1), 13. 10.1145/3099583

Salomon, R. (1996). Reevaluating genetic algorithm performance under coordinated rotation of benchmark functions. *Bio Systems, 39,* 263–278. doi:10.1016/0303-2647(96)01621-8 PMID:8894127

Sang, H. Y., Duan, P. Y., & Li, J. Q. (2018). An effective invasive weed optimization algorithm for scheduling semiconductor final testing problem. *Swarm and Evolutionary Computation, 38,* 42–53. doi:10.1016/j.swevo.2017.05.007

Saremi, S., Mirjalili, S., & Lewis, A. (2017). Grasshopper optimisation algorithm. *Theory and Application Advances in Engineering Software, 105,* 30–47. doi:10.1016/j.advengsoft.2017.01.004

Saxena, A. (2019). A comprehensive study of chaos embedded bridging mechanisms and crossover operators for grasshopper optimisation algorithm. *Expert Systems with Applications*, *132*, 166–188. doi:10.1016/j.eswa.2019.04.043

Sayah, S., & Zehar, K. (2008). Modified differential evolution algorithm for optimal power flow with non-smooth cost functions. *Energy Conversion and Management*, *49*(11), 3036–3042. doi:10.1016/j.enconman.2008.06.014

Schmidt, J., Gröller, M. E., & Bruckner, S. (2013). VAICo: Visual analysis for image comparison. *IEEE Transactions on Visualization and Computer Graphics*, *19*(12), 2090–2099. doi:10.1109/TVCG.2013.213 PMID:24051775

Sencer, S., Oztemel, E., Taskin, H., & Torkul, O. (2013). Bayesian Structural Learning with Minimum Spanning Tree Algorithm. *Proceedings of the International Conference on Information and Knowledge Engineering (IKE) (p. 1). The Steering Committee of The World Congress in Computer Science, Computer Engineering and Applied Computing (WorldComp).*

Senthilnath, J., Vipul, D., Omkar, S. N., & Mani, V. (2012). Clustering using levy flight cuckoo search. *Proceedings 7th International Conference on Bio-Inspired Computing: Theories and Applications, Advances in Intelligent Systems and Computing*, pp. 65–75. LNCS, Springer India.

Senthilnath, J., Omkar, S. N., & Mani, V. (2011). Clustering using firefly algorithm: Performance study. *Swarm and Evolutionary Computation, Elsevier*, *1*(3), 164–171. doi:10.1016/j.swevo.2011.06.003

Seok, L. K., & Woo, G. Z. (2017). A new structural optimization method based on the harmony search algorithm. *ComputStruc April 2004; 82*(9–10), pp. 781-798.

Shabanzadeh, M., Sheikh-El-Eslami, M. K., & Haghifam, M. R. (2015). The design of a risk hedging tool for virtual power plants via robust optimization approach. *Applied Energy*, *155*, 766–777. doi:10.1016/j.apenergy.2015.06.059

Shahidehpour, M., Fujisawa, Y., & Maeda, Y. (1990). Multi-stage generation scheduling by neural networks. *Proceedings of the Workshop on Applications of Artificial Neural Network Methodology in Power Systems Engineering*, pp. 66–70. Clemson, SC.

Sharma, V., Pattnaik, S. S., & Garg, T. (2012). A review of bacterial foraging optimization and its applications [IJCA]. *International Journal of Computers and Applications*, 9–12.

Shayeghi, H., Shayanfar, H., & Azimi, G. (2009). STLF based on optimized neural network using PSO. *Iranian Journal of Electrical and Computer Engineering*, *4*, 1190–1199.

Shi, Y. (2011a). Brain storm optimization algorithm. In Y. Tan, Y. Shi, Y. Chai, & G. Wang (Eds.), Advances in Swarm Intelligence, ser. Lecture Notes in Computer Science, 6728 (pp. 303-309). Berlin, Germany: Springer. doi:10.1007/978-3-642-21515-5_36

Shi, Y., & Eberhart, R. (1998). Parameter selection in particle swarm optimization. In Evolutionary Programming VII, Lecture Notes in Computer Science, 1447, 591-600. Berlin, Germany: Springer. doi:10.1007/BFb0040810

Shi, H., Chen, L., Xu, Z., & Lyu, D. (2019). Personalized location recommendation using mobile phone usage information. *Applied Intelligence*, *49*(10), 1–14. doi:10.100710489-019-01477-6

Shindo, T., Xiao, J., Kurihara, T., Morita, K., & Jin'no, K. (2015, May). Analysis of the dynamic characteristics of firefly algorithm. *Proceedings 2015 IEEE Congress on Evolutionary Computation (CEC)*, (pp. 2647-2652). IEEE. 10.1109/CEC.2015.7257215

Shi, Y. (2011b). An optimization algorithm based on brainstorming process [IJSIR]. *International Journal of Swarm Intelligence Research*, *2*(4), 35–62. doi:10.4018/ijsir.2011100103

Shi, Y. (2014). Developmental swarm intelligence: Developmental learning perspective of swarm intelligence algorithms [IJSIR]. *International Journal of Swarm Intelligence Research*, 5(1), 36–54. doi:10.4018/ijsir.2014010102

Shi, Y., & Eberhart, R. (1998). A modified particle swarm optimizer. *Proceedings of the 1998 IEEE Congress on Evolutionary Computation (CEC1998)*, (pp. 69-73). 10.1109/ICEC.1998.699146

Shi, Y., & Eberhart, R. (1999). Empirical study of particle swarm optimization. *Proceedings of the 1999 Congress on Evolutionary Computation (CEC 1999)*, (pp. 1945-1950). 10.1109/CEC.1999.785511

Shi, Y., & Eberhart, R. (2001). Fuzzy adaptive particle swarm optimization. *Proceedings of the 2001 Congress on Evolutionary Computation (CEC2001)*, (pp.101-106). 10.1109/CEC.2001.934377

Shi, Y., & Eberhart, R. (2008). Population diversity of particle swarms. *Proceedings of the 2008 Congress on Evolutionary Computation (CEC 2008)*, (pp. 1063-1067). 10.1109/CEC.2008.4630928

Shi, Y., & Eberhart, R. (2009). Monitoring of particle swarm optimization. *Frontiers of Computer Science*, 3(1), 31–37. doi:10.100711704-009-0008-4

Shoults, R., & Sun, D. (1982). Optimal power flow based on P–Q decomposition. *IEEE Transactions on Power Apparatus and Systems*, 101(2), 397–405. doi:10.1109/TPAS.1982.317120

Shu, S., Mo, L., & Wang, Y. (2019). Peak shaving strategy of wind-solar-hydro hybrid Generation System Based on Modified Differential Evolution Algorithm. *Energy Procedia*, 158, 3500–3505. doi:10.1016/j.egypro.2019.01.920

Shvaiko, P., & Euzenat, J. (2013). Ontology matching: State of the art and future challenges. *IEEE Transactions on Knowledge and Data Engineering*, 25(1), 158–176. doi:10.1109/TKDE.2011.253

Sierra, M. R., & Coello, C. A. C. (2005). Improving PSO-based multi-objective optimization using crowding, mutation and -dominance. *Proceedings International Conference on Evolutionary Multi-Criterion Optimization (EMO 2005)*, (pp. 505-519). Guanajuato, Mexico. Berlin, Germany: Springer. 10.1007/978-3-540-31880-4_35

Silva, N. B., Tsang, R., Cavalcanti, G. D., & Tsang, J. (2010). A graph-based friend recommendation system using genetic algorithm. *Proceedings 2010 IEEE Congress on Evolutionary Computation (CEC)* (pp. 1-7). IEEE.

Silva, L. A., Bezzera, J. B., Perkusich, M. B., Gorgônio, K. C., Almeida, H. O., & Perkusich, A. (2018). Continuous Learning of the Structure of Bayesian Networks: A Mapping Study. In F. U. Grande (Ed.), *Bayesian Networks - Advances and Novel Applications* (pp. 1–15). Paraíba, Brazil: Intechopen.

Silvia, N. S., & Analía, A. (2009). Building an expert travel agent as a software agent. *Expert Systems with Applications*, 36(2), 1291–1299. doi:10.1016/j.eswa.2007.11.032

Singh, A., & Sahay, K. B. (2018). Short-Term Demand Forecasting by Using ANN Algorithms. *Proceedings International Electrical Engineering Congress (iEECON)*. IEEE. 10.1109/IEECON.2018.8712265

Singh, D. A. A. G., Leavline, E. J., Valliyappan, K., & Srinivasan, M. (2015). Enhancing the performance of classifier using particle swarm optimization (PSO)-based dimensionality reduction. *International Journal of Energy, Information, and Communications*, 6(5), 19–26.

Singh, D., & Singh, S. P. (2001). A self-selecting neural network for short-term load forecasting. *Electric Power Components and Systems*, 29(2), 117–130. doi:10.1080/153250001300003386

Sinha, A., Korhonen, P., Wallenius, J., & Deb, K. (2014). An interactive evolutionary multi-objective optimization algorithm with a limited number of decision maker calls. *European Journal of Operational Research*, 233(3), 647–688. doi:10.1016/j.ejor.2013.08.046

Sivasubramani, S., & Swarup, K. S. (2011). Multi-objective harmony search algorithm for optimal power flow problem. *Electrical Power Energy Systems*, *33*(3), 745–752. doi:10.1016/j.ijepes.2010.12.031

Son, L. H. (2016). Dealing with the new user cold-start problem in recommender systems: A comparative review. *Information Systems*, *58*, 87–104. doi:10.1016/j.is.2014.10.001

Sorn, D., & Rimcharoen, S. (2013). Web page template design using interactive genetic algorithm *Proceedings Computer Science and Engineering Conference (ICSEC)*, 201-206. 10.1109/ICSEC.2013.6694779

Sousa, T., Soares, J., Vale, Z. A., Morais, H., & Faria, P. (2011). *Simulated annealing metaheuristic to solve the optimal power flow. Proceedings 2011 IEEE power and energy society general meeting, 1-8.* doi:10.1109/PES.2011.6039543

Spears, W. M., Green, D. T., & Spears, D. F. (2010). Biases in particle swarm optimization. [IJSIR]. *International Journal of Swarm Intelligence Research*, *1*(2), 34–57. doi:10.4018/jsir.2010040103

Storn, R., & Price, K. (1997). Differential Evolution – A Simple and Efficient Heuristic for global Optimization over Continuous Spaces. *Journal of Global Optimization*, *11*(4), 341–359. doi:10.1023/A:1008202821328

Subbaraj, P., & Rajasekaran, V. (2008). Evolutionary techniques based combined artificial neural networks for peak load forecasting. *World Academy of Science, Engineering, and Technology*, *45*, 680–686.

Suganthan, P. N., Hansen, N., Liang, J. J., Deb, K., Chen, Y. P., Auger, A., & Tiwari, S. (2005). *Problem definitions and evaluation criteria for the cec2005 special session on real parameter optimization. Technical report.* Nanyang Technological University.

Sun, X., Chen, C., Wang, L., Kang, H., Shen, Y., & Chen, Q. (2019). Hybrid Optimization Algorithm for Bayesian Network Structure Learning. *Information*, 1-16.

Sun, C., & Lu, S. (2010). Short-term combined economic emission hydrothermal scheduling using improved quantum-behaved particle swarm optimization. *Expert Systems with Applications*, *37*(6), 4232–4421. doi:10.1016/j.eswa.2009.11.079

Sun, C., & Lu, S. (2011). Quadratic approximation based differential evolution with valuable trade off approach for bi-objective short-term hydrothermal scheduling. *Expert Systems with Applications*, *38*(11), 13950–13960.

Sundaram, R. K. (1996). *A First Course in Optimization Theory.* Cambridge University Press. doi:10.1017/CBO9780511804526

Su, W., Wang, J., & Roh, J. (2014). Stochastic energy scheduling in microgrids with intermittent renewable energy resources. *IEEE Transactions on Smart Grid*, *5*(4), 1876–1883. doi:10.1109/TSG.2013.2280645

Su, X., & Khoshgoftaar, T. M. (2009). A survey of collaborative filtering techniques. *Advances in Artificial Intelligence*, *2009*(1), 4.

Swain, R. K., Barisal, A. K., Hota, P. K., & Chakrabarti, R. (2011). Short-term hydrothermal scheduling using clonal selection algorithm. *Electrical Power and Energy Systems*, *33*(3), 647–656. doi:10.1016/j.ijepes.2010.11.016

Tahier, T., Marie, S., Girard, S., & Forbes, F. (2019). Fast Bayesian Network Structure Learning using Quasi-Determinism Screening. *HAL*, *2*, 14–24.

Talbi, E. G., Jourdan, L., Garcia-Nieto, J., & Alba, E. (2008, March). Comparison of population based metaheuristics for feature selection: Application to microarray data classification. *Proceedings 2008 IEEE/ACS International Conference on Computer Systems and Applications* (pp. 45-52). IEEE. 10.1109/AICCSA.2008.4493515

Tan, Y., & Zhu, Y. (2010) Fireworks algorithm for optimization, in Advances in Swarm Intelligence, ser. Lecture Notes in Computer Science, Y. Tan, Y. Shi, and K. C. Tan, Eds. Springer Berlin Heidelberg, 6145, (pp. 355-364). doi:10.1007/978-3-642-13495-1_44

Tang, K., Li, X., Suganthan, P. N., Yang, Z., & Weise, T. (2010). Benchmark Functions for the CEC'2010 Special Session and Competition on Large-Scale Global Optimization. Technical report, 1-23.

Tan, Y. (2015). *Fireworks Algorithm: A Novel Swarm Intelligence Optimization Method*. Springer. doi:10.1007/978-3-662-46353-6

Tan, Y., Yu, C., Zheng, S., & Ding, K. (2013). Introduction to fireworks algorithm. [IJSIR] *International Journal of Swarm Intelligence Research, 4*(4), 39–70. doi:10.4018/ijsir.2013100103

Tarik, B., & Zakaria, E. (2019). Best Feature Selection for Horizontally Distributed Private Biomedical Data Based on Genetic Algorithms. [IJDST]. *International Journal of Distributed Systems and Technologies, 10*(3), 37–57. doi:10.4018/IJDST.2019070103

Tharwat, A., Houssein, E. H., Ahmed, M. M., Hassanien, A. E., & Gabel, T. (2017). MOGOA algorithm for constrained and unconstrained multi-objective optimization problems. *Applied Intelligence*, 1–16.

Ting, W., Qiang, Y., Zhejing, B., & Wenjun, Y. (●●●). (2103). Coordinated energy dispatching in microgrid with wind power generation and plug-in electric vehicles. *IEEE Transactions on Smart Grid, 4*(3), 1453–1463.

Tizhoosh, H. (2005). Opposition-based learning: A new scheme for machine intelligence. *Proceedings of the Int Conference on Computational Intelligence for Modelling Control and Automation*, pp. 695–701. 10.1109/CIMCA.2005.1631345

Tong, S., & Koller, D. (2001). Active Learning for Structure in Bayesian Networks. *Proceedings International joint conference on artificial intelligence, 17*(1), pp. 863-869. Lawrence Erlbaum Associates.

Trelea, I. C. (2003). The particle swarm optimization algorithm: Convergence analysis and parameter selection. *Information Processing Letters, 85*(6), 317–325. doi:10.1016/S0020-0190(02)00447-7

Troiano, L., Birtolo, C., & Cirillo, G. (2009). Interactive Genetic Algorithm for choosing suitable colors in User Interface. *Proceedings of Learning and Intelligent Optimization, LION3*, 14–18.

Turgeon, A. (1981). Optimal short-term hydro scheduling from the principle of progressive optimality. *Water Resources Research, 17*(3), 481–486. doi:10.1029/WR017i003p00481

Valian, E., Mohanna, S., & Tavakoli, S. (2011). Improved cuckoo search algorithm for feedforward neural network training. *Int. Jour. of Artif. Intellig. & Applications, 2*(3), 36–43. doi:10.5121/ijaia.2011.2304

Van den Bergh, F., & Engelbrecht, A. P. (2004). A cooperative approach to particle swarm optimization. *IEEE Transactions on Evolutionary Computation, 8*(3), 225–239. doi:10.1109/TEVC.2004.826069

Van Rijsberge, C. J. (1975). *Information Retrieval*. Butterworth, UK: University of Glasgow.

Venkatesh, P., & Lee, K. Y. (2008). Multi-objective evolutionary programming for economic emission dispatch problem. *Proc. IEEE PES Gen. Meeting*, Pittsburgh, PA, Jul. 2008. 10.1109/PES.2008.4596896

Victor, P., Cornelis, C., Teredesai, A. M., & Cock, M. D. (2008). Whom should I trust?: the impact of key figures on cold start recommendations. *Proceedings of the 2008 ACM symposium on Applied computing* (pp. 2014--2018). ACM. 10.1145/1363686.1364174

Vieira, S. M., Mendonça, L. F., Farinha, G. J., & Sousa, J. M. (2013). Modified binary PSO for feature selection using SVM applied to mortality prediction of septic patients. *Applied Soft Computing*, *13*(8), 3494–3504. doi:10.1016/j.asoc.2013.03.021

Viktoratos, I., Tsadiras, A., & Bassiliades, N. (2018). Combining community-based knowledge with association rule mining to alleviate the cold start problem in context-aware recommender systems. *Expert Systems with Applications*, *101*, 78–90. doi:10.1016/j.eswa.2018.01.044

Vlachogiannis, G., & Lee, K. Y. (2008). Quantum-inspired evolutionary algorithm for real and reactive power and reactive power dispatch. *IEEE Transactions on Power Systems*, *23*(4), 1627–1636. doi:10.1109/TPWRS.2008.2004743

Vose, M. D. (1999). *Simple Genetic Algorithm: Foundation and Theory*. Cambridge, MA: MIT Press.

Vozalis, M., & Margaritis, K. G. (2004). Collaborative filtering enhanced by demographic correlation. *AIAI symposium on professional practice in AI, of the 18th world computer congress*.

Vozalis, M. G., & Margaritis, K. G. (2007). Using SVD and demographic data for the enhancement of generalized collaborative filtering. *Information Sciences*, *177*(15), 3017–3037. doi:10.1016/j.ins.2007.02.036

Wang, H., & Zhang, H. (2018). Movie genre preference prediction using machine learning for customer-based information. *2018 IEEE 8th Annual Computing and Communication Workshop and Conference (CCWC)*, 110-116.

Wang, D. F., Han, N., Liu, Z., & Dong, S. M., & Jiao. (2002). Modelling the circulating fluidized bed boiler using RBF-NN based on immune genetic algorithm. *Proceedings of the First International Conference on Machine Learning and Cybernetics*, 2121–2125. 10.1109/ICMLC.2002.1175413

Wang, G.-G., Deb, S., & Coelho, L. (2015). *Elephant Herding Optimization*. IEEE. doi:10.1109/ISCBI.2015.8

Wang, H., Wang, W., Cui, L., Sun, H., Zhao, J., Wang, Y., & Xue, Y. (2018). A hybrid multi-objective firefly algorithm for big data optimization. *Applied Soft Computing*, *69*, 806–815. doi:10.1016/j.asoc.2017.06.029

Wang, J., & Liu, S. (2018). Novel binary encoding water cycle algorithm for solving Bayesian network structures learning problem. *Knowledge-Based Systems*, *150*, 150. doi:10.1016/j.knosys.2018.03.007

Wang, K. Y., Luo, X. J., Wu, L., & Liu, X. C. (2013). Optimal coordination of wind-hydro-thermal based on water complementing wind. *Renewable Energy*, *60*, 169–178. doi:10.1016/j.renene.2013.04.015

Wang, P., Zhu, Z., & Huang, S. (2013). Seven-spot ladybird optimization: A novel and efficient metaheuristic algorithm for numerical optimization. *The Scientific World Journal*, *2013*. doi:10.1155/2013/378515 PMID:24385879

Wang, Y., & Tang, Y. (2019). A Recommendation Algorithm Based on Item Genres Preference and GBRT. *Journal of Physics: Conference Series*, *1229*(1). doi:10.1088/1742-6596/150/1/012053

Wei, H., Sasaki, H., Kubokawa, J., & Yokoyama, R. (1998). An interior point nonlinear programming for optimal power flow problems whit a novel structure data. *IEEE Transactions on Power Systems*, *13*(3), 870–877. doi:10.1109/59.708745

Weise, T., Zapf, M., Chiong, R., & Nebro, A. J. (2009). Why is optimization difficult? In Nature-Inspired Algorithms for Optimisation, Vol. 193 of Studies in Computational Intelligence, pp. 1-50. Berlin, Germany: Springer. doi:10.1007/978-3-642-00267-0_1

Werner, T. G., & Verstege, J. F. (1999). An evolutionary strategy for short-term operation planning of hydro-thermal power systems. *IEEE Transactions on Power Systems*, *14*(4), 1362–1368. doi:10.1109/59.801897

Whitley, D., Gordon, V. S., & Mathias, K. (1995). Lamarckian evolution, the Baldwin effect and function optimization. *Proceedings International Conference on Parallel Problem Solving from Nature*, 5–15 (Springer).

Wilson, D. C., Smyth, B., & Sullivan, D. O. (2003). Sparsity reduction in collaborative recommendation: A case-based approach. *International Journal of Pattern Recognition and Artificial Intelligence*, *17*(5), 863–884. doi:10.1142/S0218001403002678

Wolpert, D., & Macready, W. (1997). No free lunch theorems for optimization. *IEEE Transactions on Evolutionary Computation*, *1*(1), 67–82. doi:10.1109/4235.585893

Wong, K. P., & Wong, Y. W. (1994). Short-term hydrothermal scheduling part 1: Simulated annealing approach. *IEE Proceedings. Generation, Transmission, and Distribution*, *141*(5), 497–501. doi:10.1049/ip-gtd:19941350

Wood, L., Nicol, G., Robie, J., Champion, M., & Byrne, S. (2004). *Document Object Model (DOM)*. Level 3 core specification.

Wood, A. J., & Wollenberg, B. F. (1994). *Power generation, operation, and control*. New York: John Wiley & Sons.

Wu, S., & Chow, T. W. S. (2007). Self-organizing and self-evolving neurons: A new neural network for optimization. *IEEE Transactions on Neural Networks*, *18*(2), 385–396. doi:10.1109/TNN.2006.887556 PMID:17385627

Wu, T., Yang, Q., Bao, Z., & Yan, W. (2013). Coordinated Energy Dispatching in Microgrid With Wind Power Generation and Plug-in Electric Vehicles. *IEEE Transactions on Smart Grid*, *4*(3), 1453–1463. doi:10.1109/TSG.2013.2268870

Wu, Z., & Chow, T. W. S. (2013). Neighborhood field for cooperative optimization. *Soft Computing*, *17*(5), 819–834. doi:10.100700500-012-0955-9

Xiao, L., Wang, J., & Yun, W. (2008). A novel localization algorithm based on received signal strength for mobile wireless sensor networks. *Proceedings of International Conference on Microwave and Millimeter Wave Technology*, Vol. 1, (pp. 92-95).

Xin, J., Chen, G., & Hai, Y. (2009). A particle swarm optimizer with multistage linearly-decreasing inertia weight. *Proceedings International Joint Conference on Computational Sciences and Optimization.* 10.1109/CSO.2009.420

Xu, P., Wang, Y., Cheng, L., & Zhang, T. (2010). Alignment Results of SOBOM for OAEI 2010. *Proceedings of the 5th International Conference on Ontology Matching (OM-2010)*, (pp. 203-211). Shanghai, China: CEUR-WS.org.

Xue, X., Chen, J., & Yao, X. (2019). Efficient User Involvement in Semi-automatic Ontology Matching, IEEE Transactions on Emerging Topics in Computational Intelligence, pp. 1-11.

Xue, B., Zhang, M., & Browne, W. N. (2012). Particle swarm optimization for feature selection in classification: A multi-objective approach. *IEEE Transactions on Cybernetics*, *43*(6), 1656–1671. doi:10.1109/TSMCB.2012.2227469 PMID:24273143

Xue, X., & Chen, J. (2019c). Using Compact Evolutionary Tabu Search Algorithm for Matching Sensor Ontologies. *Swarm and Evolutionary Computation*, *48*, 25–30. doi:10.1016/j.swevo.2019.03.007

Xue, X., & Chen, J. (2019d). Optimizing Ontology Alignment Through Hybrid Population-based Incremental Learning Algorithm. *Memetic Computing*, *11*(2), 209–217. doi:10.100712293-018-0255-8

Xue, X., Hang, Z., & Tang, Z. (2019b). Interactive Biomedical Ontology Matching. *PLoS One*, *14*(4), 1–13. doi:10.1371/journal.pone.0215147 PMID:30995257

Xue, X., & Liu, J. (2017a). Optimizing Ontology Alignment through Compact MOEA/D. *International Journal of Pattern Recognition and Artificial Intelligence*, *31*(4). doi:10.1142/S0218001417590042

Xue, X., & Liu, J. (2017d). Collaborative Ontology Matching Based on Compact Interactive Evolutionary Algorithm. *Knowledge-Based Systems*, *137*, 94–103. doi:10.1016/j.knosys.2017.09.017

Xue, X., Tsai, P., & Feng, G. (2017b). Efficient Ontology Meta-Matching Based on Metamodel-assisted Compact MOEA/D. *Journal of Information Hiding and Multimedia Signal Processing, 8*(5), 1021–1028.

Xue, X., & Wang, Y. (2015a). Ontology alignment based on instance using NSGA-II. *Journal of Information Science, 41*(1), 58–70. doi:10.1177/0165551514550142

Xue, X., & Wang, Y. (2015b). Optimizing Ontology Alignments through a Memetic Algorithm Using both MatchFmeasure and Unanimous Improvement Ratio. *Artificial Intelligence, 223*, 65–81. doi:10.1016/j.artint.2015.03.001

Xue, X., & Wang, Y. (2016). Using Memetic Algorithm for Instance Coreference Resolution. *IEEE Transactions on Knowledge and Data Engineering, 28*(2), 580–591. doi:10.1109/TKDE.2015.2475755

Xue, X., & Wang, Y. (2017c). Improving the Efficiency of NSGA-II based Ontology Aligning Technology. *Data & Knowledge Engineering, 108*, 1–14. doi:10.1016/j.datak.2016.12.002

Xue, X., Wang, Y., & Hao, W. (2014b). Using MOEA/D for optimizing ontology alignments. *Soft Computing, 18*(8), 1589–1601. doi:10.100700500-013-1165-9

Xue, X., Wang, Y., & Hao, W. (2015). Optimizing ontology alignments by using NSGA-II. *The International Arab Journal of Information Technology, 12*(2), 175–181.

Xue, X., Wang, Y., Hao, W., & Hou, J. (2014a). Optimizing Ontology Alignments through NSGA-II without Using Reference Alignment. *Computer Information, 33*(4), 857–876.

Xue, X., & Yao, X. (2018). Interactive Ontology Matching based on Partial Reference Alignment. *Applied Soft Computing, 72*, 355–370. doi:10.1016/j.asoc.2018.08.003

Xu, L., & Chow, T. W. S. (2010). Self-organizing potential field network: A new optimization algorithm. *IEEE Transactions on Neural Networks, 21*(9), 1482–1495. doi:10.1109/TNN.2010.2047264 PMID:20570771

Xu, S., & Rahmat-Samii, Y. (2007). Boundary conditions in particle swarm optimization revisited. *IEEE Transactions on Antennas and Propagation, 55*(3), 760–765. doi:10.1109/TAP.2007.891562

Yalcinoz, T., Altun, H., & Hasan, U. (2002). Environmentally constrained economic dispatch via neural networks. IEEE *6th AFRICON Conference in Africa*, 923–928. George, South Africa. 10.1109/AFRCON.2002.1160037

Yang, X. S. (2009, October). Firefly algorithms for multimodal optimization. *Proceedings International symposium on stochastic algorithms* (pp. 169-178). Berlin, Germany: Springer.

Yang, X. S. (2010b). In M. Bramer, R. Ellis, & M. Petridis (Eds.), Firefly Algorithm, Levy Flights, and Global Optimization. Research and Development, Intelligent Systems XXVI (pp. 209–218). London, UK: Springer. doi:10.1007/978-1-84882-983-1_15

Yang, C., Ji, J., Liu, J., Liu, J., & Yin, B. (2016). Structural learning of Bayesian networks by bacterial foraging optimization. *International Journal of Approximate Reasoning, 69*, 69. doi:10.1016/j.ijar.2015.11.003

Yang, J. S., & Chen, N. (1989). Short-term hydrothermal coordination using multi-pass dynamic programming. *IEEE Transactions on Power Systems, 4*(3), 1050–1056. doi:10.1109/59.32598

Yang, P. C., Yang, H. T., & Huang, C. L. (1996). Scheduling short-term hydrothermal generation using evolutionary programming techniques. *IEE Proceedings. Generation, Transmission, and Distribution, 143*(4), 371–376. doi:10.1049/ip-gtd:19960463

Yang, X. S. (2008). *Nature-inspired Metaheuristic Algorithms*. UK: Luniver Press.

Yang, X. S. (2010). A new metaheuristic bat-inspired algorithm. Proceedings *Nature inspired cooperative strategies for optimization (NICSO 2010)* (pp. 65–74). Berlin, Germany: Springer. doi:10.1007/978-3-642-12538-6_6

Yang, X. S. (2010). *Nature-inspired metaheuristic algorithms*. Cambridge, UK: Luniver Press.

Yang, X. S. (2010a). Firefly Algorithm, Stochastic Test Functions, and Design Optimization. *International Journal of Bio-inspired Computation, 2*(2), 78–84. doi:10.1504/IJBIC.2010.032124

Yang, X. S. (2013). *Recent Algorithms and Applications in Swarm Intelligence Research*. Hershey, PA: IGI Global.

Yang, X. S. (Ed.). (2013). *Cuckoo search and firefly algorithm: Theory and applications* (Vol. 516). Springer.

Yang, X. S., & Deb, S. (2009, December). Cuckoo search via Lévy flights. *Proceedings 2009 World Congress on Nature & Biologically Inspired Computing (NaBIC)* (pp. 210-214). IEEE. 10.1109/NABIC.2009.5393690

Yang, Y., & Zhang, L. (2013). Dynamic path planning of mobile beacon for localization in wireless sensor network. *Proceedings of International Conference on Wireless Communications and Signal Processing*, (pp. 1-5).

Yan, X., & Quantana, V. H. (1999). Improving an interior point based OPF by dynamic adjustments of step sizes and tolerances. *IEEE Transactions on Power Systems, 14*(2), 709–717. doi:10.1109/59.761902

Yao, F., Dong Z. Y., Xu, Z., Iu, H. H.-C., & Wong, K. P. (2012). Quantum-Inspired Particle Swarm Optimization for Power System Operations Considering Wind Power Uncertainty and Carbon Tax in Australia. IEEE Transactions on Industrial Informatics, 8(4), pp. 880-888.

Yao, F., & Xu, Z. (2012). Quantum-inspired particle swarm optimization for power system operations considering wind power uncertainty and carbon tax in Australia. *IEEE Transactions on Industrial Informatics, 8*(4), 880–888. doi:10.1109/TII.2012.2210431

Yao, X., Liu, Y., & Lin, G. (1999). Evolutionary programming made faster. *IEEE Transactions on Evolutionary Computation, 3*(2), 82–102. doi:10.1109/4235.771163

Yashen, L., Jeremiah, X. J., & Johanna, L. M. (2016). Emissions impacts of using energy storage for power system reserves. *Applied Energy, 168*, 444–456. doi:10.1016/j.apenergy.2016.01.061

Yildiz, A. R. (2013). Cuckoo search algorithm for the selection of optimal machining parameters in milling operations. *International Journal of Advanced Manufacturing Technology, 64*(1-4), 55–61. doi:10.100700170-012-4013-7

Yin, X., Cheng, L., Wang, X., Lu, J., & Qin, H. (2019). Optimization for hydro-photovoltaic-wind power Generation System Based on Modified Version of Multi-Objective Whale Optimization Algorithm. *Energy Procedia, 158*, 6208–6216. doi:10.1016/j.egypro.2019.01.480

Yong, Y., Sun'an, W., & Wanxing, S. (2002). Short-term load forecasting using artificial immune network. *Power con 2002 International Conference on Power System Technology Proceedings, 4*, 2322–2325. 10.1109/ICPST.2002.1047199

You, T., Rosli, A. N., Ha, I., & Jo, G.-S. (2013). Clustering method based on genre interest for cold-start problem in movie recommendation. *Journal of Intelligent Information Systems, 19*(1), 51–77.

Yuan, C., Malonean, B., & Wu, X. (2011). Learning Optimal Bayesian Networks Using A* Search. NSF grants IIS-0953723 and EPS-0903787, 21 IJCAI. Barcelona, Spain.

Yuan, X., Tian, H., Yuan, Y., Huang, Y., & Ikram, R. M. (2015). An extended NSGA-III for solution multi-objective hydro-thermal-wind scheduling considering wind power cost. *Energy Conversion and Management, 96*, 568–578. doi:10.1016/j.enconman.2015.03.009

Yu, B., Yuan, X., & Wang, J. (2007). Short-term hydro-thermal scheduling using particle swarm optimization method. *Energy Conversion and Management*, *48*(7), 1902–1908. doi:10.1016/j.enconman.2007.01.034

Yusup, N., Zain, A. M., & Latib, A. A. (2019, March). A review of Harmony Search algorithm-based feature selection method for classification. [IOP Publishing.]. *Journal of Physics: Conference Series*, *1192*(1). doi:10.1088/1742-6596/1192/1/012038

Zaitoun, N. M., & Musbah, J. A. (2015). Survey on Image Segmentation Techniques. *Proceedings of International Conference on Communication, Management, and Information Technology*. Elsevier.

Zelinka, I. (2004). SOMA-self-organizing migrating algorithm. In G. Onwubolu, & B. V. Babu (Eds.), *New Optimization Techniques in Engineering* (pp. 167–217). Germany: Springer-Verlag. doi:10.1007/978-3-540-39930-8_7

Zengin, A., & Tuncel, S. (2010). A survey on swarm intelligence based routing protocols in wireless sensor networks. *International Journal of Physical Sciences*, *5*(14), 2118–2126.

Zhang, Q., Zhou, A., Zhao, S., Suganthan, P. N., Liu, W., & Tiwari, S. (2009). Multiobjective optimization Test Instances for the CEC 2009 Special Session and Competition, Technical Report CES-487, University of Essex.

Zhang, Y., Liu, J., & Liu, Y. (2018). Bayesian Network Structure Learning: The Two-Step Clustering-Based Algorithm. Association for the Advancement of Artificial Intelligence, 8183-8184.

Zhang, C., Sun, J., Zhu, X., & Fang, Y. (2010). Privacy and security for online social networks: Challenges and opportunities. *IEEE Network*, *24*(4), 13–18. doi:10.1109/MNET.2010.5510913

Zhang, D., Luh, P. B., & Zhang, Y. (1999). A bundle method for hydrothermal scheduling. *IEEE Transactions on Power Systems*, *14*(4), 1355–1361. doi:10.1109/59.801896

Zhang, J., & Sanderson, A. C. (2009). JADE: Adaptive Differential Evolution With Optional External Archive. *IEEE Transactions on Evolutionary Computation*, *13*(5), 945–958. doi:10.1109/TEVC.2009.2014613

Zhang, L., Liu, L., Yang, X. S., & Dai, Y. (2016). A novel hybrid firefly algorithm for global optimization. *PLoS One*, *11*(9). doi:10.1371/journal.pone.0163230 PMID:27685869

Zhang, Q., & Li, H. (2007). MOEA/D: A multiobjective evolutionary algorithm based on decomposition. *IEEE Transactions on Evolutionary Computation*, *11*(6), 712–731. doi:10.1109/TEVC.2007.892759

Zhang, Q., & Mühlenbein, H. (2004). On the convergence of a class of estimation of distribution algorithms. *IEEE Transactions on Evolutionary Computation*, *8*(2), 127–136. doi:10.1109/TEVC.2003.820663

Zhang, S.-Z., & Liu, L. (2008). *Mcmc Samples Selecting for Online Bayesian Network Structure Learning*. Kunming: IEEE.

Zhang, W., Xie, X. F., & Bi, D. C. (2004). Handling boundary constraints for numerical optimization by particle swarm flying in periodic search space. *Proceedings of the 2004 Congress on Evolutionary Computation (CEC 2004)*, (pp. 2307-2311). 10.1109/CEC.2004.1331185

Zhang, X., Miao, Q., Zhang, H., & Wang, L. (2018). A parameter-adaptive VMD method based on grasshopper optimization algorithm to analyze vibration signals from rotating machinery. *Mechanical Systems and Signal Processing*, *108*, 58–72. doi:10.1016/j.ymssp.2017.11.029

Zhao, J. H., Fushuan Dong, W. Z. Y., Xue, Y., & Wong, K. P. (2012). Optimal Dispatch of Electric Vehicles and Wind Power Using Enhanced Particle Swarm Optimization. *IEEE Transactions on Industrial Informatics*, *8*(4), 889–899. doi:10.1109/TII.2012.2205398

Zheng, L., Pan, A., Li, G., & Liang, J. (2009). Improvement of Grayscale Segmentation based on PSO Algorithm. *Proceedings of IEEE 4th Int. Conference on Computer Science and Convergence Information Technology.* 10.1109/ICCIT.2009.68

Zheng, S., Janecek, A., & Tan, Y. (2013). Enhanced fireworks algorithm. *Proceedings of 2013 IEEE Congress on Evolutionary Computation, (CEC 2013)*, (pp. 2069-2077). Cancun, Mexico: IEEE. 10.1109/CEC.2013.6557813

Zhong, W., Liu, J., Xue, M., & Jiao, L. (2004). A multiagent genetic algorithm for global numerical optimization. *IEEE Transactions on Systems, Man, and Cybernetics. Part B, Cybernetics, 34*(2), 1128–1141. doi:10.1109/TSMCB.2003.821456 PMID:15376858

Zhou, A., Zhang, Q., & Jin, Y. (2009). Approximating the set of Pareto-optimal solutions in both the decision and objective spaces by an estimation of distribution algorithm. *IEEE Transactions on Evolutionary Computation, 13*(5), 1167–1189. doi:10.1109/TEVC.2009.2021467

Zhu, Z., Ong, Y. S., & Dash, M. (2007). Markov blanket-embedded genetic algorithm for gene selection. *Pattern Recognition, 40*(11), 3236–3248. doi:10.1016/j.patcog.2007.02.007

Zielinski, K., Weitkemper, P., Laur, R., & Kammeyer, K. D. (2009). Optimization of power allocation for interference cancellation with particle swarm optimization. *IEEE Transactions on Evolutionary Computation, 13*(1), 128–150. doi:10.1109/TEVC.2008.920672

Zitzler, E., Laumanns, M., & Thiele, L. (2002). SPEA2: Improving the strength Pareto evolutionary algorithm. *Optimization and Control with Applications to Industrial Problems.* (pp. 95-100). Berlin, Germany: Springer.

Zitzler, E., & Thiele, L. (1999). Multiobjective evolutionary algorithms: A comparative case study and the strength Pareto approach. *IEEE Transactions on Evolutionary Computation, 3*(4), 257–271. doi:10.1109/4235.797969

About the Contributors

Shi Cheng received the Bachelor's degree in Mechanical and Electrical Engineering from Xiamen University, Xiamen, the Master's degree in Software Engineering from Beihang University (BUAA), Beijing, China, the Ph.D. degree in Electrical Engineering and Electronics from Liverpool University, Liverpool, United Kingdom, the Ph.D. degree in Electrical and Electronic Engineering from Xi'an Jiaotong-Liverpool University, Suzhou, China in 2005, 2008, and 2013, respectively. He is currently a lecturer with School of Computer Science, Shaanxi Normal University, Xi'an, China. His current research interests include swarm intelligence, multiobjective optimization, and data mining techniques and their applications.

Yuhui Shi received the PhD degree in electronic engineering from Southeast University, Nanjing, China, in 1992. He is a chair professor in the Department of Computer Science and Engineering, Southern University of Science and Technology, Shenzhen, China. Before joining Southern University of Science and Technology, he was with Electronic Data Systems Corporation, Indianapolis, IN. His main research interests include the areas of computational intelligence techniques (including swarm intelligence) and their applications. Dr. Shi is the Editor-in-Chief of the International Journal of Swarm Intelligence Research. (Kuruge Abeyrathna - Contributing Author) Darshana is a PhD research fellow at the University of Agder. He completed his BSc in Mechatronics Engineering at AIT university, Thailand in 2015. Then he directly joined to the Big Data research group at Thammasat University, Thailand for his MSc studies and graduated in 2017. His research interests are in Artificial Neural Networks, Data Mining, Optimization, and Operations Research. Currently, at CAIR, he is working on a project which develops a global grid that facilitates real-time compilation, management, and analysis of spatio-temporal data.

* * *

Alexander Alfimtsev received the B. S. and M. S. degrees in computer science from the Bauman Moscow State Technical University (BMSTU), Russia, in 2003 and 2005 respectively, and the Ph. D. degree in 2008. He is currently a Professor of Information systems and telecommunications at BMSTU. He is also a Member of the International Institute of Informatics and Systemics, USA. He has 70 scientific papers, including 5 patents for inventions. His main research interests include the use of machine learning methods in human-computer interaction and computer vision.

Dhinesh Babu L. D. received BE in Electrical & Electronics Engineering and ME in Computer Science & Engineering from the University of Madras. He received his PhD from VIT. He is currently an Associate Professor in the School of Information Technology and Engineering at VIT, Vellore, India. He has served as the head of the Software Engineering Division at VIT. He has around 20 Years of experience in teaching and research. His research interests include Big Data Analytics, Machine Learning, Recommender Systems, Complex Network Analysis, Cloud Computing and Software Engineering.

Junfeng Chen received the PhD degree from the College of Control Science and Engineering, Zhejiang University, Hangzhou, China, in 2011. Currently, she is an associate professor in the College of IOT Engineering, Hohai University, Changzhou, China. Her research interests include swarm intelligence, artificial intelligence with uncertainty, cooperative coevolution, data mining techniques, and ontology matching technique. She is a member of IEEE and ACM. She won ICSI 2016 excellent paper award and was awarded the sponsorship of the Jiangsu Overseas Research & Training Program for University Prominent Young & Middle-aged Teachers and Presidents, China.

Veena Desai received her B.E. degree in Electronics and Communication Engineering from Karnatak University, India, and M.Tech. degree in Computer Networks Engineering from Visvesvaraya Technological University, India. She received her Ph.D. degree in Electronics and Communication Engineering from the Visvesvaraya Technological University, India. Her research interests include computer networks, wireless networks and cryptography. She is a member of IEEE and Computer Society of India (CSI). She has published a book chapter, twelve refereed journal papers and twelve refereed conference proceedings papers.

Nassima DIF is a PhD student at Djillali Liabes University.

Zakaria Elberrichi is a professor at Djillali Liabes University. Head team Web Intelligence and Data Mining.

Donatella Giuliani graduated in Physics at University of Bologna (Italy) in 1982 and attended a Master in "Theory and Applications of Computational Machines" at University of Bologna in 1983. From 1984 to 1988 she worked as Software Analyst for Geoseismic Data at Aquater Spa, a company of ENI Group. From 1988 to 1992 she was employed as Software Analyst in Cartographic and Photogrammetric Data at Ecobit Spa (Italy). Since 1992 she is professor of Mathematics of MIUR. She graduated in Mathematics (2000) at University of Camerino (MC), developing research activities on shape analysis and models of biological structures using non-Euclidean geometry. In 2001 she received a Master degree in "Methodologies of e-learning" at University of Florence, Italy (2001). Since 2003 she worked as a teacher of Statistics at University of Bologna. In 2009 she received a Philosophical Doctorate in Mathematics and Statistics in Computational Sciences (MaSSC) at University of Milano, with research applications on computational methods and morphological analysis in Neuroimaging in cooperation with IRCCS Institute Fatebenefratelli (Brescia). In 2015 at University of Bologna, she received a Master degree as trainer for teaching of Mathematics.

Sunanda Hazra was born in 1991 at Indas, Bankura, West Bengal, India. He received a B.E Degree in Electrical Engineering from University Institute of Technology (The University of Burdwan), Burdwan, West Bengal, India in 2012; a M.Tech Degree in Electrical Engineering from West Bengal University of Technology, West Bengal, India in 2014 and currently pursuing Ph.D from MAKAUT as well as he is working as a Lecturer in the department of Electrical and Electronics Engineering, Central Institute of Plastics Engineering Technology, Haldia, West Bengal, India. His field of research interest includes Economic emission load dispatch, Renewable Energy, Solar-Wind-Hydro-Thermal scheduling and evolutionary computing techniques.

Chawalit Jeenanunta holds a B.Sc. in Mathematics and Computer Science, and M.Sc. in Management Science from University of Maryland. He received his Ph.D. in Industrial and Systems Engineering from Virginia Polytechnic Institute and State University. He joined Sirindhorn International Institute of Technology, Thammasat University, Thailand as a lecturer and now he is an associate professor. He was a chair of Management Technology curriculum, Head of School of Management Technology, Deputy Director for Building, Ground and Properties. He is also a head of Logistics and Supply Chain Systems Engineering Research Unit (LogEn) and the head of the Center for Technology Transfer of Industry 4.0. His Research interests are in area of applications of operations research, and innovation. He received research funding from Thailand Research Fund, Institute of Developing Economies and Japan External Trade Organization (IDE-JETRO), Economic Research Institute for ASEAN and East Asia (ERIA), PTT Logistics and Electricity Generating Authority of Thailand (EGAT).

Yuri Kalgin graduated from Bauman Moscow State Technical University (BMSTU) in 2001 with honor and Moscow State Linguistics University in 2006. Today he is a senior teacher at the Faculty of Linguistics of BMSTU. He has published 11 articles and 5 booklets in the field of pedagogy. Pedagogy and teaching methods of foreign languages as well as artificial intelligence methods are of his scientific interests.

Shahab Wahhab Kareem earned his BSc in Control and Computer Engineering from the University of Technology Baghdad in 2001, and MSc in Software Engineering from Salahadeen University in 2009. He is currently a PhD research in Yasar University Izmir, Turkey. His research interests include Machine learning. He is a lecturer at the Information System Eng. (ISE) Department (2011-present).

Raghavendra V. Kulkarni received his B.E. degree in Electronics and Communication Engineering from Karnatak University, India, and M.Tech. degree in Electronics Engineering from the Institute of Technology, Banaras Hindu University, India. He received his Ph.D. degree in Electrical Engineering from the Missouri University of Science and Technology, Rolla, USA. His research interests include the development of wireless sensor network applications using computational intelligence tools. He is a senior member of IEEE, a life member of the Indian Society for Technical Education (ISTE), a member of the IEEE Computational Intelligence Society (CSI), and a member of Computer Society of India (CSI). He has published a book chapter, over twelve refereed journal papers and sixteen refereed conference proceedings papers.

Vaishali R. Kulkarni received her B.E. degree in Computer Science and Engineering from Karnatak University, India, and M. Tech. degree in Computer Science and Engineering from Visvesvaraya Technological University, India. She is pursuing her Ph.D. degree in Computer Science and Engineering from the Visvesvaraya Technological University, India. Her research interests include wireless sensor networks, computational intelligence, swarm intelligence, fuzzy logic, and neural networks. She is a member of IEEE, a life member of the Indian Society for Technical Education (ISTE) and a member of Computer Society of India (CSI). She has served as invited reviewer, session chair and author in international conferences and journals. She has published refereed journals papers and conference proceedings papers.

Nirmala M received her Bachelor's degree in Electronic Science from the University of Madras and Masters in Computer Applications from Madurai Kamaraj University. She received her M.Tech in Computer Science and Engineering and PhD from VIT. She is currently an Associate Professor in the School of Information Technology and Engineering at VIT, Vellore. Her research interests include Data Analytics, Social Computing, Sentiment Analysis, Databases, Data mining and Data Warehousing.

Mehmet Cudi Okur received his BSC in Statistics from Ankara University and MSc in Applied Statistics from Reading University .He obtained the PhD degree in Applied Statistics from Ataturk University. He has served as research assistant,lecturer and professor at Computer Engineering and Software Engineering departments of Ege, Eastern Mediterrenaen and Yasar Universities. He is currently working as a full-time professor at DEpartment of Software Engineering, Yaşar University.His research interests include databases,data mining, data analytics & computational statistics.

Moumita Pradhan received her BTech degree in Computer Science and Engineering from JIS College of Engineering College, Kalyana (under West Bengal University of Technology), India, in 2005 and MTech degree from NIT,Durgapur, West Bengal, India in Operation Research and Business management in 2009. Her area of research includes hydrothermal scheduling, economic load dispatch and soft computing techniques. Presently she is working as an Assistant Professor in the Department of Computer Science and Engineering, Dr. B.C. Roy Engineering College, Durgapur, India.

Quande Qin received PhD degree in Management Science and Engineering from School of Business Administration, South China University of Technology, Guangzhou, China. Currently, he is a lecturer in the College of Management, Shenzhen University, Shenzhen, China. His current research interests include swarm intelligence, evolutionary optimization and their applications in management and economics.

Provas Kumar Roy obtained PhD degree in Electrical Engineering from National Institute of Technology Durgapur in 2011. He received his Master degree in Electrical Machine in 2001 from Jadavpur University. He finished his Engineering studies in Electrical Engineering from Regional Engineering College, Durgapur. Presently, he is working as a Professor in Electrical Engineering Department at Kalyani Government Engineering College, India. He was the recipient of the Outstanding Reviewer Award for International Journal of Electrical Power and Energy Systems (Elsevier) in 2018, Engineering Application of Artificial Intelligence (Elsevier) in 2017, Renewable Energy Focus (Elsevier) in 2018, Ain Shams Engineering Journal (Elsevier) in 2017. He has published more than 120 research papers.

Six research scholars have obtained their Ph.D. degree under his guidance and 10 students are perusing their Ph.D. under his guidance. His research interest includes economic load dispatch, optimal power flow, FACTS, automatic generation control, radial distribution network, power system stabilizer, image processing, machine learning, evolutionary computing techniques, etc.

Sergey Aleksandrovich Sakulin graduated Bauman Moscow State Technical University (BMSTU) in 2001. He is an associated professor at BMSTU, IU-3 department. He has 30 scientific papers. Scientific interests lie in the fields of expert knowledge formalization and visualization.

Takuya Shindo received his B. Eng., M. Eng., and Dr. Eng. degrees in Electrical Engineering from Nippon Institute of Technology, Saitama, Japan in 2003, 2011, and 2014, respectively. His research interests are in meta-heuristic algorithms. In 2014, He joined the department of Electrical and Electronics Engineering, Nippon Institute of Technology, Saitama, Japan, where he is Assistant Professor.

Akash Sikarwar is an undergraduate student in computer science engineering. His research interests are in machine learning, data science and computational intelligence.

Zhou Wu is a full professor in Chongqing University (CQU), China. Before joining in CQU, he worked as a Senior Research Fellow in University of Pretoria, South Africa, from 2012 to 2015. He has been focusing on multidisciplinary areas, energy/building information modeling, intelligent optimization/control, and game theory. He is a member of IEEE, ACM and CAA. He published more than 80 peer-reviewed papers on Science Advances, IEEE Transaction on Industrial Informatics, Applied Energy, and other top journals. Furthermore, he has engineering experiences on Measurement & Verification (MV) energy efficiency projects, and holds several relative patents.

Xingsi Xue received the B. S. degree in Software Engineering from Fuzhou University, China in 2004, the M. S. degree in Computer Application Technology from Renmin University of China, China in 2009, and the Ph.D. degree in Computer Application Technology from Xidian University, China in 2014. He is a professor at the College of Information Science and Engineering, Fujian University of Technology, and the director of Intelligent Information Processing Research Center, Fujian University of Technology. He is also the kernel members in Intelligent Information Processing Research Center, Fujian Provincial Key Laboratory of Big Data Mining and Applications, Fujian Key Lab for Automotive Electronics and Electric Drive at Fujian university of Technology. His research interests include intelligent computation, data mining and large-scale ontology matching technology. He is a member of IEEE and ACM, and won 2017 ACM Xi'an Rising Star Award and IIH-MSP 2016 excellent paper award.

Index

A

Artificial Bee Colony 3, 46, 78-79, 85, 116, 119, 124-125, 163-164, 419
Artificial Bee Colony Algorithm 79, 85, 124, 419
Artificial Neural Networks 63-65, 71

B

Backpropagation 63-64, 66, 73-75
Bacterial foraging optimization 116, 119, 125, 140
Bat Algorithm 43-44, 49-50
Bayesian Network 139-143, 146-147, 155
Benchmark Function 103, 111, 218, 226
boundary constraints 217-218, 222, 226, 230, 234-243, 246, 316, 330-331, 346, 361
Boundary Constraints Handling 217-218, 222, 230, 234-243, 246, 330, 361

C

Chaos 45, 105, 108
Cognitive Diversity 243, 317-320, 332, 335-336, 338, 344, 346-347, 349-350, 352-353, 359-360
Cold start 195-200, 206, 211
Combined economic emission dispatch 384
Contour Gradient Optimization 247, 249, 253-254
Cuckoo Search 44, 116, 119, 126, 163, 419
Cultural Algorithm 384, 393, 401, 415, 417, 426, 429

D

Developmental swarm intelligence algorithm 278
Differential Evolution 2, 49, 81, 161, 163, 248, 252, 340, 379, 384, 393, 400
Diversity 32, 47, 52, 108, 111-112, 161, 217-218, 220-221, 230-234, 237-243, 246, 254, 278-279, 281, 285-287, 304, 312-314, 316-322, 331-332, 335-338, 340, 344-347, 349-360, 365-379

Dt 413

E

Economic Load Dispatch (ELD) 2, 165, 383
Elephant Swarm Water Search 139, 141, 144
Emission 1-6, 13, 15, 50, 160-167, 169-173, 179, 183-184, 186-187, 383-384, 386, 393, 396-397, 399-405, 413
Emission tax 2, 5-6, 15
Evolutionary Algorithm 27-29, 31, 38, 140, 160, 247, 249, 346, 392
Exploitation 10, 43, 45-47, 52, 55-56, 79-80, 86, 89, 92, 119, 145, 166, 174-175, 177, 217-221, 223, 230, 234, 237-242, 246, 278, 281, 285-286, 312-314, 316-317, 319-320, 323, 330, 338, 340, 344, 346, 350, 363, 369, 379, 391
Exploration 3, 10, 43-46, 55-56, 80, 91, 144-145, 147-149, 155, 166, 174-175, 177, 217-221, 223, 226, 230, 234, 237-238, 240-241, 246, 278, 281, 285-286, 312-314, 316-317, 319-320, 323, 338, 340, 344, 346, 350, 365, 379, 389, 426

F

Firefly Algorithm 44-45, 48-49, 78, 80-81, 92, 100-101, 104, 419
Fireworks algorithm 277-282, 287, 289, 292-295, 298-300, 302-308

G

Gaussian Mixture Model 78-80, 82, 86, 88, 93, 95
Gender 195, 197, 199-200, 202-203, 205-206, 211
Gene Selection 43-47, 49-50, 52, 54
Genetic Algorithm 2, 4, 29, 35, 44, 64, 108, 116, 118-119, 123, 161, 165, 195-196, 199-200, 203, 211, 248, 340, 346, 379, 383, 420
Genre 197-204, 206, 211

Global Search 10, 103, 110-111, 120, 145-148, 155, 174, 248, 272, 289, 332
Grasshopper optimization Algorithm (GOA) 1, 4, 160
Grey wolf optimization 382, 384-385, 389, 392

I

Image Segmentation 78-80, 95, 120
interactive Multi-Objective Evolutionary Algorithm 27, 31, 38
Invasive Weed Optimization 415, 417

L

Local Search 9-10, 46, 79, 86, 89, 96, 103, 110, 112, 133, 144-147, 149, 174, 248
Localization 415-424, 428, 433-434

M

matrix norm 354-355
Metaheuristic Algorithm 87, 89, 92, 392, 415, 419, 426
Metaheuristics 2, 43-46, 51-56, 58, 64, 144, 392
Meta-heuristics 2, 393
Mobile Anchor 415-416
Multi-objective hydro-thermal scheduling 385
Multi-verse Optimizer 45-47

N

normalized population diversity 345, 354, 365, 369, 379

O

Ontology Alignment Evaluation Initiative 27, 34
Oppositional based GWO 382, 385
Optimal power flow (OPF) 160
Optimum shift 277, 304

P

Parameter 3, 31-32, 45, 48, 78, 83, 103-105, 108, 110-112, 128, 142-143, 148-149, 177, 182, 186, 224, 226, 252, 257, 265, 270, 272, 278, 280, 285, 313, 321, 323, 328-330, 361, 363, 416, 427-428
Particle Swarm Optimization 2-4, 35, 44, 51, 63-65, 81, 102, 163-164, 217-219, 246, 248, 251, 312-314, 331, 333-336, 338, 340, 344-347, 349, 353, 384, 401
Pigeon Inspired Optimization 139-140, 148
Population Diversity 217-218, 220-221, 231, 239, 243,

246, 278, 281, 285-287, 304, 312-314, 316-317, 320-322, 331-332, 336-338, 340, 344-347, 349-351, 353-355, 365-379
Position Diversity 217-218, 221, 232-234, 237-243, 246, 317-320, 332, 335-336, 338, 344, 346-347, 349-352, 355-357, 359-360
Premature Convergence 2, 32, 45-46, 217-219, 242, 246, 278, 312-313, 316, 332, 337, 344, 346
Probability distribution function (PDF) 169
Prohibited operating zone 383, 389, 414

Q

Quasi oppositional based learning (QOBL) 1

R

Ramp rate 188, 383, 385, 388
Recommender system 195-197, 199, 211
Refinement 43, 45-46, 48, 52, 56, 58, 246, 312-313, 344
Renewable Wind Energy 1, 5, 15-17, 21

S

Search Performance 100-101, 108-112, 294
sensor ontology matching 27, 34
Short-Term Load Forecasting 71
Structure Learning 139-143, 146-147, 149, 155
Swarm Intelligence (SI) 1, 22, 44, 46, 80-81, 100, 140, 277-279, 304, 312, 346, 417, 419

T

t-dominance rule 27, 32-33, 38
Trilateration 415-418, 421, 423, 428, 434

U

User Experience 211

V

vector norm 354, 357
Velocity Diversity 243, 317-320, 344, 346-347, 349-352, 357-359

W

Wind energy (WE) 4, 164-165
Wireless Sensor Network 416

Ensure Quality Research is Introduced to the Academic Community

Become an IGI Global Reviewer for Authored Book Projects

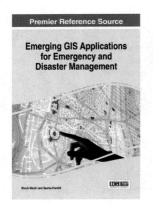

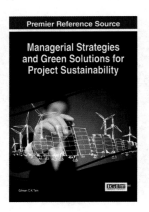

The overall success of an authored book project is dependent on quality and timely reviews.

In this competitive age of scholarly publishing, constructive and timely feedback significantly expedites the turnaround time of manuscripts from submission to acceptance, allowing the publication and discovery of forward-thinking research at a much more expeditious rate. Several IGI Global authored book projects are currently seeking highly-qualified experts in the field to fill vacancies on their respective editorial review boards:

Applications and Inquiries may be sent to:
development@igi-global.com

Applicants must have a doctorate (or an equivalent degree) as well as publishing and reviewing experience. Reviewers are asked to complete the open-ended evaluation questions with as much detail as possible in a timely, collegial, and constructive manner. All reviewers' tenures run for one-year terms on the editorial review boards and are expected to complete at least three reviews per term. Upon successful completion of this term, reviewers can be considered for an additional term.

If you have a colleague that may be interested in this opportunity, we encourage you to share this information with them.

Are You Ready to Publish Your Research?

IGI Global offers book authorship and editorship opportunities across 11 subject areas, including business, computer science, education, science and engineering, social sciences, and more!

Benefits of Publishing with IGI Global:

- Free one-on-one editorial and promotional support.
- Expedited publishing timelines that can take your book from start to finish in less than one (1) year.
- Choose from a variety of formats including: Edited and Authored References, Handbooks of Research, Encyclopedias, and Research Insights.
- Utilize IGI Global's eEditorial Discovery® submission system in support of conducting the submission and blind review process.

- IGI Global maintains a strict adherence to ethical practices due in part to our full membership with the Committee on Publication Ethics (COPE).
- Indexing potential in prestigious indices such as Scopus®, Web of Science™, PsycINFO®, and ERIC – Education Resources Information Center.
- Ability to connect your ORCID iD to your IGI Global publications.
- Earn royalties on your publication as well as receive complimentary copies and exclusive discounts.

Get Started Today by Contacting the Acquisitions Department at:

acquisition@igi-global.com

Printed in the United States
By Bookmasters